Ac]

MW00608734

A comprehensive list of the sources that fed this biography would be long, indeed. Some of them weighed in with comments that merited only a paragraph, others were more pivotal and explicit.

Archived over the course of many decades, sources include friends and acquaintances of Carrie and Debbie, their directors, producers, co-stars and fellow actors, gossipy rivals, and ex-husbands and former boyfriends such as Hugh O'Brian (in Acapulco).

Darwin Porter, a long-time Hollywood insider, found the following people particularly helpful during his compilation of this mother/daughter saga:

Rock Hudson, Christopher Jones (in Ireland), Elizabeth Taylor (in Gstaad), Bette Davis, Lana Turner, Gordon MacCrae (in Indiana), Lex Barker (in Rome), Shirley MacLaine, Gene Kelly, Fred Astaire, Vic Damone (in Florida), Ann Miller and Mickey Rooney (in New York), Barry Sullivan, Jean Hagen, Donald O'Connor, Pier Angeli, Celeste Holm, Dan Dailey, Tony Randall (he didn't like Debbie), Dick Hanley, Glenn Ford (he adored her), Cliff Robertson ("reticent but revealing"), Greer Garson (oh, so kind), Shelley Winters ("I resent Debbie"), and Paul Lynde ("I loathe the bitch").

Special thanks go to Rudy Render, her longtime friend and musical director, to Robert Wagner and especially to Eddie Fisher for their interviews with other journalists and their memoirs.

Darwin is especially grateful to the people of El Paso during his long-ago visit when he talked to a number of people who had known Debbie, her brother Billy, "Minnie and Roy," plus other members of the Reynolds family.

Most of all, we dedicate this book to Debbie Reynolds and to Carrie Fisher. Carrie was a very public source for events that transpired within her life. She wrote multiple memoirs, and delivered candid interviews on television. Her stage shows were confessionals, always presented with candor and honesty.

Frank Sinatra was of no help, but he kept his Rat Pack apprised of his dynamics with Debbie. Dean Martin and Sammy Davis, Jr. were not the most discreet repository of secrets.

One notable exception who consistently slammed the door on requests for interviews was Debbie's longtime friend and companion, obviously for reasons known only to herself.

Contents

CARRIE FISHER & DEBBIE REYNOLDS

PRINCESS LEIA & UNSINKABLE TAMMY IN HELL

"Celebrity is just obscurity waiting to happen."
—Carrie Fisher

"Marrying Debbie Reynolds was the worst mistake of my life"
—Eddie Fisher

"Eddie Fisher is like a needy, dependent person. I don't know what to compare him to. He's like an elevator that can't find the floor."
—Debbie Reynolds

"When mother heard I was heavy into LSD, she did what every sensible parent would do. She phoned Cary Grant."
—Carrie Fisher

"Had I snared King Baudoin of Belgium, I might have become queen and also First Lady of the Congo, which he then controlled."
—Debbie Reynolds

"I love her and I never loved you."
—Eddie Fisher telling Debbie why he's dumping her for Elizabeth Taylor

"Debbie Reynolds has more balls than any five guys I know. She pretends to be sweet and demure, but at heart, she's Hard-Hearted Hannah."
—Columnist Earl Wilson

"Debbie just smiles that sweet smile, but you know those wheels are turning, pushing her forward to the next heavily plotted step. She's the last person we will have to worry about. Whatever the disasters, she lands on her feet."
—Louis B. Mayer

Biographies that Focus on the Ironies of Fame
www.BloodMoonProductions.com

Award-Winning Entertainment About
How America Interprets Its Celebrities

What is Blood Moon Productions?

"Blood Moon, in case you don't know, is a small publishing house on Staten Is-land that cranks out Hollywood gossip books, about two or three a year, usually of five-, six-, or 700-page length, chocked with stories and pictures about people who used to consume the imaginations of the American public, back when we ac-tually had a public imagination. That is, when people were really interested in each other, rather than in Apple 'devices.' In other words, back when we had vices, not devices."

—The Huffington Post

CARRIE FISHER & DEBBIE REYNOLDS
PRINCESS LEIA AND UNSINKABLE TAMMY IN HELL

Darwin Porter & Danforth Prince

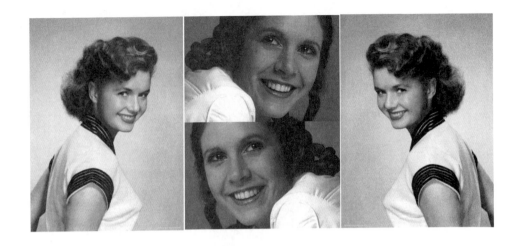

Carrie Fisher & Debbie Reynolds
Princess Leia and Unsinkable Tammy in Hell

Darwin Porter and Danforth Prince

www.BloodMoonProductions.com

Manufactured in the United States of America

ISBN 978-1-936003-57-0

Cover Designs by Danforth Prince

PREVIOUS WORKS BY DARWIN PORTER
PRODUCED IN COLLABORATION WITH BLOOD MOON

BIOGRAPHIES

Rock Hudson Erotic Fire

Lana Turner, Hearts & Diamonds Take All

Donald Trump, The Man Who Would Be King

James Dean, Tomorrow Never Comes

Bill and Hillary, So This Is That Thing Called Love

Peter O'Toole, Hellraiser, Sexual Outlaw, Irish Rebel

Love Triangle, Ronald Reagan, Jane Wyman, & Nancy Davis

Jacqueline Kennedy Onassis, A Life Beyond Her Wildest Dreams

Pink Triangle, The Feuds and Private Lives of Tennessee Williams, Gore Vidal, Truman Capote, and Famous Members of their Entourages.

Those Glamorous Gabors, Bombshells from Budapest

Inside Linda Lovelace's Deep Throat, Degradation, Porno Chic, and the Rise of Feminism

Elizabeth Taylor, There is Nothing Like a Dame

Marilyn at Rainbow's End, Sex, Lies, Murder, and the Great Cover-up

J. Edgar Hoover and Clyde Tolson
Investigating the Sexual Secrets of America's Most Famous Men and Women

Frank Sinatra, The Boudoir Singer. All the Gossip Unfit to Print

The Kennedys, All the Gossip Unfit to Print

Humphrey Bogart, The Making of a Legend (2010) , *and*
The Secret Life of Humphrey Bogart (2003)

Howard Hughes, Hell's Angel

Steve McQueen, King of Cool, Tales of a Lurid Life

Paul Newman, The Man Behind the Baby Blues

Merv Griffin, A Life in the Closet

Brando Unzipped

Katharine the Great, Hepburn, Secrets of a Lifetime Revealed

Jacko, His Rise and Fall, The Social and Sexual History of Michael Jackson

Damn You, Scarlett O'Hara, The Private Lives of Vivien Leigh and Laurence Olivier (co-authored with Roy Moseley)

FILM CRITICISM
Blood Moon's 2005 Guide to the Glitter Awards
Blood Moon's 2006 Guide to Film
Blood Moon's 2007 Guide to Film, *and*
50 Years of Queer Cinema, 500 of the Best GLBTQ Films Ever Made

NON-FICTION
Hollywood Babylon, It's Back! *and* **Hollywood Babylon Strikes Again!**

NOVELS
Blood Moon,
Hollywood's Silent Closet,
Rhinestone Country,
Razzle Dazzle
Midnight in Savannah

OTHER PUBLICATIONS BY DARWIN PORTER
NOT DIRECTLY ASSOCIATED WITH BLOOD MOON

NOVELS

The Delinquent Heart
The Taste of Steak Tartare
Butterflies in Heat
Marika (*a roman à clef based on the life of Marlene Dietrich*)
Venus (*a roman à clef based on the life of Anaïs Nin*)
Bitter Orange
Sister Rose

TRAVEL GUIDES

Many Editions and Many Variations of *The Frommer Guides,
The American Express Guides,* and/or *TWA Guides, et alia* to:

Andalusia, Andorra, Anguilla, Aruba, Atlanta, Austria, the Azores, The Bahamas, Barbados, the Bavarian Alps, Berlin, Bermuda, Bonaire and Curaçao, Boston, the British Virgin Islands, Budapest, Bulgaria, California, the Canary Islands, the Caribbean and its "Ports of Call," the Cayman Islands, Ceuta, the Channel Islands (UK), Charleston (SC), Corsica, Costa del Sol (Spain), Denmark, Dominica, the Dominican Republic, Edinburgh, England, Estonia, Europe, "Europe by Rail," the Faroe Islands, Finland, Florence, France, Frankfurt, the French Riviera, Geneva, Georgia (USA), Germany, Gibraltar, Glasgow, Granada (Spain), Great Britain, Greenland, Grenada (West Indies), Haiti, Hungary, Iceland, Ireland, Isle of Man, Italy, Jamaica, Key West & the Florida Keys, Las Vegas, Liechtenstein, Lisbon, London, Los Angeles, Madrid, Maine, Malta, Martinique & Guadeloupe, Massachusetts, Melilla, Morocco, Munich, New England, New Orleans, North Carolina, Norway, Paris, Poland, Portugal, Provence, Puerto Rico, Romania, Rome, Salzburg, San Diego, San Francisco, San Marino, Sardinia, Savannah, Scandinavia, Scotland, Seville, the Shetland Islands, Sicily, St. Martin & Sint Maarten, St. Vincent & the Grenadines, South Carolina, Spain, St. Kitts & Nevis, Sweden, Switzerland, the Turks & Caicos, the U.S.A., the U.S. Virgin Islands, Venice, Vienna and the Danube, Wales, and Zurich.

BIOGRAPHIES

From Diaghilev to Balanchine, The Saga of Ballerina Tamara Geva

Lucille Lortel, The Queen of Off-Broadway

Greta Keller, Germany's Other Lili Marlene

Sophie Tucker, The Last of the Red Hot Mamas

Anne Bancroft, Where Have You Gone, Mrs. Robinson?
(co-authored with Stanley Mills Haggart)

Veronica Lake, The Peek-a-Boo Girl

Running Wild in Babylon, Confessions of a Hollywood Press Agent

HISTORIES

Thurlow Weed, Whig Kingpin

Chester A. Arthur, Gilded Age Coxcomb in the White House

Discover Old America, What's Left of It

CUISINE

Food For Love, Hussar Recipes from the Austro-Hungarian Empire,
with collaboration from the cabaret chanteuse, Greta Keller

AND COMING SOON, FROM BLOOD MOON

Playboy's Hugh Hefner
Empire of Skin

A Word About Phraseologies:

Since we at Blood Moon weren't privy to long-ago conversations as they were unfolding, we have relied on the memories of our sources for the conversational tone and phraseologies of what we've recorded within the pages of this book.

This writing technique, as it applies to modern biography, has been defined as "conversational storytelling" by *The New York Times,* which labeled it as an acceptable literary device for "engaging reading."

Blood Moon is not alone in replicating "as remembered" dialogues from dead sources. Truman Capote and Norman Mailer were pioneers of direct quotes, and today, they appear in countless other memoirs, ranging from those of Eddie Fisher and Debbie Reynolds to those of the long-time mistress (Verita Thompson) of Humphrey Bogart.

Of course, some people have expressed displeasure in the fact that direct quotes and "as remembered" dialogue have become a standard—some would say "mandatory"—fixture in pop culture biographies today.

But in the case of this book, the conversations we've transcribed derive from the authors' recollections, and from the recollections of the people they interviewed. They were not accumulated as word-for-word transcripts, but as retellings that accurately evoke the intentions, nuances, and essence of what was said at the time.

With thanks for your interest in our work, and with a sense of grace and charity to all parties noted in this book, living and dead, from

Danforth Prince
President and Founder
Blood Moon Productions

RAISED ON A DIET OF JACKRABBITS AND RATTLESNAKES, AN IMPOVERISHED EL PASO TOMBOY MORPHS INTO

MISS BURBANK

OF 1948

MGM AND WARNERS WANT HER FOR A

SCREEN TEST

BUT HER CHURCH WARNS HER MOTHER THAT SHE'LL BURN IN THE FIRES OF HELL

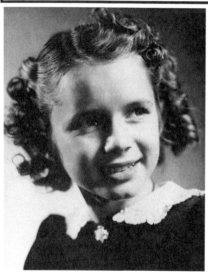 

"As a little girl from Texas, I knew I was not beautiful—cute, perhaps, certainly not an ugly dog. Who would think I would grow up to marry an idolized singer worthy of being stolen from me by that fabled beauty, Elizabeth Taylor?"

"I never thought I'd win when I entered the Miss Burbank contest of 1948. What I wanted was a free blouse given to all girls who competed. My dad thought my entering was a joke. But here I am, with a crown, robes, and throne borrowed from the wardrobe and props department at nearby Warner Brothers. Not only that—the fools even offered me a movie contract."

In El Paso, Texas, it was the last night of March in the year 1932. Beginning around 8 that evening, and continuing into the pre-dawn hours, a sirocco-like wind had sent gusts into the area from the enveloping Chihuahuan Desert. It powered the movement of tumbleweeds that rolled across the oil-streaked frontyard of a two-room shanty in back of a gas station.

Inside the sparsely furnished bedroom, Maxene Reynolds, nicknamed Minnie, was entering the last hours of her pregnancy. When she was eighteen, two years before, she'd given birth to a son, Billy. Her husband, Ray, 26, had stayed up with her most of the night planning at any moment to rush her to the emergency room of the local hospital.

She was a devoted, almost fanatical, member of the Church of Nazarene, with its strict, even Draconian, religious mandates. The hillbilly pastor there, who had migrated from the hills of Kentucky, had imbued her with superstitions. He'd warned her that infants born on the upcoming April Fool's Day were sentenced to a life of turmoil, pain, and sorrow.

Her "gut instinct," as she called it, told her that she was giving birth to a baby girl. Before Billy had been put to bed that night, she'd told him, "Son, you're going to have a baby sister." He was too young to know what she was really predicting.

Ray had already made his feelings clear: "I don't want another snotty-nosed kid in this house. I can hardly put food on the table for three of us." On many a late afternoon, right before sunset over the desert, he wandered there with his rifle and returned home with a jackrabbit. After skinning, it, he handed it over to Minnie to cook over a hot plate, since they didn't have a stove.

There was also no running water in the shanty, except in the sink of a toilet in back of the garage, which was used by all the station's patrons and always carried the strong stench of urine.

During the night, Minnie and Ray used a chamberpot, flushing its contents down the gas station's toilet stool every morning.

Before she gave birth, Minnie had argued with Ray about what to name their child, as-

Debbie's parents, Maxene and Ray Reynolds.

Maxene's flapper-length skirt was a departure from her usual more modest, more covered-up dress code.

2

suming it would be a girl. He preferred Maxie Pearl, but she wanted to call her Mary Frances. As a devout Nazarene, she nearly always gave in to the wishes of her husband, saying, "The man who wears the pants rules the roost." But on this occasion, she held out for Mary Frances and got her wish.

She was rushed to the hospital around 6AM on the dreaded April Fool's Day. In the years to come, her family called the baby girl "Sis," and she kept the name of Mary Frances throughout her years in school, only changing it later in Hollywood when she was renamed "Debbie Reynolds."

Except for some oil-rich millionaires and some ranchers with large acreage, Texas had been severely wounded in the Great Depression that had swept across the land. As Butterfly McQueen might have said in a high-pitched voice in *Gone With the Wind*, "It was no time to be birthing babies."

During the day, Ray worked at the gas station, mending cars and tinkering under the hoods of many a vehicle that had long outlived its dependable days on the road. In front of the station, resting on bricks, was a wheel-less Model-A, long stripped of all of its usable parts.

Two days after delivering her second child, Minnie, in a feedsack dress, was out pumping gas again and washing layers of grime blown in from the desert off windshields.

Winters in El Paso were bitterly cold. At night, the Reynolds family huddled around a coal-burning, pot-bellied stove, the only heat source in their shanty. Sometimes, the wind was so strong it hurled an object against one of their window panes, breaking it. Always short of money, Ray replaced the glass with cardboard.

Windy blasts from the desert were often severe. One afternoon, Mary Frances was battered when she collided with a giant tumbleweed that the wind seemed to aim at her directly, immersing her in its tangle of thorns, its spiny claws digging into her arms and legs and scratching her face, causing her to bleed. The more she fought against its fury, the more she injured herself. Finally, she broke free of its embrace, watching with relief as the monster tumbleweed was carried away on another wind current and into the desert. She arrived back at the shanty all bloodied.

American Gothic, painted in 1930 by Grant Wood, revealed grain-belt sobriety and the steadfastness of the American spirit better than anything ever depicted on canvas.

Debbie emerged from such a stern, unforgiving world.

3

In spite of their dire poverty, Minnie would always insist that the Reynolds family was middle class. In contrast, Debbie Reynolds, years later, would say, "If we were middle class, what was lower class? Those sleeping in the desert with the coyotes?"

The bleak landscape around their shanty was hazardous. Pregnant rattlesnakes would produce broods even more poisonous than the scorpions which sometimes invaded their shanty. With his rifle, Ray often shot a reptile in the head, his family then being served fried rattlesnake meat for supper.

After a year, Ray lost his job at the gas station, as customers had dwindled to barely enough to sustain its owner, who thereafter worked alone. He had lost his modest home in a mortgage foreclosure and needed to move his family into the shanty occupied by the Reynolds.

Left homeless, Ray was very inventive, getting work repairing other homes, some no more than shanties. He moved his family into the shelters he was at the time restoring or repairing. When there was no roof, they lived in the cellars of these houses. When they were ready, he moved his wife and two children into the next house he restored. But as the Depression deepened, he found no more restoration work, because nobody had any money.

Franklin D. Roosevelt had campaigned for and won the presidency of the United States the year Mary Frances was born. He launched a program for the poor called the Works Progress Administration (WPA). Ray got a job with the WPA which paid two dollars a day, twice what he'd made at the filling station.

In 1932, when she was six months old, Mary Frances, the future Debbie Reynolds, faced a camera for the first time, not knowing that she'd become one of the most photographed women of the 20th Century.

In the upper photo, at age 3½, she stands before their shanty with her devoted brother, Billy, posing for a portrait of two Depression-era kids.

He saved enough money to move his family into another shanty, this one on Magnolia Street, which had the cheapest houses. The neighbors of the Reynolds were called "chicanos," of mixed Mexican and Indian ancestry. Many of these families had originally fled to El Paso, crossing the Rio Grande during the Mexican revolution of 1910.

After the WPA job folded, Ray got another position as a carpenter for the Southern Pacific Railroad. That lasted for five months. Out of work, he could no longer afford rent on the Magnolia Street shanty.

With nowhere to go, Minnie arranged for them to move into her family home, which was a three-room shanty occupied by Mary Frances' Grandpa and Grandma Harman and their four sons. The Reynolds moved in, ten people sharing one bathroom.

In a memoir, Debbie wrote: "My brother and I slept with our heads at the top of the bed, and my young uncles at the foot of that bed. I woke up every morning with toes in my nose."

Sometimes in the late afternoon, Ray would take the hand of Mary Frances and walk down to the railroad tracks to watch the freight trains rumble along.

He told her that one day, he'd ride those rails to California, the land of milk and honey, where he'd go to work and earn enough money for a home there so he could send for Minnie and the kids. "The day will come when you've eaten your last jackrabbit, your last rattlesnake."

Back home at night, Minnie and Mary Frances sat out on the un-screened front porch, enjoying the moonlight, since the inside of their shanty was like living in a furnace. Waiting for the night to cool down, Minnie sometimes fashioned locks of her daughter's hair into spit curls.

Mary Frances wandered by herself down to the railway tracks. She, too, dreamed of going to California, land of movie stars and palm and orange trees. There, she might grow up and follow her dream of becoming a gym teacher.

At the tracks, she often looked on in fascination at

Though not specifically of either Debbie or her brother Billy, this photo depicts equivalent children with their goats in rural Texas during the Depression-ravaged 1930s. Life was hard, money scarce.

the homeless, shabbily dressed men, and sometimes women, who rode the rails, going from town to town looking for a meal or some work. At times, the El Paso police descended, handcuffing some of the men and hauling them off to jail, with the intention of running them out of town.

Sometimes, a mother, often with children in tow, would show up at the backdoor of the Harman shanty begging for food. Grandma Harman always kept a pot of beans and rice on the stove. She'd fill up a tinplate and have Mary Frances take it out to the starving itinerants.

One day, a tall, handsome, bearded stranger knocked on their back door. As she remembered it, "He was poorly dressed, his shirt in tatters, but I had never seen such a good-looking man in my life. He stood tall and proud, in spite of his poverty, and he had a well-muscled body. He'd been in construction, but had been laid off and couldn't find work."

"I had never met a man this beautiful until I went to Hollywood and found myself shaking the hand of Robert Wagner," she said. "I brought him a pail of water so he could wash the dirt off his face, and then I took him a tinplate of rice and beans, which he devoured. Before he left, he kissed my hand in gratitude. It gave me goose bumps. I found it thrilling I'd never felt a man's lips on my body. My father never kissed me."

***

"My mother prayed night and day," Mary Frances said. "We went to church all the time—prayer meetings on Wednesday, prayer suppers on Friday, perhaps a Saturday afternoon church picnic. Long sermons on Sunday morning after I attended Sunday school."

To go church, Minnie sewed two gray dresses—one for herself, another for Mary Frances. It was forbidden for women to wear red, yellow, or green. Blue was acceptable, but only in its darkest shades. Many of the older women, especially those who had lost their husbands, showed up in black. To bring some color into the church, Minnie and her daughter sometimes picked wildflowers in the fields. They were abundant after heavy rainfalls.

Founded in the 19th century, the Church of the Nazarene was one of the strictest of the Protestant sects. Alcohol and gambling were strictly forbidden, as were cigarettes. Any form of dancing, including harmless square dances, was also taboo.

When she was fourteen, Minnie had secretly entered a Charleston contest and won the first prize, which included an award of ten dollars. When her father found out about it, he "horsewhipped" his daughter.

As long as she lived, Grandpa Harman told his granddaughter, "Mary

Frances Reynolds, don't you ever dance. If you do, you'll burn in hell's fire."

"Don't worry, Grandpa," she answered. "I don't even know how to dance."

Singing, however, providing that it was strictly religious in its focus, was all right. Minnie found that her daughter had a reasonably good voice, and the pastor at the church also allowed her to precede his sermon with a little song at the altar. She got up every Sunday and delivered a rendition of songs that included "Jesus Loves Me, This I Know."

Billy and Ray did not go to church with Minnie and Mary Frances. Billy wanted to grow up to be a baseball star, and Ray was an excellent player himself. The only day they had free to play the game was on Sunday.

Reacting to that, the pastor of their church visited them late one Saturday afternoon, informing them that it was against the teachings of their church to play baseball on God's day. Faced with a choice of church or baseball, Billy and Ray chose baseball.

Hard as it might seem to imagine, one of the entertainment industry's hippest and most sophisticated performers emerged from the morally rigorous context of the evangelical Christian sect known as the Church of the Nazarene

Depicted above are the accumulated faithful of an equivalent congregation in Little Rock, Arkansas in 1938, around the time of the sect's influence over Maxene and Ray. Strict rules as imposed on Debbie by her mother included no dancing, no fripperies, and no nonsense.

In addition to her regular church, Minnie took her daughter to every big revival held under a big tent, pitched by *Elmer Gantry* types who came to El Paso to rant about the fire and brimstone that awaited sinners. That was followed by passing out the collection plate, most often to men and women in the audiences who could hardly spare a quarter.

In addition to learning how to sing, Mary Frances was taught how to "cuss," as it was called. Her Uncle Owen had once served in the Coast Guard, where he'd picked up "a sailor's vocabulary." He taught his niece a number of curse words.

One Saturday afternoon, some grim-faced ladies from the Nazarene Church gathered for a quilting bee with Minnie. At one point, Owen sent Mary Frances in to address the ladies after coaching and rehearsing her in a handful of obscenities. To the assembled church ladies, she said, "God damn it, Mommie, *some-of-a-bitch* and holy shit!"

When the ladies departed in horror, Mary Frances received "the whipping of my life."

Years later, Debbie Reynolds, who always seemed squeaky-clean on screen, shocked her audiences at public appearances by using such words as "Fucking," "Asshole," and "Prick."

Sadly, Mary Frances was not allowed to see a movie. From her girlfriends, she'd heard so much about Hollywood. But the congregation of the Nazarene Church was forbidden to go to one of the movie houses in El Paso, two of which showed only Mexican films.

However, after school, she visited the theaters, which always had large posters outside displaying the latest films. She'd stop and stare at the posters and would remember them years later. Her favorite had been Greta Garbo and Robert Taylor performing in *Camille* in 1937. "Both of them looked so beautiful. I didn't realize that a man and a woman could look that gorgeous."

She was always given a penny to put into the collection plate, but she sometimes managed to steal a dime, the cost of a movie ticket, as part of the process. Although it was forbidden, she sneaked away to watch stars of the

California Dreaming....In vivid contrast to the austerity of Depression-ravaged El Paso, Debbie worshipped at the temple of love, romance, and GARBO, depicted above with Robert Taylor in *Camille*.

1930s emote on the screen.

The first experience Mary Frances ever had outside El Paso was to the Mexican city of Juárez, directly across the Rio Grande. Before they got there, Minnie had warned her it was a wicked hellhole that would one day be destroyed by God the way he'd demolished Sodom and Gomorrah.

"I saw painted women walking the streets of town, smoking cigarettes," Mary Frances recalled. "Young men standing on street corners shouted things at them in Spanish. Some of them were drinking from bottles of what they called *cerveza.*"

She would always remember one woman forever. She wore a fiery red dress showing off a great deal of her bosom, and she heavily coated her mouth with lipstick and the area above her eyes with mascara. She stood on red high heels. But what caught Mary Frances' attention were the large ornaments that dangled from each of her ears. She'd never seen such earrings until she sat through her first Carmen Miranda movie. "As she walked, this Mexican whore wickedly swayed her hips," Mary Frances said. "I would not see that walk again until I went to see Marilyn Monroe in *Niagara* in 1953."

Before leaving Juárez, the Reynolds family witnessed a catfight between two women over a tall Mexican cowboy. Mary Frances heard the word *cabróna* ("bitch") shouted, but at the time, didn't know what it meant.

***

As related in her first memoir, Mary Frances, age six, was introduced to sex…well, sort of. As she was walking past the garage adjacent to her shanty, she heard the sounds of boys giggling inside. She wondered what kind of game they were playing. Unknown to her at the time, the two boys inside the darkened garage were masturbating. She opened the door only slightly, peering inside, then decided to enter to find out what was happening.

As she did, two boys grabbed her and began tickling her and yanking at her dress. One of them pulled the dress up to her chest. As she struggled to free herself, she screamed for help. Her brother Billy heard her call.

He rushed over and tore into the garage, pulling the boys off her. Grabbing her arm, he yanked her along as she was crying, back into their shanty. He told Minnie what had happened, blaming everything on his sister for going into that garage in the first place. Minnie warned, "Curiosity killed the cat."

She fetched a pail of water to wash the dirt off her daughter. "Boys are wicked. They want only one thing from a girl and often will stop at nothing to get it. Never trust a boy. Never be caught alone with one. He'll attack you!"

This was disappointing news to her. As a tomboy, she wanted to play with Billy and his friends, but was always rejected.

Not only would they not let her join in the fun, the boys tormented her, pulling at her pigtails or twisting her arm. Once, three boys tied her up and forced her into a large hole in the rear of the house. There, they began shoveling dirt over her body, as if planning to bury her alive. Terrified, she screamed out once again, and once again, Billy came to her rescue. "For a girl," he said, "you sure know how to find trouble."

In the days ahead, that almost became a prophecy. One afternoon, as she was walking home from school, two high school boys, no more than sixteen or seventeen, pulled up beside the curb in a souped-up jalopy. "Hi, I'm Stevie," said the boy in the passenger seat. He was a handsome, blonde-haired boy with a friendly smile. The driver was a boy about the same age, who had darker skin and didn't say anything. The blonde asked her, "Wanna go for a ride?"

She told them she'd be thrilled to do that. Whereas Billy's friends would not let her join in their games, here were two older boys inviting her for a ride into the country.

En route away from town, Stevie offered her a stick of chewing gum, which she loved. It was a treat usually denied to her.

She sat between the two boys, chewing her gum—"and feeling just great," she recalled. Outside of town, the driver turned down an old dirt road that led through a forest. At one point, he stopped the car.

To her shock, Stevie unzipped his pants, producing an erection, which in a memoir, she described as a "tall thing sticking up."

He ordered her to "lick it," comparing its taste to that of a lollipop. She'd seen her young uncles and her brother nude, since they shared the same quarters, but she'd never seen a man at full mast.

He offered to hold her chewing gum while she serviced him.

"It won't hurt," Stevie assured her. "You'll like it."

She did as she was instructed.

Years later, when she recalled this milestone in her life to friends in Hollywood, she said, "As all of you know, it didn't taste like a lollipop at all. But I fulfilled the request. One thing I've learned over the years: All you have to do with a hot teenager is to give a few licks, and they're shooting off like a rocket to the moon."

Without having said a word, the driver drove Stevie and her back into town, letting her off five blocks from her home. She chose not to mention the incident to her mother.

Three months later, she heard a story going around El Paso about Stevie, the same boy who'd offered her "a taste of the lollipop." He'd taken an eight-year-old girl to Juárez. His father tracked him down and drove Stevie to the desert, where he castrated him and left him to die. Fortunately, he was discovered by a motorist and rushed to the hospital. He'd spend the rest of his life missing one vital part of his anatomy.

When Minnie repeated the story, Mary Frances said, "Oh, Mommy, that's the same boy who had me lick his thing."

Minnie became hysterical, storming around the shanty screaming. "She didn't blame me," Mary Frances said. "But I learned my lesson well. Beware of boys who unzip their pants and ask you to do things to their thing."

***

The Southern Pacific Railroad had been forced to lay off Ray Reynolds, but by 1939, business was returning to its pre-Depression levels. The company had liked his work, and he was offered a job as a carpenter in Los Angeles if he would move west.

Since the job outlook remained bleak in El Paso, he made what he called "the second biggest decision of my life," the first having been his marriage to Minnie. The pay scale was still minimal, and he knew he'd have to leave his family for about a year until he saved enough to send for them.

There were tears in El Paso at the railway station when Minnie, Billy, and Mary Frances had to tell the man of the house good-bye, not certain when they would see him again.

When he arrived in Los Angeles, Ray put himself on a starvation budget, opting to send money back to El Paso to feed his family. He also set money aside with the intention of eventually sending for them. To economize, he didn't even rent a cheap hotel room, but carried a blanket to MacArthur Park every night and slept

Historians credit the growth of the railroads with the Westward expansion of America's Manifest Destiny.

During the Depression, Debbie's father wangled a job as a carpenter with the Southern Pacific Railroad, working on a locomotive akin to what appears above in this photo taken in 1937.

in the open. When it rained, he found a nest in an old storage room owned by the city. At a very cheap Mexican restaurant, he ordered a plate of rice and beans for ten cents.

At long last, on December 24, 1939, months after England and Nazi Germany had gone to war against each other, railway tickets were sent for his family in El Paso.

Mary Frances remembered the day she kissed Grandpa and Grandpa Harmon goodbye, not knowing if she'd ever see them again. She was seven years old.

The railroad had generously offered the family an entire boxcar to carry their household goods. Minnie found ample space to haul their antique Model A in the boxcar, too.

At Southern Pacific's Alhambra Station (demolished in the mid-1980s), six miles east of Los Angeles, Ray was waiting for the arrival of the Sunset Limited, hugging and kissing his wife when she descended from the train. He embraced Billy, and for the first time in his life, he planted a kiss on the brow of Mary Frances.

It had been cold and rainy the morning the family left El Paso, but the day was bright and sunny in California. She later compared it to Dorothy landing in Oz. Starring Judy Garland, *The Wizard of Oz* had just been released.

Everything she saw was foreign to her, a city of orange trees and palms. It was a warm day in Southern California, and the air was dry. Compared to Shantytown in El Paso, the new land looked fresh and clean.

Unknown to her at the time, she set foot in Hollywood during what film historians cite as its greatest year for film production: 1939.

One classic movie after another was playing at local theaters, none more notable than *Gone With the Wind,* cast with Clark Gable and Vivien Leigh playing Rhett Butler and Scarlett O'Hara.

Robert Donat would win the Best Actor Oscar that year for *Goodbye, Mr. Chips.* There were so many other great pictures, and Mary Frances wanted to see all of them, especially Laurence Olivier in *Wuthering Heights;* Mickey Rooney in *Babes in Arms;* John Wayne in *Stagecoach;* and James Stewart in *Mr. Smith Goes to Washington.* Bette Davis had released *Dark Victory;* Irene Dunne *Love Affair;* and Greta Garbo *Ninotchka.*

In her memoirs, Debbie wrote that she'd never seen a movie in her life until her family moved to California. That was not true.

Los Angeles wasn't a fantasyland, as Mary Frances found out on the day of her arrival. In their just-offloaded Model A, Ray drove them to a seedy motel, which was filled mostly with migrant workers from Mexico. Many of its rooms housed entire families. Later, Ray upgraded their accommodations, moving all of them into a boarding house in Glendale.

On Sunday morning, instead of going to church, Ray piled the family into his Model A and drove them around the various suburbs of Los Angeles, looking for an acre of land that was real cheap. Only once did they pass through expensive acreage when he drove across Toluca Lake, pointing out the luxurious homes of Bing Crosby and Bob Hope. It was beyond the imagination of Mary Frances that one day, she'd be befriended by both entertainers, even appearing with them.

After surveying the mansions, Ray said, "Out of our price range, unless Billy becomes the second Joe DiMaggio."

At long last, after much searching, Ray discovered a plot of land in the San Fernando Valley, which had not yet been built up in those days. The address was 1034 Evergreen in Burbank. On the block which they desired, there were only four other homes, each newly erected. A bus stop three blocks away would take one to the center of Burbank, with all its stores. Although still relatively undeveloped, the neighborhood did possess a small pharmacy and a grocery store with a very limited selection of food.

For only $250, Ray dug into his meager savings and bought the land. With a loan of $4,000 from the Federal Housing Authority (FHA), he set about building a house himself. Not only was he a skilled carpenter, but he could also install the plumbing and wiring.

For the first time in her life, Mary Frances had her own bedroom. It was no more that the size of a typical pantry, but it was hers, and she could retreat there for privacy and day-dreaming. There was even a small closet, even though she had only two or three garments to hang inside.

On her first day at school, she felt like an outcast. The rest of her schoolmates had nice, clean clothes, and she showed up in a man's shirt and Billy's hand-me-down pants. Her battered penny loafers were used and from the Salvation Army.

For food, Minnie, often with Mary

"I had arrived in the land of dreams, California. It seemed that every girl in my class wanted to grow up to become a movie star. Not me! I wanted to become a gym teacher."

"In the movies, I saw Judy Garland and Gene Kelly kissing, Van Johnson smooching June Allyson. If being a movie star meant I had to do something that disgusting, count me out."

Frances, went directly to the farmers themselves. It came as a surprise to find most of them were owned by Japanese Americans.

Half a mile away, Minnie found a farm growing Concord grapes. Once she purchased two bushels, her family devouring the succulent first batch. From the remainder, she made jams and jellies.

Their own meager grounds had once been part of an asparagus farm, and that vegetable still grew wild. "We had asparagus almost every night," Mary Frances said. "Ray brought home bushels of potatoes, carrots, or onions from other farms. All we lacked was some meat for the stewpot." They often bought liver, since most shoppers considered that meat undesirable. "It was cheap, filling, and better than rattlesnake," she claimed.

In the days before Christmas of 1940, Ray watched boxcars of Christmas trees being unloaded from Oregon. But he could not afford one, so he waited until midnight and then sneaked into a neighbor's yard and cut off a section of a hedge. Back home, Mary Frances decorated it with homemade ornaments. There was no money for presents.

Minnie discovered a local branch of the Church of the Nazarene, and she insisted that Mary Frances accompany her there every Sunday. Later, they'd join Billy and Ray in North Hollywood Park for a picnic lunch and to watch them play baseball.

Mary Frances remembered the first time the family went to the beach at Malibu, and she gazed upon the Pacific Ocean. She was already an expert swimmer, and—despite her mother's objections—she saved money from babysitting at 35¢ an hour, and bought herself a one-piece bathing suit in royal blue. She wore that Jantzen so much, it developed a hole in its seat.

In Burbank, Debbie became a Girl Scout for life. World War II was raging.

"As a scout, I not only sold cookies, I led paper drives. We collected bottles, got the deposits. All the money we made, we donated to the War Relief. We were afraid the Japs would invade California."

On rare occasions, the family went on budget camping trips in the desert or to the mountains in the distance.

Billy had joined the Boy Scouts, and Mary Frances followed in his footsteps. In her first year, she won forty-two out of a possible 100 Girl Scout merit badges. Even as a girl, she proclaimed, "When I die, I want to be the world's oldest Girl Scout."

***

Every day on the way to school, Mary Frances passed the formidable pink walls of Warner Brothers. A bustling city within a city, it turned out gangster pictures starring Edward G. Robinson, Humphrey Bogart, George Raft, or James Cagney. For women, it offered Bette Davis movies, or else Olivia de Havilland. Ronald Reagan could be counted on for B movies, and Errol Flynn, whether playing Captain Blood or Robin Hood, was the king of swashbucklers. It seemed that every girl in her class, except Mary Frances herself, wanted to be a movie star, perhaps the next Betty Grable or Lana Turner. "I was just too plain to ever think I could be a movie goddess," she said.

She didn't want to watch heavy dramas, preferring comedies and musicals instead. Betty Hutton soon became her favorite actress, and throughout her reign in the 1940s, Mary Frances never missed a zany Hutton movie.

Sometimes, she'd sit in the movie house and watch "the blonde bombshell" through three showings. Hutton had a vigorous vocal technique and perfect comedic timing, and was loud and raucous on screen, with unforgettable brio and brass.

At home, Mary Frances imitated Hutton's routines, and found she was a natural at impersonations, something she would do as a performer for the rest of her life. In time, she would perfectly imitate such stars as James Stewart, Bette Davis, Zsa Zsa Gabor, and especially Mae West.

Mary Frances' favorite movie star was Betty Hutton. One critic wrote, "Hutton belted, hoofed, grinded, smirked, goofed, and mugged. If not a bombshell, she's at least a hand grenade."

Mary Frances learned Hutton's routines and delivered a dead-on impression, launching a lifelong knack for impersonating famous stars from Mae West to Zsa Zsa Gabor.

By now an ardent fan, Debbie drew up a list of her favorites—not just Hutton, but Judy Garland, Betty Grable, Fred Astaire, Frank Sinatra, Gene Kelly, June Allyson, and Rita Hayworth.

The Girl Scouts periodically put on shows, and she was asked to appear in them.

The first time she went on stage was to impersonate Hutton. She'd seen her play Dorothy Lamour's manic roommate in *The Fleet's In* (1942), starring William Holden. Mary Frances perfected her number, "Arthur Murray Taught Me Dancing in a Hurry." After she'd performed it, the audience clapped wildly.

When she wasn't being a Girl Scout or doing impersonations, she fought the bullies in the schoolyard. Even though they were much bigger than she was, she battled them like a tigress, on one occasion pulling out a boy's hair. "I stood four feet, eight inches, and I weighed only sixty-two pounds, but I was like a stick of dynamite. I found out that boys have a vulnerable spot. Grab their little balls and squeeze with all your might. I practically castrated many a boy. I also socked them, stomped them, grabbed their heads and butted them together, and pounded their noses until the blood gushed. Thanks to my Uncle Owen, I could cuss better than any boy in the schoolyard."

"Even at an early age, I was a virtual Olympic athlete," she recalled. "Bar work, the rings, triple flips, back flips, front flips. No mere boy was my equal. Even though I was a midget, I became the captain of the basketball team. I was so short I could run between a boy's legs and emerge to hit the basket."

"There was one real bully, Jimmy somebody, who wouldn't let me alone, always pestering me, pulling my hair and hitting me. One afternoon, I went on our grounds and slowly gathered a quart jar of worms. The next day at school, I poured the squiggly creatures all over him. He looked like he was

"My first official date was to the school prom. Jerry Odens was tall and good looking. Minnie bought me this second-hand black dress and added the pink tulle and black net. The gold sandals cost $1.99."

"When Jerry took me home, I warned him, 'No funny business. I'm not that kind of gal.'"

Debbie (center) plays the French horn, a tune on which she later considered for performance during the Miss Burbank contest.

being eaten alive by worms. In the future, Jimmy gave me wide berth when he saw me coming. I told him the next animal attack on him would be a nest of deadly baby rattlers."

"At that stage of my life, boys were someone to beat up, not to love," she said. "Minnie told me that boys were dirty and wanted to do dirty things with girls. I'd already had a sexual experience when I was six, when that young Texan ordered me 'to lick it.'"

At Girl Scout camp, she experienced her first menstruation. "I thought I was going to bleed to death. It really scared me. I was too afraid to tell mother, so I kept it a secret. Sex education at the Reynolds house did not exist."

"I don't think my mother was very sexual at all," she said. "She and Daddy had the room next to mine, and the walls were thin. He would demand sex, and force her, against her will, to submit. Instead of sounds of ecstasy, all I heard was her crying during the actual act itself. She must have hated it."

***

After the Japanese attack on Pearl Harbor on December 7, 1941, a major change swept across Burbank. President Franklin D. Roosevelt ordered the arrest of all Japanese Americans living in the area. They were rounded up in their homes, corralled into trucks, and transported to concentration camps, their farmlands seized. During the war, they were assigned shanties to live in.

In their places, new settlers, many drawn to employment at the Lockheed war plant, migrated to the San Fernando Valley, erecting homes on the farmland taken from the Japanese.

Burbank was growing overnight, and its rapid growth and fast changes were baffling to Mary Frances. Even the movie studio began turning out war propaganda movies. She read that some of her favorite stars, including Robert Taylor, Clark Gable, and James Stewart, had joined the military.

At night, her family blanketed their windows, the people of Burbank fearing a Japanese bombardment.

Early one evening, Ray took both Billy and Mary Frances to Hollywood to see all the changes, including the recently established USO and the Hollywood Canteen. It had been founded by Bette Davis and John Garfield to entertain servicemen, many of whom were departing for unknown destinations in the Pacific theater of war, some never to return.

The Reynolds brood strolled along the Strip between Hollywood and

Sunset Boulevards, which swarmed with men in uniform. Almost overnight, honky-tonks had opened to cater to these young men, along with pinball parlors and photo galleries. Many servicemen were snapping "final pictures" to send back to their families in the Middle West or wherever. Dances were held to sell war bonds, and Hollywood was turned into an entertainment mecca of a different stripe, replete with amusements that included more than just films.

One arena was opened to view from the street, and Mary Frances stared in fascination at all the dancing going on. She remembered one sailor "who might put Fred Astaire to shame."

Years later, she would claim she did not know how to dance until she began to make pictures. That was not true. Her schoolmates back in El Paso remembered her first date with a boy, Jerry Odens.

A classmate, Sue Broy, recalled, "I saw Mary Frances and Jerry jitterbugging, and they were fantastic. They also could do the Lindy and were the best foxtrotters on the floor—in fact, they won several dance contests at school."

Dancing maneuvers that Mary Frances wouldn't do involved any step that involved intimate body contact. "Some girls in my class let boys dance so close to them that their things go hard," she said. "I never wanted that to happen to me. If, in the future, I ever took up with a boy, and that is highly doubtful, I will want a guy who is honest and true, one who will adore me and treat me fairly, and who will not demand sex like my daddy does to my mother. I know from her crying and groaning that sex is very painful for a woman to endure, much less a girl. Frankly, sex should not be performed by some boy to give him a thrill, but only when a man and his wife want to have a child."

***

Mary Frances was "sweet sixteen" on May Day, 1948, when she and her friend, Norma Harris, strolled down Magnolia Boulevard in Burbank. Both girls stopped in front of Clark's Dress Shop, which displayed postwar summer fashions which neither of them could afford. In a corner of the window was an advertisement touting the upcoming Miss Burbank contest, sponsored by the Chamber of Commerce and Lockheed Aircraft, which at the time employed many of the local residents.

Any girl entering the contest would receive a white silk blouse and a scarf. At Recreation Hall, she signed up and was given the clothing items, although she had no intention of actually competing. "Burbank is filled with beautiful girls," she told Norma. "I wouldn't stand a chance."

18

At dinner with her family that night, she announced what she'd done.

"Girl, you must be joking," Ray said. "A beauty contest? *Miss Burbank?* Just who do you think you are? Betty Grable?"

She confessed she had entered the contest only as a means of receiving the scarf and blouse.

He pondered that for a minute before announcing, "Then you've got to go through with it. Otherwise, you'd be a liar and a cheat."

She gave in to his demand. The contest called for both beauty and talent. Previously, she had saved up enough money to buy a Jantzen bathing suit, but had worn it so often that she'd worn a hole in the seat. Minnie volunteered to patch it for her.

For the talent part of the contest, Mary Frances thought she might play "Pomp and Circumstance" on the French horn, which she'd done so well before.

She was told that she had to wear high heels on the stage, and she didn't own a pair. On a visit to the home of the best-dressed girl in her school, Patty Hockensmith, she borrowed a pair of chunky shoes with four-inch heels. At the time, they were jokingly known in Hollywood as "Joan Crawford fuck-me shoes."

She set about learning to walk in these towering high heels. At first, she tottered around the living room, nearly toppling over several times. She was hampered by the fact that she wore a size two and Patty a size four, but she was determined, fearing that she'd fall down on stage.

On the night of the contest, her friend, Jerry Odens, told her that two talent scouts, one from MGM, another from Warners, were judges. He was referring to Solly Baiano from Warners and Al Trescone from MGM. The third judge, Ruth Birch, was an independent talent scout.

Mary Frances stood in the wings as thirty-two girls performed. Two of the contestants tap-danced, as if trying to be the next Eleanor Powell or Ann Miller. Another delivered a scene once depicted by Katharine Hepburn in *Little Women* (1933).

Finally, the last contestant, #33, was called, and Mary Frances, wobbling on her high heels, came onto the stage with a Victrola. She lip-synched "I'm a Square in the Social Circle," giving her best Betty Hutton impersonation. [*The ever bubbly Hutton had sung the song in her film,* The Stork Club, *released in 1945.*]

Shortly after her performance, even though the audience roared its approval, she was seen attempting to exit from the Recreation Hall, but one of the contest's organizers stopped her, saying that none of the contestants could leave until the winner was announced.

She was the most shocked person in the auditorium when she heard the announcer proclaim, "Miss Mary Frances Reynolds is Miss Burbank of 1948." For the next two weeks, she reigned as the Queen of Burbank, appearing in parades and festivities.

Baiano and Trescone met her at the end of the contest, each wanting her to submit to a screen test. After the flip of a coin, Baiano won for Warner Brothers. "I think I can sell her to Jack Warner, although he's not putting many people under contract these days."

The next day, Baiano put through a call to Ray, her father, asking him if he, or perhaps her mother, would bring Mary Frances to Warners for a screen test. Ray had never seen a movie, not one movie, in his entire life, and he didn't know what a screen test was. He claimed he would talk it over with Mary Frances and his wife.

That night, in the middle of dinner, he turned to Mary Frances. "I got a call from this guy at Warners. He wants you to walk up the street and make a screen test. It seems that some of those jerks think you should be in the movies. Why, I don't know."

"I've never heard anything so ridiculous," Minnie said.

"What can you do in pictures?" Ray asked. "Ride a horse as a Texas cowgirl?"

"I play the French horn," she answered. "The conductor of the Burbank Youth Symphony Orchestra says I'm pretty good at 'Pomp and Circumstance.'"

"Just a minute," Minnie interrupted, slamming her fork down against her plate. "No one asked me what I think about Mary Frances signing a movie contract. I'll have to talk to the pastor or a deacon at the Church of the Nazarene. I don't want any daughter of mine sentenced to the eternal flames of hell's fire!"

"In borrowed high heels, two sizes too big, and in a worn-out bathing suit, I strutted my stuff in the Miss Burbank contest of 1948."

"I'd worn a big hole in the seat. Minnie had to sew it up; otherwise, the audience would have seen my naked ass."

Chapter Two

MGM CHRISTENS ITS NEWEST STARLET

DEBBIE REYNOLDS

ALTHOUGH SHE REGULARLY DATES AGGRESSIVE HOLLYWOOD WOLVES, SHE REMAINS CHASTE

DEBBIE *"BOOP-BOOP-A-DOOPS"* AND *"ABA DABA DABBAS"* HER WAY TO STARDOM & A MILLION RECORD SALES

When MGM teamed Debbie with Carleton Carpenter for a new version of that 1914 song, "Abba Dabba Honeymoon," no one knew what a spectacular success it would become. "That little bitty number of mine and Carleton horsing around the swing on the back porch became a showstopper. It was embraced by a new generation and sold more than a million records."

When Carleton saw this picture of Debbie and himself, he said, "In case anyone asks, I'm the cute one."

After Sunday services at the Church of Nazarene, Minnie privately approached Deacon Turnbill to ask him if her daughter, Mary Frances, should sign a movie contract with Warner Brothers.

Even though Burbank was a neighbor of what he called "the city of sin" (Hollywood), Turnbill was far removed from it. A gray-haired man of 60, he wore an overly starched white shirt and a suit he'd purchased in 1925 as his "Sunday-go-to-meeting" outfit.

"Warner Brothers will turn your daughter into a modern-day Jezebel," he warned her. "She'll be forced, like the whore of Babylon, to service the male stars, such hideous creatures as Edward G. Robinson. Behind the walls of that studio, I hear there's an orgy going on day and night. If you sign your underaged daughter to work for Warners, we'll have to talk about excommunicating both of you from our church."

With that pronouncement, he turned and walked away.

Although a devout Christian herself, Minnie was not as harsh as Turnbill. She decided Warners couldn't be the Sodom he'd envisioned, and she called Solly Baiano and set up an appointment at the studio.

He invited her to visit at 2PM the following day and was waiting at the gate to show her around. As she later reported, "I didn't see one single orgy." Warners was a bustling factory, turning out movies. She saw many carpenters like her husband building sets. Actors who were dressed up like cowboys and Indians passed her by, as did young girls in late 19th Century show business costumes. She spotted some "pirates" rushing by, and thought that perhaps Errol Flynn was making another one of those swashbuckling pictures like *Captain Blood* (1935).

She reported to her husband over dinner that the studio looked like a safe environment. She'd been taken to a small, one-story building that served as a schoolhouse for Warner contract players, some of them stars, who'd gone to work in pictures before finishing high school. She was introduced to Lois Horne, the school mistress, her gray hair twisted into a bun, who assured Minnie that Mary Frances would find Warners a welcoming place.

"I'll see that your daughter is looked after," Horne promised. "Also, I'll make sure she behaves herself."

In a $12 gray dress with a purple sash purchased at Lerner's, Mary Frances arrived at the gates of Warners where Baiano waited for her. He showed her around the studio, where she spotted Virginia Mayo walking by.

Mary Frances was introduced to Sophie Rosenstein, who taught acting and had just worked with Doris Day, coaching her on her first picture. The pop art blonde and band singer was making her screen debut in *Romance on the High Seas* (1948).

Before leaving Warners that day, Rosenstein gave her a script to take home to rehearse. It was an excerpt from a recent release, *One Sunday Afternoon*, a remake of *Strawberry Blonde* (1941), starring James Cagney, Olivia de Havilland,

and Rita Hayworth.

On the day of her test, although Mary Frances thought she'd have to appear on camera, the test consisted of a reading before Warner executive William Orr, the son-in-law of Jack Warner. *[Orr was married to Joy Page, Jack Warner's stepdaughter.]* Orr found Mary Frances "cute as a bug's ear—perky, sweet, innocent-appearing, perhaps virginal." After her reading, she asked if she could put on a record. Orr granted permission, and when the music started, she lip-synched "Murder, He Says," one of Betty Hutton's rowdy numbers. He didn't like her raucous delivery, and asked her to sing the song in her natural voice, which she did, *a cappella,* and he liked her rendition.

A screen test was scheduled for two days later. Mary Frances sat before a camera and was asked questions about her life. Then, as the cameras continued to roll, she performed three short scenes from previous Warners films.

Baiano phoned Minnie four days later, telling her that Warners was ready to sign a seven-year contract. Mary Frances was in the other room, listening in. She was horrified to hear her mother put her down. "She can't sing. She can't dance. She certainly isn't beautiful." Although none of those negatives was true, Mary Frances had to muffle her tears.

Nevertheless, Minnie walked down the street to the Warner's gate two days later, ready to sign the contract since Debbie was still a minor. She was astonished to learn that Mary Frances would make $65 a week. Her husband brought home only $50 a week. The Warners salary would rise to $75 a week in six months.

Both mother and daughter were informed of the Coogan Bill, a California law that had been legislated in 1939 in response to the plight of child actor Jackie Coogan. He had earned millions of dollars, only to discover, when he became an adult, that his parents had spent almost all of his money. In the well-publicized aftermath of that discovery, the law now demanded that some 15 percent of every underaged actor's earnings would be invested in a trust until the child reached adulthood.

That night at dinner, Ray approved the terms. "Those movie people are nuts. If they want to throw away their money on my daughter, they're welcome to do so."

On her first day as a contract player for Warners, Mary Frances learned that she'd have to spend three hours a day "book learning" with the formidable Miss Horne.

After school, and since there was no immediate film work for her, she wandered around the lot.

"All week, I had stars dancing in my eyes," Mary Frances recalled.

She doubted if she'd ever be a movie star, and still planned to become a gym teacher. She was told the studio had a gym, and she wandered over to it. There, she saw Kirk Douglas training to play a prizefighter in *The Champion* (1949). He was being taught how to box by Mushy Callahan, the former Middleweight Boxing Champion of the World.

As Douglas was resting between rounds, he spotted Mary Frances watching him and ordered her out of the gym.

One morning, when she reported to the little schoolhouse, Miss Horne ordered her to go to Steve Trilling's office. He was in charge of casting, and she rushed to see him in hopes he'd cast her in an upcoming movie.

Trilling informed her that she had to get rid of that name, Mary Frances, "Frances is identified with those Talking Mule movies, and Mary is too common and usually associated with the mother of Jesus," he said. "Our producer, Delmer Daves, recently had a daughter he named Debbie, not Deborah. I want that name for you. From now on, you'll be Debbie. We're still working on your last name."

After that was settled, Trilling told her that Jack Warner wanted to meet her, and that he would walk her over to his office.

She'd once seen him arrive in his shiny Rolls-Royce the color of elephant skin. The moment he got out of his car, two security guards flanked him for his transit into his office.

When Trilling reached his outer office, he turned Debbie over to two secretaries, who escorted her down the hall into Warner's office.

There, she found the mogul on the phone. He glanced up, only to signal her in. The secretaries then departed, after she was shown to a seat. Warner was balding, with a thin mustache. She heard him say, "Like hell we will. No way, Bette!" Then he slammed down the phone.

Jack Warner signed Debbie to a contract, but did not appreciate her talent and soon let her go.

She wondered, "Could that have been Bette Davis on the other end of the line?"

He looked at her for the first time. "Well, Kid, Steve told me you're now Debbie. But the Reynolds has to go. I think I'll name you Debbie Morgan. Dennis Morgan is one of our biggest stars, and I'll borrow his last name."

"Mr. Warner, sir, I can live with the Debbie tag, but I refuse to give up my daddy's name."

That act of defiance might have gotten her kicked out of his office, but

**GIRL WANTS BLOUSE
---GETS FILM CONTRACT**

Because she wanted a blouse, Mary Frances Reynolds, 18, Burbank High School student, won a beauty contest, became "Miss Burbank of 1948"—and a motion picture actress.

Her seven-year contract with Warner Bros. Studio was approved yesterday by Superior Judge Clarence M. Hanson, who ordered her to invest 20% of her earnings in government bonds. The pretty brown-haired girl participated in the beauty contest during "Burbank on Parade," annual civic event. Incidentally, she won the blouse that lured her into participation.

She expects to continue her education at the high school, she said, and is now in the A-11 grade. In addition she will be trained in dramatics at Warner's to prepare for her career.

She is a drum majorette with Burbank's Junior Grenadiers Band.

Miss Reynolds lives with her parents, Mr. and Mrs. R. F. Reynolds, of 1034 N. Evergreen St., Burbank.

This is the first newspaper article about Debbie and the movies. Thousands upon thousands more would follow her for the rest of her life.

When she saw this picture of herself, she winced. "I don't look like a budding movie star—more like one of the Dust Bowl refugees who fled to California."

he seemed to admire her spunk. "OK, if it means that much to you. But whatever your billing, I'll always call you 'The Kid.'"

At the end of their ten-minute meeting, Warner picked up the phone and asked his secretary to get Trilling on the line. As soon as he came on, Warner barked, "Put this kid in a picture…anything."

The next day, Trilling spoke to her. "Debbie Reynolds, we're rushing you into a film that's already being shot. It's the latest Bette Davis picture."

That night, Debbie could hardly sleep, thinking about appearing with the Queen of Warner Brothers. Only later did she learn that Davis was being dethroned. She'd seen her in *The Little Foxes* (1941) and *Now, Voyager* (1942), and had gone to *Dark Victory* (1939) at a revival theater.

Over dinner, she'd announced to her family, "In my first picture, I'm going to be co-starring with Miss Bette Davis."

As she learned the next day, it wasn't exactly a co-starring role.

***

Debbie was very disappointed to learn that she would be uncredited in *June Bride* (1942), and would appear only at the end of the film as the girlfriend of one of the young men attending the wedding of Jeanne Brinker (Barbara Bates). "If you blink, you'll miss me," Debbie said.

The property had been around for a long time. The script had been acquired by Paramount, who later sold it to Jack Warner for $25,000. Davis and Robert Montgomery ended up as the romantic leads, although Janis Paige and Betty Hutton had been considered for the role of the magazine editor, too, and both Fred Astaire and Cary Grant had been offered the part of Davis' love interest.

For the June issue of their women's magazine, *Home Life*, Montgomery and Davis journey to Crestville, Indiana to craft a feature story. They immediately realize that the dreary, old-fashioned Brinker home has to be redecorated before anything can be photographed, as it's dowdy and filled with Victoriana kitsch. Madcap antics ensue, and the wedding is almost called off.

Debbie had long been fascinated by the screen image of Davis, and she asked Joe, the lighting man, to let her climb up the rungs of a ladder and onto an overhead catwalk to better watch Davis and Montgomery emote twenty feet below in a love scene.

In spite of their personal objections to each

Although Robert Montgomery and Bette Davis personally loathed each other, they had to make love on the screen in *June Bride*.

In time, Davis and Debbie would become close friends, but their first encounter was a total disaster.

other, the two stars played out their love scene most effectively. Suddenly, Debbie's foot slipped and made a clanking sound against the railing.

Davis pushed Montgomery away and glared upward. "Who in the fuck is up there?" she shouted in that much-imitated voice of hers. "Come down at once! This is a closed set."

Joe whispered to Debbie, "Beat it, kid!"

She scrambled down the ladder, nearly falling, and fled through the nearest door before shooting resumed.

She later wrote, "That commanding voice of Miss Bette Davis frightened the hell out of me. She was going to kill me. I was going to be fired, machine gunned, destroyed, and hung on the wall as a trophy."

In spite of fairly good reviews, *June Bride* flopped at the box office, and did absolutely nothing for Debbie's fledgling career. It also hastened Davis' farewell to Warners, which occurred the following year after the disastrous release of *Beyond the Forest* (1949; *"What a dump!"*)

***

Warners didn't want to waste any money on its new juvenile, now officially billed as Debbie Reynolds. According to the terms of her contract, she could be laid off for a period of up to six weeks beginning six months after its debut. Because they had no work for her, the studio availed itself of that option.

William Orr phoned her, reminding her that Warners had the right to renew her contract any day it wanted to. "As soon as we get a role for you, I'll be in touch. Call this a hiatus."

She really didn't mind, and returned to her life as Mary Frances, going back to school in Burbank. But her girlfriends didn't welcome her—in fact, they were jealous and snubbed her. Many of her schoolmates, especially the pretty ones, wanted to become movie stars and resented her for her good luck.

With Christmas soon approaching, Mary Frances went to the local J.C. Penney's and applied for a job. She was given one in the blouse department, which had a special section for Girl Scouts, selling uniforms and other accessories. She was put in charge of that section.

She had been working in the store for only two weeks before Steve Trilling from Warners' casting department tracked her down. "We've got a role for you, Debbie," he said. "It's a good little part in the next June Haver musical. You'll love it. Report for work with us tomorrow."

Quitting her job at Penney's, she went to Warners the next morning and was introduced to David Butler, the director, all 300-plus pounds of him. "He made Sydney Greenstreet look like Skinny Minnie," she said.

The Daughter of Rosie O'Grady, released in 1950, starred the new singing sensation, Gordon MacCrae, with his rich baritone voice, as the male lead, Tony

Pastor.

The title role was cast with June Haver, a blonde-haired singer and dancer whom 20th Century Fox had groomed to be "the next Betty Grable." However, she lacked the pinup girl's sex appeal.

Warners' answer to Gene Kelly, Gene Nelson, was cast in *Rosie O'Grady* as Doug Martin. Debbie watched in awe as he performed a dance number. "The guy's terrific," she said.

The supporting role of Dennis O'Grady went to actor James Barton, who had three daughters: Haver as Patricia, Marcia Mae Jones as Katie, and Debbie as the youngest, Maureen. It is Patricia who wants to sing and dance in vaudeville, eventually getting romantically involved with Tony Pastor (MacRae).

Jack Rose had specifically written the role for Debbie, who would appear in 19th Century costumes. The song, "The Daughter of Rosie O'Grady," had been written in 1917, but most of the other songs were specifically created for the film.

One afternoon, Gordon MacCrae visited Debbie's dressing room, inviting himself to come in. He shut the door behind him and offered to share with her a delicious lunch with fresh fruit someone had packed for him. As she was eating a banana, his arm ever so gently embraced her, as his lips moved closer and closer to hers.

Suddenly, "that stern prune," her teacher, Lois Horne, threw open the door, demanding that MacCrae leave at once. "She's jailbait, you jerk!" she shouted at him. "Get out or I'll report you to Jack Warner."

Leaving his lunch behind, he fled, and from then on, gave Debbie wide berth. She later said, "Gordon has such an engaging personality, and he's got that rich voice. And he's so good looking. A girl could do worse, surrendering her virginity to Gordon. I just knew he'd be gentle."

Ever since she was a girl, she'd always had fine hair through which her ears protruded. "I looked like an elf in some photos."

On the set of *The Daughter of Rosie O'Grady*, in the middle of a scene, Butler seemed to think so, too, and abruptly, he called a halt to filming. He yelled for the makeup man to come and apply some kind of glue to pin Debbie's ears back. After he worked on her for a while, shooting resumed. But the intense heat of the lights melted the liquid adhesive and out popped those elf-like ears. Once again, makeup was summoned, and once again, the same thing happened. Finally, by the third take, her ears stayed glued in place.

June Haver and Gordon MacRae in *The Daughter of Rosie O'Grady*.

On screen, the dashing MacCrae fell in love with June, but offscreen, he pursued "jailbait Debbie."

Learning of her plight, Horne gave her the name of a plastic surgeon, Dr. MacDougal, and she set up an appointment for Debbie to see him. Two days later, she was in his office. Under sedation, she had the cartilage in the back of her ears removed. Minnie drove her home all bandaged, and for three days, she suffered agonizing pain until it went away. When the bandages came off, her ears no longer protruded, and no director would ever complain about them again.

Debbie was advised that she needed an agent. It was recommended that she sign with the Louis Schurr Agency, which represented a number of stars, mainly Bob Hope. At the agency, Wilt Melnick was assigned to oversee Debbie's career.

"Wilt entered my life just at the right moment," Debbie said. "I needed someone in there pitching for me. I got the news that Mr. Jack Warner, the jerk, wasn't going to pick up the option on my contract. Stardom seemed more elusive than ever."

When Al Trescone, a talent scout for MGM, heard that Warners wasn't going to retain Debbie, he got in touch with her himself. He'd been one of the judges who bestowed on her the title of Miss Burbank of 1948, and had been impressed with her bouncy style and talent.

He remembered her lip-synching and doing a perfect imitation of Betty Hutton. Just such a role had recently opened at MGM in a new musical entitled *Three Little Words*, a film that was scheduled for a release in 1950.

Throughout the rest of her life, Debbie recalled the morning she arrived at the fabled studio of Metro-Goldwyn-Mayer, which boasted of having "more stars than there are in heaven."

Those dazzling personalities ranged from Clark Gable to Robert Taylor, from such beauties as Hedy Lamarr to a very young Elizabeth Taylor. The studio was ruled by the formidable Louis B. Mayer, whom some defined as "The King of Hollywood," although that title was also used for Gable.

Debbie walked onto the lot as the tumultuous war-torn 1940s were coming to an end and as the 1950s were just beginning. Panic was sweeping through the studios as movie attendance started to drop as increasing numbers of Americans were sitting at home watching shows on the "little black boxes" in their living rooms.

Even so, MGM was bustling with activity as Debbie passed one sound stage after another.

Debbie met with Jack Cummings, the director of *Three Little Words*, who

Debbie *(right)* was a lesser star, one of the three O'Grady sisters, shown here with June Haver *(left)* and Marcia Mae Jones *(center)*.

28

introduced her to Eddie Mannix, the second most powerful executive at the studio. She also met Burt Grady, who headed talent at MGM. "*Three Little Words* is going to star Fred Astaire and Red Skelton," Grady told her. "In my first evaluation of Fred, I wrote of his screen test. 'Can't act, can't sing, can dance a little.'"

After chatting with the men, Debbie did the same Betty Hutton number she'd performed in the Miss Burbank contest. The men seemed to like it.

Mannix invited her to lunch in the MGM commissary. There, Mayer sat at his reserved table in a far corner, starting his meal (as always) with chicken soup based on his mother's own recipe.

In time, she'd learn that Mannix at MGM was known as "The Fixer." His main job involved camouflaging the private peccadillos of MGM stars, especially when they got into trouble.

"You've got something," Mannix told her. "I don't know what it is, but it's something."

Over a corned beef sandwich, she learned what *Three Little Words* was about. Astaire would play Bert Kalmar, with Red Skelton cast as Harry Ruby. These two Tin Pan Alley song-writing partners had been famous during the first half of the 20th Century.

"We'll need you to lip-synch the squeaky, high-pitched voice of Helen Kane," Mannix told her.

"Who is she?" Debbie asked. "Never heard of her."

"She was once famous, born in the Bronx back in 1904," Mannix said. "Her hit song was 'I Wanna Be Loved By You'" An animator, Grim Natwick used that voice in his creation of the popular cartoon character, Betty Boop. You'll have to learn to sing '*boop-boop-a-doop*'"

"I can do that," Debbie answered. "just watch me go."

Within the week, she was offered a two-week gig at $350 a week. That would very shortly lead to her signing a seven-year contract.

On the first day of the shoot, she met her co-stars. Skelton was most amusing, and she remembered him as "the funniest man I ever met." One critic said, "Red is strictly a baggy pants clown. He fidgets, he mugs, he puffs out his cheeks and crosses his eyes, and his mop of red hair is always in disarray."

In contrast, she found Astaire the epitome of grace and elegance, both on and off the screen. "His dancing defies gravity," she said.

Dressed in a sailor suit, Debbie watches Fred Astaire *(left)* and Red Skelton play a tune on a piano that's about to be carted away in a truck.

She also met the film's two leading ladies. Vera-Ellen was a brilliant dancer, but not a singer. With the understanding that her singing voice was dubbed by Anita Ellis, she evolved into the perfect dance partner for Astaire, having learned to emulate his incredible dance steps and follow his choreography.

The Titian-haired Arlene Dahl was arguably the greatest beauty at MGM during the 1950s. Debbie found her dazzling with Lex Barker, her boyfriend, the movie Tarzan. He showed up to escort Dahl to lunch. "When God created Adam," Debbie said, "he must have looked like Lex. What a man!"

Debbie had one scene, filmed on a congested sidewalk, with Astaire and Skelton, who bash out a tune they're composing on a piano that's about to be carted away in a truck. Astaire is singing the words to "I Wanna Be Loved By You." Debbie chimes in with her *"Boop-boop-a-doop."*

In another scene, she appears with Carlton Carpenter, performing the entire Helen Kane song—lip-synching it. She found Carpenter a delight, and they became life-long friends. A talented actor, a former nightclub magician and Broadway actor, he was "goofily charming, lean and lanky." On screen together, they shared a marvelous camaraderie, singing "I Wanna Be Loved By You." They'd go on to a bigger performance together.

***

At MGM, when the stars (or would-be stars) weren't working, they attended classes designed to improve their performances on film—ballet (which Debbie failed), singing lessons, modern dance, and "stretching."

She concluded that none was better at stretching that Cyd Charisse, her leg pointing skyward over her head. Vera-Ellen was her high-octane competition. Tap-dancing Ann Miller, always in great shape, was a regular student, and a good one. Arriving in a leotard and diamonds, "Zsa Zsa Gabor couldn't do anything right," Debbie said. "I talked to her and learned to imitate her Hungarian accent." On rare occasions, when they weren't otherwise working on other projects, Ava Gardner, Lana Turner, and Grace Kelly showed up, too.

For "book learning" (as Debbie continued to call it), the number of pupils in MGM's little red brick schoolhouse had

In a scene with Carleton Carpenter, Debbie had to pantomime Helen Kane's high-pitched voice in the number, "I Wanna Be Loved By You."

When Louis B. Mayer saw the rushes, he said, "I like the way her eyes light up. Sign her!"

narrowed to only three: Debbie herself, Elizabeth Taylor, and Claude Jarman, Jr., who had co-starred with Gregory Peck and Jane Wyman in *The Yearling* (1946).

In class, Debbie met and talked with Elizabeth, an actress who was destined to play such a large role in her future.

Addressing Debbie, Elizabeth said, "I know you know who I am. But who in hell are you?"

"Debbie Reynolds, a bit player in *Three Little Words,* a picture being made with Fred Astaire. I've got a contract."

"Count yourself lucky," Elizabeth replied. "Mayer is kicking star after star out on their asses. Hollywood's glory days are coming to an end, but I'm still here, and so is Ava Gardner plus a few others."

"I'm surprised that Mayer wanted me," Debbie admitted. "I'm not that good a dancer, and I can't really sing. But I do a great Betty Hutton impersonation."

"What a thrill that must be," Elizabeth said, sarcastically. Then she looked at Debbie carefully, as if evaluating her. "You're hardly a sex symbol. You're no challenge to Ava...or to me. Of course, being a contract player has its advantages. There are a lot of hot men working at MGM or at rival studios. I'm currently in love with Peter Lawford, but dating Nicky Hilton."

"I've seen Lawford a few times driving his Cadillac convertible on the lot with a surfboard sticking out the window."

"Stay away from him," Elizabeth warned. "I staked him out first. If you want to get laid, try Mickey Rooney. He'll fuck anything that wiggles."

"I'm not interested," Debbie said. "I'm not into boys all that much. I've seen a few who are good lookers, though. But I don't understand men."

"Who does?" Elizabeth answered. "You and I might become friends...sort of. For me, nothing destroys a friendship more than a girl chasing after a man I've already earmarked for myself."

"You'll have no competition from me," Debbie said. "You're only the most beautiful girl in the world."

"I know that," Elizabeth said. "And I'm so fucking bored with hearing it. Frankly, if chasing boys is not your hobby, what is?"

"I'm in the Girl Scouts."

"Oh, Debbie, you are so square, but adorable. We'll see if two people as radically different as you and I can get along."

***

MGM ordered Debbie to take acting lessons from the studio's "resident dragon," Lillian Burns (also known as Lillian Burns Sidney), the most famous acting coach in the history of Hollywood. Like any rising young starlet, Debbie was already being trained in dancing, diction, walking, talking, smiling, and singing, and even being coached in how to pose for a photographer.

Grace Kelly once said, "A star's image was all-important. A starlet had to be taught how to enter a room, how to exit a room, and how to be camera ready at all times, since you didn't know when a photographer would jump out and take your picture. Pity the poor teacher who had to coach some of the girls in etiquette. Before signing with MGM, some of them had been waitresses in hash houses, strippers, prostitutes, or country maidens milking cows."

Before she met Burns, Debbie had talked to MGM swimming star, Esther Williams, an actress sometimes referred to as "Neptune's Daughter," by the studio's publicity department. According to Williams, "I pity you for having to takes lessons from that bitch, Lillian Burns. She's a journey into hell. She comes from the school of acting that one size fits all, forgetting that some women are taller, thinner, fatter, or younger than she is. She demanded that all five feet, eight inches of me behave like a feisty little poodle with quick, jerky movements. That's not my style, baby. She tells you, when you're trying to convey anger, make your nostrils flare and let your eyes bulge out from your head like Joan Crawford does."

"I was prepared to face a tarantula," Debbie said. "But Lillian and I bonded. In time, she was like a mother to me, calling me her daughter. She helped me a lot. I was so inexperienced. Her speaking voice evoked Bette Davis. She was a tiny woman, but in her theatricality, she was larger than life. Of course, she was very demanding, very stern, but it was for my own good."

As she was leaving Burns's class one afternoon, Debbie met Howard Strickling, head of MGM's publicity department. He introduced her to Clark Gable. "He was a little worse for wear," she said, "but I was looking up into the face of Rhett Butler."

"You're a tiny little thing," he said, patting her head. "Just how old are you?"

"I just turned seventeen," she said.

"I lost my virginity when I was fifteen to this 57-year-old woman in Cadiz, Ohio. What's your status?"

She remembered "turning red" all over. No adult male had ever asked her such a thing. Normally articulate, she became tongue-tied. "I finally managed to stammer, 'I'm not that kind of gal.'"

"Too bad," he said before walking off with Strickling. She'd always dreamed of meeting Clark Gable, but without any clue that their encounter would turn out like it did.

Acting coach Lillian Burns Sidney was one of the most powerful women at MGM, with a direct line to Louis B. Mayer.

"She picked which girls would get star treatment," Debbie said. "For some reason, she shone her light down on me. She became the great mentor of mine, a kind of Mother Superior, advising me which roles to take, which men to marry."

32

"What was he really like?" she wondered. "Some dirty old man?"

An hour later, she entered the commissary for a hamburger. She had not had time to eat her packed lunch and the sandwich meat had turned rancid in the hot California sun.

At a far table, she spotted Gable dining with Nancy Davis, a starlet. MGM was a rumor mill in those days, and word had spread that Nancy wanted to marry Gable and go live on his ranch.

"I bet Gable didn't ask her about *her* virginity," Debbie said, ruefully, "In those days, Nancy Davis was known as the Fellatio Queen of Hollywood. I didn't know what fellatio meant, so I looked it up in a dictionary, finding out that I had performed fellatio on a 17-year-old boy when I was only six. Maybe I should have told Mr. Gable that."

At any rate, in a few weeks, Elizabeth Taylor had informed her that Gable had dropped Nancy, and she was in hot pursuit of Ronald Reagan. "Ronnie seduced me when I was jailbait, and now he's Nancy's consolation prize," Elizabeth said.

***

Before filming began on Debbie's next picture, Louis B. Mayer sent word that he wanted to receive her in his office. She trembled in fright at the news, since she'd heard he was a terrible man and could make or break a star's career on a whim, as he'd done with John Gilbert and so many others.

Beginning in his outer office, two secretaries walked her down a "quarter mile hall" to the large oaken doors that opened into his inner office. It was a mammoth place, painted in ivory. He was short, only five feet five and portly, sitting behind what must have been the largest desk ever made. Perhaps because he was short, the desk was mounted on a platform so that one had to look up to him.

A former junk dealer, he'd entered the entertainment industry by buying up Nickelodeon arcades. He made his first big money when he obtained the rights to distribute D.W. Griffith's *The Birth of a Nation* (1915) on the eastern seaboard. The film was controversial in that it portrayed the Ku Klux Klan in a heroic light.

However, as head of MGM, he demanded wholesome family fare—"no perversions." He told his producers, "Americans go to the movies to be entertained, not disgusted. Out in that dark audience,

"I was terrified when I was ushered into the cream-colored office of MGM's Louis B. Mayer. He could pluck an unknown out of a line-up and make her a star. He could also destroy a career."

"The highest paid man in movies, he was labeled a bigoted vulgarian, but he gave me my big break and made me a star in spite of my limitations."

they can dream."

Behind his wire-rim glasses, he carefully evaluated Debbie, as he'd once done to Greta Garbo, Clark Gable, Norma Shearer, Judy Garland, Joan Crawford, and Mickey Rooney.

He was a busy man, but took time out to make small talk, asking her how she was doing in her classes. But he soon grew impatient and got to the point: "I've decided to give you a good little part, your most substantial to date, in a romantic comedy by Dorothy Kingsley. She's our best writer. The picture is *Two Weeks with Love*. Do well in that movie, and I can tell you that you will have a brilliant career at MGM."

"Thank you so much!" she stammered.

A secretary knocked on the door and entered. "Mr. Mayer, Robert Taylor is waiting in the outer office."

For the first time, Mayer stood up. "If you have any problems here, know that my door is always open to you. Now goodbye and good luck."

The secretary had taken her arm, and was escorting her out. Debbie managed to call back to Mayer, "I'm most appreciative!"

***

Two Weeks with Love, set for a 1950 release, starred the singing sensation Jane Powell, with Ricardo Montalban, "the Mexican heartthrob," as her leading man. Debbie soon learned that her part wasn't quite as substantial as Mayer had indicated.

The film focused on the Robinson family, who head out of New York for a vacation at "Kissimee in the Catskills," a resort hotel. Love strikes both of the Robinson sisters, Powell as Patti and Debbie as Melba.

She had been impressed with Powell ever since she'd seen her in *A Date with Judy* (1948), co-starring Elizabeth Taylor and Robert Stack. Powell's most memorable footage had captured her singing "It's a Most Unusual Day."

Debbie found Powell the cheeriest of movie sopranos, with a bird-like voice. She was almost as wholesome as Debbie herself. She'd been told to wear flats, because Powell was an inch shorter than she was.

Debbie met her future rival in love, Elizabeth Taylor, at MGM's little schoolhouse:

"She looked like such a sweet, innocent little girl, but she had this potty mouth," Debbie said. "I heard she'd been seduced by older actors like Ronald Reagan when she was trying to get the role in *That Hagen Girl* that ultimately went to Shirley Temple."

"She and Robert Taylor had an affair during the making of *The Conspirator*. I never dreamed that in our future, I'd become involved in a love triangle with her."

It was during her filming of *Two Weeks With Love* that Powell received news that she had been cast in *Royal Wedding* (eventually released in 1951) opposite Fred Astaire and Peter Lawford. June Allyson had dropped out because she was pregnant. Her role had then been transferred to Judy Garland, who had to bow out because of illness. Debbie had heard about the script and told her family, "If something happens to Jane, here I am! Debbie Reynolds to the rescue!"

On the set of *Two Weeks with Love,* Debbie met her director, Roy Rowland, and renewed her relationship with Jack Cummings, who had produced *Three Little Words.* Rowland was married to Ruth Cummings, the sister of the producer.

The male star, Ricardo Montalban, was MGM's resident Latin Lover, a major competitor for that Argentine heartthrob, Fernando Lamas. Montalban chatted briefly with Debbie, talking about Hollywood's penchant for changing the names of its wannabe actors. "When I hit town in 1943, the studio wanted me to change my name to Ricky Martin."

Of all the members of the cast, Debbie bonded most with the veteran actor, Brooklyn-born Louis Calhern, who played her father. The year he worked with Debbie was the grandest of his career, having received an Oscar nomination for playing Oliver Wendell Holmes in *The Magnificent Yankee* (1950). Other roles included Buffalo Bill in *Annie Get Your Gun* (also 1950) alongside Debbie's favorite actress, Betty Hutton. Calhern also starred opposite Marilyn Monroe as her double-crossing lawyer and sugar daddy in John Huston's crime drama, *The Asphalt Jungle* (also 1950).

Born in Texas in 1902, the elegant Ann Harding was cast as Debbie's mother. Harding had been a big star in the 1930s when RKO promoted her as its answer to the MGM superstar, Norma Shearer. Harding had previously graced the screen with such leading men as Laurence Olivier, Ronald Colman, Leslie Howard, and Gary Cooper.

In *Two Weeks with Love*, Debbie was once again teamed with Carleton Carpenter, each of them assigned to interpret a popular song. Originally written in 1914, it had become famous over the years for its chorus:

"Although Jane Powell and I were very different types, we were often seen as rivals," Debbie said. "Yet through it all, we maintained a friendship, and in the future, I would ask her to replace me on Broadway in *Irene*."

"Louis B. Mayer called us 'his little canaries,'" Debbie claimed. "He was known to seize one of his starlets and order her to his ivory-colored office for seduction. But Janie and I escaped his net. He didn't consider us sex symbols. Ann Miller was more his type."

Aba daba daba daba daba daba dab,
Said the chimpie to the monk;
Baba daba daba daba daba dab a dab,
Said the monkey to the chimp.

Some naïve observers speculated that Carpenter and Debbie were romantically involved. That wasn't true. Whenever Carpenter needed "arm candy" to appear with him at premieres or other events, he showed up with the actress Joan Evans.

Nearing the end of a brilliant film career, Busby Berkeley was tagged to oversee the project's dance numbers. In the 1930s, during his heyday, he had become celebrated for his large, lavishly costumed casts whose dance choreographies spun into complex geometric patterns.

By now, however, Berkeley—a chronic alcoholic—was usually intoxicated before 10AM. The crew strapped him to the boom camera so he wouldn't fall to the ground when it was elevated.

Rowland, the film's director, was not known for throwing lavish Hollywood parties, but on the occasion that he actually hosted one, during the filming of *Two Weeks with Love*, he invited Debbie.

She was dazzled by all the big stars there, and went around the rooms introducing herself to everyone. "I wasn't shy," she recalled.

Once again, Debbie was teamed with Carleton Carpenter, this time in *Two Weeks With Love.*

According to her co-star, "She (Debbie) was Miss Personality in person, cute as a bunny, and I don't mean a Playboy type bunny. Jack Cummings, our producer, liked the way we looked together."

"Originally," he said, "the character of Melba was supposed to be a short, chubby kid with a crush on me. Deb got the role, and she was anything but chubby. I was tickled that we'd get to team up again. We really hit it off, onscreen and off."

Lena Horne sung for the guests that night, and she and Debbie bonded.

She invited Debbie for lunch in her dressing room the following day. "I was asked not to lunch in the commissary, where they serve *café au lait* as a drink. When it's the color of a woman, that's a different story," Horne said with a touch of bitterness. She had recently learned that her dream role, that of a mulatto, Julie LaVerne, in the 1951 film, *Show Boat*, had gone to her friend, Ava Gardner.

"For Lena, it was always 'Stormy Weather,'" Debbie said.

***

Debbie's greatest exposure to a mass worldwide audience occurred at the 1951 Academy Award presentations in Los Angeles. To her surprise, even though she was still a relatively unknown starlet, she was selected to present the Oscar for that year's Best Cinematography.

Perhaps she didn't know that she could have gone to MGM's wardrobe department and been assigned a spectacular gown to wear for that occasion. Instead, she went to Lerner's Department Store in Burbank, where for $12 she bought a strapless evening gown with a beaded bodice. Instead of wearing a diamond necklace like Zsa Zsa Gabor and the other female stars, she unpretentiously tied a red ribbon around her neck.

One of the hosts of that year's Oscar ceremony, Fred Astaire, her recent co-star, had been selected to introduce her. First, though, he brought on Marilyn Monroe. Debbie was so dazzled by her look in a low-cut ball gown that she didn't even hear why Astaire was introducing her.

"That's a tough act to follow," she said to a security guard standing nearby.

After Monroe exited from the stage, Astaire announced, "Please welcome the most talented and most delightful Miss Debbie Reynolds." The orchestra struck up "Younger Than Springtime," as she walked out onto the stage, "shaking all over." In spite of her nervousness, she read the list of nominees, presenting the Oscar for the year's best cinematography to W.M. Guthrie and Robert Surtees.

Backstage, she encountered Monroe. There was no need for an introduction. "Your gown is fabulous," Debbie told the blonde star.

"And yours, honey, is so precious!" Monroe said. "It would be the highlight of your high school's senior prom. A little advice: If you're going to become a big MGM star, you've got to look sexy." Then Monroe sauntered off.

Debbie watched her go, deciding she was still perfecting "The Walk" that would eventually make her famous.

Fred Astaire introduced both Marilyn Monroe and Debbie at the 1951 Academy Award presentations. Monroe told Debbie she needed to dress sexier to make it on the screen.

"I was coming along," Debbie said. "Within three years, *Modern Screen* would name me that magazine's most popular. Runners-up were Grace Kelly, number two, followed by Elizabeth Taylor, number three. Eat your heart out Marilyn! You came in number six, after Doris Day and June Allyson!"

***

It seemed that every day, or on any night, Debbie met a movie star (or stars), either on the MGM lot or at private parties, to which she was now being invited.

Roy Rowland, her director, hosted a party for Noël Coward, who was on another visit from London. He'd come to the party with his longtime friend, Clifton Webb, whom he'd first met in Davos, Switzerland, on a skiing holiday in 1924.

"Somehow, the most sophisticated man in London and the most sophisticated man in Hollywood liked me," Debbie said. "Heaven knows why. By one o'clock, Noël was at the piano, Clifton doing a little dance, and there was me singing. A friendship among the three of us was formed that night, and I never really understood why. I was so naïve and innocent that maybe they found me amusing."

Debbie agreed to have lunch with Webb and Coward a few days after the party. Over a meal, they gossiped, laughed, and told amusing stories until 2:30PM. As it happened, Coward had already invited Webb to one of his homes near Ocho Rios on the northern coast of Jamaica for a week-long holiday. He surprised Debbie by asking her to go along, and she was flattered by the invitation. But first, she had to check with Minnie.

Minnie had taken to hanging out in the wardrobe department of MGM, and she must have asked some of the wardrobe mistresses there if they felt it safe for her teenage daughter to fly away. She suspected that Coward and Webb might be "dirty old men."

The chief wardrobe mistress assured her that Debbie would be perfectly safe with either gentleman. "If anything, Noël and Clifton have eyes for each other." Then she moistened her index finger and rubbed her eyebrow, an old-fashioned way of signaling that someone was homosexual.

Landing in Jamaica after the long transit from California, Debbie was put into a waiting taxi with a black driver, who drove them to Firefly, Coward's new vacation retreat at St. Mary, some 20 miles east of Ocho Rios. Here, Coward had entertained Errol Flynn; Elizabeth the Queen Mother (i.e., Elizabeth Bowes-Lyon, the wife of King George VI and the mother of Queen Elizabeth II); Vivien Leigh, Laurence Olivier, and Katharine Hepburn. Another re-

Even before the sophisticated gloss she later acquired, young Debbie survived (and thrived) among the *über*-sophisticates of the final days of the British Empire.

During a little known period of her life, she was the extended houseguest at the home, in Jamaica, of the darling of café society, Noël Coward *(right photo above)*.

Coward's other houseguests included Clifton Webb *(left photo above)* and in a separate, unrelated incident, Queen Elizabeth, the Queen Mother, who had lavishly praised "his talent to amuse."

cent guest had been Princess Margaret Rose.

"Adlai Stevenson was vacationing in Port Antonio, so I invited him, too," Coward told Debbie. "His clothes and manner were a bit offputting, very common. J. Edgar Hoover is spreading the rumor that he's a secret homosexual. Yet he told us that he plans to challenge General Eisenhower for the U.S. presidency."

Debbie loved Jamaica and its people, and she took delight in the setting of Firefly, near the seacoast, with the Blue Mountains on the distant horizon. That Friday morning, Coward arranged for his driver to take her to the open-air market in Port Maria. There, she discovered all sorts of handicrafts along with strange fruits. Locals were dressed in every color of the rainbow. One husky Mandingo-like man, heavily muscled and rather handsome, whispered to her, "Come away with me. I'll make love to you all day. White women don't know what lovin' is like 'til they've been made love to by a Jamaican man."

She politely turned down the offer.

At twilight, she sat with Webb and Coward beside the pool, watching the sun go down. The air became fluttery with fireflies, which had prompted Coward in the naming of his house. On another evening, she spotted Webb and Coward holding hands as they walked along the beach.

Later that night, she recalled Webb being in a sad mood, a condition that Coward called *La nostalgie du temps perdu,* suggesting he was living in the past, recalling both of their glory days in the 1920s and 1930s. "All my friends have died," Webb said.

Coward warned, "There is no future living in the past."

Debbie then chimed in, "I don't have much of a past to remember."

After her return to Hollywood, Debbie accepted an invitation to the home of Peter Lawford. Privately, she asked him about homosexuality, a subject with which he was vastly familiar. "I sort of get it," she said. "But I don't, really. How do they make love?"

He explained sodomy to her, leaving out fellatio. "That must be awfully painful."

"Millions of straight people practice it, too," he responded.

"As long as I live, I'll never let any man do that to me," she said.

***

Debbie had been getting up at 4:30AM to take the bus from Burbank to Culver City so she'd be on time to report to makeup at MGM. Ray had taught her how to drive his car, and at long last, he decided that it was time for her to own her own auto, now that she was old enough to get a license.

For $50 he bought her a four-door Chevrolet and overhauled the motor himself. With chintz left over from her living room curtains, Minnie upholstered the seats, and brother Billy painted it an emerald green.

Behind the wheel of her own car, she felt independent for the first time in her life, anxious for the day when she could move out and into her own private apartment. The engine made so much noise that security guards at the studio asked her to park outside the gates so as not to interrupt shooting on the sound stages.

In the meantime, Minnie made arrangements with the Los Angeles School Board to allow Debbie to graduate from high school in Burbank. It was clearly understood by the administrators at MGM's Little Red Schoolhouse that both she and Elizabeth Taylor would have to take their final exams downtown at University High. Elizabeth eventually graduated from that school, but during some of her sessions there, she was mobbed by autograph seekers. As a less famous "also ran," Debbie spent time at Burbank High School as part of the logistics associated with earning her diploma.

America had entered the Korean War, and soldiers were being shipped from California to the warfront. The USO was busy again, and MGM's publicity department asked Debbie if she'd perform for the men in uniform. She went first to Travis Air Force Base, driven there by MGM's new singing star, Howard Keel. "I was already in love with him ever since I'd seen him opposite Betty Hutton in *Annie Get Your Gun*. I'd heard a rumor that he'd seduced a very mature Marilyn Monroe when she was only thirteen, but he was a perfect gentleman around me—not even a kiss."

Onstage, 1950, in Korea, Debbie entertains the troops.

Lower photo: Reprising, in North Asia, her *Abba Dabba Honeymoon* hit with Carleton Carpenter

Arthur Loew, Jr. joined the performers. He was the grandson of Adolph Zukor, the founder of Paramount Pictures, and his father, Arthur Loew, Sr., was president of MGM. Elizabeth told Debbie that she and Arthur had had a brief affair before she "surrendered" him to Janet Leigh.

To entertain the airmen, Joey Bishop performed a comedy *schtick,* and Debbie joined with Carleton Carpenter to sing "Abba Dabba" and "Row Row Row," their second recording from the movie *Two Weeks with Love*. She also sang her solo number, "I Wanna Be Loved By You."

On another of Debbie's USO tours, the chief star was Paul Robeson, an African American singer who had once been a major football player. As a performer, he had a powerful, deep bass voice. His biggest hit was "Ol' Man River," which he'd sung in the 1930s production of *Show Boat* on Broadway. He later became one of the leaders of the Civil Rights Movement.

Back on the homefront, Debbie wanted friends her own age, and Ray reluctantly agreed to let her invite people over. Her first guest was her ballet teacher, who always wore red pants and pink shoes when he was going out. When he arrived in Ray's living room, he shocked Debbie's father, who had been reared in homophobic Texas. Ray immediately retreated to his bedroom and would not come out to dinner. When Debbie went in to retrieve him, he demanded that she, "Get that god damn faggot out of this house."

When she was seventeen, she said goodbye to her brother Billy. He'd been drafted and was undergoing basic training at Fort Ord in Monterey, along with fellow soldiers who included actors Richard Long and David Janssen.

For her USO show, she was accompanied by a talented African American piano player, Rudy Render. Back in Burbank, she invited him for dinner with her family. He arrived just as the family was sitting down for their meal. When Ray saw that he was black, he got up and left the table. Later that night, he told Debbie, "First, a faggot. Now a nigger. Is that all you can bring home?"

Later, when Render was seriously injured in an automobile accident, Debbie moved him into their converted garage, which had a small bed and a kitchenette. Minnie and Debbie looked after him. When Debbie went overseas, Ray gradually began to tend to Render himself. Somehow, his prejudices, in time, melted away, and he later referred to Render as "my second son."

By 1950, Debbie was entertaining the troops in South Korea. There she witnessed "some of the most horrific scenes of my life." Day after day, she tried to comfort young men who had been severely wounded, many of them never to recover.

"The suffering, the agony, the moaning, the smell of death," she said. "Often, I'd have to retreat to the toilet to vomit, but I always emerged with a smiling face."

Many friends came and went throughout Debbie's long life, but she and Rudy Render developed a lifelong friendship. He was an excellent musician and often accompanied her, musically.

"I saw the boyfriends come and go, as well as the husbands. None of them really worked out for poor Debbie."

From Korea, Debbie flew back to Los Angeles in December of 1951, wanting to be home for the Christmas season. But first, MGM ordered her and Carleton Carpenter to go on the road to promote *Two Weeks with Love*, beginning in Washington, D.C. "We got god damn tired of *Abba-Dabba*-ing," she said. "A big star, perhaps Phil Silvers, would be the main attraction, and Carleton and I would be the opening act."

"Abba Dabba" sold more than a million records, zooming up to Number 5 on the *Billboard* charts. Debbie got a $15,000 royalty check.

Ray Reynolds flew to El Paso to spend several weeks with his relatives. With her new riches, Debbie ordered a crew to install a swimming pool in their backyard. Conspicuously over scale, it was the same size as the floor plan of their house.

For its inauguration one Sunday afternoon, she invited her newly minted friends. One was Farley Granger, a handsome young actor who was Samuel Goldwyn's "Golden Boy." He arrived with his date, Shelley Winters, who had recently made *A Place in the Sun* (1951), co-starring Montgomery Clift and Elizabeth Taylor. Debbie's battles with Winters lay in her distant future.

That weekend, Ray returned from El Paso to find that Debbie had bought him not only a set of golf clubs, but a shiny red 1951 MG convertible. He chastised her for spending her money, but accepted the gifts. He hated the pool, however. As soon as Debbie moved out, he ordered a crew to fill it in with dirt.

***

Debbie was sent the script of a new MGM romance, *Mr. Imperium* (1951). Lana Turner had been cast as the female lead after Greer Garson turned it down. In it, Lana was to play a nightclub singer who becomes a major movie star, and falls in love with an European prince who becomes a king.

Horribly miscast, and far too old, Ezio Pinza, the celebrated Italian opera singer, played Lana's love interest. A reporter wrote, "Whoever came up with that idea obviously thought a sour pickle and ice cream made a delightful taste sensation."

Debbie was disappointed in her small part, which showcased none of her talents. Most of her scenes would be with Marjorie Main, of Ma and Pa Kettle fame. In the plot, Main runs a boarding house in the Italian Alps, to which Pinza and Lana retreat. In her operation of the inn, Main is assisted by Debbie, her niece, who had lost both her parents, but found this surrogate mother in the wake of their deaths.

Debbie found Main's voice one of her most distinctive features. In addition to her trademark—an "owl's nest" hairdo, a style she retained throughout her career—Main had a distinctive voice redolent with Americana. Debbie agreed with the assessment of the older actress's critics, who defined Main's voice as "strident, galvanized, raucous, gritty, stentorian, gravelly, cindery, gruff, and raspy."

On the set of *Mr. Imperium*, Lana and Debbie became confidantes and lifelong friends. Lana admitted that she "detested the script, but I can't complain. Dan Hartman, who wrote it, is also my director, and Edwin H. Knopf, his co-writer, is the god damn producer."

At the time, Lana was married to her third husband, Bob Topping, the tin plate heir. She said she took the role because she needed the money, as Topping had gone through all of his money and was now devouring hers with his gambling debts.

Debbie later reflected: "Lana, Doris Day, and I had something in common. Each of us married men whose main talent was spending all the millions we'd accumulated with hard work and dedication."

Lana had something else to confide: When shooting began in June of 1950, she was three months pregnant. "Since I need the money, I'm not telling Hartman."

Debbie admired Pinza's rich, smooth, and sonorous voice. For nearly a quarter-century, he'd been a star at New York's Metropolitan Opera. His biggest Broadway success had occurred in *South Pacific* opposite Mary Martin. He'd sung one of Debbie's favorite songs, "Some Enchanted Evening," during the run (1949-1954) of that musical.

Eddie Mannix at MGM had hailed Pinza as "The Great Lover."

"He was anything but," Debbie said. "Both Lana and I thought he was a ladykiller but only in his mind. He was always pinching my bottom. Lana suffered an even worse fate. He groped her every chance he got."

According to Debbie, "Lana complained to me constantly

The cast of *Mr. Imperium* included *(top photo)* Marjorie Main (aka "Ma Kettle"), with Debbie interpreting the role of her surrogate daughter.

In the lower photo, Lana Turner and Debbie became lifelong friends after this movie was made.

Insert photo is of Ezio Pinza, the so-called great lover that Lana denounced as "Mr. Garlic Breath."

about their love scenes, labeling him 'Mr. Garlic Breath.'" She also called him 'The man with the Roquefort teeth.' He devoured these cheese pastries and lived off garlic."

"When he kisses me on camera," Lana told Debbie, "he sticks his garlic-coated tongue down my throat. Once, when he did that to me, I ran from the camera and retreated to my dressing room, where I vomited. Morning sickness and garlic breath—it's all too much for me."

"It was during the making of *Mr. Imperium* that I heard about rough sex," Debbie claimed. "Both Elizabeth (Taylor) and Lana seemed to be into it, although I'm still not sure exactly what it is. Sometimes, when Lana sat with me in makeup, I noticed some bruises on her and, on one occasion, a black eye. Makeup did what it could to conceal it. She told me these assaults came not from her husband, but from her boyfriends."

Debbie remembered Marjorie Main as "being so much fun. But she had serious bladder trouble. In the middle of a take, she'd have to bolt to the toilet. Between her pee breaks and Lana's fighting off Pinza, it was a tense atmosphere."

A widow and a secret lesbian, the eccentric Main had married Stanley Krebs, who had died in 1935. She always carried around his ashes.

At lunch one day with Debbie, she placed the urn containing her late husband's ashes on the table, and ordered lunch both for herself and "for Stanley."

On weekends, Main drove to her modest home in Palm Springs, placing Stanley—or what was left of him—on the front seat.

Late one Friday afternoon, just before Debbie waved her goodbye, Main told her, "I'm really pissed off at Stanley. I caught him flirting with Lana, and I gave him hell. How could he possibly go for Lana Turner, when he's got me?"

Radio City Music Hall in Manhattan had booked *Mr. Imperium* for a long run—that is, until its producers sat through a private screening. These New York executives immediately canceled the booking. When it was shown in select theaters across the country, it flopped. Since none of the critics had blamed Debbie for the movie's failure, she was disappointed but not devastated to the degree that Lana and Pinza were.

***

As an MGM starlet, Debbie had become well known even before co-starring in *Singin' in the Rain.* Her smiling face appeared in magazine after magazine, including *Modern Screen, Photoplay,* and *Motion Picture Screen Stories.* Once a month, she visited MGM photographer Virgil Apgar to pose for publicity photos.

She was also ordered to give fan magazine interviews, especially with the two leading gossip columnists of Hollywood, Louella Parsons and Hedda

Hopper. Each of them was formidable, but in very different ways. Other, less fearsome, columnists Debbie would cultivate included James Bacon, Sheilah Graham, and Mike Connolly.

Parsons was called the most powerful woman in Hollywood, and her column, published in the periodicals controlled by William Randolph Hearst, appeared in some 200 newspapers. "She can make or break a starlet like you," the publicity department warned Debbie.

The night she met Parsons was at the home of Lana Turner. Parsons was a plump brunette with liquid brown eyes. She thought of herself as a "glamour gal," even though she clearly wasn't. She reserved her fury for such stars as Greta Garbo, Orson Welles, Vivien Leigh, Charlie Chaplin, Katharine Hepburn, and the likes. But she had her favorites, none more famous than Clark Gable.

The two most influential gossip mavens of Tinseltown were Hedda Hopper (*left*) and Louella Parsons.

"Hedda was the Bitch of the World," Debbie said. "She could praise you one minute, then become an attack dog the next. She once told me I should marry Tab Hunter to squelch those gay rumors about him."

"Darling Louella was such a dear," Debbie continued. "So sweet to you. But when I ceased to be America's Sweetheart, I feared she was going to cut out my liver and eat it raw. She was as bloodthirsty as Hedda."

As they talked, Parsons ordered tumbler after tumbler of "water," which was actually vodka. A Hollywood hostess like Lana knew that when Parsons said water, she meant vodka.

After a long, but rather vague chat, Parsons rose to her wobbly feet and tottered off. She left behind a large wet spot on the sofa. Lana later informed Debbie that Parsons suffered from a bladder malfunction. To Debbie, she appeared intoxicated and scatterbrained, but reading her column the next day, it appeared that she had radar in her ears. "She picked up the most indiscreet gossip from the other side of the room," Debbie said.

A week later, Debbie was introduced to Parsons' potent and frequently poisonous rival, Hedda Hopper, at a party at the home of Louis B. Mayer.

Debbie later claimed that to her, Hopper evoked the images of both Gypsy Rose Lee and June Havoc. "She wore this outrageous picture hat and a lavender gown. I was soon to learn that she was known as 'The Bitch of Tinseltown.'"

Politically, she was to the right of Attila the Hun, and was both anti-Semitic and anti-black. Even though she had a gay son, actor William Hopper, she was also one of the town's most notoriously vocal homophobes.

Seated with Debbie on the sofa, Hopper began to probe her, as was her custom: "And what kind of star do you want to be, little girl?"

45

"The next Betty Hutton," Debbie blurted out.

"That makes sense," Hopper said. "A good choice. Even though she's had a hit, *Annie Get Your Gun*, Hutton is just too temperamental and too crazy to last. I hear through the grapevine that she may be dumped in the months ahead. Of course, you'll have to dye your hair blonde instead of your present unappealing color."

"That's too bad about Hutton," Debbie said. "I wish her well. I do a great impersonation of her."

Hopper kept eyeing her skeptically, as if not knowing what to make of her. "Are you dating anyone seriously?"

"Not really, just some studio dates."

"Let me warn you about some of the guys being escorts," Hopper said. "Arthur Loew, Jr. is a real wolf. He's been making it with Liz Taylor and Janet Leigh. John Drew Barrymore, Jr. is a psychotic. Tab Hunter and Rock Hudson are *bona fide* homosexuals. Hugh O'Brian will have your panties off on the first date. Robert Wagner is cute, but I keep hearing conflicting stories about him, some rather disturbing."

"I haven't dated any of those guys," Debbie said. "Actually, I'm just back from Jamaica. I was with Clifton Webb and Noël Coward."

"Perhaps you know by now that those two are the biggest pansies in the entertainment industry…notorious, in fact."

"Avoid Joan Crawford," Hopper continued. "When she's not fucking every stud in Hollywood, from Clark Gable to that attorney, Greg Bautzer, her lez streak comes out. Likewise, when Ava Gardner isn't screwing anything in pants, she, too, goes the lez route. On occasions, she's been known to pick up whores on Santa Monica Boulevard. Marilyn Monroe follows the same pattern as Ava. She's lez at least one night a week. She and Barbara Stanwyck had a torrid affair when they made *Clash by Night* (1952)."

"I could believe that about Marilyn, but I find it hard to believe it about Ava," Debbie said.

"Believe it, my dear. Hedda knows all the secrets."

"Nearly all the crop of pretty boys coming up are either homosexual or bi," Hopper continued. "Tony Curtis is bi. Although he denies it, Robert Stack is also bi. Marlon Brando is bi. But Monty Clift is 100% queer. A harmless escort would be Roddy McDowall, but don't let him get near one of your boyfriends."

"What about Peter Lawford?" Debbie asked. "He seems nice."

"That limey from London has had everybody—you name them: Rita Hayworth, Noël Coward, Judy Garland, Van Johnson, plus virtually every studio messenger boy at MGM, along with call boys and beach bunnies. If you do make it with him, at least you won't get pregnant. He prefers oral sex."

Debbie remained polite, but found Hopper tiring and didn't go for her line of conversation. After two hours, she retreated from the party.

The next day, when she encountered Elizabeth Taylor at MGM, she told her, "Hedda Hopper has given me a lesson on Sex Education 101."

"She's nothing but a fading whore herself," Elizabeth said. "She once thought of herself as blonde and beautiful, and was a screen actress. In one forgotten film, she actually played Mona Lisa. It's not well known, but Hedda will give a young actor good publicity in exchange for a 'poke.'"

***

In October of 1951, MGM assigned Elizabeth Taylor and Debbie the task of flying to Washington to represent the studio at a celebration of the 50th anniversary of the American Movie Theater. The other industry representatives also commissioned to attend the event weren't familiar to Debbie. They included Adolph Zukor, the CEO of Paramount.

At the official ceremony, President Harry S Truman welcomed them to Washington, and made some remarks. After the ceremony, he invited the representatives from Hollywood to join him at the White House for drinks. His wife, Bess, did not come down to greet them. "That means I can slip an extra bourbon or two," Truman whispered to Debbie.

After a few drinks, Truman played the piano for them, inviting Debbie to sing "I Wanna Be Loved by You." She later said, "I was accompanied on the piano by the most famous man in the world, who had dropped the atomic bomb on Japan. Imagine such a thing!"

She also recalled that Truman was the first of many presidents she'd meet over the years. "I thought John F. Kennedy would come on to me, based on his reputation, but he merely shook my hand. It was a different scenario with my fellow Texan, Lyndon B. Johnson. He made a pass at me, but I didn't accept it. I didn't want to piss off Lady Bird."

***

Part of Hollywood royalty, with links to both MGM and Paramount, the rich playboy, Arthur Loew, Jr., phoned Debbie and asked her for a date. She was flattered and accepted. Loew had recently ended affairs with both Elizabeth Taylor and Janet Leigh, who by now was preoccupied with Tony Curtis.

"I not only got invited to visit Harry Truman at the White House, but when I was married to Eddie Fisher, he invited us to visit him at his home in Independence," Debbie said.

"He had named Eddie his favorite G.I. He told me I was one lucky gal to make off with a guy like Eddie."

Loew was on the prowl again, and remembered having met Debbie before. She was in awe of dating such an important player within the Hollywood elite, and was eager to go out with him, although Hedda Hopper had warned her that he was one of the biggest wolves in Tinseltown.

"He wasn't the prettiest boy in Hollywood," she said. "No competition for Curtis, Rock Hudson, or Tab Hunter, much less for that divine Robert Wagner. But Arthur was charming—almost charismatic."

Loew's interest in Debbie came and went within a period of ten days. Joan Collins lay in his future. She was already sending out her "siren call" in his direction.

On their first date, Loew took her to La Rue's, an upscale French restaurant operated by Billy Wilkerson of the *Hollywood Reporter*. He assured her that they would get written up in Wilkerson's column the next morning. "It's publicity both for his restaurant and for us."

Within a glittering world of crystal chandeliers and silver, they passed the first booth. Upholstered in gold-colored leather, it contained Humphrey Bogart, sitting alone. Loew told her the booth was always reserved for Bogie, La Rue's most faithful VIP patron.

The waiter appeared to take their drink orders. She became the only patron there that night who ordered milk, Loew preferring two gin martinis.

The menu was entirely in French, so she pointed to escargots as an appetizer. They were served without shells, in a casserole, and she ate them, later almost vomiting when she learned they were snails. For a main course, he recommended *Tournedos La Rue*, served with white truffles.

After dinner, he drove her up into the Hollywood Hills to a lookout point where lovers gathered to neck. As he moved toward her, she pushed him back. "Hedda Hopper told me you were a wolf."

"Don't I deserve at least a kiss?" he asked her.

"Is this a sing-for-your-supper kind of date?" she asked. "Okay…one kiss."

A compromise was reached. She would give him another kiss, but only after he took her back home to her doorstep. He agreed, and she thought that was the last she'd ever see of him. But on Evergreen Street, he asked for another date two nights hence.

As they were seen around town, Hopper wrote that she predicted marriage in their future. During the short time Loew was with her, she found he knew everybody who was important in town. "No

For a while, Debbie dated Arthur Loew, Jr., "The Prince of Hollywood" and the heir to the founders of MGM and Paramount.

"I made a mistake," she said. "I didn't put out. So I lost him to Joan Collins, Eartha Kitt, and James Dean. Arthur was versatile in his sexual partners."

one noticed me. Everybody was sucking up to Arthur."

She was swept into glittering nights at Ciro's, the Mocambo, or Cocoanut Grove. "Arthur seemed to be on the guest list of every Hollywood party." Producer Joe Naar invited them to a raucous Hollywood party, where she hung out with what she later called "a prehistoric gathering of the Rat Pack, minus Humphrey Bogart and Judy Garland."

He dated her a few more times, before he eventually realized that she didn't feel comfortable in upscale restaurants and chic night clubs. He therefore let her plan the agenda for one of their upcoming dates: She wanted to be taken to Barney's Beanery for chili, perhaps a hamburger. It had been serving those dishes since 1927 to Clara Bow, Clark Gable, Jean Harlow, and John Barrymore. The sign over the counter read "FAGOTS *(sic)* KEEP OUT!"

He then took her to see the film version of *A Streetcar Named Desire* (1951), where the performances of Marlon Brando and Vivien Leigh awed her. She could hardly imagine she'd get to know them in the years ahead. The night ended at Will Wright's Ice Cream Parlour.

Loew could not go on settling for merely a chaste kiss, and eventually, he moved on to other lovers. Elizabeth Taylor had maintained their friendship even after she had broken off their love affair. At MGM, in makeup, she updated Debbie on Loew's new lovers, both of whom were unknown to her. One was the African American singer from South Carolina, Eartha Kitt; the other a former hustler, the rebellious young actor, James Dean.

***

Debbie never knew how John Barrymore, Jr. got her phone number, but he called and asked her for a date. She was flattered to get an invitation from the heir to the throne of the "Royal Family of Acting." He was her same age, born to John Barrymore, "The Great Profile," and the actress Dolores Costello. John Jr. was also the nephew of Lionel and Ethel Barrymore.

When Debbie went out with him, he'd already made four pictures—two in 1950 (*The Sundowners* and *High Lonesome*), and two in 1951, *Quebec* and *The Big Night*.

Unlike Arthur Loew, who liked chic clubs and restaurants, John preferred simple evenings, a movie followed by pizza at Encino's and a walk along the beach.

"John Barrymore, Jr., the son of 'The Great Profile,' was a very intense young man," Debbie said. "He seemed to know he could not live up to the reputation of his father, acclaimed as one of the great actors, at least when he was young and before he turned into a Hollywood drunk."

"My dating of John Jr. ended when I invited him for a sleepover at our house, and Ray kicked him out in the middle of the night."

He spoke a lot about the Barrymores, and seemed to be living in the shadow of his celebrated father. He told her that his parents separated when he was 18 months old. "Dad wasn't there for me when I was growing up."

"Dad told me he lost his virginity at the age of fifteen to his stepmother, Mamie Floyd," John claimed. "He's had every woman from Tallulah Bankhead to Carole Lombard."

He quoted his father's advice to him about women: "Don't trust any of them as far as you can throw Fort Knox. They're all twittering vaginas."

"The few times I saw him, he was always intoxicated," John said. "For a while, he lived with that hellraiser, Errol Flynn. When he had to pee, he rarely made it to the toilet. In a room full of people, he'd retreat to a corner. Once, he rushed into the women's toilet and pissed away. A woman came in and chastised him, 'Mr. Barrymore, this is for ladies!' He whirled around, shaking his penis at her, and said, 'So, madam, is this.'"

Once, when they visited a tavern in Malibu, both of them ordered cokes. During their time there, he made several trips to the men's room, and she later realized he must have been taking drugs. Driving her back to Burbank, he often put his head out the window as if he were going to throw up. He complained that he was nauseated and might not be able to drive back home.

He asked her if he could sleep over. At first, she thought he was suggesting going to bed with her, but he explained that he'd be fine if he could sleep on the sofa in her living room.

Minnie greeted them at the door and after assessing that he was ill, invited him to sleep on the couch, getting him a glass of warm milk, some sheets, and a blanket.

Ray had been asleep at the time, but when he got up to go to the bathroom, he discovered John, horizontal, on the sofa. He ordered him out of the house at once.

He pleaded with Ray, "I'm too sick to drive. Please let me stay." Debbie and Minnie begged Ray to relent, but he virtually kicked John out the door anyway.

The last Debbie saw of John was him staggering out of her house. He never phoned for another date, but she read about his future escapades in the newspapers. On several occasions, he was arrested for drunk driving, for speeding, and for violent and abusive behavior toward his first wife, the actress, Cara Williams. The couple had a son, John Barrymore III.

A decade later, Debbie dined at Trader Vic's, a *faux* Polynesian restaurant in Manhattan. She looked up from her table to be greeted by John. At first, she didn't recognize him, as he'd aged a lot and had a beard.

He spoke of that night her father kicked him out of his home in Burbank. "Actually, I wasn't sick—it was all an act. My plan was to wait until everybody was asleep. Then I was going to slip into your bedroom and take your virginity. Obviously, that scheme didn't work."

"I'm sure I missed a big thrill," she answered, sarcastically.

He looked down at her and then walked on.

[In 1975, during John's marriage to his third wife, Jaid, the couple became the parents of actress Drew Barrymore.]

***

MGM did not have a lot of young, eligible bachelors with whom to arrange publicity-seeking studio dates for its starlets. *[John Ericson, Richard Anderson, and Rod Taylor were possible candidates.]* So the publicity department arranged dates for its female stars with rising actors from other studios. Consequently, a date was set up between Debbie and Rock Hudson, then under contract to Universal.

When he arrived at her doorstep, she was stunned by how tall he was. "I think he was at least ten feet towering over me," she said. "Of course, I'm exaggerating, but not that much. To talk to him, I had to look toward the sky."

In addition to being tall, Rock was one of the handsomest men she'd ever met. Before getting a contract at Universal, he'd been a truck driver until he was discovered by the (predatory) gay agent, Henry Willson, who always put his wannabe actors on the casting couch before signing them. Rock told Debbie, "My real name is Roy Fitzgerald."

"He was Mr. Beefcake (a new word I'd learned)," she said. "Not just tall, but solidly built, wavy-haired, and with a dazzling smile. He wasn't stuck up like Tony Curtis, but down to earth. He loved to laugh and told amusing stories—often dirty. I didn't admit it to him, but I'd never seen him on the screen. When I first met him, he was making a movie called *Iron Man* (1951) with Jeff Chandler, the actor with the premature gray hair."

Rock was filled with optimism for his future in films, in spite of what he admitted were several awkward appearances on screen.

"As an actor, I'm compared to a wooden Indian," he said. He took her to the Cocoanut Grove, where photographers snapped their picture as they entered. She spotted Judy Garland sitting with Peter Lawford at a distant

It all began on a studio-arranged date whose purpose involved generating publicity for up-and-coming stars such as Debbie Reynolds and "that handsome hunk," Rock Hudson.

The two clicked as friends and began a lifelong relationship, often dishing their other lovers with each other.

The only possible conflicts that arose (and none of them was ever too serious) was when they found themselves dating the same guy.

table. Even the mysterious Howard Hughes was there, escorting the beautiful Lana Turner.

"It was a grand evening of entertainment," she said. "But I forgot who was performing that night. It might have been Vic Damone."

"All evening, Rock was the perfect gentleman—no hanky panky under the table."

A sexy blonde stopped at their table. "It was Marilyn Monroe, whom I'd met on Oscar night," Debbie said. "She smiled at me, but bent down and kissed Rock on the lips."

"Give me a ring, sweetie," Marilyn told him.

"Obviously, he'd known her before, maybe as David knew Bathsheba," Debbie said. "He gave no details as Marilyn staggered toward the ladies' room with that walk of hers, for which she should have been arrested. I watched her later, when she came and joined the table of Darryl F. Zanuck from Fox. She was the only woman present at a table otherwise occupied by six men in business suits, probably from the New York office. I just hoped poor Marilyn would not have to service all of them before the night was over."

After dinner and the show, it was time to return to Burbank. Transportation was not a problem. A studio limousine had picked them up and taken them to the Cocoanut Grove, and was later waiting to deliver them back to their homes.

"He didn't put the make on me all night," she said, "unlike some guys. Besides, I was just too short and he was just too tall. It would have been impossible for our bodies to have fitted together."

"Thanks for being the perfect escort," she said.

"I think you're charming," he said. "A lot of fun. Some day—sooner than later—I'm sure you'll meet your Prince Charming and live happily ever after."

"I sure hope so," she answered.

Then he glanced at his watch and kissed her lightly on the cheek. "Gotta run. I've got a hot piece waiting for me at home."

***

It was at this time in her life that Debbie faced two milestones, one romantic, the other professional.

She would be offered a movie role that would immortalize her in cinematic history, and Prince Charming, "the man of my dreams," walked into her life.

Chapter Three

DEBBIE IS CAST IN HOLLYWOOD'S GREATEST MUSICAL,
SINGIN' IN THE RAIN
("I CAN'T SING, AND I CAN'T DANCE,")

"GENE KELLY MADE ME BLEED. I WAS A VIRGIN AT THE TIME."
[DEBBIE'S STATEMENT WAS ACCURATE, BUT COYLY MISLEADING.]

IN ONE OF PARIS' MOST EXPENSIVE HOTELS,
DEBBIE SCORES A HIT WITH **JOLTIN' JOE DiMAGGIO** AT BAT

SWINGING IN MEXICO WITH THE KING OF THE JUNGLE
"SEXY LEXY" BARKER ("ME TARZAN, YOU DEBBIE")

Just past her 19th birthday, Debbie Reynolds in her first starring role burst onto the scene in MGM's 1952 *Singin' in the Rain*.

"Louis B. Mayer forced me onto Gene Kelly, the co-star of the picture. He wanted a dancer, and I wasn't one, but I could learn...and damn it, I showed that fucker. Oh, my poor bleeding, aching feet. The role was more painful than childbirth."

Robert Wagner, as Debbie Reynolds admitted years later, "was the only man I ever really loved. My deepest regret is that we never married. Of course, he never asked me. I thought he was the most beautiful man who ever set foot in Tinseltown. Instead of R.J., I made three nightmarish choices in husbands."

R.J. first met Debbie at a party when she had signed with MGM, under Louis B. Mayer, and he had signed with Darryl F. Zanuck at Fox. He even dared to date the mogul's daughter, Susan Zanuck.

The first time Debbie went out with this "heartthrob" (as she called him) was on a double date arranged by their studios. She had just completed *Two Weeks With Love*. In *With a Song in My Heart*, (1952), with Susan Hayward cast as the tragically heroic singer, Jane Froman, R.J. had played a brief role as a shell-shocked soldier to whom she sings.

Debbie saw the movie three times before leaving the theater. "I decided then and there that R.J. was the man I was going to marry and have three children—two boys who looked like him and a girl who, poor thing, looked like me."

R.J.'s appearance in *With a Song in My Heart* brought tons of fan mail into Fox. Zanuck told him, "I'd better make you a star, boy. All those matinee idols of the 1940s are getting a bit long in the tooth and not able to reliably get it up, as opposed to the old days when they each had three conquests a night."

Zanuck also said, "I hear that outside your dressing room door is the most crowded place on the Fox lot—telephone operators after work, secretaries, starlets, each hoping you'll give them a poke."

Years later, Debbie wasn't quite sure which boy escorted her that night during that double date with R.J. She didn't remember the name of his date, either. "All I knew was that I had eyes only for him. What a great looker. What a good dresser, immaculate, clean-cut, all American. He was one classy guy, the most perfect of the male species. He was only two years older than me, but twenty years older in terms of sophistication, style, and manners."

After that double date, R.J. phoned Debbie late the following morning and asked her out. "This time it'll be a real date," he said, "not one arranged by the studio."

"What about the girl you were with last night?" she asked.

"Who? I don't remember any other girl. I was

Hollywood moguls predicted that Robert Wagner (R.J.) would fade with the stardust memories of the 1950s and all those "pretty boys" like Tab Hunter and Troy Donahue.

Debbie could have told them differently. This "gorgeous heartbreaker" would survive into the 21st Century.

"He was the man of my dreams, but ended up in the bed of that Natalie Wood," Debbie said. "Not that it did her any good."

out with you. That's why I kept gazing into your eyes all night."

He wanted to meet her in the lobby of the Roosevelt Hotel on Hollywood Boulevard, almost opposite Grauman's Chinese Theater. It dated from the 1930s and had been visited by virtually every movie star since then.

When she talked about it with her father, he refused to allow her to drive into Hollywood in her car. He demanded that R.J. drive to Burbank and pick her up, and that he deliver her back home by 11:30PM. *[That involved an hour's drive from his home in Bel Air to Debbie's house, and then another hour's drive back.]*

If her memory served, he took her to Musso & Frank Grill on Hollywood Boulevard, which had been launched in 1919, and had fed every star from Charlie Chaplin to Gloria Swanson. Under old oak beams, she ordered roast chicken with cranberry dressing and rissole potatoes, which came to $2.50, plus another 35¢ for bread and butter pudding.

After that, they went to Olvera Street in downtown L.A., which was like a quickie trip to Mexico. He bought her a pair of *huaraches* (hand-woven sandals) as a gift to her. Then, urgently out of time, they had to begin their transit back to Burbank, where Roy was impatiently waiting up.

She got a light kiss on the lips that night, but on subsequent dates, he became more amorous, "always pressing his luck to the limit," she said. "R.J. was not used to getting turned down."

"We went to Hollywood parties, where he seemed to know everybody. As a teenager, he'd caddied for Clark Gable, Bing Crosby, and Cary Grant at the Bel Air Country Club.

One night, having met R.J.'s parents and finding them delightful, Debbie got permission to stay over at the Wagner family's home. She slept with his mother, Hazel, that night, and R.J. joined his father in the other bedroom.

Gradually, Debbie came to know a lot about "God's gift to women," as she called him. As the years went by, she heard of his A-list of Hollywood seductions: Joan Crawford, Yvonne de Carlo, Tina Sinatra (they were engaged), Mona Freeman, Lori Nelson, Jean Peters (who later married Howard Hughes), Terry Moore (who claimed to have married Hughes aboard a yacht at sea), Linda Christian (Mrs. Tyrone Power), Stefanie Powers, Elizabeth Taylor, even sultry Lana Turner.

"Debbie and Robert Wagner made the perfect couple, or so it seemed," claimed Gene Kelly, who knew both of them. Fan magazines at the time hailed her as "The Girl Next Door," and labeled him as "The All-American Boy."

Both of them still lived at home with their parents. Debbie's press agents at MGM seized on the romance, as did those of Wagner at Fox, hoping that the two would wed. One agent told her, "You and R.J. make hot copy."

Although accounts differed, R.J. had been spotted by the notorious gay talent agent, Henry Willson, who preferred handsome young men whom he "auditioned" on his casting couch. He was famous for coming up with new, catchy names for his stars, although R.J. refused to alter his birth name. In addition to several others, Willson "created" Rock (Hudson), Guy (Madison), and Troy (Donahue). Collectively, they became known as "the pretty boys of the 1950s." Debbie always wondered if R.J. ended up on Willson's casting couch, but was too embarrassed to ask.

Although aging as a matinee idol when Debbie met him, Tyrone Power still exuded masculinity and male beauty.

"He was the matinee idol of my movie-going in the 1940s," Debbie said. "If I were into older men, Ty would be at the top of my list. He was as good looking as Robert Taylor mistakenly thought he was."

In those days, Debbie was the virtual president of what those gossip mavens, Hedda Hopper and Louella Parsons, defined as the "No Necking League" [aka "The 'No Sex Before Marriage' League"]. It's not that R.J. didn't try to seduce her. He did. Of course, he could have had more sex than he needed, but perhaps he viewed Debbie as a challenge. At any rate, he kept dating her and kissing her, going as far as he could.

"Debbie was crazy about me, and I loved her," Wagner said. "But I never tumbled all the way like I did with other women. I've always been a little more casual about life than she was, and I wasn't sure we'd mesh together."

Once, after an encounter of R.J. and Debbie with Gene Kelly, her future co-star, Kelly said, "Those love birds made the perfect match. I thought I heard the sound of wedding bells, although they were very young. She was *The Girl Next Door*. He was *The Boy Next Door*. They were a couple that could only have been spawned in America."

"No one could play a homosexual bitch better than prissy Clifton Webb," said director Otto Preminger, who cast him as Waldo Lydecker in *Laura* (1944).

When he was cast in *Titanic* (1953), Robert Wagner played his son aboard the doomed ocean liner.

As Webb confided to composer Cole Porter, "I wanted R.J. for my lover—not my son. Alas, our co-star, Barbara Stanwyck, sank her painted nails into him instead."

Debbie got permission from Roy and from Minnie to attend a weekend house party on Lake Arrowhead. It was the home of Watson Webb, who worked in the film department at Fox as "the head cutter." The 14-room home was surrounded by beautiful grounds and had a small dock equipped for boating and water skiing early on most mornings, when the water was smooth.

The guest of honor that weekend was another

Webb, Clifton, who had become her friend after that trip to Jamaica. She was also introduced to the dashing matinée idol of the 1930s and '40s, Tyrone Power. He was there with his French wife, Annabella, although the pair seemed on the verge of divorce.

Debbie went over beautifully with her fellow guests, entertaining them with her impersonations, which included everyone from Zsa Zsa Gabor to Barry Fitzgerald.

The next day, down at the dock, she had a long chat with Power. She would later write, "Tyrone Power, as a star, was right up there with Clark Gable and Gary Cooper. And being in his physical presence was almost overwhelming. He was so beautiful, so charming, so gentle, so sensitive, so kind—to everybody." Yet she didn't want to get carried away, since her heart belonged to R.J.

She told him that she'd heard Clifton Webb asking the host if he would assign R.J. to his bedroom. "I don't know if that request was granted, but do you think Clifton has a crush on R.J.?"

"I'm sure he does. Who doesn't have a crush on this divine boy? I know I do." Then he smiled enigmatically.

Had she heard right?

After that weekend, R.J. and Debbie continued to date. Professionally, their careers were taking off, hers with an offer to star as the female lead in *Singin' in the Rain* and his to play the lead in *Beneath the 12 Mile Reef* (1953) with Terry Moore and Gilbert Roland.

In makeup, early one Monday morning at MGM, Elizabeth Taylor asked Debbie if she'd surrendered "it" yet to R.J.

"No, and it's damn hard turning him down," Debbie answered. "He can be so persistent, and he's so appealing. Actually, I've had him several times in my dreams. I want him to be my husband, not my lover."

"Better surrender it, girl," Elizabeth said. "His banana should meet your cherry to make a banana split at some point. Half the girls in Hollywood, and all of the gay guys, are after R.J. He's at the age when a young man is at his sexual peak, and he has to get it from someone. Better it be you than some slut like me."

"Elizabeth, you're anything but a slut," Debbie responded.

"I was just being dramatic. Actually, though, I'm not a scarlet woman. Color me purple. Frankly, I could go for R.J. myself."

And so she did one day.

***

At the Watson Webb party, Tab Hunter had been a surprise guest, joining Debbie and Robert Wagner as the youngest guests there. She'd met him casually in 1949, but on Lake Arrowhead, she got to know him better and liked him

57

a lot.

She hoped, however, that her host, Watson Webb, wouldn't assign him as R.J.'s roommate. She'd heard from R.J. that Hunter was the "prettiest of the pretty boys" in gay agent Henry Willson's "stable of young colts."

In some ways, Debbie thought Hunter was a far more attractive male animal, with a better body, than R.J. But that didn't mean she was going to make a play for him, since she knew he was homosexual, and at that point, her heart still belonged to R.J.

She'd seen Hunter in his debut film, *Island of Desire* (1950) in which he, cast as a Marine, was stranded on an island with the luscious, but older, Linda Darnell. One critic claimed that, "The movie is a dud, but it's worth the admission to see Tab Hunter's magnificent body on display."

After the party at the Webb estate on Lake Arrowhead, Debbie and Hunter began to date. She found him a reliable "fill-in" when R.J. was otherwise occupied. She suspected he had some mysterious affair going on.

The first time Hunter "dated" Debbie was in the summer of 1952, when billboards across Los Angeles were displaying his body in *Island of Desire*.

At a premiere, photographers practically stampeded to take their pictures, the captions billing them as "America's Sweethearts." One columnist, not knowing that Hunter was a homosexual, suggested that marriage was in the offing.

As Hunter recalled, "Everybody was glamourous that night, except for me with my too short pants on my rented tux and the junk heap I drove to get there."

He and Debbie stood behind John Wayne, Gregory Peck, and their women, waiting for their elegant cars to be retrieved from a back lot and returned to whomever had originally deposited them. Hunter's vehicle—an unpaid-for-1941 Ford coupé "that smoked like Oscar Levant"— arrived at the end of the red carpet. He compounded his embarrassment by having to hand the parking attendant an I.O.U. for one dollar because "I was that broke."

On subsequent dates, the couple adopted a somewhat bizarre hangout, the New Folies Burlesque in downtown Los Angeles, "whooping and hollering" at the strippers.

Hunter claimed that of all the young starlets he dated in his early career, only

"Tab Hunter had the body, and he had the looks," Debbie said. "He also had the perfect physique and oodles of charm. I was his 'arm candy' at premieres, but never more than that. He batted for the other team."

Debbie and the actress Lori Nelson endured as friends.

***

One spring morning, Debbie was summoned once again to the ivory-colored office of L.B. Mayer. From behind his platform desk, he looked her up and down "like I was a slave on the auction block" (Debbie's words). She would always remember the sunflower yellow vest he wore on that bright day.

He wasted no time getting to the point of the meeting. "A surprise is coming your way," he said. "I'm casting you in a musical starring Gene Kelly and Donald O'Connor. We don't have a title yet."

She was flabbergasted, remembering, "I was thrilled but also horrified at the challenge. Kelly and O'Connor meant singing and dancing. They were two of the best in the business. Could I do it? I didn't let Mayer know how scared I was."

"I can't dance," she confessed.

"You'll dance!" he responded in his most commanding voice.

He was buzzed by his secretary, Ida Koverman, who announced, "Mr. Kelly is on his way."

Within minutes, Debbie was shaking his hand, finding him "looking more than a little puzzled."

"Gene, I have just surprised Debbie and now I have the same surprise for you," Mayer said. "I'm casting this girl in your next musical as the leading lady."

He turned to her and evaluated her harshly. "Do you sing? Do you dance?"

"Not really," she answered. "A little jitterbugging, the fox trot."

"Can you do a time step?"

She claimed she could, and performed before him, doing a "waltz clog"— not the time step.

His face reflected his disapproval. "What about the Maxi Ford?" he asked.

"Sure, I drive my own car."

"You're one mixed-up girl. A Maxi Ford is a dance step."

It was Kelly's favorite dance step, known among dancers as "the traveling time step."

Kelly then turned to Mayer. "What are you doing to me, L.B.?" he asked.

"The girl stays in the picture," Mayer said in his most demanding voice. "Case closed."

Years later, Kelly dismissed Debbie's account, claiming, "Ever since I saw her do the 'Abba Dabba Honeymoon' number in *Two Weeks With Love*, I wanted her for the role of Kathy Selden. Also, there was never any meeting in Mayer's office."

In direct contradiction, Ida Koverman, who had arranged the meeting of Debbie, Mayer, and Kelly, said, "She told the truth. Gene did not."

"So I got the role and Kelly could do nothing about it, even though he was the biggest star at MGM in those days," Debbie said. "But he got his revenge on me by working me nearly to death. Fortunately, Arthur Freed, the producer, adored me, and he was the biggest musical bigwig at the studio."

Freed imported a lot of young male dancers and choreographers from Broadway to help him stage his musicals. Collectively, they become known as "the Freed Unit." One day, Debbie was walking with Esther Williams and Red Skelton, with whom she had appeared briefly in *Three Little Words* (1950). On the MGM lot, they passed a bed of pansies blooming in the California sun. "Look, ladies," Skelton said: "A bed of pansies otherwise known as the Freed Unit."

In yellow raincoats and boots, even an umbrella, Debbie and her *Singin' in the Rain* co-star, Gene Kelly, were ready to let it pour. "I was terrific in the musical except for my voice. I hated the way I sounded."

Freed assigned the Brooklyn and Bronx-born screenwriting team of Betty Comden and Adolph Green to come up with a scenario for the musical. They didn't know the title of the film, nor who the stars would be.

Freed had told them he was considering Howard Keel, the new singing sensation who had co-starred with Betty Hutton in *Annie Get Your Gun* (1950). Fred Astaire was another possibility.

But these actors were tossed aside when Gene Kelly wanted to star in the musical and also to co-direct it with Stanley Donen.

Jean Hagen delivers her most memorable performance in *Singin' in the Rain*, playing the squeaky-voiced Lina Lamont, whose career would be wrecked at the dawn of the talkies.

At the premiere of her latest picture with Kelly, she is supposed to sing. Behind the curtain, Debbie's Kathy Selden supplies the sound as Hagen lip-synchs. Midway through the illusion she's trying to create, Kelly pulls the curtain to reveal to the audience whose voice they're actually hearing.

Before Debbie was cast, Freed surveyed possible stars on the MGM roster. Kathryn Grayson had the best voice, but having been born in 1922, she was considered—according to the standards of her day—as a bit too long in the tooth for an *ingénue*. "I want someone fresh-faced and innocent-looking. An actress like Pier Angeli meets that criterion, but she's wrong for the part. June Allyson might have done it ten years ago, although she's hardly innocent, called MGM's nympho in residence. Jane Powell looks the part, but her voice is too operatic."

Finally, Freed's choice narrowed down to Debbie. "From what I hear from the boys who date her, she is still innocent. Apparently, her Dad guards her pussy like Fort Knox. Perhaps if a guy gets lucky, he can kiss her on the cheek at her doorstep. Her Dad is waiting inside the door to see that his daughter meets her 11:30PM curfew."

Then Freed came up with a title, naming it after one of his biggest song hits, "Singin' in the Rain," which had been performed in one of MGM's first talking musicals, *The Hollywood Revue of 1929.*

Neither Comden nor Green liked the title. "What does it mean?" she asked. "Except for one song interlude, it has nothing to do with our story."

The plot for *Singin' in the Rain* took place during the awkward transition, beginning in 1929, when studios switched from the Silents to the "Talkies." Its setting evoked the end of the Roaring Twenties, the era of the flapper, best portrayed on the screen by Clara Bow and Joan Crawford. It was a time when young people danced the Charleston, and the shimmy came into vogue. Victorian dresses and long hair were tossed aside for bobbed hair and short dresses showing "gams." It was also the era of bootleg "hootch" and a stern-faced President, Calvin Coolidge.

The picture dealt with the dilemma of many stars who did not have voices that recorded well. A major casualty of those changing times was John Gilbert, a matinee idol of the 1920s and the former lover of Greta Garbo. His voice recorded as too high-pitched. Many other 1920s stars did not make the transition to talkies, although Gilbert struggled on in a few pictures before his early death. The vamps of the silent screen, Gloria Swanson and Pola Negri, soon became *passée.*

Debbie would never forget the first day she was summoned to his office. He told her she owed a big debt to Mayer for getting her the role. "He was a major force in my career, too, and one day you'll sing his praises if *Singin' in the Rain* makes you a major star."

The interview lasted for about half an hour. Near its end, Freed came out from behind his desk. Suddenly, without warning, he unzipped his pants and exposed an erection. Apparently,

Arthur Freed was a great lyricist. His talent graced hits which included *The Wizard of Oz, Meet Me in St. Louis,* and *Singin' in the Rain.*

When he summoned Debbie to his office, he told her, "I have a treat in store for you." Then he unzipped his pants and displayed his erect penis.

he'd been fondling himself behind his desk.

She gasped but said nothing. "I didn't know whether to play it cool, or else scream and run." She pretended a greater maturity than she actually had. "Did he want me to treat it like a lollipop or not?" Finally, she told him, "It's certainly something to admire."

After a few seconds, he returned to his desk and dismissed her.

She later learned that Freed was known as "The Flasher" at MGM and had a fondness for exposing himself to teenage girls.

In her autobiography, *Child Star*, Shirley Temple wrote that she was only twelve when Freed unzipped for her and exposed his penis. "I was innocent of the male anatomy, and I giggled. That infuriated him. He told me to get the hell out of his office."

Debbie found Stanley Donen, the co-director of the picture, much easier on her than that stern taskmaster, Kelly. Donen was also a producer and choreographer, and he'd directed both Kelly and Sinatra in the musical *On the Town* (1949).

One day, Elizabeth Taylor arrived on the set of *Singin' in the Rain*. At first, Debbie thought her friend wanted to take her to lunch in the commissary. As it turned out, she had a date with Donen. He appeared, kissing her on the lips, lingering for quite a while before he turned to Debbie and invited her to join them.

Over their meal, Elizabeth confessed that she and Donen were conducting a secret affair. It had begun when he started to direct her in *Love is Better Than Ever* (1952). "I asked Stanley to prove the validity of the title—and did he ever! This is a dark secret, so don't blab. He's divorcing Jeanne Coyne, your dance teacher, and plans to marry Marion Marshall. In the meantime, he's got me."

[After her marriage and ultimate divorce from Donen, Marshall became the second wife of Robert Wagner, Debbie's all-time crush.

"Oh, what a tangled web lovers in Hollywood weave," Debbie said.]

Having begun his career on Broadway as a chorus boy, Stanley Donen, a South Carolina native, had just completed the musical *Royal Wedding* (1951), starring Fred Astaire and Jane Powell.

In time, he would be linked to one of Debbie's alltime favorite musicals, *Seven Brides for Seven Brothers* (1954) with Howard Keel and Jane Powell, who had nabbed a role that Debbie coveted.

***

Decades later, looking back at her tumultuous life, Debbie claimed that the most difficult ordeals in her life included mastering the choreography and interpersonal complications of *Singin' in the Rain* and giving birth to Carrie Fisher.

On her 19th birthday, she began a three-month period of rehearsals at MGM to master the dance steps needed. Kelly showed up on the first day to teach her some steps himself, including the Maxi Ford.

In the beginning, he seemed quite patient with her, telling her that he resisted taking dance lessons when his mother enrolled him at the age of eight. "I was constantly getting beaten up by school bullies who called me a sissy. I dropped out, but resumed when I was fifteen and big enough to fight back."

He demonstrated some of the more difficult dance steps himself. "His legs were like pistons, and his thighs were as strong as Hercules," Debbie said. "I can't vouch for other parts of his anatomy."

Unlike Freed, Kelly detested Mayer, calling him "a ruthless bastard. He has this veneer of benevolence and self-righteousness. But that fools no one except maybe an innocent little thing who was Miss Burbank of 1948."

He introduced her to a trio of talented dancers and choreographers who would be her teachers in the weeks ahead: Jeanne Coyne, Ernie Flatt, and Carol Haney.

Coyne's divorce from their co-director, Stanley Donen, had come through. Ironically, in 1960, she would marry Kelly. "That's keeping it in the family," Debbie said.

Haney later choreographed *The Pajama Game* on Broadway, and eventually, Flatt became the choreographer for *The Carol Burnett Show*.

Kelly dropped in every three days or so to see how Debbie was doing with her lessons. "At no time did I get one word of praise, one word of encouragement. He was a hell of a taskmaster, always criticizing. At times, I wanted to bash the fucker in the face. Instead of that, after he'd left one day, I bashed in a mirror on the set in my frustration. He was talented, yes, but a shit as a human being."

The lessons dragged on and on, and she found them increasingly difficult, but worked hard to master all the steps. One day, after her instructors had left for lunch, she crawled under a piano and began to sob. Suddenly, she looked up and saw only a pair of pants and shoes. They were worn by Fred Astaire, whom she'd met during the filming of *Three Little Words*.

He coaxed her out of her nesting place and took her to a neighboring sound stage, where he was rehearsing with Hermes Pan, the best-known choreographer in Hollywood.

She witnessed how even the master

Fleeing from crazed and screaming autograph-hunting fans, Gene Kelly, as movie idol Don Lockwood, jumps into a car piloted by a young starlet, Kathy Selden (Debbie).

Without knowing it, this intruder would launch her into stardom at the dawn of the Talkies.

of the dance found certain steps difficult and only achieved his idea of perfection after grueling mistakes and revisions of his movements. "As much as I detested Kelly was how much I liked and respected Fred. He urged me to go back and master those damn steps, and I did."

***

At long last, Debbie was given the script of *Singin' in the Rain* to read. She was to play starlet Kathy Selden. Kelly was cast as Don Lockwood, a matinee idol of silent pictures, who was most often teamed with his leading lady, Lina Lamont (Jean Hagen), a beautiful but vain, vacuous, cunning, and shallow silent screen star.

The film's second lead was played by Cosmo Brown (Donald O'Connor), Don's best friend. All of them worked for the same fictional studio, Monumental Pictures.

To escape from a mob of his screaming fans, Don flees after a premiere at Grauman's Chinese Theater and jumps on a trolley car, from which he leaps into an open jalopy driven by Kathy.

As her car with its unwanted passenger moves down the street, she mocks his silly screen stardom and claims she is a serious stage actress.

Days later, the studio boss, R.F. Simpson (Millar Mitchell), summons his cast and crew to present a demonstration of how a musical number would be staged in a talkie. In the center is a huge mock wedding cake. The demo opens with dancing girls circling the cake.

To Don's amusement, Kathy (Debbie) pops out of that mock cake right in front of him. She may be a serious actress, but as a means of paying the rent, she's got to take whatever job she can in the meantime.

Kathy (Debbie) is humiliated when he learns she's only a chorus girl. At the end of the number, she confronts him. Furious, she picks up a cake and tosses it at him. He ducks and the cake hits Lina Lamont, who is elegantly dressed and made up, directly in the face. She screams in panic.

Before filming began, Kelly wondered if Debbie would be able to hit Hagen in one take. As a skilled Girl Scout, who knew how to throw a ball, she assured him she could. Just in case, he lined up four cakes. Jean was prepared to get smashed several times. If so, she'd have to retreat to her dressing room at the end of every take and change into a fresh duplicate gown.

"Debbie got me right in my face on the first round," Hagen said. "I was forever grateful to her for being such a good shot. I pitied those people in silent films who were always getting a creamy cake thrown in their face. Now I know what it feels like."

While shooting a scene with Don (the plot includes the filming of "a movie within the movie"), Lamont defiantly informs him that she maneuvered to get Kathy fired. After searching for her, he finds Kathy still at Monumental Pictures, but working on another film.

Within the film, all these flirtations occurred after the 1927 release of *The Jazz Singer*, in which Al Jolson is heard singing. *Singin' in the Rain* is a spoof of the turmoil unleashed upon the entertainment industry in the late 1920s when movies went from silent to sound. The (fictitious) head of the fictitious studio (Monumental), R.F. Simpson (Millard Mitchell), decides to turn the latest Lockwood/Lamont vehicle, *The Duelling Cavalier*, into a talkie. However, Lamont's voice is grating and comes with an adenoidal, whiney-sounding New York accent. Her voice—its tonalities, intonations, and pronunciations—is disastrous, and the movie is beset with a lot of other difficulties.

Don and Cosmo want to rename it *The Dancing Cavalier,* and they ask Kathy to (secretly) dub the disastrous voice of Lamont.

At the premiere of *The Dancing Cavalier,* the audience clamors for Lamont to sing. Don and Cosmo decide to double-cross her. Out front, Lamont is lip-synching Kathy's voice from behind the curtain. Kathy is actually singing (ironically, in the film, Debbie's voice is also dubbed). The curtain is raised, and Lamont is exposed, meeting ridicule and mockery from the audience. Horrified, she flees in disgrace, her film career over. Don proudly announces to the audience who the real star of the picture is.

The movie ends showing Don and Kathy kissing in front of a billboard announcing their latest picture—*SINGIN' IN THE RAIN.*

***

In addition to Kelly, Donald O'Connor as Cosmo Brown was Debbie's other co-star. "We adored each other the day we met and became instant friends," she said.

At the age of 12 in 1937, he'd appeared with Bing Crosby in *Sing You Sinners*. After a brief movie career as a juvenile, he moved to Broadway, but was lured back to Hollywood in 1941.

In 1949, he became a footnote in movie history by appearing in the lead role in *Francis*. Released in 1950, it was the first in what became a series of silly but commercially successful films about a soldier befriended by a talking mule. His talents were wasted as he starred in one talking mule picture after another.

"Donald could dance almost as well as Kelly," Debbie said. "Keeping up with those two guys was impossible for me."

One day, Marilyn Monroe appeared on the set and gave O'Connor "a slurpy wet one." (Debbie's words). As she looked on, Monroe informed him, "I just want to get acquainted as only I know how. It's been announced that we're going to co-star in the Fox musical, *There's No Business Like Show Business* (1954). Oh, yes, that dyke, Ethel Merman, is in it, too."

Originally, Kelly didn't want Jean Hagen cast as Lina Lamont. To portray the silent screen star with the squeaky, irritating voice, she was greatly inspired by the performance of Judy Holliday in her Oscar-winning role of Billie Dawn in *Born Yesterday* (1950).

When Debbie met her, Hagen was fresh from her success in the *noir* crime drama, *The Asphalt Jungle* (1950), in which she competed with another blonde, Marilyn Monroe. She told Debbie, "I think Marilyn is too much of a caricature to ever go big in the movies."

"I love the very talented Jean Hagen," Debbie said, "But she sure was no fortune teller."

Ironically, of all the stars who appeared in *Singin' in the Rain*, Hagen was the only one who would be nominated for an Oscar—in her case, as Best Supporting Actress of the year. *[She lost to Gloria Grahame for her performance in* The Bad and the Beautiful *(1952) opposite Kirk Douglas and Lana Turner.]*

Hagen had made her film debut in the classic *Adam's Rib* (1949), co-starring Spencer Tracy and Katharine Hepburn. She became even better known when she played the wife of Danny Thomas in the hit TV series, *Make Room for Daddy* (1953-56).

A future star, Rita Moreno, had a small role in *Singin' in the Rain* as Zelda Zanders, "the Zip Girl," a close friend of Lamont.

Debbie met Mae Clark, who had an uncredited role as Lamont's hairdresser. Because of financial difficulties, she was taking whatever roles came her way. Back in the 1930s, she was a big star, achieving screen immortality when James Cagney smashed a grapefruit in her face in the classic gangster flick, *The Public Enemy* (1931).

***

Not just the acting, but the musical numbers made *Singin' in the Rain* memorable. Debbie performed "You Are My Lucky Star" from the play, *Broadway Melody of 1936*. However, the song was cut, Debbie complaining, "It was in too high a key for me." The footage was saved and later was inserted into the context of *That's Entertainment III* released in 1994.

The dance number, "Good Mornin'" in *Singin' in the Rain*, remains one of the most memorable in movie history, even though it was "living hell" for Debbie to perform. In the photo above, she energetically dances with Donald O'Connor (left) and Gene Kelly (right).

"When I was told I had to dance with those two hoofers, each of them among the best in the business, I felt there was only one way out for me: Go into the kitchen, shut the doors and windows, and turn on the gas, dying slowly and painlessly from carbon monoxide."

In another scene, the camera descends from a crane overhead, and Donen ordered Kelly to kiss Debbie passionately. "He took me in his arms, holding me tight. Suddenly, I felt a foot of tongue down my throat. I'd never been French kissed before, and I found it disgusting. I reacted in horror and gagged. I wanted to throw up. I was stunned that a thirty-nine-year-old man would do that to a teenage girl. It was vulgar!"

Debbie's first number was "All I Do Is Dream of You" from the 1934 Broadway hit, *Sadie McKee*. "Kelly told me to make my taps sharp and clear, so it was recorded on a sound stage with a wooden floor. He popped in during rehearsals and criticized virtually every move I made. Talk about giving a teen gal confidence!"

It was during this shoot that Debbie heard the ground-shaking news that Louis B. Mayer had been booted off the lot. His replacement was Dore Schary. Her new boss was said to go in for message pictures instead of frilly and frothy MGM musicals, the kind Mayer liked and the type that Debbie was hoping to star in in the 1950s.

Kelly told her he'd heard that "Schary doesn't like cutie pies like Debbie Reynolds and Jane Powell." Consequently, she feared for her future at MGM.

Of all the song-and-dance numbers, the hardest for Debbie was "Good Morning" from *Babes in Arms* (1939), a film that had starred both Judy Garland and Mickey Rooney. It had been inspired by a Broadway play with the same name from 1937.

"Kelly insisted we do that couch scene a hundred times," she said. "We started at 8AM. By nightfall, my feet were bleeding. At 11PM, I collapsed on the set and had to be taken home in an MGM ambulance."

In Burbank, an alarmed Minnie summoned the family doctor, who ordered two days and nights of complete rest. Calls came in from MGM demanding that she return to work at once, but Minnie was adamant and followed the doctor's orders.

Ironically, after that ordeal, Kelly ended up liking the first take after all.

Returning to the studio, Debbie was summoned to makeup. The artists there had been told to make her look like a flapper from the 1920s. "They plucked my eyebrows but assured me that they would grow back. They penciled in thin lines of mascara, which was the style of that day. Regrettably, my eyebrows never grew back. That's why I always travel with my eyebrow pencil wherever I go. The same thing happened to Lana Turner when she was an MGM starlet."

O'Connor executed one of the great solo numbers in the history of Hollywood musicals when he performed "Make 'Em Laugh." Although it was saluted at the time as an original song, it bore a striking resemblance to Cole Porter's "Be a Clown" used in the Arthur Freed-produced musical, *The Pirate* (1948).

In it, O'Connor danced, sang, and clowned, using every trick in his vaudeville background. This time, it was he who collapsed after the final take. He entered the hospital for five days, his condition hindered because he'd smoked four packages of Camel cigarettes between takes.

After seeing the final cut, Freed suggested to Kelly, and he agreed, that the movie needed a big dance number before it could be released. Cyd Charisse, who had previously performed at the *Ballet Russe de Monte Carlo*, was brought in to dance with Kelly. He didn't need to teach her to dance.

The role played by Cyd Charisse (*left in the photo above*) was that of a long-legged beauty in a green-sequined dress with a Louise Brooks hairdo. She vamps her way through the most dramatic and self-consciously *avant-garde* sequence in the film.

Together, she and Kelly created a memorable, sexy number, a combination of music and dancing.

It was a difficult shoot, made even more so when Charisse had to appear with streamers of Chinese silk fifty feet long attached to her shoulders. A high-velocity wind machine was needed to keep the streamers airborne.

The musical highlight of the film was the title song performed by Kelly. As his biographer, Clive Hirschhorn wrote: "He abandons himself to a California cloudburst, kicks and stamps at a gutterful of water, climbs halfway up a lamppost, arms outstretched, water pouring onto his face as he defied adversity. The number is an apotheosis of his art and the climax of an adventurous film career."

Kelly later said he had a horrible cold and was running a temperature of 103°F. "I feared I was going to catch lethal pneumonia with all that cold water raining down on me."

[Debbie later acquired many of the costumes from Singin' in the Rain, *and displayed them when she opened a hotel in Las Vegas, hoping one day to feature them in a museum devoted to costumes from classic films.*

She always remembered her bleeding feet and used that for comedy in her act years later in Las Vegas.

She confessed to her audiences, "During the making of Singin' in the Rain, *Gene Kelly made me bleed. I was only a teenager at the time. And a virgin."*

Of course, the hip Vegas audience assumed that she meant that he penetrated her hymen.]

When *Singin' in the Rain* opened, it received modest success and generally got good reviews. Debbie experienced the first reviews of her life, and most critics seemed to think she handled the role of Kathy with verve, brightness, and skill.

It became the tenth-highest grossing movie of the year in the U.S. and Canada, but MGM was disappointed, having anticipated it would be their big grosser at the box office that year.

Debbie, Kelly, and O'Connor were not nominated for an Oscar. As mentioned, Jean Hagen was nominated for Best Supporting Actress. The following year, however, Arthur Freed won a Best Picture Oscar for *An American in Paris* (1951), which had also starred Kelly.

The greatest praise came perhaps from Frank Sinatra, who would in time be the co-star in a movie with Debbie. "All film musicals before and since *Singin' in the Rain* look a bit Neanderthal by comparison. What an imagination Gene Kelly has—always at fever pitch. You could heat New York City with the fire of his creative candle!"

Over the decades since its opening, *Singin' in the Rain* has been discovered by each new generation and hailed in most circles as the best film musical of all time.

In 1989, the U.S. Library of Congress selected it for preservation in the National Film Registry. It also topped AFI's "Greatest Movie Musicals" list and was ranked as the greatest American motion picture of all time in its updated list of movies in 2007. In 2017, *Sight & Sound* magazine listed it among the 50 greatest films of all time, *Singin' in the Rain* placing 20th.

***

For the Hollywood premiere of *Singin' in the Rain*, Robert Wagner was Debbie's escort. The glamourous and photogenic couple made a dazzling entrance just a week after she'd celebrated her 20th birthday. In a dress designed by Helen Rose, Debbie smiled and smiled for the cameras, then "smiled some more."

Consumed by stage fright at the debut of her first star role, she held R.J.'s hand tightly when the theater went dark. On the screen, Debbie, along with Gene Kelly and Donald O'Connor, excited the audience with their dancing talent and the sheer verve of their performances. As "The End" flashed across the screen, Debbie turned to R.J. "I'm a star at last!"

After that glittering event, she was disappointed that R.J. didn't call for the next two weeks. She phoned his parents to see if he were ill, but they were vague as to his whereabouts.

"Are these little desertions part of married life?" she asked Elizabeth Taylor.

"Get used to it, baby," she answered. "On my wedding night, my first husband, Nicky Hilton, left me alone in our honeymoon suite and ran off with two whores."

When another handsome, virile young actor, Hugh O'Brian, phoned and asked her to accompany him to a gala event, she accepted. Once again, she called on Helen Rose to design a gown for her.

Marion Davies, the former move star and mistress of William Randolph

Hearst, was hosting a fabulous party at her Beverly Hills mansion, to which she had invited the elite of Hollywood.

Ostensibly, the party was to honor the gay crooner, Johnnie Ray, who was the hottest singing sensation in America at the time, rivaling Eddie Fisher.

She and O'Brian showed up at the gala and wandered through the elegantly furnished room of Davies' Mediterranean-style villa stuffed with art and antiques.

Before arriving on the doorstep, Debbie knew little about Davies, except for what R.J. had told her. "She is the unofficial empress of Hollywood," he said. "Or at least she used to be, when she was shacked up with Hearst."

The couple was introduced to Captain Horace Brown, formerly of the Maritime Service. Davies had wed him after the death of Hearst, Brown becoming the only man she ever married.

She had decorated the main rooms downstairs to evoke the décor of such popular Manhattan clubs as El Morocco, the Stork Club, and "21."

"Hugh and I wandered into a stunning A-list of stars," she said. "As I looked on, he was kissed by Ava Gardner, Lana Turner, Joan Crawford, Merle Oberon, even Dinah Shore and countless others. I got a kiss and congratulations from Clark Gable, Gregory Peck, and Jack Benny, to name a few. Some of the men kissing me, I'd never met before."

O'Brian and Debbie gravitated to "El Morocco," where within the hour the hostess herself made a dazzling entrance. "I would always remember Davies," Debbie said. "She was laden with diamonds and rubies, including the longest teardrop earrings I would ever see. This mistress thing seems to reap rich re-

When sexy Hugh O'Brian (Wyatt Earp) was handed this publicity still of himself, he exclaimed, "Hot damn! And hot again! Do I ever look hot!"

Debbie seemed to think so, too, and began to date this ex-Marine, a man of machismo and action.

Hugh O'Brian escorts Debbie to a lavish party at the home of Marion Davies. Later that night, he made one thing clear to her when he parked near her house:

"You can keep that chastity belt on, but you're not getting out of the car until I get off. There are other ways to do it without my having to pork you."

wards."

"Hugh was a doll, and it was one of the most memorable nights of my life. I even danced with Gable, but he preferred Kay Spreckles as a partner and would soon marry her. Diana Dors, the blonde British bombshell, was there with her stud lover, Tommy Yeardye. In the powder room, she confided that Yeardye was 'hung like a horse.' I don't know what I was supposed to do with that data."

Broderick Crawford was drunk and practically grabbed my vagina," Debbie said. "How did I handle such an assault? "I congratulated him on his Best Actor Oscar for *All the King's Men* (1949)."

When Brown introduced Davies to Debbie, she found her fascinatingly refreshing. They chatted for a few minutes, Debbie discovering she had a potty mouth and a sense of rowdy humor. She was known to say outrageous things to the likes of teetotaler Calvin Coolidge, whom she got drunk; Sir Winston Churchill ("I hear you have the biggest dick in the British Empire"), and Albert Einstein ("Why don't you get a haircut?").

"Miss Davies, who soon became Marion, was the most notorious woman in California," Debbie said. "She called Hearst 'Droopy Drawers,' and according to rumor had had a series of affairs: Rudolph Valentino, Gable himself, Charlie Chaplin, Leslie Howard, and even Joseph Kennedy when he was not otherwise occupied with Gloria Swanson."

"I saw *Singin' in the Rain* and I just adored your performance," Davies said. "I lived through that era when the silents learned to talk. I had this god damn stutter. I was told to put a pebble in my mouth. During a scene, I swallowed the fucking thing— and that was the end of that. Fortunately, I had another hole I could use to get rid of it."

A chorus girl in the *Ziegfeld Follies*, blonde, spunky Marion Davies was plucked from the dancing lineup and turned into a movie star by press baron William Randolph Hearst.

One of the brighter lights of silent films, she was caricatured but immortalized as Dorothy Comingore in Orson Welles' *Citizen Kane* (1941), one of the greatest movies of all time.

At the end of the party, Debbie, with O'Brian at her side, thanked Davies for the invitation. "She looked Hugh up and down as if she might devour him," Debbie said.

Then she turned to Debbie. "This stud here looks like a rugged type of guy who knows what a woman wants and is ready, willing, and able to give it to her."

"I'll find that out later tonight," Debbie said, deliberately provocative to a *grande dame* who was shock proof.

Her departing words to Debbie were, "I like to entertain at home. That way no one can kick me out on my ass."

On the way out, she ducked into the

powder room for a final relief. There, she spotted Louella Parsons of the leaky kidneys. More congratulation for *Singin' in the Rain*. The gossip maven was drunk. "I see you're here with another man tonight. Wait until that little cutie, Robert Wagner, finds out about this."

"R.J. and I have no commitment," Debbie said. "We're not going steady. We see other people."

"That's for sure!" Parsons said. "Maybe you're too young for him. I hear he likes *older* women, at least at this stage in his life."

That was the first clue Debbie had that R.J. was seeing someone on the side. What older woman? Could it possibly be Doris Duke, the tobacco heiress, who owned Falcon Lair, the former home of Rudolph Valentino? She was known for seducing the latest round of Hollywood "hotties" such as Marlon Brando. Maybe she'd discovered R.J.

En route to Burbank, O'Brian found a secluded spot with a view of Los Angeles and pulled off the road. As she recalled, "He wanted a heavy makeout session. He was very aggressive, but didn't hurt me. At first, I gave in to him until things began to get out of control. I told him I didn't go all the way. He claimed he was desperate for relief. All of a sudden, he unzipped his pants and whipped out an erect penis. He masturbated while feeling one of my breasts."

"By the time I got home, I had escaped a deflowering, and Hugh didn't have blue balls, a term I'd recently learned. I thought he'd never see me again, because I knew he wanted more."

[Debbie was wrong about that. From that unlikely night in the city, a life-long friendship between O'Brian and Debbie would last until both of them died in 2016.]

***

For a 1952 release, Tony Curtis starred as an Arab prince in *Son of Ali Baba*. For the rest of his life, he would be ridiculed for a line he really didn't say in that movie. He owed that mockery to Debbie, who articulated it during an appearance on the Jack Paar show.

"Jack, did you see this new guy in *Son of Ali Baba?*" she asked. "Tony Curtis, he calls himself. Actually, he's Bernard Schwartz of the Bronx. He was hilarious. He tells Piper Laurie, "Yonder lies the castle of my *fodda.*"

The audience burst into laughter. The actual line was "Yonder, in the valley of the sun, is my father's castle."

"She was ridiculing my Bronx accent, perhaps by calling me Bernard Schwartz. She revealed an anti-Semitic streak in her. Maybe I'm hypersensitive on the topic. To my everlasting regret, her mockery haunted me for years. When I was introduced to people like Hugh Hefner, his first line to me was 'Yonder lies the castle of my *fodda.*' And so it went for the rest of my life. I'll owe Debbie for that."

"Instead of going after her unpenetrated vagina," he continued, "I married

Janet Leigh, her rival. Eat your heart out, Debbie!"

[Curtis' feelings about Debbie would change when later, they co-starred together in The Rat Race *(1960).]*

***

In 1952, MGM released *Skirts Ahoy!* in which Debbie appeared only in a cameo. Since the 1940s, it had been a practice of the studio to ask its contract players to make brief appearances in a film. Sometimes, the audience burst into applause at the sight of a familiar screen face.

Producer Joe Pasternak put together the package of this musical about three young women who were motivated to join the WAVES for different reasons. They were played by Esther Williams, the star of the picture, Joan Evans, and Vivian Blaine. An all-star cast featured Barry Sullivan, Keefe

> "Bobby Van and I did a show-stopping song-and-dance number in the Esther Williams' film, *Skirts Ahoy*," Debbie said.
>
> "But she upstaged us in that poster by hiking her skirt up to her cooze."

Brasselle, Billy Eckstine, and Keenan Wynn, with Debbie and Bobbie Van sparkling in a song-and-dance specialty number.

Many critics pointed out that Van and Debbie made "the right combination," evoking her movie appearances with Carleton Carpenter.

***

Debbie's next picture, *I Love Melvin* (MGM, 1953), was a lightweight comedy that reunited her with Donald O'Connor, her friend and co-star from *Singin' in the Rain*. Both of them knew that the plot was threadbare, and the only reason they were teamed was because they'd been so terrific together in *Singin' in the Rain*.

The story line, such as it was, provided an excuse to link several musical numbers together. "MGM was good at that," Debbie said.

Shot on location in New York City, *I Love Melvin* is the story of Melvin Hoover, a lowly photographer's assistant for *Look* magazine. *[Now defunct,* Look *competed during its heyday with* Life *magazine.]*

In it, Debbie was cast as a small-time actress, Judy Schneider. Una Merkel played her mom. Judy is set to marry Harry Flack (Richard Anderson), the boring heir to a paper box company.

Suddenly, Melvin enters her life. He exaggerates his position on *Look* and promises the ambitious starlet he'll get her on the magazine's cover. George Wells was both the director and co-writer. He was known to Debbie since he'd penned the Astaire picture, *Three Little Words,* in which she'd appeared briefly. The director was Don Weis, who'd had a long career at MGM, working with such stars as Bob Hope, Lucille Ball, Sal Mineo, and Red Skelton. He was even better known as a television director involved with such TV series as *The Twilight Zone* and *Fantasy Island.*

Debbie's guiding light was neither Wels nor Weis, but the famed dancer and choreographer, Robert Alton, a major figure on Broadway and in Hollywood musicals from the 1930s on. He had not only discovered Gene Kelly, but he'd had several collaborations with Astaire and designed such Hollywood musicals as *The Harvey Girls* (1946) with Judy Garland, and *Show Boat* (1951) with Ava Gardner, Howard Keel, and Kathryn Grayson. He'd also worked with such stars as Betty Grable, Marilyn Monroe, and Vera-Ellen.

Although Debbie also performed a second rendition of "A Lady Loves to Love" in a farmlike setting, the more sophisticated and formal version was used in the movie's final clip. The farm footage was saved, however, and later inserted into *That's Entertainment III,* the 1994 documentary film released by Metro-Goldwyn-Mayer to celebrate the studio's 70th anniversary.

Alton had Debbie perform a dangerous number where, amazingly, she was configured as a football thrown about by two teams. Fortunately, she'd been trained in gymnastics and finished its filming without injury. During rehearsals, her double had broken her arm.

***

During her filming of *I Love Melvin* in New York City, Debbie was sent on a publicity junket to Yankee Stadium. When she got there, she was introduced to a shy, quiet man, Joe DiMaggio. As the star player for the New York Yankees, he'd made his last appearance as a ballplayer in September of 1951. During his 13-year career, he became best-known for his 56-game hitting streak, a run of skill and luck that unfolded in the early 1940s.

Debbie poses for "shutterbug" Donald O'-Connor in their second co-starring roles together in *I Love Melvin* (1953).

"Donald and I became great friends for life except for one big blowup years later. No, we never made it, but that didn't stop him from trying over the years. He was one runty but talented little horndog, but I adored him....sometimes."

"Of course, I met him two years before that shameless hussy, Marilyn Monroe, dug her red-painted claws into all that male flesh. She was totally wrong for him. I predicted the marriage would not last as long as a plucked wildflower. I could have been the kind of wife this Italian macho man needed and wanted. However, Joltin' Joe was not gone from my life forever."

[As Debbie predicted, the DiMaggio-Monroe marriage had a short life span. They eloped to San Francisco in January of 1954, but after nine months, Monroe asked celebrity attorney Jerry Giesler to file for divorce on the grounds of mental cruelty.

After making Tammy and the Bachelor for Universal in 1957, Debbie flew to London with her husband, Eddie Fisher, who was booked into the Palladium. She didn't expect to see much of him, so she invited a girlfriend, Jeanette Johnson, a sports enthusiast and physical education teacher, to accompany them.]

Fisher wanted to remain in London for a few more days, so Johnson and Debbie flew to Paris with the understanding that they'd rendezvous there with him later.

Booked into a suite at the Crillon in the heart of Paris, Debbie met the designer, Joseph Picone, head of the Evan Picone Fashion House. He invited Jeanette and Debbie to join his wife and himself for dinner within the *Belle Époque* splendor of Maxim's.

Picone told Debbie that a surprise guest would be joining them. About twenty minutes later, she looked up to see Joltin' Joe himself headed toward their table. He kissed Debbie on the cheek. "I swooned," she said. "the moment his lips touched my skin."

During the course of the dinner, Picone and Johnson did most of the talking. DiMaggio was reserved, although Debbie noticed he kept glancing at her.

"Until I met him, I'd never been so aroused by a male animal. He was giving off vibes to make me excited. Jeanette knew all about baseball, and she spent most of the evening reviewing Joe's career highlights. At the end of the dinner, he asked me where I was staying. It seemed he was at the Crillon, too. How convenient."

"In my big dance number from *I Love Melvin*, the brilliant choreographer, Robert Alton directed me in my first glamourous dance number on the screen," Debbie said.

"I sang and danced to 'A Lady Loves to Love.' I wore a sequined outfit with a large net skirt forming a train. Dressed in top hats lined with scarlet silk, a lot of good-looking gay dancers (at least I thought they were gay) surrounded me."

"Marilyn Monroe ripped off my number when she performed 'Diamonds Are a Girl's Best Friend' in *Gentlemen Prefer Blondes* (1953)."

Back at her suite, Debbie reviewed her phone messages, most of them from members of the French press. Before midnight, while Johnson was in the shower, a bellboy delivered a manila envelope from DiMaggio marked PERSONAL AND CONFIDENTIAL.

She opened it and was shocked to see that it contained a full frontal nude of DiMaggio, snapped as he showered, no doubt in the Yankee's locker room.

"I gazed upon a watery Joe, taking in the view of him in all his uncut splendor."

[That frontal nude, widely available on the internet, was published in Blood Moon Production's scandal-soaked exposé of love, lust, and dementia, Hollywood Babylon, It's Back *(2008).]*

Debbie scribbled in a note to Johnson, "See you later, alligator," and hurried to DiMaggio's suite.

The world will never know what took place in the suite of the baseball star, but she was seen leaving his room at around 4AM the next morning.

It was Monroe herself who spread the assertion that "Debbie had Joe before I did."

Marilyn Monroe and Debbie had something in common: Both of them knew what lay hanging below that brief outline of pubic hair belonging to Joe DiMaggio. The photo above shows him nude under the shower of the locker room at Yankee Stadium.

***

In November of 1952, MGM asked Debbie to go on a publicity junket to Mexico City to celebrate two occasions: the opening of the studio's South of the Border branch, and the inauguration of Mexico's newly elected president, Adolfo Ruiz Cortines.

The columnist Hedda Hopper, in exchange for publicizing the opening

"I was used to meeting big-name stars," Debbie later told O'Connor. "But nothing like Joltin' Joe or the Yankee Clipper. I'd met Tyrone Power, but I thought Joe was the handsomest man I'd ever encountered. He had a rugged masculine appeal, more than such pretty boys as Tab Hunter and Robert Wagner."

"I was still in love with R.J., but for sheer raw sex appeal, Joe sent shivers up my spine."

of MGM's Mexican branch, went along for a free vacation. Debbie was accompanied by flame-haired Rhonda Fleming and one of her favorite actresses, Celeste Holm, who developed a friendship with Debbie during this jaunt.

Debbie also requested that her father, Roy Reynolds, be allowed to join the troupe, along with her high school friend, Jeanette Johnson, a physical education teacher, a profession to which young Debbie had once aspired.

During the southbound airplane ride, Debbie sat in a front-row seat with Holm, getting to know her personally. She had long admired her screen performances, including her Oscar win for *Gentleman's Agreement* (1947) opposite Gregory Peck. She'd also been nominated for an Academy Award for her roles in *Come to the Stable* (1949) opposite Loretta Young, to whom she was often compared, and again with Bette Davis in *All About Eve* (1950).

"Celeste Holm became my dear and trusted friend beginning with a publicity jaunt to Mexico," Debbie said. "I was starting to mess around, and I needed someone to have girl talk with...about men."

"She lent a sympathetic ear and never judged me, unlike our fellow tour group member, Miss Hedda Hopper."

"On that trip to Mexico, Celeste became like the big sister I never had, and soon I was sharing my secrets with her. At the age of twenty, I was beginning to have secrets that needed to be covered up. God forbid that my father heard about them. He still treated me like I was a thirteen year old."

The inauguration of President Cortines attracted a huge audience gathered in front of the Palace of Fine Arts in Mexico City on December 1, 1952. "I was too short to see what was going on," she said. "Suddenly, this Greek god picked me up and hoisted me onto his broad shoulders. It was Lex Barker, the most beautiful man who ever played Tarzan. At the time, he was divorcing Arlene Dahl and went on to marry Lana Turner."

After the ceremony, Barker invited Debbie to go with him to a reception for Cortines and later, to have dinner with him. That night at around eight o'clock, both of them were introduced to Cortines, who was born in 1890, making him the oldest of all Mexican presidents. He would live in history as the president who granted women the right to vote.

Johnson and her father were dining in another part of town, so she was free for a romantic candlelit dinner with Barker, whom she later dubbed "Sexy Lexy."

"I drank champagne for the first time in my life, and it made me giddy," she said. She had long been aware that Barker had a cult following that consisted not just of women, but of legions of gay men as well, many of whom viewed him as the best-looking man on the planet.

Over dinner, she discovered that this handsome hunk was no jungle man, but a well-educated, smooth, and sophisticated male with courtly manners. The son of a wealthy Canada-born building contractor, Barker attended Princeton, where he played on the football team. He later dropped out to join a theatrical troupe.

"After dinner, he invited me to go up to his hotel suite with him, and I was so intoxicated I accepted. For some reason, I was not afraid."

To Holm, she confessed what had happened that night: "He stripped off his clothes in front of me and tried to get me to take off my own, but I held out. I'd seen nude men before in El Paso, but nothing like Lex. One night in years to come, I heard Arlene talking about his big package."

"Hoping to satisfy him, I went down on him, like that high school boy, Stevie, had taught me in the woods near El Paso when I was only six years old. When he blasted off in my mouth, I wanted to spit it out, but he made

"Lex Barker was blonde and devastatingly attractive, towering over me at 6'4", the same height as Rock Hudson. He was the first man I met who could have charmed the panties off me."

"I was intent on keeping my virginity until I got married, but what red-blooded woman could resist the sex appeal of this Adonis? How could Arlene Dahl have ever let him go?"

me swallow it. Then he shocked me. He went down on me. I didn't know men did that to women. I thought it was only what women did to men, or men did to other men. It really felt good. He begged me to spend the night, but I couldn't. I got back to my own hotel at three in the morning. Fortunately, Roy was still asleep."

***

While Debbie was in Mexico City, Hedda Hopper followed her around until Debbie managed to shake her. "She was a dangerous woman and could destroy a girl's career, so I had to be careful."

The columnist was even older than the Mexican president, having been born in 1885, the daughter of a Quaker butcher. "When I was an actress at MGM, L.B. Mayer insisted I lie on his well-worn casting couch. Before he got booted out of MGM, did he force you onto that damn couch?"

"He did not. Maybe he knew I wasn't that kind of girl."

"Don't try to fool me, kid," Hopper answered. "I have it on good authority that you were seen leaving Lex Barker's suite before dawn."

"That's a damn lie," Debbie said. "I don't know where you heard such filth. It was my former schoolmate, Jeanette Johnson, who visited Barker's room. We look a bit alike."

"Oh, I see," Hopper replied. "That's your story. I don't believe a word of it, but I won't print the item. You'll owe me one. But one day, girl, I'll be devoting entire columns to your exploits. All stars get involved in a scandal at some point in their lives."

Before the official opening of MGM's offices in Mexico City, Debbie had four days off, and used it for a beach holiday in Acapulco. There, she, along with Holm, spent time swimming in shark-infested waters with their newly minted friend, the handsome Olympic champion, Bob Mathias.

At the time, Acapulco was in its heyday as the favorite vacation retreat of Hollywood stars. Merle Oberon, the reigning duenna of the resort, must have read in the papers about the arrival there of Debbie with Holm, because she called their hotel and invited them to a gala party she was hosting the following night.

The next morning, Debbie had to go to a local fashion house and be fitted into a gown for the occasion. She and Holm made their entrance into Oberon's lavish villa. Although she'd aged since she'd made *Wuthering Heights* in 1939, Oberon was still a dazzling beauty.

She took Debbie's hand and introduced her around. Oberon's Hollywood friends already knew Holm. Debbie met Gary Cooper, who in turn introduced her to his companion, Barbara Stanwyck. They were there filming *Blowing Wild* (1953) with the Mexican actor, Anthony Quinn.

"Hedda Hopper, 'The Bitch of the World,' looked like a combination of June Havoc and the stripper, Gypsy Rose Lee," Debbie said.

"Well dressed and always well groomed, she hid under a ridiculous picture hat, thinking she was God Almighty. For a long time in Hollywood, she was always making and breaking stars. "

"I had to put up with her, and our relationship over the years went down a rocky road, but she was powerful, so I had to keep brown-nosing her."

"Stanwyck chose not to shake my extended hand and diverted her eyes elsewhere," Debbie said to Holm. "Do you think she's jealous of me because I'm young?"

"She's jealous of you because she's having an affair with your cute little boyfriend, Robert Wagner," Holm said.

Debbie was shocked, not believing what she'd heard. "You're a very honest person, but this time I can't believe what you just said. R.J. and Barbara Stanwyck? My God, she's old enough to be his grandmother, or at least his mother."

"Believe it!" Holm said. "Clifton Webb is also in love with Wagner, but R.J. prefers Stanwyck. As you know, all three of them are starring in *Titanic* (1953)."

Dazed by the revelation, Debbie was suddenly aware that the very tall Gary Cooper was hovering over her. "Wanna dance, little girl?"

She was swept up in his arms, as they danced to a Mexican orchestra. "He held me closer and closer. He was so tall, and I was so short. He was virtually rubbing that big thing of his in my face. The dance floor was very dark, and he unzipped his pants and placed my hand inside. I couldn't believe it. No wonder he was called the Montana Mule. I got the feel of my life before I returned him to Stanwyck, who glared at me."

***

Years later, during the late 1970s, at a dinner at the home of dancer Tamara Geva, Celeste Holm discussed her enduring friendship with Debbie with the senior author of this book, Darwin Porter. "It has survived because I know that the real woman behind all that virginal sweetness and light that she presents to the world. She'd like you to believe that she never had sex outside of her three marriages. But many Hollywood wolves raided the henhouse, finding Debbie ripe for plucking—that's *plucking*, darling. Rhymes with."

"When she's not posing for the camera being Tammy," Holmes continued, "she's one tough little cookie, very realistic about life. Don't get me wrong. I adore her, and she knows I don't buy that virginal act. Tammy could be had. Let me tell you about the time both of us made a movie with Frank Sinatra."

Barbara Stanwyck played R.J.s mother in *Titanic*, but in real life, she became his lover after her divorce from Robert Taylor.

As Wagner later confessed, "I took Barbara home from a party. I saw this magical look of desire in her eyes. We danced in her living room and drank champagne. I left at dawn. Our love affair lasted for four years."

Chapter Four

DEBBIE ADAPTS & ACQUIESCES TO HER
HOLLYWOOD IMAGE

BIDDING FAREWELL TO HER "ALLTIME DREAMBOAT," ROBERT WAGNER, SHE ENGAGES WITH EDDIE FISHER

WHO TOOK HER VIRGINITY? WAS IT FISHER? WAS IT SINATRA?

Half the trees in Canada were cut down to make newsprint for the romance of Eddie Fisher and Debbie Reynolds, dubbed "America's Sweethearts." Through hysterical coverage from almost a dozen movie rags and the mainstream press, the world learned of the day-by-day courtship of this handsome singer and this beautiful, bubbly MGM star.

Decades later, their daughter, Carrie Fisher, said, "They graced the tabloids of the day, so adorable, so ogled by an array of eyes. So cute and cuddly and in some way charmingly average...the Brad Pitt and Jennifer Aniston of the late 1950s, only slightly more so."

After the success of *Singin' in the Rain*, Debbie had hoped for stronger roles in musicals and romantic comedies, theatrical opportunities that would better showcase her talents. Her wish did not come true. She went from "one silly little picture to another" (her words), often co-starring with older actors such as Dick Powell and Frank Sinatra.

On some occasions, she didn't get the lead, but "played second fiddle" to such stars as Jane Powell. For the most part, these films were released during the final years of the 1950s, when MGM musicals were going out of style.

The studio was impressed with Bobby Van and Debbie in their cameo appearances in *Skirts Ahoy!* It was decided to co-star them together in *The Affairs of Dobie Gillis*, released in the summer of 1953.

Arthur Loew, Jr., whom Debbie had briefly dated, was the producer of *The Affairs of Dobie Gillis*, and he granted her star billing, a position she would not get again until she shot *Tammy and the Bachelor* at a competing studio (Universal) in 1957.

Debbie and Van, who was married at the time to starlet Diane Garrett, became "great pals," as she claimed. "He was full of energy, and, as a dancer, he could jump around like a pogo stick."

Bob Fosse, the talented dancer and choreographer, was also in the cast. "He was brilliant and gave us great advice in our dance numbers, then retreated to his dressing room, where he entertained a series of starlets. I later found out what the 'big attraction' was."

***

Jack Cummings had previously cast Debbie in *Three Little Words* and in *Two Weeks with Love*, and he also gave her the lead in his next musical, *Give a Girl a Break*, released by MGM in 1953. Its producer was Stanley Donen, whom Debbie had met during his affair with Elizabeth Taylor.

"I faced stiff competition with three of the best dancers in Hollywood," Debbie said. *[She was referring to Marge and Gower Champion and Bob Fosse.]*

The plot was already familiar to movie goers. A temperamental star of a new Broadway musical walks out, leading eventually to an unknown being cast to replace her. Ted Sturgis (Gower) is the benefactor who supports the replacement, suggesting that the producers should "Give a Girl a Break"—hence the movie's title. In this case, it was Debbie in the role of novice Suzy Doolittle. Ted

Max Schulman, a writer and humorist, was known for the TV and short story character (Dobie Gillis) he had created. Schulman wrote about young people in collegiate settings, having carefree times and falling in love.

His character of Dobie Gillis became the subject of a series of short stories later compiled into an anthology entitled *The Many Loves of Dobie Gillis*. Later, Schulman borrowed from this material to fashion a screen play for Van and Debbie, entitled *The Affairs of Dobie Gillis*.

is shocked when his former dance partner and lover, Madelyn Corlane (Marge Champion), shows up to try out.

Complicating matters, composer Leo Belney (Kurt Kasznar) wants ballerina Joanna Moss (Helen Wood) for the unfilled part. Bob Dowdy (a "gofer" portrayed by Fosse) is enchanted by Debbie as Miss Doolittle.

Expect the usual ups and downs. Long before the end, the audience already knows that—despite some setbacks—Debbie will eventually win the role, and that love will triumph between Marge and Gower, and between the "gofer" (Fosse) and Debbie.

She and Fosse performed beautifully together onscreen. Off screen was different. She later described working with him as "one of the worst experiences of my life."

"Fosse and Gower were fierce competitors," she said, "each dancer trying to outdo the other."

During the filming of the previous movie he'd made with her, Fosse had ignored Debbie off screen. Now, during the crafting of *Give a Girl a Break,* when he began paying her unwanted attention, she wished he had continued to snub her.

"I never met a man, before or after, who was so proud of his endowment," she said. "He would come up behind me and press 'God's gift to womanhood' into my back when I was seated. It was rock hard. It was obvious that he wasn't wearing a dance belt. I tried to push him away, as I was feeling every inch of it. It was like a foot long, or so it felt. One day, he came into my dressing room and exposed himself. I kicked him out."

"Our director, Stanley Donen, seemed smitten with Fosse," Debbie claimed. "He was so awed by his talent that he followed him around like a lovesick puppy. In one of our love scenes, all the camera saw was his face. In another

Debbie *(left)*, Bob Fosse, and Marge Champion in *Give a Girl a Break*.

Throughout the course of filming Fosse frequently tried to impress Debbie with the size of his endowment.

scene, he managed to capture my left ear. I went to the front office when the guys there watched the footage. They agreed with me, and ordered Donen to reshoot our scenes."

Even after he'd exposed himself to her, Fosse kept pressing his erect but covered penis up against her. Finally, she went to a men's store in Culver City. There, she asked the sales clerk "for a very, very large jockstrap, the biggest you've got."

When he looked perplexed, she said, "It's to hold up my boyfriend so his thing doesn't droop halfway down his leg."

The next day, she placed the mammoth jockstrap in Fosse's locker. After that, she never again had to face his "prodigious appendage."

"Frankly, I think Fosse needed a woman who had something the size of the Grand Canyon. If I'd given in to him, I'm certain that I would have bled to death."

During the brief period when Debbie was a contender for key role she eventually lost to Jean Simmons, the noted Shakespearean actor, Sir John Gielgud, tutored her in Shakespearan techniques.

***

After some lackluster roles, Debbie was delighted to learn that she was the number one choice to play the lead in MGM's upcoming dramatic comedy, *The Actress* (1953). "[It was] my first chance to play a real dramatic part. I would get to star opposite Spencer Tracy, who would be cast as my disapproving father, objecting to my going out onto the wicked stage."

It was based on an autobiographical screenplay entitled *Years Ago*, by Ruth Gordon, and it would eventually be directed by George Cukor.

Awaiting a screen test, Debbie studied the script, which called for the portrayal of an aspiring actress, Ruth Gordon Jones. In addition to her father, there would be scenes

Debbie always regretted "the role that got away," in *The Actress* (1953), a flavorful account of Ruth Gordon's experience in Massachusetts in the early part of the 20th Century and her dream of becoming an actress.

The role went to Jean Simmons (right). Spencer Tracy played the film's irascible father, Teresa Wright the mother.

84

with the very talented Teresa Wright, cast as her mother As a college boy in pursuit of Debbie, Tony Perkins would make his film debut.

She was instructed to report to MGM Monday morning for her screen test, with the understanding that it would be directed by Cukor himself. "I was terrified. After all, he had directed such stars as Katharine Hepburn, Greta Garbo, and Joan Crawford, and for a while, he had helmed Vivien Leigh and Clark Gable in *Gone With the Wind* (1939) until MGM fired him."

Several scenes were shot during the screen test, and when it was over, Cukor congratulated her. He wrote Gordon: "I think we've got the right girl. Debbie has real charm (a mighty rare commodity among younger actresses), temperament, individuality, pathos, and humor. What the hell else do you want? I even pulled in John Gielgud to help her with the Shakespeare passages."

Debbie moved ahead with costume fittings, makeup tests, and hairdressing. The following week, an MGM messenger boy came to tell her that Dore Schary wanted to see her at once in his office.

"I was frightened," she said. "Louis B. Mayer liked me, but Schary, according to rumor, referred to me as 'that silly little girl from Burbank.'"

"When I walked down the long corridor to his office, I was shaking. Once he summoned me in, he glared harshly at me. He didn't waste words."

"Cukor wants you for the lead in *The Actress*," he said. "I do not! You're wrong for the role. I've recast it with Jean Simmons in the lead. She's a real actress and, as you know, was even nominated for an Oscar for her performance opposite Olivier in *Hamlet* (1948). She's also coming out this year in *Young Bess* (1953) and *The Robe* (also 1953). She'll be brilliant as Ruth Gordon, not some cutie pie mugging on camera. That's it. You're out. Don't worry. I'm sure we'll turn up with some fluff for you to amuse popcorn eaters. I'm busy. Good morning."

As it worked out, Debbie in summer theaters in 1953 and 1954, performed in Gordon's stage play, *Years Ago*. "The role suited me just fine, and I got rave reviews."

Dore Schary, the new head of MGM, didn't like Debbie. "Mayer liked those frothy, silly musicals. I do not," he snapped.

He summoned Debbie to his office: "You're not going to star in *The Actress*. You'd fuck up this movie. I'm giving it to a real actress: Jean Simmons."

***

Robert Wagner *[widely known as "R.J."]* and Debbie were still dating, perhaps less intensely than before. They had been going together for a year and a half with no talk of marriage.

Privately, Alan Ladd told his gay friends, "R.J. is

the handsomest and sexiest young man in Hollywood." As far as it is known, Ladd never came on to his dream man. However, he did invite R.J. and Debbie to spend a weekend with him on his ranch in San Fernando Valley.

On other occasions, the couple pursued athletic endeavors such as swimming, water skiing, or else a game of tennis where she often beat him.

They were frequent visitors to the home of Clifton Webb and his overly protective mother, Maybelle. "She may have been prettier in her day, but when I met her, she looked like an aging Clifton in drag," Debbie said.

Webb had made *Stars and Stripes Forever* (1952) with R.J. and soon would be co-starring with him again.

"As gay as a goose, Clifton just worshipped R.J.," Debbie claimed. "He practically drooled over him. It was one of the most powerful crushes in Hollywood. But R.J. said he'd never made a pass at him."

"I loved the way R.J. kissed, although my responses were shy and tentative," she said. "Like any red-blooded American boy, he had more on his mind than a quick kiss inside the front door at the end of the night. He always held me close when we were dancing, and I felt the 'impression' of his body against mine. It frightened me. One night, he dropped by my house to tell me he was going on location in northern California to make *The Silver Whip* (1953) with Dale Robertson and Rory Calhoun."

Later, Debbie confessed, "It was on that night, with him going away tomorrow, that I decided then and there was the time he was going to screw me. At long last, the cherry would be popped. I sent out age-old signals that this female was ready, willing, and able to be deflowered."

"Amazingly, he did not pick up on my signals. If he had only asked, or given me some signal, I would have said yes. But he did not."

On location, he wrote to her, saying, "Maybe after this picture is wrapped, I'll be able to win you because I am sure I love you."

As he later said, "Between the time I wrote that and the time I returned to Hollywood, life happened."

Wagner was immediately cast in *Titanic* (1953), starring Barbara Stanwyck and Webb. "The sexual chemistry between Barbara and me was evident in our first scene together," he claimed. "I was twenty-two and she was forty-five."

"On our first date, I ended up leaving her house at dawn," he said. "But I was back the next night. Our coming together—no *double entendre* intended—was like gangbusters. She was good in the kitchen and even better in the boudoir. For the next four years, we became part of each other's lives. She was very loving, very caring, very involved with me—and highly sexed."

"As for Debbie, we saw each other on two or three dates when I needed to appear with a girl on my arm at some premiere. She was still Debbie, the Virgin Queen. Our relationship became part of the stardust memories of yesterday."

In 1954, Debbie announced, "I no longer have any desire to be a gym teacher." That was the year *Modern Screen* magazine led off with her being the most popular female star of the year, followed by Grace Kelly, Elizabeth Taylor, Doris Day, June Allyson, Marilyn Monroe, Ann Blyth, Janet Leigh, Jane Powell, and Pier Angeli.

Some of the most popular male stars that year included Rock Hudson, Marlon Brando, Tony Curtis, Tab Hunter, Robert Wagner, and William Holden.

For her next picture that year, MGM lent her out to RKO at the request of that studio's owner, the fabled aviator and eccentric billionaire, Howard Hughes. The arrangement was for the filming of yet another romantic comedy, *Susan Slept Here* (1953).

Dick Powell was an unlikely choice as Debbie's leading man. Having been born in 1904, he was fifty years old at the time he was called upon to play love scenes with Debbie.

Shot in Technicolor, the movie was based on a play of the same name by Alex Gottlieb and Steve Fisher.

As the lead, Mark Christopher, Powell was cast as a thirty-five-year-old screenwriter, suffering from writer's block after winning an Oscar for his previous work. On Christmas Eve, Sam Halon (Herb Vigran), a vice squad sergeant, arrives on his doorstep with Susan Landis (Debbie), a rambunctious seventeen-year-old who is fighting, kicking, biting the cop, and screaming. Abandoned by her mother, she'd been arrested for hitting a sailor over the head with a beer bottle.

Mark is trying to write a script about juvenile delinquency, and the cop suggests that during the holidays, he use Susan as a guinea pig to learn more about vagrant youth up close and personal.

At first, he is reluctant to take her in until he learns that she'll be sent to jail if he doesn't. As the plot develops, Susan gradually begins to fall in love with her "captor." This is observed by his long-time *fiancée*, Isabella Alexander (Anne Francis), the daughter of a U.S. Senator.

Francis had never looked more glam-

"Howard Hughes, of all people, came up with the ridiculous idea that I play a juvenile delinquent who falls in love with Dick Powell, an actor thirty years older than me," Debbie said. "I always felt that Dick had the sex appeal of Percy Kilbride—that's Pa Kettle to you."

"But Powell must have had something below the belt, because Marion Davies, Ginger Rogers, Ida Lupino, and Evelyn Keyes went for him. He ended up marrying June Allyson after John F. Kennedy dumped her."

ourous than she did as the *femme fatale* in *Susan Slept Here*. She appears in stunning contrast to tomboy Debbie, and would go on to greater success in the upcoming classic, *Forbidden Planet* (1956).

To save Susan from jail, Mark impulsively marries her in Las Vegas, but doesn't plan to consummate the marriage. After she's been rehabilitated, he asks his lawyer to begin proceedings to have the marriage annulled.

Glenda Farrell was cast as Maude Snodgrass, Mark's secretary. In the 1930s, she'd been a star player at Warners, most often cast as a squinty-eyed, wise-cracking dame. In *Little Caesar* (1930), she played a gangster's moll, and she became quite famous in a series of roles, cast as an intrepid ace reporter, Torchy Blaine.

Before she met the producer, director, and cast, Debbie was asked to rendezvous with Howard Hughes at his home. His reputation had preceded him. Joan Crawford claimed, "He would fuck a tree."

As a spectacularly wealthy bisexual with enormous power in Tinseltown, he'd seduced, among many others, Gary Cooper, Cary Grant, Tyrone Power, Errol Flynn, Bette Davis, Marilyn Monroe, Rita Hayworth, and even Katharine Hepburn, during a period when she thought he was on the verge of marrying her.

Debbie pulled up at his estate in her 1932 Chevy that was falling apart. That didn't daunt Hughes at all. Despite his status as a billionaire, he also drove a shabby car and dressed in ragged, baggy clothes.

She was leary about seeing him alone in his house, as he was said to specialize in young girls with large bosoms.

Lana Turner, Hughes' former lover, told Debbie that the aviator had been known to seduce five or six young women a day. "But it's kind of chaste because he likes sex only one way. His favorite way is oral, both the giving and receiving."

In a memoir, Debbie discreetly omitted most of the dirt about what happened as the evening progressed.

"If I had been dedicated to my career, I would have plopped down on his casting couch with my dress up. But I found him a bit creepy. I just couldn't go for it."

"As I retreated to the door, he followed me out all the way to my car. I told him I'd work hard to make a good movie. He handled the rejection like a true gentleman—in fact, he was kind and polite. He waved goodbye as I headed out of the driveway in my dilapidated junk heap."

The next day, she was called in to meet her producer, Harriet Parsons, the daughter of Hollywood's leading gossip columnist, Louella. Harriet was one of the first women film producers in Hollywood, known for such notable classics as *I Remember Mama* (1948), and *Clash by Night* (1952), co-starring Barbara Stanwyck and Marilyn Monroe, in which the older bisexual actress seduced the younger blonde starlet.

Debbie found Harriet "very friendly, perhaps too friendly. She invited me for a weekend at her home, promising we'd have a lot of fun. I was not interested in her kind of fun, since she was a known lesbian."

As she later told Dick Powell, "First, the owner of the studio comes on to me, then the producer. That leaves just the director."

"Welcome to show business, kid," Powell said. The two became good friends, a relationship that lasted for years.

The director, Frank Tashlin, had no interest in Debbie, perhaps because he'd recently taken a new bride, Mary Costa. He had been a gag writer for Lucille Ball and the Marx Brothers.

Among his credits as a cartoon animator was a 1937 satire *The Woods are Full of Cuckoos*, in which he had caricatured Powell with a bird named "Dick Fowl." In the 1930s, the actor had been a crooner in movie musicals, appearing on occasion with his second wife, Joan Blondell.

In the middle of filming *Susan Slept Here*, Powell invited her to visit his ranch in Amber Hills, set on 43 acres in the Mandeville Canyon section of Brentwood, outside Los Angeles. There, she was entertained by his wife, June Allyson, whom Debbie knew casually from MGM.

After lunch, while Powell went to attend business associated with his ranch, Allyson told Debbie, "Louis B. Mayer saw my screen test. He said, 'She isn't pretty. She certainly isn't sexy. She sings fairly well. She doesn't dance all that well, either. But she's got something—sign her.'"

Debbie was somewhat aware of Allyson's reputation at MGM, where she was known for having had affairs with Lt. John F. Kennedy and with Ronald Reagan, a good friend of her husband.

Maybe it was the film's title, *Susan Slept Here*, that seemed to encourage some of its key decision-makers to hit on then-*ingénue* Debbie.

Upper photo is Harriet Parsons, the film's producer, lower photo is of RKO's billionaire owner, the notoriously promiscuous Howard Hughes. Although Debbie adroited deflected their personal interest, each wanted to link her casting to her performance in bed.

The star, a known alcoholic, took Debbie on a tour of the house, and on the second floor, invited her to take in the view of the valley from a balcony. As Debbie did, Allyson emptied the contents of a flower vase into a glass and started to drink what Debbie soon realized was vodka, part of a secret supply she was hiding from her husband and the other members of her household.

Allyson, by now intoxicated, then spoke candidly, perhaps with the belief that she could trust Debbie to be discreet.

"Dick is full of shit," she said: "I mean that literally. He was born without a sphincter which, of course, is the muscle controlling bowel movements. He has no bowel control, so he takes medication—first to induce constipation, then a laxative to purge himself."

She also confessed that she was in love with two other actors—Dean Martin and Alan Ladd. "I don't plan to leave Dick, but to conduct secret affairs on the side, often in my dressing room. I'm just crazy for Alan and Dean, but I come home at night to Dick for more dick."

When Powell befriended Debbie, he was devoting most of his time to "the little black box." In association with partners who included Ida Lupino, David Niven, and Charles Boyer, he had founded Four Star Television. His ranch would later be used as a backdrop for the ABC-TV series, *Hart to Hart* (1979-1984), starring Robert Wagner, Debbie's sometimes boyfriend.

Powell's partner, David Niven, showed up late Sunday morning to spend the night. In his movies, the British actor projected an image of a suave, dry, urbane, upper-class sophisticate.

When Debbie met him, he was involved as a player in one of the most controversial films of 1953, *The Moon Is Blue*, with William Holden and Maggie McNamara, and directed by Otto Preminger. It was a saucy sex comedy about a young woman flaunting her virginity. Although evaluated as outrageous by some critics at the time, it was tame by today's standards.

Niven surprised Debbie by telling her that she had been seriously considered for the role before it was cast with McNamara.

"I had no idea," she said.

"You would have been terrific," he told her. "And I hear that you're still a virgin, but I'm not asking for confirmation."

Throughout the rest of the day, he flirted with her, but she was getting used to that kind of attention from older males.

"June Allyson taught me to project an image of sweetness and light regardless of what was going on behind the scenes," Debbie said.

"She had been America's Sweetheart in the 1940s, a role I was now assuming. Privately, June was a drunk and a nymphomaniac."

At the Oscar Awards ceremony in 1974, David Niven was surprised onstage when a streaker flashed across the stage, interrupting his speech.

Niven said, "Imagine a jerk showing his 'shortcomings' to the world."

"These grandfather guys sure come on strong," Debbie whispered to Allyson later in the afternoon.

"You're preaching to the choir," Allyson said. "Dick is even older than David."

Niven was known to have lived with the priapic Errol Flynn, and the two actors had jointly hosted the most notorious house parties and boating trips in Hollywood. Niven had seduced Ava Gardner, Rita Hayworth, Norma Shearer, Ginger Rogers, Loretta Young, and even Mae West.

He'd also had affairs with two of the world's richest women: Woolworth heiress Barbara Hutton and tobacco heiress Doris Duke.

He followed Debbie into the kitchen and came up behind her, pressing his body into hers like Bob Fosse had done. "Hedy Lamarr compared it to a beer can," he whispered in her ear.

She broke from him. "Mr. Niven, I don't drink beer. I tasted it once and spat it out."

That night, she locked the door to her bedroom.

***

MGM, with the cooperation of the State Department, decided to send Debbie, Carleton Carpenter, and Pier Angeli— an Italian actress who MGM was billing as "The Little Garbo"—on a whirlwind 30-day publicity tour of South America.

It was designed as a good will/good neighbor tour, with stopovers at each of the Loew's theaters. Debbie was excited. Since she'd studied Spanish for two years in high school, she wanted to put her limited knowledge of the language into practice. It was on this trip that she cemented a life-long friendship with Angeli.

Panama was the first stop. There, they entertained U.S. servicemen, before flying to Columbia. *Singin' in the Rain* had been a big hit in South America, and crowds in all the capitals lined the streets shouting *"DEBBIE, DEBBIE, DEBBIE"* and *"PIER, PIER, PIER."*

Columbia was a highlight. It seemed that the entire population of Medellin turned out in the street to greet them. Riding in an open convertible, Debbie said she felt like a queen as clusters of orchids were thrown at her. "It was like a purple rain," she said.

At movie houses, Carleton and Debbie sang and danced. But Angeli protested to Debbie, "I can't sing. I can't dance." Debbie taught her a simple dance routine to get her through her stage appearances, each of which terrified her.

In private, Angeli never wore makeup, with the understanding that whenever she'd been scheduled for an appearance before a camera, an MGM makeup artist would work his or her magic on her. In Columbia, for the first time, Angeli attempted to apply it herself.

When Debbie saw the results, she laughed. "Pier, you look like a clown. Ringling Brothers went thataway." She taught her new friend how to apply makeup.

"Debbie was as cool as a cucumber," Angeli said. "Every day, she'd wake me up in the morning."

"Let's go shopping," Debbie said.

The trip was tiring, but Debbie was full of energy, as they flew on to promotional gigs in Ecuador, Venezuela, Brazil, Bolivia, Paraguay, Uruguay, Chile, and Cuba.

Wherever they went, they were invited to society balls, and each of the American embassies threw receptions for them. In Chile, they got invited to the presidential palace to meet the newly elected president, Carlos Ibáñez del Campo. "Fortunately, Ibáñez spoke Italian, so Pier became our translator."

As part of a publicity junket, Debbie toured through South America with the Italian starlet, Pier Angeli.

During their flight back to California, the two young actresses were unaware that in just a few months, both of them would be competing for the same boyfriends, each with disastrous results.

If the trip had a downside, it was in Buenos Aires. "Amazingly, even though the country was in the midst of a Perón uprising, crowds turned out to greet us," Debbie said. "Armed soldiers were around every corner and even guarded our bedroom doors at night. Parts of the capital were under siege, and we were very frightened."

All in all, the trip had been a big success, and both MGM and the State Department were pleased with the results. During the plane ride home, Angeli and Debbie laughed and talked in first-class seats. The two young actresses seemed unaware of the oncoming storms that men like James Dean, Eddie Fisher, and Vic Damone would bring to their lives.

***

For her eleventh film role, Debbie was offered the third lead in MGM's *Athena,* a romantic comedy, with music, set for release in 1954. Never in her young career had she ever rejected a script, but she hated her role as Jane Powell's sister.

She phoned the producer, Joe Pasternak, objecting to her lackluster part. "How long do I have to go on living in Jane Powell's shadow?"

"You have a contract, so you've got to do the picture...or else," he said "You will be the third lead in your next picture after *Athena.* Guess who the star is? Jane Powell."

[Actually, Powell almost didn't get the role.

Elizabeth Taylor had lunch with Debbie the following Saturday. "MGM originally offered me the role of Athena," Elizabeth said. "Esther Williams was brought in as my replacement, but soon, she announced she was pregnant. I predict that Athena is going to be a fucking dud. Your role is not important, so you won't get blamed. I think that in a few months, sweet little Jane Powell will be shown to the MGM gate as ungraciously as Clark Gable was."]

The following Monday, Debbie reported to work for a script reading with her co-stars and their director, Richard Thorpe. He had helmed her in the Fred Astaire picture, *Three Little Words* (1950).

He introduced her to the other members of the cast. The attractive British actor, Edmund Purdom, had the romantic lead. Other members of the cast included singer Vic Damone, Linda Christian, Louis Calhern, Evelyn Varden, and Steve Reeves.

Purdom played a conservative lawyer, Adam Calhorn Shaw, who wants to run for the Senate, avoiding any scandal. He's engaged to a beautiful and sophisticated, but somewhat chilly society lady, Beth Hallson (Christian).

His life is about to change after he meets Athena Mulvian (Powell). She's energetic and eccentric, coming from a family of teetotalers and vegetarians, each with a religious devotion to astrology and numerology.

Athena is immediately smitten with Purdom, and shows up at his home unannounced the next day to mulch his sickly peach trees. At the end of her task, she kisses him and makes clear that she intends to make him her husband, a role he'd be suited for, she says, based on her numerological calculations. She also decides that his close friend, singer Johnny Nyle (Vic Damone), would be an ideal mate for your younger sister, Minerva (Debbie).

In addition to Powell and Debbie, there are five other sisters: Niobe, Aphrodite, Calliope, Medea, and Ceres. Their eccentric grandparents are Ulysses Mulvian (Louis Calhern) and his wife, Salome (Evelyn Varden).

Part of the plot involves their grandfather training a group of bodybuilders, each a contestant in an upcoming Mr. Universe competition. It's clear that the most likely winners are Ed Perkins (muscleman Steve Reeves) and Bill Nichols (Richard Sabre).

Expect the usual rocky road to romance between Adam and Athena, including a breakup with his girlfriend, Beth. Grandma foresees difficult times ahead, but at the end of the picture, Athena arrives at Adam's house for a reconciliation, offering to cook him ham and eggs for breakfast. She is a firm believer in the theory that "Love can triumph over the stars."

Thorpe assigned the casting department at MGM to round up a dozen or so of the young men with the best bodies in Hollywood. The gay members of the department were only too eager to begin scouting. "The casting couch must have been worn out," Debbie quipped.

She met Reeves, the only muscleman in the film who would attain stardom. Eventual winner of the real-life Mr. Universe contest, he'd already won the Mr. Pacific, Mr. America, and Mr. World competitions, and would go on to other roles in sword-and-sandal epics in the U.S. (including *Hercules*; 1958, which propelled him to stardom) and in Italy.

Meeting Debbie, he made the inevitable pass, telling her, "There's one muscle I haven't introduced you to yet."

"Save it for some gay director," she told him. "Incidentally, you can't increase its size with exercise."

Most of the singing in *Athena* went to Powell, in part because of her operatic voice. Although she didn't know it at the time, her "type" at MGM was going out of style, whereas Debbie's film career was just getting started.

In songs, Debbie was assigned "Imagine." She also performed "I Never Felt Better" with Damone.

"I found Edmund charming and ever so gracious and good-looking," Debbie said. "I could have gone for him myself if Linda Christian hadn't already staked him out. The year I worked with him (1954) was the career highlight of his life."

She was referring to two other movies he released that year: *The Student Prince* and *The Egyptian*.

Born in Brooklyn to Italian immigrants, Damone became a popular singer in the 1950s, almost a rival of Eddie Fisher. His best-known songs were "You're Breaking My Heart" (a number one hit on *Billboard)* and two number four hits—"My Heart Cries for You" and "On the Street Where You Live" from *My Fair Lady.*

There was never any romance between Debbie and Damone, although she suspected they might have had an affair if she'd sent the right signal. However, she quickly transformed it into a sisterly relationship and became his confidante, often learning more personal data than she cared to know. He was alleged to have told Purdom, "I like to shock Debbie because she is so easily shocked, perhaps virginal."

"Vic was handsome, a very talented singer, and from what I heard, a raging Romeo," Debbie said. "He often spoke to me of his girlfriends, of which he had quite a few. I heard in graphic detail what he'd done the night before."

"Vic was the first man who ever talked to me about pubic hair," she said. "R.J. never talked about his pubic hair with me, although I felt his hard penis rubbing up against me."

"Vic liked redheads, and I soon learned why. It was a big thing with him that a woman have red pubic hair. I'm sure he wondered if Maureen O'Hara or Arlene Dahl had a red bush. We both knew that Rita Hayworth didn't, because the studio dyed her hair. We suspected that Rhonda Fleming, the flame-haired Queen of Technicolor, had red pubic hair. Perhaps we should ask Ronald Reagan about that, since they were making pictures together."

"I was very shocked when Vic married Pier Angeli," Debbie said. "Pier and I had changed from our street clothes into bathing suits for a dip in my pool, and, as I noticed, she did not have red pubic hair. Vic must have married her for other reasons."

***

"My mother, Minnie, developed a crush on Eddie Fisher before I did," Debbie claimed. She never missed one of his 15-minute shows, *Coke Time with Eddie Fisher,* broadcast on NBC beginning in 1953.

Debbie was always going somewhere and rarely sat through one of Fisher's broadcasts. Minnie constantly praised the singer to Debbie. "He is so sweet, so adorable. Too bad he's Jewish, or else he might be a possible husband for you."

"Please, mother, you know I'm in love with R.J.," Debbie protested.

As she recalled at the time, "Eddie was the heartthrob of America, bigger, even, for the moment, than Frank Sinatra, bigger than all of them until Elvis came along. Eddie made nearly thirty gold records and was known as 'The Jewish Sinatra.'"

Born to Russian Jewish immigrants, he had begun his roller-coaster ride in the slums of Philadelphia, leading him to a tumultuous life of fame and fortune, drug addiction, and sorrow.

A Depression-era kid, he'd begun his singing in an alleyway, trying to lure customers to buy vegetables at a stand run by his Papa. As he grew older, he appeared in talent contests and sang at *bar mitzvahs* and at local fairs.

At the age of fourteen, he got his first big break, singing on radio in his home city of Philadelphia for $25 a week. That was also the year he lost his virginity, seducing a neighborhood girl named Tootsie Stern.

He gravitated to Manhattan and eventually appeared at the Copacabana "which launched me into Dreamland. I was no longer the skinny little Jewish kid from Philly."

With his strong and melodious tenor, his boyish charm, and his good looks, he went on to win millions of fans, mostly young girls, who shouted and cried at his concerts, screaming, "EDDIE! EDDIE! EDDIE!" Bobbysoxers adored him like they had once flocked to Sinatra concerts during the war.

Called "The Coca-Cola Kid," he plunged into a reckless lifestyle devoted to fame, money, and women. In time, before he succumbed to drugs and depression, he seduced some of the world's most celebrated women. In a memoir, he admitted to affairs with such sex symbols as Kim Novak and Mamie Van Doren. In bed with Marlene Dietrich, she advised him never to marry an actress.

Merle Oberon lured him into her much-used bed, and he also seduced Ann-Margret, Stefanie Powers, and such singers as Edie Adams, Dinah Shore,

Michelle Phillips, and Abbe Lane. Sue ("Lolita") Lyon told him she wanted him to go to bed with her to learn whether his sexual prowess matched that of Richard Burton

He even had an affair with Judith Campbell Exner, when she was not sleeping with President John F. Kennedy or with mob boss Sam Giancana in Chicago.

Include an array of Broadway or Las Vegas showgirls, and the list rises dramatically, thanks in part to a madam in Hollywood who arranged sexual liaisons among her girls and male stars.

Fisher's romance with Debbie began in June of 1954 on the set of *Athena*. He'd come to see Joe Pasternak, its producer, who wanted him to star in Debbie's next picture, *Hit the Deck* (1955).

She had heard that he'd told a reporter for *Modern Screen*, "Of all the young stars of Hollywood, I would most want to meet Debbie Reynolds."

"I find Eddie sort of cute," she said. "But at the time, I was hardly overwhelmed by him like I was with R.J." (Robert Wagner).

He told her that he was in town for his big opening at the Cocoanut Grove at the Ambassador Hotel in Los Angeles. The next day, he obtained her private phone number from Pasternak and called her at home.

Minnie picked up the receiver to hear a voice identifying itself as Eddie Fisher. Thinking he was a prankster, she quipped, "Yeah, and I'm Lauren Bacall. Do you want to speak to Bogie?"

Fisher finally convinced her that he was the real thing by warbling some lines from two of his favorite songs. Putting down the receiver, Minnie went screaming through the house for Debbie. "It's Eddie Fisher on the phone. He wants to speak to you."

After a brief chat, Fisher invited her as his guest to a ringside table at the Cocoanut Grove

Although behind the scenes on the set of *Athena*, there was a lot of horseplay with members of the good-looking weighlifting corps, on the surface, at least, the venue was one of unrelenting wholesomeness.

Depicted above are one of the couples (Edmund Purdom and Jane Powell) whose squeaky-clean interchanges helped to define the parameters of the script.

During their filming of *Athena*, the female leads (Debbie and Jane Powell) discovered that they shared the same April Fools' event: Their birthdays.

As such, the studio provided a cake and photographers to record the celebration.

on his opening night. He told her he'd have his best friend, Mike Todd, call on her and drive her to the event. She eagerly accepted his invitation.

For her gala night out, Debbie phoned Helen Rose, persuading her to design a red lace gown for her. She already had a string of pearls, but asked Jane Powell if she could borrow her ermine jacket. Before Todd's arrival, she spent two hours in a Burbank beauty parlor getting a complete makeover.

Even Roy, her father, was impressed. "As I live and die, I do believe my little Texan tomboy has become one of those Hollywood glamour gals. I hope you don't turn into a whore like the rest of 'em."

She rehearsed her arrival at the Cocoanut Grove, the most glamorous club in Southern California, usually filled with movie stars. For decoration, the owners had purchased all the artificial palm trees recycled from the set of Rudolph Valentino's most famous film, *The Sheik*. The club's decorator had added *papier-maché* coconuts and toy monkeys whose eyes lit up.

Bing Crosby had been discovered here one night by Mack Sennett. During the heyday of the Roaring Twenties, Joan Crawford had won the most Charleston contests.

Her escort downtown, Mike Todd, was just a name to her. She knew little about him, and, of course, it was beyond her wildest dreams, that he would become a pivotal figure in her life. Fortunately, before he drove to Burbank to pick her up, she'd found a magazine article in the beauty parlor and read about him.

Born to Polish Jewish immigrant in Minnesota, he was one of nine children in

Debbie, emoting with Steve Reeves in this scene from *Athena*, thought the muscle-bound Hercules "was the most perfect male specimen on the planet. He was the role model for our health-crazed musical, *Athena*, and for the bodybuilding fad that engulfed Southern California."

In association with the filming of *Athena*, Debbie, who had harbored dreams of becoming a physical education teacher, swings into action on a bar between two well-muscled studs, each a Mr. Universe candidate.

a poor family. As a boy, he was always a rebel, getting expelled from the sixth grade for running a game of craps.

For three years in the late 1940s, he'd been married to actress Joan Blondell. He'd had a lot of high profile romances: Marlene Dietrich, Evelyn Keyes (Scarlett O'Hara's younger sister), stripper Gypsy Rose Lee, author Anita Loos, and actress Jean Simmons.

He was living at a super-hectic pace, comedian Joe E. Lewis claiming, "Mike belongs on a runaway horse."

He was rumored to have killed his first wife, a student, Bertha Freshman.

CHEESECAKE: Ann Miller (left), Debbie (center), and Jane Powell, wistfully reviewing the status of their love lives in *Athena*

BEEFCAKE: *Athena* probably marked the debut of America's perception that Southern California had evolved into the nation's centerpiece of bodybuilding and male beauty, as displayed in this publicity shot for the film.

Never in my life would I ever be surrounded by such glorious symbols of masculinity," Debbie said. "Ever the show-off, I even flexed my muscles to these hunks."

The notoriously promiscuous Lana Turner once told Debbie how she evaluated men during her tours through Muscle Beach: "I look first at how they fill out the pouch in their bathing suit. Then I take in their manly chests, settling a bit on their faces, before gazing upon their magnificent thighs."

In 1944, he'd produced Mae West's controversial *Catherine Was Great*. By then, the press was calling him "America's most flamboyant, headstrong, and cocksure showman since Billy Rose."

He was directly responsible for the Ma and Pa Kettle hit series of movies in the early 1950s. When Debbie met him, he was working to perfect Todd AO, a widescreen process designed by the American optical company.

He was also creating his most famous work, *Around the World in Eighty Days*, which would premiere in 1956. One of the most expensive cinematic productions at that time, its cost, as pegged to equivalent values of today, would be $52 million.

Debbie later told Jane Powell that *en route* to the Ambassador Hotel, "Mike tried to feel me up. He told me he didn't believe I was a virgin, and said 'You've been kicking around Hollywood too long to pull that act on me.'"

"Right there and then, I had it out with him," she said. "As Eddie's best friend, I didn't want to play hanky-panky with him. I told him I wanted to be his friend, too, but we had to be friends, not lovers, not a man and a girl who hit the sack behind Eddie's back. He took it very well. I also told him he wasn't my type."

In a memoir, Fisher claimed that both Evelyn Keyes and Todd arrived to drive Debbie to the Grove, but as Debbie remembered it, she met Todd and Keyes on another night at the Grove, not at Eddie's opening.

"I arrived at the Cocoanut Grove with my cherry intact," she said. As promised, she was seated at a ringside table. Her friend, Pier Angeli, was two tables away. Debbie waved at her, noticing that she didn't have an escort. Debbie chatted with Dan Dailey, Jeff Chandler, and Gordon MacCrae, noticing that Joan Crawford was there, trying to put the make on crooner Johnnie Ray.

Linda Christian with Edmund Purdom in 1962. They had fallen in love during their filming of *Athena* with Debbie.

Each of them was miserable in their respective marriage, hers to Tyrone Power. "We were two people longing for love, with so much to give to each other," Christian said. "He kissed me softly and put his arms around me. We were both in need of love and understanding."

Vic Damone and Debbie Reynolds starred together in *Athena*.

"I fell in love with his velvet baritone," Debbie said. "It was intimate and rhapsodic. He never got into my treasure chest, but he groped it a lot. Personally, he was a real devil, and a wife abuser, and had a rough life. Two of his wives, including Pier Angeli, committed suicide."

Todd whispered to Debbie, "According to rumor, Johnnie's got a big one, and Joan wants to enjoy it."

"But he's gay," Debbie said.

"That never stopped that bitch," he answered.

During the first show, Fisher directed all his romantic ballads at Debbie. She was immensely flattered. Later, she recalled, "I think that was the night I fell in love with Eddie Fisher."

At the end of the first show, he joined Todd and Debbie at table, much to the delight of photographers who collectively gathered into an unofficial kind of press corps every evening at the Grove.

Without Debbie noticing it, Angeli was fuming. She had been designated (and invited) as Fisher's date that night, and now she was being ignored. Again without Debbie noticing, she got up and headed toward the exit, sobbing as she left.

When Debbie excused herself to visit the powder room, Crawford took the seat next to Fisher, inviting him to dump Debbie and go home with her. According to Fisher, "I guess she struck out with Johnnie Ray. She promised me that we'd make love all night."

"I was finding out that famous women viewed me as a valuable commodity," Fisher said. "It seemed that all of them wanted to get into my pants, even the men. Before I went on, Jeff Chandler had visited my dressing room. Rock Hudson had dumped him, and he wanted to make a cowboy picture with me. He asked me to go home with him that night, so we could rehearse some cowpoke scenes to-

When Debbie met Eddie, he was one of the most famous pop icons of his era, known for his singing and for his associaion with "the American Empire's" most famous beverage.

In the boom years after World War II, it was making inroads to new markets worldwide. As its spokesperson, pop singer and youth Icon Eddie Fisher became almost as famous as the soft drink itself.

gether. I'd been around the block. I knew what he wanted. I told him, 'Jeff, we're both Jews, and Jews don't make good cowboys.'"

At the end of the evening, Fisher drove Debbie all the way back to Burbank. At her doorstep, with Roy waiting inside, he kissed her on the cheek. She kissed him back, before hurrying inside.

"I thought Debbie and I would make the ideal couple—she, the All-American Girl, me, the Boy Next Door. The press would eat it up. Lots of publicity for both of us. She was very real, very natural, quite bright, pretty enough without being terribly sexy, and very talented, although hardly in the major leagues like me. She was getting a little too old for those silly teenager roles."

Fisher later told Todd and others, "Debbie is a *shiksa*, and doesn't every Jewish boy dream of *shiksa* pussy? Later, of course, we marry nice Jewish girls and settle down, have a family, and do all those good things. But for some reason, I preferred to fuck *shiksas*, since I had too much respect for Jewish girls."

***

After that night at Cocoanut Grove, "Two dozen of the world's most beautiful roses" arrived on Debbie's doorstep in Burbank. "I didn't really need to read the card, as I knew they must be from Eddie." He phoned later that day and invited her to a second night of his performance.

This time, he sent a limousine for her and no escort. However, at a ringside table, she was seated with Marlene Dietrich and two songwriter friends of Fisher's: Dick Adler and Jerry Ross, who were said to be helping Dietrich with her stage act.

Dietrich was polite but distant, and Debbie had heard rumors from Louella Parsons that she had once had an affair with Fisher, but she couldn't believe it, telling Parsons, "Eddie, I think, likes young girls. Marlene was a waitress at the Last Supper. What handsome young man would want to make love to a woman that old?"

"Robert Wagner and Barbara Stanwyck, for one," a drunken Parsons had responded.

Debbie looked startled, and finally agreed with the columnist. "You've got me there, Louella. *Touchée!*"

A bisexual, Joan Crawford at first tried to seduce Debbie—and was rejected.

Eventually, their relationship endured and then evolved into a lifelong friendship.

Golden Age Superstar Marlene Dietrich was known for her exotic and sultry glamour, and as a voracious sexual predator:

"My friend, Barbara Stanwyck, and I often have to teach these Hollywood juniors like Robert Taylor (for her) and Eddie Fisher (for me) how to make love."

"Whereas Barbara and I have sex without gender preference, the poor dears are such amateurs. They are so timid and afraid of homosexuality.".

For as long as Eddie's gig lasted, six whole weeks, that same limousine was sent all the way to Burbank to retrieve Debbie and return her. She never knew who would be joining her at ringside, his guests ranging from Gene Kelly to Donald O'Connor, her co-stars in *Singin' in the Rain.*

She often dropped into Fisher's suite after the show. He had been booked into the best suite at the Ambassador, and sometimes room service arrived with a late supper.

"Every night, he pressed me to have sex with him, but gave in to me when I asked that he hold back. After all, it was the Eisenhower era, and good girls didn't put out."

"I admit, our lovemaking was growing more passionate," she confessed to friends such as Donald O'Connor. "Yes, he continued to French kiss me. When Gene Kelly had first done that to me, I almost puked. But I became very turned on by Eddie's golden tongue. We came very close some nights to performing the dirty deed, but I always left the Ambassador just in time."

One night, he was more amorous than before," claiming he couldn't hold out," she said to O'Connor. "Over my protest, his one hand traveled all the way to Alaska while he masturbated himself."

The next day, a messenger boy arrived at her doorstep carrying a small package from the best jewelry store in Beverly Hills. She opened it to discover a red-velvet box containing an exquisite diamond-and-pearl bracelet.

"I apologize," the card said. "It was only because I love you so much that I can't restrain myself sometimes."

On Fisher's final night at the Grove, he invited every member of Debbie's family to sit at ringside. Roy turned down the invitation. "I'm not going to stay awake half the night to hear a Jew boy sing. If I want to hear someone croon, I'll play a Hank Williams record."

"Through Eddie Fisher, I got to know Mike Todd," Debbie said. "He was overpowering, very narcissistic, and demanding, an absolute control freak and a tyrant. He had a volatile temper and was known to manhandle women, especially Elizabeth Taylor. She seemed to like that. He once told me that Elizabeth was like one of America's pioneer women."

"Liz has even been known to pour her own champagne for breakfast," he confided.

Depicted above is Mike Todd's mistress before his involvement with Elizabeth Taylor.

She was Evelyn Keyes (Scarlett O'Hara's little sister), depicted here in a sexually suggestive publicity photo with John Payne for *99 River Street* (1953).

Minnie, however, was thrilled by the invitation and so was Grandma Harman, who was in Burbank on a visit from El Paso. "It was a grand evening, and Eddie almost charmed the pants off Grandma and Minnie. They swooned like school girls," Debbie said.

The following night, Fisher picked her up and drove her to the Mocambo, where they sat with Mike Todd and Evelyn Keyes for the opening of comedian Joe E. Lewis.

Earl Wilson, who was a columnist for the *New York Post,* was on one of his many visits to Hollywood. He was the first columnist to present Debbie with the big question. "When are you and Eddie Fisher going to tie the knot?"

She told him, "We're just friends."

***

The following night, actress Lori Nelson and Debbie decided to cook a dinner for Fisher and his close pal, Joey Forman. The two men had grown up together in Philadelphia. The dinner had gone pleasantly enough, as the quartet laughed and talked.

As all of them sat in Nelson's living room after dinner, Fisher handed Debbie a crumpled piece of Kleenex. "At first, I thought it was something he'd blown his nose in. But as I opened it, I discovered a large emerald-cut diamond ring, the type I'd seen Marion Davies wear when Hugh O'Brian took me to her home for a party."

"What?" she gasped, so astonished she didn't know what to say.

"Isn't eleven karats enough for you, gal?" Forman asked.

"Eddie, I can't take this," she protested unconvincingly. "It's too expensive, and I hardly know you…*yet.*"

Don't be silly," he said. "It's an engagement ring. I've staked you out. You're my girl now. Put it on your finger. It'll keep the wolves away when I'm on the road."

"He hadn't asked me to marry him," Debbie recalled. "I guess the ring was supposed to do that."

At midnight, before driving her back to Burbank, he asked her if she'd spend the night with him at his suite at the Ambassador. "You can tell Minnie you're overnighting with Lori."

"Oh, Eddie, I want to, but I need to get to know you better. Can't we postpone it a little bit more?"

"Okay, gal, if that's the way you want it. But I warn you: I can't hold out forever. I want you to be my wife, and I want to make love to you for the rest of our lives."

"I want you to be my husband," she said, "but not tonight."

"I'm one hot-blooded boy, and I have my needs," he protested.

That night, as he pulled up in front of her father's house in Burbank, "I let him fondle my breasts," she confessed. "It got so heated he took it out and

103

masturbated with his free hand, the other hand becoming 'the fondler.'"

As she later confessed to Evelyn Keyes, "He even took some of his semen and rubbed it on my lips, then French kissed me. If any other man but Eddie had done that, I would have bolted from the car after hitting him on the head. But since he was my husband-to-be, I guess the kiss was okay, but damn messy."

"During the time I got to know Debbie, we did everything together," Fisher claimed. They were beginning to attract attention from the press. "It took quite a while for Debbie to put out. But I had to have sex. My libido was on fire in those days, and thousands of girls went for me bigtime. During my dating of Debbie, I had sex at least once a day. When I returned to the Ambassador, a bimbo was waiting, often a lovesick fan. I'd kiss Debbie good night and then rush off for some heavy action with some hot *puta.*"

"Even though I had certain reservations about Debbie, we had a lot of fun in the beginning," he said. He recalled the times they went water skiing on Lake Arrowhead, swimming on the beaches of Malibu, attending bullfights in Tijuana, dining at Chasen's, arriving at chic Hollywood parties at the homes of such stars as Alan Ladd or Gregory Peck, and visiting Palm Springs for the weekend with Minnie as the chaperone.

"We were falling in love, perhaps her with me more than me with her," he said. "A disturbing thought emerged. "She and I had nothing in common when the fun things were over and we sat around. During those quiet times with nothing to do, I watched television. Marlene Dietrich and I could sit for hours talking about life and love. Not Debbie. She hadn't lived enough. We also came from completely different backgrounds. She was born into a fundamentalist Christian family, and I grew up in a Jewish household in Philly. She told me she hadn't seen a Jew until she moved to California."

"As the weeks went by, I began to notice a difference in our personalities. Unlike my stage appearances, I was shy and more reserved in private. She was a ham, always having to perform. At a Hollywood party, someone like Judy Garland sang for guests, Debbie had to follow and try to do one better, although Garland is a tough act to follow. She loved the spotlight. I hate to say this, but, as time went by, I concluded that her life was just one long performance."

***

With an eleven-karat diamond ring on her finger, Debbie decided she had to meet Robert Wagner and come to some kind of understanding about their relationship, or lack thereof.

She had once selected him as the young man to take her virginity, only she never got around to telling him. She was certain he would have been most willing.

Without phoning, late one morning, she drove from Burbank to his parents' home in Bel Air, just hoping he would be there. As she pulled into his driveway, she spotted him on the lawn. She was relieved, knowing she didn't have to get involved with his parents for this showdown.

During her drive to Bel Air, she had fantasized about how the dialogue with him would go. As regards the eleven-karat diamond ring she was wearing, she imagined that his reaction might be something like: "Debbie, you can't marry that singer guy because I'm in love with you. I've finally decided I can't live without you. I'm too much in love. I want you to be my wife, the mother of my children."

Her fantasy did not live up to reality. As she exited from her car, he smiled at her but did not rush to kiss her like he usually did. As the morning sun was beating down, he motioned for her to come and sit with him on a white-painted wooden bench under a shade tree.

At first, he sat with her in silence, not even looking at her, but staring vacantly at the grass. He didn't attempt to hold her hand as he usually did. She made her wearing of the eleven-karat diamond obvious.

"Getting married?" he casually asked. "Someone I know, perhaps? Bing Crosby, Clark Gable? Perhaps James Stewart? Certainly not Cary Grant. He's still chasing after me. Errol Flynn, no doubt. Maybe someone younger, like Rock Hudson. Surely not Tab Hunter?"

"Stop kidding around R.J.," she said, in a voice harsher than she meant. "I'm engaged to Eddie Fisher."

"Tell me something I don't already know," he said. "You've been kicking around Hollywood long enough to know it's hard to keep a secret. Everybody knows you were sitting at ringside every night during his gig at the Grove."

"Eddie and I have promised to be true to each other," she said.

"You mean, like Frank Sinatra and Ava Gardner?" he asked.

"No, I don't mean that and you know I don't." She studied his face for some kind of regret at losing her, but found nothing of the sort. If anything, he seemed to be feeling a kind of relief.

"I hope you and Eddie will be very happy and will raise a brood of eight little Fishers, each able to sing like him or dance and mug like you."

Then he rose from the bench, signaling an end to their conversation. He glanced at his watch as if late for another rendezvous. "I'm glad you came over. I have a confession to make myself. Up to now, I've slowly stopped seeing you and with a damn good reason. My heart belongs to another. I'm very much in love."

"I think I know who," she said. "Hollywood, as you know, is a very small town with a lot of gossipy mouths."

"It's certainly not Clifton Webb, although he'd like that very much, I'm sure. I'm in love with Barbara Stanwyck, a mature kind of love, hardly puppy love."

"If so, you'd be the puppy and she'd be the bitch," she said, sarcastically. Then, without saying another word, she ran toward her car sobbing. As she pulled out of his driveway, she looked back at him one final time. He stood on his lawn the way she'd encountered him, but now he looked bewildered.

She knew it was time to move on and into the arms of another handsome young man. R.J. would forever remain the boy who got away.

On looking back at what happened that morning, he said, "There was a time in my life, when I was very young, and when Debbie was even younger, that I loved her. But I never tumbled all the way. I guess I knew in my heart of hearts that there were a lot of other women waiting for me to seduce them."

***

The hot days of July, 1954, descended over Southern California as Debbie was told by Joe Pasternak to stand by for another MGM musical. In the meantime, Fisher had signed a contract to perform at The Sands in Las Vegas. He flew there days before her arrival so he could rehearse and stage his performance.

Debbie was invited for opening night, which she would attend with her fellow guests, Louella Parsons and songwriter Jimmy McHugh. Although Fisher was already in residence within a suite at The Sands, he booked his honored guests in suites at the Desert Inn, some distance away.

On the morning of Debbie's arrival, a "Las Vegas Rag" (her contemptuous name for a local newspaper) had printed a gossipy item about Fisher, claiming that a showgirl was seen leaving his suite at 6AM.

Debbie didn't confront Fisher with this item because she refused to believe it. After all, even though they were not having sexual intercourse, he had promised to be "true blue" to her. She'd been warned that gossips like to destroy relationships between stars even before they'd really begun.

Without giving a reason why, Fisher had asked Debbie to remove her eleven-karat diamond and keep news of their engagement a secret, especially from Louella Parsons, her traveling companion. But in a moment of weakness, she showed the columnist her engagement ring.

In November of 1953, gossip maven Louella Parsons was a guest on the popular TV game show, *What's My Line?*.

Sour-looking, she appeared sober, clad in pearls and an expensive fur, trying to disguise her very recognizable voice. Perhaps her sour look came from her attempts to control her weak kidneys.

She was the first columnist to expose the romance of "Eddie and Debbie."

The next day, Parsons defined them in print as "America's Sweethearts," and the label stuck for months. The press picked up the item and began running stories about "Eddie and Debbie."

"Louella really started an avalanche of publicity." Fisher said. "Good publicity for me. In those days, she liked me a lot, and I called her 'Mom.'"

In the wake of Parson's column, all her rivals joined in to publicize the romance, especially Hedda Hopper. Their romance headlined many a column, including those of Dorothy Kilgallen, Walter Winchell, Earl Wilson, Leonard Lyons, Ed Sullivan, Harrison Carroll, James Bacon, and Mike Connolly, who was always "bitchy" to Debbie.

On July 5, the "Eddie & Debbie" love story moved across the wire services of United Press and the Associated Press.

"Every time I went out the door, I was mobbed by reporters," she said. "At first, I loved all the attention, but it became a bit of a drag when some women reporters followed me into the toilet."

Fisher, too, welcomed the publicity, and every seat was booked for his appearance at The Sands.

After one late show, which Debbie did not attend, Zsa Zsa Gabor approached him. "She invited me back to her suite, promising that I needed a real woman to make a man out of me, not some little *ingénue* like sweet Debbie Reynolds."

"Too late, Zsa Zsa," I said. "Marlene Dietrich has already made a man of me."

By the time Fisher's gig ended, *Time* magazine had defined his involvement with Debbie as "The world's most refreshing romance." That month, five national magazines splashed cozy pictures of the "lovebirds" on their covers.

After kissing Fisher goodbye, Debbie flew back to Los Angeles with Parsons. After each of his final three appearances in Vegas, Fisher entertained a different showgirl in his suite every night, so he was not sexually deprived by Debbie's absence.

After his return to Los Angeles, he dated Debbie during his second night in town, pleading exhaustion on the first night back. He was to give a concert at the Hollywood Bowl, which had sold tickets to all 20,000 of its seats. He was that popular, and his romance with Debbie had made him an even more valuable commodity at the box office, as he knew that it would.

For his appearance at the Bowl, he arranged for two distinguished escorts for Debbie, songwriter Irving Berlin, and General David Sarnoff, his boss at NBC and the founder of RCA.

In those days, Fisher was always surrounded by an array of male cronies, notably Eddie Cantor, who had always claimed to have discovered the singer. Called "the Apostle of Pep," Cantor was a performer, comedian, dancer, singer, actor, and songwriter. On TV, Debbie had watched his eye-rolling song-and-dance routines as he sang such hits as "Makin' Whopee" or "How Ya Gonna

Keep 'Em Down on the Farm (After They've Seen Paree?)."

Cantor kissed Debbie and wished her all the happiness in the world. "Eddie is like my son, my beloved son. I worship the boy."

Backstage, she hugged and kissed Fisher before he went on stage. He introduced her to his manager, Milton Blackstone. Like Col. Tom Parker with Elvis Presley, Blackstone took fifty percent of all of Fisher's earnings, from both his records and from his live shows.

"He was as cold to me as an Arctic wind," Debbie said. "It was obvious that he didn't want Eddie to marry me."

She also met a shadowy figure in Fisher's life, Dr. Max Jacobson, who gave her "a clammy handshake. He hovered in the background of Eddie's life, not wanting publicity. He looked sinister to me, like a Vincent Price character in a murder movie."

She soon learned that Jacobson accompanied Fisher to every performance and was, in fact, his doctor.

"Is something wrong with Eddie?" she asked Joey Forman, his friend.

"He gives Eddie vitamin shots before every performance. They boost his energy level."

She later queried Fisher about this mysterious doctor. "Oh, it's nothing much," he said. "Vitamins. Female hormones."

"What are you trying to do?" she asked. "Grow breasts?"

"Don't worry your pretty little rabbit head about it," he answered. "I've got everything under control."

The next day he announced to Debbie that he was flying to London for a three-week engagement. "I had to call Joe Pasternak this morning and tell him I won't appear with you in *Hit the Deck*." The role went to Tony Martin.

Before he flew out of Los Angeles, he had his most serious talk with Debbie. He was under great pressure from his friends not to marry her. One night, sitting in her backyard beside her pool in Burbank, he discussed some possible problems.

"You know, of course, I'm Jewish, and you were brought up in a fundamentalist Christian family. Minnie still drools over me, but Roy makes it obvious that he doesn't get off on having a Jew for a son-in-law. You've not met my family in Philly. They're very Jewish."

They also faced another dilemma. Whereas she wanted to remain in Hollywood and make movies for MGM according to the terms of her contract, his Coca-Cola shows were being taped for NBC in New York City.

Her suspicion was confirmed when he quoted Blackstone's objections to their upcoming marriage. His agent had told him, "You've got the world by the tail. You're selling millions of records, and you've got millions of fans, mostly teenage gals. You're also hauling in millions. "Even though every one of those screaming bitches wants to be your sweetheart, Miss Burbank of 1948 isn't putting out."

"If you marry Cutie Pie, their dreams will be shattered, and they'll turn to some other handsome, unmarried crooner with a good voice. Vic Damone comes to mind. Do you want to throw your career away for some *shiksa* pussy? *DO YOU?*"

"Two people who love each other as much as we do should be able to work out their problems," she said, dismissing his concerns.

The next day, she heard that *The Daily Sketch* in London had broken the news that she would be escorted to England by Fisher, but that was not part of her plans.

"We were the hottest news in the world in the romance department," she said. "We beat out Frank and Ava. Our phone in Burbank was ringing off the wall with calls from reporters. I ordered an unlisted number. I told Minnie I was too famous to be listed in the damn phone book."

The day before Fisher flew away, he had a final date with her. After he retrieved her in Burbank, he presented her with another gift, a toy poodle named "Fanny" which he had named after his latest hit song.

That night they dined in a quiet tavern overlooking the beach at Malibu. Each talked about how much he or she would miss the other.

As a farewell gift, he presented her with an exquisite diamond-and-gold wristwatch from Lecoultre, which made some of the finest timepieces in the world. "There are only three of this particular watch made. One is owned by the Queen of England; another is in the possession of the wife of Charles de Gaulle. As of tonight, you own the third watch, my little rabbit, Mary Frances. You can use it to time the hours that I'm away, as you wait for my return."

During his transit to London, on a stopover in New York, he phoned her daily before inviting his Broadway showgirl *du jour* to spend the night in his suite at the Waldorf Astoria.

She didn't hear from him again until he arrived in the English port of Southampton on August 7, 1954, where a limousine was waiting to drive him into London.

He sent her a cable, declaring his everlasting love, and added some additional information as a postscript: Aboard the *Queen Elizabeth*, he had gone nude into the ship's steam room. There, he confronted Noël Coward sitting naked on a marble slab. After appraising Fisher's ass, he politely asked, "Let me pat it, dear boy."

***

For one brief, shining moment, Debbie was told that she might be cast as the lead in her next MGM musical, *Hit the Deck*. At the time that he held out that promise, Joe Pasternak said he'd previously assigned the lead roles to Jane Powell and Tony Martin, with Debbie taking third billing, in a configuration equivalent to what she'd had with Powell in *Athena*.

Pasternak had been disappointed by Powell's reception in *Athena*, which had bombed at the box office. For a while, he had considered firing her.

Dore Schary, however, was not enthusiastic about the idea and told the producer to stick with Powell. Pasternak, therefore, had to shatter Debbie's dream. He phoned her to inform her that Powell would retain the lead "with you playing second fiddle."

Tap-dancing Ann Miller and big band leader Tony Martin, two of the co-stars of the feel-good musical extravaganza about life in the Navy, *Hit the Deck*

Roy Rowland, who had directed Debbie before, had already assembled an all-star cast, each member of which was a famous name with recognition at that time (the mid-1950s) in Hollywood history: Vic Damone, Walter Pidgeon, Gene Raymond, Ann Miller, Russ Tamblyn, Richard Anderson, Jane Darwell, and Alan King.

Powell, Damone, and Miller weren't in the best of moods, as word was that each of them would not have their contracts renewed by MGM, which was desperately cutting back after suffering massive losses of profits, mainly because of the increasing popularity of television.

Then *Variety* announced that players who included song-and-dance man George Murphy; Bobby Van, Debbie's former co-star; Jack E. Leonard; and Vera-Ellen would appear in cameos, but they were dropped from the cast at the last minute.

Hit the Deck had originated as a Broadway musical, *Shore Leave*, in the 1920s. First National had filmed it as a silent picture in 1925. RKO purchased the rights to it in 1930, and by 1936 had adapted it into a musical, *Follow the Fleet*, with Fred Astaire and Ginger Rogers. MGM bought the rights in 1947, but waited until 1955 to release it as *Hit the Deck*. Sonya Levien and William Ludwig drastically rewrote the script, but retained some of the songs from the Broadway musical, including such standards as "Sometimes I'm Happy," "I Know That You Know," and "Hallelujah." Hermes Pan, Fred Astaire's longtime choreographer, was retained as the project's dance director.

The story follows a familiar plot line involving sailors on leave, evoking *On the Town* (1949) with Frank Sinatra and Gene Kelly.

The chief boatswain's mate, Bill Clark (Tony Martin), on shore leave, goes to a night club where his longtime fiancée, Ginger (as portrayed by Ann Miller), is the star performer. She's been engaged to him for six years, but her patience has come to an end and she breaks it off.

Rico Ferrari (Damone) goes home to find his mother, Kay (as portrayed by the singer, Kay Armen), being amorously pursued by a florist, Mr. Peroni (J. Carrol Naish). Then Rico falls in love with Susan (Jane Powell) after he breaks up her romance with an aging jerk, Wendell (Gene Raymond).

Meanwhile, Danny Xavier Smith (Russ Tamblyn) discovers the charms of Carol Pace (as portrayed by Debbie). Both Powell and Tamblyn are cast as the children of a stern father, Rear Admiral Daniel Xavier Smith (i.e., Walter Pidgeon).

Expect the usual plot devices—sailor falls for girl; sailor loses girl; sailor gets girl in the final reel. After a lot of complications, Tony Martin, Tamblyn, and Damone win their girlfriends, making for a happy ending.

Debbie was most impressed with Tamblyn as her boyfriend and admired his talent as a dancer, ever since she'd seen him in *Seven Brides for Seven Brothers* (1954).

"We had a number in *Hit the Deck*, 'The Devil's Fun House.' It took three days to shoot, and I ended up battered, beaten, and black and blue all over. But Russ was a doll, and I adored him. Too bad he didn't ask me to marry him. I would have."

In spite of her trying to steal Powell's role, the two performers retained their friendship throughout the course of filming.

Damone was showing increasing interest in Debbie's friend, Pier Angeli. Both were Italian, and she thought they'd make an ideal couple. How wrong she was!

Debbie had long been impressed with the singing voice of Tony Martin. Ironically, he'd appeared in the first version of their movie, *Follow the Fleet* with Astaire. He was married to dancer Cyd Charisse, whom Debbie knew from the set of *Singin' in the Rain.*

Her friend, Lana Turner, had raved about Martin's prowess as a lover.

It was during the filming of *Hit the Deck* that Debbie began a lifetime friendship with Ann Miller, whom she dubbed "the best tap dancer in Hollywood his-

Debbie, in *Hit the Deck* as the Navy's sweetheart, was indeed an amusing musical comedienne.

In reference to her performance, and perhaps with a twinge of regret, she said, "There I was, surrounded by four gorgeous men in blue, each a doll. But then Eddie Fisher showed up on the set to claim me."

tory." Like Debbie, she'd been born in Texas, her father a criminal lawyer who represented such notorious gangsters as Machine Gun Kelly and Baby Face Nelson.

At the age of thirteen, she'd been discovered by Lucille Ball and signed to a contract at RKO, eventually landing at MGM and appearing in some of its great musicals of the 1940s, including *On the Town*.

Gene Raymond, married to Jeanette MacDonald at the time, was a romantic lead in the 1930s, but was now reduced to smaller roles such as the foppish womanizer he played in *Hit the Deck*.

The first day he met Debbie, he reminded her that he'd worked with bigger stars, and even listed them: Loretta Young, Humphrey Bogart, Jean Harlow, Clark Gable, Bette Davis, Carole Lombard, and Joan Crawford. She got back at him. "Of course, you played with them, but could only bask in their reflected glory. That's why you'll be forever known as Mr. Jeanette MacDonald."

As one reviewer put it, *"Hit the Deck* is cute and so unforgettable you'll not remember one scene the next day." It lost about half a million at the box office.

***

Frank Sinatra had returned to MGM after a six-year absence to make *The Tender Trap* by humorist Max Shulman and Robert Paul Smith. The title came from an Oscar-nominated song (*Love Is) The Tender Trap* by Jimmy Van Heusen with lyrics by Sammy Cahn.

For his leading lady, Sinatra asked for Debbie to play the innocent young starlet, Julie Gillis, with supporting players Celeste Holm and David Wayne.

Cast as a womanizing theatrical agent in Manhattan, Sinatra is 35-year-old Charles Y. Reader. He's living in a bachelor's dream world with beautiful women coming and going from his apartment, cleaning and cooking for him and even walking his dog. The plot leaves out what other chores these women might be doing for him. The girls are Poppy (Lola Albright), Helen (Carolyn Jones), and Jessica (Jarma Lewis).

His longtime companion is Sylvia Crewes (Holm), whom he might marry one day, or maybe not. She is a worldly and wise musician whom he has long neglected. Joe McCall (Wayne) arrives on the scene, having left his wife Ethel and his children back home in Indiana. He's been best friends with Charlie since kindergarten. Since Charlie is neglecting Sylvia, he begins to date her.

At an audition, Charlie meets Julie Gillis (Debbie), who temporarily wants to break into show biz before retiring at the age of 22 to be a wife and mother. She resists the advances of this older man, but soon is falling in love with him.

At this point, the audience knows what's going to happen. Joe will give up Sylvia and go back home to his wife and children, whereas Sylvia, age 33, will at last find a man who wants to marry her.

112

Charlie attends her wedding, and encounters Julie standing nearby. Sylvia tosses him her bridal bouquet, and he catches it. He also proposes marriage to Julie, kisses her, and it's THE END.

Debbie had several lunches with David Wayne during the shoot. "I picked his brain for every tidbit I could find about Marilyn Monroe,"

A lot of people didn't realize it, but Wayne appeared in four films with Monroe, more than any other actor. They included *As Young as You Feel* (1951), *We're Not Married* (1952), *O'Henry's Full House* (1952), and *How to Marry a Millionaire* (1953).

Debbie worked smoothly with Holm, her close friend. Over lunch, the older actress told her, "I've known Frank (Sinatra) a very long time. No, not that way. Better watch out, gal. He's got that lean and hungry look in his eye, and they're trained on you. You won't be his first virgin."

"I'm in love with Eddie; but I find Frank mesmerizing," she said. "I guess I'd have to say yes, if he insists. After all, he is *the* Frank Sinatra. I don't want to go down in film history as the only woman who turned down Sinatra. Zsa Zsa Gabor told me she rejected him one night in Palm Springs, and he didn't take no for an answer. She claimed he raped her."

"Frank is a better kisser than Eddie," she claimed. "Of course, Frank has had more experience, everyone from Marilyn Monroe to Judy Garland, from Elizabeth Taylor to Lana Turner. He downplays his affairs, at least to me. He claimed that if he had as many seductions as he's given credit for, he'd be in a jar in the Harvard Medical School."

She cooperated fully with her director, Charles Walters, whom everybody in the cast and crew called "Chuck."

At first, she'd been intimidated to work with such an es-

"When a Lothario turns forty, he likes 'em young," Frank Sinatra told his friend Celeste Holm on the set of *The Tender Trap*. In that movie, he falls for ingénue Julie Gillis, played by Debbie.

"You know more about how to please a lady than any man on the Eastern Seaboard," she coos to him on camera. Then she asks, "How many girls are there in your life?"

Those words might have been uttered by Debbie during one of her real life conversations with Ol' Blue Eyes.

teemed director, who had recently won the Best Director Oscar for *Lili* (1953), starring Leslie Caron. He'd also helmed many of the biggest MGM musicals, including *Good News* (1946) and *Easter Parade* (1948). Before working with Debbie, he had guided such stars as July Garland, Fred Astaire, Gene Kelly, June Allyson, and Esther Williams.

He'd even directed Joan Crawford during her return to MGM in 1953 when she starred in *Torch Song*. He was set to direct Kelly and Sinatra, along with Grace Kelly, in *High Society* (1956). Holm predicted that both Sinatra and Crosby would fall in love with the blonde goddess.

Debbie had met the producer, Lawrence Weingarten, only once and did not try to ingratiate herself with him this time. After all, he was the producer who had denied her the lead role in *The Actress* with Spencer Tracy, assigning it to Jean Simmons instead. When she met him, he'd just produced *Rhapsody* (1954) with Elizabeth Taylor.

Sinatra, not the director, was the stern taskmaster on the set. "All of us had to know our lines and be camera ready with all our movements," Debbie said. "Frank got it right on the first take, and he demanded that of us. He was a real pro, except on Monday morning when he was recovering from the wild partying of the previous weekend. I really didn't know the status of his marriage to my friend, Ava Gardner. She didn't talk about it and neither did Frank."

Behind the scenes, she found Sinatra a bit intimidating, but told the press, "He is fabulous to work with, sweet and lighthearted." No one had ever associated him with those words.

After a long slump in his career as a recording artist, Sinatra had made a comeback, winning the 1953 Best Supporting Actor Oscar for *From Here to Eternity*. "He was working again in feature films and recording once more," Debbie said. "I told him he was going to be bigger and better than ever."

Often, after work on a Friday, Sinatra would join fellow Rat Packer, Humphrey Bogart, aboard his boat, the *Sirocco*, and sail to Catalina Island.

She claimed she always wanted to be invited, but never was. At least that's what she wrote in a memoir. Holm recalled it differently, and remembered that Debbie did sail once with Sinatra and Bogie to Catalina

At MGM, Ann Miller, with her "machine gun" taps and breathtaking spins, danced into Debbie's life to become her confidante.

"I was supposed to be the keeper of her secrets, but I didn't do a good job of it," said the gossipy dancer.

while Fisher was in London. Bogie's wife, Lauren Bacall, was not on board. Debbie was introduced to his mistress, Verita Thompson, who was in charge of his hairpiece.

On this cruise, Sinatra began calling Debbie by his nickname for her, "Schweetie," which he deliberately pronounced "with a Liberace lisp."

It will never be known exactly what happened between Debbie and Sinatra during that waterborne transit to Catalina. Verita Thompson later claimed that her lover, Bogie, assigned Debbie to Sinatra's cabin, just assuming they were having an affair.

A week later, another friend and confidante to Debbie, Ann Miller, decided to throw what she called a "hen party," inviting some of the stars with whom she worked at MGM, notably Janet Leigh, Lana Turner, and June Allyson.

Tap-dancing Ann Miller was never known for her discretion, and she revealed what Debbie had told her about Sinatra.

"She confessed to having sex with Frankie, although she claimed she was still a virgin and waiting for Eddie to do the dirty deed. Apparently, he masturbated against her vagina after performing oral sex on her. If she is to be believed, she performed oral sex herself at the age of six on a seventeen-year-old boy in El Paso."

The glamorous "hens" at the party debated whether that form of seduction consisted of losing one's virginity. "I mean both of them had a climax, maybe more than one," Miller said. "I'd say she lost her carefully guarded cherry to Frankie."

Lana Turner disagreed. "What Frank and Debbie did I call heavy petting. A woman can't lose her virginity until a man penetrates her."

Miller quipped, "You should know, doll,"

The stars did not concur on whether or not Debbie lost her virginity on a technicality. The talk quickly shifted to when each of them lost hers. Turner claimed that her seducer was Artie Shaw on her honeymoon night. Leigh cited a student, Kenneth Carlyle, whom she married at age 14. Allyson revealed her first time was with a gay chorus boy on Broadway in 1938 when they worked on the musical *Sing Out the News*.

Miller topped them all, citing Louis B. Mayer when she was just a teenager.

In print, at least, Debbie never revealed what she and Sinatra did in bed during that trip to Catalina. But she did write about his warning her not to marry Eddie Fisher.

"It's a hard life for a singer, and especially for his wife. On the road for most of the year, a crooner is not an ideal family man. If you have children with a guy like that, he'll not only neglect you, but not be a real father to kids. If he's hot, like Eddie and me, girls just throw themselves at us in very town. No red-blooded singer can remain faithful to his wife when faced with such temptation."

"I love Eddie, and I want to chance it," she said. "Sure, it's a risk. Let's face it: All of life is a risk."

"Okay, doll, but remember: You were duly warned," he said.

As she later told Miller, "I know Frank meant well, warning me about future heartbreak. But I'm in love and on top of the world."

She didn't feel on top of the world when she saw the first screening of *The Tender Trap*. Her only comment was, "It was more fun to make than it was to watch."

***

After Eddie Fisher's return to New York following his gig in London, press interest in his romance with Debbie seemed more intense than ever. "The faucet had been turned on full blast, and there was no way to shut it off," he said. "If Debbie had any doubts, she didn't express them to me."

Almost daily, Fisher's friends urged him not to marry her, the main objections coming from his manager, Milton Blackstone. He frankly admitted, "I hate the little bitch."

"Milton, god damn it, I think you're jealous," Fisher charged. "You're a single man who runs my life down to the most minute detail. You even see to it that I have clean underwear. Very suspicious."

Marvin Cane, a song publisher, chimed in with his objection. "You're insane to think of marrying little Miss Burbank. My Cadillac is waiting outside the door. I left the engine running. Let's get the hell out of town before you make the mistake of your life."

The most serious and potentially threatening objection came from the executives of Coca-Cola, sponsors of his TV show. A chief executive warned him, "Your upcoming marriage will damage your career. You stand to lose a lot of your fan base, which consists of young girls, all big Coca-Cola drinkers. As the sponsor of your show, we might have to drop you."

He faced more objections when he flew into Los Angeles and took Debbie out on his first free night. He found her thrilled with the prospect of marriage and spent most of the evening talking over the big wedding she was planning, which, ironically, was eerily similar to the foundation of the plot of the upcoming movie she'd been assigned, *The Catered Affair* (1956).

On Eddie's second night back, Lauren Bacall threw a big party for him at her home, where Humphrey Bogart was slowly dying of cancer. Most of the Rat Packers were there, including Peter Lawford, Dean Martin, and Sammy Davis, Jr. Wearing pajamas and a silk robe, Bogie came downstairs and spent part of the evening with them. Before retiring, he delivered his opinion of their upcoming nuptials. "Listen to your papa, you two silly kids. This marriage thing will never work. You two will head for the divorce court an hour after you exchange marriage vows."

To that, Fisher responded, "Advice from a man of experience, who has gone to the altar four times, is much appreciated."

The next day, Fisher met with his mentor, Eddie Cantor, who labeled Debbie, with some accuracy, "the Iron Butterfly."

"Don't even think of marrying her," the comedian warned. "She'll ruin your life and your career. But if you're determined to go through with it, I'll throw you an engagement party."

During Fisher's reunion with his best friend, Mike Todd, the producer jerked him by the collar. "Listen to me, you little Jew bastard, you marry the scheming little hussy, and I'll deliver the second cut to your dick, and this time it'll be more than taking a bit of foreskin. Maybe I'll even deball you."

That same day, *Star* magazine predicted that Fisher would eventually make a wonderful husband, but cautioned, "Not now! He's got a lot more living and loving to do before he's domesticated."

Fisher's needle-happy doctor, Max Jacobson, was one of the few who didn't object to his marrying Debbie. It soon became clear that he hoped to add her as his patient, getting her hooked, like Judy Garland, on his "vitamins."

"My two best buddies from my early days in Philly, Joey Forman and Lenny Gaines, also denounced Debbie, calling her a dingbat and a phony," Fisher claimed.

Meanwhile, many of Debbie's fans were sending her letters begging her not to marry Fisher. The most frequently asked question was, "Do you want your children to be half-Jew?"

In spite of her intimate sexual involvements with Sinatra, Debbie insisted that she went to her honeymoon bed a virgin, and perhaps in a narrow technical sense, that was true. But in a memoir, Fisher contradicted her claim.

Debbie still used the word "deflowering." In her case, that deflowering took place shortly after Fisher flew back to Los Angeles from his engagement in London. It had begun as a dinner date, followed by "heavy petting" in his car as it was parked in front of her home in Burbank. It was becoming so intense that he told her he couldn't wait any longer. "Either you give in to me, or tomorrow, I'll announce to all the newspapers that the engagement is off."

She was horrified at the threat of that kind of publicity, as she seemed to be enjoying her title as a member of "America's Sweetheart Couple."

Reluctantly, she invited him to the little poolhouse in her backyard, used for family and friends as a dressing room. It contained a cot for unexpected overnight house guests, and a small toilet. As he later confessed in print, "The sex was terrible. We were like two robots. There was no tenderness. It was completely physical and did not feel that great."

He later reflected on sex with his wife-to-be, as opposed to previous affairs—"and much better sex"—with Marlene Dietrich, Judy Garland, and Merle Oberon.

He even told friends who included Dean Martin that in London, his sexual partner had been Princess Margaret's lady-in-waiting. "I came very close to fucking Margaret Rose herself," he bragged. "Had I been able to prolong my stay in London, I'm certain that the British Royalty might have had its first Jew prince marrying into the blue bloods."

Fisher confided to Joey Forman, who knew Debbie, that "I'm faced with a dilemma: I fear I'm marrying a woman I don't really know and one that I don't enjoy having sex with—and you, of all people, know how much I like to have sex. The world is practically demanding that I marry her, even though it might seriously damage my career."

"I guess after all the forests of Canada were denuded to create newsprint hawking our upcoming marriage, I'll have to go through with the god damn ceremony. I dread it. Perhaps she'll be a good mother to our children, which I prefer to bring up in the Jewish faith. For sex, I can get all I want outside the home. I'll be away on the road most of the year, so I will hardly have to depend on Miss Debbie for sex. No one will say I'll be sexually deprived, even though married."

He was due to report to NBC and had other engagements in New York, so he flew there and invited Debbie to fly there later. Without his knowing it, she purchased a separate ticket for Minnie, who flew to Manhattan to act as a chaperone. He planned to continue his seduction of Debbie, hoping that the sex would get better. During their time in New York, he occupied a suite at Essex House, but booked Debbie and Minnie too into a suite at the Madison.

On his third night in town, his mother, Katherine Fisher, flew to New York and had dinner with her prospective in-laws. She had divorced Eddie's father, Joseph Fisher, and had remarried Max Stupp, who ran a grocery market.

Fisher took all of them to dinner and was very critical of his (biological) father. "Papa insulted my mother, humiliated her, ridiculed her, and even beat her. She had to leave him. I still love him, but he was one rotten husband."

He turned to Debbie. "I promise I won't beat you unless I catch you with another man." Then he smiled: "I'm just joking."

The next night, Debbie and Minnie attended a recording session at NBC Studios to watch Fisher sing before the cameras. Afterward, they dined with Jennie Grossinger, who ran the most famous resort in the Catskills, then known as "The Borscht Belt" because of its heavy reliance on Jewish guests. She had been one of the first hotel owners to appreciate Fisher's talent and to book him for performances.

The following night, Debbie had her first major confrontation with the hysteria of Fisher's fame. They arrived by limousine for his concert at the Palisades Amusement Park in New Jersey. To control the surging crowds, one hundred extra policemen were hired as security guards.

When Debbie began her exit from the limousine, the crowds, mostly composed of hysterical teenage girls, surged toward the vehicle, booing Debbie. The suspicion that Fisher might marry her didn't set well with this crowd.

After he jumped out and made his way through the adoring crowds, someone on the security staff advised the chauffeur to drive on, taking Debbie with him, fearing it would be dangerous for her to confront the hostile crowd.

Over dinner that night, she told Fisher that she found the crowd "monstrous."

"Better get used to it, kid, if you marry me."

That Sunday night, he appeared on *The Ed Sullivan Show,* and she went with him and once again faced screaming crowds, young teenagers adoring Fisher but hostile to her for taking their heartthrob away from them.

The show, broadcast across America, was followed by an evening at the Stork Club. Minnie remained behind at the Madison.

Joan Crawford arrived stag. After she entered the room, she caught Fisher's eye. He immediately asked her to join Debbie and himself at table.

At first, Debbie was cool to the screen idol, because she'd heard that she and Fisher had once sustained a torrid affair. But she found Crawford gracious and charming, and a lifelong friendship was formed that night.

Two hours later, after they said good night to Crawford, Fisher told Debbie, "The way Joan doted on you, it's obvious that she wants to fuck you. She's part lez."

"Don't be silly," Debbie chastised him. "How in hell can a woman fuck another woman?"

***

Whenever she could break free of MGM, which wasn't often, Debbie flew to New York. Discreetly, Fisher would slip her into his suite at Essex House. As he told his pal, Joey Forman, "The sex didn't get much better. She's very unresponsive. Just lies there."

During one of her visits, he rented a car and drove her to Philadelphia to meet his family. So far, she'd only met his mother, Katherine, but on this trip, she was introduced to Max Stupp, the grocer, Fisher's stepfather. She also met his four sisters and two brothers. "I was the only Gentile in the crowd that weekend," she said. "The extended family came in to meet the *shiksa,* a word I'd only recently learned. Many of them had thick Jewish accents. Obviously from the Old Country."

"A few of his aunts and uncles, whomever, were a little too frank with me, telling me they wished that Sonny Boy would marry a nice Jewish girl, settle down, and raise nice Jewish children."

Like a harbinger of things to come, "Eddie and Debbie" announced their official engagement on the same day that Joe DiMaggio and Marilyn Monroe told the world that they were separating. Both of those news items were carried on frontpages around the world.

Even though he objected to Fisher marrying Debbie, Eddie Cantor threw an engagement party, inviting 500 guests from the A-list, including everyone from Groucho Marx to Jack Benny. Benny would later give her advice about her first gig in Las Vegas. She found him "adorable," polite, and cuddly. She liked Marx except for his habit of wet-lipping her during prolonged kisses on her mouth. He would later speak of her in his act, telling Dick Cavett in 1970, "I've known Debbie Reynolds for seventy-five years."

On another show, he claimed he visited her in the hospital, hoping "to get to the truth about her chest. I've been tricked by too many gals who have falsies or padded bras. From what I felt, Debbie's are real."

Years later, Debbie said, "He pissed me off at the time, although as the years went by, I laughed it off. Today, I live in Beverly Hills and my boobs live in San Diego."

Many of the major stars of MGM showed up at Debbie's engagement party, including Judy Garland, Frank Sinatra, and Ava Gardner. Elizabeth Taylor could not make it.

In the middle of the party, Edward G. Robinson approached her, telling her how much he had admired her legs in *Singin' in the Rain.* "In spite of my ugly face, I, too, have some of the most beautiful legs in Hollywood."

Gordon MacCrae was there. After a few drinks, he, too, came over to her. He hadn't seen her since the making of *The Daughter of Rosie O'Grady* (1950). He told her, "You were sweet sixteen when I first came on to you. Now that Eddie has broken you in, how about giving another singer a chance at the goodies?"

"I'll take a raincheck, handsome," she said. "From all I hear, I'm missing out on something really good."

Fred Astaire talked to her. He'd been so helpful and encouraging of her in the past. "I want to co-star in a movie with you as my dancing partner."

"I'd like that, too, but Ginger Rogers is a tough act to follow."

George Burns arrived with his wife, Gracie Allen. "At his age, he came on to me," she said, "calling me 'doll' and saying that he could still cut the mustard. Who ever heard of cutting mustard?"

Pier Angeli appeared on the arm of Vic Damone, with whom Debbie had made two movies. She spoke to each of them on separate occasions. "Now that I've met Vic, I've forgiven you for stealing Eddie Fisher from me."

Later, when Debbie was alone with Damone, she said, "You told me you were turned on only by women who are red down below."

"I still am, and I'm considering taking Pier to a beauty shop where, in the back room, some hairdresser can give her a pubic dye job. Incidentally, I never learned about the color of your pubic hair?"

"Ginger," she answered. "Named after Ginger Rogers." Ann Miller arrived late, kissing Debbie on both cheeks and wishing her well. "I just talked to Eddie. He told me that after you kids get married, he's going to force you to give up your career. Is that true?

"Hell, no!" she answered. "I'm going to make him quit singing and stay home and raise our kids. I want him to learn to cook and change diapers. If I walk in the door in the late afternoon and find one speck of dust anywhere, he'll face hell."

At the end of the party, its host, Cantor, asked Debbie to join him on the terrace. "I wish you and Sonny Boy well, but I still think you're making a mistake. He can extend his career by another three or four years as America's heartthrob if he postpones marriage. Surely, you don't want to deny him that. He's at his peak right now, and this time in show business may never come again. Besides, Eddie is not ready to settle down. Too many wild oats to sow."

"I'm sure you've already talked to Sonny Boy about this," she said. "The decision is up to him. And thanks for the party."

The gay columnist, Mike Connolly, also attended. He later told friends, "Miss Reynolds delivered an Oscar-winning performance, greeting every guest, all 500 of them, showing off her $50,000 diamond engagement ring, clinging to Eddie's arm, smiling, forever smiling, and gushing all over the room. Who knows what that one really thinks? She tells everyone she wants to be a *June Bride*, the name of that old Bette Davis clunker in which Miss Reynolds appeared on the screen for two seconds, which is about all I can stomach of her goo."

A photographer from *Life* had attended the party, and his magazine published a four-page spread on the event.

"I was with Eddie in California, in New York, and in Philadelphia, but I didn't feel I really know him," Debbie told Pier Angeli. "I feel at times I'm engaged to a stranger who leads an entirely different life when he's not with me. I hear a lot of gossip—that's Hollywood for you. Even when he is with me, he's distracted by a hundred other things, everybody pulling him in a direction different from the altar. He's very career minded, you know."

"Oh, Debbie," Angeli said, "Let's face it: You're the most career-minded actress in Hollywood yourself."

Just when she privately began to question the idea of marriage to Fisher, he came through with some unexpected surprises. Being a Jew, he did not celebrate Christmas, but he knew that the Reynolds family did. On Christmas Day, 1954, he arrived on their doorstep in Burbank with gifts for the entire family, presenting Debbie with a sheared nutria coat.

She thought that was her gift, but then he took her hand and led her out the front door. There, parked on the street, was a shiny new 1955 Ford Thunderbird, hot off the assembly line. In fact, such a model had not been delivered to the showrooms yet. Fisher had hired someone to drive it from Detroit to California.

"I was so overwhelmed, I burst into tears."

After New Year's, Fisher had to fly back to New York. But he phoned every day. Once, he sent a telegram: "JUST PICKED UP A MAGAZINE AND DIDN'T SEE YOUR PICTURE OR MINE EITHER. WHAT ARE WE GOING TO DO?"

As she drove around in her sporty red Thunderbird, Debbie pondered her upcoming marriage. Based on that telegram, she wondered if he were marrying her just for the avalanche of publicity their romance was generating. Every one of his live performances was sold out, and all of his records were hits.

She shared her concerns with Ann Miller. "Do you think Eddie's in it just for the publicity?"

"Have you ever thought that you, too, might also be in it for the publicity?" Miller asked. "All in all, last week, you got five or six movie offers, more than any other actress in Hollywood. This avalanche of publicity seems to be working for your career, too."

"I'm certainly not in it just for that," Debbie protested.

"I adore you, gal, but maybe you are and don't realize it yet."

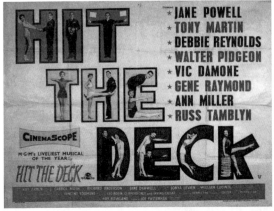

A publicity poster for *Hit the Deck* called for its stars, including Debbie, to contort themselves into shapes that corresponded to the letters. In the lower of the two illustrations above, Debbie appears in the "C," and, with her co-star Russ Tamblyn, in the "E" as well.

These antics and more were part of a feel-good musical that managed to make life in the U.S. Navy seem like a constant round of feel-good, endlessly wholesome, family-friendly fun.

Chapter Five

WEDDING BELL BLUES

PUBLICITY MACHINES AND TABLOID RAGS GO CRAZY

"Marrying Debbie Reynolds Was the Biggest Mistake of My Life"
—Eddie Fisher

DEBBIE GETS UP CLOSE AND PERSONAL WITH JAMES DEAN, ("HE'S MESMERIZING"), THEN LOSES THE FEMALE LEAD IN *REBEL WITHOUT A CAUSE*

One reason Eddie Fisher and Debbie Reynolds might have so effectively captured the imagination of the public is that they were so photogenic...everyone's fantasy of the ultimately fun, hardworking, and wholesome all-American romance. Postwar America and the newly emerging TV generation loved it, as well as any product or consumer good they opted to market.

In the weeks before her marriage to Eddie Fisher, Debbie had more on her mind than getting a husband. She spent time fretting about the future of her career.

When their contracts were not renewed, the biggest stars at MGM were rapidly fading from the scene. After twenty-five years as the King of Hollywood, Clark Gable had driven off the MGM lot for the last time without any particular fanfare.

One by one, the stars were disappearing, including the former reigning beauties, Lana Turner and Ava Gardner. June Allyson and Van Johnson, once billed as America's Sweethearts, were let go. Mickey Rooney had been MGM's box office champion throughout the late 1930s and early '40s. No more. Brusque goodbyes were extended to Andy Hardy. As for Judy Garland, after having made millions for MGM in all those hit musicals of the 1940s, she was shoved out the gate as studio brass agreed, "The old MGM musical is on life support."

Debbie, however, was retained, MGM seeing her as a possible money maker in the new crop of romantic comedies sweeping America in the mid-50s. Even if they didn't have scripts that were immediately suitable for her, MGM reasoned that it could always lend her out, at a profit, to other studios.

That actually came true: In the immediate years to come, RKO requested her services, as did Universal, Paramount, 20th Century Fox, Columbia, and even Warner Brothers, the studio that, years earlier, had briefly put her under contract.

***

When Fisher returned to Los Angeles, Debbie arranged for him to accompany her to MGM, where they were shown a pre-release screening of *The Tender Trap*, the movie in which she had co-starred with Frank Sinatra. Later, during dinner, Fisher had little to say about the film, spending most of the evening discussing his own competitive relationship with Sinatra.

"I used to think of myself as the next Sinatra," he claimed. "He'd been a skinny kid from Hoboken who made it big, and I was a skinny kid from South Philly who was also making it big. Most teenage girls want to hear me sing instead of Frankie. He reminds them of their fathers."

"Frankie should hate me out of pure jealousy," Fisher said. "But he doesn't. We're still pals." He related a story that had been told to him: One night in Manhattan, Sinatra passed a theater near Times Square where Fisher was billed as the new singing sensation. Lines to buy tickets stretched way down the block, just as they used to do for Sinatra in the 1940s.

As he walked past some of Fisher's fans, one of the nastier girls jeered at him, calling out, "You're washed up!" Another teenager screamed at him, "Ol' Blue Eyes! Time to get some grandfather specs."

"The big stars who once pursued Frankie are now after me!" Fisher said. "To name only a few, Zsa Zsa Gabor, Hedy Lamarr, Lucille Ball. He's got me beat in one department. He's a damn good actor. Not me, baby!"

In March of 1955, Fisher told her that he'd be flying to London for an appearance at the Palladium. To his surprise, she begged to go along, and he reluctantly agreed, even though "I had a lot of hot numbers to call, and I didn't need a lot of extra baggage," as he described to his manager, Milton Blackstone.

Not only did he allow Debbie on board, but Minnie insisted on tagging along, too.

"I thought I might use the time abroad to get to know Eddie better," Debbie said. "Such was not the case. We were hounded by the press all the time we were there. I couldn't even slip away to Eddie's suite, because Minnie was watching me like a hound dog on my trail."

In his act, Fisher was allowed to introduce Debbie to a standing ovation from his approving audiences. The British tabloids had written extensively about their romance. Together and onstage, they sang, "A Man Chases a Girl." [Fisher and Debbie each knew it well, having previously recorded it, an Irving Berlin number known for its coy and collisional tag line, "until she catches him."]

He also slipped her into his act when a Royal Command Performance was staged at Blackpool, the tackiest summer resort in England. Fisher stood in line to greet Queen Elizabeth and Prince Philip. Although he begged the managers to let Debbie stand with him, she was excluded because she had not been officially registered in the line-up.

As Philip shook his hand, he whispered into Fisher's ear, "You're not really going to marry that girl, are you?"

Fisher stammered, "Yes, I am, Your Highness." Philip merely nodded before moving on. "I didn't even know he knew anything about America's Sweethearts, much less have an opinion about our upcoming marriage."

***

Back together in Los Angeles during part of that summer, Fisher and Debbie spent more time together than they ever had before.

Walt Disney invited them to Disneyland in Anaheim, where he asked them to join him in a convertible ride down Main Street. As they rolled past crowds on both sides, the Sweethearts waved at their applauding fans.

The hysterically publicized couple seemed to be on everyone's list of honored guests. Fisher had long suspected that Debbie's devotion to him in public was part of her act. "In private, things between us seemed to be cooling down," he said. "It was months before our marriage, and we had sex on occasion, but it was still without passion. She could have been watching TV or reading a book while I pounded away, trying to please her…and myself."

"We were always caught up in a whirlwind," she said.

Sinatra invited both of them to join about a hundred other celebrities to a July 4th concert in San Diego where their mutual friend, Judy Garland, performed at a benefit for the Exceptional Children's Foundation. Transportation for many of the invited guests, including Fisher and Debbie, was aboard a specially chartered deluxe bus.

On the bus, Debbie made the rounds, talking to Gary Cooper, Peter Lawford, Ronald and Nancy Reagan, Donald O'Connor, Dick Powell, June Allyson, David Niven, Dean Martin, Lauren Bacall, Humphry Bogart, Lana Turner, Betty Grable, Harry James, and James Stewart.

At the benefit, on stage, Sammy Davis, Jr., performed with Martin, their act followed by Betty Hutton, who "pissed off" Garland. She was furious that Hutton had been booked on the same bill. *[Garland had been fired from* Annie Get Your Gun *and replaced with Hutton.]*

The hyper-energetic Hutton told the audience, "I'm Betty Hutton, the real thing…and not a Debbie Reynolds impersonation."

To celebrate Fisher's 27th birthday on August 10, Mike Todd and his mistress, actress Evelyn Keyes, gave a bash in his honor.

Upstaging all the guests, Marlene Dietrich made a spectacular entrance in a white silk suit that looked as if it had been tailored for a man. She sang *Lili Marlene* for the guests, dedicating this World War II favorite to Fisher.

Debbie knew that Dietrich had already seduced Fisher, and it soon became obvious that Dietrich had had an affair with Todd. A Hollywood underground "rag" had printed that Dietrich, Todd, and Fisher had sustained a three-way during the week they spent as guests of Sinatra in his villa at Palm Springs.

***

As Fisher and Debbie moved deeper and deeper into the summer of 1955, pressure from friends mounted, some telling him to drop Debbie, others urging him to continue his plans for the wedding.

"After all that god damn publicity, I feared I'd have to walk down the aisle, even though I had cold feet," Fisher said. "I suspected that she might be marrying me for career advancement—that's the kind of gal she was. Other stars were falling by the wayside—even big stars, lots of them—but Debbie intended to stay on top as MGM's little darling."

"Finally, I told her I wanted to postpone the wedding, dashing her hopes to become a June bride." Instead of delivering that bomb up front and personal, he preferred to phone her with the news.

By now, however, even Milton Blackstone feared a backlash ("Your fans will turn against you") if "Sonny Boy" walks out on Debbie. Fisher began to wonder if he and Debbie had become victims of their own massive publicity.

Some members of the press began to sense "blood in the water." (Debbie's words.) Stories were filed, including one headlined "Trouble in Paradise." It suggested that Fisher and Debbie had agreed to see other people, although there was no such pact.

Louella Parsons was still supportive of their romance, writing in her column, "If those two darlings aren't in love, then neither was Romeo and Juliet."

One reporter learned that Fisher had canceled his reservation for the honeymoon suite aboard the S.S. *United States*. That same day, Coca-Cola notified him that it would not be moving his television show to Hollywood. That meant that he and Debbie would have to continue being separated for long periods of time.

Then MGM sent Debbie on a tour of South Korea to entertain the U.S. servicemen there. *En route* back to Los Angeles, she became sick from "some bug I picked up," and had to be hospitalized when her plane landed in Honolulu.

The press wrote unflattering stories about Fisher's not rushing to Hawaii for a bedside vigil over his stricken bride-to-be. "Even at this point, it was apparent that Debbie was going to get the good press in our relationship. Me, the villain!"

Finally, Fisher and Debbie were together again, healthy and in California. Together they opted to escape to a little house in the dreary town of Desert Hot Springs. The winds were so strong, they reminded Debbie of El Paso.

Away from the prying eyes of the press, they talked seriously about their upcoming problems and the predictable trouble they might encounter.

Blackstone warned them, "You kids have gone too far down the road to turn back now. The press will crucify Eddie if he doesn't go through with it. His bookings will dry up, and he may even lose his TV show. His career will be in jeopardy."

"Like a doomed man sent to the gallows, I walked the last mile," Fisher said. "Or was about to. Did I love her? Does anybody really love anybody else, except in the movies?"

***

Eddie Fisher and Debbie could not agree on many things, especially the date of their wedding—or even if there were going to be a wedding. Whereas she wanted a big Hollywood splash "with tons of press," he preferred a more subdued ceremony back East, attended mostly by family and close friends.

"I was very weak and timid in those days, allowing people to push me around—shove, really," Fisher said. "But I decided to take a stand like a man. I demanded that the wedding, if it were to take place at all, be held on the grounds of Jennie Grossinger's wonderful resort in the Catskills, an easy drive from New York."

Debbie claimed that she was "grossly disappointed," but relented to his demands. She feared that if she didn't, there would be no wedding at all.

No sooner had he set the date in September of 1955 than he realized it was Yom Kippur, a sacred Jewish holiday. "No devout Jewish man would wed on a day like that, especially to a *shiksa*," Fisher said.

He phoned Debbie on the West Coast, informing her that he couldn't marry her on Yom Kippur, a holiday of which she had never heard. "She became hysterical and started to scream at me over the phone. I finally got her to cool off, and assured her I'd reschedule it as soon as possible."

Having agreed on a revised wedding date, Debbie flew from the West Coast to New York on September 17, a Friday. She had been warned not to alert the press. When she was spotted at the airport, she told a reporter that she had come to watch the Rocky Marciano-Archie Moore fight, a not very convincing excuse, since she'd never shown the slightest interest in boxing.

She was still clinging to the myth of her virginity. She wrote, "Premarital sex in the Dark Ages of the 1950s was considered immoral and cheapened a woman in the eyes of society."

In his 1981 memoir, Fisher claimed he'd already seduced her on several occasions. She later did admit that she'd had sex with him at the Essex House in New York right before the wedding.

Although in years to come the prospective bride and groom each attested to differing versions of their premarital sex life (or lack thereof), they did agree on one thing, and that was how disappointing the sex act had been.

She claimed that when he'd first seduced her, she found the act "quick and mechanical. It wasn't uncomfortable and it wasn't wonderful. It wasn't anything I had dreamed about or read about or thought it would be. He seemed to be going through the motions, never cuddling, never kissing, not even holding me."

At Essex House, he kept a small apartment, since he was in New York so often. He did say later that they engaged in premarital sex. But, as he told Blackstone, "It was not memorable."

When she woke up the next morning, she found a note from him. He had an early-morning session with executives at CBS. She claimed, "I was left feeling cold, lost, and frustrated."

Blood tests were needed, so Fisher took her to the office of Max Jacobson, whom he continued to mockingly refer to as "Dr. Needles."

By now, the reputation of this notorious doctor was known to Debbie, as was his list of celebrity clients. Over the years, Jacobson had administered amphetamines and other medications, some of them addictive, to Humphrey Bogart, Lauren Bacall, Ingrid Bergman, Yul Brynner, Maria Callas, Leonard Bernstein, Truman Capote, Montgomery Clift, Rosemary Clooney, Cecil B. De-Mille, Judy Garland, Nelson Rockefeller, Elizabeth Taylor, Tennessee Williams, and Elvis Presley. In September of 1960, Jacobson would begin giving injections to John F. Kennedy.

Debbie refused to allow Jacobson to draw samples of her blood, insisting that his nurse do it instead. The nurse then drew blood from her.

Fisher, however, had no objection to Jacobson's drawing a sample of his blood, in the aftermath of which the doctor gave him a "big boost" injection.

After that, Fisher, reacting to the amphetamines, drove Debbie to the Catskills, where accommodations had been arranged for them on the grounds of Grossingers. Milton Berle had agreed to turn over his two-room cottage, a building he maintained on the grounds of the resort, to the future honeymoon-ers. As part of their sojourn, they stopped off to obtain a marriage license at a small courthouse in the Catskills.

Plans had evolved so quickly that Debbie had not been able to buy a wed-ding gown. She phoned her mother in Burbank and asked her to go the MGM wardrobe department to borrow the wedding dress she'd worn in *The Tender Trap*. Minnie drove over and retrieved the white lace "ballerina length" outfit with the full skirt. Carefully boxed, she flew with it to New York aboard a plane with her husband, Roy, and with Debbie's older brother, Billy.

A few days before the wedding, Fisher, without telling Debbie, wanted to call off the wedding completely. Milton Blackstone, his manager, arrived on the scene. "You've got to marry the scheming little publicity hound," he heat-edly told Fisher. "Men down through the ages have married women without being in love."

Also before the ceremony, Joey Forman, one of Fisher's most enduring friends, remained adamantly opposed. "Come with me, you dumb kumquat. I'll drive you to Manhattan where you can book us a suite at the Waldorf As-toria. On your dime, rich boy. We'll spend a week auditioning a bevy of Broad-way babes. I'll take your rejects."

At Grossingers, the Sunday night before the wedding, the future honey-mooners had had a stressful day. "We hardly spoke to each other, saying only a good night," he said. "She retired to her bedroom, and I slept alone. I didn't wake up until ten the next morning. After shaving and showering, I knocked on her door. It was locked. There was no answer. I feared that something had happened to her. Had she committed suicide?"

Fisher exited from the cottage and ran out onto the grounds. There, he en-countered Paul Grossinger, Jennie's husband. "Something's happened to Deb-bie," he shouted. Paul rushed to the cottage and broke glass to enter her room, finding her sprawled out on the floor, apparently unconscious.

He immediately phoned his brother-in-law, a doctor visiting the resort from Manhattan. The doctor rushed to revive Debbie and could find nothing wrong. He ordered her back into bed to rest, and had room service deliver her some hearty chicken soup.

Later, Fisher wondered if Debbie had been putting on some sort of act for reasons known only to her. "You never knew with her…I mean, what she was up to. All her life, before or behind the cameras, she was always carrying on a drama, with or without a script. She got my attention all right."

***

As the sun was setting over the Catskills that Monday evening, the wedding ceremony was conducted in the newly built home of Jennie Grossinger's daughter, Elaine Grossinger Etess. For the event, Jennie had ordered her pastry chefs to create a six-tiered wedding cake five feet high and three feet wide, a mammoth confection that could feed 250 people.

Debbie's parents and her brother, Billy, were in the front row, seated next to Fisher's biological father, whom she met for the first time. Because of traffic delays, Fisher's mother and stepfather arrived an hour late, and sat on the opposite side of the room.

Judge Lawrence Cooke presided. Right before the ceremony, he told Debbie, "I'm so nervous, I'm shaking all over."

"I'm the one who should be nervous," she answered. "I've never had sex before," which was not true.

"The bride looked radiant," Fisher said, years later. "In fact, the most beautiful I'd ever seen her. Of course, I looked pretty gorgeous myself. Half the teenaged girls in America thought so, at least those not hung up on Pat Boone. Debbie seemed to be imitating Elizabeth Taylor in her movie, *Father of the Bride* (1950), the one where Spencer Tracy played her father."

Jeanette Johnson, who had been Debbie's gym teacher in high school, was her maid of honor. As the mother of the bride, Minnie looked on with pride, whereas Roy remained skeptical. He later complained that he felt uncomfortable in a room full of Jews.

Overruling Debbie's objections, Fisher denied access to the wedding—which he wanted to remain private—to photographers from Manhattan. In deference to his wishes, Elaine had confined them to the basement of her home, where waiters plied them with liquor, with the understanding that after the

"Don't let the wedding day smiles fool you," Eddie Fisher said. "Long before Debbie and I were married, I began to understand the woman I had fallen in love with was not the person I knew. Knowing that, why did I marry her? Why didn't I just walk away?"

"I think there is only one possible answer to the question: I don't have the slightest idea."

ceremony, Debbie and Fisher would restage their wedding ceremony for the press.

Judge Cooke had ended the ceremony on an odd note: "The world had bad news last week." Apparently, he was referring to reports that President Dwight Eisenhower had had a heart attack.

As Debbie was leaving the room, Fisher's mother, Katherine, came up to her. "Just give a little and take a little, and your life will be a happy one."

"I'll try to be a good wife to Eddie and a good mother to his children," Debbie promised. She later told her maid of honor, "Maybe sex in a marriage is not all that important."

What had been designated as their honeymoon cottage—a secluded farmhouse far removed from reporters and photographers—was about four miles away.

On her honeymoon night, the bride complained of a headache and retired to the lone bedroom upstairs. Drinking heavily, Fisher remained on the sofa watching television. By the time the station went off the air, he had passed out.

He woke up the following morning at around 8AM. Hearing nothing from the upstairs bedroom, where his bride had spent their honeymoon night, he decided to go jogging.

"I started out slow, but as I went along, I found myself breaking into a run," he said. "I wanted to flee from that cottage. I ran and ran until I had no breath left in me. I collapsed in a meadow, where a breeze was blowing down from the mountain. I lay there on the ground for about two hours, not wanting to get up and move into my life."

"Finally, I knew I could not stay there forever, so I picked myself up off the ground. This time, I walked very slowly back to our so-called honeymoon cottage, not knowing if Debbie would be there or not. She was not, but had left a note for me."

Eddie,

Having breakfast with my folks before they have to fly back. I took the car. I'll return later. Jennie is having the staff prepare us a picnic basket with a lot of goodies. See you around."

It was signed *"Mrs. Eddie Fisher alias Debbie Reynolds."*

***

"My honeymoon with Mr. Eddie

Fisher was just glorious," Debbie said, sarcastically. "He took me to a Coca-Cola bottlers' convention in Atlanta, surely what every girl dreams about."

The soda company executives were hoping to capitalize off Debbie and Fisher as America's sweethearts, perhaps unofficially using her as an unpaid spokesperson.

She killed that idea at her first meeting with the press in Georgia. After Fisher delivered his usual plug for the soft drink, she chimed in with "I don't drink Coca-Cola. It's bad for the teeth. Makes them yellow. I'm a milk drinker myself."

At first, the witnesses around her assumed she was joking, thinking she was just being a cute, wisecracking comedy star. But Fisher knew she was serious, and he was furious, later charging, "What in the fuck are you doing? Trying to sabotage my most profitable gig?"

Along with Debbie, he was slated to appear as an entertainer before the convention of Coca-Cola bottlers and their wives. As she recalled, "The master of ceremonies reminded me of the future sitcom *All in the Family*. He was Archie Bunker in the flesh."

In his public address, he first extended a warm welcome to "This little bundle of cuteness, Miss Debbie Reynolds, and her new groom, our spokesman, Eddie Fisher. They've been married only three days, and they hauled themselves out of their honeymoon bed to be with us here today. They are welcome to our marvelous club, which, as you know, is off-limits to niggers and Jews."

"Obviously, the shithead didn't know that Fisher was a Jew," she said.

When it came time for her to speak, she stunned the audience: "We broke all the rules today. You see, in this wonderful club of yours where no Jews are allowed, you made an exception for my very Jewish husband, and I appreciated that. As you can see, he's not black. Perhaps next year you'll invite Louis Armstrong."

The audience sat in stunned silence.

After Atlanta, Debbie and Fisher flew to Miami, where they stayed at the Thunderbird Motel. Fisher later related to Blackstone and others what Debbie told him about her sexual preference.

"Don't get the wrong idea," he said. "There was no confession of lesbianism. That would come later. She told me that when it came to sex, she preferred it oral instead of intercourse. She revealed that once, when she worked at RKO, Howard Hughes invited her to his house and told her he also liked it oral."

"Later, I heard some crap that she preferred oral sex because of some incident in El Paso when she was only six years old and got involved with a seventeen-year-old boy. I could live with her choice. What red-blooded male would turn down a good blow job? I figured I could get what Sammy Davis, Jr. called *poontang* from any number of girls."

Also according to Fisher, "She told me she wanted to have two or three children, which meant that on occasion, we would have to have sex the old-fashioned way."

After their wedding, since she was not due at MGM right away, she returned with Fisher to his apartment at New York"s Essex House. As America's Newlywed Sweethearts, they were invited to Yankee Stadium to watch the Dodgers play the Yankees in the World Series.

An announcer broadcast their presence in the stadium, where nearly all 40,000 of the baseball fans stood up to cheer them. "Did this ever happen to Joe DiMaggio?" she asked Fisher.

She traveled with him the following week to South Bend, Indiana, where Fisher had been charged with the official opening of another Coca-Cola plant. "With my career on hold, I felt like I was being hauled around like a piece of luggage."

During her time in the Middle West, she experienced a highlight of her marriage to Fisher. He escorted her on a pre-arranged visit to Independence, Missouri, to see Harry S Truman and his wife Bess. "Truman was very nice to me," Debbie said, "but I got the impression he'd never seen one of my movies." As it turned out, the ex-president had been a fan of Fisher's, calling him "my favorite G.I."

At first, Fisher seemed nervous about calling on Truman, and he told Debbie why: "I briefly dated his daughter Margaret. But at this party, I deserted her and left with Virginia Warren, the daughter of Earl Warren, the Chief Justice of the Supreme Court."

After their travels through the Middle West, they settled back into his apartment at Essex House, where Debbie became quickly bored. She started going out with male friends, often those visiting from Hollywood, who took her to clubs and Broadway plays whenever Fisher was busy, which was most of the time. The gay actor, Roddy McDowall, was a frequent escort. Fisher always maintained, "He'd rather be dating me than Debbie."

In January of 1956, Debbie was ordered to report back to work at MGM to shoot a new movie, *The Catered Affair,* in which she'd been suggested for the third lead once again. She'd heard rumors that the director and producer disagreed on casting her, one wanting her for the role, the other opposing it. She didn't know which of the two wanted her. She'd also heard that the producer disagreed about who to cast as the female lead, Bette Davis or Thelma Ritter.

They did agree, however, on who they'd assign as the male lead, both of them wanting Ernest Borgnine, who had won an Oscar for *Marty* (1955). He had played a Bronx butcher who doesn't plan to fall in love, but does.

***

The Catered Affair (MGM, 1956) began as a teleplay episode of the *Philco Television Playhouse.* The star had been the very talented Thelma Ritter, who had scored such a big hit with her performance as the cynical, sharp-tongued Birdie opposite Bette Davis in *All About Eve* (1950). In *The Catered Affair,* as a downtrodden Bronx housewife, Ritter played Aggie Hurley, who dreams of having a big wedding for her daughter, something she'd long fantasized about but which had been denied her.

The teleplay by Paddy Chayefsky had followed in the wake of his huge success in the film *Marty,* which had brought a Best Actor Oscar to Ernest Borgnine in 1955 and made him a star.

In that competition, Borgnine beat out James Dean, Spencer Tracy, Frank Sinatra, and James Cagney. Dore Schary, the new boss at MGM, wanted him to play the male lead in *The Catered Affair* as Tom Hurley, a beleaguered taxi driver who had been saving up for years to purchase a taxi medallion and be independent. Aggie wants him to blow everything he'd saved on her daughter's wedding, a catered affair.

The producer was Sam Zimbalist, who was far better known for his major adventure films such as *King Solomon's Mines* (1950) with Stewart Granger and *Quo Vadis* (1951) with Robert Taylor, both of which had received an Oscar nomination for Best Picture.

The director, Richard Brooks, had just helmed *Blackboard Jungle* (1955), a box office hit dealing with juvenile delinquency, starring Glenn Ford. Both Brooks and Zimbalist agreed on the casting of Borgnine, who not only could act, but looked the part, with his gruff voice, Machiavellian eyebrows, and gap-toothed Cheshire cat grin.

Whereas conflicts were raging over the casting of both the mother and daughter, there was also a lot of upset about the selection of a scriptwriter. Schary wanted Gore Vidal to adapt the Chayefsky play for the big screen.

In raging opposition, Zimbalist claimed, "That faggot will turn a poor Bronx housewife into a version of Margo Channing in *All About Eve*. He's an American aristocrat. What does he know about kitchen sink drama in the Bronx? As a *prima donna* bitch himself, he'll make Aggie a *prima donna* bitch."

Siding with Schary, Brooks defended Vidal as a writer and won that round.

Vidal admitted that Chayefsky "had the perfect ear for proletarian speech. I was content to be, in those days, Trigorin to his Chekhov. Also, I was literarily eccentric in that I never wrote about 'the little people.'"

Then there was a bitter dispute over who would play the female lead role of Aggie. Chayefsky had told the press, "My teleplay is an unfocused piece, in which the first act is a farce, the second act a comedy-drama, and the third abruptly drama. There aren't a dozen actresses who could make one piece out of all that. Miss Ritter, of course, did."

Indeed, it made sense to offer Ritter the chance to transfer her television success onto an equivalent role on the big screen, but Dore Schary, the MGM boss, said, "I adore Thelma, but she's not box office. Bette Davis wants the role, and I'm going to give it to her."

Zimbalist protested that Davis would be miscast. However, after her "exile" in Maine, she had returned to Hollywood with an expanded waistline and thickened jowls, and was showing signs of aging, characteristics which fitted the role of Aggie.

Zimbalist feared she'd repeat all those legendary mannerisms she'd played out in previous roles, including her "smoking a cigarette and eating up both her leading man and the scenery."

Davis had another view, wanting to show Hollywood her versatility. The year before, she'd played Elizabeth I in *The Virgin Queen*. She hoped that by shocking viewers as the Bronx housewife, she'd win another Oscar.

She was still bitterly disappointed that she'd lost the Best Actress prize for *All About Eve*, the award having gone to Judy Holliday for her comedy, *Born Yesterday* in 1950.

Another conflict between the producer and director arose over the casting of the young bride-to-be, Jane Hurley. Both Zimbalist and Schary wanted Debbie, who, up to then, was primarily known for her appearances in romantic comedies.

As Debbie herself revealed, "Dore and Sam wanted me for only one reason: Not because of any great acting ability, but to capitalize off my fame as Eddie's sweetheart."

Even so, she felt that the role was right for her. "God damn it, I knew more about growing up poor than any of those mother fuckers."

Then Brooks came up with an unusual actress to play the role. By now, Margaret O'Brien, the famous child actress of the 1940s, was a late teenager around eighteen years old. She was trying to make the transition from child actress to more mature roles, and Brooks felt she'd be terrific as Jane. But neither Zimbalist nor Schary were impressed, and eventually demanded that Debbie be cast, overruling Brooks' preference for O'Brien.

The supporting cast was agreed upon without debate. Barry Fitzgerald would play the lovable old Uncle Jack Conlon, who lives with the Hurleys. His girlfriend, Mrs. Rafferty, would be portrayed by Dorothy Stickney. Jane's

In *The Catered Affair*, Ernest Borgnine, Bette Davis (center) and Debbie fight it out at the table in a dreary Bronx kitchen.

Bette wants to spend their life's savings on a big wedding for her daughter, but husband Borgnine wants a taxi medallion.

prospective groom would be essayed by the Australian actor, Rod Taylor, cast as Ralph Halloran.

Davis confided to Debbie that the role of the low-brow Bronx housewife would be one of the biggest challenges of her long career, a chance to play against type. She worked with Brooks, asking him for guidance if she showed any of the mannerisms of films associated with her in the late 1930s or '40s.

"She developed a powerful crush on Brooks," Debbie said.

"I'm a pushover for sexy, strong, and handsome men," Davis said. "Perhaps I've found another director like William Wyler to guide me in my future roles."

Of course, Debbie knew that Brooks had no erotic interest in Davis, and, in fact, would go on to marry the beautiful English actress, Jean Simmons.

Debbie regarded the making of *The Catered Affair* as one of the most humiliating experiences of her life. "Brooks rode me all day long. He mocked my acting, calling me Debbie Dimples, Miss Hollywood, and even Eddie Fisher's Baby Doll."

One scene called for her to cry on cue, and she was unable to do that. Brooks attacked her viciously in front of cast and crew. Having tangled with many a director herself, notably Mike Curtiz, Davis comforted the younger actress in her dressing room. Beginning that afternoon, the women developed a mother-daughter relationship that lasted for the rest of their lives.

Of course, there would be an occasional disagreement. But whether she was right or wrong, Debbie always apologized and was reinstated into Davis' good graces.

[One night in 1985, Davis told her, "You are the daughter I always wanted, not Miss B.D. Hyman, whom I have cut out of my will."

When she read her daughter's scathing memoir, My Mother's Keeper, *Davis claimed that book almost caused her to have another stroke. "At least Joan Crawford wasn't alive to read that dreadful exposé of*

According to Debbie, "To prepare for her role, Bette Davis took playing Aggie very seriously. I even went with her to help her buy her own wardrobe. We took a taxi to a seedy area of downtown Los Angeles, where she purchased dresses from a secondhand clothing store."

Someone from the press learned of this, and filed a story the next day that "a bankrupt Bette Davis, one of the stars of Golden Age Hollywood, was seen shopping for clothes in a thrift shop in downtown Los Angeles. How the once-mighty have fallen!"

her, Mommie Dearest, *by that ungrateful adopted daughter of hers, what was that dreadful child's name again? Christina or some such shit?"]*

One scene with Debbie on *The Catered Affair* had gone well until Brooks noted that she was wearing her eleven-karat engagement ring from Fisher. He walked over to her and slapped her hard, sending her running sobbing to her dressing room.

He turned to Borgnine: "Little Miss Dimples is playing a poor little girl from the Bronx, yet she's wearing a large diamond ring worth a king's ransom. What is she? A high-priced hooker on the side? I'll have to reshoot the whole damn thing."

Barry Fitzgerald was the scene stealer of the picture. Debbie delighted in meeting him, and he even taught her how to imitate his engaging Irish brogue, which in time she would use in her impersonations on TV or on the stage.

Aggie to her daughter: "You're gonna have a big wedding whether you want one or not!"

He confided to her, "I've been a lifelong bachelor, but that doesn't mean I won't pinch the fannie of a pretty little vixen like you from time to time—so watch out!"

In an almost unprecedented development in 1944, he was nominated for both Best Actor of the year as well as Best Supporting Actor, all for the same picture, *Going My Way.* His co-star, Bing Crosby, won the Best Actor Oscar, with Fitzgerald garnering the Best Supporting Actor award. Sadly, *The Catered Affair* was the Irishman's last film. He was to die in Dublin in 1961 at the age of 71.

The Catered Affair opened to poor reviews and did not do well at the box office. A typical attack appeared in *The New Yorker:* "The movie is a confused and wearying account of a family squabble in the Bronx. In the role of the mother, Bette Davis is done up to resemble a fat and lonely house-

Debbie found Rod Taylor "devastatingly attractive in the most masculine of ways."

He would marry three times, which was not uncommon for a star. What was not commonplace, as she soon learned, was that for a while, he lived in Malibu as the lover of Rock Hudson, who was to appear in two of his films.

wife, but even so, she conveys the impression that she's really a dowager doing a spot of slumming in the Bronx."

Another critic wrote that she played Aggie Hurley "like a slumming Queen Elizabeth in the Bronx."

When the Academy Awards were announced, Davis was not on the list of contenders. She phoned Debbie and sobbed. "The role was probably my last chance to win an Oscar."

Debbie tried to convince her that there would be other roles, other awards. Weeks later, both of them sat watching the Best Actress Oscar go to Ingrid Bergman for her comeback picture, *Anastasia* (1956).

When it came to awards, Debbie fared better than Davis. The National Board of Review voted *The Catered Affair* one of the best movies of 1956, and Debbie won its Best Supporting Actress honor.

***

When Debbie had to go to Hollywood to film *The Catered Affair,* Fisher flew there with her to set up housekeeping.

To welcome her back to the West Coast, Mike Todd staged a large reception, complete with Mexican bands, on the grounds of the well-manicured gardens in back of a mansion he'd rented on South Carolwood Drive. He invited only those on the Hollywood A-list. "I got kisses from everybody from Gary Cooper to Dean Martin, from Frank Sinatra to Samuel Goldwyn and David O. Selznick," Debbie said. "Lucille Ball arrived with Desi Arnaz, when he fed me a foot of Cuban tongue when he kissed me. Edie Adams was there with Ernie Kovacs."

Until then, Coca-Cola had refused to let Fisher film his TV show in California, but the soda company finally relented and let him shoot the program in Hollywood. His first appearance was with Eddie Cantor. Milton Blackstone decided that Fisher would get better ratings if he did a number with Debbie as a means of profiting from the massive publicity the newlyweds had received.

Her contract with MGM, which paid her $450 a week, denied her the freedom to appear on television without permission from the studio. In an attempt to resolve that conflict, she made an appointment with Benny Thau, an MGM executive, scheduling it for the

MGM executive Benny Thau refused to allow Debbie to appear on television as part of Eddie Fisher's show. He insisted that doing so would be a violation of her contract with the studio.

She nonetheless defied him. After she appeared with her husband as his sidekick in one of his programs on "the little black box," Thau was enraged—and vengeful.

afternoon. "I didn't want to intrude on his mornings," she said. "In those days, Nancy Davis (later Reagan) was going to his office in the morning to give him blow jobs."

"When I met him, he was so cold he pissed Arctic ice," Debbie said. "He absolutely refused to let me go on television. I later agreed with Eddie that I'd appear on his show anyway, and to hell with that bastard, Thau."

Debbie's rage against Thau was mirrored in her animosity toward Blackstone, Fisher's agent. "Blackstone was a tough cookie in business," she said. "I was rehearsing this number with Eddie, and he noticed that I wore a white diamond cross. He walked over to me and demanded that I remove it. 'It shows you hate Jews!' he charged."

She relented to his demand, later telling Fisher, "I hate that son of a bitch."

"He said virtually the same thing about you," Fisher claimed, "but he leaves out the 'son of' and just says 'I hate that bitch.'"

Thau saw the episode he had forbidden on TV. In its aftermath, the following Monday, he summoned Fisher—not Debbie—into his office. "You're telling people all over town that you want to be a movie star. For going against my wishes and for putting Debbie in your show, I'll see that all studios will close their doors to you."

Fisher, of course, was devastated, and the newlyweds fiercely argued in the aftermath.

They had rented a lavish home set on a hundred acres on a hillside in the Pacific Palisades. It was the former residence of MGM's "Boy Wonder," Irving Thalberg, and his wife, the former queen of MGM, Norma Shearer.

"It was true what Thau said," Fisher claimed. "I did want to become a movie star, but I ran into a lot of resistance. I got a role on TV, opposite Margaret O'Brien, the former child star, in *Romeo & Juliet*. I gave her her first screen kiss. But watching myself perform, I decided that as a movie star, I was to acting what Sir Laurence Olivier was to pop music."

The prospect of remaking *The Jazz Singer* (1927) was dangled before him. "The story of my life," Fisher said. "A poor little Jewish boy who dreams of becoming a hot shot star. But the part went to a Lebanese, Danny Thomas. Go figure that!"

Fisher was also up for the role of a soldier in a World War II drama, *The Young Lions* (1958), with Marlon Brando and Montgomery Clift. "My role went to my buddy, Dean Martin," Fisher said.

"I also wanted to do Budd Schulberg's *What Makes Sammy Run?*, the story of the ultimate Jewish hustler. I could draw upon Blackstone for inspiration for that one, but the deal fell through."

The nights he spent at home were mostly with his card-playing cronies. Many of their games, on which they often placed ten-thousand dollar bets, lasted until dawn. According to Debbie, "My only job was to bring these hungry boys sandwiches where they neither thanked me or looked up. Marilyn

Monroe, when married to Joe DiMaggio, had the same duty in her marriage."

"As for sex, forget it," she said. "One night I begged him to come to bed and do his duty as a husband."

"I'm busy right now," he called to her. "Start without me. I'll be in later."

"What was he suggesting?" she wondered. "Masturbation?"

It wasn't always boring. Sometimes, Fisher would kick out his card-playing cronies and invite a glittering array of stars. On many a night, they entertained Tony Curtis and Janet Leigh, Edie Adams and Ernie Kovacs, Dean and Jeanne Martin, George Englund and Cloris Leachman, and, inevitably, Mike Todd and his mistress, Elizabeth Taylor.

At some of the parties, especially when a singer was invited, Debbie would perform a duet with him or her. Her partners ranged from Ethel Merman to Noël Coward, from Frank Sinatra to Judy Garland. "Eddie never joined in," Debbie said. "He always looked sullen. The guests loved it, but Eddie resented my performing."

"In the house alone with him, he was often moody," she said. "Sometimes he'd go for days without speaking. Often, he was gone all day and all night, coming in at four o'clock the following morning with no explanation as to how he'd spent the night. I heard rumors that he was screwing around, especially when he went to Las Vegas."

Fisher's disapproval of her performing live before guests reached a crescendo one night at Mocambo. Dean Martin was on the stage kibbitzing and clowning around, and he invited Debbie to join him. "We had the audience screaming in hysteria, all of them except Eddie. He sat glaring at me."

On the way home in the early hours of the morning, he attacked her. "You were just plain awful. A fucking bore. You embarrassed me in front of Hollywood. To think that a class act like myself would marry a little goofball like you...By the way, I hear you and Martin were fucking."

As the days went by, his attacks mounted. She began to lose her self-confidence. "Judy Garland can sing. Debbie Reynolds cannot. Imogene Coca is a great comedienne. You're not even a mediocre one."

In desperation, she called Martin, hoping he would give her some reassurance. "He's jealous of us because he has absolutely no sense of humor. Frank Sinatra can kid around. Eddie cannot. Savvy Sammy is a riot. Not Eddie. He can sing a bit, but Sinatra, Perry Como, and Vic Damone are better, even that Pat Boone. He's jealous of all of them."

"I couldn't look to my parents as role models," Debbie said. "Their marriage lasted for fifty-seven years, but they spoke to each other only for forty-two of those tumultuous years."

"To please Debbie," Fisher said, "I built a swimming pool in the rear garden, even though it was a rented property. She'd constructed one for her parents in Burbank. Nothing I did seemed to make my bride happy. She was living lavishly in Norma Shearer's house and spending my income."

He gave her $2,500 a week to run the house, but he suspected that she was stashing much of that money, along with her $450-a-week salary, in her name at a bank.

"She certainly wasn't spending it on food," he said. "The refrigerator was always bare. One night when my friend, Joey Forman, came over, I wanted him to stay for dinner, but she'd warned the cook not to feed him and to keep the liquor cabinet locked."

On another night, he asked his friend, Lenny Gaines, an actor and comedian he called "the funniest man on earth" to stay over for dinner. Debbie objected, claiming, "I have only two steaks in the fridge."

According to Fisher, "Sometimes Minnie cooked a casserole and brought it over: Otherwise, I think we would have starved to death."

In a memoir, Fisher wrote that he never understood why his wife was that concerned about money. "She had never been poor growing up, had never gone hungry like I was."

Apparently, he knew nothing about her young days in Texas, when the Reynolds family lived miles below the poverty line.

"My bank account was open to one and all," he said. "I was very generous, spending as fast as the cash poured in. She stashed every dollar away that she could get her greedy little hands on. Money and sex, or the lack thereof, became our greatest source of friction."

"I managed to get along with her father, Roy, and we often played cards," Fisher said. "I knew he was an anti-Semite, but he kept that prejudice to himself. Her mother was a god damn bitch, always interfering in our lives and causing trouble. She was the classic horror mother-in-law. When I heard she was visiting Debbie, which was far too often, I retreated to this whorehouse in downtown Los Angeles, where the madam had a bevy of gals waiting for me to fuck."

Debbie constantly complained to Fisher's mother, Katherine, about how much money he was sending to her, his divorced father, and all of his siblings.

"He needs money for us so we can build a house of our own and have children," Debbie said. "If he provides for everybody else, there will be nothing left for our own brood."

Even Mike Todd warned Fisher, "Sonny Boy, you can't support the entire world. You should reduce Debbie's weekly maintenance fee from $2,500 a week to $300."

"It was true," Fisher said. "The more money I gave my family, the more they wanted. My siblings always needed more for dental work, hospital bills, help with a mortgage, a new car—you name it. One of my brothers wanted a nose job because people told him his nose looked like Tony Bennett's—not mine. I guess my money-grubbing family and even myself thought the gold-laden money train would continue forever to pull into the station with a sack of money for everybody."

"I never asked Eddie for money," Katherine said. "I was grateful for whatever he could provide. When I visited Debbie and him, I could see how unhappy Sonny Boy was. He never said anything to me, but I could see it in his face. If only he'd married a nice Jewish girl. It was obvious to me he'd trapped himself into this hideous marriage. They put on a good show in front of the press, but that marriage was a sham."

***

Pier Angeli and Debbie remained friends, but another man was about to move into their lives. Each of them would become involved with this handsome and charismatic, but mysterious figure. His name was James Dean.

Since she was a married woman, Debbie told only some of her closest friends about her involvement with this controversial actor, sharing intimate details with Judy Garland, Ann Miller, and Celeste Holm. But never to Angeli, who was having a much more torrid relationship with Dean.

In fact, whereas Debbie's relationship with Dean remained a dark secret, his affair with Angeli would become fodder for the tabloids.

***

Originally entitled *The Blind Run*, a "youth-in-angst" saga, the film, *Rebel Without a Cause* (1955), had a long, tortuous launch.

Dr. Robert Lindner had written a book in 1943 during his stint as staff psychiatrist at the Federal Penitentiary in Lewisburg, Pennsylvania. Warners purchased the rights to it in 1946, and in the late 1940s, it was conceived as a vehicle for Marlon Brando. Although that actor even submitted to a screen test for it, the project never got off the ground. After the success in the 1950s of such juvenile delinquency movies as *The Blackboard Jungle*, Warners revived *Rebel*.

Its director, Nicholas Ray, wanted to film it, and he hired Stewart Stern, who had written the script for Pier Angeli's debut film *Teresa* (1951).

James Dean was cast as Jim Stark, the alienated young hero in *Rebel Without a Cause*.

"Jimmy and Stark had something in common," said director Nicholas Ray. "Both of them want to belong, yet feared belonging. Dean understood the character, including Stark's conflict of violent eagerness and mistrust, the intensity of his desires, his fear, all of which could make him at times arrogant and egocentric. I felt Dean could capture the character behind all this and depict Stark's desperate vulnerability."

Thus, Stern set out to bring the tormented story of the alienated teenager, Jim Stark, to the screen. A seventeen-year-old new kid on the block, he arrives at Dawson High where he is taunted by a tough street gang.

James Dean signed for the starring role right before Christmas in 1954. At that time, *Rebel* was envisioned as a Grade B movie in black and white, a kind of exploitation film about juvenile delinquency, which was all the rage across the country.

Ray briefly considered casting Margaret O'Brien, the former child star at MGM, as Judy, the female lead. Among others, Dean was dating Lori Nelson at the time, and he recommended her instead. But after thinking it over, Ray decided that neither actress would be right for the part.

Ray went on to claim that MGM "was trying to push Debbie Reynolds onto me, since the studio had no immediate role for her and she was under contract. "If *Rebel* turns out to be a musical, Debbie would be perfect."

Margaret O'Brian was cursed by her success as a child actress and was desperately searching for more adult roles

"I've met her," Dean said sarcastically. "She is the least likely juvenile delinquent in Hollywood. Maybe we might make it work if you recycle 'Abba Dabba Honeymoon' for the film."

Another candidate for the role, as it was originally conceived, was the *über*-blonde, Jayne Mansfield, whose widely publicized super-structure measured 40"-24"-36". Dean said, "As Judy, Jayne would be 'busting out all over.'"

Ray said, "I considered the casting of Mansfield a hallucination. When she came in, I didn't even bother to put film in the camera."

Based on the film's original script, the casting of Mansfield may not have been as outrageous as Ray had claimed. In the first draft, Judy was to have played a "teenage slut" who, early in the film, is arrested for solicitation. Mansfield, with the proper wardrobe and leeway, could easily have convinced audiences that she was a young prostitute.

But Jack Warner ordered a rewrite. In the final version, Judy is being disciplined by police for breaking curfew.

In the meantime, Dean had switched his own casting preference for the character of Judy to Car-

The studio was pushing sex kitten Jayne Mansfield onto Nicholas Ray for the role of a teenage slut (as the script was then written).

Ray called it "the most outlandish suggestion of the decade."

roll Baker, whom he had known from the Actors Studio in Manhattan.

Jack Warner, who controlled the film's financing, had long regretted letting his option on Debbie's contract expire. "She slipped away from my stable of stars and went to make money for that shithead, Louis B. Mayer. I want her for the role of Judy," Warner said.

But Ray opposed the choice, having settled on Natalie Wood. In spite of the age difference between them, they were engaged in an off-the-record affair.

Yet Warner still insisted on Debbie, thinking she could help with the exploitation of the movie because of the massive publicity that she'd generated by marrying Eddie Fisher.

In a memo that Warners issued on March 22, 1955, he placed Debbie at the top of the list of contenders for the role of Judy, followed by second-tier choices, Natalie Wood and Carroll Baker, plus a dozen other far less well-known actresses, including Kathryn Grant (later, Mrs. Bing Crosby).

Many executives at Warners thought Wood was too young for the role and that Debbie would be more convincing. Wood was born in 1938, Debbie in 1932.

Eric Stacey, Warner's production manager, issued a memo. "No actors should be assigned to *Rebel Without a Cause* unless they are at least 18 years old. Older actors who can play teenagers should be cast. Debbie Reynolds might be ideal because she looks so young, especially with the right wardrobe and makeup. A minor cannot work at night except under emergency conditions, and then not after 10PM—and on this picture, approximately 80 percent of the scenes take place at night."

"But I wanted Natalie," Ray told his associates. "I was fucking her at the time Warner was trying to force Debbie Reynolds onto me. But playing along with Warner's wishes, I wanted to test Debbie in some scenes with Jimmy, so I summoned both of them to my bungalow at the Chateau Marmont."

Before emoting in front of Ray as Judy, Debbie read Stewart's description of her. "At sixteen, she's in a panic of frustration regarding her father—needing his love and suffering when it is denied. This forces her to invite the attention of

Debbie would probably have been fabulous in the "juvenile delinquent" role (Judy) eventually awarded to Natalie Wood. But to her deep disappointment, she couldn't shake the wholesome image with which she was associated. Nicholas Ray simply didn't want her.

In the final cast, Sal Mineo (left) is secretly in love with James Dean, pictured above in the lap of Natalie Wood.

other men in order to punish him."

She dressed for the role of Judy, making herself up to look like a high school senior. She wore a pair of blue jeans, as did Dean himself.

"At first, I was nervous because I thought Ray was judging me harshly," Debbie said. "I knew he didn't want me for the role. I also heard that Jimmy wanted Carroll Baker. I was no Actors Studio graduate like her."

"My first reading with Jimmy was awkward. He held back. Neither Ray nor Jimmy helped me, since both of them wanted me to fail."

"I felt I could identify with Judy in the script," she said. "The character seemed to express something hidden in me, especially the mother who did not understand me and the old and distant father who would not even kiss me. I could sink my teeth into Judy and play her. Who knows? I might even win an Oscar."

"Suddenly, something happened," she said. "I think I stirred up something in Jimmy. Without any help from the script, Ray commanded us to play a love scene like teenage lovers. Boy, did I let loose. I was determined to get that god damn role. I became a high school slut. Jimmy relaxed—and how! He started to wrestle me on the floor. Both of us seemed to forget all about Ray. He was tackling me. Quite by accident, I felt his erection. That really turned him on. We were about to rip off each other's panties until Ray called 'CUT!'"

"Jimmy had stirred up some long-suppressed passion in me, and I was left on the floor, unsatisfied," she said.

"Jimmy left and Ray told me he'd stay in touch. Feeling unfulfilled about everything, I headed back to Burbank to wait for a phone call that might never come."

One biographer later wrote that Debbie wasn't interested in *Rebel,* having no interest in dramas and preferring instead to stick to musical comedies. She was misquoted as saying, "I want lighthearted parts."

"That statement was not at all true," she said. "Whoever wrote that didn't take into account that I was playing a serious role in a Bette Davis movie, *The Catered Affair.* I'd been told that MGM musicals were dying out. I knew that to survive in my career, I had to switch to more dramatic roles, showing my versatility. I also thought Jimmy and I would make a terrific screen team. I'd seen him in *East of Eden,* and he was compelling. What an actor!"

***

Debbie's friendship with Pier Angeli had begun when the two of them, along with Leslie Caron, were known as "The New White Hopes for MGM." Its once-spectacular stars of yesteryear, Greta Garbo, Joan Crawford, and Norma Shearer, had faded away.

"Pier and I often dated the same men before our [*respective*] marriages," Debbie recalled. "John Barrymore, Jr. and Arthur Loew Jr. come to mind. We called them 'hymen busters.'"

In spite of their rivalry over men that they both dated, Debbie and Angeli remained best friends. "Pier's datebook was more filled than mine," Debbie said. "Among others, she went from Kirk Douglas to Paul Newman to James Dean, and then ended up marrying Vic Damone, my co-star in two movies."

Paul Newman made his big screen debut in the Biblical epic, *The Silver Chalice* (1954) alongside co-stars Pier Angeli and Virginia Mayo. During filming, Newman launched an affair with Angeli, even though he had a wife and kids in New York and was also seeing Joanne Woodward on the side. He was drawn to the *petite* Angeli's fragile, prim, shy, and romantic charms.

One day, James Dean dropped by the set for a reunion with Newman, who had been his rival for roles in New York and, according to rumor, his occasional lover. Back East, both men had been known as bisexuals.

As Debbie noted, "Pier began a balancing act between Jimmy and Paul. She had affairs going on with both of them, and even took them home to meet her overpowering mother, Mrs. Luigi Pierangeli.

The mother objected to both men, to whom she fed Italian dinners on separate occasions, of course. A stern Catholic, she insisted that her daughter drop Newman because he was a Jew. She found fault with Dean, too, labeling him a "degenerate."

When Newman returned East, Angeli saw more of Dean. Over lunch one day in the commissary with Debbie, Angeli talked about Dean and her feelings for him. "Before we got down to the heavy stuff, Pier told me how she stayed rail thin: She had a small piece of raw hamburger for lunch and two raw eggs."

"Jimmy is different from all the rest," Angeli said. "He loves music. He loves it from the heart, the same way I do. We have much to talk about. It's wonderful to know such an understanding man. We go to the beach, where we just sit or fool around like college kids. We talk about ourselves, our goals, our problems, movies, acting, about life and death. We are most *simpatico* with each other."

Nicholas Ray met Debbie one more time at Warners, where he invited her to lunch. At the time, Jack Warner was still insisting that Debbie play Judy in *Rebel Without a Cause*. [*He was aware of James Dean's affair with Angeli.*]

"Jimmy is intensely determined not to love or be loved," Ray said. "He's fascinated, absorbed at times, with anything new—be it beautiful, bizarre, perverted, not so perverted. Whatever. If a woman

Troubled Pier Angeli. Her private anguish seemed to match that of James Dean.

146

like Pier thinks she's the only one in his life, she will find out differently. He also has other women and many men in love with him."

Angeli and Dean were last seen in public together at the premiere of Judy Garland's *A Star Is Born* in September of 1954.

Debbie was surprised when Angeli announced her engagement to Vic Damone on October 4, 1954. "She never told me about him. For a while, I thought he was going to marry Elizabeth Taylor."

[Hedda Hopper had written, "Fickle Elizabeth Taylor has fallen in love again, this time with a handsome young crooner, Vic Damone, who is giving Frank Sinatra's fading career a push toward oblivion."

But when Damone was drafted into the U.S. Army, Elizabeth dropped him, telling associates, "I'm not the type of gal to wait around until Johnny comes marching home."]

Helen Rose, Debbie's favorite designer, threw a bridal shower for Angeli at her home in Beverly Hills in November of 1954. Debbie whispered to Rose, "I can't believe Vic is marrying Pier. He told me on the set of *Athena* that he only likes women with red pubic hair. Of course, he went for Liz (Taylor) and she certainly doesn't have red pubic hair!"

The wedding of Vic Damone to Pier Angeli took place on November 24, 1954, in Hollywood at St. Timothy's Catholic Church.

[Ironically, this would be the same church where seventeen years later, Angeli would be buried after committing suicide.]

Six hundred star-studded guests showed up for the wedding ceremony, including Debbie. A legend still persists that Dean, astride his Harley-Davidson and wearing a black leather jacket, was spotted across the street from the church as *confetti* rained down on the newlyweds as they exited from the church after the ceremony.

The roar of a motorcycle engine could be heard by members of the wedding party. Debbie swore she saw Dean speed away. As one reporter wrote, "Jimmy, looking like Marlon Brando in *The Wild One* (1954), roared down the street and out of Pier Angeli's life forever."

Dean later told his best friend, William Bast, "That wasn't me. As a bizarre joke, I hired this guy to impersonate me, knowing that at a distance, no one could make out my face behind the goggles. Shame on you, Willie, for thinking I'd be dumb enough to actually show up myself. Surely you don't think I'm that dumb?"

Debbie remembered calling on Angeli long after her honeymoon, when she was pregnant with their son, Perry, named after Perry Como. "I knocked, but she wouldn't let me come in until I forced my way in. There, I found out why she was refusing entry. Her face was swollen, and Damone had given her a black eye. I was so outraged I begged her to leave the bastard. But she was too afraid of him."

In the years ahead, Debbie saw Pier less frequently. "When they divorced in November of 1958, her marriage to Damone was riddled with violence, charges and counter-charges, and court battles over custody of their son, Perry.

In 1962, the Italian beauty married bandleader Armando Trotajoli, but they divorced in 1966.

Later, after her divorce from Trotajoli, Angeli moved back to Italy, where her awful mother had her committed to an insane asylum. There, she suffered "hell on earth" and was sexually abused by both male and female caretakers. Eventually, she returned to L.A., hoping to resume her movie career. That didn't work out.

Angeli told Debbie, "Jimmy Dean is the only man I ever loved deeply like a woman should love her man. I never loved either of my husbands the way I loved Jimmy. I would lie awake in the same bed with my husband, but wish it were Jimmy there. I had to separate from my last husband because I don't think that someone can be in love with one man—even if he is dead—and live with another."

[In September of 1971, Debbie was greatly saddened to learn that her dear friend had died from an overdose of barbiturates at her apartment in Los Angeles at the age of thirty-nine.]

***

When Debbie was still in the running to play Judy in *Rebel Without a Cause*, she had dinner one night at Pier Angeli's home. Later, the two actresses talked in private.

Debbie confessed that if she got the role of Judy, she feared that Dean would act circles around her. "He'll make me look like an amateur. I think Judy should be a bit sexy, but not like Jayne Mansfield. In the beginning, she was set to play Judy. Let's face it, for the 1950s, big boobs seem to be the attraction of the day—not just Mansfield, but Marilyn Monroe, Mamie Van Doren, and all the other cows."

"That leaves us out, and certainly Natalie Wood, too," Angeli said. "If she plays Judy, wardrobe will have to pad her bra and make her wear a butt pad, too."

Dean had confided to Nicholas Ray that "Debbie is the cleanest, sweetest-smelling gal I've ever seduced. She's as fresh as a morning glory any time of the day. She's small and delicate and her soft body just melts into mine. Almost more than the sex act itself, I enjoy arousing her to the point where she's completely under my spell. Until her, no woman, nor man for that matter, has ever surrendered to me completely. But I'm going to end this affair before it gets too serious."

"Why in hell?" Ray asked.

"Because I could fall in love with her, and that is the last thing on my agenda. I plan to live a very long life, and falling in love is not on my wish

148

list."

One night at a party at the home of Tony Martin and Cyd Charisse, Debbie had a long, confidential talk with her friend and confidante, Ann Miller. The tap-dancing star got more details about Debbie's involvement with Dean than any other confidante. Later, according to Miller, "It seemed that Debbie liked to have Dean make love to her a hell of a lot more than Eddie Fisher."

"Eddie might kiss you on the mouth, but Jimmy kisses everything—your throat, your breasts, your shoulders, and on and on," Debbie confessed. "A rainstorm of kisses, perhaps more like a hurricane. His tongue doesn't just kiss, it sloshes. But he can also be a gentle nibbler, particularly on a woman's nipples. At a woman's ear, he's like a cobra snaking his tongue around the lobes, searching for prey."

"With his soft caresses, he arouses me more than any man before, not that there have been enough of them for me to make an accurate judgment. I enjoy every minute of his love-making. I never imagined that sex could feel that good. In penile dimensions, he's an average man, but that's the only thing average about him."

"Jimmy seems to undress a girl just by looking at her," Debbie claimed, as cited later by Miller, "There's something explosive about him, something hard to define. He marches to a different drummer from the rest of us. Also, as an actor, he comes from a different planet. He's completely different from all the pretty boys of the 1950s, including R.J. Jimmy has a smoldering allure that draws women to him, and a hell of a lot of men, too, or so I hear. He seems to appeal equally to both sexes."

"With R.J., I was attracted to his eyes. But Jimmy's most alluring facial feature is his mouth and how he moves it. I've come to think of him as a male Marilyn Monroe. He also has this 'Little Boy Lost' quality—what girl can resist that?"

"I read somewhere that he is 'wily, controlling, beautiful, seductive, and sexually ambivalent,' and I agree he is all those things…and more. God, I'm getting carried away talking about this guy, and I haven't even been cast opposite him yet."

Miller's advice was, "To hell with the movie. Forget Eddie Fisher. Go for it. How often do you think a guy like Jimmy will enter a girl's life again?"

On another night at a party, Debbie had a girl-to-girl talk with Jean Hagen, her co-star in *Singin' in the Rain*. In reference to Debbie, Hagen later said, "She seemed thrilled at the idea of making *Rebel Without a Cause* with James Dean. She even thought they might evolve into the ideal screen team for the 1960s, sorta like Clark Gable and Joan Crawford in the 1930s, or Spencer Tracy and Katharine Hepburn in the 1940s."

"I find Jimmy mesmerizing," Debbie confessed. "The boy just oozes sex appeal. Eddie Fisher has a voice but no sex appeal beyond that. Let's face it: Rock Hudson, Tab Hunter, and Robert Wagner are gorgeous dreamboats.

Imagine a girl looking at a picture of Eddie Fisher in a bathing suit and comparing it to one with Tab Hunter showing flesh. Tab would obviously be more appealing."

Debbie was more or less geared up to shoulder the role of Judy in *Rebel Without a Cause* until one morning, a story appeared in *Variety* that described how Ray had won the casting battle and had offered the role to his preferred choice, Natalie Wood.

Debbie burst into tears and ran to her bedroom.

"That god damn little bitch has all the luck," she complained. "She gets not only R.J., but becomes Jimmy's new co-star too. She'll have to wear bracelets to cover up her deformed left wrist."

On September 30, 1955, Debbie and Angeli desperately phoned each other when they learned of Dean's fatal car crash on the way to Salinas, in his new Porsche Spyder Speedstar convertible.

"I don't know if the poor boy ever loved anyone—maybe not even himself," Debbie said.

***

The executives at RKO were eager to capitalize off the avalanche of publicity generated by the marriage of Eddie Fisher to Debbie Reynolds. A memo went out: "Find a script for America's sweethearts—and do so at once."

In a distant corner of a storage area associated with Vintage Films, *Bachelor Mother* was rediscovered and recycled. In 1939, it had been a star vehicle for Ginger Rogers and David Niven. A team of writers, the most famous of which was Norman Krasna, came up with an updated script for the 1950s, *Bundle of Joy*, set for a release just before Christmas of 1956.

Fisher and Debbie were offered the respective starring roles. In an attempt to gauge their onscreen chemistry, and with the hope and intention of pairing them together in future pictures, RKO requested a screen test. RKO learned that Debbie was pregnant. *[Whereas in the movie, she discovered a baby on the stoop of her townhouse, in real life, she was having her own child.]*

Debbie and Eddie Fisher were cast in *A Bundle of Joy*, a remake of a movie that had been a huge hit back in 1939, *Bachelor Mother*.

It had starred David Niven and Ginger Rogers, who discovers and subsequently adopts an abandoned baby.

As the plot unfolds, everyone, including Niven, mistakenly believes that the baby is her own biological child.

Debbie's pregnancy meant that she had to be filmed behind counters, or wearing a large fur coat, or else holding a baby in front of her as a means of concealing the fact that the future Carrie Fisher was growing inside her.

Eddie Fisher was horrified by his fear that the strain on Debbie would induce a miscarriage. His fear was amplified when she had to appear in an athletic scene with male dancers tossing her over their shoulders. He tried to stop the filming of the scene,

calling out, "Are you crazy? You're going to lose our baby!" Then at one point, he accused her of deliberately trying to sacrifice the life of their unborn infant. "The Iron Butterfly," as she was to an increasing degree being called, continued the scene, which required great dexterity.

***

In the early days of the shoot, Fisher was delighted to have been cast as the star of a major motion picture. "My dream was coming true. I wanted to follow in the footsteps of my idol, Frank Sinatra, in being a crooner who could also be an actor in major films."

She reminded him that he had a voice, but that he lacked Sinatra's acting talent and experience. "Faced with the reality of that, Eddie slapped me for the first time. He could not face the truth."

The newly married couple continued to argue and fight throughout the rest of the shoot.

Norman Taurog, their director, had been born in the last year of the 19th century and had emerged as a battle-hardened screen veteran, who broke into films in 1920. At the age of 32, he'd won a Best Director's Oscar for *Skippy* (1931).

He'd also helmed many of the great stars of Golden Age Holly-

Eddie Fisher holds a baby boy in his arms as he confronts Debbie in a pivotal scene from *Bundle of Joy*.

During their co-starring performances, tension, competition, and resentment broke out both on and off the screen. In other words, it was art reflecting life.

151

wood, including Mickey Rooney and Judy Garland, and in time, he would direct six Martin and Lewis films as well as nine movies starring Elvis Presley.

Unfortunately, despite Fisher's crippling insecurities, they couldn't count on the director to help him through his scenes. "We didn't know it at the time he directed us, but Norman was in the early stages of Alzheimer's disease," Debbie said. "Not that much was known about that illness at the time. That explained his constant memory losses and why he repeated the same instructions over and over again. Sometimes, after a scene was wrapped, he'd forget about it and order us to shoot it again, thinking it was for the first time."

Taurog and Krasna had written the original screenplay for *Bachelor Mother* in 1939. He was called in as a script doctor for recycling *Bundle of Joy*.

Debbie was left with nothing but unpleasant memories of her filming of *Bundle of Joy* because of her constant bickering with Fisher. "I tried to help the jerk with his scenes. He was completely inexperienced and flubbed one scene after another. He was just too arrogant to listen to advice from anyone, especially me."

In the film, she plays an unmarried sales clerk, Polly Parish, working in the hat department of a large department store, owned by J.B . Merlin (Adolphe Menjou). He is the father of Dan Merlin (Fisher). Polly is fired because she "oversells hats" to women who don't really want them and soon return them to the store.

Despondent, she walks in despair back to her apartment. On the steps of an orphanage, she discovers an abandoned baby in a blanket. The staff there is alerted and, of course, assume that the unmarried Polly is the boy's mother and that she's ashamed to have had a child out of wedlock.

Ginger Rogers had played the role more convincingly in the film's original version, but Debbie tried, working hard and like a true professional, unlike Fisher.

Expect the usual complications in this screwball comedy. As the store's owner, J.B. Merlin, Menjou concludes that his son, Dan, is the father of the boy, and that his long-cherished wish to have a grandson has at last been granted. Taking charge of the situation, he encounters the usual obstacles. In the meantime, Dan falls in love with the reluctant Polly. Eventually, he wins her heart, concluding with a proposal of marriage.

Other key roles were played by Tommy Noonan, Nita Talbot, Una Merkel, Melville Cooper, and Mary Treen, each of them familiar screen faces to audiences of the 1950s.

Debbie had watched Menjou on the screen in any number of movies. He'd been making them since 1914, back in the silent era, and had even starred with Rudolph Valentino in his most memorable film, *The Sheik* (1921). He'd worked with such greats as Charlie Chaplin, Gary Cooper, Greta Garbo, and Marlene Dietrich, and interpreted Fisher as "the most untalented little shit ever appearing on the screen." However, he found Debbie hard-working and very professional.

While shooting the film, Debbie lunched with John Wayne and Edmund Grainger, the producer of *Bundle of Joy*. He and the Duke had maintained, over the years, a long and lucrative association.

When Grainger was called away for about thirty minutes, Wayne shocked her with a confession, whose contents were in vivid contrast to his macho screen image.

"If you're turned on by me, like hordes of other women, you'll have to be the aggressor, since women scare the hell out of me. I tried once to be a philanderer like my friend, Gary Cooper, but it made me feel cheap and dirty."

"You're safe with me," Debbie assured him.

It seemed that everybody, both the critics and the movie-going public, were disappointed with *Bundle of Joy*. Unfavorable comparisons to the original were inevitable.

Fisher and Debbie attended its world premiere at the Capitol Theatre in New York on December 19, 1956. It had by this time evolved into a fund-raiser for refugees of the disastrous Hungarian Revolution which, after about a month of violent protest against oppression by the Soviet regime, had ended in a humiliating defeat in October of 1956.

Midway through the film, Fisher rose from his seat to go stretch his legs in the theater's lobby. According to Fisher, "To the embarrassment of some of my friends, they encountered me when they, too, were sneaking out of the theater. Each one made up a quick excuse *[for their early departure]* and told me how great I'd been on the screen."

"I was obviously terrible, and everybody knew it. I was also forced to attend the premiere in Los Angeles. Making the fucker was painful enough. Sitting through it a second time was pure torture."

***

During the filming of *Singin' in the Rain,* the director, Stanley Donen, threw a party, inviting Debbie, who came unescorted. At the gathering, Donen introduced her to Van Cliburn, the greatest pianist in the world at the time.

The unlikely pair immediately bonded, chatting pleasantly with each other. He was only twenty years old, but had been playing the piano since he was three. He told Debbie that his mother, a pianist herself, had insisted he start at that early age.

"My parents didn't want me to go into the movies," she told him. "They thought all movie stars were wicked."

"Are they?" he asked.

"No, just me." He laughed at that remark and hugged her.

After the party, he drove her home and escored her to her doorstep. "Don't invite me inside to make love to you," he warned her. "If you were Tab Hunter, my tongue would be handing out. But since you're a woman, no way."

He hugged and kissed her good night.

She later said, "I found him adorable, and I appreciated his candor about his sexual preference."

When Debbie and Eddie Fisher were making *Bundle of Joy,* Van Cliburn, who was in Hollywood at the time, came onto the set where she introduced him to her husband. Cliburn was otherwise spending hours every day rehearsing for his upcoming concert debut at Manhattan's Carnegie Hall.

Eddie admired his music. After he learned that he was staying at a hotel, he invited him to come and live with Debbie and himself. The pianist eagerly accepted.

Fisher later recalled, "At first, I was worried that this charismatic musician might put the make on Debbie when I was out of the house. But right after he moved in, I learned he was gay. If anyone had to protect his virginity, it was yours truly."

"Once in our house, he'd sit at my piano playing sonatas, complete symphonies, some of the most beautiful music ever written, for six hours a day. I couldn't believe it: In our living room, Debbie and I had the greatest pianist in the world entertaining us."

"He wasn't always at the piano," Fisher said. "He liked to swim in our pool, and I joined him. In our changing room, I stripped down in front of him and paraded around a bit to give him a chance to see what was dangling. He was a real gentleman. He looked, took in my junk, but didn't grope."

Two nights later, he told me that his great dream was to play for Elizabeth Taylor. I was surprised. Here was this artist who had played for kings and heads-of state, but he wanted Elizabeth to hear his music."

"I told him I'd invite hi-mover, but he claimed my piano wasn't suitable. He'd only play on this grand piano he pre-

In Eddie and Debbie's living room, Van Cliburn performed a special concert for their guest of honor, Elizabeth Taylor, who arrived in a lavender gown with pink accessories. As Louella Parsons might have written, "She never looked lovelier."

The music of his private concert drifted through the open windows and was loud enough for the neighbors to hear it.

Fisher later wrote, "When I opened the front door, I was greeted with the entire population of Beverly Hills on my lawn. I invited Van Cliburn out to take a bow, and the crowd roared their approval."

Depicted above is Van Cliburn in 1958 being congratulated by Soviet strongman Nikita Khrushchev after winning the Tchaikovsky Piano Competition in Moscow at the height of the Cold War

ferred. I told him I could arrange that. Damn it. I had to remove a set of three windows to get that piano into our living room. But some workmen pulled it off, and Van Cliburn had his piano."

"The following night, Elizabeth arrived at our house alone for dinner," Fisher said. "After our lovely meal, all of us went into the living room to listen to him play. Debbie raised all the windows to let in the night air."

"Listening to the world's greatest piano music and looking at the world's most beautiful woman was one of the greatest gifts I ever received."

[From that night forward, Debbie and Van Cliburn rarely saw each other, but spoke on the phone, keeping each other up to date on their romances, their heartbreaks, and their careers. "I could always share my disappointments with him. As for him, he had nothing but professional success and failed romances."

She was thrilled at his success in 1958 when, at the age of 23, he won the inaugural quadrenial International Tchaikovsky Piano Competition in Moscow. All of this took place against the backdrop of the Cold War.

Over the years, she watched as he entertained presidents from Harry S Truman to Barack Obama, as well as presidents or crowned heads of other countries, too. Time magazine likened him to "Horowitz, Liberace, and Elvis Presley, all rolled into one."

Like Debbie, Cliburn, too, became involved in a scandal. In 1998, his domestic partner of seven years, mortician Thomas Zaremba, filed a palimony suit against him, wanting part of his estate after they separated.

Both a lower court and the appellate court in Texas tossed the case, asserting that the state did not allow palimony suits to go forward unless there had been a written agrement laying out, in advance of the "divorce," the financial terms of an ultimate separation of the partners.

A few weeks before he died in 2013, Cliburn phoned Debbie to tell her he was suffering from bone cancer.

"I cried when I put down the phone," she said. "He was such a special genius. Americans will always remember him as the Texan who conquered Russia. I will forever miss him. I should have married him instead of Eddie. At least he would not have left me for Elizabeth Taylor, if only because he was not her type."]

***

My marriage to Debbie Reynolds was not a happy experience," Fisher told his close friends Jerry Lewis and Joey Forman. "The trouble began when we cut the wedding cake. After that, the marriage went south."

"On my honeymoon in Georgia, I came to realize I'd not married a woman, but a show business act. She was always on camera, even if there was no camera. She never turned off her motor and became a person. Always acting, always the comedian, always putting on a show."

"Image meant everything to her. Her career was her entire life. That little Texan coyote was determined to get ahead at any cost. Our life was lived to be

155

played out for the media, which gushed about our fabulous marriage."

"The character she projected to the world was a complete phony. She was anything but sweetness and light, longing for a loving husband and a house full of kids."

"An hour or so after we'd vowed to be true to each other for eternity, our marriage began to crumble," he said. "On my third night of wedded bliss, I met this cute little number, who worked for Coca Cola, and we got it on. Throughout my entire marriage, I turned to other women for sexual gratification, which I was not getting from Miss Debbie. Okay, I admit it, I was not a perfect husband and even a rotten father. But no man is perfect."

"Once," Fisher said, "driving to the studio, we got into an argument about Jesus. Debbie insisted he was a Jew. He was not Jewish, probably not even circumcised. The argument got so violent, I kicked her out of my car. She had to walk to RKO to shoot scenes that day. We spoke to each other only on camera. Jesus was not a Jew. Everybody knows that except Debbie."

"No matter what I said, she would start an argument. We never agreed on anything. Our arguments often became vicious, as both of us tried to hurt the other. Deep into her pregnancy, she told me I was not the father, saying that the true dad was Robert Wagner. Yet in the press, we were the ideal couple."

"We were two different people, not compatible. My friends didn't like her, and I didn't like her friends. My manager, Milton Blackstone, continued to call her 'the little schemer who's using you just for publicity.'"

"What have you learned from this marriage?" Blackstone asked him.

"I learned that no man on the face of the earth should marry little Miss Debbie Reynolds if he wants to keep his balls intact. She'll snip them off."

"From the outside, our life seemed glamorous and star-studded," Fisher said. "We entertained William Holden and Judy Garland. Jerry Lewis was often at our house, and we at his. He fucked around as much as I did."

"Debbie would be thrilled when Bette Davis came to dinner," he said. "She was nothing but a washed-out, ugly old drunk who would sit there and make drool eyes at me whenever Debbie left the room. Joan Crawford had a pretend relationship with Debbie, although this fading star of yesterday secretly resented Debbie for her youth and beauty. I had once fucked Crawford, and away from Debbie, she sent signals that she was ready for some repeat action."

"We were friends with Rory Calhoun and his wife, Lita Baron. He was fucking, among others, Marilyn Monroe, with whom he'd made two movies. He was also screwing Rock Hudson. He suggested to me that I needed for the sake of variety some man-on-man sex. I liked him a lot, but didn't want to go that far. I admit that on a few nights, I was tempted, when I'd had too many of Max Jacobson's injections and lost control of my impulses from time to time."

"When not fighting about sex, Debbie and I had epic battles about money," Fisher said. "I tried to get her to file a joint income tax return with me, but she adamantly refused, even though my accountants figured I could save $300,000 in taxes."

"I know I shouldn't have, but I called her a stupid bitch that night. She gave me the slap of my life. I hated her so much that for days, I could not stand to look at her. If she came into a room, I got up and left, locking myself in my study."

To make matters worse for an increasingly depressed Fisher, Coca Cola canceled his television show in February of 1956. "I was no longer the Coca Cola Kid. I began singing in night clubs more frequently, especially in Las Vegas, where I set for myself the goal of seducing every showgirl in Nevada. Of course, Frankie, or Dean Martin, had beat me to most of them. I heard one of the favorite games of these hot-to-trot cuties was comparing my sexual technique to that of Frankie or Deano."

"Through it all, I was growing up," he said, "becoming more sophisticated. But like living in a time capsule, Debbie was still promoting her image as the Girl Next Door. I wondered how long she could go on pulling off that bullshit. During our marriage, I heard rumors she was not actually fucking some guys, but rewarding a few of them with one of her blow-jobs."

Through the ups and downs of her marriage to Fisher, Debbie put up a brave front. Such was the case when the two of them appeared on Edward R. Murrow's *Person to Person* TV show.

"On the air, she indicated she was impatient to finish the show so she could rush back to the bedroom with me," Fisher said. "It was very flattering, picturing me as a stud. But we were hypocrites, selling a false image to the media. If we were America's Sweethearts, then America was in one god damn hellhole. Of course, like all images, we would soon be toppled from our Valentine throne. Robert Wagner, Debbie's longtime crush, and Natalie Wood would replace us, also toppling the romantic image of Tony Curtis and Janet Leigh. Like me, Tony was fucking around a lot behind Janet's back. In his case, with both sexes."

In spite of their deteriorating marriage, Debbie and Fisher purchased a home for their soon-to-be enlarged family. It was an elegant English Tudor-style house with three bedrooms in Beverly Hills.

Debbie was not fooling every member of the press. Some columnists were becoming more realistic about her, especially Earl Wilson, the New York-based gossip monger.

"To put it bluntly," he privately said, "Debbie Reynolds has more balls than any five guys I've ever known. She pretends to be sweet and demure, but at heart she's Hard-Hearted Hannah."

On October 26, 1956, Carrie Frances Fisher was born. Debbie experienced "incredible pain" in bringing her into the world. More pain was to come as her troubled daughter grew up.

Defying all memory records for a one-day-old, Carrie later wrote about the day of her birth.

"All the doctors in the delivery room were bussing around my mother's pretty head, saying, 'Oh, look at Debbie Reynolds asleep—how pretty.' All the nurses ran over to my father, saying, 'Oh, look, there's Eddie Fisher. Look at him' So when I arrived, I was virtually unattended."

***

Recovering from child birth, Debbie was eager to return to work.

Since there was no immediate role for her at MGM, Universal had come up with a script for her. It was entitled *Tammy and the Bachelor,* and it had a title song, "Tammy," to which she would be forever associated, even into her eighties.

For the camera, Debbie and Eddie Fisher, all smiles, tried to hold onto their image as "America's Sweethearts." They weren't that and actually never had been.

According to Eddie "At a party at the Dorchester Hotel in London, I met Laurence Olivier and his wife, Vivien Leigh. I'd always thought of them as this gorgeous couple, really in love with each other. I had to laugh at that. That night, they weren't even talking to each other. They could barely look at each other."

"I'd believed the stories I'd read about their loving relationship just as completely as other people believed stories about my wonderful marriage to my beloved Debbie. Beloved, hell! My marriage to this vixen was a god damn sham!"

Chapter Six

SWITCHING PARTNERS

MICHAEL TODD'S DEATH IN A FIERY PLANE CRASH PLUNGES
"DEBBIE'S QUARTET" INTO A ROMANTIC ROUNDELAY AND A
TABLOID FRENZY

TAMMY'S IN LOVE

DEBBIE'S HIT RECORDING BECOMES THE ANTHEM WHOSE SYRUPY
RESIDUE WILL HAUNT HER FOR THE REST OF HER LIFE

The paparazzi snapped hysterically as the "Todds & the Fishers" arrived at Epsom Downs. Tragedy and scandal lay in their immediate futures, but this was a happy occasion. One picture caption identified Elizabeth as "Mrs. Hilton Wilding Todd."

[By the end of her life, she'd be known as "Mrs. Hilton Wilding Todd Fisher Burton Burton Warner Fortensky."]

"On my outings with Mike, Elizabeth, and Eddie, I was the odd man out (or woman, in this case)," Debbie said. "I was extra baggage. Privately, I called Eddie, Mike, and Elizabeth 'The Unholy Trio,' or else 'The Love Triangle.' Mike was in love with Liz; she was in love with Mike; and Eddie was in love with both of them. A cozy romance. God only knows what the three of them did on those weekends when they left me at home and went off together."

Debbie and Eddie Fisher had been spending a weekend in their little vacation home in Palm Springs during the final days of her pregnancy. They retreated there whenever they could get away for a short holiday, which was rare. Fisher had spent most of the day playing golf with Dean Martin and some of his card-playing cronies. She expected she'd have to confront yet another night of high-stakes poker.

She had been alone throughout most of the day. By mid-afternoon, she began to feel dizzy and feared that that signaled the beginning of labor pains. Fortunately, in a lucky coincidence, her physician, Dr. Levy, was also in Palm Springs that weekend, something she learned when she heard him that morning being interviewed on a local talk-radio program. As she got worse, she contacted him to report her dizziness and what she thought were the early stages of labor pains.

During her phone dialogue with her doctor, she asked him to retrieve Fisher from one of the local golf courses and bring him back at once.

When he got there, Fisher seemed distracted and alarmed and ran about frantically. For some reason, the doctor determined that she should deliver the baby not in Palm Springs, but at his hospital in Los Angeles. Fisher immediately agreed to drive Debbie back to Los Angeles, with the doctor in the car, even though Debbie feared that she'd have to give birth in a moving vehicle. Fortunately, they arrived in time.

Before she was rolled into the delivery room, Fisher uttered the final (prebirth) words she remembered: "I hope it's a boy. I'll call him Eddie Fisher, Jr."

He was disappointed an hour later when Dr. Levy emerged into the waiting room and told him, "It's a girl, a healthy baby girl."

"Oh, shit!" Fisher responded.

By the time he was allowed to see Debbie, who was recovering in a hospital bed, Dr. Levy must have told her what her husband had said. Her first words to him were, "I'm so sorry to disappoint you. Why is it that a man always wants to have boys—and not girls?"

"Forget it," he answered. "The important thing is that you survived."

"I almost didn't," she said. "I've never felt more pain in all my life. Why didn't God design the male body to bear children—not the weaker sex?"

"Don't give me that!" he said. "Women are the stronger sex. They even live longer than men. You're tough, so don't pretend."

Back at their home, Debbie, still in a weak condition, began to feel that the birth of Carrie Frances Fisher on October 26, 1956 might heal the wounds of their dysfunctional marriage.

"For a change, Eddie was in a good mood around the house," she claimed. "He had reason to be. Not only was he the father of a beautiful baby girl, but his recording of 'Cindy, Oh Cindy,' had become a big hit."

RKO released ads that once again promoted its recent film, *Bundle of Joy,* which had opened to financial failure. Now, with all the publicity about the birth of Carrie, the picture was re-released and audiences flocked to see it.

Fisher didn't share Debbie's enthusiasm about the status of their marriage, later writing, "Even the joy of having Carrie didn't bring us closer together."

His good spirits didn't last for long. He became morose, sitting for hours at a time beside their pool. Once, when she was passing through the living room, she heard him sobbing out by the pool all by himself.

"I was glad when Milton Blackstone came up with more work for me," he said. "It gave me the chance to get out of the house. Regardless of who was visiting, even Jerry Lewis, Debbie always had to put on a show by pulling out one of her tits and insisting on breast-feeding Carrie. I found that disgusting. She was like some mammal, a cow, feeding its young."

During the weeks following Carrie's birth, he was gone most of the time, either working or playing golf with his cronies. "Right from the beginning, I became an absentee father. Years later, when I met Elvis Presley, we chatted pleasantly, even though the fucker knocked me off the charts. He told me when he got married, after serving in the Army, that he could no longer have sex with his wife once she'd given birth."

"That finishes a woman off for me," Elvis said. "Stretches their pussy out of shape and makes their tits fall."

"I couldn't agree with you more," Fisher said. "By the way, I didn't think that rock 'n roll was here to stay."

Even though he was critical of Debbie, Fisher complimented her on being a good mother to Carrie, although she often had to leave her with the maid or with Minnie.

"That mother-in-law of mine huddled over our house like a locust. I couldn't stand the bitch, but she did take care of Carrie during those early years because Debbie was always making a picture. Minnie became, in fact, a surrogate mother."

Debbie's memory of those early years differed remarkably from his. She wanted her public to hear a different version. "I breast-fed her and Eddie would sit with me, looking at mother and daughter like a proud papa. He loves the baby, and he loves me. I felt we had attained what was needed for a happy marriage—a family."

"But he got really pissed off at me when I told him the allowance he was giving me of $2,500 a week simply would not be enough. I needed at least another $500 a week for the care and feeding of Carrie."

"Can't you produce enough milk to feed her?" he asked in anger before storming out the door.

"He flew that weekend to San Francisco without luggage and when he came back, he didn't tell her where he'd been or what he'd done.

As he admitted later, "I was ripe for a love affair. And it was about to happen with a beautiful Las Vegas showgirl."

Debbie had been friends with producer Ross Hunter and his lover, Jacques Mapes, a set designer she'd met during the filming of *Singin' in the Rain.* The two men often had dinner at her home in Burbank.

When Hunter decided to make *Tammy and the Bachelor,* which Universal had scheduled for a 1957 release, Mapes recommended Debbie for the title role. After discussing it with her at her home, Debbie agreed to return to films after having given birth. She'd play a seventeen-year-old "swamp girl" who lives with her grandpa on a rickety houseboat on the Mississippi River overlooking the coastline of Louisiana.

She had long admired Hunter, applauding him for preserving some of the romance and glamour of Golden Age Hollywood in his films such as *Magnificent Obsession* (1954) with Jane Wyman and Rock Hudson.

"Ross could do romantic comedies, melodramas, and musicals. I'd heard rumors that he put Rock Hudson through his paces on the casting couch before making him a star opposite Ronnie Reagan's ex-wife, Jane. but every producer in Hollywood has a shadowy side. I hope he didn't make Jacques jealous."

Hunter had told her, "I give the public what it wants: A chance to dream, to live vicariously, to see beautiful women, jewels, gorgeous clothes, and to experience melodrama. The way life looks in my pictures is how I want life to be.I don't want to hold a mirror up to life as it really is."

"A man after my own heart," Debbie answered. "That's the kind of movies I want to make myself, preferably opposite some dreamboat like Rock Hudson."

Tambrye ("Tammy") had been created by Cid Ricketts Sumner in his 1948 novel, *Tammy Out of Time.* Many years would pass before it reached the screen.

A lawyer turned screenwriter, Oscar Brodney was hired by Hunter to adapt the novel into the script for a feature film. He'd had recent success in 1953, writing the screenplay for *The Glenn Miller Story,* starring James Stewart and June Allyson. For his effort, Brodney was nominated for an Academy Award.

The son of a Jewish watchmaker, Joseph Pevney was the producer of *Tammy.* An ex-actor turned director, he had recently made *Female on the Beach* (1955) with Joan Crawford and Jeff Chandler.

Pevney presented her with *Tammy and the Bachelor's* final script, which Hunter had given to him. She'd never bothered to read the novel.

Tammy is being "raised" by her grandpa, a moonshiner named John Dinwitty. Her best friend is a goat named Nan. Although she dreams of life beyond the swamp, she's well-adjusted to her present realities.

One day, a small plane crashes into the river nearby. To the rescue rush grandpa and Tammy. They discover a handsome young pilot within the airplane's ruined cockpit. He does not seem to have suffered any bodily injury, but he remains unconscious for a full day.

Tammy undresses him (but not on camera) and puts him to bed, where she nurses him back to health with tender, loving care. This is the dream man of her fantasies.

When he regains consciousness, she gives him some of Nan's goat milk to restore his health. His name is Peter Brent, and he lives with his family in a mansion some distance away. Its name is Brentwood Hall.

Before he departs, he tells Tammy that if anything should happen to her grandpa, she is welcome to come and live with his family. Weeks later, Dinwitty is arrested by the sheriff for distilling and trafficking in bootleg liquor. Left alone, Tammy and Nan, the goat, set out toward Brentwood Hall...and Peter.

When she finally arrives at his estate with her goat, a dance rehearsal is being hosted by Peter for his young friends, including his girlfriend, Barbara Bissle, who is beautiful, sophisticated, and glamorous.

Peter misunderstands the situation, jumping to the conclusion that her grandpa is dead. He invites her in to meet his family, Professor Brent and his tense and somewhat neurotic wife. Tammy also meets Peter's eccentric Aunt Renie, who lives in the house, along with the lovable African American cook, Osia.

Expect the usual romantic or comedic complications: A glamorous girlfriend who's jealous of Tammy; a predatory pursuit of her by his best friend; her virtual adoption by Peter's eccentric aunt; her winning over of Peter's par-

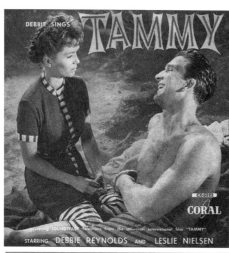

In most movie posters of the 1950s, it was the female star who posed for cheesecake. But not in these photos advertising *Tammy*.

Debbie's co-star, Leslie Nielsen, strips for the beefcake shots.

ents; crop failure; and, at the end, Peter's realization that he's in love with Tammy just as she's in love with him.

Jay Livingstone and Ray Evans wrote the title song, "Tammy," which, as the titles rolled, was sung by the Ames Brothers. It's the lament of a naïve and sentimental teenaged girl, and Debbie sings it later in the movie. That it became a major hit, and that it would spark a string of sequels was beyond her wildest dreams.

She was enthralled when she met her leading man, Leslie Nielson. A native of Saskatchewan, he was six years older than her, and very handsome. He'd served in the Royal Canadian Air Force during World War II. Before that, he'd been a disc jockey with dreams of becoming an actor.

In time, he would play 220 different characters, both in the movies and on TV. When she met him, he'd made his film debut in a 1956 sci-fi thriller that has since become a cult classic, *Forbidden Planet,* one of the seminal and most enduring examples of its genre.

Tammy would be the last movie wherein he'd play a bona-fide romantic lead. Despite his hopes of becoming known as a serious dramatic actor, his *forte* became deadpan comedy roles in films that included *Airplane!* (1980) and *The Naked Gun* (1988).

According to Debbie, "When he and I made *Tammy,* he hated his role, calling it silly. He also felt that my character of Tammy was ridiculous. His dream was to replace either Marlon Brando or James Dean on the screen. He was all hung up on Method acting, the type of performer that Actors Studio was churning out. He challenged Hunter on every line, wanting to know its true purpose and his character's motivation for saying it. What a fucking bore!"

"Not only that, but he had an annoying habit of going around carrying a portable, hand-held fart machine. He liked to come up behind a woman, press the button, and make it seem like she'd blasted off like a rocket. He did that to me several times until I gave him a good slap. He was such a joker, pulling that stunt on everybody. I finally told him that when he dies, he should state in his will that he wanted the words, 'LET 'ER RIP!' engraved on his tombstone."

"I proved what a brilliant Method actor I was when the director told me that I was to look into Debbie's eyes as if I was falling in love with her."

"I felt no love for her in this silly little movie and with that silly little show-off."

164

[Amazingly, and as unlikely as it seems, Nielsen had those exact words carved into his gravestone in November of 2010 when he was interred at the Evergreen Cemetery in Fort Lauderdale.]

Crusty old Walter Brennan, whose distinctive voice she learned to imitate, was cast as Grandpa Dinwitty. She thought he must have been born in Arizona or New Mexico, and was surprised when she learned that he was from Massachusetts. He'd won a Best Supporting Actor Oscar in 1936, 1938, and 1940, making him only one of three actors to win a trio of Academy Awards. He'd gotten his start in films alongside another newcomer, the then-recently renamed John Wayne (aka Marion Robert Morrison).

Usually cast as a grumpy old man, Brennan had co-starred with Humphrey Bogart, Henry Fonda, and Gary Cooper, plus with an array of other bigtime stars.

Another member of the cast, Mala Powers—playing Peter's poised, stylish, and somewhat cynical girlfriend—was a beautiful native of San Francisco. She became deeply jealous of Debbie both on and off the screen. "I didn't like her bubbling personality. I had been in show business since I was seven. If felt I had the looks and talent for super-stardom, especially after I'd played Roxane in *Cyrano de Bergerac* (1950), the film that brought Jose Ferrer an Oscar."

"After that," Powers continued, "I was part of a USO tour through Korea, where I contracted a rare blood disease that nearly killed me. I came back to face a dwindling film career and later turned mainly to teleplays. I was one of those young hopefuls of the 1950s who came to Hollywood seeking stardom, like Debbie. But the North Star never shone down on me like it did on her. Not only that, but the show-off even snatched up that very cute, very adorable Eddie Fisher. Some girls have all the luck."

The portly Louise Beavers—a great favorite of Debbie, who seemed to have been utterly devoid of racial prejudice—played the cook, Osia. Beavers had actually been born in Ohio and had to learn to speak with the dialect of a stereotypical Southern Negro.

"Many people in my own race attack me for playing subservient roles to white folks," Beavers said.

Tammy is in love with that handsome hunk Leslie Nielsen, but her pet goat, Nan, comes between them.

165

"To hell with them. I play the damn parts, I don't live them. In private, I'm a lady and go anywhere in my mink coat, even if the weather is too hot."

Her main competitor was Hattie McDaniel. Beavers told Debbie, "Every day I wake up, I curse MGM for casting Hattie as Mammy in *Gone With the Wind*. It was a part I desperately wanted."

Sidney Blackmer and Fay Wray were cast as Peter's parents, Professor and Mrs. Brent. A native of North Carolina, born in 1895, Blackmer almost made a career out of playing President Theodore Roosevelt. Debbie had seen him on a Broadway stage in William Inge's *Come Back, Little Sheba* (1950). To Blackmer's regret, when that play was adapted into a film, his role was re-assigned to Burt Lancaster.

For years, Fay Wray had been a big star, but was now reduced to minor roles. "She'd achieved screen immortality by getting carried away in the arms of that mighty gorilla in *King Kong* (1933), the best of those beauty-and-the-beast thrillers," Debbie said.

Debbie was disappointed by *Tammy and the Bachelor's* initial failure at the box office. At the time, it was beyond her wildest dreams that her recording of the song, "Tammy," would generate a second chance for the movie at the box office.

"With 'Tammy,' I achieved my own screen immortality," Debbie said.

***

Walter Brennan played Tammy's moonshining grandpa in *Tammy and the Bachelor*. "I respected his talents, but he was a right-winger from hell."

He told her, "Niggers were content with their status in life until a lot of commie agitators stirred them up with all this civil rights hogwash."

Debbie bonded with Mildred Natwick, cast as Aunt Renie, who supported her both on and off the screen.

"She was one of the great character actresses in Hollywood—warm, witty, and with that quavering voice which later assured her roles in all those spinster and biddy parts."

It went unreported at the time, but during the making of *Tammy and the Bachelor*, Debbie developed a crush on the handsome young actor, Craig Hill. In the movie, portraying Peter's best friend, he pursued Tammy romantically (some said, predatorily).

As a means of garnering publicity for his star, Henry Willson and the MGM publicity department arranged "studio dates" for Hill with a series of up-and-coming starlets or with established actresses who included Debbie. Thus, he functioned as the then-unmarried Debbie's escort at gala parties or premieres.

On one occasion, he accompanied her to a screening of the 1952 remake of *What Price Glory*, a war film, set in World War I that starred James Cagney. *[An earlier version with slightly different premises, and more closely based on a 1924 play by Maxwell Anderson, had been released in 1926.]*

"I went out with Henry [Willson's] boys because I needed an escort to attend certain galas when Eddie was away for weeks at a time,," Debbie said. "Of course, I knew that they were homosexuals. They weren't fresh, and they were fun...sweet guys. They never came on to me, like all the straights I dated. Hugh O'Brian comes to mind. When I was seventeen, and still a virgin, I couldn't stand getting mauled when they took me home. Hands all over me, grabbing anything they could. All the gay boys I dated, including Tab Hunter and Rock Hudson, were nice to me. Some of us even became good friends."

In Robert Hufler's biography, *The Man Who Invented Rock Hudson*, Hufler described a date between Hill and Debbie where Willson functioned as the chauffeur. In his black Cadillac, he drove them from one publicity event to another. She started to worry about what the agent had imbibed that evening.

"It was raining and it was obvious to me that Henry was on something," she claimed. "He was more than intoxicated. He was stinking drunk and at the wheel. I feared for my life with this reckless driver. I demanded that he stop and let me out of the car. He obeyed and slammed on the brakes somewhere on Mulholland Drive. I got out even in the driving rain."

About a quarter mile away, she

Craig Hill had a small role in *Tammy*.

At the time, he was one of the stallions in the stable of the gay talent agent, Henry Willson, who was known for "manufacturing" and renaming such newbie wannabes as Rory Calhoun, Guy Madison, and (most famously) Rock Hudson.

spotted a little roadside café and called her father, Roy, in Burbank and asked him to come to rescue her.

Hill and Debbie went out on a few more dates, but never again with Willson as the driver.

At a reunion with Hill, during the filming of *Tammy & the Bachelor* and over lunch, she noted a change in him. He had become uncharacteristically and rather aggressively flirtatious. "Had he quit 'batting for the other team,'" she wondered, "and trying to assert himself as a straight man?"

Ross Hunter filled her in on Hill. He was still one of "Henry Willson's boys" and having a sometimes affair with Rock Hudson. He was also living with the handsome young actor, John Carlyle, who later wrote a memoir, *Under the Rainbow: An Intimate Memoir of Judy Garland, Rock Hudson, and My Life in Old Hollywood* (2006).

Debbie learned that before taking up with Carlyle, Hill had had an affair with Marlene Dietrich (of all people) during one of her gigs in Las Vegas.

According to Debbie, "I realized then that he must be bisexual. I was a married woman, at least in name only. Eddie was a married man, too, although he didn't act like one. Craig had only a small part in *Tammy*, but we became great friends. Even though he was not needed, he showed up on the set and often visited me in my dressing room. We lunched together in the commissary. We were seen together so much that some people thought Craig, not Nielson, was my new leading man."

Hill later admitted, "Debbie and I realized that our relationship was no more than a brief fling. I went home to John (Carlyle) at night."

Ross Hunter, their director, was aware of Hill's interest in Debbie. He, too, was attracted to Hill, "but I let Debbie have him. My calendar was heavily booked. I knew that Eddie wasn't much of a husband, and Debbie deserved a little fun. I don't think their involvement ever got serious. Let me put it this way: She gave Craig 'lip service.'"

***

For many months, Debbie and Fisher had dined, danced, gone swimming, vacationed in Palm Springs, attended premieres or Hollywood parties, whatever, with producer Mike Todd and his mistress, Evelyn Keyes. Debbie had first seen her on the screen as Suellen, one of the O'Hara sisters in *Gone With the Wind* (1939). Often, Todd spent evenings talking about the movie he was producing, *Around the World in Eighty Days* (1956).

Before taking Keyes as his mistress, he'd entered, in 1927, into an ill-fated marriage to Bertha Freshman, who had died in 1946. After that, he married (1947-1950) actress Joan Blondell, whom he'd "poached" from Dick Powell.

A cocksure, flamboyant showman, he had a long list of celebrity seductions, including ending up in Mae West's bed when he'd produced, in 1944, her controversial play, *Catherine Was Great* .

Some of his other high-profile seductions included Marlene Dietrich and stripper Gypsy Rose Lee, as well as author Anita Loos, heiress Lorraine Manville, dancer Muriel Page, and lots of actresses, most notably Marilyn Monroe and Jean Simmons.

Todd was Eddie Fisher's role model. If the producer ordered steak for dinner, so did Fisher. He had an enormous influence on Fisher's career and personal life. On some nights, Todd would stop playing poker and say to Fisher, "C'mon, lets go out and find ourselves some broads." Fisher dutifully followed along.

He even imitated his mentor by falling in love with Elizabeth Taylor.

Debbie was an eyewitness to the beginning of the Todd/Taylor romance. It all began in July of 1956 when Todd and Keyes invited her, along with Fisher, to a Sunday barbecue at their home in the Hollywood Hills. The swim party included some three dozen guests in swimwear. Among them was the gay gossip columnist Mike Connolly, who spread the whispered rumor that Fisher was in love with Todd and that Debbie was a closeted lesbian "with the hots for her former gym teacher."

Elizabeth showed up with her second husband, the British actor Michael Wilding. She had already revealed to Debbie that her marriage to him was on the rocks and that the two of them shared different bedrooms.

As Debbie noted, Wilding did not join the swimmers, but wandered to the bar in the living room, obviously despondent, in part because of his failing marriage.

Elizabeth and Todd, however, seemed to be having a good time. Attired in a very revealing white bathing suit, she lay on a pink air mattress adjoining his, a gaudy chartreuse. They were only inches apart as they chatted and laughed.

Positioned some distance away, on side-by-side *chaises longues*, Debbie and Fisher eyed the couple. He whispered to Debbie, "I don't like her legs. I could never go for a dame like that."

As she later said, "When your husband says that about a woman, his wife had better watch out."

After the barbecue, Todd walked

In this picture, Evelyn Keyes was no longer playing the virginal Suellen, Scarlett O'Hara's younger sister. She'd grown a bit slutty.

She once told a reporter, "Mike Todd dumped me for Elizabeth Taylor. But who do you think is the love of Elizabeth's life? Mike Todd or Richard Burton?"

"Neither of the above, she continued. "The love of her life is Elizabeth Taylor."

Fisher and Debbie out to their car. "He was beaming," Fisher said. "I'd never seen him so lit up, and I'd known him when he was attracted to a *Titanic* filled with women."

"As I sat behind the wheel with Debbie at my side," Fisher continued, "I looked out the car window and said to Todd, "Don't kid me, you fucking Jew bastard. You've fallen in love with Elizabeth Taylor."

"Who hasn't?" Debbie chimed in.

"Guilty as charged, judge," Todd said. "Sentence me to a life of total ecstasy."

Fisher admitted in a memoir that right from the beginning, he, too, had been attracted to Elizabeth.

"She's such a god damn spoiled brat," he said *en route* home after the barbecue. As time went by, he told Debbie, "I find it hard at times to like Elizabeth. She can be a real pain in the ass."

"The man protests too much," Debbie said. "Maybe you would like a piece of that ass."

"Shut your fucking trap, Tammy, or I'll belt you one," he threatened.

Two days after the swim party, Elizabeth got a call from Todd, asking her to visit him at his office in the Thalberg Building at MGM.

Later that afternoon, she called Debbie to tell her what had happened: "I was sitting in his outer office with my feet up on a table, drinking a Coke, and he rushed in and picked me up by my arm. Without a word, he practically dragged me out of the office and down a corridor. He shoved me into an elevator, still not speaking, just marching along breaking my arm. He took me into this deserted office. He sort of plunked me down on a couch and pulled a chair up to me. He started in on this spiel that lasted about a half hour without a break."

"He told me he loved me and that there was no question about that. 'We're going to be married,' he said. I looked at him the same way I imagine a rabbit looks at a mongoose. All kinds of things went through my mind. I thought he was stark, raving mad. I had to get away from this lunatic."

"Then he joined me on the sofa and took me in his arms. His tongue kissed me for at least five minutes. When he broke away for air, he told me very forcefully, 'From now on, I'm the only man you're gonna fuck!'"

The maternal Elizabeth Taylor is pictured with an infant and its father, the British actor Michael Wilding.

"We had a lovely, easy life, simple and quiet. Two babies were born; otherwise it was more of an older brother-sister type of relationship," she said.

***

Just three weeks after that Sunday barbecue, Evelyn Keyes phoned Debbie. "Our hanging out together is over," the actress said. "Mike's left me for Miss Taylor."

"When a man wants to leave, he leaves," Keyes said. "You really can't stop him and don't even try. One day, if Eddie ever leaves you, it won't be for Elizabeth, of course, but for someone he finds more alluring."

It was ironic that Keyes said that. When Fisher ultimately left Debbie, it would be for Elizabeth Taylor.

Only an hour after talking to Keyes, Elizabeth phoned Debbie to tell her that she and Wilding had filed for legal separation, with her seeking custody of their two sons. Until they sold their home, they would continue to live under the same roof, "but separately," Elizabeth assured her.

"Instead of Eddie and I hanging out with Mike and Evelyn, there was a change in our social life," Debbie said. "Our dining and dancing partners were now Mike and Elizabeth. As a trio, they were a heavy partying gang. I never was."

During the early days of the Todd/Taylor romance, Debbie became friends with Dick Hanley, Elizabeth's gay secretary. Never known for his discretion, he kept her abreast of all the gossip.

[Despite Todd's marriage to Elizabeth, he phoned Keyes late one night and suggested that he wanted her to continue as his mistress on the nights he was away from his wife. According to Keyes, "He was furious when I moved to Paris and married Artie Shaw." Their marriage occurred in 1957. The bandleader had previously been married to both Lana Turner and Ava Gardner.

In 1959, after Todd's death, Keyes encountered her rival, Elizabeth, at a Hollywood party. "Maybe it was a good thing that he dumped me," Keyes told the star. "An advantage was that I'd no longer have to smell the stench of his cigar. I would no longer be kept awake all night while he and his raucous buddies played gin rummy. Unlike you, I might not have gotten the flu and would have been aboard that fatal flight with him. In that case, I would no longer be inhabiting the earth. So in essence by running off with my boyfriend, you may inadvertently have saved my life."]

Elizabeth Taylor fell into early maternity with husband Michael Wilding, but with Mike Todd, husband No. 3, she was Princess Elizabeth.

It seemed inevitable that a womanizing Eddie Fisher would make the cover of *Confidential*, the leading scandal magazine of the 1950s. In September of 1956, that *exposé* rag published a cover story entitled EDDIE FISHER & THE THREE CHIPPIES. Beside the headline, they ran a picture of his smiling face grimaced into a wink.

Debbie was horrified to read the revelations, although the charges made in the article took place during the spring of 1952 when the singer was still in uniform and long before he married her.

The venue for the exposé, as written by Philip Barker, was the Book Cadillac Hotel in Detroit, where Fisher was touring for the U.S. Army during a recruitment drive. His companions were three baseball players from the Detroit Tigers, plus a series of "luscious lassies" (a euphemism which translated at the time as "prostitutes").

The article alleged that Fisher, seated with his companions in the living room of his suite within that hotel, tapped a blonde on the shoulder and invited her into the bedroom. She emerged an hour later with a smile on her face. Fisher then ambled over to a redhead and repeated his action. According to Barker's account, "Private First Class Eddie brought the redhead back into the living room, and she looked dazed and happy. He deposited her on the sofa and strode nonchalantly over to a brunette, telling her, 'You're next!'"

An hour later, as the brunette emerged from Fisher's bedroom, she sighed, telling the athletes, "Boy, I'd support this guy forever if he'd let me. Fisher is the greatest ever!"

One baseball player was very impressed, telling everyone in the room, "This kid could obviously give transfusions to tigers."

Barker concluded by writing something catty that Debbie's personal experience had already disproven: "All three of the little Detroit doxies are willing to bet their bankrolls on one thing: Debbie Reynolds *must* have had a wonderful honeymoon."

Fisher denied the story, but faced a dilemma: "What was I going to do, sue *Confidential* and be forced to prove that I wasn't a great lover?"

In October of 1961, Debbie herself was featured on the cover of *Confidential*, the subject of an embarrassing *exposé*.

***

Since Todd and Elizabeth Taylor were together almost every night, there remained the issue of her divorce from Michael Wilding.

On November 14, 1956, Elizabeth's lawyers filed papers in a California court asking for a divorce. The charge was extreme mental cruelty. Wilding would have to pay no alimony and would get fifty percent of the proceeds from the sale of their home, which was worth around $200,000 on the market at that time.

"For Elizabeth, getting involved with Mike Todd also meant getting into Eddie Fisher's crotch," Dick Hanley recalled. "The two men were glued at the hip. Unknown to the public then, or even now, was that Fisher had been sexually involved with Elizabeth even before she married Mike Todd."

"Wilding had first-hand evidence of this affair, and I kept Debbie informed," Hanley said. "She pumped me dry for any detail I knew. Actually, I viewed the Todd/Taylor/Fisher liaison as a *ménage à trois*. Who, on any given day, was fucking whom? So who was plugging Debbie? I was never certain, but I knew that on occasion, she was slipping around and seeing Sinatra, but never in public. Perhaps they were just holding hands and listening to his records. I once heard Debbie throw up to Fisher that Sinatra was ten times the singer he was. That sure pissed him off."

At two o'clock one morning, Todd and his gin rummy cronies were planning to continue playing until dawn, as stakes were the highest ever for this beer-swigging, cigar-smoking lot.

Elizabeth grew bored, and Todd ordered Fisher to drop out of the game and take her home, where Wilding was still occupying the guest room.

"They talked until around four o'clock in the morning," Wilding later told Stewart Granger and Jean Simmons. "I heard them. Finally, I went to sleep. At around eleven o'clock the following morning, a call came in from Benny Thau at MGM. He said it was urgent that he speak to Elizabeth. When I knocked on the door of the master bedroom, Eddie answered it. His face was covered with shaving cream, but nothing else covered him."

Embarrassed, Wilding called to Elizabeth, "It's Thau on the phone. Some emergency at MGM."

"Okay," shouted Elizabeth. "Tell the fucker I'm coming. First, I've got to take a piss. And shut the god damn door."

When Fisher brought Elizabeth back to Todd's Beverly Hills mansion for a late luncheon the next day, Todd said, "I hope you two lovebirds had a good time."

"EDDIE FISHER AND THE 3 CHIPPIES" in *Confidential* marked the first exposure of the singer's "sexcapades."

Throughout the latter years of the 50s, tabloids would devote rivers of ink, forests of trees, and miles of column inches to revelations and speculations about Debbie, Elizabeth, and Eddie.

The singer later said that after lunch, Todd practically dragged Elizabeth off to his upstairs bedroom. "If you want to get fucked, let a real man do it," he told her in front of Fisher.

Before Elizabeth's marriage to Todd, there were other intimate sightings of Elizabeth with Fisher. A waiter at the Beverly Hills Hotel later said he delivered a room service dinner to them late one night in a suite that Fisher had booked.

"Fisher was in the nude in the living room listening to his own records, and I could see Taylor in the bed since the door was open," the waiter claimed.

Of course, as an MGM star, Debbie had known Elizabeth far longer than Fisher and Todd. "We were only surface friends, and we had no deeper a relationship than Peter Pan had with Cleopatra. She was not a woman's woman, but always gravitated to men such as Roddy McDowall or Peter Lawford. Often these men were gay."

After a few dates as a quartet, Fisher began to criticize Debbie for lacking glamour. "Why can't you dress up like Elizabeth? She always looks fabulous… and very sexy. You come off like the leader of a Girl Scout pack."

The first time Debbie and Fisher invited Elizabeth and Todd to their home for dinner, the evening ended in violence. That Saturday night, the couple shocked Debbie, but not Fisher.

"Mike knocked her to the floor, I mean he really clobbered her," Debbie said. "She screamed but rose to her feet and walloped him right back, He dragged her by the hair as she screamed at him and kicked him, He succeeded in dragging her across the room. I went running after him, jumping on his back to help her. The two of them were slapping each other. My heart was pounding. The next thing I knew, they were wrestling on the floor, kissing and making up. I'm left standing there like the cop on the beat in a wife-beating case where the cop gets it. They both got mad at me for interfering."

Elizabeth said, "Debbie, you're such a little Girl Scout. Grow up!"

"In spite of the rough stuff, I envied Elizabeth and Todd," Debbie said. "They always seemed to be having a good time. What did I have with Eddie? He told me I wasn't funny, was awful between the sheets, and couldn't make chopped liver. You're just a cute little girl with a turned-up nose. Nothing less, nothing more."

In December of 1956, Elizabeth filed papers to divorce Wilding, but in California, it would take a year before their final decree was granted.

Before Christmas, Todd rented a yacht in Nassau Harbor and took her on a cruise. She tripped and took a bad fall, seriously injuring her back.

Debbie said, "Ever since I've known Elizabeth, she was always having back problems. But this time, it was different. She was flown to New York in a private plane."

After a series of tests, Dr. John Lattimer, one of New York's leading orthopedic surgeons, told Todd that his wife-to-be would require a delicate operation. Several of her spinal disks had been crushed. Her left leg was numb and had started to atrophy. There was grave danger of paralysis and, possibly, amputation.

During a four-hour operation on December 8, 1956, the doctor had to remove dead bone right down to the spinal cord's nerve center. He then surgically removed bone from her hip and pelvis, out of which he fashioned "little matchsticks" that he assembled into a cluster that later calcified into a unified whole. After two months of recovery, this mass of bone fragments had fused into a six-inch "hybrid" component within her spinal column, allowing her to walk again.

The pain was so great that at times she would pass out. She required care around the clock.

Fisher took Debbie on a flight from Los Angeles to New York, where they visited Elizabeth in the hospital. She immediately shared her fears with them and updated them on her grave condition.

When Todd came into the room, he delivered a bombshell. "I just learned this afternoon that my twenty-four year old bride-to-be is going to have our baby. An out-of-wedlock baby. The press vultures will really tear into that. Her doctors have warned her that she's not up to giving birth."

"I was told that having the baby might leave me permanently crippled," Elizabeth said, "and that I might have to spend the rest of my life in a wheelchair. But god damn it, I'm going to have Mike's kid."

Debbie tried to talk her out of it, but she refused to listen. "I'm tougher than I look," Elizabeth said.

"Whatever his faults, no one could say that Mike Todd was dull," Debbie said. "When he came into a room, he dominated it. He was like some prizefighter with a potty mouth that put Elizabeth's tongue to shame. He smoked stinking cigars, and he spent money even when he didn't have it."

"I've never been poor," he told Debbie. "Only broke."

"Eddie was his adoring acolyte," she said. "I often had fights with him, claiming he loved Todd more than he did me."

She agreed with Evelyn Keyes that Todd was like a character created by Damon Runyon.

"He doesn't have the world's biggest dick," Keyes told Debbie, "but he convinces any woman he does. He has millions one week, then loses the pot of gold the following week."

At first, Todd's bluntness took me by surprise," Debbie claimed. "The first time Eddie and I dined with Elizabeth and him, he was chewing his steak. He put down his knife and fork and looked over at Elizabeth."

"I plan to fuck you real good after I finish this damn steak," he said to her.

She giggled. "Right here in the restaurant? Can't you keep it zipped up until we get home?"

Early in 1957, Fisher signed a contract to appear at the Tropicana, the newest and glitziest hotel in Las Vegas. His act would be backed up by "the most beautiful young showgirls in the gambling mecca."

"They were gorgeous, absolutely gorgeous, and I knew I could have my pick," he told Mike Todd, who had advised him not to work Vegas because of its connections to organized crime. "The ugliest girl in the bunch had been named Miss Australia," Fisher said.

Since the terms of his contract had granted him approval of looks, comportment, and wardrobe of everyone in his act, he minutely inspected each of their costumes. "There wasn't much to inspect," he jokingly said. "I think their scanty costumes consisted of inserting a pearl into their navels. At one point, they were choreographed to dance around me. I had a difficult time suppressing my hard-on."

Even though he asked her not to, Debbie flew into Vegas with Carrie, then six months old, on her lap.

Most of the showgirls in the chorus line-up were beauties from either Britain or Australia, many of them long-legged "refugees" from the Lido in Paris. All of them were quite tall, and they were adorned with fanciful headdresses that made them seem even taller. Wearing those headdresses caused for balancing skill to keep them from toppling over.

In an agreement with the show's choreographer, Debbie inserted herself into the show's lineup, planning a surprise entry without telling Fisher. She slipped backstage and put on a costume with a gold lamé top.

The towering headdresses made each of the girls look eight feet tall, Debbie at five feet, put on one of the headdresses and, in a surprise appearance on stage, "sabotaged" (his words) Fisher's singing of "Cindy, Oh Cindy."

As he sang his current hit, at first he didn't now why the audience was laughing until, to his horror, he realized what all the hysteria was about. "Debbie looked like a midget, and with her mugging freak show, she ruined my act with her gag. I admit that the audience loved it. I could have killed her. She just couldn't resist being the center of attention, even if it were my act. She threw off my performance. I never got back on track, and even forgot some of the lyrics to some of my hit records. Thanks, Debbie!"

"My most 'blessed event' was when she and Carrie flew back to Los Angeles. I was damn glad to get them out of town. The reason? I had fallen in love."

After her unexpected appearance in his act at the Tropicana, Fisher later wrote: "There was no single event that marked the end of our marriage. I didn't stomp out angrily one day and never came back. There just came a time when I could barely stand to be alone with her. We were wrong for each other. I knew I had to get away from her."

After Debbie and Carrie flew out of Las Vegas, Fisher later admitted that he fell in love with Pat Sheehan, an eighteen-year-old girl who worked at the Tropicana in Las Vegas. The affair with "the most beautiful girl I'd ever seen" lasted for the good part of a year.

He first spotted Sheehan when she was standing in the wings watching him sing his hit song, "Oh! My Papa." The following night and the night thereafter, he spotted her again standing in the wings giving him a come-hither smile—"and I knew what that meant. She was hot for me. I felt the same way about her."

On the third night, he came offstage and shook her hand, looking deeply into her blue eyes. "Of course, I had no way of knowing at the time that she had joined Bing Crosby's long list of lovers. Except for Pat, my fellow crooner dated from the A-list. To name a few, Joan Bennett, Ingrid Bergman, Joan Blondell, Joan Caulfield, Frances Farmer, Miriam Hopkins, Betty Hutton, Grace Kelly, Dorothy Lamour, Mary Martin, and—after she dumped Ronald Reagan—Jane Wyman. Inger Stevens told me she became ill from the stress that man caused her."

"When I found out she was also Bing's girl, I was not surprised. The gals at Tropicana had a code word. Instead of calling themselves 'kept women,' they preferred to claim that their sponsors provided them with 'scholarships.' One of the British girls was shacked up with Jackie Gleason. She said her fantasy was to phone him one night when she was fellating me. I turned down the offer."

"As my affair with Pat grew more intense, she told me I was a better lover than Bing," Fisher said. "That was music to my ears. She also told me he couldn't stand my guts. Could he be jealous? He was a cruel bastard, as I learned from his son, Gary. He was drunk the night we flew from Casablanca—remember that old movie with Bogie?—to Paris. He told me his dad beat hell out of his sons."

Before he married Debbie, Eddie Fisher was a *schmaltzy* boy balladeer whose cleancut romantic style "roared in like a rocket," playing almost constantly on jukeboxes of the 1950s.

However, the advent of *rock 'n roll* and Elvis Presley, as well as the Debbie *vs.* Elizabeth scandal, sent his career crashing back to earth.

"My father is a god damn cocksucker," Gary told Fisher. "I want to slit his throat. Slit the jugular vein and suck out his blood like a vampire. That's how much I hate him"

Eventually, Debbie through some means learned of his affair with the teenaged showgirl, yet never confronted him with his infidelity. Over lunch one day with Dick Powell, her former co-star, she spoke about it. "I'm glad someone takes care of Eddie's sexual drive, so I don't have to bother."

Sheehan lived in a trailer on the outskirts of Vegas. Fisher usually drove her home from work when both of them were through at the Tropicana, and he often spent two hours or so with her. One morning he left her trailer at 4AM. At the time, he was driving his shiny new, easy-to-spot black Cadillac, a gift from his manager, Milton Blackstone.

Suddenly, he was rammed by another car driven by a woman, who was seriously injured and had to be rushed to the hospital. He claimed that his Cadillac was totaled. "The only safe spot had been the driver's seat, and I emerged from the wreckage with only a bruise or two. Fortunately, Pat was not in the passenger seat or she would have been killed. That would have ended my career. Imagine the headlines."

During his eight-week engagement, he spent nearly every night with Sheehan in her trailer. One night at the Tropicana, Dean Martin came onstage to perform a duet with him. "You seem to have a steady piece stashed somewhere," he said to Fisher after the show. "I have three such pieces myself, and those gals keep me drained."

"At the end of my gig, I could not bear to break it off with Pat," Fisher said. "So I rented her an apartment in Hollywood and moved her there. My affair with her continued through most of the final months of my marriage to Debbie—that is, until I met Elizabeth Taylor. Pat wanted to marry me, but I told her that Debbie would not give me a divorce. She threatened to leave me if I didn't marry her—and eventually she did."

"You won't believe this, but after that, Pat resumed her affair with Bing. That was to be expected. The surprise came when she married his son, Dennis. Talk about a family affair."

"I cheated on Debbie before I met Pat, but after our breakup, I cheated like gangbusters, often two or three gals a day. I even screwed one of her best friends. Up to then, I thought she was a dyke and was carrying on a lesbian affair with my wife. I still think that. But after just one night with her, I was convinced that she was not exclusively a lesbian, but a bisexual."

"When I was out of town, which was most of the time, and my pal Sinatra was in Hollywood, he always phoned Debbie, or so I was told," Fisher claimed. "I heard that from Dean and other sources. Ol' Blue Eyes wanted to continue whatever they had going when they made *The Tender Trap*. I don't know if she accepted his invitations or not. I suspect she did."

"'After all,' she once said. 'What gal can turn down Frank Sinatra?' Debbie was always very discreet, as she had that image to maintain. She never admitted to any affairs, but she had them. Unlike her, I was honest about the girls I loved. Unless they had husbands, the public would be shocked to learn how many Hollywood wives were hot to trot."

***

Mike Todd was horrified at the bad publicity that might be generated once the press learned that Elizabeth was carrying his out-of-wedlock baby. Through his lawyers, he urged her to get a quickie divorce out of state, thereby avoiding the one-year residential requirement that divorce at the time required in California.

At first, Michael Wilding balked at the plan, but relented after Todd offered him a cash settlement of $200,000. Not only that, but he was given all of the proceedings from the sale of the Benedict Canyon house that he co-owned with Elizabeth, instead of the 50% that he had been promised. "Money talks," Todd told Elizabeth.

Meanwhile, after leaving her hospital bed, Elizabeth flew with Todd to Mexico City, even though she was still in great pain because of her back injury. Before leaving New York, she phoned Debbie at her home and asked her if she'd fly south for the wedding to be her maid of honor. "I'm flattered," Debbie told her." She learned that Todd had already selected Fisher as his best man, and that the festivities would take place in Acapulco.

In Mexico, Todd and Elizabeth, as they later related to Fisher and Debbie, ran into complications in their attempts to acquire both a divorce for Elizabeth from Michael Wilding, and a marriage license for Elizabeth and Todd. "We were viewed as an immoral couple, and judges running for re-election didn't want anything to do with us," Elizabeth said. "But Mike came to the rescue with lots of lots of pesos."

The divorce finally granted, Todd faced the often hostile press, announcing that he would marry Elizabeth on February 2, 1957.

In anticipation of the wedding, accommodations were arranged within a private villa in Aca-

Eddie Fisher's lover in Las Vegas, showgirl Pat Sheehan, was once billed as NBC's answer to Marilyn Monroe.

She took drama lessons from Debbie's best friend, Agnes Moorehead.

According to Eddie, "In exchange for the lessons, I think Pat had to put out for Agnes."

Pat Sheehan was the lover of Bing Crosby, but later married his son Dennis (see above). She and Debbie once vied for millionaire Bob Neal.

After her divorce from Dennis, she had affairs with Rod Taylor, Frank Sinatra, Cantinflas, and Jack Cassidy.

pulco, with the understanding that it contained separate bedrooms for the increasingly alienated best man and matron of honor. When Debbie and Fisher flew in for the ceremony, they left Carrie back in California in the care of her nanny.

Todd ordered one hundred bushels of orchids, along with 15,000 yellow gladioli. He also stocked fifty cases of champagne, and, for the wedding feast, imported baby lobsters, cracked crab, and tureens of Iranian caviar shipped over from pre-Castro Cuba.

Debbie met with the jazz band flown in from New York, and the men agreed to rehearse "Tammy" with her. She also met with the English-speaking bandleader of the local mariachi band Todd had hired. "I became a labor negotiator," Debbie said. "All of them wanted more money, but settled for one-fourth of what Todd was paying the New York guys."

She also met with the trio of head chefs Todd had hired to supervise a staff preparing the shellfish along with an array of Mexican specialties. For the first time, she tasted roast chicken in chocolate sauce. She even received a shipment of sports shirts Todd had had custom-made for the guests. Women were to wear a shirt with the initials ETT emblazoned on it, the men with the initials MT.

One afternoon, Debbie supervised the installation of kerosene torches to light the night. "I hope they don't set the damn place on fire. Mike is getting just too fucking carried away." The more she hung out with Todd and Elizabeth, the more potty-mouthed Debbie became, a trait that would follow her for the rest of her life.

On the day of the wedding, Todd had the kitchen staff cut hundreds of coconuts in half. At the last minute, in lieu of using standard champagne stems, waiters filled the coconut shells with bubbly, and handed them out to guests as drinks.

Todd introduced Debbie to Cantinflas, the most famous comedian in Mexico. Little did she know that by 1960, she would be appearing in a movie with him. At his own expense, as recognition for his friend and mentor, Mike Todd, in whose recent film he had played such a prominent role, he had arranged the largest display of fireworks in the history of Mexico.

With all the arrangements in place, Fisher and Debbie joined Elizabeth, who had been carried from her bed to a *chaise longue* beside the pool. She was wearing the skimpiest of bikinis. Debbie noted that her husband was eyeing all that ample display of flesh, especially her breasts. "They were so much bigger than mine," Debbie said.

Elizabeth told them that Todd could find no rabbi who would marry them, and he had gone to Mario Lepotogui, the mayor of Acapulco, who was willing to officiate at a civil ceremony.

On her wedding day, Elizabeth retreated to her bedroom with Debbie, who helped her wash and set her hair. Before dressing, Debbie helped her strap on a back brace because she was still in pain.

Debbie's favorite designer, Helen Rose, had created a stunning baby blue chiffon wedding dress for Elizabeth. Then she showed Debbie her wedding gift from Todd, an $80,000 diamond bracelet. Debbie learned that in addition to that, Todd had given her two movie theaters in Chicago, plus 40% of all the revenues earned worldwide by *Around the World in Eight Days.*

"He's got this wonderful private plane he's renamed *Lucky Liz,*" she told Debbie. "He says I will bring him good luck."

The wedding was set for eight o'clock, and the guests waited impatiently for an hour before Elizabeth agreed to be carried down the aisle by two beefy security guards. "I trailed along," Debbie said, "feeling more like a bridesmaid than a matron of honor."

Dick Hanley stood near Debbie during the ceremony, and both of them noted that Elizabeth was intoxicated. Debbie whispered to him, "The Todd baby will probably be born an alcoholic."

At the reception, Debbie sang "Tammy," and Fisher delivered his rendition of "The Mexican Wedding Song."

Later, Debbie sat beside Elizabeth at the table, fulfilling her requests from the buffet. "She got going with the Mexican specialties, including hot tamales, tortillas, tacos, guacamole, and green-boned fish. That was followed by roast pig on a spit, which made her all greasy-mouthed. Instead of a slice of the wedding cake, she went for large helpings of the lemon-and-peach chiffon pie."

Later, Elizabeth developed stomach cramps, blaming it on "the tainted cracked crabs."

At the reception, Todd was too busy to spend any time with Debbie, although he did come over to give Elizabeth a kiss. He turned to Debbie and said, "I see the world as a place to plunder, and Liz as the woman to bag the loot I bring home."

The next morning, Debbie and Fisher were invited to join the newlyweds at eleven o'clock for a gathering around their

At the wedding ceremony of a pregnant Elizabeth Taylor to Mike Todd, he announced, "I'm staging the wedding of the century."

During his preparations for the wedding, Todd must have imagined he was producing a movie on the scale of *Around the World in Eighty Days.*

Since Elizabeth was still confined to bed, he asked Debbie to supervise the final preparations, including the music, the cuisine, and the decorations.

"For the first time in my life," she said, "I felt like a movie producer myself, lavishly handing out wheelbarrows of pesos."

swimming pool. Debbie was surprised to come upon the honeymooners lying entirely nude in the glaring sunlight.

Drinking champagne, Todd invited Debbie and Fisher to remove their clothes and join them. Whereas Fisher stripped down, Debbie retreated inside the house. "I was just too modest for this kind of Hollywood decadence," she later said. Through a picture window, she eyed them at the pool as they chatted and laughed.

She was again surprised when Todd had to urinate. "He walked over to the water and pissed in his pool," Debbie said. "A bit casual for my taste. After that, I made a point of not going swimming in his pool in Beverly Hills ever again."

When Elizabeth came back, fully undressed, into the living room, having had her spirits lifted by Fisher and Todd, she called her Mexican maid to bring her her robe. She invited Debbie to join her on the sofa, as Todd and Fisher had gone upstairs.

"Being married to Mike is all sweet craziness," she said to Debbie. "He translates the most impossible life I've lived on the screen into reality. He has a big heart and an incredible gift of showmanship. Every time I let out a big fart, he uses the occasion to honor me with another diamond. I know that he seems rough and tough, even gruff, on the surface, but it's just an act. He's a gentle man until he beats the shit out of me, which I call 'foreplay.' Every woman should have a Mike Todd in her life."

Two security guards came into the room to carry Elizabeth upstairs for some much-needed bed rest. She promised to join the party for a late lunch "after my siesta."

Then Hanley came into the room to discuss the evening's dinner plans with Debbie. Todd was hosting a party at a chic restaurant in Acapulco, to which she and Fisher were invited. Increasingly, Elizabeth's secretary was becoming Debbie's *confidant*.

"Mike and Elizabeth are like a candle burning at both ends," Hanley told her. "That candle is destined to flicker out. Such intensity, such fire, cannot go on forever."

***

During the last days of spring, 1957, Fisher got another booking at the Palladium in London and made plans to fly there with his usual entourage. Members, by now, included the ever-faithful "Dr. Needles" (Max Jacobson).

For romance, Fisher had been maintaining an ambitious fixation: Princess Margaret Rose of Kensington Palace. During a previous trip to London, he had circled her as she flirted back at him. Their relationship had never developed beyond that point.

One night at a gala in Mayfair, she had approached him with a request to dance with her. "I turned her down because I was just too nervous. I stammered like a schoolboy. But she sent a signal that she was definitely interested in me, and on this trip I planned to go after her. Talk about dating from the A-list! To me, Margaret was second only to going after the queen herself."

As it turned out, no romance ever developed between Fisher and Margaret, although one paper headlined a story THE PRINCESS AND THE SINGER.

Once again, Debbie heard of his upcoming trip to London, and invited herself to go along with him, although he made it clear that he didn't want her. Since Debbie knew she'd be alone throughout most of the trip, she asked her former gym teacher, Jeanette Johnson, to accompany her.

During the previous weeks, Debbie had been despondent over the box office failure of *Tammy & the Bachelor.* Her recording of the song "Tammy" had not been released when the movie opened.

But when the syrupy, sentimental song was released, it became an instant hit. "Every radio station in America seemed to be playing it," she said. Universal had pulled the picture from general release, but then re-issued it when "Tammy" became a success. After an unsuccessful launch, Debbie's film went on to make millions for Universal.

On the *Billboard* charts, she was competing against Jerry Lee Lewis, Paul Anka, Buddy Holly, and—lest we forget—Elvis Presley. Congratulations poured in from many quarters, "except one, my own husband, Eddie, the holder of 27 gold records. He was really jealous of me. He hardly spoke to me."

For years, he'd been RCA's most visible and most successful recording star—that is, until Elvis came along. Fisher predicted that rock 'n roll was a mere passing fad and that it would soon disappear. How wrong he was.

"Eddie's career peaked in the early 1950s," Debbie claimed. "I think all that 'Eddie & Debbie' romantic dribble kept him in the public eye. He owed it all to me. By the time I took up with him, his heyday was behind him."

Fisher watched with jealousy and dismay as "Tammy" shot up to become the number one song in the country. For three entire months, it topped the *Billboard* charts. Wherever Debbie went, she was asked to sing "Tammy," such requests continuing until the final years of her life.

After London and a stopover in Paris, Fisher and Debbie were invited to vacation at Villa Florentina, a luxurious retreat nestled in gardens at the *über*-chic community of Cap Ferrat on the French Riviera. Todd was paying $20,000 a month to rent the villa.

"I adored my times with Mike and Elizabeth," Fisher said.

In the seventh month of her pregnancy, Elizabeth didn't seem to mind when Todd exposed her breasts, asking Fisher to admire their size. "All three of us were casual about flaunting our nudity, although little Miss Prim and Proper (Debbie) retreated inside the villa with that gym teacher friend of hers," Fisher said.

During their takeover of Villa Florentina, illustrious guests dropped by for a swim. They included Gary Cooper, David Niven, and William Holden. Todd asked Cooper to arrive by himself, "because I can't stand that god damn wife of yours." *[Todd was referring to Veronica ("Rocky") Balfe Cooper, a minor Hollywood actress and East Coast socialite with extensive experience in California and in Paris. Married in 1933, their marriage lasted, with many adulteries, until Cooper's death in 1961.)*

Debbie confided to Jeanette Johnson that she wished "she had become Mrs. William Holden instead of Mrs. Eddie Fisher."

The highlight of the trip was when Prince Rainier and Princess Grace invited all of them to a gala event at their palace in Monaco. Todd rented a stretch limo for the 30-minute east-bound transit from Cap Ferrat. On their way there, Fisher gossiped about a conversation from his show-biz past: "Bill Holden told me that Grace was an easy lay, having fucked everybody from Ray Milland to Bing Crosby, even Clark Gable. I met her at a party and asked her for a date the following night. She gave me a light kiss on the lips and told me she'd like nothing more, but that she was going to Europe in the morning. She ended up in Monaco, and the rest is history."

"One night when Mike and I were gambling in Monte Carlo," Fisher asserted, "I was surrounded by beautiful girls coming on to me. But I didn't take advantage, since Mike was on a winning streak, and he wanted me to be with him as his good luck charm."

"When we drove back to his villa, I was super horny and needed relief. That night, I committed an unthinkable act: I screwed my own wife, the result of which appeared nine months later."

Debbie's account of the seduction was different: "I wanted another baby for Carrie, so she wouldn't grow up as an only child. I loved having a brother like Billy, and I wished the same for Carrie."

"I was waiting for Eddie when he returned from Monte Carlo," she said. "Mike retreated upstairs to be with Elizabeth. Eddie was not a drinker, but I lured him into having two ice cold beers. The drinks made him intoxicated. I lured him to bed upstairs and came on to him real strong. It took some doing, but I

HRH Margaret Rose. *[Detail of a larger portrait by Cecil Beaton.]*

"Her Royal Highness really flirted with me, and made it pretty obvious that she wanted me to plug her," Fisher claimed. "But I felt in her august presence, I'd be too nervous to get a hard-on."

got him erect. He entered me suddenly and it all seemed over in about twelve seconds."

"When the dirty deed was done, Eddie collapsed into a drunken stupor. I scooted up to the headboard and propped my legs up against it all night. I wanted every molecule of that sperm to go deep into my body. I stayed that way until Jeanette and I flew to Madrid the next morning."

According to Fisher, "It was a chilly goodbye when I saw Debbie and her gym teacher friend off to Spain. I never liked her friend. I don't care for women with mustaches."

"If someone ever makes a movie of my life with Debbie, it won't be called *Bundle of Joy* like that turkey in which we co-starred. It should be entitled *The Razor's Edge.*"

"I heard that Debbie and Jeanette Johnson attended the bullfights in Madrid," he said. "I think Debbie liked watching bulls get stabbed in the ring. Locals, I heard, considered bull testicles a delicacy. I'm sure she devoured them on many an occasion. I could just see her munching down on some *cojones.*"

Shortly after her departure, Fisher flew in the opposite direction, landing in Tel Aviv, where he later claimed, "I was treated like King David, and was surrounded by beautiful girls. My mother would be proud of me. I settled down with a Jewish girl at least for the night, although I didn't think that was what mother meant whenever she lectured me on the subject."

Some of the women he bedded were soldiers with guns. One was a best friend of Moshe Dayan's daughter and another was the private secretary to David Ben-Gurion, the primary founder of Israel and its first Prime Minister. "Danny Kaye was said to have screwed her before I got to her—that is, when he wasn't pumping Laurence Olivier."

After her sojourn in Spain, Debbie and her friend flew back to Los Angeles before Fisher winged in from Israel. When he arrived at home, he discovered she'd moved his clothes into their guest bedroom.

Two days later, they were sitting in the office of his attorney, Mickey Rudin. "In a nutshell, Debbie demanded everything—the house, its furnishings, alimony, child support—you name it. The price of my freedom came high, but I was willing to pay it to get rid of her."

A week later, she fainted while shopping at Saks in Beverly Hills. She was rushed to her doctor, who examined her, pronouncing her pregnant.

After delivering her announcement to Fisher, he exploded in fury. "You're trying to ruin my career. You know I was planning to leave you, and now I can't. I can see headlines about me abandoning America's Sweetheart when she's pregnant. You trapped me that night on the Riviera, you scheming bitch."

"I wanted to get the hell out that very afternoon," Fisher said, "but for the sake of my career, I had to stay. I would come and go as I pleased, and never again would I darken her bedroom door. I'd spend my nights with other women, many of whom were practically begging me to go to bed with them.

Eddie Fisher was in big demand as a lover."

Her account differed from his own: "When I told Eddie that he was going to have a boy, he was overjoyed. He changed almost overnight and became not only a devoted husband but a great father to Carrie. I just couldn't believe it."

She had a reason for not believing his assurances. Later, he dismissed some compliments she'd expressed about him to Todd as "a Tammy fantasy."

To keep up appearances, he found a larger house for his dysfunctional and fast-expanding family, a four-bedroom structure on Conway Avenue in Holmby Hills. "I never intended to live there myself."

"I soon joined the club of pregnant Hollywood wives," Debbie said. She recalled one event where expectant mothers gathered, an occasion attended by those rival gossip mavens, Louella Parsons and Hedda Hopper.

Debbie spent much of her time there chatting with the former MGM starlet, Nancy Davis, now married to Ronald Reagan. She was expecting her second child, who turned out to be Ron Reagan, Jr.

"Nancy and I didn't talk much about Ronnie," Debbie said. "As a subject, he was just too dull. I knew she had chased after Sinatra and wanted him to marry her, but had settled for Ronnie instead. Sinatra had chased after me, so Nancy and I dished him."

On February 24, 1958, Todd Fisher was born, his father naming him after Mike Todd. When Debbie and her infant boy arrived at their new house in Holmby Hills, Mike Todd and Elizabeth Taylor were the first visitors. "Mike was delighted that our kid had been named after him," Debbie said.

On August 6, 1957, Elizabeth, at peril to her body, had given birth to Frances ("Liza") Todd.

"It was a happy time for all of us," Debbie said, foresaking the truth. "We were two loving couples with children. Eddie was elated to become the father of a boy. I felt that all of our

RAINIER AND GRACE

"I never got to screw Grace Kelly like a lot of my buddies, such as William Holden," Fisher said. "I heard from a lot of guys that she was a hot piece. Gary Cooper told me she appeared like a cold fish until you got her panties off—and then she was a firecracker. I kissed her and asked for a date. She was all for it, but had to give me a raincheck since her first visit to Monaco was scheduled for the next day."

problems for the four of us would soon be behind us, and we could lead happy, productive lives."

Three weeks later, fate intervened, changing their lives forever.

***

Mike Todd invited both Fisher and Debbie to a small birthday party for Elizabeth on February 28, 1958, a celebration of her 26th year. Only a select group of friends received invitations, including David Niven and his wife, Hjordis. Art Cohn was also invited, as he and the host had been working on Todd's biography, *The Nine Lives of Mike Todd*, a book published posthumously, with additional edits by and contributions from Cohn's widow.

Todd uncorked the first of many bottles of vintage champagne and insisted that a nondrinker like Debbie have at least one glass. "It made me tipsy," she said.

Debbie listened with a certain envy as Todd raved about the performance Elizabeth was giving in the current film adaptation of Tennessee Williams' *Cat on a Hot Tin Roof*, playing Maggie the Cat opposite Paul Newman. "A sure-fire bet," Todd told Debbie.

He also told her he had big plans for his wife, including starring her in an upcoming epic, *Don Quixote*, to be shot in Spain. John Huston had agreed to play Quixote chasing windmills across the plains of La Mancha, with his faithful sidekick, Sancho Panza, a role that Mickey Rooney wanted to play.

"I wish I had a powerful man like you backing me in my career," she confessed. Todd did not respond, perhaps viewing that as criticism of his best friend.

In his living room, Todd cornered Fisher and Debbie and invited both of them to fly with him to New York to attend a Friars Club Roast at the Waldorf Astoria, one that would honor him as "Showman of the Year."

Debbie was shooting a picture called *This Happy Feeling*, and could not get away. Fisher also had a conflict in his schedule, one that called for him to shoot a Chesterfield commercial in Greensboro, North Carolina.

Fisher, however, would be free to fly to New York aboard a separate plane and following a different route, joining Todd in time for the roast as a co-occupant of his hotel suite. "At the roast, I'll see that you're seated next to Sir Laurence Olivier," Todd said. "It'll be a class act."

Fisher had already asked Sammy Cahn to write *risqué* lyrics to the "Around the World in Eighty Days" theme as a musical joke he'd deliver during the roast.

Yet before Todd's scheduled departure for the event in Manhattan, Elizabeth—stressed from the prolonged shooting of *Cat on a Hot Tin Roof*—developed a severe case of bronchitis, with a temperature of 102° F.

She wanted to go, but Todd refused to let her. He invited her director,

Richard Brooks, instead, but he turned Todd down.

The AP reporter, James Bacon, had originally accepted an invitation to travel with Todd to the event, but an hour before the scheduled departure, he called Todd and bowed out. "I urged him not to fly," Bacon later revealed to Debbie. "It was the worst night I could remember in Los Angeles, with torrential rain, thunder, and 'second coming' lightning."

"Mike always did live on the edge," Debbie said. "Never afraid to take a chance." He'd once told her that *Lucky Liz*, a single-engine Lockheed Lodestar, could fly through any storm. In honor of Elizabeth, he'd painted the bedroom aboard his plane with a shade of violet that matched her eyes. "He was such a romantic," Debbie said.

As Debbie learned later, her friend and confidant, Dick Hanley, Elizabeth's secretary, was going too. At the airport, however, Todd rescinded his invitation, telling him, "Elizabeth's sick and needs you to take care of the kids."

Elizabeth later told Debbie what happened when she saw Todd before he left for the airport aboard his ill-fated flight. "He may have had a fear that something dreadful might happen. He came into my bedroom and kissed me goodbye five times before leaving. I pleaded with him not to go, but he assured me he'd be safe."

"The night was very Macbethian," she recalled. "I knew he didn't want to leave me."

From the airport, he called her for the last time. "I love you, Lizzie Schwarzkopf. You're beautiful, doll. Remember, save those sugartits for your loving man."

***

Embarking on the final flight of his life, Todd flew out of Burbank Airport at 10:11pm on March 21, 1958.

He had promised Elizabeth that he would telephone her from Albuquerque, New Mexico, where his pilot planned to stop for refueling. It was a call that never came in. He also promised to call from Kansas City, where he planned to pick up Jack Benny for the ongoing segment of the flight to New York. Throughout the course of that evening, aircraft throughout the region encountered heavy thunderstorms, lightning, and strong headwinds.

A report of what happened next was made available on April 17, 1959, nearly a year later, by the Civil Aeronautics Board (CAB). An urgent message was received from *Lucky Liz* by the night air traffic controller at Winslow, Arizona. The pilot, William S. Verner, requested clearance to climb to an altitude of 13,000 feet. *Liz* was flying at 11,000 feet, and its wings were icing. The controller granted the request.

The next time it was heard from, the *Liz* sent a radio message to the air controller at Zuni, New Mexico, reporting that it had climbed to 13,000 feet, that it had been caught in a violent storm, and that its wings were still icing. It was the last radio transmission from the doomed aircraft.

At Grants Airport control tower in Grants, New Mexico, an air controller reported seeing a brilliant illumination of the March sky. At first, he thought it was a spectacular flash of lighting. However, an Air Force pilot, flying a B-36 through the same night sky, sent an air-to-ground communication, notifying the control tower that a plane had exploded. As revealed in the delayed CAB report, the time of the explosion was 2:40am.

Spiraling out of control after the shutdown of its single engine, *Lucky Liz* had plunged to earth through a thick fog and burst into flames.

A CAB agent concluded, "The right master engine rod had failed in flight and the right propeller was feathered. Complete loss of control of the aircraft followed, and the plane then struck the ground in a steep angle of descent."

One contributing factor to the pilot's loss of control was that the plane was overloaded. It had a weight limit of 18,605 pounds, but was actually carrying 20,757 pounds at takeoff. The extra tonnage contributed to the failure of the flight. The situation was aggravated by surface ice on the wings and engine. The anti-icing system was inadequate.

Todd's plane went down in the Zuni Mountains of New Mexico some twelve miles southwest of Grants. The bodies were scattered over a two-hundred yard, snow-covered crash site.

At daybreak, a search party in New Mexico discovered the plane wreckage, which had turned into a funeral pyre for Todd, Cohn, and both pilots, Verner and co-pilot Thomas Barclay.

Although the bodies had been charred beyond recognition, Todd's corpse was initially identified because his skeleton was still "accessorized" with the gold wedding ring he'd worn since his marriage to Elizabeth.

Later, when his ring was returned to her, she had it melted down and re-shaped for her finger. "I wore it every day until someone else who loved me told me to take it off. I have had two great loves in my life. Mike Todd was the first."

***

The AP reporter, James Bacon, may have been the first person in Los Angeles alerted to Todd's death. An AP stringer in Grants, New Mexico, called Bacon to check up on him. "Your name was on the passenger list. I wanted to make sure you were still alive."

Shocked, Bacon explained that he had canceled at the last minute. After getting details, he immediately called the Los Angeles Bureau of the Associated Press. Within fifteen minutes, news of the crash was flashed around the world. Most news reports of Todd's death gave his age as forty-eight. Actually, he was fifty-three years old at the time.

Morning programs on the U.S.'s East Coast and in London were interrupted to broadcast the breaking news.

Even though millions of people around the world already knew about Todd's death, Elizabeth did not. At around 5AM, after a restless night, she'd fallen into a deep coma after taking sleeping pills.

MGM was notified and immediately, one of its executives, Benny Thau, phoned Dick Hanley, asking him to break the news to Elizabeth before the wire services started ringing her. He called Dr. Kennamer and asked him to drive to her home with him. When the men arrived, a maid told them that Elizabeth was still asleep upstairs.

Dr. Kennamer suggested that he and Hanley wake her up and tell her of Todd's death.

As Elizabeth later recalled to Debbie, "It was the most traumatic moment of my life."

She had just awakened when the men entered her room. She screamed, "No, he's not!" even before they spoke.

***

Debbie had risen early that morning and was sitting at her dressing table, removing the rollers from her hair. She'd heard from Fisher that night after he'd landed in Manhattan to sing at the roast for Todd.

At Debbie's door stood a distraught Frank, her Mexican houseman, who had once worked for Todd. "He's dead," he said in a quiet voice barely audible. "Mr. Todd is dead. His plane went down somewhere over New Mexico."

"It can't be!" she shouted at him, not believing what he'd said. "Not Mike! Not dead!"

Immediately, she switched on the small radio on her bedside table. The news was being broadcast at that very moment. Not only was Todd dead, but so was Cohn and the pilot and co-pilot. "My god!" she said to Frank. "Eddie and I might have been on that plane if we'd accepted Todd's invitation."

She immediately tried to get through to Fisher at the Waldorf-Astoria. Jim Mahoney, his press agent, had already broken the news to him. She spoke to him before Fisher came on the phone. "The poor guy's been crying his eyes out. I've never known him to suffer such grief. Mike was so close to him, more than any father could be."

When Fisher came on the line, she extended her sympathies. He told her he was taking the next plane out of New York headed for Los Angeles.

Debbie responded, "I'm going over to Elizabeth's to see what I can do. If I can't comfort her, I can at least take care of her children."

He shouted at her, "Don't you dare do that! Stay away! Don't go there!" Then he slammed down the phone.

She was bewildered as to why he would object to her trying to help, and decided to defy him and go anyway. It was only a twelve-minute drive down Sunset Boulevard to Schuyler Road in Beverly Hills.

Before she could enter the Todd residence, she had to fight her way through an army of photographers and reporters. Elizabeth's security guards recognized her, and escorted her through the gates.

In the foyer, Hanley rushed to embrace her, as did Sydney Guilaroff, Elizabeth's favorite hairdresser. Then Michael Wilding appeared to embrace her as well.

Everyone in the foyer suddenly heard a screech from the top of the stairs. There stood Elizabeth in a sheer white nightgown, screaming, "No! No! It's not true! It's not true! Oh, Mike!"

"I'll never forget the look of terror and anguish," Debbie recalled. "That face—ashen, her violet eyes desperately sad, her hair askew and wild—yet she was incredibly beautiful, even in tragedy. And that piercing scream of agony as she called out Mike's name…"

She began to descend the steps. On the way down, she screamed once again, "No, not Mike! Not Mike!" Then she bolted toward the door.

Both Kennamer and Hanley ran after her to bring her back in. They carried her up the steps, where Debbie was standing on the landing. "She looked at me, but I don't believe she knew who I was. She was too far gone and heavily medicated. I didn't say anything to her. I didn't know what to say."

When Debbie returned to the foyer, she heard Elizabeth's two sons, ages three and five, crying. She rushed to

Had he survived, Mike Todd would undoubtedly wished that he'd flown aboard a conventional commercial flight instead of aboard his doomed private aircraft which, on previous flights, had taken him, with Elizabeth, to Moscow.

DID YOU KNOW? That the golden couple agreed for their likenesses to be featured in an ad for TWA, back when that airline (and the happy couple too) were flourishing.

Reporters noted the ironies of the name (*The Lucky Liz*) associated with her late husband's doomed aircraft.

their room to comfort them. They didn't understand what was going on and seemed terrified.

"When I looked up, I saw Wilding enter the room," she said. "After all, he was the father. He hugged and kissed his sons. He smelled of liquor, and I sensed that neither he nor Elizabeth were in any condition to look after such young boys. I asked if I could take them home with me, and he agreed. Todd's daughter, Liza, was in the care of a nanny."

***

Immediately after he arrived at the airport in Los Angeles, Fisher took a taxi to see Elizabeth. He was one of the very few people allowed to visit her bedroom.

He told his press agent, "Debbie is always intruding on my act, and I want her to stay out of this. It's not her job to comfort Elizabeth—but mine. Elizabeth doesn't even like Debbie all that much. She is always butting in. She tries to be the star of every show. But I'm not going to let her."

Much later, Debbie was surprised when Elizabeth extended an invitation to both Fisher and her for dinner at her house. She wanted to thank Debbie for looking after her young sons.

Elizabeth ate almost nothing at dinner, but drank a lot of champagne. After about an hour, she asked both Debbie and Fisher to come up to her bedroom. In it, Hanley had piled boxes of mail and telegrams from all over the world.

"Read these two to me that Hanley fished out," Elizabeth requested.

Debbie read the first telegram. It was from the White House. "The President and I extend our deepest sympathy." It was from Mamie Eisenhower.

The second was from Clark Gable, who had lost his great love, Carole Lombard, in a plane crash in 1942. "I know what it's like to lose someone you love," he wrote. At that point, Fisher suggested that Debbie should return home at once to look after the children. He would take over the processing of Elizabeth's telegrams.

In the foyer, as Debbie was leaving, she encountered Hanley, who said, "Elizabeth told me she was contemplating suicide by overdosing on sleeping pills. But then Eddie arrived, and she said he gave her a reason to live."

He left out some additional information which Elizabeth had also told him: "Eddie claims he's always been in love with me," Elizabeth had confessed to Hanley.

Fisher returned back to his home early the next morning, at 4AM, slept for only five hours, showered, and then rushed over to visit Elizabeth again. His only words to Debbie were instructions to take care of Elizabeth's sons and his daughter, Carrie, whom he had been neglecting. A nanny was looking after Todd.

When Debbie next saw her husband, he informed her that he was flying to Chicago with Elizabeth for the funeral. "You can't go," he said. "The kids need you."

***

Still harboring his longstanding crush on Elizabeth, her aviator suitor of yesteryear, Howard Hughes, finally connected with Elizabeth on the phone. Very generously, he offered her the use of one of his TWA jets to fly her to Todd's funeral in Chicago and then back to Los Angeles. She willingly accepted his offer and thanked him profusely.

During the flight to Chicago, the crew remembered Elizabeth clinging desperately to Fisher, and cuddling up protectively in his arms. The pilot later said, "Those two clung to each other like long lost lovers."

Ashen and veiled, Elizabeth disembarked from Hughes' TWA plane in Chicago. On the ramp, she was supported by her brother, Howard, and her doctor, Rex Kennamer. Dick Hanley followed them, carrying her two large purses.

Her arrival at Chicago's airport was greeted by some 2,000 fans, screaming her name and clamoring for an autograph, which she would not have given under any circumstances. A limousine whisked her to the Drake Hotel in Chicago, where a suite had been prepared for her. It was filled with flowers from friends and from fans expressing their sympathy.

Michael Todd, Jr., with his wife, Sarah, had met Elizabeth at the Chicago airport. He had gone ahead to make the funeral arrangements.

The next day police estimated that some 20,000 frenzied fans lined the funeral route to Todd's grave site. It was believed that this was the largest turnout since Bugs Moran gang members were buried in the wake of the 1929 St. Valentine's Day Massacre.

Some of the more crazed fans showed up along the funeral route not to commiserate with Elizabeth, but to scream and shout for Fisher. They were the more dedicated members of his Chicago fan club. Many of them brought their record albums for him to autograph. Of course, in these circumstances, he could not grant such requests.

Designer Helen Rose flew to Chicago with Elizabeth's "widow's weeds"—a black mink wrap, black leather gloves, a black suit trimmed with broadtail fur, a black vel-

193

vet cloche hat, and a black veil that left her scarlet-painted lips visible.

Elizabeth specifically had not invited Montgomery Clift, the gay actor who had been her "long lost love, the man who got away." Nonetheless, she spotted his face in the milling crowds. He was horrified at the mob threatening her. "They were noisy and vengeful," he said. "I saw envy in their faces, hatred, and bleakness."

Defined during its aftermath by Hanley as "a Todd extravaganza," the funeral of Michael Todd took place on March 25, 1958 at the Jewish Waldheim Cemetery in Zurich, Illinois, outside Chicago.

Fans ate potato chips and popcorn, trashing the cemetery with their garbage. Untamed children crawled over the Jewish tombstones. Hot dog vendors peddled snacks and drinks to the mob.

At Todd's grave site, which was covered with a black tent, Elizabeth bowed before the bronze casket containing his charred remains. "I love you, Mike," she said, sobbing. "I will love you for eternity. There will never be another."

As Rabbi Abraham Rose conducted the Orthodox service, his voice was drowned out by fans shouting, "LIZ! LIZ! LIZ!"

A photograph of the young weeping widow, supported by Fisher, was flashed around the world. In Hanley's words, "Eddie had become a surrogate for Mike. Michael, Jr. was yet another surrogate. Elizabeth had two men in her life, both of whom were in love with her."

Later, Fisher told Debbie that the funeral was "an agonizing ordeal—I didn't think I'd get through it." Like the widow, he knelt before the casket and sobbed. "I've lost the only real friend I ever had."

Hanley stood nearby, mesmerized by the scene of the weeping Elizabeth with Fisher. "Eddie was behaving more like a widow instead of as a best friend," he later said. "I had heard only rumors about the intimacy of Eddie and Mike. It was not a traditional male/male friendship. They were asshole buddies in more ways than one, or so I heard."

As the police tried to clear a pathway for Elizabeth back to her waiting limousine, unruly spectators tried to break through the cordon of police, hoping to tear off pieces of her clothing. One woman with a camera ripped off her veil, saying, "Listen, bitch, I want a picture of your tear-soaked face."

Fisher managed to push her inside the limousine, whereupon they discovered that the driver was missing—lost in the crowd. The mob surrounded the car. Some of the young men began to rock the vehicle, trying to force her to come out and to pose for pictures. She screamed, fearing the limousine would be toppled over. It took eight policemen to force the crowd to stand back from the limo. The driver finally appeared.

As she recalled, "Hordes of people swarmed like insects all over the limo so we couldn't see out the window."

It took an hour for the police to clear a pathway for the limousine to leave the cemetery and take Elizabeth back to the Drake. Once there, she met privately with Clift. The confrontation did not go well, as she had not wanted him to come to Chicago.

From the living room of her suite, Fisher heard Clift and Elizabeth exchanging angry words. Then Clift stormed out of her bedroom, slamming the door behind him. As he was leaving, he turned to Fisher, who later told Debbie what happened. "Monty reached to kiss me. I thought it would be a kiss on the cheek, a condolence kiss. What I got was his tongue down my throat."

"I've always had a crush on you," he told Fisher. "Come and stay with me when you return to New York."

"Are you going to take him up on that offer?" Debbie asked. "I think you two guys would make a cute couple."

"Always the joker," he answered, sarcastically.

As soon as was reasonably possible, Elizabeth, with Fisher at her side, departed from Chicago along with their guests. At the airport, in the wake of this grotesque funeral, they boarded Hughes' plane for the flight back to Los Angeles.

Throughout most of the flight, Elizabeth, in front of everyone, huddled with Fisher, his arms protectively around her. He shared a memory of Todd with her:

"Mike told me that most young boys in America grow up wanting to become President of the United States. But Mike told me his life-long wish was to marry Elizabeth Taylor."

***

At this time in her life, Debbie had little to sing about except for her children, Carrie and Todd. Nonetheless, she accepted an invitation to sing "Tammy" at the annual Academy Awards presentation. To that effect, she arrived at the Pantages Theater in the late afternoon to rehearse the number with an orchestra.

When the time came for her to perform, she said she was "filled with grief and loss. I didn't want that to show, so I tried my best. It was all I could do to keep from crying as I sang this romantic song of an innocent girl."

When it was over, she didn't wait around to see who won the Oscars, but rushed home to tend to her children.

Waiting for her was Michael Wilding, who had been sleeping on the sofa in her living room. Without a real invitation, he had moved into their home, ostensibly so that he could be near his sons.

"His favorite place was on a stool by the bar," she said. "Eddie and I, both non-drinkers, never stocked much booze. He drank everything in sight, and I had to call for liquor deliveries."

"Night after night, he indulged in this fantasy that after Todd's death, Elizabeth was certain to take him back. I didn't believe that for a moment. Michael was a man in late middle age and a drunkard. Elizabeth was still young and vital. I felt she'd go on to have future husbands. For all I knew, she'd be getting married to some young stud when she was seventy or beyond."

"Mike Wilding was a very forgiving sort and didn't seem to resent she'd taken up with Todd before divorcing him. I guess for a man to love Elizabeth was to love her forever. Eddie certainly was showing an amazing devotion to her."

"After two weeks, I had had it with Mike," she said. "I wanted him to get on with his own life. Elizabeth phoned me and told me she was ready to take her children back, and I hugged and kissed them as they left."

"It caused me pain, but I asked Mike to go," she said. "I wanted to get on with my life with Eddie. Let things return to normal, if you could call our married life normal. He told me that Elizabeth still needed him, and he was spending his time with her and neglecting his own children...and me."

"And then one night he told me that Elizabeth had flown to New York, leaving her children in the care of two nannies."

According to Debbie, "The next morning, I came into the guest room to give Eddie his fresh laundry. I was shocked to see him packing two suitcases. He told me he was booked on a flight to New York."

"Perhaps you'll have the time to see Elizabeth there," Debbie said to him.

"If I can spare the time," he answered.

"When will you be returning," she asked.

As he headed out the door, he said, "I don't really know. I have several things in the works. Tell our babies goodbye for me."

As she later wrote, "Eddie decided to follow Elizabeth to New York. The rest, as they say, is history."

***

The first mention in the press about the growing *liaison* between Fisher and "The Widow Todd" appeared in a column by James Bacon. He was alive only because at the last minute, he'd turned down Todd's invitation to fly with him aboard *Lucky Liz*.

Bacon wrote, "Our boy singer, Eddie Fisher, performed the most dangerous duty known to man. He dried a widow's tears."

Chapter Seven

Eddie Fisher Telling Debbie
Why He's Dumping Her for Elizabeth Taylor:

"I LOVE HER
AND I NEVER LOVED YOU"

Debbie's Newest Role:
Abandoned Wife and Mother

Her Brush With the Future King of Belgium
(Queen Debbie, First Lady of the Congo?)

Mating Games
Her Movie Characters Reflect the
Coy Seduction Rituals of the 50s

Making her first public appearance after the death of Mike Todd, Elizabeth flew into Las Vegas to attend Eddie Fisher's opening at the Tropicana. When Debbie heard of that, she, too, flew to Vegas in spite of her husband ordering her not to.

That night, he was torn between two lovers, one current (Elizabeth), and the other, Debbie, still his wife but hardly his lover any longer.

Debbie's next picture, *This Happy Feeling,* released in 1958, involved her as a loan-out to Universal. The title didn't match her mood. "If anything, I was depressed."

Its producer, Ross Hunter, had cast her in *Tammy & the Bachelor,* and he was hoping for a repeat success. A film adaptation of a play by F. Hugh Herbert entitled *For Love or Money,* Hunter intended to benefit from her rendition of the film's theme song, "This Happy Feeling," hoping that it would morph into a pop song hit equivalent to that of "Tammy."

For its cast, he'd lined up a formidable list of upcoming stars combined with some of the favorite performers of yesterday. Her two leading men were Curt Jurgens and John Saxon, backed up by Alexis Smith, Mary Astor, Troy Donahue, and Estelle Winwood.

On her first day back on the Universal lot, she met her director, Blake Edwards. He seemed more interested in his upcoming film, *Operation Petticoat* (1959) than he did with his present assignment. His biggest hits, such as *Breakfast at Tiffany's* (1961), and those Pink Panther successes, lay in his future, as did his marriage to singing star Julie Andrews.

From the moment he was first introduced to Debbie, he addressed her mockingly as "Tammy," and was frank in admitting he would have preferred a different actress in her role, although he refused to name his choice. "Ross insisted on casting you, because he's hoping to have another hit like *Tammy,* He's even going to advertise our picture as "THAT TAMMY GIRL IS BACK!"

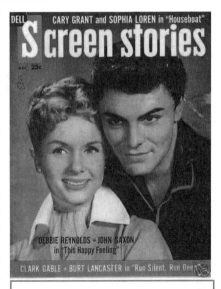

"For a man directing a so-called comedy, Edwards seemed more depressed than I was," she said. "My life was coming unglued, but I didn't know what his problem was. Ross told me that although Blake was married, he lived in the closet. Ross would know, I guess. Takes one to know one."

Edwards had co-written the screenplay of *This Happy Feeling* with Herbert, author of the play on which the film was based. Alexis Smith, portraying an actress, Nita Holloway, is

When fans saw this picture of Debbie and heartthrob John Saxon, readers thought it was the beginning of her latest romance.

Actually, they were promoting their latest film, *This Happy Feeling.*

198

in love with Preston Mitchell ("Mitch"), a character portrayed by Curt Jurgens. The character he plays has retired from the stage but Nita wants to lure him back to Broadway to play the father of a new teen idol, Tony Manza (Troy Donahue).

Mitch lives next door to the handsome, rather dashing and much younger Bill Tremayne (John Saxon). Bill borrows his car one night to go to a party where he meets a pert and pretty little secretary, Jane Black (Debbie).

Later, he offers to drive her back home in a rainstorm, during which he becomes too amorous for her taste. She bolts from the car and arrives on Mitch's doorstep. He invites her to dry off, and he even offers her a bed for the night. The next morning, Nita arrives and concludes that her aging beau has had an affair with "this cute little bundle of energy."

Expect the usual romantic complications between Bill (Saxon) and Jane (Debbie) who get together again and fall in love. Mitch goes back to Nita (not that he ever left), and also returns to Broadway to appear with her on stage.

On the final day of shooting, Edwards approached Debbie and pronounced *The Happy Feeling* "a total mess. Don't you agree, Tammy?"

In a memoir, she claimed she found Edwards "funny and creative, so talented, one of a kind. It was so much fun doing scenes with him."

She was being officially kind. In reality, she told friends she detested working with him, as would her friend, Rock Hudson, in the future when he made *Darling Lili* (1970) with Edwards directing him and his co-star, Edwards' then-wife, Julie Andrews.

Born in Bavaria in 1915, Jurgens had been an actor on the stage in Vienna. In 1944 he was sent to a Nazi internment camp in Hungary, labeled as "politically unreliable," which, indeed (at least from the Nazi's point of view) he was. After the war, he became an Austrian citizen.

As a film actor, Jurgens was often cast as a soldier in war movies. Debbie had seen him in Roger Vadim's *Et Dieu…créa la femme (And God Cre-*

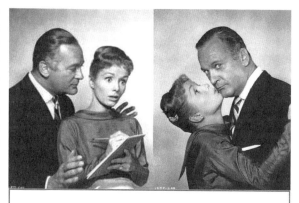

"As a romantic lead, Curt (Jurgens) and I were completely wrong for each other," Debbie said.

"Talk about chemistry—we had none. I admired his taste and continental sophistication, especially when he invited me to his beautifully furnished home. But as a sexual partner, I would be as much attracted to him as I would to my grandfather in Texas."

ated Woman; 1957).

"I was a midget standing next to Curt, as he towered over me at six feet, four inches, the same height as my pal, Rock Hudson," Debbie said.

"John Saxon and Troy Donahue, my co-stars, had been members of what the gay talent scout, Henry Willson, called 'my stable of pretty boys.' She knew that both Willson and Ross Hunter had put Rock on the casting couch. She didn't know if Saxon or Donahue had suffered the same fate. "Troy for sure, but John, I doubt."

An Italian American, Saxon had been born Carmine Orrico in Brooklyn. Willson had discovered him when he'd appeared, at age 17, on a magazine cover. Debbie had seen him in only one film, *Unguarded Moment* (1956), with Esther Williams.

"When I met John, he was getting 3,000 fan letters a week, mostly from lovesick teenage girls. After working with me, he would go on to co-star with Sandra Dee, that cute little girlish bug who followed me in a *Tammy* sequel, with disastrous results."

[Nearly half a century would go by before Debbie and Saxon co-starred in a play, Love Letters, by A.R. Gurney. The play opened at El Portal Theater in North Hollywood, and drew many of Debbie's former co-stars or else friends from her past.]

Debbie also met Willson's other "pretty boy," Troy Donahue, born Merle Johnson. He told her, "I'm sometimes mistaken for Tab Hunter. But I tell fans, 'I'm the straight one.'"

"Troy was about as straight as a crooked mountain road," she said. "When I met him, he was having an affair with Rock, who gave me the lowdown: 'Great cocksucker, tiny dick.' Troy tried to come on to me. I told him, 'Troy, you must be kidding.'"

"My competition for Curt in the film was Alexis Smith," she said. "Troy was just pretending to flirt with me. Alexis was serious. She had the hots for me, but I told her I didn't go that route. I think her union with her fellow actor, Craig Stevens, was a lavender marriage. There were a lot of those in Hollywood."

At the flickering twilight of an illustrious career, Mary Astor was given the small and thankless role of Miss Tremaine. In the 1930s and '40s, she had played, among other roles, bitchy vixens and wicked *femme fatales,* immortalizing herself in *The Maltese Falcon* (1941) opposite Humphrey Bogart.

Cast as Mrs. Early, character actress Estelle Winwood was a chicken-necked, wobble-voiced old crone born in 1883 in England. "I adored her," Debbie said. "She was the best friend of Tallulah Bankhead. She told me, 'Tallulah has a great heart, but it rarely beats in the right place.' She played a flakey housekeeper in our film. If Edwards had given her a bigger role, maybe *This Happy Feeling* would have made some money."

***

In the wake of the death of Mike Todd, Eddie Fisher had become the constant companion of his widow, returning to his home only to shower and change his clothes. He checked to see that his children were all right before heading out the door once again. In passing, he curtly informed Debbie, "Elizabeth is still overcome with grief over Mike's death. She needs me. See you."

On April 14, 1958, Debbie was told that Elizabeth had returned to work at MGM to complete her performance as Maggie the Cat in *Cat on a Hot Tin Roof* opposite Paul Newman.

On one occasion, Debbie herself visited Elizabeth on the set and received her thanks for caring for her two sons. On another day, she asked Debbie to take both of her sons to the doctor, a task she gladly handled for her.

Even before the Taylor/Fisher/Reynolds scandal became public news, many Hollywood insiders, including drama coach Lillian Burns Sidney, was aware of what was going on. She said, "Eddie was a shy, self-effacing man. But his public persona had little to do with the man behind the mask. He had neither talent nor personality. His taste in women ran from bimbos to showgirls."

"The only truthful thing he said to me was that his marriage to Debbie was not the ideal couple depicted in all those glossy movie magazines. Their marriage right from the beginning ran out of gas. She confessed to me that she'd tricked him into seducing her so she could have her second child, Todd Fisher."

In June of 1958, Fisher was booked for a six-week return engagement at the glitzy Tropicana in Las Vegas. Although he didn't want Debbie to fly in for his opening night, she did anyway, leaving their children in the care of a nanny.

Elizabeth also decided to fly in on opening night, which would mark her first appearance since Todd's death. Laden with jewels, she made a glittering entrance into the hotel's nightclub, receiving a standing ovation. Her escorts were her former beau, the wealthy playboy, Arthur Loew, Jr., and Mike Todd, Jr., who was rumored to be "comforting" her when Fisher wasn't available.

"After the show, Eddie was hostile to Arthur, whom I had dated, and also to Mike Junior," Debbie claimed. "Was he jealous? Didn't he realize that a woman as man-crazed as Elizabeth would start to date after she recovered from Todd's death?"

In a memoir, Fisher admitted that he was jealous of Loew. "I had become possessive of Elizabeth. I guess I was falling in love with her, but couldn't admit it, even to myself."

Later that night at the Tropicana, it was not Loew who was seen entering Elizabeth's suite, but Fisher, along with Dr. Max Jacobson. He had given Fisher injections before his opening act. Since Elizabeth had been complaining of sleepless nights, he asked the doctor to visit her and give her injections to make her sleep.

The following morning after a good night's sleep, Elizabeth flew back to

Los Angeles aboard a different plane from Debbie's. The following night after Fisher's second show, she phoned him late. "Eddie, as soon as you fly back, you and I have got to talk. It's very important. I can't explain on the phone."

Back home again, Debbie, in the wake of Fisher's Vegas engagement, threw him a 30th birthday bash at Romanoff's, inviting only two dozen guests, one of whom was Elizabeth. Debbie had arranged for Fisher to sit between them.

But Elizabeth didn't show up. However, she called the restaurant midway through the celebration, and explained to Fisher that she was having her period and didn't feel well.

She asked him to come by the following day and see her, giving him her new phone number. She told him she had temporarily moved into Loew's house with her children. En route home that night, he revealed to Debbie that Elizabeth was living with Loew.

Debbie told her friend, Jeanette Johnson, "At least having Elizabeth living with Loew will take some of the burden off poor Eddie, who has been seeing her every night. I'm not paying any attention to rumors that claim that they're having an affair. Romantically speaking, he's not her type."

"He imitates Todd with all those long cigars, and a lot of other crap, but he's only a dime store version of Todd, merely the mock, not real turtle soup."

"Frankly, I don't think he could satisfy a woman like Elizabeth in bed. Let's face it: She's a world-class *femme fatale*. If she marries again, I think it'll be to a real rugged type, perhaps that Welsh actor, Richard Burton, or even Victor Mature, with whom she's had an affair already."

When Fisher arrived at Loew's house the following day, he found Elizabeth beside the pool. Dressed in a champagne-colored bathing suit, she was playing with Liza, Todd's daughter.

As he later wrote, "Our eyes met and that was it. Not a word was spoken. I was in love with Elizabeth. Before I left that day, she gave me Mike's gold money ring."

The next day, when he showed up to take her for a drive, she told him that Loew was away on business. He drove her to Malibu with Liza. "Watching Liza play, she held my hand, eventually taking it and pressing it against her breasts. We kissed, most passionately."

That night in Loew's bed, Eddie Fisher's affair with Elizabeth Taylor was launched. "Sex became almost a daily thing with us," Fisher later confessed.

As a means of keeping up appearances, Elizabeth and Fisher often invited Debbie along for the early part of the evening. As a threesome, they were seen at such places as La Scala, where they dined. "I wanted to deceive the press," he said. "As well as my wife. I had been Mike's best friend, and it was only reasonable that I would try to console his widow."

According to Fisher, "We frequented the Polo Lounge, often dragging Debbie along, although Elizabeth found much of her talk boring. Sometimes under the table, I'd run my hand up Elizabeth's dress. Just for me, she made a point of not wearing panties. No one, especially Debbie, seemed to think we were in love. How dumb can a wife be? Both Elizabeth and I knew we could not go on forever concealing our love for each other."

***

A widely read New York columnist, Earl Wilson, was the first to describe, in print, the romance of Eddie Fisher and the recently widowed Elizabeth Taylor. He'd seen them dancing cheek to cheek in Manhattan at the Harwyn Night Club. "Eddie is now a sort of escort service for Liz," he wrote. "She is no longer mired in the Gothic gloom following the death of Mike Todd in a plane crash."

"After that item, all hell broke loose," Fisher said.

Walter Winchell, an even more popular columnist, practically had Fisher filing for divorce so he could marry Elizabeth.

The news quickly reached Debbie. In one morning alone, she received three phone calls from "well-meaning friends," offering their sympathy. She decided for the moment to ignore the press speculation and "put on a brave front."

The singer and actress, Edie Adams, married to Ernie Kovacs, had invited Fisher and Debbie to a small dinner party at her house.

Debbie told her that Fisher was not available so Adams suggested she go with her neighbors, Dean and Jeanne Martin. They willingly agreed to take her. She told Jeanne, "I want to arrive with friends so I won't look like the lonely widow going to a party."

While Jeanne was still getting dressed, Martin pulled into Debbie's driveway to pick her up. While he was still inside her foyer, she quickly realized he'd been drinking. As always, when he was around her alone, he became sexually aggressive, almost as if obligated, like his friend, Frank Sinatra, to make the inevitable pass. He surprised her when he said, "I want you to get revenge on that little Jew bastard you married—you know, the one who calls himself a singer."

"And how do I do that?" Debbie asked, knowing the answer.

"By making out with me," he said.

Martin was serious but not all that serious. She held him off for the moment. "Jeanne is waiting, I'm sure," she said, heading for the door.

At the party, although she was aware that her fellow guests had heard about the

Dean Martin was always on the make for Debbie any time they were alone.

203

items in the New York gossip columns, no one said anything to her. "My clue was that no one ever mentioned Eddie at all."

Later that night, after the party, Martin dropped his wife, Jeanne off at the door to their house and then drove over to Debbie's. She bid him a good night, but he asked to come inside for a glass of water.

"Dean Martin? Drinking water? I can't believe that," she said. No sooner was in the door than he grabbed her for a deep-throated kiss.

She pushed him away. "Let me go, Deano. If you're that hot, you've got a wife waiting across the street."

"Now that you're deprived of a husband, you're gonna have to get it from somewhere, and I'm called 'Ever Ready.'"

After turning him down, she gave him only a brief kiss on the cheek and bid him good night. After checking on her children, she went to her own bedroom to get some sleep. But first she decided to place a late-night call to Fisher at the Essex House in Manhattan. She made repeated calls, but got no answer. She knew that Elizabeth was staying in a suite at the Plaza, having read that she had purchased an entirely new wardrobe for a trip to her native England. It was after 2AM when Debbie decided to call Elizabeth at the Plaza. The operator there told her that Miss Taylor was not accepting phone calls.

A mistress of disguised voices, Debbie came up with another scheme. She pretended to be a telephone operator calling from Los Angeles. "It's urgent that Dean Martin get in touch with Eddie Fisher. Mr. Martin was told to call him in the suite of Elizabeth Taylor."

The operator at the Plaza put through the call.

Fisher's sleepy voice came through. "Deano, what in the fuck are you calling me for at this hour?"

"It's not your friend, Deano. It's your wife, Debbie Reynolds. Put Elizabeth on the phone."

Fisher stammered with some made-up excuses until he finally admitted the truth. "I'm flying back to Los Angeles tomorrow. We'll talk about it then."

"Don't bother," she said, slamming down the phone.

Even though she hadn't revealed her true feelings during her conversation with him, she later admitted, "I was floored that Eddie was in bed with Elizabeth. I felt numb all over, my mind a blank at first. It was like I was floating in space somewhere."

"I didn't blame Elizabeth. Eddie is such a needy person. He's so dependent, and I guess she found that 'little boy lost' quality appealing. She was probably providing him with what he didn't get at home. I suspected that it was more than just sex, although I'm certain there was plenty of that, too."

"Eddie doesn't seem to know what he wants. He's like an elevator who can't find the floor. I don't think he ever took the time to figure out who he is. Perhaps all those injections from Dr. Needles kept him up there somewhere heading for some hellish place like Jupiter, never falling to earth."

Unlike what he'd promised on the phone, Fisher did not fly back to California but extended his stay with Elizabeth. The romantic duo headed to Grossinger's Resort in the Catskills, with the understanding that Eddie would be dedicating the resort's new swimming pool. Although they hid away in Jennie Grossinger's house, the press quickly learned of their whereabouts.

Privately, Jennie was skeptical of the latest affair of her favorite singer, who had, for several years, been like a son to her. She told her friends, "Frankly, I think Eddie is biting off more than he can chew. I prefer Debbie Reynolds to Miss Taylor. Debbie is much friendlier both to me and to my staff. But whatever my dear boy decides to do, he knows I have his back."

After that Labor Day weekend in the Catskills, the whole world seemed to learn of the Fisher / Taylor affair.

On September 8, 1958, the *Los Angeles Herald-Express* headlined a story— EDDIE FISHER DATING LIZ TAYLOR. That revelation got more play than Nikita Khrushchev threatening atomic retaliation against the United States if it attacked Red China.

At around the same time, although the Soviets had launched Sputnik, Alaska had voted for statehood, and Dr. Martin Luther King, Jr. had been arrested in Alabama, newspapers were obsessed with "Liz & Eddie" as they had once been with "Eddie & Debbie."

Thousands of Elizabeth's fans were outraged that she had not spent a year mourning the death of Todd.

As the news broke, and for weeks to come, reporters and photographers virtually camped out in front of the home that Debbie had once shared with Fisher. To avoid them, he had to slip around to the backyard with his friend Joey Forman and enter through the kitchen door. When he got there, he smelled one of his favorite foods, lima bean soup, cooking on the stove. "I couldn't believe it," he told Forman. "Debbie expects to save our marriage by offering me a bowl of lima bean soup."

Inside their living room, he confronted her. "Welcome home," she said.

"Cut the shit!" he barked at her, as Forman stood behind him. "Face the facts, girl. I love Elizabeth, and I never loved you. It's over, kid."

Forman chimed in. "Eddie's right. He always told me he never loved you."

"Shut your god damn face, you stupid jerk," she yelled at Forman. "And get the hell out of my house."

"Joey stays, bitch." Then Fisher turned to his friend. "Go to the guest room and start packing my essentials." He turned back to her. "I'll have Joey drive over later to get the rest of my possessions. I'll be living with him in his apartment on Sunset Boulevard. You remember the movie, *Sunset Blvd.*, don't you, Debbie? Norma Desmond living in the delusions of yesterday, not able to face the reality of today? I want a divorce, as soon as it can be granted. Got that?"

"I'll never give you a divorce," she threatened. "We have two children to raise. Aren't you even going to go in to see them?"

"In time. I've got more important things on my mind now." He headed for the guest room as she raced in tears upstairs to what had originally been defined as their bedroom.

Fisher had to face reporters long before Debbie did. "My marriage to Debbie had ended long before I became involved with Elizabeth."

In contrast, when Elizabeth encountered rumors of her affair with Fisher, she shouted, "Those reports are garbage!"

When Debbie read her remark, she quipped, "It's garbage all right."

By now, the Fisher/Taylor affair had become a world-wide news event. The leading newspaper of Stockholm ran the story under the headline: BLOOD THIRSTY WIDOW LIZ TAYLOR VAMPIRES EDDIE FISHER.

Their mutual friend, the musician, Oscar Levant, quipped to the press, "Just how high can Eddie Fisher stoop?"

A London newspaper summed up Debbie's dilemma: ERRANT HUSBAND, WRONGED WIFE & WICKED WIDOW.

Some reporters took delight in making puns, including the *New York Mirror:* "The storybook marriage of America's Sweethearts, Eddie Fisher and Debbie Reynolds, skidded on a series of curves—Liz Taylor's."

"Harlot" was one of the kinder words used to describe Elizabeth. She was also called "a viper, a cannibal, a barbarian, and a man-eater." Magazines such as *Photoplay* urged the public to boycott her films, which they did not. *Cat on a Hot Tin Roof* became a big box-office hit. She was denounced in newspaper editorials throughout the country, and one fire-and-brimstone pastor in Los Angeles urged his congregation to burn her in effigy.

Hedda Hopper, long a supporter of the Fisher/Reynolds sweetheart image, got through to Debbie, who told her, "Eddie wants to be a movie star. He married me. Then he left me for an even bigger movie star. I'll give it a year at the most. I know Elizabeth. She'll toss him aside for bigger game. Eddie will be yesterday's baloney sandwich."

Privately, Hopper referred to Elizabeth as "That bitch! That slut!"

When Elizabeth returned to Los Angeles, Hopper phoned her.

She's had three mates, now she is on her 4th—her best friend's spouse.

This page from one of the pulpy tabloids reflected America's point of view at the time. "Eddie is deplorable, and Liz is a harlot."

Her remark became infamous: "Mike Todd is dead. I'm alive! Maggie the Cat is alive. What do you expect me to do—sleep alone?" She could no longer deny the romance she'd recently denounced as garbage. "To put it bluntly," she told reporters, "Eddie is not in love with Debbie Reynolds—and never has been. Only a year ago, they were headed for the divorce courts. But he called it off when he learned she was going to have her baby. She got him drunk and tricked him into her bed, where he had not slept in months. I'm not taking anything away from Tammy because she never really had him."

In a phone call to Hopper's rival, Louella Parsons, Debbie said, "I always knew Eddie would leave me for another woman. I never dreamed it would be Elizabeth Taylor, who was my friend during her marriage to Mike Todd. Mamie Van Doren, perhaps, but not Elizabeth Taylor!"

An MGM publicist, Rick Ingersoll, said that Debbie faced a public relations choice. "It was time for her to portray herself as the good and faithful wife opposite Elizabeth's role as a homewrecker. As I knew she would, she went for the sympathy vote, brilliant in her depiction of the deserted wife and mother whose husband was stolen by a brazen Jezebel."

He also claimed, "Debbie was not nearly as hard-boiled as Elizabeth Taylor. Frankly, she seemed rather fragile. She blamed MGM and its publicity department for siding with Elizabeth because she was a bigger money-maker for the studio than Debbie's sweet little pictures, a case of Maggie the Cat battling Tammy. The scandal might destroy Fisher's career, but it was making Elizabeth the most sought-after movie star in the world. Many studios also wanted to star Debbie in pictures. Because of the world-wide publicity, she was in demand as well."

Privately, even President Eisenhower voiced his opinion, telling his wife, Mamie, and some of his aides, "Elizabeth Taylor and Eddie Fisher are moral outlaws, and, I suspect, Democrats."

The time had come for Debbie to make her carefully staged appearance before the photographers and reporters camped out on her doorstep. She carefully made herself up for the occasion, in Tammy drag, with safety pins for Todd's diapers attached to her white lace blouse.

Emerging from her house to face a barrage of press, she demurely told the men, "I still love Eddie. I'm trying to arrange a face-to-face with Elizabeth, but she won't return my calls. I'm hoping, even at this late point, to save my marriage. My babies need a father. I took Eddie to a marriage counselor, but it did no good. He wouldn't listen. It's like he's fallen under Elizabeth's spell."

Most reporters fell for Debbie's script. One staffer from *Variety* claimed that Elizabeth was a "spoiled, materialistic, and scandalous woman—a home wrecker whose selfish needs and hedonistic sex drive know no limit. In contrast, Debbie is a deserted but still loyal wife, dedicated to her philandering spouse and the welfare of her children."

Privately, Debbie told her friends, "I have to face reality. I have lost Eddie to the world's most beautiful woman. Elizabeth is a Venus's-flytrap, me a little daisy."

For weeks, Debbie felt isolated and alone. When friends called, she often told them, "I guess I wasn't woman enough for Eddie. At least he didn't desert me for one of those Vegas bimbos he used to screw. He left me for the most famous movie star in the world."

Years later, when Richard Burton, then married to Elizabeth, said, "Before they wither, Elizabeth's breasts will topple empires."

"How could I, a little Texas tomboy, growing up in El Paso near the Mexican border, compete with Cleopatra?" Debbie asked in 1965.

As she told her friend, Camille Williams, "I was not a woman of the world, and that was what Eddie desired, a passionate creature like Elizabeth, a man-devouring vixen. She offered champagne and caviar, and I came up with lima bean soup. But he isn't well matched for her. Our little Jewish singer has a lot to learn about women. She'll destroy him, both the man and his career. Wait and see."

Quite by accident, she ran into Sara Taylor, Elizabeth's mother, on the MGM lot. Sara told her, "My daughter and Eddie think they can live their lives loving Mike Todd and consoling each other. Both of them are living in the past, trying to keep Todd's memory alive. Their relationship is doomed to failure, as it was right from the start."

Debbie was at the studio that day to have MGM make her failed marriage official and not just speculation in the press. She joined her lawyer, Frank Belcher, and went into the office of Howard Strickling, who handled emergencies of MGM stars along with his co-worker, publicist Eddie Mannix. The men were called "The Fixers."

Strickling had been called in by Louis B. Mayer to handle such "indiscretions" as the murder of Paul Bern (Jean Harlow's husband); the studio-directed drug addiction of Judy Garland; and even the murder of Ted Healy (creator of *The Three Stooges*) at the hands of Wallace Beery.

Debbie and Belcher met with Strickling for an hour. Later that day, he faced the press with a brief announcement. "Debbie Reynolds and Eddie Fisher have separated. No further action is being taken at this time." He opted not to answer any questions.

By now, the Taylor/Fisher/Reynolds love triangle had become the most controversial marital news since King Edward VIII (later known as the Duke of Windsor) abdicated his throne to marry "the woman I love," Wallis Simpson.

In a candid confession of regret, Debbie said, "I should have married Bob Wagner. We were in love. Perhaps I was more in love with him than he was with me. But that little two-timer, Natalie Wood, came into his life when not bedding Elvis Presley or Warren Beatty. Ironically, years later, Elizabeth got to bed Bob herself. It seems that no man is ever safe from her clutches."

Voracious reporters knew where Debbie and her children were living. But where were Elizabeth and Fisher?

It was only in 1990 that the world learned where they'd been hiding. Edie Adams, a friend of both Debbie and Fisher, published a memoir, *Sing a Pretty Song*, in which she claimed that Elizabeth and Fisher came to live with her and her husband, Ernie Kovacs.

It was from that hideaway that Fisher phoned Debbie to inquire about their children. He told her he was getting death threats from the Jew-hating KKK and was being mailed Haitian voodoo dolls with pins embedded in their hearts. Elizabeth was also getting death threats and had beefed up her security guards as protection for her children.

"I'm carrying a loaded revolver, but I don't know how to use it," Fisher told Debbie.

She responded, "I'm not getting any death threats, but hundreds of letters are arriving at MGM for me. Lots of them are from the Deep South, states such as Georgia and Alabama. My fans claim that next time I should marry a good Southern Baptist Christian—not some Jew with a beak nose."

"Thanks for the update," Fisher said sarcastically.

Three days after Strickling's announcement, Debbie made her own statement to the press: "I am deeply shocked over Eddie's desertion of not only me, but his babies, Todd and Carrie. He and I had never been happier than we were during the past year. He is a great guy and a loving father. The separation deal that was ironed out was not my idea."

At the end of 1958, *Motion Picture* magazine published the results of its annual poll. In terms of reader interest, fans named Elizabeth Taylor as its most enticing subject, with the newly single mom, Debbie Reynolds, coming in in second place.

Because of the scandal, Fisher's career would never recover. In contrast, Debbie's earning power zoomed from $75,000 annually to more than one million dollars, and Elizabeth's take-home pay quintupled.

***

With her separation from Eddie Fisher now official, Debbie returned to something she loved more than marriage—her career. "My fans were clamoring for Tammy to return to the screen," she said. "They wanted to see her in action again, preferably in a romantic comedy." That was exactly what MGM had in store for her with *The Mating Game*, set for a 1959 release.

Her leading man would be Tony Randall, and her parents would be played by Paul Douglas and Una Merkel, with veteran actor Fred Clark in a supporting role as Randall's boss.

The script by William Roberts was based on a British novella, *The Darling Buds of May*, written by H.E. Bates and published in 1958. It was adapted into a British TV miniseries (1991-93) starring Catherine Zeta-Jones in the role that Debbie had interpreted on the "big screen" years before.

Before shooting began, Debbie met with her producer, Philip Barry, Jr., and the veteran director, George Marshall. Barry was mainly known for his work in TV, turning out such hit shows as *The Goodyear Playhouse*.

Marshall certainly knew how to direct a comedy, having helmed Laurel and Hardy in some of their classics, and he'd also worked with Bob Hope, Will Rogers, Jerry Lewis, and W.C. Fields.

Debbie had seen his 1939 *Destry Rides Again* with Marlene Dietrich and James Stewart. *[After her affair with Stewart, she had to undergo an abortion.]* Debbie had gone to the movie three times, learning to perform a hilarious impersonation of Dietrich singing her standard, "See What the Boys in the Back Room Will Have."

Marshall would work on another picture with Debbie entitled *How the West Was Won*.

During a meeting with Marshall and Barry, Debbie said, "I don't think a five-year-old would believe that I could fall for a man like Tony Randall. I know him. Please, if we've got love scenes, keep them to a minimum."

Years later when Randall was one of the leads in a long-running hit TV series, *The Odd Couple*, in which he played Felix Unger, Debbie quipped, "Randall and I were the original odd couple when we co-starred in a comedy."

In the year of their movie's release, Randall also co-starred with Rock Hudson and

AMATEURS! *Learn from her!*
EXPERTS! *Study her technique!*

M-G-M REVEALS HOW
DEBBIE REYNOLDS
WINS
TONY RANDALL

Based on Debbie's revised status as a mature, consenting, divorced mother of two, she capitalized off her recognition as a "nice but no longer virginal woman who been done wrong" by an errant husband,"

Hollywood at last began marketing Debbie as a girl who, under the right circumstances, might say "yes."

Ironically, the man they paired her with in *The Mating Game* was the notoriously fussy Tony Randall.

Hipsters throughout Hollywood guffawed at the combo.

Doris Day in *Pillow Talk*. "Rock told me that Randall came on to him," Debbie claimed. "I had begged Ross Hunter to cast me in that movie opposite Rock, but he was set on Doris."

The Larkins, Pop and Ma (as portrayed by Douglas and Merkel), are country people living on a farm with their tomboy daughter Mariette (Debbie). They anger their snobbish neighbor, Philip Ober (Wendall Burnshaw). Vengefully, since they had never been known to file a tax return, he reports them to the Internal Revenue Service.

At the IRS, Oliver Kelsey (Clark) sends his aide, Lorenzo Charlton (Randall), to Maryland to investigate the Larkins. His audit is complicated by the fact that for decades, Pop has usually bartered and traded with his neighbors, without any attempt at record-keeping, for whatever his family needs.

While he's on the farm, as part of an unlikely romance, Lorenzo falls for Mariette, even though he pressures the Larkins with the results of an audit that demands that they pay the IRS an "estimated tax" of $50,000. Pop, however, produces a receipt from the Union Army for 30 horses which Yankee soldiers "confiscated" during the Civil War. Over the decades since then, with interest included, the Larkins are owed $14 million.

Pop generously rejects the idea of filing a counter-claim for that amount, but a grateful U.S. government agrees to not bill them for the amount they'd previously claimed, or for any future tax bills either. Lorenzo and Mariette presumably will get married and live happily ever after. After all, it's a romantic comedy, and it made fairly good money at the box office.

During the making of the film, Debbie bonded with Una Merkel, who had, decades before, been an *ingénue* in silent films and later achieved major success in the talkies of the 1930s. She'd often appeared as the wisecracking best friend of such stars as Carole Lombard, Loretta Young, and Jean Harlow.

Marshall had directed her with Dietrich in *Destry Rides Again,* especially in preparation for their famous "cat fight" which became one of the most iconic scenes in the history of the cinema.

Merkel also played the elder daughter of W.C. Fields in *The Bank Dick* (1940). She told Debbie, "Both Marlene and Fields tried to get into

As Debbie matured as an actress, she abandoned the virginal mystique that had served her so well in her early films.

Here she is on the set of *The Mating Game* with Carrie and Todd, clearly demonstrating that even if the man who'd sired her children had flown the coop, she was still a loving and attentive mother.

my pants."

Debbie worked with Paul Douglas in the final months of his life, during the course of his marriage to his fifth wife, the actress, Jan Sterling. Debbie had admired him in the 1949 movie, *A Letter to Three Wives*.

Near the end of the shoot, he told Debbie that director Billy Wilder had offered him one of the leads in the upcoming film, *The Apartment*. But two days before shooting began, he died of a heart attack, the role eventually going to Fred MacMurray.

After making a movie with Randall, Debbie still didn't think of him as a great screen lover, but she found him amusing and delightful as a friend. They developed a relationship that lasted for years.

She later wrote about an amusing incident that occurred during the making of the movie when her dressing trailer stood next to his, separated only with a thin common wall.

One afternoon, between takes, she was reading one of the latest stories, headlined "DEBBIE STEALS LIZ'S HAPPINESS," about the Elizabeth/Eddie/Debbie love triangle. In it, she was chastised for not granting Fisher a divorce.

"Tony loved opera," she said. "Between takes, he would always break into song from one of his favorite arias. He had at least fifty arias he loved."

As she was reading the latest newspaper stories about her, her own trailer began to "shake, rattle, and roll."

"At first, I thought it was another one of those California earthquakes. Tony's baritone voice could be heard through all the thumping."

She decided to get up and check what was going on next door. Moving to a position directly in front of the entrance to his dressing room, she threw its door open without knocking. "To my shock, I came upon Tony Randall, jaybird naked, jumping up and down on the sofa in his trailer. I was taken back by the size of his equipment. It was a huge thing, from the looks of him, I always thought he might be a Princess Tiny Meat. Not Tony!"

Later, she wrote that she had once commented on Bob Fosse's thing. "I didn't want my fans to think I was a size queen like Lana Turner. Size is a preoccupation in Hollywood whenever gals get together. The penis size of their various lovers is always the topic of the day. Mil-

It started with a car: Debbie and Glenn Ford ensnared in ownership of a plaything they can't afford.

ton Berle once told me he had the largest in Hollywood and even offered to display it for me. I turned down the offer. Joan Crawford, however, an expert on the subject, told me that the actor, John Ireland, had the biggest. One day, when I have the time, I'll take along a ruler in my purse to end this Berle/Ireland controversy."

***

George Marshall, who had just directed Debbie in *The Mating Game,* was assigned to helm her in her next romantic comedy where she'd play the female lead in *It Started With a Kiss* (1959). Its production had already been scheduled by MGM as an upcoming release in Metrocolor and CinemaScope. The wide screen would take advantage of the scenic landscapes of Spain, where much of the film was shot.

Its producer, Aaron Rosenberg, hired Charles Lederer to write the screenplay. Glenn Ford was cast as Joe Fitzpatrick, an Air Force staff sergeant and a Korean War veteran.

At a society raffle in Manhattan, he meets Maggie Putnam (Debbie), a dancer and model who is staffing a booth there, hoping to meet and marry a millionaire. She persuades him to buy a raffle ticket, although he has little hope of winning the grand prize, a red, custom-built Lincoln Future concept car.

He's more interested in her than in the automobile. He finds her sexy and appealing, and he pursues her. In what was called the briefest courtship in movie history, he marries her. She's wearing his wedding ring. But to her chagrin, instead of living with a millionaire, she'll be expected to live on his $340-a-month paycheck from the Air Force. After a torrid honeymoon, the Army sends him to a U.S. military base in Spain, where, as his wife, she's summoned to join him to begin their married life.

Before she can join him, Joe is announced as the winner of the custom-built car. Debbie doesn't inform him of his win right away, intending instead to break the news as a big surprise after she joins him in Spain. *[The Air Force agrees to ship the car to him through the port of Cádiz.]*

Not realizing that he's won the car, Joe jumps to the conclusion that the "surprise" is that Maggie is pregnant. Could it be? So soon after their impulsive wedding?

He stands with her in Cádiz, watching as his shiny new car is unloaded and uncarted. He is stunned, adoring the car as he embarks with Maggie on a brief honeymoon, touring through some of the wonders of Andalusia *en route* north. Along the way, they draw the attention of adoring crowds of Spaniards who are dazzled by the spectacular vehicle.

But trouble arises when he returns to his base. Visiting congressmen Charles Meridan (Harry Morgan) and Richard Tapped (Edgar Buchanan) wonder how an enlisted man can afford such a luxurious vehicle. Joe's commanding officer, Major General Tim O'Connell (Fred Clark), warns him that U.S. military personnel have been told not to promote the image of Americans as snobbishly rich.

More complications ensue, including the revelation that Joe and Maggie will face a mammoth income tax bill of $17,000 on the car.

The super glamourous Marquesa Marion de la Rey (Eva Gabor) becomes enamored of Joe. At the same time, Spain's most dashing matador, Gustavo Rojo (Antonio Soriano), develops a crush on both Maggie and for Joe's shiny new vehicle, which he offers to buy.

[Based on the visibility generated by this film, Soriano developed a fan base, especially from gay men who appreciated his virile charms. In their bedrooms, many of them posted publicity pictures of him as a matador dressed in a tight-fitting "suit of lights."]

Since it's a romantic 1950s comedy, fans could expect a happy ending. The Marquesa turns Joe back over to Debbie, and the amorous matador ends his pursuit of Debbie, but purchases the automobile. Joe and Maggie reconcile themselves to a relatively modest lifestyle, and she soon evolves into the dutiful spouse of a U.S. airman.

In a memoir, Debbie revealed that during a rehearsal in her dressing room, "Glenn decided I was kissable and came after me. I ran around and around the room several times, until I got tired. Finally, I stopped, and he crashed into me, knocking me down."

She drew the curtain on what happened next, as she did on virtually all of her romances outside of wedlock. So although her subsequent affair with Ford was obliquely hinted at in several gossip columns, it never made the scandal magazines.

As she later told her girlfriends back in California, "The picture was aptly named *It Started With a Kiss*. The first time Glenn kissed me off screen—yes, with tongue—I fell madly in love with him, even though I didn't want to. He was the sweetest-smelling man I'd ever met. To put it bluntly, he was good enough to eat. God, I'm getting vulgar."

In the 1940s, Ford had been one of Debbie's favorite leading men, and now, she could turn over in bed and look directly into his handsome face. He was the ideal leading man both in weepies and in romances, and he brought a genial and relaxed sincerity to the screen. In the words of one critic, "Glenn Ford can be a brooding menace, heroic, taciturn, wise, foolish, amiable, dull, or sardonic."

At the time that Debbie first worked with him, and he romanced her, he was at the peak of his career, appearing on *Quigley's List of Top Ten Box Office Champions*.

As Ford later confided to his best friend, William Holden, and others of his cronies, "Debbie couldn't get enough of me. She told me she didn't know a woman could have an orgasm until I gave her her first. Fortunately, I was coming to an end of my affair with Eva Gabor when I met Debbie, so jealousy was not an issue since Eva had met a new beau in Spain."

In 1959, Ford was in the process of divorcing his wife, Eleanor Powell, the former tap-dancing star of movies in the 1930s. The couple had married in 1943 and had produced a son, Peter.

"I began a heavy dating of Debbie in Spain," Ford revealed, "taking her to flamenco clubs, hidden Spanish restaurants in the old town, a dinner party hosted by Ava Gardner, and long, lovely, romantic weekends touring such historic towns as Segovia and Toledo."

Although this scene between Debbie and Glenn Ford in bed was filmed by two working actors "in character" on a film set, it was also a depiction of what was going on between them off screen.

"I didn't mean to fall for Glenn at this troubled time of my life," Debbie said. "I told Jeanette Johnson and others that I found him irresistible. What woman could resist him? But I felt I had to protect my image, that of the abandoned wife. After all, I had kids to support because I knew I couldn't count on Eddie."

"Elizabeth was massively attacked for falling for Eddie so soon after Todd's death. I didn't want to look like some Vegas whore running off with another man hours after my spouse deserted me. Otherwise, my fans would feel it was all an act...I mean, my role of the abandoned wife."

Ford told his longtime friend and director, George Marshall, "I fell in love with Debbie and asked her to marry me, but she's holding me off on wedded bliss. She wants the bliss without the wedding. I don't think she really loves me. This is a bit vain to say, but I think she's in our relationship just for the sex, and she's getting plenty of that."

As Marshall knew so well, many stars had had sex with Ford without wanting marriage. Such was the case with Joan Crawford and Rita Hayworth, who had sustained an affair with Ford for years, ever since they'd co-starred together in *Gilda* (1946). Barbara Stanwyck had had an affair with Ford, and so had Margaret Sullavan when they had co-starred together in *So Ends Our Night* (1941).

These women had called him back time and time again for repeats, all except Marilyn Monroe with whom he'd had only a brief fling. Starlet Linda Christian had praised his sexual prowess, claiming he was far better than her husband, Tyrone Power, though not as good-looking.

215

When he'd made *A Stolen Life (1946)* with Bette Davis, she had come on to him, but he had rejected her. Forever after, she'd referred to him as "that shithead."

"While shooting in Spain, I had to go into the bullring with a real bull," Debbie said. "I also had another bull chasing me, Glenn Ford, but I ran faster. Don't get the wrong idea. I'm crazy about him, but only as a friend."

When Ford heard she was denying their affair, he told Marshall, "Debbie is still playing Tammy, perhaps forever."

In Spain, heavy rains shut down production for four straight days. Eva Gabor knocked on the door of Debbie's dressing room, claiming, "I feel so alone waiting around to begin shooting. May I come in?"

Debbie immediately adored her Hungarian accent, and imitated her for years in her future stage appearances. Eva always claimed, "I think she sounds more like Zsa Zsa than me."

It was during their first long talk that Debbie learned that Eva herself had been romantically involved with Ford ever since they had co-starred in *Don't Go Near the Water* (1957). She'd had a crush on him after seeing him in *Gilda*. "Glenn was one of my greatest lovers, *dahlink*," Eva told Debbie. "In bed, he's not a hard-driving, demon stud, but has tender qualities like a late teenager trying to please a damsel. He is so endearing with his wonderful masculine aroma that is so intoxicating. Glenn was the second greatest lover of my life after Tyrone Power."

"Glenn was very generous with his magnificent body, allowing me to explore every nook and cranny. He is also a great kisser."

"Stop it!" Debbie said. "You're turning me on."

Eva confessed that she was seeking a new husband, and that Ford would

In yet another example of the percolating sexual giddiness flourishing in Hollywood in the 1950s, Eva Gabor, the youngest of the fabled bombshells from Budapest, had been a lover of Glenn Ford *(upper photo)* since they'd co-starred together in an earlier film.

But on the set of *It Started With a Kiss*, he was spending his nights with Debbie, since Eva had moved on to another lover.

not commit himself. Therefore, she had moved on to another lover. "I want you to meet him. He's an absolute doll, a handsome young stockbroker from Wall Street with plenty of money."

Both Eva and Debbie were staying at the Palace Hotel in Madrid. The following night, she invited Debbie to come with her to her nearby suite to meet Richard Brown, who was to become her next husband.

He wasn't in the bedroom or in the living room of the suite. With Debbie trailing her, Eva opened what turned out to be the door to the bathroom. "*Dahlink*, meet my new beau."

There was Brown, nude in the bathtub without bubbles.

"Don't stand up," Debbie hastened to add.

After greeting him, she and Eva retreated into the living room. "You could clearly see that submarine in the water. That's why I'm attracted to him. As Zsa Zsa would say, it hangs down all the way to Honolulu."

"So it does," Debbie said. "Some girls have all the luck."

"So, you see, we can be friends. You can pursue Glenn. Maybe he'll marry you."

***

On April 2, 1959, the day after Debbie celebrated her 27th birthday, she returned from Spain after completing the location shooting of *It Started With a Kiss*. The final scenes were to be shot in the studio at MGM.

Back in California and united, Ford and Debbie often spent the night together. "Unlike Eddie, who couldn't do a god damn thing around the house, Glenn was a dreamboat both in and out of bed. He could do plumbing, wiring, even air conditioning. When there was a leak in my roof, he climbed up there and repaired it himself, claiming he had once worked as a roofer. He even installed some plate glass windows for me."

He told her when he first came to Hollywood, he'd been a stable boy for Will Rogers. "Once, when he walked into his stable and stepped in a stallion's big, smelly dump, he fired me."

Ronald Reagan married Nancy Davis in March of 1952. Flanking them in this wedding photo are his best friend, Bill Holden (right) and his wife, actress Brenda Marshall.

Before the marriage of Reagan and Davis, Debbie and Glenn Ford had been frequent guests of the couple, always with Bill Holden in tow.

Romantically, during pillow talk, Ford and Debbie often discussed what their future as a married couple might be like: "We'd rise from our bed and head for the studio, where we might be co-starring together in a series of romantic comedies, like Doris Day and Rock Hudson," Ford said.

As a lover, he was the master in bed, giving her instructions about what he liked. "My hot spots begin with my ears and extend to my big toes."

Sometimes, they went out, but never in public. On three different occasions, they visited their mutual friends, Ronald and Nancy Reagan. One night, William Holden was there without his wife. Ford and Holden had been best friends ever since they had co-starred in *Texas* (1941).

"Bill had been drinking heavily, and Nancy suggested we drive him home," Debbie said. "On the way there, Bill hinted that Glenn and I should have a three-way with him. I gathered that these two handsome hunks had done that with the same woman on more than one occasion. Glenn seemed up for it, but I turned down these two horny devils, although it sure did sound like fun."

"Throughout Glenn's future affairs and marriages, I never cracked the enigma of this darling Canadian," she said. "At least, like Eva, I got to enjoy the most romantic sex of my life."

"But I figured he might not make the ideal husband," she said. "He couldn't resist looking at and patting every good-looking woman he met. He loved women. He liked to play with them, touch them everywhere, and flirted shamelessly with them, whether they were married or not. Even during some of his future marriages, he still came to me on certain nights."

"Glenn and I continued to talk about our futures, even though I knew I would probably never become the next Mrs. Glenn Ford. Maybe I could have domesticated him into a loving, faithful, adoring husband, but I seriously doubt that. Not only would we be friends for decades, but we'd even make another romantic comedy. At least I got to play the role of his wife on screen."

***

On May 20, 1959, UPI moved a story across its wires that ended up in a number of newspapers across the country, even the *Salt Lake City Desert News & Telegram*.

HOLLYWOOD—Bachelor King Baudouin of Belgium met an array of glamourous movie stars Tuesday, but he seemed to have eyes only for Hollywood's newest bachelor girl, Debbie Reynolds.

The 28-year-old ruler twice had the petite beauty as his table partner over lunch, and as a party date that night, His Majesty and Miss Reynolds danced into the early morning hours at a party Thursday night in his honor. The event didn't break up until 2AM, about half an hour after Miss Reynolds left. He was seen walking her to her car and whispering in her ear.

Debbie's royal romance had started on the final days of her shooting *It Started With a Kiss* on the MGM lot. The publicity department phoned Ford and her, asking them, as a team, to welcome a royal visitor to the set. It was King Baudouin of Belgium on his three-week tour of America. She was thrilled at the prospect of meeting royalty. She had been told that his favorite movie had been *Singin' in the Rain*.

"I felt like a princess when I got to shake his hand," she said. "He was handsome, standing tall and lanky and reminding me of Jimmy Stewart in his heyday. I had learned he was only two years older than me. Right in front of Glenn's jealous eyes, he devoted all of his attention to me, and he was so polite, so charming, so exciting. When he took my hand, he held it for so long I blushed. The rattlesnake-eating, El Paso tomboy was turning into Cinderella with her Prince Charming, except he was a *bona fide* king."

MGM had planned an elegant luncheon for the king in a private dining room, where he was seated between Debbie and Ford. Other guests included Frank Sinatra, Gina Lollobrigida, and Eva Marie Saint. "He was polite to the other guests, even Glenn, but after his introductions to them, he had eyes only for me," Debbie said.

That night, director Mervyn LeRoy, the discoverer of Lana Turner, hosted a private A-list party for the Baudouin at his ranch-style house in Bel Air.

Before going there, Debbie boned up on just who His Majesty was, at least some of his background so she wouldn't appear ignorant of his history.

Born in 1930, the seductive young monarch was the elder son of King Leopold III and his first wife, Princess Astrid of Sweden. Baudouin's mother had died in an automobile accident when he was five years old, in 1935. After Leopold's abdication in 1951, Baudouin had ascended the throne, becoming the fifth King of Belgium.

He would also become the

On the set of *It Started With a Kiss*, Glenn Ford (right) and Debbie received a royal visitor, King Baudouin of Belgium.

"Right in front of Glenn's jealous eyes, His Highness flirted shamelessly with me," Debbie said.

last Belgian king to be the sovereign of the Congo, which was still a colony of Belgium when he ascended to the throne. The Congolese called their young king *Mwana Kitoko*, meaning "beautiful boy."

At the LeRoy home, the director welcomed Debbie with open arms, as he had admired her work. In 1963, he would award her the lead in his next picture, *Mary, Mary*. He had asked her to come alone so that she could be the king's date for the evening.

For the gala occasion, Helen Rose already had a lime-green gown designed, which Debbie wore with an ermine jacket. "I was practically the only single girl there," she said. "Everybody there was married, especially Robert Wagner and that hussy, Natalie Wood. I had time to chat with the couples before the king arrived, especially Kirk Douglas and Anne Buydens and Dick Powell and his nympho wife, June Allyson."

Thirty minutes after she'd walked in the door of the ranch-style house, she heard a commotion out front. Escorted by police officers on motorcycles, Baudouin had arrived with his security guards and an entourage of eight limousines.

LeRoy had hired a band for the evening, and Baudouin danced every dance with Debbie, whom he held closely in his princely arms. "He was a bit tall for me, but I got to lean into his chest to feel the beat of his heart, which was thumping. I was flattered. I was turning him on, and he could have the pick of any pretty girl in Belgium."

Sometime during the course of the party, with the understanding that he'd slip away from his security forces, Debbie and the king agreed to meet the next day at a secluded café in Culver City.

"I enjoyed the following day when I could play hooky from my bosses at MGM, and he could be free of all those 'handlers' of his."

In anticipation of their rendezvous, she had told him to bring a bathing suit for an outing to the beach in Malibu. "No one recognized us that day. His face wasn't known to Americans, and Miss Debbie Reynolds knew how to disguise herself if she wanted to."

At a secluded spot on the beach, the king and the movie star enjoyed a few hours of sun and surf before retreating to a beach house being rented at the time by Rock Hudson and the Australian actor, Rod Taylor. Hudson had offered it to the king and to Debbie for "a little love in the afternoon like the kind that the aptly named 'Rod' and I have. Enjoy!"

Later, she confessed to Hudson, "His Majesty and I made love all afternoon, and I was transported to heaven. Let's call it more than a royal poke. It was extended lovemaking. I could really go for His Highness. At first he was so sweet, so gentlemanly during the fuck but, as we progressed, he got more and more aggressive. He became wild with excitement. I still have the hots for Glenn, but I also dig Baudouin."

Back in Los Angeles, a sense of panic had broken out among Baudouin's handlers. The king was missing. MGM publicity informed its executive, Benny Thau, of the development, and at the same time told him that Debbie had not shown up on the set that day. She, too, was missing.

It didn't take Thau long to figure out what had happened. He tried to calm the nerves of Baudouin's entourage, explaining that Debbie had driven their leader either up the coast or perhaps to Palm Springs for some "sightseeing." He apologized profusely for this indiscretion, and suggested that it would be better for everyone to keep this out of the newspapers.

The sun was setting when a very sexually satisfied Debbie drove Baudouin back to his hotel, returning him at last to his security forces. Before he exited from her car, he kissed her hand. "Until we meet again, Sweet Lady."

Once it was determined that the king was safe, Debbie faced the fury of the chief of his security contingent. "He turned out to be a real shit," she told Hudson. "He reminded me that I was a commoner and, as such, was not allowed to socialize with or travel with the king."

His father, King Leopold, married a commoner after his first wife died, and it created a scandal throughout Belgium. "We will do everything to prevent His Majesty from falling into the same trap," the security chief told Debbie.

At MGM the next day, Thau came to Debbie's dressing room and delivered a stern lecture, threatening her with suspension "if you ever pull a stunt like that again."

"Benny, don't get so fucking hot under the collar," Debbie said. "You can't blame a gal for trying out for another role."

"What role are you talking about?" he asked.

"That of Queen of Belgium and First Lady of the Congo. Not bad for Little Miss Burbank of 1948."

[During Baudouin's reign, the colony, formerly known as the Belgian Congo, became independent. Patrice Lumumba became the newly independent nation's prime minister.]

"Even though I was too common for a king, I got one more chance at Baudouin," Debbie told Hudson.

The final stop of Baudouin's North American tour was scheduled for New York,

In December of 1960, Baudouin was married in Brussels to Doña Fabiola de Mora y Aragón.

For years after the fact, Debbie remembered her liaison with Baudouin with nostalgia and a sense of "what might have been."

where a lavish party was being hosted in his honor at the Waldorf Astoria. It was widely understood that it would be attended by a lot of dignitaries, including the Mayor of New York.

Having wrapped *It Started With a Kiss,* and with time on her hands. Debbie secretly flew to New York, where she crashed the party. Even though she hadn't received an invitation, security let her go into the ballroom, after she threatened to create a scene if they didn't.

When Baudouin spotted her in another stunning gown by Helen Rose, he gravitated to her right away. "He danced all his dances with me."

At around midnight, as the party was winding down, he whispered to her to meet him in his suite in half an hour, after he'd bid goodnight to the other guests.

Back in Hollywood, she phoned Hudson with news: "I got to spend the night in Baudouin's arms, perhaps for the last time. It was a deep probe, if you get my drift. He is the man for me. To hell with Eddie Fisher. And if the king asks me to fly to Brussels., I'll even tell Glenn (Ford) to go fuck himself. But that's not gonna happen, and both of us know it. The king knows it, too."

[She was a bit sad to read a story in the newspaper dated December 15, 1960. In Brussels, the king had married Dona Fabiola de Mora y Aragón. "She became his consort, not me. Poor me. Lucky girl. However, their marriage in time became a sort of tragedy. He desperately wanted an heir to the throne, but all five of her pregnancies ended with miscarriages."

"I could have given him children, even a son. After all, I produced Todd. The Belgian crown passed to his younger brother, Albert II, when darling Baudouin died in the summer of 1993, perhaps never knowing the happiness he could have found with me. Such a dear, dear man. Even though I'm a commoner, I could have learned to be a regal queen, perhaps taking lessons from Liz."

No doubt she was referring to Queen Elizabeth II of Great Britain — and not Elizabeth Taylor, who was only a queen on the screen when she was cast as Cleopatra.]

***

"During my final years as an MGM contract player, my co-stars and I were always welcoming kings, queens, and princes to the lot. Royals wanted to meet movie stars during their visits to Hollywood. We were considered movie royalty. Forgive the lack of modesty in my saying that. Ironically, I got in-

According to Debbie, "Although I had married a Jew, after the marriage ended, I indulged in some heavy petting with a handsome Arab, King Hussein of Jordan. I felt this 'iron bar' in his pants."

volved with yet another royal highness during the making of *It Started With a Kiss*," Debbie said. "It was King Hussein of Jordan."

When he arrived on the set, both Ford and Debbie formally greeted him. Almost immediately, he told them that his two favorite movies were *Singin' in the Rain* and *The Teahouse of the August Moon*, each of which he had ordered to be shown on several occasions in his royal palace in Jordan.

Ford smiled politely. What Hussein didn't know was that *Teahouse* was his least favorite movie, because he'd had an ongoing and rather bitter feud with his co-star, Marlon Brando, whom Ford had labeled "an arrogant prick."

Although Debbie didn't know a lot about Hussein before his arrival, the publicity department at MGM filled her in on his biography. They also loudly warned her not to create a royal scandal as she'd done when she ran off with King Baudouin without telling anyone.

She learned that after the abdication of Hussein's father, Talal, in the summer of 1952, the seventeen-year-old Hussein had ascended to the throne. When he met Debbie, he had recently divorced his first wife, Dina bint Abdul-Hamid, whom he'd married in 1955. Before his death in 1999, he would marry four times and father eleven children.

Over lunch, he described to Debbie and Ford that he was not one of the oil-rich royal princes, as his country was rather barren of natural resources. "During one cold winter, when I was a child living with my family in Amman, my sister, Princess Anna, died of pneumonia because we couldn't afford to heat our big palace."

He also told fascinating stories about his dynasty, which Debbie claimed "were straight out of *Arabian Nights*." In 1916, his namesake, Hussein bin Ali, had led an Arab revolt against the Turkish forces of the Ottoman Empire. Hussein asserted his status as the 40th direct descendant of Muhammad, and that he was a son of the Hashemites who had ruled Mecca for 700 years, making it the oldest dynasty in the Muslim world.

For his lunchtime appointment, he appeared in MGM's commissary wearing a regal dress uniform with gold shoulder emblems and medals on his chest.

"He was short, like me," Debbie said. "I found him charming and rather flirtatious. He certainly had an eye for the ladies. He didn't pay much attention to Glenn, and when he did, he inadvertently insulted him. When speaking of *Teahouse*, he spent most of the time praising Brando's performance."

"He was no Baudouin, but I liked him immensely," she said. "When Glenn was called back to the set, I stayed on in the commissary chatting with him. He kept telling me how beautiful I was, more beautiful than any royal princess he'd ever seen. He invited me to dinner in his hotel suite that evening at nine."

She spent two hours getting dressed for the occasion. Helen Rose rushed to finish a champagne-colored gown she'd been working on.

"I appeared at Hussein's door and was let in by a security guard," Debbie said. "The gown had plunging *décolletage* without showing my nipples. After all, I wasn't Jayne Mansfield letting it all hang out tits and all. I have breasts, but not milk jugs."

The next day, she phoned Rock Hudson, her *confidant* in all matters sexual. "I had to talk to somebody," she said, revealing what had transpired the previous evening between Hussein and herself.

"The dinner was divine, and so was he. I thought seduction was in the cards, but it did not lead to intercourse. However, we did indulge in heavy petting that would have resunk the *Titanic*." [*Ironically, she'd made a reference to the doomed ocean liner that would later form part of the plot of* The Unsinkable Molly Brown.]

"I never got to see what color his silk drawers were," she confessed to Hudson. "But I did get to see him without his shirt. He's a real breast man. As a little baby, he must have drained his mother dry sucking on her tits."

She admitted to having arrived at a strange insight during their love-making: "I thought of Eddie, who is a Jew, as you know, and of Elizabeth, who converted to Judaism. In some perverse way, I was getting revenge, making out with an Arab. I know that's ridiculous, but that's what crossed my mind at the time."

"You mean to tell me that you didn't unzip him and have a close encounter with the royal prick?"

"No, but I felt it a few times. Unlike 'Long John' (a reference to Baudouin), it was a bit on the short side but like a bar of iron. I could have pressed my clothes with it. While working over my breasts, I think he erupted in his pants. That's the reason we didn't go all the way."

After that, she never saw Hussein again, but other Middle East royals lay in her future. In a memoir, she gave only "vanilla" descriptions of her close encounters with some of them, referring to them as "magic carpet rides" to the mysteries of the East.

***

Almost daily, pressure was mounting on Debbie to grant Eddie Fisher a divorce in Nevada so that he and Elizabeth Taylor would not have to wait for a year to marry, as defined by California law.

On her last day at MGM shooting *It Started With a Kiss,* a reporter confronted her: "Last night, Elizabeth Taylor claimed you were wrecking her life and Eddie Fisher's life by not going ahead with your divorce."

She brushed him aside, even though she sensed the tide of public opinion was beginning to shift against her. She decided that the time had come for her to agree to divorce her husband, who seemed desperately in love with the "siren of the screen." At this point, there was absolutely no hope of a reconciliation. Also, at the time, she was deep into a continuation of her affair with Glenn Ford, who was at the time still in the throes of a divorce from Eleanor

Powell.

On the day she agreed to free Fisher, she sarcastically remarked, "God forbid that I should deny Elizabeth Taylor another lover." Privately, she said, "Elizabeth will chew up little Eddie Fisher and spit him out. As a father, forget it," she said. "Eddie didn't even drop in to see Carrie and Todd. They were very young. I'm not sure at this point they even knew they had a dad."

Her family members were very supportive, Minnie and Roy visiting frequently and helping with the grandchildren. Her brother Billy moved into the basement room of her house and agreed to stay there as long as she needed him.

In Las Vegas, Fisher was appearing at the Tropicana when news came that Debbie had agreed to give him a divorce. On his opening night, after hearing the news, he came on stage and sang the Eddie Cantor standard, "Makin' Whoopie." As he sang "another bride, another June, another sunny honeymoon," the spotlight focused on a dazzling Elizabeth Taylor, who was prominently positioned in the audience, laden with diamonds, rubies, and emeralds.

She later told the press, "I've signed to do two more films. After that, I plan to desert the movies and become a housewife and mother forever." The news stunned and disappointed her fans.

After his opening night performance, Fisher threw a party for his friends at the Hidden Well and Ranch outside town, which he was renting for $500 a week. He invited a list of VIP guests, along with his usual friends and cronies. Ronald and Nancy Reagan arrived, as did Rock Hudson and Tony Curtis, who were sharing a double bed in a suite at the Tropicana.

Fisher had visited both of the male stars earlier that day in their suite. Hudson invited him to come into the bedroom "for some fun with Tony and me." Fisher turned down the offer, asking "for a raincheck."

Debbie had reason to worry about Fisher making any alimony payments. Not only was he spending nearly all of his money on Elizabeth, he was losing heavily at the dice tables of Vegas. Leaving out a lot of the personal details, Hudson brought her up to date on what was going on since he'd just visited with Fisher and Tony Curtis in Las Vegas.

"By the way," he said. "Tony wants to make a movie with you."

"Bring it on," she said. "I think we'd make a great screen team, but you and I would be even better."

"I'm sure that will happen one day, too," Hudson promised.

***

Hudson had not exaggerated about Fisher being a spendthrift. He had gone through his cash reserve quickly, giving Elizabeth a $270,000 diamond bracelet, a diamond-studded evening bag, and a $500,000 emerald necklace from Bulgari.

On February 19, 1959, Debbie arrived at the Superior Court in the heart of Los Angeles with her attorney, Frank Belcher, and her loyal friend, Camille Williams.

Before the judge, Debbie testified that Fisher "has treated me in a cruel and inhuman manner." She also claimed that he had taken up with "a notorious woman" without naming her. "This has caused me great pain and embarrassment. I think I should be granted a divorce on the grounds of abandonment, if nothing else."

A 48-page settlement agreement was presented to the court, and the judge approved it and granted the divorce decree to "Edwin Jack Fisher and Mary Frances Reynolds." Each party would be free to marry in one year. The next day, Debbie faced banner headlines: DEBBIE GETS MILLION DOLLAR SETTLEMENT.

She was granted both of their homes in Hollywood and a much more modest vacation house in Palm Springs. She went on to assert that she would receive $36,000 a year for the first two years, followed by $30,000 a year after that until she either remarried or died.

[Fisher, according to Debbie, paid only two of these annual payments before informing her that he had run out of money. NBC canceled his television show, and, in essence, he would have to spend the next few months, perhaps longer, as the "kept boy" of Elizabeth. She had financial woes of her own, since Mike Todd had emptied their bank accounts with his extravagance.]

But both Elizabeth and Fisher didn't want to wait for a year to get married. He begged Debbie to agree to a "second" divorce in either Nevada or Mexico, but at first she stubbornly refused. "I just didn't feel like it," she claimed. Privately, she told Williams and other friends, "I hate Eddie Fisher."

But eventually, she decided to "wash that man right out of my hair." On May 12, Fisher, with Debbie's approval, appeared in a Las Vegas courthouse before Judge David Zenoff. After a twelve-minute hearing, he was granted his divorce from Debbie and now was free to marry Elizabeth.

Debbie was told that her divorced husband and his bride-to-be went immediately to the marriage bureau in Las Vegas's Town Hall and applied for a marriage license. The happy couple were wed in a civil ceremony in the courthouse, followed by a "blessing" in the Temple Beth Shalom.

Mike Todd, Jr. was Fisher's best man, and Elizabeth's sister-in-law, Mara Taylor, was her matron of honor. Fisher wore a dark business suit with a white yarmulke, and she appeared in a stunning green chiffon dress designed by Jean-Louis.

Honored guests included Eddie Cantor, her hairdresser Sydney Guilaroff, and her secretary Dick Hanley. Benny Thau, representing MGM, fretted that Elizabeth's high standing at the box office would be threatened.

After the wedding, Elizabeth told the press, "I've made the right choice in a man. Eddie and I will grow old together. Our honeymoon will last thirty or forty years. Let me tell you something: A career makes a poor bedfellow on a cold night."

In Hollywood, Debbie responded to reporters asking her about her former husband's new wife with this: "So the widow Todd has married again: The union will probably last eight months, if that. After all, I'm sure she'll marry again, many, many times. Perhaps she'll go after some married man. Stewart Granger or Robert Taylor, come to mind. I'm sure she's checked out each of them before. Okay, boys, let's wrap it. The soap opera's over. Time to move on. Next chapter!"

As time went by, Fisher became increasingly bitter toward Debbie. "She is the girl next door all right, but only if you live next door to a totally self-centered, totally driven, insecure, untruthful phony."

One night, as a means of recovering from her divorce blues, Debbie phoned Rock Hudson and asked him to accompany her to the chic, star-studded restaurant, Chasen's. She wanted to appear again before the world as a divorced woman getting on with her new life, not the weeping, deserted spouse.

Hudson and Debbie were shocked that evening by the presence there of some of their fellow diners: Fisher and Elizabeth were sitting at the best table, conspicuously holding hands. Several tables away, Michael Wilding, Elizabeth's second husband, was

"At long last, I got to marry the man of my dreams from back in the 1950s," Debbie said. "At least I married him as part of the plot of my latest film, *Say One for Me.*"

In the top photo, she's depicted auditioning for a stage show, and in the middle photo, she's shown as a movie bride marrying the character played by R.J.

In the lower photo, she's being guided in prayer by Bing Crosby, who's playing a priest.

there with some starlet. At yet another nearby table sat Elizabeth's first husband, hotel heir Nicky Hilton with actress Terry Moore.

"At least all of us sat at separate tables that night," Debbie said. "No communal tables for that whoring crowd."

***

At first, Debbie was titillated when producer-director Frank Tashlin phoned her to tell her that she'd been assigned the female lead in his next picture, *Say One for Me*. MGM was lending her to 20th Century Fox for this 1959 release. Tashlin had previously helmed her in *Susan Slept Here* (1953).

She was surprised, then somewhat taken aback, to learn that Bing Crosby and her former "flame," Bob Wagner, would be her leading men. She'd have to sing a duet, "Say One for Me," with Crosby, and sing and dance with Wagner, who was hardly a song-and-dance man. Would this project become an example of miscasting?

Wagner stirred up romantic memories, even though both of them had gone their separate ways. She told her girlfriends, "I don't want to sound too dramatic, or too poetic, but my love affair with Bob belongs to the stardust memories of yesterday. We were both young, just starting out in the business. I hear he's taken up with some actress—what's her name?"

Debbie knew perfectly well who Natalie Wood was.

She confessed in a memoir that RJ still reminded her of "my fantasy life. But he wasn't that interested, so get over it, Debbie. During the making of the film, I kept mostly to myself, since I was going through a divorce. I still had a crush on R.J., and I do to this day. There is no man more terrific."

She knew Tashlin had been an animator and that he continued his involvement in the production of a well-known comic strip, signing his name to it as "Tish Tash." He'd also written gags and screenplays for the likes of the Marx Brothers, Lucille Ball, and both Bob Hope and Red Skelton. He'd also worked on six of Jerry Lewis' early solo films, including *The Geisha Boy* (1958).

Her reunion with Tashlin ended badly when he bluntly told her, "Bing didn't want you for the role. He said you're not a real singer."

"I never pretended to be," she said. "Who does he think he is to judge me? Frank Sinatra? Now that's a crooner who really knows how to sing."

After reading the script of *Say One for Me* by Robert O'Brien, Debbie knew this wasn't going to be another *Singin' in the Rain* for her. Her role was that of Holly LeMaise, the daughter of an oldtime vaudevillian. She is forced to take a job as a showgirl in a nightclub to pay the medical bills of dear old dad, who has fallen ill.

The featured entertainer at the nightclub is Tony Vincent (Wagner), a playboy chasing after all the showgirls, who usually give in to him because of his dashing good looks. But when the new girl arrives, Wagner turns his attention to the sweet, innocent-looking Holly, and begins to pursue her with seduction on his mind.

Holly is one of the parishioners in the church of Father Conroy (as portrayed by Bing Crosby), whose church is in the theater district of Manhattan. After attending one of the shows at Tony's club, he's horrified that the womanizer might be trying to corrupt little Holly.

The usual complications and entanglements ensue, but we're heading for a happy ending with this one, as the priest ends up officiating at the wedding of Holly and Tony as THE END flashes on the screen.

When she saw the finished product, Debbie told her friends, "Holly marries Tony in the movie. I should have married R.J. I'm sure Natalie Wood is far more experienced in bed than I am. But R.J. could teach me all the ways I could sexually satisfy him. I'm a fast learner. One night at a party, Steve McQueen confided to me that he never saw what was so great about Natalie. 'She's lousy in bed,' he said."

Crosby had played the role of a priest before, and far more convincingly. In *Going My Way* 1944), he'd won the Best Actor Oscar.

Wagner claimed that he didn't like working with Tashlin, but he felt "I was not so bad as a singer and dancer. Of course, I was no Fred Astaire."

He revealed that "Debbie was going through a rough time in her life in the middle of divorcing Fisher. She kept mostly to herself, retreating to her dressing room at the end of the shoot. She was fragile, so I spent most of my free time with Bing talking golf."

Tashlin said, "I'd heard that R.J. had the hots for Debbie, and I expected him to make frequent trips to her dressing room to plug her. But not once did I see him go after her."

According to Wagner, "When I made that movie with Debbie, I was spending my nights enjoying the Hollywood social scene with Natalie."

Tashlin asked Debbie if she were jealous that Natalie got her man. "What can I say?" she answered. "She got him, I didn't. At the time I was foolishly wearing a chastity belt, and Natalie was giving it away to every man who could get it up in Hollywood, from Jimmy Dean to Nicky Hilton, from David Niven to Frank Sinatra. She even got Raymond Burr to fuck her, and he's as gay as a goose."

At its premiere in June of 1959, *Say One for Me* was panned by *Variety:* "Something went wrong in this film's development. Box office will have to depend on the marquee names of Bing Crosby and Debbie Reynolds. At least Crosby's voice is still there, and Debbie is…well, Debbie."

The *Hollywood Citizen News* found the movie "sometimes monotonous, a photodrama with music." Bosley Crowther of *The New York Times* wrote that "Bing will never make Monsignor. He'll always be a parish priest."

Historically, *Say One for Me* was listed in the 1978 book, *The Fifty Worst Films of All Time.*

Although Crosby had objected to working with Debbie, she won him over with her professionalism and dedication to her role. He even agreed to give her a quote for the record sleeve of her first album, entitled *Debbie*. He was mild in his praise, however. "I listened to this beautiful album Debbie Reynolds has etched for Dot, and found myself captivated and enchanted."

Privately, Debbie told Tashlin, "I think Bing was attracted to me, enough to pinch my ass. But he's a bit old for me. Grace Kelly, Dorothy Lamour, and Jane Wyman are welcome to him."

***

One night with her latest picture wrapped, and a new one not begun, Debbie sat in her living room. "I don't think I've ever been as lonely in my life. But my calendar was about to fill up…and how!"

An hour earlier, she'd received a call from Joan Crawford who invited her for dinner the following night, an invitation Debbie accepted. After watching Jack Benny on television, she decided to turn in early, having already put Todd and Carrie to bed.

At around 10:30PM, her phone rang, and she picked up the receiver, thinking it might be Fisher calling to inquire about the welfare of his children. He hadn't phoned for weeks, and Carrie often looked out the living room window into their driveway, thinking he might pull up at any minute.

On the phone was a very distinctive voice she recognized from years of moviegoing. "It's Bob Mitchum. Debbie?"

"Bob?" What a surprise. Is something wrong? I hope you're calling to tell me I'm the co-star of your next movie."

"Maybe someday. Something else has come up. Right now, my car is just ten blocks from your house. Can I drop in?"

She hesitated only a moment. "I guess…if you want."

Chapter Eight

DEBBIE'S "NEW NORMAL"

As a Desirable, Ambitious, & Hard-working

HOLLYWOOD ENTERTAINER

Divorced, Famous, and Single, She's Out and About with Some of the World's Richest & Most Eligible Bachelors

Robert Mitchum, a Pimp for Howard Hughes, Defines His Rape of Debbie as "Consensual Sex"

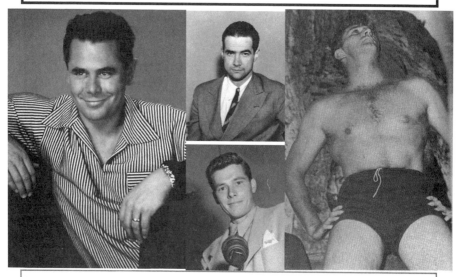

Free at last from Eddie Fisher, Debbie Reynolds was at the peak of her beauty and sexuality as she set out to hook up with some of the most desirable men in Hollywood. Some of them were movie stars, others handsome enough, but very, very rich.

These included Glenn Ford (left), Howard Hughes (top photo center), Nicky Hilton (lower photo center), and Robert Mitchum (right).

From afar, she had fallen in love with Ford when he co-starred in *Gilda* (1946) with love goddess Rita Hayworth, playing a twisted hero and misogynist who may also have been shacked up with George Macready..

Way back in 1953, Howard Hughes at RKO had originally wanted Robert Mitchum to co-star with Debbie in *Susan Slept Here*. He had refused. "I don't dance," Mitchum had informed its director, Frank Tashlin. "I sing a bit, but I'm not doing it. Get Dick Powell."

In retaliation for his refusal, RKO had put him on suspension until he agreed to return to the studio and accept his next assignment.

Now, several years and many films later, as he sat across from Debbie in her living room, enjoying another drink, (he'd had several before arriving), she found him strangely appealing, primarily because of his sly wit, self-deprecation, and refreshing candor. "I look like a shark with a broken nose," he said. "Some jerk wrote that I have lizard eyes and an anteater nose."

"I've always found you very handsome on the screen," she said. "And I'm not alone. you have fan clubs all over America. I wish you'd made *Susan Slept Here* with me. Nobody could believe that Dick Powell and I were a romantic couple. Some critics thought he came off like a child molester because he was so much older than me."

Mitchum's reputation had preceded him. Though married to the long-suffering Dorothy Spence, he was known for sleeping around. In time, he'd sustain affairs with Lucille Ball, Rita Hayworth, Shirley MacLaine, and maybe Jane Russell. Rumor had it that when he first arrived in Hollywood, he was a male hustler, his major means of support being Clifton Webb. His boss at RKO, Howard Hughes, was also rumored to "have the hots for Mitchum."

Once at a party, Debbie had asked Jane Greer about the link between Mitchum and Hughes. Greer

Rugged Robert Mitchum was known for lighting up, but he didn't always smoke regular tobacco.

"Robert Mitchum is not for the faint of heart," Debbie claimed. "He was a raging drunk, womanizer, pot smoker, rapist, calypso singer, and a trench-coated *film noir* movie star with a huge, uncontrollable ego."

In the lower photo, he's throwing a hand grenade in his depiction of *The Story of G.I. Joe* (1945)

had co-starred with Mitchum in the memorable *film noir*, *Out of the Past* (1947).

"I think Bob is a fantasy alter ego for Howard," Greer told Debbie. "Whereas Howard has always doubted his masculinity, Bob seems completely assured of his. Women gravitate to Bob like bees to the sweet nectar of an aromatic flower. Deep down, Howard suspects that women come on to him only because of his money and power, which is so often the case."

Debbie's former co-star, Dick Powell, had told her that he thought Hughes lived vicariously through Mitchum. "He admires Bob's super cool attitude toward women."

Mitchum had confessed to Powell that, "All the broads throw themselves at me, but frankly, I don't give a god damn if they do or not. If they want what I've got, fine; otherwise, they can go fuck themselves. I'm not going to beg for it."

"Howard spent a fortune wooing Ava Gardner," Powell said. "He gave her jewelry, cars, free airline tickets. But all Bob had to do was snap his fingers, and Ava came running."

Debbie wasn't surprised when Mitchum asked if he could roll a marijuana cigarette. All of Hollywood, and much of America, too, had heard of his arrest on September 1, 1948, following a drug raid on Ridpath Drive in Laurel Canyon. He was arrested with actress Lila Leeds, described by columnist James Bacon as "one of the most beautiful women in Hollywood—looks like Lana Turner, only cuter."

As punishment, a judge had sentenced him to sixty days of intensive labor at the Wayside Honor Farm in Castaic, California, some 42 miles north of Los Angeles.

Out of curiosity, Debbie wanted to know what it was like working with Marilyn Monroe on the picture, *River of No Return* (1954).

"Marilyn's okay," he said, "but she didn't have to go and tell some nosy reporter that I had bad breath and was a lousy kisser. I've known her for years. I first met her when she was Norma Jean, and I worked at the Lockheed Aircraft Factory with her first husband, Jim Dougherty."

Without actually confirming it, Mitchum suggested to Debbie that he'd seduced Marilyn when she was only a teenager—and a married one at that.

As the hands of a grandfather clock moved into the early morning hours, he had not yet revealed why he was visiting her at this hour. Did he want to seduce her, or was he but an agent serving the interests of Hughes, who was known for chasing after recently divorced women.

"Howard wants to drive you to Las Vegas this weekend," Mitchum told her. "It seems he wants to talk over a movie deal, a real dramatic part with top-notch roles for both of us. I'm not suggesting any casting couch. This is a legit deal."

"I'd be most interested," she said. "Surely, I don't need to tell you that at this point in my career, I don't have to lie on anyone's casting couch."

"I already know that. There's no casting couch involved with me. That doesn't mean I wouldn't like a roll in the hay with you. You're a real cutie, and I know you're not a virgin, certainly not after living with Eddie Fisher. So stop acting like one."

"I'll take you up on that meeting with Hughes, but I'll turn down the roll in the hay."

"In that case, I need something else," he said. "I'm too high to drive without killing myself or someone else. Can I rent your guest room for the night?"

"That's reasonable," she said, "since Eddie no longer sleeps there. He left behind a pair of pajamas."

"Don't need them," he said. "I sleep jaybird naked."

"Suit yourself," she said. "I'll show you the room."

She had fallen into a deep sleep when she heard a knock on her door at around 4AM. "It's Bob," he called out. "Can I come in?"

'Oh, Bob, go back to bed. Get some sleep."

Without an invitation, he threw open the door. In the light of the hallway, he appeared naked and aroused. "I'm horny," he said, moving toward her bed.

What happened next is the subject of some dispute, one of those "he said, she said" kind of encounters.

Later, she told her confidantes that "Bob raped me. Suddenly, he was on top of me, a big load. I'm tiny. He overpowered me."

Mitchum presented a different story: "I raped her for only a minute. After that, she was urging me on. She enjoyed it. A man can tell. I mean she *really* enjoyed it. After all those months of not getting any from Fisher, she was hungry and, as is well known in Hollywood, I have meat for the poor."

***

During their early years as Hollywood starlets, Debbie and Terry Moore were friends. Moore had achieved early success when she was nominated for a Best Supporting Actress Oscar for her role in the 1952 film, *Come Back, Little Sheba*, starring Shirley Booth and Burt Lancaster. Debbie's early success, as the world knows, was her starring role in *Singin' in the Rain* (1952)

On their first visit to Las Vegas in 1953, Debbie and Moore had stayed at the Desert Inn, the desert abode of Howard Hughes who occupied an entire floor for himself and his frequently changing en-

Starlet Terry Moore received an Oscar nomination for her role in *Come Back, Little Sheba* (1952), a role that Debbie had coveted.

But was she really married to Howard Hughes?

tourage. He had arranged for their use of a suite, as he was having an affair with Moore.

"Terry was one busy gal in those days," Debbie claimed. "She had three men on the string: Hughes himself; Nicky Hilton, the hotel heir and first husband of Elizabeth Taylor; and Bob Neal, the Maxwell House heir and one of America's most eligible bachelors."

"Since Terry was dating all three, I wondered how she kept her social calendar straight," Debbie said. "One night she didn't, and I had to cover for her with Hughes."

Although she maintained an uneasy friendship with Moore, Debbie was jealous of her for reasons not associated with Hughes. When Moore had been a player in *Beyond the 12-Mile Reef* (1953), rumors flew that she was having a torrid affair with her co-star, Robert Wagner, for whom Debbie still harbored a crush.

Without checking with Wagner, the publicity department at 20th Century Fox released some hasty feature stories about their romance, betting that they'd be good for box office. Later, Fox released some fabricated (and completely false) news about their engagement.

Debbie continued her hidden resentment of Moore for years until she read Wagner's 2008 memoir, *Pieces of My Heart.* It revealed that throughout the filming of *Beneath the 12-Mile Reef,* Wagner was still living with, and in love with, Barbara Stanwyck. Simultaneously, Moore was having an affair with Hughes, and eventually became pregnant with his child.

"Terry was very weepy when she told me of her condition," Wagner said. "So both of us were blindsided by all this engagement nonsense. Terry was not in love with me, and I was not in love with her. Frankly, I was livid at Fox for trying to railroad us into marriage. Perhaps they'd learned of Terry's pregnancy and were trying to rush us to the altar."

Eventually, the story died a natural death. "My marriage to Terry did not happen," Wagner said. "Neither did that baby of hers."

The romantic publicity helped the movie. Eventually, it grossed $4 million at the box office, and Wagner's salary rose from $350 a week to $1,250.

"I never knew if all those tales about the romantic involvements of Terry were true or not," Debbie said. "If so, she had some classy boyfriends. One was 'Mr. Cocksman,' Greg Bautzer, when he wasn't screwing Lana Turner or Joan Crawford."

Also according to Debbie, "Moore was also rumored to be carrying on with Prince Mahmed Pahlavi, the brother of the Shah of Iran. In a touch of irony, I scored an upmanship with her on that one. I got to hang out with the actual Shah of Iran. Terry was also rumored to be involved with Henry Kissinger, that ugly old toad who was Richard Nixon's Secretary of State."

Moore confided many strange stories about Howard Hughes's eccentricities to Debbie. She was said to have lost her virginity to him, and also to have married him in 1949 aboard his yacht in international waters off the coast of Mexico. When Hughes died, she got a large settlement from the estate. "We were never divorced," Moore claimed.

"When I got to know Howard, I asked him if he had really married Terry," Debbie said. "He told me it was just a mock ceremony at sea with no legal binding."

Moore also told Debbie that Hughes would insist that she wash her hands for more than ten minutes at a time, since he had this fetish about cleanliness. He also was fascinated by her bowel movements and wanted complete reports. And in the event that she couldn't remember when she'd passed her last bowel movement, he'd give her laxatives and supervise her "progress."

None of these stories ever tempted Debbie to get personally involved with Hughes.

"Terry also moved in on Elizabeth Taylor's territory," Debbie said. "Or should I say Elizabeth's 'abandoned territory?'"

She was referring to Moore's affair with football star Glenn Davis, who had been one of Elizabeth's early lovers. And, as mentioned, Moore began an affair with Nicky Hilton shortly after Elizabeth divorced him.

There was another irony: Moore's third husband (1959-72) was Stuart Warren Cramer III, who had previously been married to the actress Jean Peters. Eventually, Peters became Hughes' final wife. "Tinseltown gets pretty incestuous at times," Debbie said.

At the Desert Inn in Las Vegas, Hughes had reserved a beautifully furnished suite and arranged to have it filled with flowers, turning it over to Debbie as a means of welcoming her to the gambling mecca of America. An invitation was waiting for her to dine with Mitchum and Hughes at eight that evening.

As Mitchum had promised, Hughes discussed the idea of teaming them together in a film, mainly because they were such different types. Someone had sent him a script about a couple who meet in Vegas, fall in love, and get married. The script went on to relate how, after her groom installed her back in his home town in Indiana, the ex-showgirl tries to adjust to life on the farm and his ultra-religious and moralistic parents. The drama pivots around how two very different people in love make adjustments for each other "with a lot of compromises along the way" (Hughes' words). The script idea intrigued Debbie more than it did Mitchum.

After dinner, Mitchum excused himself, saying he had a hot date. Debbie suspected it was with the blonde-haired actress Gloria Grahame, whom she knew only slightly. Before dinner, she'd seen them having a drink together in the bar. Mitchum's affair with Grahame had begun when they had co-starred together in *Crossfire* (1947).

At one point, she'd been married to Nicholas Ray, the director. But when he returned to their home one afternoon and found his wife in bed with Tony, his 13-year-old son, he kicked him out and later divorced her. In time, Grahame married Tony and had two sons with him, thereby defining him as stepfather to his own stepbrother, who was only ten years younger than Tony.

***

Should Debbie be added to Howard Hughes' long list of movie star seductions? Apparently, the answer is yes. Columnist James Bacon called him "Hollywood's greatest swordsman."

Hughes' movie star lovers included Bette Davis, Carole Lombard, Billie Dove, Yvonne De Carlo, Ava Gardner, Kathryn Grayson, Jean Harlow, Susan Hayward, Veronica Lake, Katharine Hepburn, Gene Tierney, Lana Turner, Ginger Rogers, Rita Hayworth, Shelley Winters, and inevitably, Marilyn Monroe. One of his lovers, Paulette Goddard, said, "Howard would have five or six girls a day."

As a bisexual, Hughes also seduced some of the leading men of Golden Age Hollywood, including Clark Gable, Robert Taylor, Errol Flynn, Gary Cooper, Guy Madison, and both Cary Grant and his lover, Randolph Scott.

Debbie never provided any particularly fulsome details about her involvement with Hughes. She did state, however, that she was "the perfect type for Howard. He liked young girls with big breasts like Terry Moore. My breasts were never the equal of Jane Russell in his famous movie, *The Outlaw* (1943), but it was obvious that he found me very appealing."

The next day, a hotel maid told Mitchum that Debbie had not slept in her bed in her own suite. She'd spent the weekend in Hughes' quarters.

In a memoir, Debbie wrote that "Howard taught me to play craps. We stood together in the casino at the Desert Inn for two hours. He didn't bring me any luck. I didn't win a damn cent, but it was fun. I stuck to one-dollar chips, so was hardly known as a big spender like my former husband. Howard didn't even buy one chip, even though he was the richest man in America."

In time, Debbie became well acquainted with Moore's other two boyfriends, Nicky Hilton and Bob Neal. She'd actually started to date Neal, that rich Texan with the Maxwell House fortune, before she met and married Eddie Fisher. "Minnie wanted me to marry Bob."

She would resume her relationship with Neal in the wake of her divorce. She also became intimate with his best friend, Nicky Hilton. But those two handsome hunks would have to wait until after she made another picture with

Glenn Ford, during the filming of which she would resume her affair with him.

***

Debbie was delighted when director George Marshall reteamed her with Glenn Ford in *The Gazebo* (1959) for MGM, a CinemaScope black comedy. It was a story about a couple being blackmailed.

Debbie's longtime designer, Helen Rose, was hired to create her wardrobe. Based on those outfits, Rose would later be nominated for an Oscar for Best Costume Design.

"Helen made me look gorgeous in my role as Nell Nash, a Broadway star, married to Glenn, who played my husband, Elliott, a television writer and director."

"I was in my post-divorce blues, looking for love in all the wrong places with all the wrong men, and Glenn was in the throes of an agonizing divorce from that tap dancer he'd been married to for sixteen long years." Debbie was referring to her "competition," Eleanor Powell, the mother of his son, Peter.

Powell was going to gain custody of their son according to the terms of their divorce. "That's not all she's getting," Ford told Debbie. According to California's divorce laws, she'd receive half of their communal property, valued at around $750,000, plus their home on Cove Way and an annual payment of $40,000 for six years. After that, the yearly alimony would be lowered to $30,000 for the rest of her life. In addition, she would receive $250 a month in child support.

Debbie read in the paper that a reporter had asked Powell if she'd return to the screen. "I don't know," she told him. "I'm now forty-seven years old, and I feel like eighty-nine."

The Gazebo had originated in 1958 as a play on Broadway starring Walter Slezak. The comedy had been written by Alec Coppel and Frederick Brisson (i.e., Mr. Rosalind Russell).

Ford told Debbie that at first he didn't think the play would make a good film, but he finally approved the script by George Wells, who had been hired by producer Lawrence Weingarten. Six years later, Weingarten would cast Debbie in *The Unsinkable Molly Brown* (1964). He had long been a supporter of her career, having cast her oppo-

In this publicity shot from *The Gazebo*, Debbie kisses her co-star Glenn Ford. "In real life, I did more than kiss him."

site Frank Sinatra in *The Tender Trap*.

Debbie assured Ford, "We'll make it work, and we won't have to hide the sexual chemistry between us. In case a gal hasn't told you yet, you're all man!"

In *The Gazebo*, Elliott is being blackmailed by Dan Shelby (voice of Stanley Adams) over nude photographs taken of Nell when she was eighteen. Elliott fears that if they're leaked to the press, it will destroy his wife's Broadway career.

But as the blackmailer's demands for money grow larger and larger, Elliott decides that there's only one alternative, and that involves shooting him when he arrives for his latest payment. In the dark, Elliott fires a gun at him and then conceals the body in a concrete foundation for an antique gazebo that Nell has recently acquired and which is awaiting reassembly in their garden. Much of the plot spins around Elliott's attempt to keep the body hidden, especially from the building contractor, Sam Thorpe (as played by John McGiver).

The plot grows more and more convoluted, even involving a kidnapping of Nell by The Duke (Martin Landau) and Louis the Louse (Dick Welles). Believe it or not, there's a happy ending to all this mess. It turns out that the audience has been tricked: Elliott didn't murder the blackmailer after all.

Throughout the shoot, Debbie did what she could to cheer up Ford, and he spent many nights at her house, in her bed, making love to her.

For a while, he had lived in the same house with his estranged wife, each occupying separate quarters. But he'd moved out and went to live in a converted garage on the grounds, a building that has once belonged to Charlie Chaplin. It was now occupied by his mother, Hanna Wood Ford.

"I had to spend the night at Debbie's after she put her kids to bed, since I couldn't very well take her home to mother," Ford claimed.

In several of Debbie's pictures, she met big stars of yesterday, many of them reduced to accepting small parts in films. She accurately predicted that same fate for herself.

James Kirkwood, Sr. and ZaSu Pitts were cast as Mr. and Mrs. MacGruder. Both of them had been big stars in the silents. Pitts had even been the star of the infamous silent film, *Greed* (1924), directed by Erich Von Stroheim.

Kirkwood, too, was a noted actor. He'd also been the lover of Mary Pickford and had married another silent screen star, Lila Lee, who had co-starred with Rudolph Valentino in *Blood and Sand* (1922).

The Kirkwoods had produced a gay son, James Kirkwood, Jr. (1924-1989) who would go on to win a Pulitzer Prize for his involvement in the authorship of the hit Broadway musical, *A Chorus Line* (1975)

Regrettably, all of the scenes with Pitts and Kirkwood were deleted from the final print by Marshall.

Carl Reiner was cast in *The Gazebo* as Harlow Edison, the district attorney. At the end of the shoot, he told Debbie he was flying to New York to work on a screenplay.

When he returned to Los Angeles, he gave her a copy of it to read. In bed that night, she read it twice, thinking it would make a wonderful film comedy, with the lead role ideal for her.

She phoned producer Ross Hunter the following day and pitched *The Thrill of It All* to him. He seemed intrigued, and she drove to his home and presented him with the script. She'd more or less forgiven him for not casting her opposite Rock Hudson in *Pillow Talk,* the choice having gone instead to Doris Day.

"Do you known what Ross, the gay blade, did?" she later asked her friends. "He gave my role in *The Thrill of it All* (1963) to Doris Day. She is hard to hate, but let's put it this way: I don't exactly adore her for taking my roles. Not only that, but she gets to play love scenes with that hunk, James Garner."

Debbie would not forever be denied an on-screen romance with Garner. Within the decade, she'd be co-starring with him in *How Sweet It Is!*

***

In the future, Debbie would consider marrying Ford, but his constant involvement with other women caused that dream to simmer down into a sustained friendship. When the romantic torch fizzled, their friendship remained. As age overtook them, they evolved into calling each other "Pa" and "Ma."

At one point, however, both Ford and Debbie were considering a trip down the aisle to the altar and "dumping our spouses." In the meantime, a certain Marilyn Monroe lookalike (or wannabe) intervened.

Debbie was referring to Liz Renay, the author of a hot memoir, *My First 2,000 Men,* in which she described her affair with Ford.

Renay, as stated in her own autobiography and to anyone who'd listen, made it a point to seduce as many male actors from the A-list as she could. They included, over the course of a busy lifetime, Clark Gable, Errol Flynn, and Burt Lancaster. She also took time out for sex with B-picture actors (Lawrence Tierney, Forrest Tucker, and Dan Duryea) too. Renay was also the gun moll of mobster Mickey Cohen, and at one time had to serve time in prison for refusing to

Starlet Liz Renay was hailed as Hollywood's ultimate star fucker.

"If I guy couldn't get Marilyn Monroe, he called me," she said. "I was the next best thing." She entitled her memoirs *My First 2,000 Men.*

At the time that Glenn Ford was seducing her, he was also having an affair with Debbie.

testify against him.

One evening Debbie confronted Ford about his ongoing affair with Renay, telling him, "Oh, Glenn, you could have done better than this low-class whore."

[She was saddened when she learned about Ford's final years. Before his death in 2006, he was confined to bed. She advised his son, Peter, to affix depictions of naked breasts onto his ceiling "so that it will give your dad some pleasure."

Peter did not follow her advice.]

***

"My uncle back in El Paso had taught me to talk dirty—I mean, really filthy—and I took to it like a pig to shit. Rock Hudson became the only person I could really talk dirty to. He loved it and shot back as good as it got. I liked nothing more than dishing men to him, and he told me shocking stories about movie stars who are supposedly straight but lived in the closet. For a long time, our favorite man to dish was Tony Curtis, who had been his lover before he married my friend, Janet Leigh."

"The Kid from the Bronx," Tony Curtis was a self-admitted "big bag of nothing put together with spit and glue" when he first arrived in Hollywood. A hopeful starlet, Debbie was one of the first actresses he met there.

"All of us were just kids really—not just Debbie but Marilyn Monroe and Rock Hudson too. Marlon Brando and I became real close, and moved in together, which sparked a lot of rumors."

"In the beginning, I was not close to Debbie, because I was dating Janet Leigh, and she and Debbie had become friends at MGM. I didn't want her to know too much about what I was up to, fearing she'd go and blab to Janet."

"If Debbie liked you, she'd let you run around with those WASP friends of hers like Gene Kelly and Henry Fonda. But if she didn't like you, you'd be shipped to Siberia or to a concentration camp. Because Debbie and Janet were friends, she accepted me, though always considering me a bit of a smart ass."

"That Debbie gal was a real firecracker, a talented actress with many good qualities unless you stood in her way. Then she'd cut off your balls and stew them in chili sauce for breakfast."

"I wasn't having any sexual fantasies about Debbie in those early years," he said. "I went around with a lump in my pants all day until I ran into Marilyn Monroe, Piper Laurie, Yvonne De Carlo, Mona Freeman, or else Mamie Van Doren. They could always bring quick relief."

"The guys went after me, too, considering me a cute trick with a body beautiful. Orry-Kelly, Cary Grant's old lover, really fell for me during a costume fitting. He later told Marilyn that I had a better-looking ass than she did. Debbie found that story amusing."

According to Curtis, "One night, Debbie brought Danny Kaye to a party at the home where Janet and I lived. Kaye and I were both Jews from New York, and I thought we'd bond. But he was real sarcastic with me. Right in front of Debbie, in a mocking reference to my costume in *Some Like It Hot*, he asked, 'Do you always appear on screen in high heels?'"

"What a shitty remark," Curtis answered. "I knew he was referring to rumors that I was gay. He was the gay blade, screwing Laurence Olivier and half the cute extras in his pictures. I knew he was sexually attracted to me, and was covering it up with sarcasm. Later that evening, I asked Debbie never to bring him to my home again."

"Actually, Debbie was jealous of Janet and me, although pretending friendship," Curtis claimed. "Before, Janet and I had been America's Sweethearts. But when she married Fisher, they took over the title. But after they lost it, Janet and I were restored to our throne until we lost it at the time of our divorce in 1962."

"Debbie wouldn't admit it, but she was insanely jealous of Elizabeth Taylor—and not just because she'd taken her husband away from her. She envied her beauty and her bigger tits."

"You never understood where you stood with Debbie, as she waxed hot and cold from one day to the next. Fisher told me she was a secret lesbian, although I saw no evidence of that. I did, however, warn Janet not to be left alone in the same room with her. In some ways, Debbie reminded me of that shit, Jerry Lewis...always demanding, always wanting to be in control, always the center of attention."

"It wasn't until the making of *The Rat Race* that sparks flew between Debbie and me, and I don't mean the angry kind," Curtis said. "I'd never fucked her until we made that movie. Nearly every one of my leading ladies had surrendered their honeypot to me, Debbie being the exception."

In a memoir, Curtis wrote, "We snuggled together quite nicely during our kissing scenes, and I spent a lot of time hanging out in her dressing room."

That observation was corroborated by their director, Robert Mulligan, who said, "Those sparks between Debbie and Tony turned into a bonfire when we shot *The Rat Race*. She'd been a tough shell to crack, because she'd been kicked around a lot in Hollywood, and she was standoffish at first. But she gave in. When they weren't needed on the set, they spent hours together in her dressing room."

As Curtis himself claimed, "Debbie was no longer mocking me for saying '*fodda.*' Instead, she was calling out pre-orgasm, 'Sock it to me, Daddy-Oh!'"

***

Producers William Perlberg and George Seaton decided that Debbie and Tony Curtis would make a good screen team in their upcoming movie, *The Rat Race*, set for a release by Paramount in 1960.

A Jew born in Poland, Perlberg had been a fur trader before becoming a personal assistant to Harry Cohn at Columbia. Of Swedish descent, Seaton had grown up in the Jewish section of Detroit, defining himself as "a Shabas goy." [*i.e., From the Yiddish, this translates roughly as a Gentile who, on the Sabbath or on holy days, performs tasks that are forbidden to rigidly Orthodox Jews.*]

In partnership with Perlberg, Seaton would achieve his greatest film triumphs, including such classics as *The Song of Bernadette* (1943) with Jennifer Jones; *The Miracle on 34th Street* (1947), and *The Country Girl* (1954), which brought Grace Kelly a Best Actress Oscar.

From Playwright Garson Kanin, Perlberg and Seaton bought the screen rights for *The Rat Race,* a script that Kanin had developed with his wife, Ruth Gordon.

Robert Mulligan was hired as the director, and he was just months away from helming his greatest hit, the humanistic drama, *To Kill a Mocking Bird* (1962). A former marine in World War II, he'd once written editorials for *The New York Times* before pursuing a career in television.

By 1959, the year he'd worked with Debbie, Mulligan had won an Emmy for his direction of *The Moon and Sixpence,* marking the TV debut of Laurence Olivier. At around the same time he was plotting separate projects for Tony Curtis and Rock Hudson.

A few years later, Debbie went to Mulligan asking if she could play the female lead in *Love With the Proper Stranger* (1963) starring Steve McQueen. He turned her down, preferring her rival on screen and off, Natalie Wood.

Mulligan told Debbie that in *The Rat Race,* she'd play a dance hall hostess dancing with men from the streets of Manhattan who wanted to hold a girl up close while paying a dollar for the privilege.

In preparation for the role, Debbie went to a costume shop near Times Square in Manhattan and bought "some whorish clothes and a blonde wig. I looked like Mamie Van Doren on a bad night."

That afternoon in her new drag, she was hired by the manager of a dance hall on Eighth Avenue. "I wore this sleazy red

Tony Curtis was Debbie's leading man in *The Rat Race*. According to Debbie, "I met his wife, Janet Leigh, when I went to work as a starlet at MGM, and I liked her. At first, I didn't like Tony and mocked his Bronx accent."

"He later spread the lie that he and I had a thing while shooting the film."

Her director, Robert Mulligan, confirmed Curtis' claim.

strapless that showed off my tits," she said. "No one knew I was Debbie Reynolds, movie star, although one drunk told me I looked like that gal in *Singin' in the Rain*, although not as pretty."

Her first dance partners were three sailors on leave, and, as she recalled, "they got their money's worth. After all those months at sea, they were hot and ready to go. They'd rented a room up the street at a fleabag and asked me to go there with them. I told them, 'I'm not that kind of gal.'"

Her most amusing partner was a guy named Joe, who worked at a deli. "He smelled of sour pickles, herring, and salami. His head came up to my nose. He also weighed about 300 pounds."

The plot of *The Rat Race* has Peter Hammond, Jr. (as portrayed by Curtis), arriving on a Greyhound bus in Manhattan from his native Milwaukee. His dream is to find work as a jazz saxophonist.

Renting a cheap apartment, he encounters Peggy Brown (Debbie), who is being evicted from those quarters for failure to pay back rent.

Since she is penniless, he lets her stay with him in the apartment with a promise of no hanky-panky. Together, they attempt to make it in the big, cruel city, surviving *The Rat Race* on whatever jobs they can find.

Rehearsing with "freelance" jazz artists who are later revealed as scam artists, Pete is sent out for coffee with a promise that they'll include him as a member of their ensemble for one of their upcoming music gigs. During his absence, they betray him by disappearing with his instruments. Shortly thereafter, a three-month booking emerges for a job playing with a dance band aboard a cruise ship, but he has no saxophone.

Learning of his plight, Peggy goes to the sleazy owner, Nelly Miller (as interpreted by Don Rickles) of a night club, and offers to prostitute herself to some of Miller's male clients in exchange for a loan of $600. She has no intention of becoming his whore, but she has the money to buy the instruments that Pete will need for the seagoing gig he'll now be able to accept.

A lot of complications get aired before Pete returns from his gig aboard the cruise ship. He reappears in time to rescue Peggy from becoming an "irretrievably fallen" woman. Predictably, they fall in love. Before the end of the picture, they've reconciled themselves to

"I was a bit intimidated to work with Don Rickles, known for his biting sarcasm. But I found him rather kind when not 'on.'"

"On screen, he was an abusive club owner, trying to turn me into a prostitute. Off screen, he was more gentle."

"'I'm scared shitless,' he told me. 'Afraid I'm going to fuck up my role.'"

struggling together with the knowledge that they may not have a lot of money, but they have each other.

Veteran actor Jack Oakie played the third lead of "Mac," an empathetic bartender. He is best remembered for portraying Napoléon in Charlie Chaplin's *The Great Dictator* (1940), for which he was nominated for an Oscar as that year's Best Supporting Actor.

Don Rickles ("the master of the insult") played the malevolently corrupt nightclub owner. Frank Sinatra called him "bullet head." In response, Rickles said to him, "Make yourself at home—hit somebody."

When he met Debbie, Rickles quipped, "Still trying to pull off that virgin act? I hear that at the latest orgy, you were on the bottom of the pile."

Mulligan said: "I had a great time working with Tony and Debbie. In front of the camera, they were real pros. Off camera, they were in her dressing room fucking. Our film was shot in forty-six days. Tony mastered the saxophone. He'd had practice when he played a saxophone player in *Some Like It Hot* (1959) with Marilyn Monroe."

In his evaluation of *The Rat Pack,* the film critic for *The Financial Times* wrote: "That their innocence remains creditable is due more to the playing of Tony Curtis (a delightful and increasingly subtle actor) and a newly audacious Debbie Reynolds than to the writing."

***

In September of 1959, during her filming of *The Rat Race,* Debbie was asked to appear as a guest on *The Tonight Show,* hosted at the time by the controversial and notoriously temperamental Jack Paar. Publicity-wise, she was still recovering from the aftermath of the Fisher/Taylor/Reynolds scandal.

Before she agreed to go on as a guest, she hammered out an understanding with the producer that neither of them would discuss Fisher or Elizabeth. The producer had urged her instead to "keep it light, keep it funny."

"That I can do," she said.

After being introduced to the audience by Paar, her opening moments were awkward. "Some tie you're wearing," she said, looking at his out-

In a riotous scene from *The Tonight Show,* Debbie tried to strip her host, Jack Paar, evoking raucous laughter from millions of late-night TV viewers.

In this shot, she and Paar were composing themselves, adjusting their clothing after the burlesque.

rageous necktie colored Halloween orange and shocking pink.

He removed it and handed it to her. Then she checked his wardrobe once again. "Your tie doesn't match the handkerchief." Then he removed the handkerchief from his pocket and handed it to her, too, but she stuffed it back into the pocket of his jacket.

On the air, she then described her experience working as a dime-a-dance girl near Times Square as a preparation for her role in *The Rat Race*. She invited him to get up from behind his desk and dance with her. Mostly they clowned around on the floor as she took the aggressive lead. He had a hard time keeping in step with her.

After he sat down, he asked, "Were you that rough with Eddie Fisher?"

The subject that had previously been agreed upon as taboo had been raised, and as she admitted later, "I was dumbstruck." For a moment, she didn't know how to respond. Then, impulsively, she crawled under his desk and reached up for him, yanking at his jacket, pulling him under the desk with her.

Then she began stripping him, first his jacket, which she tossed on the desk. Then came his shoes and socks, even the wastepaper basket in what she was broadly suggesting was an act of rape she was committing on him.

The audience was roaring with laughter. She ruffled up her dress to suggest he'd gone for her breasts. She then unbuttoned his shirt.

"Want me to take it off?" he asked.

"No need for that," she said. "Let's get up." The audience was still laughing, and she knew her impromptu comic *schtick* had been a hit—and seen by millions out there in TV land.

Their striptease made headlines the next day: DEBBIE GOES WILD, and DEBBIE STRIPTEASES PAAR.

***

Before she met and married Eddie Fisher, Debbie had casually dated a handsome, wealthy Texan, Robert (Bob) Neal, the Maxwell House heir. In Hollywood, along with his best friend, hotel heir Nicky Hilton, Neal had a reputation as a playboy. Eleven years older than Debbie, "with fifty years more experience" (her words), he'd been a Marine during World War II and had a strong, muscled body. When not in Texas, he lived in one of the homes he owned in Beverly Hills, Palm Springs, and on the beachfront in Malibu.

"In those days, I wasn't putting out," Debbie said. "How dumb could you be? I probably lost Robert Wagner because I held onto my virginity. At the time I was dating Bob Neal, I also dated another Bob, my beloved R.J. Minnie thought both of them would be great catches, preferring Neal because he had all that coffee money."

"Bob Neal was the first man who ever gave me jewelry," she said. "For my birthday, he presented me with a lavish gift, a little cross studded with diamonds. It was expensive, but I knew he could afford it."

Neal came back into Debbie's life after she divorced Fisher. "I was delighted when he wanted to be with me again. Perhaps he had to tear himself away from such bombshells as Marilyn Monroe or Jayne Mansfield. By this time, I had lost my virginity if you call going to bed with Eddie Fisher losing your virginity. In other words, I was putting out."

She remembered one time in Las Vegas when she was dating Neal. "I was feeling like 'The Girl About Town.' Not exactly an easy lay, but I could be had if the right man came along. My fellow Texan, Bob, was my kind of man. There's something about men from Texas. Just ask any gal in Hollywood."

"One night, we were motoring along the Strip in Vegas, and Bob spotted a car behind us. He told me, 'We're being tailed.'"

"We drove for about a mile, and the car following us never lost us, even when Bob stepped on the gas. Finally, he slammed on the brakes, got out of the car, and stormed over to confront two men in the vehicle in back of us. I was afraid he might get killed or beaten up. I heard him shouting at the men. When he came back to our car, he told me that the men were from the security forces of Howard Hughes."

"You must have dated Hughes at some point," he said. "Sometimes, when he has a girl, the fucker thinks he owns her, that she's his exclusive property. He likes to know what one of the girls he's seduced is up to. In Los Angeles, he keeps five or six girls on retainer, never visiting them for sex, but supporting them and giving them a house to live in. He's a throwback to *Arabian Nights* when men had harems."

He told her, "You know, Hughes bats for both teams. My friend Nicky (Hilton) is hung like a horse, and on occasion, he lets Hughes give him a blow job. Hughes chased after Elizabeth Taylor for months, giving her a box of jewelry. I think his ultimate fantasy would have been to have a three-way with both Nicky and Elizabeth."

Debbie's greatest period of intimacy with Neal occurred when she took a month off from MGM for a much-needed rest. From Winthrop Rockefeller, she rented a beach house along Waikiki in Hawaii, and flew her children and her parents there for a vacation with her.

Somehow, Neal heard of this, and he, too, flew to Hawaii to join her. "The first time we hit the beach, he wore a male bikini, the kind they wear on the French Riviera. I kidded him, telling him, 'I know it's for real, but most people will probably think you stuffed a sock in there.' He was flattered."

During the second week of her holiday in Hawaii, he rented a yacht with a crew and invited her to sail through the Hawaiian archipelago. Her parents remained behind to tend to Carrie and Todd. On their first night at sea, he had a lavish Hawaiian dinner prepared, which they consumed on the moonlit deck. She even drank champagne until it made her giddy.

"It was a romantic night, and I wanted to become Mrs. Robert Neal. He'd never been married before. Too busy playing the field. I thought he was taking me on this cruise to propose marriage to me. No proposal ever came, however. But I got some of the best loving I'd ever had…Texas style, that is."

On the first night after he'd seduced her, she woke up in his stateroom. He was not there. After showering, she got dressed in shorts and a halter top and wandered on deck to find him.

"I couldn't believe it. He was standing there completely nude. In the yellow-red sun, he looked glorious. Rich people, I have found, are very casual about nudity, having grown up stripping down in front of servants. He looked perfectly relaxed, happy to be with me."

"Come here, goddess," he called to her. "I want to kiss you like you've never been kissed before."

"There was a slight taste of sea salt on his lips," she said. "Delicious."

Suddenly, a servant appeared on deck with Neal's bathrobe. "It's time for breakfast, sir," he said, holding the robe up for Neal to slip on.

"Breakfast, the day itself, and all the days that followed that week were glorious," she recalled to Rock Hudson. "Perhaps the most glorious of my life. The nights…what can I say? I enjoyed love-making from the man who knew how. From my very limited experience, I found most men don't really know how to hit a woman's hot spots. Certainly not Eddie. Poor Elizabeth. After Mike Todd, she must feel deprived."

"On my last day at sea, I knew I had to return to my children and my parents. I didn't really want to. My desire was to sail for days island-hopping, beach-going, with romantic dinners and even more romantic nights, each with Bob in my arms. I could get lost forever in the islands with Bob. But there's a thing called reality. After two months, Eddie had stopped the alimony payments, and I was now the family's chief breadwinner. I had to get back to work, even if the pictures being offered to me were crappy."

Back in Hollywood, she dined with Rock Hudson, and shared stories about her recent adventures with Neal. He brought her up to date on his string of lovers, then showed her a story from United Press International. It named the four most desirable bachelors in the

Debbie's romance with Bob Neal even made the cover of a trade-industry magazine.

A famous playboy, he was the heir to the Maxwell coffee fortune. The headline blared, "Debbie's 10 Nights with Bob Neal: FROM DATES TO DIAMONDS TO DANGER!"

world. The men named included Howard Hughes, King Baudouin of Belgium, Marlon Brando, and coffee heir Bob Neal.

"My god, I've seduced three of the men on that list," she said. "Imagine that!"

"And I've had Marlon Brando," Hudson chimed in. "To my surprise, I found I had twice as much as he has."

She waited and waited but Bob Neal never called again, even though he'd told her he'd spent the most glorious week of his life with her in Hawaii.

"Instead of Bob, he sent his best friend, Nicky Hilton, a very different type of man from Bob. I think I took up with Nicky only because he'd been married to my rival, Elizabeth Taylor. After all, she was seducing my first husband. Why not go after HER first husband? A bit perverse of me, wouldn't you say?"

Bob Neal, however, was not completely gone from Debbie's life. When she was filming *What's the Matter with Helen?*, a film with that "atrocious" Shelley Winters, Debbie decided to track down the Texan for an encore performance.

***

If anyone's reputation had preceded him, it was that of playboy Nicky Hilton, the hotel heir. One afternoon, without telling Debbie goodbye, Neal flew to Texas on business. He'd had a date with Debbie to take her to the Cocoanut Grove to hear Sammy Davis, Jr. that Saturday night.

To her surprise, Nicky showed up on her doorstep instead, hauling with him three dozen long-stemmed yellow roses. He'd been taken there in a marron-colored, chauffeur-driven limousine.

She recognized him at once from his pictures in all the movie magazines when he had become the first husband of a very young Elizabeth Taylor. Among many others, he'd also been dating her friend, Terry Moore. Unknown to Debbie at the time, he was also having an affair with Zsa Zsa Gabor, his former stepmother when she

On May 6, 1950, a teenaged Elizabeth Taylor married the socialite and hotel heir, Nicky Hilton. *Tout Hollywood* turned out for the wedding, but the couple filed for divorce five stormy months later.

Debbie said, "Elizabeth got Nicky Hilton before I did, but I got Eddie Fisher before she did."

Years later, after the residue from *l'affaire Fisher* had simmered down, Debbie found Hilton (for a brief period, at least) enticing when he showed up on her doorstep "young, rich, handsome, and hung."

was married to his father, Conrad Hilton.

When he wasn't dating Moore, he was seen with the French actress, Denise Darcel, or else with Jeanne Crain, perhaps with socialites like Kay Spreckles (the future Mrs. Clark Gable) or Hope Hampton.

Without knowing that Debbie would date him in the future, Moore had bragged about his sexual prowess. "He has absolutely the largest penis—wide as a beer can and much longer. To make love with him is like fornicating with a horse."

In contrast, Elizabeth had told Debbie that her brief marriage to Nicky was "horrendous."

"I had heard he was an abusive drunk, but he was the perfect gentleman the night he escorted me to the Grove to hear Sammy, and we certainly went in style," Debbie said.

At the Grove, the difference in their heights was awkwardly obvious. He rose to a height of more than six feet, with broad shoulders, an athlete's waist, brown hair, and rather sad eyes.

Nicky was the eldest of his three brothers, each of them an heir to the vast Hilton Hotel chain. He was certainly the best-dressed man at the club. Debbie learned he had all his suits tailored at the most chic men's store on Savile Row in London.

As she sat across from him, she remembered what her friend Zsa Zsa had said about him: "He's a great charmer but he possesses the capacity for even greater cruelty. He pretends to be a devout Catholic, but instead, he is self-righteous, pushy, and dictatorial. He always has to have his own way with a woman."

Debbie saw none of that side of him on their first date. "I found him fun-loving and warm-hearted. Many famous guests came up to our table. He seemed to know everybody. Peter Lawford, a close friend of his, sat down and joined us for a drink. So did Frank Sinatra and Dean Martin. The Rat Packers were there in full force."

After their time together at the Grove, he drove her home and settled for a light kiss on the lips. "It made me tingle all over," she confessed. "Elizabeth had him, and I figured that if I made the right moves, he'd be mine. At least I'd have 100,000 beds to sleep in in all those hotels."

He made a date with her for the following evening, with the understanding that they would attend an A-list gala at his father's hotel, the exclusive Bel-Air Hotel. Although he'd been officially designated as its manager, he rarely showed up for work.

The day before the event, she fretted about what to wear. She need not have worried. At two o'clock that afternoon, her doorbell rang, and two packages arrived for her. Nicky had called Helen Rose, who had spent all night rushing to finish a dusty pink chiffon gown for her. Another smaller package contained a gift, the most expensive piece of jewelry she'd ever been given.

Her eyes were dazzled by a pair of diamond earrings with dangling pearls.

That night at the gala, she stood by Nicky's side as he welcomed some of the top movie stars of Hollywood, including Cary Grant, John Wayne, and Gary Cooper. Many of the guests were friends of Conrad Hilton, his father. They included Texas oilmen, industrial tycoons, CEOs, senators, and even fading members of the European aristocracy.

Arriving late was the man who made all this possible, Conrad Hilton. He towered over Debbie.

Although like his son, he had on a beautifully tailored suit, he wore a tacky-looking tie bearing illustrations of three of his hotels. "Hello, little girl," Conrad said to her. "I heard you were like me, growing up po' in Texas and having rattlesnake for dinner."

"Something like that," she answered.

"Now I own hotels and you're a god damn movie star," he said. "We Texans know how to get ahead in this world." Then he patted her on the head. "Now, girl, I want you to promise me something. You be good to my boy."

"I will," she vowed.

She kept her promise that night. After the gala, Nicky invited her to his elegantly furnished suite, the best in the hotel. Privately, he referred to it as his "fuck pad." As he sat across from her, speaking in his soft Texas drawl, his dark brown eyes suggested mischief and desire. According to rumor, he'd had affairs with many women, even men when he was in the Navy during World War II. If gossips were to be believed, he'd been having sex without any particular preference for gender since he was fourteen years old. It was said that, just after puberty, a family maid had seduced him at his family's mansion in Texas.

When she returned to her home on Monday morning, after her weekend with Nicky, she phoned Rock Hudson: "Having sex with Nicky is like giving birth to a baby. Not only that, but he rests inside you until he's ready for another round of pounding."

"Don't get me excited," Hudson told her. "What's his private phone number?"

That Tuesday night, Nicky took her to dinner at Conrad Hilton's sixty-four room mansion in Bel Air. Conrad was there with tap-dancing Ann Miller, Debbie's friend from her early days at MGM. Formally dressed butlers wearing tails served drinks followed by a lavish pheasant dinner. Maids in black uniforms with frilly aprons were there, too, responding to every request.

While Conrad remained for a nightcap with his

Homespun and straightforward, Conrad Hilton was a sort of Gary Cooper type, rough and rugged, with a ten-gallon hat, boots, and spurs, none of which seemed coordinated with his tailored suit.

favorite son by one of the mansion's fireplaces, Miller and Debbie said good night to one another in the hallway. "Guess what I heard tonight?" Miller whispered, giggling, into Debbie's ear: "Conrad's brother told me that he, Conrad, and Nicky have three feet of cock among the three of them, but he wasn't going to tell me how it was distributed. Go, girl, go!"

Debbie spent some time that evening in Nicky's bedroom, admiring the artwork, the lavish furnishings, and the bathroom fixtures in fourteen-karat gold. Nicky knocked on the door before entering, even though it was his bedroom. "He was so polite," she said.

As she later confessed, "He was the perfect lover, so considerate. I think all those stories of his brutality were exaggerations. Hollywood gossip."

When Dick Hanley, Debbie's friend and Elizabeth Taylor's private secretary, heard that she was dating Nicky, he phoned her. "He's a Dr. Jekyll and Mr. Hyde personality," he warned. "Right now, you're seeing the best side of him. The one he presents to the world until you get to know him. He beat me severely one night and raped me. He's a compulsive gambler. Conrad pays off his massive gambling debts in Vegas. Not only that, Nicky beats up women, and he's an alcoholic. He's also a heroin addict and sex maniac. It doesn't matter if his partner is a man or woman, as he believes that all cats are grey at night."

"What you say may be true, and you've never lied to me, but are you telling me this just because you want to reserve him for yourself?"

"Oh, come on, Debbie. You know I don't have a chance with him, although I'd endure any beating if he wanted me to come and live with him as his secretary."

"I knew it!" she said. "I'm never wrong about these things."

The following weekend, she accepted an invitation to spend the weekend with him at the Hilton family's vacation retreat on Lake Arrowhead. Beside the lake, amid a landscape illuminated with moonlight, he presented her with a diamond ring and asked her to marry him. He was candid about the origin of the ring. "I was going to give it to Elizabeth, but the bitch, a real spoiled brat, filed for divorce before I could add it to her collection."

"I couldn't believe I had heard right," she later said. "The heir to the Hilton hotel chain proposing marriage to little ol' me. A gal who grew up in a Texas shantytown. But there were complications. He wanted me to join the Catholic church and to promise to raise any children we had as Catholics. My daddy didn't like Catholics, and I was reluctant to commit to another faith like that, but I promised to do so, even though it was a vow I knew I would not keep."

"Of course, Elizabeth converted to Judaism, but she was no more committed to that religion than I was. If I married Nicky, that would really sock it to those coyotes, Elizabeth and Eddie Fisher, the shit."

After their time together beside Lake Arrowhead, Nicky flew her to Las Vegas and housed her within another lavishly furnished suite. That was the first time she'd ever seen him "get stinking, staggering drunk. He had suffered heavy losses at the dice tables. But he told me, 'Conrad will pay the boys off.'"

After the passage of many hours, and as the evening grew late, Nicky disappeared. She thought he might have stumbled back to his room to sleep off the many drinks he'd consumed. But he was not there, either. She undressed and got into the bed alone, rapidly falling asleep. The long dreary evening had been exhausting.

At around 3AM, he returned to the suite and barged into her bedroom, turning on the lights. He looked half dressed, with his coat off, his tie unfastened, and his shirt unbuttoned. "Let's have some fun," he called out to her.

Behind him were two Vegas showgirls—hookers on the side—he'd picked up in the bar.

"They were dressed in just enough clothing not to get arrested for nudity," Debbie recalled.

"I've brought the party with me," he said to her, moving toward the bed.

"Debbie Reynolds! I can't believe it's you!" said one of the hookers. "Can I have an autograph?"

Horrified, Debbie jumped out of bed and grabbed her robe. "I'm packing my clothes and getting the hell out of here." Then she pulled off the diamond ring and threw it at him.

As she later confessed to Hudson, "I wasn't allowed to escape. He had the whores hold me down while he raped me. It was brutal. He spat in my face as he did it. Everything I heard about Mr. Hyde was coming true. I was left bleeding."

"After the assault, I fled down the hall and called management," she said. "They got me another suite and woke up the house doctor. I had not been seriously injured, even though I was in pain. He gave me a sedative, which put me out until that afternoon. As soon as I could, I booked the next flight to Los Angeles. My luggage had been packed by someone and was resting by the door. Goodbye, Nicky Hilton. Goodbye forever."

She later said, "Nicky seemed to recover quickly from my desertion in Vegas. I heard through the gossip mill that he was seen the following weekend in Manhattan sharing a hotel suite with some hookers."

As time went by, Nicky never learned to control his violent rages. His addiction to alcohol and gambling intensified.

Most of Elizabeth's Taylor's biographers gave him rough treatment. David Bret wrote, "Handsome but virtually devoid of charisma, (Nicky) Hilton had many male lovers from his days in the Navy. Back in Hollywood, he often had black or Jewish lovers, who would have to listen to his virulently racist or anti-Semitic ranting when he'd had too much to drink. He later had affairs with Natalie Wood and Marilyn Monroe, and treated them both badly. He was convinced that one of these mistreated lovers or a vengeful partner might kill him, so he kept a loaded gun on his bedside table, with a rosary wrapped around it for good luck."

***

Debbie's friendship with Judy Garland dated from her early days at MGM when she was already its major singing star. In 1950, their friendship intensified when Garland was fired by MGM from the title role of *Annie Get Your Gun*. The part was subsequently awarded to Betty Hutton, the personality that Debbie loved to imitate above all others.

Garland and her latest husband, Sid Luft, lived with three children in a large house on Mapleton Drive, two blocks from Debbie.

Luft was often away, and Garland could not stand to be alone, so she frequently called Debbie after she put her children to bed.

In the wake of her divorce from Fisher, on many a night, Debbie, too, was alone. As she confided to Garland, "It doesn't make much difference being married or not. On most nights during my marriage to Eddie, I was home alone, too."

Garland spent many an evening with Debbie complaining about her marriage to Luft. As a girl, Liza Minnelli, her daughter with Vincente Minnelli, remembered hearing shouting matches coming from her mother's bedroom at night.

"He constantly complains of my heavy drinking and pill popping," Garland told Debbie. "I know he's fucking other women when he goes away on those so-called business trips of his. When he's home, he fills the house with these creepy friends of his. All they seem to talk about is betting on horses. Mostly he fights with me about the debts piling up. Or why I got fired from MGM. On many a night, I should have phoned the police and had him arrested on assault and battery charges."

Although Liza would sometimes sneak downstairs to spy on them as they sang and danced to music in the living room, most nights were traumatic. As Debbie noted, Garland suffered from frequent headaches, and she would have sudden, inexplicable fears such as when

"Armies have marched over my battered body," Judy Garland confessed to Debbie during one of their "till-dawn-breaks" vigils.

In the photo from 1957 depicted above, Garland prepares to go onstage.

Garland was downing pills at the time, telling Debbie, "I've had some of the same guys you've had, including Eddie Fisher and your current beau, Glenn Ford. Mario Lanza had garlic breath, and Peter Lawford is strictly an oral artist."

In reference to those pills, Garland said, "I hate them. The wake-up pills are the worst, because they make me hop around like a Mexican jumping bean."

thunder and lightning streaked the sky, probably because of some emotional trauma she had suffered during childhood.

"She had this feeling of her own impending doom," Debbie said. "There had been suicide attempts. She feared she'd lost her voice, that she'd never be able to work again. She was convinced she'd never reach her 50th birthday. She was a poor, tortured soul during the wee hours of the morning that Frank Sinatra used to sing about."

On many a night, she spoke of the troubled and failed relationships in her life, and of her marriages to musician David Rose and Vincente Minnelli. "My marriage to David went on the rocks because he was repulsed by my frequent requests for him to perform cunnilingus on me. I aborted his child. I also aborted the child of Tyrone Power when he refused to marry me. The same thing happened to my friend Lana Turner. Goodbye to Ty, and goodbye to his child. I was set to marry Artie Shaw, but Lana married him instead. As I predicted, it was a disaster."

In contrast, Garland had nothing but kind words for her homosexual friends. Their mutual friend, Rock Hudson, sometimes visited Garland at night to keep her company when Debbie wasn't available. Garland said that her father, Frank Gumm, had been a homosexual, as was her second husband, Minnelli. "He wore more lipstick than I did."

Her list of lovers was long, and on many a drunken night, she told amusing stories about them.

She discussed playboy Aly Khan ("Rita Hayworth was welcome to him"); the fabled attorney Greg Bautzer ("One of Hollywood's greatest cocksmen"); Yul Brynner ("His head isn't the only head he's got"); Frank Sinatra ("I know you've had him too"); Orson Welles ("He claims he makes actresses fall in love with him and that he's the Lillie Langtry of the homosexual set"); and Mario Lanza ("He claims his singing comes right from his balls").

Garland did not discuss her lesbian affairs, but they were well known throughout MGM and later confirmed by many of her biographers. Her main involvements were with Kay Thompson, the writer and cabaret star; and with her personal publicist, Betty Asher; and with Ethel Merman.

The sexual revelation that most disturbed Debbie was Garland's confession that she'd had an affair with Eddie Fisher.

"Please spare me the details," Debbie said. "Just one question: Was it during my marriage to the shit?"

"Yes," Garland answered, rising to her feet. "Let's drop the subject. I've got to pour myself another drink."

During her intimate times with Garland, Debbie was still involved on occasion with Glenn Ford, "with considerable time off between engagements" (Debbie's words).

She learned that Ford and Garland had had an affair. She asked him about it one night. He answered, "It was a long time ago. I met her in Santa Monica

255

when she was part of the Gumm Sisters act."

Long after Debbie's affair with Ford faded into an enduring friendship, she learned that in 1963, Garland and Ford had been seeing each other and having a torrid affair that lasted for several months.

Over dinner one night, she asked Ford about it. "She wanted to marry me, but I knew it wouldn't work out. She had too many problems, and I have problems of my own. During the white heat of our affair, she often cried herself to sleep in my arms."

In Ford's living room, Debbie noticed that he had placed a large photograph of Garland with a note still attached. It read, "Glenn, dear one, now I can look forward and see the beauty of the sun and the moon and the love you give to me. You have my heart and I adore you. Judy."

Debbie's reaction? "I noticed that he didn't have MY picture on display."

"When Judy sang her classic, 'The Man That Got Away,' she was dreaming of Glenn. I, too, sometimes sang her song at home after Glenn stopped dropping in to see me, and after he stopped loving me. He went on to other loves, other wives, but he left Judy and me with a lot of stardust memories of 'what might have been,' the saddest phrase in the English language."

***

The singer, Margaret Whiting, it is believed, may have been the first to suggest to Debbie that they could turn chic Hollywood parties into fund-raising events for charity.

That had led in 1955 to the formation of The Thalians, dedicated at first to raising money to support children from broken homes who were often abused and emotionally disturbed. The group took its name from Thalia, the Greek muse of comedy and idyllic poetry.

By the late 1950s, Whiting and Debbie, among others, lured some of the biggest names in Hollywood to lend their support. Actors who included James Stewart and Frank Sinatra contributed, as did such movie goddesses as Rita Hayworth and Lana Turner. Gene Kelly, Bing Crosby, and Bob Hope also became major donors.

When Whiting moved to New York City, Debbie became president, and the Thalians raised millions to construct the Cedars Sinai Hospital. Today, the group, based in Mission Hills, California, deals mainly with military veterans with emotional and/or mental trauma.

The annual Thalian Ball was a major fund-raising event, and Debbie was asked to approach Harry Karl to underwrite the cost of the ball, with help from Conrad Hilton and Alfred Bloomingdale.

A multi-millionaire shoe manufacturer, Karl, in Debbie's view, was considered "the most free-wheeling, high-spending *habitué* of Hollywood's café society." Beautiful women, expensive restaurants, lavish tips, he was the last of the big-time spenders.

In 1958, Karl donated a quarter of a million dollars to the City of Hope, a cancer research center in Los Angeles. That would be worth about $2 million in 2017 currency.

Zsa Zsa Gabor had dated Karl and told Debbie, "He wanted me to marry him, but I never will, *dahlink*. He gives away millions to charity. As his wife, I would expect those millions to be spent buying diamonds for *me*."

Debbie's first introduction to Karl had been at an exclusive Hollywood party where he arrived with his wife, actress Marie McDonald. Debbie had known her since the early 1950s when they had both worked for the USO.

She had broken into show biz by entering and winning beauty pageants, holding such titles as "The Queen of Coney Island," and later "Miss New York State." In Hollywood, she appeared in a number of B pictures, and competed with Betty Grable for the title of pinup queen of World War II.

McDonald is mainly remembered for starring in the 1945 screwball comedy, *Getting Gertie's Garter*. Like Debbie, she had also co-starred in a film with Gene Kelly, *Living in a Big Way* (1947).

In that same year (1947), McDonald had married Karl, one of the seven times she'd wed. Right before her marriage, she had been dumped by gangster Bugsy Siegel.

During the course of her marriage to Karl, McDonald suffered four miscarriages. Eventually, the couple adopted a son, Harrison, nicknamed "Bo," and a daughter, Denice. In time, Debbie would become their stepmother.

In 1954, in Nevada, McDonald divorced Karl, telling the judge that she was allergic to him. He immediately began dating flame-haired Rhonda Fleming, the screen actress.

Despite her allergy claim, McDonald remarried Karl in 1955 in Yuma, Arizona. But they separated again a few months later, as she claimed that he beat her when she was four months pregnant. After their daughter, Tina Maria, was born, they reconciled. But by March of 1958, she sued once again for divorce, this time demanding a $4

Marie MacDonald and Harry Karl are pictured during one of the few happy moments in their two turbulent marriages.

Known as "the hottest sexpot ever to emerge from the hills of Kentucky," the blonde goddess was marketed in her press and PR campaigns as "The Body."

"I ended up as surrogate mother to their brats," Debbie said. "Marie shocked me when she told me she'd always been physically allergic to Harry."

million settlement.

The next time Debbie spotted Karl, he was at the Desert Inn in Las Vegas. She'd been invited to a business dinner with Harry Cohn, the head of Columbia Pictures. Karl was seated two tables away, celebrating a rare win of $150,000 at the gambling tables. This was most unusual for him, as he was known around town as one of resort's biggest losers.

Cohn had learned that Debbie's contract with MGM was not going to be renewed. He'd told his backers that he was considering putting her under contract. "We might make four or five million dollars off her before her tits wither."

Cohn was a notorious star seducer and "starlet plugger," as he defined himself. His conquests had included big names like Lucille Ball, Marilyn Monroe, and Marlene Dietrich, but most of his women were unknowns under contract at Columbia. He demanded sexual favors from them as a "reward" for keeping them employed.

Debbie expected Cohn to live up to his reputation as a potty mouth. "Harry reeks of smut, like a berserk, unexpurgated Chaucer," her friend, Henry Mollison, told her. Debbie, however, had discovered that on her own when Cohn told her, "Lemme tell ya about show business. It's about cunt and horses!" Director Elia Kazan said, "Cohn is the biggest bug in the manure pile."

Over dinner, Debbie had to keep slapping down Cohn's hand that was trying to feel under her dress.

Jack Entratter, the owner of the Desert Inn, joined Debbie and Cohn at table, but ignored Karl's greeting. "I detest people who win in my casino. My casino is for losers."

At some point, after she returned home, Debbie planned to get in touch with Karl to solicit a contribution from him for the Thalians. Now was not the time, as she was due to fly to Mexico to appear in a cameo in a movie.

In the wake of his upcoming divorce, he placed several calls to Debbie, but did not get her on the phone. Apparently, he wanted to date her. Then, columnist James Bacon, who had spoken to Karl, ran an item in which he predicted that Debbie Reynolds would become Karl's next wife.

***

The director, George Sidney, had married Lillian Burns, Debbie's longtime acting coach, mentor, and dear friend. As a favor to him, she agreed to appear in his latest film, *Pepe*, scheduled for a 1960 release from Columbia Pictures and starring the Mexican actor Cantinflas.

Sidney had recently directed *Pal Joey* (1957) with Frank Sinatra and Rita Hayworth. He'd hired another friend of Debbie's, Dorothy Kingsley, to work on the screenplay for *Pepe* since she'd done such a good job on the script for *Pal Joey*.

As Cantinflas's co-stars, Sidney had hired Dan Dailey and Shirley Jones.

Jack Lemmon agreed to appear in drag as Daphne, the continuation of a role he'd recently played in *Some Like It Hot* (1959) with Marilyn Monroe and Tony Curtis.

Both Sidney and Cantinflas were hoping to repeat the success of Mike Todd's *Around the World in Eighty Days* with its all-star cast. To do so, they rounded up the greatest array of Hollywood players ever to appear in one film. The glittering cast included not only Debbie, but Joey Bishop, Billie Burke, Maurice Chevalier, Charles Coburn, Richard Conte, Bing Crosby, Tony Curtis, Bobby Darin, A.B. Davis (known for the character of Schultzy that she played on TV), Sammy Davis, Jr., Jimmy Durante, Zsa Zsa Gabor, Judy Garland (voice only), Greer Garson, the columnist Hedda Hopper, Ernie Kovacs, Peter Lawford, Janet Leigh, Dean Martin, Jay North (Dennis the Menace on TV), Kim Novak, André Previn, Donna Reed, Edward G. Robinson, Cesar Romero, and, lest we forget, Frank Sinatra. The veteran actor William Demarest appeared as a movie studio security guard and gatekeeper.

Cantinflas played the title role of Pepe, a hired hand on a Mexican ranch. One day, a boozing Hollywood director, Ted Holt (Dan Dailey), arrives and buys a white stallion from Pepe's boss. Even though he doesn't own the horse, Pepe loves that animal, considering it "one of my family."

Hoping to get the beloved stallion back, Pepe journeys to Hollywood, where he meets a dazzling array of movie stars. His luck changes when he wins big in Las Vegas, produces a hit movie, and meets Suzie Murphy (Shirley Jones), an actress who has fallen on hard times. With Pepe's guidance, and with the luck he brings her, he turns her into a big movie star. In the end, the stallion is returned to the ranch, and the movie ends happily.

Cantinflas was the most famous comic film actor in the Spanish-speaking world—in fact, Charlie Chaplin called him "The best comedian alive." [Actually, he was known as *"the Charlie Chaplin of Mexico."*] Today—in the U.S. at least—he is mostly remembered for his starring role in *Around the World in Eighty Days*.

"He tried and failed to duplicate the success of Todd's film," Debbie said. "Alas, Pepe was a box office disappointment, except for my cameo. Just joking, fellas. He and I did this complicated dance sequence that he had a hard time performing. His

In the film, *Pepe*, the Mexican actor, Cantinflas, falls asleep on Janet Leigh's breasts during a dance marathon.

humor is deeply rooted in the Spanish language, and American audiences just don't get it."

Debbie flew to Acapulco to film her sequence and invited her friend, Jeanette Johnson, to go with her. Both of them were invited to the rented villa that Lillian Burns shared with her husband, George Sidney. Preceded with a swim, the luncheon featured Mexican cuisine.

Throughout her career, Debbie had turned to Burns for advice. She had read in the gossip columns the erroneous report that Debbie was heavily dating Harry Karl and was on the verge of marriage. "If you marry him, you'll be making the mistake of your life."

"Marry him? I hardly know him. Don't believe what you read in the papers."

"That may be true, but my husband knows a lot of Karl's friends," Burns said. "All he talks about is marrying you, and Harry usually gets what Harry wants. Money talks.:

"Not with me, it doesn't," Debbie said. "He can dream on. I'll star in his fantasies, but not in real life. He's not exactly what you'd call handsome, and, as you know, I go for guys who look like R.J."

"He's been married several times, twice to Marie McDonald, and he's a reckless gambler. He'll go through his millions and anything you've got stashed away for your old age, too."

"Well, he's always been nice to me and to Todd and to Carrie," Debbie said.

"Stay away from him," Burns warned. "He'll fuck up his own life and yours, too."

"I will," she promised. "Right now in the god damn hot sun, I'll make a blood promise that I will never marry Harry Karl. I won't even date the bastard."

***

[After filming Pepe *with Cantinflas, the Mexican comedian was not completely gone from Debbie's life. They became longtime friends.*

When she faced bankruptcy in 1973, he purchased her apartment in Century City, which she had bought as an investment. "That extra cash came in when I desperately needed it," she said.

"Maybe I should have married Cantinflas and moved with him to Mexico. He and I could have a lot of fun talking dirty like I did with Rock Hudson. He even told me the secret of his success with women. He said that before insertion, he dripped Mexican hot sauce on the head of his penis and then plunged it into a woman. "The puta always screams with passion,"

"Are you sure?" Debbie asked. "Maybe her guts are on fire."

After her divorce, Debbie spent many evenings at home, often with her friend Camille Williams. She'd hosted parties before, but not since Fisher had left. Camille persuaded her to throw a small dinner party for a special list, and helped her draw up what Debbie later defined as a very "mixed bag."

Hugh O'Brian, Debbie's former "hot date," showed up with his current mistress, songbird Margaret Whiting, the daughter of Richard Whiting, the famous composer of popular songs. Her big gold record had been "Moonlight in Vermont" in 1943.

Lucille Ball arrived with a surprise guest, actor George Sanders, who had co-starred with her in *Lured* (1947).

Huntz Hall was an unlikely guest. Debbie used to see him in those *Dead End Kids* movies, which gave way to the *Bowery Boys* films. He and Debbie had become friends. "I bought some pot for him to smoke," she said. [*Hunt had been arrested in 1949 for possession of marijuana but his trial resulted in a hung jury.*]

She invited her former beau, Robert Wagner, who asked if he could bring Natalie Wood. Putting up a brave front, contrary to her feelings, Debbie told him, "I'd be delighted."

As a joke, Jack Lemmon showed up in the Daphne drag he'd worn in *Some Like It Hot* (1959). [*As noted earlier, he would also appear as the same character, Daphne, in the about-to-be-released* Pepe.]

Thelma Ritter arrived with her husband, Joe Moran. She and Debbie would soon be starring in *How the West Was Won*. Glenn Ford came stag

Gary Crosby (photo above) is pictured with his father, Bing, a parent he hated, as did his brothers. ""Ever since I was a little boy he abused me," he told Debbie.

Debbie herself had already made a movie with Bing Crosby, and she'd lived in fear of arousing his fury. "You could make one wrong move, and he'd never speak to you again," she said.

and had to leave early, ostensibly for a business appointment. Debbie suspected that he had resumed seeing Eva Gabor.

She sent invitations to Marlon Brando and Karl Malden, those stars of *A Streetcar Named Desire.* Malden showed up with his wife, but Brando did not appear.

Debbie had recently become friends with the film and TV producer, David Wolper, who would in time be known for such shows as *Roots, The Thorn Birds,* and *The Rise and Fall of the Third Reich.*

But the guest who dominated her evening was Gary Crosby, whom she'd met on the set of *Say One for Me,* which had starred his father, Bing Crosby, and Robert Wagner.

Previously, she had attended two performances of his singing group, *The Crosby Boys,* comprised of Gary and his brothers, Philip and Lindsay. Gary had stopped by her house that afternoon and had rehearsed two of his songs, "Play a Simple Melody" and "Sam's Song." *[Gary, with his father, had duetted with those songs on a record, which eventually evolved into the first double-sided gold record in music history.]*

Out on her terrace, as her dinner party neared its end, he asked her if he could spend the night. At first reluctant, she agreed, saying, "Why the hell not?"

Apparently, they made love that night, although she had little to say about it other than "Let Grace Kelly take Bing. I'll go for Gary."

He stayed around the following day, and both of them went swimming in her pool and had lunch together on her terrace. He said that if he ever got around to writing an autobiography, it would be entitled *In the Shadow of Other Stars.*

He cited the movie he'd just made with Pat Boone called *Holiday for Lovers* (1959). His life seemed to justify that title. He'd recorded duets with Louis Armstrong and a 45-rmp single with Sammy Davis, Jr. During military service with the U.S. Army in Germany, he'd been stationed with another singer, Elvis Presley. "I also got to appear on *The Tennessee Ernie Ford Show,*" Gary said. "Guess who the star was?"

In 1954, he starred in *The Gary Crosby Show.* "But it was only the summer replacement for my shithead father, *The Bing Crosby Show.*"

When Gary got around to publishing his memoir in 1983, it was entitled *Going My Own Way.* In it, he was highly critical of his father's emotional and physical abuse. In 1989 and 1991, respectively, both Lindsay and Dennis committed suicide by gunshot.

***

After returning from Mexico, Debbie called Karl and invited him to lunch at Stephen Crane's Luau restaurant, and he eagerly accepted. This was a choice spot for her, as Lana Turner's ex-husband never presented Debbie or her guests with a bill.

When she came face to face with Karl at table, she got a better look at him, figuring that he was older than he actually was. He was forty-five, and she was only twenty-seven, but he had turned prematurely gray, like the actor Jeff Chandler.

He certainly had a good tailor, as he looked like he'd just emerged from London's Savile Row. Actually, he confirmed that, claiming, "Prince Philip and I have the same tailor."

His hazel eyes lurked behind thick black horn-rimmed glasses. He had a penchant for alligator shoes and diamond rings. "When I buy leather goods, especially shoes, I pay extra for the skins of an endangered species."

When Lana Turner heard that her former husband, Stephen Crane, was offering free meals to Debbie and her guests, she assumed they were having an affair. A handsome, charismatic man and failed actor, he had married Lana, but dated such major stars as Rita Hayworth and Joan Crawford.

He was the father of Cheryl Crane, who in 1959 would be linked to the murder of her mother's lover, the gangster Johnny Stompanato. However, Hollywood insiders claimed that it was Lana who fatally stabbed Mickey Cohen's henchman when he threatened to carve up her face.

After lunch, Karl wrote Debbie a check for $5,000, and then asked her out for a date. She told him, "I'm still getting over my divorce from Eddie and not dating at the moment." [She had been secretly dating, but had avoided being seen in public.]

She did give him her phone number. Since he had a business appointment with a Beverly Hills lawyer later that afternoon, he ordered his chauffeur to drop her off at her house on his way to his meeting.

The following day, he phoned her after the delivery of three dozen yellow roses. Someone had told him that was her favorite flower. She put him off about a possible date, and she continued to do so during each of his future calls. Those roses kept arriving until she told him she actually liked pink roses, too, even red ones.

Finally, she invited him to her home for dinner, but there was a catch. She also included her mother and father, Minnie and Ray. She felt she could get rid of Karl because she was certain he would find the evening boring, or perhaps not want to come at all.

But he arrived promptly at eight o'clock the following evening, bringing new golf clubs for Ray, a mink stole for Minnie, and a diamond bracelet for Debbie.

He spent part of the evening wooing Minnie, even making her giggle. He then had coffee in the living room, where he talked baseball with Ray.

"He also laughed at everything I said," Debbie claimed. "He told me I was the most clever young woman he'd ever met, and he also lied and told me I was far more beautiful than Marie McDonald."

"Marilyn Monroe's sex appeal is totally artificial," he claimed. "You have genuine sex appeal, the real thing."

He called again four days in a row, and the roses were now a mixture of colors. She agreed to have a drink with him in the Polo Lounge of the Beverly Hills Hotel. He ordered champagne, and she settled for a bottle of Coca Cola. He took out a gold cigarette case and opened it, offering her a smoke. "I don't smoke," she said, noticing the beautiful diamond clip inside. She closed the lid with the clip still inside and returned the case to him. "No thanks."

After their drinks in his chauffeur-driven limousine he made "no attempt to kiss me or feel my breasts like most men," she revealed. "We rode in the back seat with a number of toys he'd purchased for Carrie and Todd."

"I want you to marry me," he told her. "I'll be a loving husband and a wonderful, giving father to your kids."

"That's very nice," she said. "But there's a problem. I don't love you."

For the next few days, he called her repeatedly, begging her to marry him. But she kept turning him down. The roses kept arriving, and a pair of dazzling diamond earrings was sent over, too. She decided to accept them. Zsa Zsa had told her, "You may turn down a man's love, but never his diamonds."

She didn't go out to dinner with him, but was shocked to learn that he had taken Ray and Minnie to dinner at three of the most expensive restaurants in Los Angeles, and he had even purchased a pearl necklace for her mother.

In September of 1959, right before Labor Day, he placed an urgent call to her. She noted a certain desperation in his voice. "This is my final request. Once again, I want you to marry me. Please say yes. I need to know *RIGHT NOW.*"

"This is so crazy," she said. "I hardly know you. You don't know me except for a few encounters. I can't commit to a marriage with a stranger, a very generous stranger, a nice man, but a stranger nonetheless."

He put down the phone without saying goodbye to her.

"That's that," she said. "He won't be calling again."

She told this to Minnie, who scolded her for letting "a good man get away, a rich one at that. He could have done so much for you and your kids."

Three days later, the Sunday edition of the *Los Angeles Herald* arrived on her doorstep. Over morning coffee, she perused the frontpage. Below the fold was the story of Karl's marriage to Joan Cohn, the widow of the recently deceased Harry Cohn of Columbia Pictures. "I just couldn't believe it," she said. "He must have married Joan that same afternoon he proposed to me. That's why he was so urgent for my answer. Well there goes this multi-millionaire philanthropist from the life of Debbie Reynolds."

How wrong she was.

Chapter Nine

CASHING IN ON HER MARITAL SCANDAL

"DAUNTLESS DEBBIE"
BECOMES ONE OF HOLLYWOOD'S HOTTEST STARS

HER SALARY SOARS

HOW TAMMY MARRIED HARRY KARL,
A MULTI-MILLIONAIRE SHOE MANUFACTURER.

DEBBIE "WINS THE WEST" IN A SPRAWLING "MANIFEST DESTINY" EPIC WITH HER SCREEN LOVER, GREGORY PECK

In their *exposé* of "the real Debbie Reynolds" in October of 1961, *Confidential* raised a question: "Did Debbie capitalize on the tidal wave of (negative) public opinion that drowned poor Eddie in the aftermath of his affair and subsequent marriage to Elizabeth Taylor?"

The magazine went on to answer its own question: Whereas the reams of hot air had chilled Eddie's career, they had transformed Debbie into an eight million dollar star.

In reference to her marriage to Harry Karl, Debbie claimed, "When I wed that ugly toad, I thought I'd struck it rich. I just love real estate, and in his chauffeur-driven Rolls-Royce, I drove around Beverly Hills checking out properties. Regrettably, and unknown to me, once I bought places, these pieces of real estate somehow evaporated once the fucker became their overseer."

Confidential, **the leading scandal magazine** of the 1950s, was the first to expose "the smallest thing that ever came out of El Paso," a reference to Debbie. In its October 1961, issue, she was the subject of the lead story on the cover: DARE YOU READ THE TRUTH: DID DEBBIE REYNOLDS HOODWINK HOLLYWOOD?

She shared the cover with an exclusive about sex-for-play film starlets who frolic for $1,600 a night, and a tantalizing *exposé* on the exiled Egyptian King Farouk, who, the magazine claimed, "likes 'em three-at-a-time."

The magazine had already exposed her ex-husband, Eddie Fisher, for cavorting simultaneously with "three chippies."

Written by Mel Snyder, the article was not an exposé of Debbie's sex life—details of which were largely unknown at the time—but of a tough, profit-driven personality who was not the sweet innocent she portrayed in public and on the screen.

It did give her credit for taking lemons and turning them into lemonade, a reference to how she handled Fisher's dumping of her for Elizabeth Taylor. The magazine maintained that she used those truckloads of publicity to turn herself into a million-dollar studio property, rising to become one of the ten most popular stars in Hollywood.

Snyder mocked her appearance when she faced reporters and photographers after it was revealed that Fisher had fled their home. "With her hair in pigtails, she appeared with baby diaper pins for Todd and a warming bag for Carrie's bottle. She wore no makeup and looked very pale, telling the press, 'It seems unbelievable to say that you can live happily with a man and not know that he does not love you.'"

Of course, that was a fabrication. She had never lived happily with Fisher. "Had she botched that appearance, she would have missed the brass ring in Hollywood," Snyder maintained. "but she pulled it off."

He referred to her as "Dauntless Debbie, a careful planner with a will of iron. This Texas Tornado has swept through Hollywood for the admitted purpose of making money. She's tight with a buck and is very shrewd in business affairs."

He even criticized her charity work, citing the Thalians, suggesting that they were a ruse to garner favorable publicity for herself. "She perpetuates the girl-next-door image that is only that…an image.'"

Her friend, dancer-actress Marge Champion, told the press, "No one gets to be a star in show business without some kind of self-preservation. You can't let everyone walk over you. Dinah Shore is one of the most beloved people in show business, but don't you think with all those magnolia blossoms that she doesn't know what's good for her. Debbie is the same way. She has a sixth sense about what is good for her."

Debbie always told the press, "My greatest joy is to be with my family." The magazine challenged that assertion, claiming that she spent almost no time with Carrie, 5, or with Todd, 3.

"She leaves home at 6AM before they are up and puts in a twelve-hour day at the studio. She gets home at around 7PM and is in bed by 8PM to get her beauty sleep before facing the cameras the next morning. She spends her days off with her large circle of friends. The children are left in the care of a nursemaid. Every now and then, Todd and Carrie are groomed and made ready for a photo op with their mother."

A reporter from the *London Sunday Express* noted that she ordered the nursemaid to deliver Carrie and Todd to the studio at 1PM where cast and crew looked on as she posed for pictures patting their heads. After fifteen minutes, she sent them back home and resumed her work.

Snyder concluded: "Every star twinkles only to see how much gold dust it can catch. Debbie strives hard to present only one side of herself to her adoring fans. She rarely makes any self-revelations. But she did once."

"If I ever get away from being just me," she said, "I'd be sure to wake up some morning hating the person I'm pretending to be."

***

When Debbie learned that MGM was lending her to Paramount to co-star with Fred Astaire, she was skeptical. "I've played every role anyone ever assigned me, but Fred—whom I adore—and I would not be convincing as screen lovers. Isn't he getting a bit wobbly to make love to me on camera? I looked it up: He was born May 20, 1899."

But when she read the script, she was put at ease. *The Pleasure of His Company* had originated on Broadway in October of 1958, the creation of Samuel A. Taylor and Cornelia Otis Skinner, who had also penned the screenplay. It was another film by producers William Perlberg and George Seaton, who had co-starred her with Tony Curtis in *The Rat Race*. This time, Seaton was the director.

The plot called for Debbie to be cast as a San Francisco debutante, Jessica Poole, whose father was a globe-trotting *bon vivant*, Pogo Poole. She hasn't seen him since he divorced her mother, Katharine (as played by Lilli Palmer).

Since her divorce, her mother has remarried a stodgy banker, a role played by Gary Merrill, an actor famously wed to Bette Davis. *[For some reason, the scriptwriters had defined that character's name as Jim Dougherty, the same name as Marilyn Monroe's first husband.]*

Debbie, as Jessica, is set to marry Roger Henderson (Tab Hunter), a cattle rancher from the Valley of the Moon in California's Sonoma County. Pogo has been invited to the wedding, where he stirs up trouble. Although Jessica (Debbie) is delighted to see him again, and he makes peace with Katharine, both Jim and Roger remain skeptical of his intentions.

Pogo tries to break off his daughter's engagement, inviting her to run away with him and see the world. He also seems to be deliberately attempting to separate Jim from Katharine.

But it all works out in the end as Pogo heads for the airport, not with either his daughter or his former wife, but with Toy (Harold Fong), the family's prized chef.

Debbie was delighted to be working with Astaire again. *[He had appeared with her in her third picture,* Three Little Words *(1950).* He'd also given her support and encouragement during her darkest hours learning the intricate dance routines for *Singin' in the Rain.*

Of course, she was not alone in considering him one of the screen greats. In a career that would span three-quarters of a century, he was named the Fifth Greatest Star of All Time by the American Film Institute. Gene Kelly had told Debbie, "The history of dance on film begins with Fred Astaire."

John Russell Taylor summed up Astaire's unique appeal: "A classic, one of a kind. There never was anyone vaguely like Fred Astaire. Critics argued about whether he could sing at all, and yet all the great popular composers, such as Cole Porter and Harold Arlen, agreed that he had no equal in the delicate art of putting over a song, even if he croaked it. And when it came to the dance, he just inhabited a different world from the others."

In reference to Astaire, Debbie said, "It was like dancing on air. I felt as light as a feather. Fred had his hand on my back. He had very long fingers. His figure was lean, athletic, and beautiful, even at the age of

In the 1950s, fan magazines such as *Screen Stories* promoted the *faux* romance of Debbie and Tab Hunter, even though their editorial staffs knew that "Tab was as gay as a Christmas goose, but gorgeous." Most likely, he was spending his nights in bed with fellow actor Anthony Perkins.

When fans saw this picture of Debbie and Hunter in tennis shorts, they asked a question: "Which one has the most shapely legs?"

sixty."

The German actress, Lilli Palmer, was intimated by the idea of dancing with him. At the time that Debbie met her, she'd divorced Rex Harrison and had married actor Carlos Thompson, "the Argentine heartthrob." As a Jew, Palmer had escaped from Germany when Hitler and the Nazis came to power.

As stated by Palmer, "The last time I danced, I ended up in a heap at the feet of those chorus girls at the Moulin Rouge in Paris."

Debbie watched as she performed a dance number with Astaire. "Unlike me, she landed squarely on his dancing feet. But he pulled it off. After that, he never allowed her to land at all. She just hung suspended in his skinny arms."

Debbie and Fred Astaire were photographed in San Francisco during the making of one of their mediocre films, *The Pleasure of His Company*. "The title was apt for how I felt about hanging out with Fred," Debbie said. "His name evoked serene agility."

He told her, "Ginger Rogers told me that I would-never make it as a movie star because of my enormous ears and bad chin line."

Debbie liked working with veteran actor Charles Ruggles, cast as her grandfather, Mackenzie Savage. "We became friends, and forever after I called him grandpa."

Tab Hunter had the fourth lead, even though he'd recently been appearing in pictures as the star. "I would have settled for tenth billing to work with a legend like Astaire," he said. "It was also great working with my old pal Debbie, the first gal I ever dated in Hollywood. One night in her parents' home in Burbank, I tried to kiss her but she backed off, telling me it would be like kissing her brother Billy."

A lot of the location shooting for *The Pleasure of His Company* was executed in San Francisco. After work, Astaire, Debbie, and Hunter often walked down the steep hill from the Mark Hopkins Hotel to dine in Chinatown.

"Tab and I were great friends, but never lovers," she said. "I always knew he was gay. I was so happy when he found a partner, a wonderful man, and settled down."

For interior shots, cast and crew returned to Hollywood, where Debbie rejoined Carrie and Todd.

"At the end of each picture, I always worried that it would be my last," Debbie said. "But soon I learned that Fox wanted me for a picture, and Paramount wanted me to return. Not only that, but MGM was preparing to cast me in two of the greatest pictures of my entire career. My professional life was great, but I didn't know where my private life was headed. I didn't feel emotionally stable enough to survive another disastrous marriage."

***

Harry Karl's marriage to Joan Cohn, the widow of Columbia's CEO Harry Cohn, lasted for only twenty-one days. Three weeks after her wedding, she filed for divorce. As mandated by their settlement, in exchange for his freedom, Karl gave her two mink coats, a diamond ring, and a million dollars.

The first person he telephoned in the aftermath of that settlement was Debbie. Her refusals to accept his calls did not deter him. He continued phoning. She did not find him attractive, and the idea of going to bed with him repulsed her slightly.

Ever since she'd dated Robert Wagner, he had been the standard by which she judged other men. She still adored male beauty, finding that Hollywood's most attractive men included Tab Hunter, Jeffrey Hunter, Rock Hudson, Tony Curtis, and Farley Granger.

But during the months following her divorce, her mind was not dominated by romance. She feared that her days as a leading lady were numbered, maybe five or six years at the most. She had bills to pay and children to support and educate.

She'd been under contract to MGM for ten years, but she felt she needed a better deal and wanted to branch out in ways that would improve the nature of both her movies and her television appearances.

Through Irving Briskin, a business manager and producer, she renegotiated her contract with MGM, agreeing to make four pictures a year for $2,000 a week.

Even though she refused to take Karl's calls, he kept phoning her for a date. In desperation, he turned to a mutual acquaintance, Sidney Korshak, a well-known Hollywood attorney, and asked him to intercede with her on his behalf. "He's eating his heart out for you," the attorney said. "Let him meet with you at least once."

The studio mogul, Harry Cohn, once shared the same wife, Joan Perry, with Harry Karl, but Karl's marriage to her lasted only three weeks.

"I had to settle a million on her. During our 'wedded bliss' I got to screw her five times. The way I figured it, that cost me $200,000 per fuck."

The photo above, snapped in 1946, shows Perry with her then-husband, the notorious Harry Cohn.

Noted for her sense of fashion, Perry is dressed in couture about as expensive as anything available on the planet at the time.

Finally, she relented and invited Karl to her house one afternoon at 2PM, claiming that she had business associates arriving at three, and that he'd have to leave before then. She viewed their rendezvous as a chance to brush him off.

He arrived right on the dot, an elaborate ceremony she witnessed through the picture window in her living room. His driver, wearing an elephant-born uniform, pulled into her driveway in a maroon-colored Rolls-Royce. He jumped out to open the rear door. Karl emerged with a large bouquet of roses, and the chauffeur carried several packages of toys for Carrie and Todd.

As Debbie settled in with him in her living room, she bluntly asked him, "Why did you marry Joan so soon after proposing to me?"

"I felt that because I was older, I didn't have a chance with a young thing like you," he answered. "Besides, I don't exactly look like Tyrone Power and Errol Flynn as they did in the '30s. Let's face it: Women don't make passes at men who wear glasses."

"I thought it was the other way around," she said.

"I hoped I might dazzle you with my money," he said, "and gifts. Let's not forget gifts like jewelry. You may not know this, but since 1952, I've taken over Karl's Shoe Stores, the largest privately owned retail shoe chain in America."

"Well, that's tempting at least," she said jokingly. "At least I wouldn't have to go barefoot in winter."

"I also feel I could be a good father to Carrie and Todd, give them everything they need, including a good education."

"That's very fine, but it still doesn't explain why you rushed into a marriage with Joan," she said.

"When you turned me down, I thought it was for the final time. I went out of my mind and acted impulsively, fearing that Joan might be my last chance. I hear you're making a lot of money on your own these days, so you hardly need to marry me for my money. It was a mistake marrying Joan, but I'm not blaming you. It was my own damn fault."

He put no pressure on her that afternoon and even exited before the 3PM deadline for the business appointment she did not have. He also didn't ask her for a future date and at the door, he merely shook her hand.

He did say, "Do you mind if I call you again in a few days?"

"I guess so," she said before shutting the door on him.

Finally, near the end of November in 1959, she went out with him on their first real date, which was to the local premiere of Tchaikovsky's ballet, *Swan Lake*.

In the same chauffeur-driven Rolls, he arrived with more toys for Todd and Carrie. She was charmed by a special piece of jewelry he presented to her, a bauble he'd commissioned from the most exclusive jewelry store in Beverly Hills. In honor of their attendance at *Swan Lake*, it was an exquisite and very expensive mother-of-pearl pin in the shape of a swan with a "neck" of glittering diamonds.

He also gave her yet another velvet-covered box, this one containing a pair of diamond earrings, almost an exact duplicate of a set he'd presented to Marie McDonald on the occasion of their second marriage.

After *Swan Lake [in reference to which she claimed, "Harry stayed awake!"]*, she began to date him two or three times a week. He even escorted her to the premiere of *The Rat Race*, the picture in which she'd co-starred with Tony Curtis. On that night, he'd arrived with fifty long-stemmed roses wrapped in a mink stole.

Her former acting coach, Lillian Burns Seaton, kept phoning her, urging her to drop Karl. "If you go ahead and marry the bastard, make sure that the diamond ring he gives you is bigger than the one he gave Marie McDonald."

***

The time had come for her to return to work for producer Jack Cummings, who had cast her in her first two pictures for MGM, *Three Little Words* (1950) and *Two Weeks With Love* (also 1950). She had also appeared in his movie, *Give a Girl a Break* (1953) with Gower and Marge Champion.

"I swooned the first time I walked on the set and saw Steve Forrest, my love interest in *The Second Time Around*," Debbie confided to her other co-star, Thelma Ritter.

"I had been the victim of adultery myself, and I knew he was married, but what is a girl to do? In my dressing room, he held me close to his body and started kissing my neck. I simply defy a woman to resist this walking streak of sex."

He had moved over to 20th Century Fox, and he wanted her to play the lead in his next film, *The Second Time Around*, the story of a young woman with children who finds a new life with another husband after losing her first one.

"I'll do it," she said, without reading the script. "Sounds like the story of my own life."

The Second Time Around, her 27th movie, was set for a Christmas (1961) release. Cummings, working with the noted director, Vincent Sherman, had lined up a diverse and talented cast headed by Debbie and co-starring Steve Forrest, Thelma Ritter, Andy Griffin, and dancer Juliet Prowse. Cast as Lucretia Rogers, Debbie played a New Yorker in 1911 who loses her husband. Over the objections of her mother-in-law, she decides to temporarily leave her children and accept a job in the Arizona territory. Her hope involved building a new life for herself and sending for her kids later. The plot came from the novel, *Star of the West*, by Richard Emery Roberts. He had fashioned the screenplay with Oscar Sault and Clair Huffaker.

After arriving in Arizona, Lucretia learns that her prospective employer has died and that the job he had offered was not available. However, a very butch Thelma Ritter, as a tough old rancher, Aggie Gates, hires her.

In the meantime, she attracts the eye of Dan Jones (Steve Forrest), the local saloon-keeper. As a romantic partner, he has already been staked out by his jealous employee, Rena Mitchell (Juliet Prowse). Rancher Pat Collins (Andy Griffin) also has an eye out for Lucretia. The villain of the film is crooked Sheriff Burns (Ken Scott).

After a series of adventures and mishaps, Debbie herself becomes the sheriff and starts to clean up the town. In the meantime, she sends for her kids back East and ends up in the arms of Dan Jones (Forrest). On posters and in ad campaigns, and in reference to the spunky character perhaps inspired by Debbie's former portrayal of Tammy, the film was eventually marketed with the tagline SHE'S TANGLING WITH HE-MEN WHO WANT TO BE FREE-MEN.

Forrest was a tall, good-looking, blonde, the younger brother of Dana Andrews, a far better-established star. Debbie had seen him on the screens of the 1940s, especially in that Samuel Goldwyn classic, *The Best Years of Our Lives* (1946).

She had met Forrest briefly in 1953 when he'd had an uncredited role in *I Love Melvin*, the film she'd made with Donald O'Connor. She told her co-star, "That Steve Forrest is about the sexiest thing walking on two legs."

"Wait till you see the third leg," he quipped.

She was startled, and it took her a moment to figure out what he meant.

"No, I'm not gay," he said. "Steve stood next to me at the urinal."

In *I Love Melvin*, Forrest had played a small uncredited role described as "Photographer Crane." At that point in his career, he was struggling for bigger roles. In 1952, he'd also appeared uncredited in *The Bad and the Beautiful*, co-starring Lana Turner and Kirk Douglas. Lana had been cast as a screen actress, Georgia Lorrison, and Forrest appears with her in a scene where she is undergoing a screen test.

Ever alert to male beauty, Lana seduced Forrest in her dressing room. "Why not?" she later told Debbie. "I've had his brother Dana, too. Sometimes, if a girl goes for one brother, she might as well fall for the other one, too."

Despite his infidelities, Forrest was a married man and had been since 1948 when he wed Christina Carilas. It became one of the most enduring marriages in Hollywood, lasting until his death in 2013.

Another major star, Jane Wyman, had also succumbed to the charms of Forrest. In her case, it was in 1953 when he'd played her son in Edna Ferber's *So Big*. "It was a case of off-screen incest," Sherman told Debbie. "After she dumped Ronald Reagan, Jane began pursuing younger men, even Rock Hudson. One of her boyfriends was once mistaken for her grandson."

During lunch one day with Sherman, Forrest told him, "The secret of a long-lasting marriage is to play around with other women. Then come back to home, hearth, and those bedroom slippers for a home-cooked dinner with your wife. Enjoying that added spice on the side will only enrich your marriage and make it last."

"You're preaching to the choir," Sherman said.

One of Hollywood's best-known directors, Sherman, too, was in an enduring marriage—in his case to Hedda Comorau, whom he'd wed in 1934. He'd had high-profile affairs with Rita Hayworth, Bette Davis, and Joan Crawford. "My leading ladies always fall in love with me."

"How about Debbie?" Forrest asked.

"I'm giving her to you as a present."

Sherman later claimed, "Debbie needed some loving. She was in the prime of her life, with her hormones raging. After being dumped by Fisher, she felt undesirable to men. If nothing else, Steve restored her confidence in her own womanhood."

"During the making of our silly western, little Miss Debbie fell in love with Steve. When he wasn't needed on the set, and she was free, he headed for her dressing room. The whole cast and crews knew what was going on. Thelma Ritter told me, 'Debbie has to get it from some place.'"

"Debbie told me herself that she felt a lot of guilt because what she was doing was strictly forbidden by the doctrines of her Church of the Nazarene, whoever the fuck they are," Sherman said. "But her guilt didn't stop her from having some fun. I understood it. That Steve guy was firecracker hot. Women couldn't resist him, especially when he wore tight pants. A gal would have to be a lesbian not to go for him."

"Actually, he was just following in the footsteps of his older brother, Dana Andrews," Sherman said. "He was known for seducing his leading

During the making of *The Second Time Around*, Debbie was pursued by a "mama's boy," as portrayed by Andy Griffith. "In time, he became America's favorite folksy sheriff, but he wasn't like that at all in private," she said.

He told her, "I lead a scandalous life, and I'm capable of doing unforgivable things. If my fans knew what I'm like, they'd turn on me in droves. I might even be arrested."

She never found out what those dark secrets were.

ladies, everyone from Gene Tierney in *Laura* (1944) to Joan Crawford in *Daisy Kenyon* (1947)."

"Steve broke Debbie's heart when he refused to divorce his wife and marry her," the director claimed. "Perhaps she was trying to pull an Elizabeth Taylor trick—that is, lure a husband away from his wife."

"At the end of our picture, Steve had to tell Debbie that it was all over between them, as he was heading home to his faithful wife. Debbie went into hiding for a while to recover. She'd really fallen bigtime for God's gift to women."

***

Debbie published two memoirs—one in 1988 and another in 2013. In neither book did she mention that her co-star had been Forrest. Instead, she claimed that Andy Griffin had been her leading man, when in fact he was the "second banana" who lost the girl. "The fact that she didn't even mention Steve's name must be proof that she was still pissed off." Sherman said.

Debbie liked working with both Griffin and Ritter. Griffin complained to Debbie that having to ride a horse "messes up my private parts." She went to wardrobe and got him extra padding to protect what he called "the nicest family jewels to come out of North Carolina."

She'd seen Griffin's breakthrough film debut in *A Face in the Crowd* (1957). In it, he played an ambitious country boy who is discovered and morphed into a powerful and unscrupulous TV star. *[Many viewers and critics interpreted the character he played as a specific reference to Arthur Godfrey.]*

During his long-running TV series, he was typecast as the good-hearted, country-wise Sheriff Andy Taylor in his long-running TV series, *The Andy Griffith Show*. (1960-68). Debbie said, "But he was so much more sophisticated and had a darker side to him that came out in some later pictures."

During the shooting of *The Second Time Around*, Debbie cemented her friendship with Ritter, "even though this tough-talking Belle of Brooklyn stole every scene with me." No great beauty,

During the filming of *The Second Time Around*, Thelma Ritter became one of Debbie's best friends.

Their friendship aroused the ire of Agnes Moorehead, who became clearly jealous of Debbie's new bonding.

Ritter was known for her comedic characters with strong New York accents. She received six Oscar nods for Best Supporting Actress, more than any other actress in that category.

Her most memorable role was that of "Birdie" in *All About Eve* (1950) with Bette Davis. Ritter also starred as Doris Day's housekeeper in *Pillow Talk* (1959) in which she drank Rock Hudson under the table.

In reference to the actress who played Debbie's "competition" in the film, Debbie said, "Juliet Prowse was given a thankless role that could have been played by dozens of other actresses. She didn't get to show off that she was brilliant as a dancer. She was trapped in our silly little western."

Sherman later said, "Steve took care of Debbie's libido during our shoot. As for Juliet, Ol' Blue Eyes, Mr. Sinatra himself, showed up on occasion for prolonged visits to her dressing room. Once upon a time, or so I've heard, he got it on with Debbie, the eternal virgin."

Upon the film's release on December 23, 1961, Bosley Crowther of *The New York Times* took time off from Christmas shopping to rush into the Paramount Theatre on Broadway at 43rd Street to see *The Second Time Around*. He filed this summation:

> *"Don't look for quality. Just go there expecting nothing more than another chance to see Miss Reynolds fluff her fine little feathers prettily; Miss Ritter play the hard-boiled softie; Andy Griffin chew the fat bucolically; and Mr. Forrest act the noble scapegrace—and you may have a pretty good time. Vincent Sherman has kept things moving on the CinemaScope and color screen."*

***

During the making of *Can-Can* in 1959, Frank Sinatra had met dancer Juliet Prowse, whose later picture, *The Second Time Around,* starred Debbie.

At the time of the singer's encounter with Prowse, she was twenty-three and he was forty-five. He'd been introduced to Prowse by their mutual

A celebrated dancer, Juliet Prowse was disappointed when, as a contract player for Fox, she was assigned this lackluster role of a saloon girl.

In this scene (depicted above), she was told to come on to Andy Griffith.

"After sharing beds with Frank Sinatra and Elvis Presley, I was supposed to have the hots for poor Andy. Ah, Hollywood."

friend, Shirley MacLaine. He dedicated his song in *Can-Can*, "It's All Right With Me," to Prowse. MacLaine later said, "Frankie seemed to be falling in love. At last, a woman who might, perhaps, make him forget Ava Gardner."

The long-legged Prowse was an Anglo-Indian dancer born in Mumbai (then known as Bombay), India, but reared in South Africa by her British colonial parents. Spotted by a talent agent in Paris, she eventually signed to play the role of one of the *ingénues*, Claudine, in *Can-Can*.

[Prowse captured the attention of the world when, during a studio tour in Hollywood in honor of the U.S. visit of the Soviet leader, Nikita Khrushchev in September of 1959, she performed a saucy version of the Can-Can. At the end of the show, in his evaluation of what he defined as yet another example of capitalistic decadence, he denounced the dancers for "showing their asses."]

After the wrap of the movie, Sinatra invited her to Las Vegas. In 1962, they announced their engagement. Several complications arose during the course of their pre-marital foreplay: During the making of *G.I. Blues* (1960), Prowse also sustained a brief but torrid affair with Elvis Presley.

During their film together, Debbie and Prowse had long talks about Sinatra, and whether the younger actress should marry him. "He's a wonderful man," Debbie said. "I practically fell in love with him, even before we made *The Tender Trap*. Had he asked me, I would have married him and surrendered my virginity. Only problem was, he never asked me, and I went on to marry that disaster, Eddie Fisher, or Mr. Elizabeth Taylor as he is now referred to."

"He wants me to give up my career, and I don't want to," Prowse told Debbie. "He wants love and marriage going together like a horse and carriage. Or so the song goes, but I want career and marriage. If I marry him and give up my career, for which I've worked so hard, he'll probably dump me in a few years and then I'll no longer be in demand in Hollywood."

"Don't worry about that," Debbie advised. "After a year or so, he'll be urging you to return to films since all your dancing around the house will probably be driving him crazy."

On four different occasions, Sinatra showed up on the set of *The Second Time Around*. He hugged and kissed Debbie each time, as if they were old friends.

Prowse had other serious reservations about marrying Sinatra, which she discussed with Debbie. "I don't think I'm in love with the man. I think I'm in love with Frank Sinatra, the legendary singer. I was more flattered by his proposal of marriage than of the actual prospect of being married to him. Perhaps I'm in love with his voice, not with the man himself. Besides, I'm close to the age of his daughter. He's also overly possessive, wanting to control every aspect of my life. At times, I think he's more like a father figure than a lover. He's got an awful temper and can explode into rage at the slightest provocation. The other night, when his spaghetti wasn't cooked right, like his mother used to do it, he threw the plate of food in the waiter's face."

"That's true, I guess," Debbie said. "He does have a bit of temper, so I've heard. But he's never revealed that side to me."

"There's another problem," Prowse said. "I know he's slipping around and dating other women, Marilyn Monroe for instance."

"That's stiff competition," Debbie said.

During one of the final times Sinatra visited the set, Prowse was appearing on camera with Steve Forrest.

Debbie kissed Sinatra lightly on the lips. "If things don't work out between you and Juliet, you can always propose to me. In case you do, I'll accept in advance. You can save money on buying me a large diamond engagement ring. I already have one I can give you to give to me."

"Sounds like a pretty good deal," he said jokingly. "I'll think it over. That diamond ring would make it more economical for me."

"Of course, you'll probably leave me for Marilyn Monroe," she said, with humor. "That would mean I'd enter the pages of Hollywood history as the dame who lost both of her husbands to Tinseltown's two sexiest goddesses, Elizabeth and Marilyn."

"Instead of me," Sinatra responded, "I think you should marry Sammy Davis, Jr. You guys are the same size. It would generate tons of publicity."

[There was a footnote to the Sinatra/Prowse affair. While appearing at the Cocoanut Grove in Los Angeles, Eddie Fisher was introduced to Prowse and was immediately attracted to her. "I found her exquisite, especially those long legs of hers. Elizabeth has dumpy legs."

Although he knew that she was "Frankie's gal," he'd also heard from Dean Martin that they had temporarily broken up during the summer of 1961.

Before Fisher started his heavy dating of Prowse, he phoned Sinatra at Claridge's Hotel in London to ask his permission.

"Go ahead, have a ball," Sinatra told him.

Walter Winchell got wind of this and ran a column headlined EDDIE/FRANK/JULIET—NEW FILM TRIANGLE.

Fisher later wrote, "The sex with Juliet was lovely, but we were both in love with other people, me with Elizabeth, she with Sinatra."

Years later, Fisher made a confession to his daughter, Carrie, who was now grown up and having turbulent affairs of her own.

"I was railroaded into a marriage to your mother, even though I never loved her. Many nights when I fucked Debbie, I was thinking of Elizabeth, even though she was married at the time to Mike Todd. I felt guilty about that."

"Except for Elizabeth, I think I'm more in love with the chase than I am with the actual conquest. When I was screwing Juliet Prowse, I was actually dreaming of Ann-Margret, with whom I was also having an affair."

"I pulled many a fast one on Debbie," Fisher claimed. "She always considered Edie Adams one of her best friends. Guess what? Edie and I often slipped around behind Debbie's back and got it on."

"So that's why you never became Father of the Year," Carrie said.]

***

Debbie's next film, *How the West Was Won,* was an inter-generational saga, a Metrocolor epic with an all-star cast and, perhaps, a sense of America's Manifest Destiny. It was scheduled for release by MGM in 1963. It would become one of the most famous films in which she appeared, as well as one of the most life-threatening she ever performed in. A sprawling drama shot on locations between Kentucky and Oregon, it was scripted to show the color and violence of the American West, incorporating 12,000 extras, more than 600 horses, a stampede of 2,000 buffalo and endless views of evocative "big sky" panoramas.

Debbie, as Lilith, facing her own "Manifest Destiny" and a hassle of life-threatening action shots, in *How the West Was Won.*

Its producer, Bernard Smith, hired three directors for five segments, each illustrating a different "chapter" in the collective lives of a family (the Prescotts) during their westward migration. *[The segments, each loosely divided and often segué-ing seamlessly into one another, included* The Rivers *(set in 1839);* The Plains *(set in 1851);* The Civil War *(1861-65);* The Railroad *(1868); and* The Outlaws *(1889).]* Spencer Tracy provided the narration.

In an attempt to lure American families from their television sets, MGM had arranged to have the picture shot for display on the curved-screen, then-innovative three-projector Cinerama process. The directors of this multi-segmented epic included John Ford, Henry Hathaway, and George Marshall. Debbie knew only one of these men, Marshall, who had previously directed her in *The Mating Game* (1951) with Tony Randall as her unlikely beau.

At MGM, she'd heard much talk about the movie, but in no way thought of herself

Debbie dreaded "working with that vicious son of a bitch," Henry Hathaway in *How the West Was Won.* He didn't mind risking the lives of his actors in many of his action-adventure films.

He told Debbie, "Having a death during the making of a film, or a possible leg amputation for an actor, is all part of the game of making movies."

as a contender for any of the roles in it. All that changed one afternoon when Hathaway phoned and invited her to lunch the following day in the MGM commissary.

She knew nothing of the plot, the segment she might be in, or a possible role for herself, but she'd heard only bad news about Hathaway, who was said to be brutal with his stars, especially actresses.

She knew he was a friend of Glenn Ford, so she phoned him for the "low-down" on Hathaway. He didn't give her a good report. "I like Henry person-ally, but when he takes over a picture, he's the son of Himmler. He's better at handling male stars—John Wayne, Gary Cooper, and Randolph Scott—than he is with women."

She already knew that Hathaway got his start in silents, and had directed many big stars such as Marlene Dietrich, Adolphe Menjou, Fay Wray, Clara Bow, and Walter Huston. Surprisingly, he'd also directed Marilyn Monroe in her first breakthrough movie, *Niagara* (1953), in which she invented her famous wiggle-walk.

"He really rides an actress," Ford said. "I don't mean he fucks them, but he makes life living hell for them. Susan Hayward once threatened to scratch his eyes out."

With that warning from her sometimes lover, Debbie approached the luncheon with trepidation. Waiting for her was a silver-haired man born in 1898, rugged and masculine, a so-called "man's director."

Hathaway explained the scope of the panoramic picture he wanted to make about the settling of the West and her possible role in it—that of a sev-enteen-year-old, Lilith, who in 1851 journeys to bustling St. Louis, where she finds work performing in a dance hall. "Well, a dance hall tart would be a break from Tammy. I'm flattered that you think a woman of 29 could be convincing as a teenager."

With great enthusiasm, he predicted that *How the West Was Won* would be a milestone in Hollywood cinematic history.

Finally, at the end of his pitch, she told him, "The movie sounds great, just great. But I'm turning it down."

"What the fuck?"

"It's not the movie itself," she said. "But you. I'm told that you're hell on wheels, especially with your female stars, who end up fighting you and ulti-mately hating you. I don't feel that you and I as a team could work together in harmony, especially on some remote location in the wild. I've even heard you're a misogynist."

"That's not true. I love women. I'm a true gentleman, a kindly soul with impeccable manners extended to the fairer sex. Think Ashley Wilkes in *Gone With the Wind.*"

His next move shocked her. He rose from the table and shouted at her, at-tracting the attention of other stars in the dining room. "You're doing the god damn picture—and that's that, you little spitfire." Then he stormed out of the commissary, heading off into the sprawling landscapes of America looking for suitable locations.

Ultimately, it wasn't Hathaway but her dear friend, Thelma Ritter, who persuaded her to accept the role. "I play Agatha Clegg. You'll be my wagon train partner as we head out to tame the West, fleeing from Indians who want to rape us and turn us into their squaws. We'll have a blast. If Hathaway gets out of line, I'll clobber him."

Finally, after many talks, Debbie said, "I'll do it. I'll stop with this 'reluctant debutante' stance I've been taking." She sent word to Hathaway, telling him, "For better or worse, I'm your Lilith."

She was astonished when she read in *Variety* who her co-stars would be, the most glittering array of names ever assembled for a Western. Such big stars as James Stewart and John Wayne led the cast, which also included Carroll Baker, Karl Malden, her friend Agnes Moorehead, Walter Brennan, Lee Van Cleef, Brigid Bazlen, Gregory Peck, Robert Preston, John Larch, David Brian, Andy Devine, Henry Morgan, Richard Widmark, Russ Tamblyn, Carolyn Jones, Lee J. Cobb, Eli Wallach, Harry Dean Stanton, and Mickey Shaughnessy. Henry Fonda, sporting a walrus mustache at the time, was cast as a Buffalo Hunter. Raymond Massey appeared in his familiar role of Abraham Lincoln.

On the set, Debbie shared a reunion with her friend, Karl Malden. He played Zebulon Prescott, the father of two beautiful daughters: Eve (as played by Carroll Baker) and Lilith (as portrayed by Debbie). Eva is attracted to a bucolic beaver trapper and fur trader, Linus Rawlings (James Stewart). Their romance gets off to a rocky start, as he doesn't want to settle down to home and hearth, preferring the fleshpots of the then-frontier settlement of Pittsburgh instead.

"I'm gonna play your dad in the movie," Malden said to Debbie. "As you know, Agnes (Moorehead) will be your ma. We leave New York State with you and with hundreds of other settlers via the Erie Canal, but we don't survive the journey. Your sister settles down on a farm in Kentucky. As Lilith, you head west for a glamourous life as a saloon girl. Expect gunfights, buffalo stampedes, a lot of stuff like that. This film will be hard to shoot. I predict two or three guys will get killed during the making of this blockbuster."

In addition to the star-studded cast, MGM hired 12,617 movie extras plus 350 Native Americans from five different tribes.

James Stewart and "the other blonde," Debbie's on-screen sister, Carroll Baker.

Debbie met with the film's producer, Bernard Smith, who gave her a copy of the long, action-studded script by James R. Webb. Smith was a famous editor of classic detective stories by such writers as Raymond Chandler and Dashiell Hammett. Previously, he'd produced *Elmer Gantry* (1960), the thought-provoking drama about a con man and a female evangelist selling religion to small town America. For his role in that, Burt Lancaster won an Oscar.

Smith told her, "I've studied your part, and I think you'll be great in it. Of course, sometimes my recommendations aren't accepted. I once suggested to Paramount's Frank Freeman that he purchase John Collier's treatments of *The African Queen* as a vehicle for Gary Cooper. Freeman told me, 'Coop's too old.' So John Huston went for it, and, as you know, Humphrey Bogart walked off with the Oscar."

"Make the picture, girl. If it fails, call me whatever name you like. H.L. Mencken labeled me 'a Jew, a moreover, and a jackass.'"

The best news that Debbie heard was that Gregory Peck would be her love interest. She had long considered him "as the most handsome actor in Hollywood, in spite of the fact that one of his ears was bigger than the other."

Cast as Cleve Van Valen, a gambler rogue, he learns that she has inherited a gold mine in California, and he heads west with her on the wagon train, which is led by a horny, wife-hunting wagon master (played by Robert Preston), who also pursues Lilith.

When Cleve learns that her gold mine is worthless, he abruptly abandons her. New and alone in a muddy boom town, she finds a job performing in a hastily erected dance hall, and opts to live in her covered wagon until she can find something better. Times are rough.

Later, she gets a job performing in the music saloon of a riverboat.

Quite by chance, Cleve is a passenger on board, and he re-enters her life. After playing the winning hand in a high-stakes poker game, he proposes to her, and together, they move to the rapidly growing city of San Francisco to seek their fortunes.

Along with the crew and other members of the cast, Debbie was ordered to report to work in Paducah, Kentucky, a small swampy city close to the junctions of four major rivers: The Tennessee, the Ohio, the Cumberland, and the Mississippi. Rising from soggy ground amid all these

Gregory Peck was Debbie's love interest in *How the West Was Won*. "Regrettably, our affair was strictly on camera," she lamented.

He told her that he'd been set to play opposite Marilyn Monroe in *Let's Make Love* (1960), but that he'd dropped out after a rewritten script had diminished his role.

"Yves Montand replaced me, and he took the title of the film literally. Off came Marilyn's panties."

282

waterways was an island infested with rattlesnakes and water moccasins. It was there that Hathaway opted to film part of his sequence. In advance of the cast and crew's arrival, he hired four Kentucky hunters with rifles and lots of ammunition to shoot and kill as many of the venomous reptiles as they could.

Remembering her poverty-stricken childhood in El Paso, Debbie made a recommendation to Hathaway: "You should barbecue some of the meat from the biggest rattlers. Makes for good eatin'."

In spite of Hathaway's promise to treat Debbie kindly, he started yelling and screaming at her from Day One, barking such orders to her as, "Get your ass over here!"

When she could take no more, she pretended to faint, shutting down production. He accused her of faking it, as crew members crowded around trying to revive her. She opened her eyes and revived herself after he apologized. She repeated that stunt three more times. For the remainder of the shooting, whenever he regressed and started shouting at her again, all she had to do on such occasions was to warn him, "I'm about to faint."

"Gregory (Peck) was more beautiful in person than he was in the movies, and he looked mighty gorgeous on the screen, too," Debbie said. "I could have gone for him bigtime. At least I got to kiss him on camera…or cameras in this case. I wanted to make it as passionate as possible, so I opened my mouth, hoping his tongue would fill the cavity. When Gene Kelly first French kissed me, I almost puked. But with Greg, I wanted more. I flubbed the scene two or three times so I'd get to have him kiss me again."

"I never got acquainted with what lurked below Greg's belt," she said. "That privilege went to such fine ladies as Ingrid Bergman and Ava Gardner. Susan Hayward got to sink her red-painted claws into all that male flesh, too, as did that whore, Barbara Payton. Lauren Bacall also went for him, and I suspect that Joan Collins also scored a home run."

Both Debbie and Peck didn't like

"Dance Hall Debbie" as a saloon girl in 1850s St. Louis in *How the West Was Won*

The Perilous West: In this souvenir photo from MGM, as she verges on panic, Debbie is hauled by a frogman from the icy waters of Colorado's Gunnison River.

Director Henry Hathaway, whose back is to the camera, supervises.

283

working in front of three cameras, part of the then high-tech Cinerama process. "I find it almost impossible to act realistically in front of a giant machine with three lenses," he told her. "You have to look at the camera instead of at the actor you're talking to. In one scene, instead of a person, I was talking to a tree off camera. That was hell."

Whereas Debbie had learned how to control Hathaway, Peck had not. "He yells. He screams. He foams at the mouth. He chews cigars all day. Who in hell does he think he is?"

Hathaway shared his opinion of Peck with Debbie. "He's a cold, indifferent actor. There is no love in him. I keep knocking on the door of his impenetrable reserve, but he never lets me in."

During the making of the movie, Debbie cemented her friendships with Carroll Baker, Thelma Ritter, and especially with Agnes Moorehead who became her dearest female friend for life.

Baker said, "I'd heard rumors that Debbie was a spoiled brat and snob. None of that was true. I found her delightful and down to earth, and we became dear friends. We got off to a strange start. One day she came to my room and announced, 'I'm a pushy broad just barging into your room to be your friend.'"

"Carroll (Baker) was a very fine actress," Debbie said. "I adored her in Tennessee Williams' *Baby Doll* (1956) where she was cast as a sexy little teenage vixen opposite Karl Malden. She was also great as James Dean's lover in *Giant* (1955). After making *How the West Was Won,* she told me that she'd been cast in the film version of Harold Robbins' *The Carpetbaggers* (1964)."

"I'll play the Jean Harlow character," Baker said, "with George Peppard doing the Howard Hughes impersonation."

Whenever possible, Hathaway preferred not to use stuntmen, which often put his actors in jeopardy. During location shooting, two members of the crew drowned, and one man had to have his mangled leg amputated.

"On two different occasions, once on a location shoot in Colorado and again in Oregon, Thelma and I were nearly killed," Debbie said. "Hathaway, the bastard, would have used the scenes of our deaths and ordered that the script be rewritten to reflect that."

In one dramatic scene, Ritter and Debbie were fleeing from rampaging Indians in their covered wagon pulled by six galloping horses. The shot took place at the "Dallas Divide," a cliff that forms a section of the Black Canyon near Telluride in Colorado. "We kept waiting for Hathaway to call 'cut,' as our horses were racing dangerously close to the cliff, and we couldn't slow them down. We faced certain death. Thelma was using every curse word she'd learned growing up on the tough streets of Brooklyn. Finally, at the last second, five wranglers slowed down our horses just before we plunged to our deaths like the scene in that future movie, *Thelma & Louise* (1991) that co-starred Susan Sarandon and Geena Davis."

Another dangerous shot for Ritter and Debbie was at another location, the Gunnison River in Oregon. She and Ritter almost drowned that day. "I was a topnotch swimmer, but Thelma was not," Debbie said.

The scene called for them to cross the fast-moving currents in a covered wagon, but in the middle of the stream, the pressure of the icy water caused the wagon to break apart. Hathaway had hired frogmen to work underwater, holding the women up so that their heads bobbed above the surface of the water.

Whereas Ritter was saved by two frogmen, Debbie was caught up in freezing currents that were racing toward a stretch of deadly rapids.

"I was wearing a long skirt and petticoats, which was almost my undoing," she said. "I thought my eyes were going to fall out of my head. I paddled frantically, but I was being forced downstream. I hit rocks that ripped my hands, causing them to bleed. Where were those god damn frogmen? I was a hundred yards downstream, bouncing over boulders like a piece of Styrofoam. Finally, 'The Frogman' appeared, a little late. Had he delayed another second or two, *The New York Times* on its frontpage would have carried my obituary, and I'm sure I would have led off the nightly news on TV."

Hathaway came to check up on them when they were out of those wet clothes and into robes, getting warmed up in a heated trailer.

His sexist remark infuriated both Ritter and Debbie. "I hoped that cold water didn't make you frigid, so I don't have to face complaints from your boyfriends." Then he barked an order to a member of the crew. "Get these gals a slug of brandy."

"You son of a bitch!" Ritter yelled to his departing back as he exited from the trailer.

By the next day, Hathaway's manners hadn't improved. Both Ritter and Debbie had to get back into wet gingham skirts and petticoats to shoot a scene that showed them emerging from the river. Since it was wet, Debbie's dress was very tight around her bosom.

Hathaway came up to her and noticed that as he checked out her breasts. "Here's our chance to get some sex into this movie. Run to the trailer. Get some ice cubes from the fridge and rub them around your nipples until they get hard. Jean Harlow used to do that in every scene before going on camera."

"The hell I will!" she said defiantly. "In case you don't know it yet, I'm not Jean Harlot" (sic).

***

Hathaway also cast Debbie in the final segment (*The Outlaws*; 1889) of *How the West Was Won*. For this segment, Debbie, again as Lilith, was transformed into a 90-year-old woman. "I had to go from seventeen to ancient, a bit of a stretch," she said.

She and Cleve (Gregory Peck) had made and spent several fortunes before his death. The widow Lilith is forced to auction off all her possessions to pay her debts. She travels to Arizona with Zeb Rawlings (George Peppard) and his wife, Julie (Carolyn Jones).

Peppard played the son of Lilith's sister Eve (Carroll Baker). The family takes the train to Arizona to oversee Lilith's remaining asset, a ranch, where they hope to make a new life for themselves.

Now a marshal, Zeb is menaced by an old enemy, outlaw Charlie Grant (Eli Wallach). Zeb had killed his brother in a gunfight. Now he is threatening to move against Zeb's family. There's a lot of action in this final segment, including a shootout and a train wreck before Lilith and the Rawlings family can travel to their new home.

Gregory Peck accompanied Debbie to see the rushes. She was rather pleased with her performance and by that of Thelma Ritter. But he was disappointed to see how his role had come out. In the aftermath of his viewing, he denounced the whole movie, defining it as "predictable and corny."

Most of the reviews, however, were quite favorable, and *How the West Was Won* went over big at the box office, garnering $50 million in receipts. Praise, of course, was not universal, one critic finding it "a saga of dim-witted bunglers who couldn't get anything right."

At Oscar time, *How the West Was Won* was nominated for Best Picture of the Year, losing to *Tom Jones*, the bodice-ripper starring a woman-chasing Albert Finney.

"Elizabeth's *Cleopatra* also lost," Debbie said with a certain glee. "I think Elizabeth's barge sank somewhere along the Nile."

How the West Was Won was also nominated for Best Art Direction, Best Color Cinematography, Best Color Costume Dressing, and Best Original Score. It won Oscars for Best Writing, Best Film Editing, and Best Sound.

The last time Debbie ever saw Peck, he told her, "Whenever *How the West Was Won* is showing on TV, I practically break a leg rushing to my set to turn it off."

***

Based on what Carroll Baker had told her, Debbie was not prepared to like George Peppard, a son of Detroit, who had scored such a big hit in Truman Capote's *Breakfast at Tiffany's* (1961). In it, he had played a male hustler.

"I thought he was a pretentious, egotistical brat," Baker claimed, "and that is just for starters. He claimed to be a bachelor, even though I knew he was married. He also had conveniently dropped seven years off his age. I got the impression that he thought he was God's gift to women."

When he didn't get anywhere with Baker, he turned to Debbie, who believed he was a bachelor. That was years before he married actress Elizabeth

Ashley. "Unlike Carroll, I thought George was indeed god's gift to women—so handsome, so virile, so charming, he was like some blonde-haired Viking God."

"I was a bit jealous when I'd learned he was going to star opposite Carroll in *The Carpetbaggers*. She just didn't appreciate this former Marine stud. Like Carroll, he had studied acting at the Actors Studio in New York, but I didn't hold that against him," Debbie said.

Before becoming a movie star, he'd been a fencing teacher, a taxi driver, and even a mechanic in a motorcycle repair shop.

Debbie had heard rumors from Rock Hudson that Peppard was bisexual. He was known to have had an affair with another bisexual actor, Paul Newman, when they had co-starred in the baseball drama, *Bang the Drum Slowly* (1956) for *The United States Steel Hour*.

"On the screen, I drooled over George's baby-faced looks and touch of menace," Debbie said. "He was so cool. The press hailed him both as the next Richard Widmark or the next Alan Ladd. Trouble was, it was the 1960s, and movie fans didn't seem to want another Ladd or Widmark."

During and after the filming of *How the West Was Won*, Debbie began a secret affair with Peppard that lasted for several months.

One day she discussed her passion for him with her confidant, Rock Hudson.

In the midst of her revelation, he interrupted her: "Slow down, gal." She had gotten carried away, asserting that Peppard in the nude must have resembled Adam right after God had created him as an occupant of the Garden of Eden.

"Hollywood is filled with beautiful men for you to pursue," Hudson said. "But stay away from George. He belongs to me. On those nights he's not banging you, he's banging me."

"That sure put a damper on my affair with George," Debbie said.

***

During the filming of *How the West Was Won*, Debbie had a torrid affair with one of her co-stars, George Peppard, although denying it in a memoir.

When he heard about it, her friend, Rock Hudson, phoned and warned her to "back off. He's my private property."

In the photo above, Peppard is shown as a hardworking male hustler opposite Audrey Hepburn, a scatterbrained call girl, in his most famous role, *Breakfast at Tiffany's* (1961), a film based on Truman Capote's *novella* with the same name.

In Debbie's third memoir, published in 2015, she was nearing the end of her life. No longer did she feel that it was important to maintain her virginal Tammy-like innocence as she'd done in her first two memoirs.

As for Peppard, she admitted that she'd had a sexual fantasy about him. But then, she knew he'd been a married man, so she didn't want to appear to be committing adultery.

"I would love to have had the courage to try for a kiss from George, but I was afraid I'd like it too much."

Rock Hudson would not have agreed, had he still been alive. "She wanted more from George than a kiss," he'd once said. "She had every inch of him—and that was plenty."

She did loosen up in her final years and became more revelatory. She admitted she found comedian Buddy Hackett particularly objectionable. One day, she went to his house to pick up Todd and Carrie, who had been playing with the Hackett children.

"He put his hand up my skirt and with the other hand felt my breasts. I had never seen anyone so rude or as sexually crazy as he was. He thought it was funny."

On another occasion, she visited Glen Campbell at his home to rehearse a duet with him that they were set to perform at a charity event for the Thalians.

"He had only started to rehearse with me when he was on top of me on the floor," she claimed. "I adore Glen, but I didn't want to be his afternoon delight. As a gymnast, I managed to escape from him."

That's not how Campbell told his cronies. "I held her down until she relented, and I didn't get off her until I'd given her a good time. I'm sure she'll want repeats. Most of the gals I screw want more."

In a candid admission in her final memoir, she admitted what Hollywood insiders already knew. "Of the many times I've been romantically involved, most of the men are not worthy of writing home about. But some have been very nice men—temporarily."

[EDITOR'S NOTE: The authors of this biography do not agree with Debbie's assessment. Some of the men she encountered were the most desirable in the country, and are indeed worthy of writing about.]

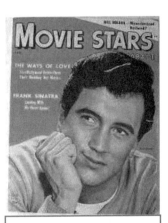

For seven years, Rock Hudson was the top box office star in Hollywood. On rare occasions, Debbie and he shared the same boyfriends.

"At one time, I thought Rock might want me as his wife in a lavender marriage that would conceal his gayness. I might have gone for that."

"After my divorce from Eddie Fisher, a lot of men phoned me; most of them already in a marriage," Debbie claimed. "Some of them were just roving wolves, but another group were guys reportedly involved in happy home life, if such a thing exists in Hollywood."

In a memoir, she didn't name these stars, although she did share amusing anecdotes about their "come-ons" to her friends.

The list of her would-be visitors is not complete but it was known to include Steve Cochran *[known around Hollywood as "the Schvantz"]*, Rory Calhoun *["I learned to fuck while in prison"]*; John Ireland *["I'm the king of Hollywood, not Clark Gable"]*; Forrest Tucker *["I call my monster 'The Chief'"]*; Fernando Lamas *["Latins are the best lovers"]*; Burt Lancaster *["I've got a leopard skin rug for you to lie on"]*; Victor Mature *["I can promise you your biggest thrill"]*; and William Holden *["For references, check with Audrey (Hepburn) or Grace (Kelly)]*.

Other callers included Audie Murphy *["Most women can't resist me"]*; Mickey Rooney *["Big things come in small packages"]*; Mel Tormé *["I'm the natural successor to Sinatra"]*; and Anthony Quinn *["Women tell me I'm easy to fall in love with"]*.

In the meantime, Debbie was going out with Harry Karl, even though she was eighteen years his junior. He was hardly her fantasy man like Steve Forrest, but she told friends such as Agnes Moorehead that he might provide security for her children and herself since he was a multi-millionaire. She also found him "sensitive and generous."

Hollywood insiders just assumed that Debbie and Karl were having an affair. Two of the premier proponents of that belief included gossip mavens Louella Parsons and Hedda Hopper.

"I don't know what Harry is doing for sex, but he's not getting it from me," Debbie told

Buddy Hackett didn't exactly put a gun to Debbie's head, "but he got in his feels over my protests."

In today's world, she could have brought a sexual harassment suit against him.

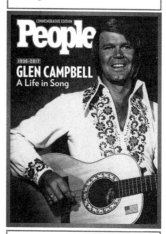

Debbie claimed that during a rehearsal with singer Glen Campbell, he wrestled her to the floor to rape her, but she fought him off.

Campbell did not agree, telling his cronies, "She was crazy for me."

Thelma Ritter and Agnes Moorehead. "Perhaps he's getting it on the side."

There were rumors that Karl was still dating screen actress Rhonda Fleming, whose red hair had once made her "The Queen of Technicolor." Eddie Fisher had heard rumors that Karl was a frequent patron of prostitutes.

Press speculation about Karl's affair with Debbie broke for the first time in one of Hopper's columns. In reference to Karl's previous marriages, she headlined it: A LETTER TO DEBBIE: PLEASE DON'T MAKE ANOTHER MISTAKE—HARRY KARL HAS ALREADY MADE FOUR.

[At a party on the night her column was published, Hopper was overheard talking to another gossip columnist, Mike Connolly, who said, "Karl is not only an old relic, but a hideously ugly man. He's also a god damn Jew. What is it with Debbie? She prefers Jews as husbands?"

"Perhaps she prefers clipped meat," Hopper answered.

"Not me," Connolly retorted, drunkenly. "I always demand that my tricks have foreskins."]

The column infuriated Debbie, and the following morning, in a rage, she drove over to Hopper's house unannounced. She barged in, passed her secretary, and confronted her, yelling, "You're nothing but an anti-Semite."

"Some of my best friends are Jews," Hopper answered. "Louis B. Mayer even tried to make a star out of me. I was warning you that you're making a big mistake by even considering marriage to Harry Karl. You should marry Glenn Ford. He's more your type."

"How dare you tell me who I can marry and who I can't!" Debbie said, her voice rising. "Who do you think you are?"

"WHO AM I?" Hopper answered. "I'm the Bitch of Hollywood, competing with Joan Crawford."

For another thirty minutes, they engaged in a fierce argument of charges and counter-charges. At one point, they decided to laugh it off. Debbie came to realize she could not antagonize the second most powerful columnist in Hollywood.

As Debbie stood up to leave, Hopper said, "If you do marry this creep, don't come to me at your divorce. All I'll do is tell you 'I told you so.'"

Debbie's last vision of Hopper was of her sitting at her typewriter with the sun pouring in on her. She was all in pink, even a pink veil. Debbie imagined that the sun was powerful enough to grow the flowers on her pink picture

Marie McDonald was billed as "The Body" for obvious reasons. She was also a "Popcorn Venus," one of the love goddesses of the 1940s, though not the equal of Ava Gardner or Rita Hayworth.

She married Harry Karl twice, causing Debbie to wonder why.

hat. Her dress, her hosiery, and her high heels were all in pink.

"Now run along, dearie," she said. "I've got a column to write. To make up with you, I'll write an attack on the marriage of Eddie Fisher to Elizabeth."

***

As part of her ongoing evaluation of Harry Karl, Debbie decided to let him demonstrate what kind of father he might be to Carrie and Todd. During the previous two summers, she had rented a four-bedroom villa in Malibu with a guest suite, which she offered to Karl.

"I really put him to the test," she said. "I liked to have my beauty sleep until nine each morning, but the kids woke up hours earlier. At 5AM, when Todd was up roaring for action, I directed him to Harry's suite."

He rose to the challenge, taking the kids to amusement parks, to children's shows, and for days at the beach in Malibu, even though he personally detested the sands. Afternoons usually ended with a visit to Will Wright's Ice Cream Parlor. Whereas Todd was not dedicated to any particular flavor, Carrie always ordered peppermint. After two weeks, Debbie said, "Harry passed the test as a father. But what kind of husband will he make?"

***

Both Karl and Debbie had been plagued with scandals originating with their former spouses.

Marie McDonald, the actress, had married and divorced Karl twice, and she still retained custody of their three children, Harrison, Denice, and the youngest, Tina.

If Debbie married Karl, she didn't want to be sucked into any more scandal. McDonald's promiscuous lifestyle frequently involved her in sordid rumors.

One of McDonald's biggest scandals occurred during January of 1957, when she mysteriously disappeared from her home in Encino. Some 24 hours later, police discovered her wandering along a desolate desert road near Indio.

She claimed at the time that "Two swarthy men, one of them brandishing a sawed-off shotgun," had broken into her home and hauled her away. "No doubt, Harry Karl is behind this," she charged.

Her statement was met with skepticism and doubt. Karl immediately branded the charges as "absurd and ridiculous."

Even so, he came under heavy suspicion, and was featured in unwanted headlines about the alleged kidnapping.

Much later, McDonald admitted to the press that she'd faked her kidnapping, hoping that the charge of abduction would incite the court to grant her a larger divorce settlement.

During a search of her home, where Michael Wilding was living at the time, the police found a copy of the Sylvia Tate novel, *The Fuzzy Pink Nightgown*. Defined as a satirical parody of Hollywood's star system, its plot spins around a movie star who was kidnapped by two men. Indeed, when McDonald was spotted by the police beside that deserted road, she was wearing a fuzzy pink nightgown. Later, she was accused of faking her own kidnapping in ways inspired by the events that transpired within the book.

"Marie is doing a hell of a lot better with her alimony than I am with Eddie. He's paying no child support at all while he lives it up with Elizabeth Taylor," Debbie said. "Marie got a million-dollar settlement from Harry—plus $50,000 a month in child support."

By the end of September, 1960, Debbie shut down the Malibu house and moved back into her home on Conway near the rear of the Beverly Hills Hotel. The place was far too small, and Karl began house hunting, since he'd become convinced that Debbie was going to marry him.

"I am hardly Tammy falling in love," she told Thelma Ritter, her first visitor. "I think I'm being a smart business woman, as I consider Harry a good investment. He owns a hell of a lot of shoe stores. Todd and Carrie will never have to go barefoot."

One night, Karl took her to Chasen's for a celebration. A decree of divorce after his three-week marriage to Joan Cohn had come through, and he was free to marry again. He claimed that Joan, in the aftermath of her divorce from him, was dating both Laurence Harvey and Tab Hunter.

"Why?" Debbie asked. "Both of those guys are gay."

She had great reservations, but she finally agreed to marry Karl on November 25, 1960 in the Beverly Hills home of his sister, Mrs. Sarah Pollock. The marriage took place at 10PM, only three hours after they announced their engagement.

Jeanette Johnson was Debbie's maid of honor, and Saul Pollock, Karl's brother-in-law, his best man. In recognition of their differing religious traditions, the double-ring ceremony was nonsectarian, presided over by the Rev. John Mills of the Little Brown Church in San Fernando Valley.

She was filming, so the honeymoon was a quickie. After a brief reception, she was driven away in Karl's Rolls-Royce by his chauffeur, arriving late at the doorstep of his lavishly furnished, five-bedroom house in Palm Springs.

If she is to be believed, she had her first sex with Karl that weekend. "It was not on the night we arrived. Both of us were too exhausted. We waited until the late morning."

Back in Hollywood, she phoned Rock Hudson, who wanted to know all the details: "It was professionally performed, rather formal. He called me 'Baby Doll' and claimed I was the only woman he'd ever loved. He got off. I didn't. At least I performed my duty and satisfied him…I think."

"Sounds thrilling," he said, sarcastically. "Personally, I'd have gone for Glenn Ford. He's a doll, and he's still got his foreskin. Why do Jewish mothers insist on mutilating the dicks of their sons?"

"How do you know that Glenn still has his foreskin?"

"I make a habit of finding out such details."

Her house on Conway could not accommodate Karl's "armada" of clothing, accessories, and "lots and lots of shoes, mostly alligator." He had to rent a suite at the Beverly Hills Hotel to handle his wardrobe overflow.

"He was the most fastidious man I've ever known," she said. "For some reason, he sent his custom-made shirts to New York to be laundered. A guy named Murray would arrive every morning at 6:30AM to shave Harry. He'd wash and blow-dry his hair, and he'd pay special attention to his mustache. That's where I came in. I used my eyebrow pencil to darken the few gray hairs growing in his mustache."

As she later confessed, "There wasn't much sex during the first weeks of my marriage. Carrie insisted on sleeping between us every night. Sex resumed when Carrie finally moved into her own bed. Harry walked around our bedroom jaybird naked. The first time Carrie saw a man's equipment, she screamed, 'Mommy, Harry's guts are hanging down. Call a doctor!'"

With her film completed, Debbie was free to take a vacation, and she and Karl flew to the Half Moon Resort at Montego Bay in Jamaica. "Every mosquito in Jamaica seemed to want Harry's blood, and I spent the nights applying lotion to his delicate skin. Finally, we cut short our vacation and flew to Miami."

There, they stayed at the Thunderbird Hotel, owned at the time by her friends, Albert and Phyllis Pollock [*no relation to Karl's sister and brother-in-law.*]

Back in California, Thelma Ritter once again was one of her first visitors. Debbie reviewed her honeymoon: "It was idyllic if a gal likes to lie awake at night listening to Harry snore. He sounds like a car with a bad muffler. If Hedda Hopper knows so much about Harry, she should have warned me about the snoring."

The construction of Karl's dreamhouse on Greenway Drive in Beverly Hills had been completed, and he moved Debbie and his new family into the split-level home, which was decorated in what she called "extreme modern." It overlooked the golf course of the Los Angeles Country Club. Even though he was not allowed to actually join the country club because he was Jewish, Karl would spend most of his days playing on the course.

The home had cost half a million dollars. She thought that he would pay for all of it, but he asked her to put up $150,000. That still left a $200,000 mortgage.

At last, Karl had plenty of closets for his virtual men's store. "Half the alligators in Florida must have been butchered to make all those shoes for Harry," she said.

Every week, he showed up with a different gift, perhaps a $5,000 Gucci purse or a $3,000 Rolex studded with tiny diamonds. A custom-made Rolls-Royce was shipped in from England to adorn their driveway.

As she told Ritter, "Maybe the sex isn't so great—Glenn Ford was a far better lover, but the gifts from Harry kept arriving. If I can survive this May-September romance, I'll own more jewelry than Marie Antoinette. Not only that, but I have a Chinese cook, a butler, and a personal maid. I've also got a cleaning woman, and every morning, sharply at 8, a laundress arrives to do all the wash. Sometimes, when I wake up in the morning, I imagine I'm Zsa Zsa Gabor."

When Mr. and Mrs. Karl entertained, he always hired violinists to accompany whomever was playing the piano, often Oscar Levant or, on a rare occasion, Van Cliburn during one of his trips to California. French champagne and Iranian caviar preceded lavish dinners.

After that, guests headed for the living room, where they were often treated to a famous entertainer "singing for their supper" (Debbie's words). "I always ended the evening with the forever-requested 'Tammy.'"

"We gave a wedding party for Jack Lemmon when he married Felicia," Debbie told Ritter. "I've rarely admitted this, but I have long had the hots for Jack. But he was too in love with Felicia to give me a tumble."

Marge and Gower Champion were given an anniversary party by the Karls. Debbie had been friends with them since they'd co-starred with her in *Give a Girl a Break.*, and Gower was set to direct her upcoming picture, *My Six Loves.*

One room of his new house was large enough for Karl to host dances, with a live band One night, Debbie noted Jennifer Jones sitting on the floor watching Ricardo Montalban dance with Lana Turner. Later, Jones told Debbie that she had fallen in love with Montgomery Clift when they had co-starred in *Indiscretions of an American Wife* (1953). "And then I found out that he was gay."

It was at these parties that Debbie began to drink for the first time, preferring vodka and 7-Up "because that way I wouldn't have to taste the liquor."

She would later describe her next move as "One of the biggest mistakes of my life, certainly the costliest." At Karl's request, she turned over all her money to him with the understanding that it would henceforth be managed by their business manager, Irving Briskin.

"I never saw any part of my salary," she said. "It went directly to Briskin. If I were short of money, Harry gave me a hundred-dollar bill to stuff into my Gucci purse. That's all I needed, as I could charge almost anything I wanted. He never complained, even when I bought very expensive gifts and clothing for Todd and Carrie, also for Ray and Minnie. I had joined all the bitches in Beverly Hills married to rich husbands."

***

Eddie Fisher and Elizabeth Taylor were in Rome when they heard of Debbie's marriage to a multi-millionaire. Elizabeth suggested that they should send her a telegram of congratulations. "Wishing you all the happiness you so *richly* deserve," the telegram read. It was signed, "Love, Elizabeth and Eddie."

Alone and back in Hollywood, Fisher attended a party at the home of Joan Cohn, Karl's former wife. Later in the evening, the former Mrs. Harry Cohn whispered to Fisher, "Wait until Debbie finds out what Harry is all about."

"I pressed her to explain that, but that's all I got," he said.

Fisher visited Carrie and Todd only on rare occasions. "Todd was shy like me, and Carrie was growing up to be pert and pretty. They called Karl 'Daddy Harry.'"

"I ran into Debbie on only one occasion, when she came home early from the studio," he said. "She chastised me for buying expensive presents for our kids."

"I have no intention of spoiling them, and that's exactly what you're trying to do," she claimed. "In case you haven't learned it yet, you can't buy love. You've got to earn it!"

The question of Todd's religion came up, since Debbie had promised to rear him as a Jew. "I reminded her of that promise," he said. "Since she'd married a Jew, I thought Todd was being raised in my faith."

"I'm not bringing him up as a Jew," she said, "because I have changed my mind. When I made that promise, I was still in love with you. I am no longer in love with you. When you married me, you promised to be faithful and true. You broke your promise to me, therefore, I'll break my promise to you."

Karl entered the room and overheard them. "Don't worry," he said. "Debbie and I are taking the children to a very nice Methodist church."

Fisher later said, "I left the house full of anger and resentment. What could I do? What right did I have to do anything? The poor little waif from El Paso was doing god damn well for herself. She was living like a queen and getting expensive presents and being driven around by a chauffeur in a Rolls. Karl built a home for them in Malibu. Their place in Beverly Hills was deluxe all the way, as was their home in Palm Springs. Debbie was sure going through the bucks. I heard rumors that Karl also lost tons of money gambling and patronizing only the most expensive prostitutes. He preferred one who had altered herself to look like Ava Gardner."

One night over drinks with Dean Martin and two other friends of his, Fisher was very candid. "I dumped Debbie because I never loved her. It cost me only a million dollars and a lifetime of being insulted by her fans. Even so, it still seems like a good deal to me. After all, Harry Karl is supporting my two children, and giving them everything they want. So that lets me off the hook. Let him be the sucker."

At one point, the conversation switched to mothers-in-law. "Maxene—the family calls her Minnie—is one pushy broad. The only thing I have against the state of Texas is that she came from there. She interfered constantly in my life with Debbie. She would have gotten between our sex organs if she could have. Oh, now that's a horrible thought."

One afternoon, when Fisher arrived unannounced to see Todd and Carrie, he learned that they were playing with other children at a neighbor's house. "Harry had been drinking, and I joined him in a coke," Fisher said. "I was startled when he confessed to me how unsatisfactory Debbie was in bed. He admitted that's why he had to pay prostitutes. He told me that Marie McDonald was a spitfire in bed."

"She couldn't get enough of my Jewish prick," Karl claimed. "Why else would I be giving her $50,000 a month?"

According to Fisher, in reference to his conversation that afternoon with Karl about McDonald, "I decided not to tell him I was already intimately familiar with 'The Body' [her nickname]. I met her when we toured together in Bob Hope's annual Christmas show. After we played the military bases, we flew to Paris for a hot weekend at the George V. She told me I was ten times better in bed than Karl. She also told me, 'You're so great as a lover. I can't imagine how Debbie Reynolds allowed you to slip away.'"

"I thought it was fair exchange," Fisher said. "He was screwing my former wife, and I was screwing his former wife."

***

On the home front, Debbie was anxious to return to work, telling Thelma Ritter, "This being a housewife and mother is one crock of shit!"

Gower Champion phoned to tell her that he'd recently cast Cliff Robertson and David Janssen in the film they were about to make, *My Six Loves*. She considered them two of the handsomest and most masculine men in Hollywood. "If I'm going to be true to Harry, I had better show up wearing a chastity belt," she confided to Gower.

Chapter Ten

Even after Two Miscarriages, Two "Impossible" Marriages, and Dance Routines that Would Kill a Lesser Performer, Debbie is

UNSINKABLE

Hollywood Buzzes With Rumors, Spread by Eddie Fisher that She's a Lesbian

The director of *The Unsinkable Molly Brown,* Charles Walters, told Debbie and Harve Presnell (right photo) that to finish the picture with dwindling funds,he was cutting their athletic, rousing dance number, "He's My Friend."

The co-stars protested, claiming that they could shoot it in one take, if multiple cameras were directed at them simultaneously.

"Harve and I pulled it off, and it became one of the most iconic dance sequences ever to appear in a Hollywood musical," Debbie said.

Debbie remembered working on the romantic comedy, *My Six Loves, as* "one great big party." Her friend, Gower Champion, was making his directorial debut. He had the script reworked four times by four different writers. One of them was Peter Funk, who had penned the novel on which the movie was based.

My Six Loves, set for an April (1963) release, marked Debbie's return to Paramount, where about a year before, she'd made *The Pleasure of His Company* with Fred Astaire. Playing opposite Cliff Robertson and David Janssen, Debbie had star billing in *My Six Loves.*

Champion had hired a stellar cast of supporting players. They included Eileen Heckart, Hans Conried, Mary McCarty, John McGiver, Alice Ghostley, Jim Backus, and Alice Pearce, who became Debbie's lifelong friend.

Cast as Janice Courtney, a major Broadway star, Debbie flees to her bucolic retreat, a leafy home in Connecticut, for a much-needed rest. Here, she discovers six abandoned children living in a shanty on her estate. She takes them in and looks after them with the help of her housekeeper, Ethel (Heckart) and the Rev. Jim Larkin (Robertson). Then her producer, Marty Bliss (Janssen), persuades her to return to Broadway.

In Manhattan one night, she learns that one of the kids is missing. Frantic, she returns home to discover the missing child. Reunited with the children and with the preacher, she decides that instead of a Broadway career, she wants to play the role of wife to Rev. Jim and mother to the brood of adorable but otherwise "unclaimed" children.

Debbie said, "Gower really wanted to succeed as a film director. I'd never seen a man so dedicated to the job and to dance itself. I visited his home one afternoon to discover that the entire first floor had been converted into a rehearsal hall, with the furniture built into the walls, leaving plenty of room for dancing. He

Debbie Reynolds

MY SIX LOVES

Debbie said, "Cliff Robertson was the handsomest and most romantic of priests, but, as far as he's concerned, I lower the curtain on our friendship."

and his wife, Marge, presented a 'concert' for me. They were real dancers. I just faked it."

She remained friends with the Champions for many years. After directing her, Gower moved on to his greatest success when he helmed the Broadway production of *Hello, Dolly!*, starring Carol Channing.

Her co-star and leading man, Cliff Robertson, was dashing and romantic. She'd been fascinated by his looks and charm ever since his film debut in *Picnic* (1955) opposite William Holden.

When she met Robertson, he had divorced his first wife, Cynthia Stone, and was yet to marry Dina Merrill, the Post cereal heiress. She had grown up at Mar-a-Lago, now the Florida vacation retreat of President Donald Trump.

One of Debbie's loves NOT implied in the movie's title was Gower Champion.

"I adored Cliff," Debbie said, "but he was a bit vain, spending more time in makeup than I did. I flirted shamelessly with him, but he was the perfect gentleman."

Before working with him, Debbie had met David Janssen before, as he'd served in the U.S. Army with her brother, Billy Reynolds, who had introduced them years before.

At the time of her reunion with Janssen, he was married to Ellie Graham and "was drinking heavily and seemed deeply troubled," Debbie said. "His marriage was going along all right, I guess, but he had this deep and abiding obsession about Clark Gable, of all people. I finally found out why."

Debbie and Janssen had a long talk one night when he told her he was of Irish-Jewish descent, the reputed son of a banker father and Berniece Graf, a former chorus girl in Hollywood. In 1930, with the advent of the talkies, she fell madly in love with Clark Gable just as his film career was taking off.

Debbie starred with David Janssen in *My Six Loves*. He was convinced that Clark Gable was his biological father.

"When I was older, my mother took me to see Gable as Rhett Butler in *Gone With the Wind*," Janssen said. "She never missed one of his movies. When I was twelve, she confessed that Gable was my real father, and that I was his bastard son."

"After we made our movie together, I saw David only infrequently," Debbie said. "I was aware that he was sinking deeper and deeper into alcoholism. He died young, at the age of forty-nine, in 1980."

She had her own tragedy after completing *My Six Loves*. While making that film, she was pregnant. This time, Harry Karl was the father. When the movie was wrapped, she and Karl flew to Europe, combining business with a vacation.

It was during her exploration of the Colosseum in Rome that she felt the fetus inside her moving. "It dropped three inches. I knew at once I had lost my child."

Back in Los Angeles, her doctor confirmed her suspicion. He ruled out a caesarean since he claimed it would greatly impair her health. After that, the story grows confused.

Although it seems reasonable that doctors could have legally removed a dead fetus from a woman's womb, Debbie nonetheless maintained that because abortion was illegal at the time, she had to carry the baby to term. Years later, she continued to maintain that she'd gone ahead and given birth to the infant, a stillborn.

She was so devastated that she asked Karl to make all the arrangements for the infant's burial.

Without discussing it with her husband, she had a lingering suspicion that "something is wrong with Harry's sperm. After all, he had all those miscarriages when married to Marie McDonald."

"From then on, I decided I would not bring, or attempt to bring, a child into the world. I told the press I planned to raise a large family. That was not true. I took precautions in the future never to get pregnant again. I had Carrie and Todd—and that was enough. I had to devote more time to my movie career before it, too, became a stillborn."

***

Still depressed over the loss of her baby, Debbie recuperated until she was ready to face the camera again. An intriguing offer had come in from Jack Warner, the mogul who had fired her in the late 1940s when she was a bit player making $60 a week.

He had acquired the rights to Jean Kerr's long-running romantic Broadway comedy, *Mary Mary*. To be shot in Technicolor, it was slated for release in October, 1953, at the Radio City Music Hall in Manhattan.

Warner made Debbie the most lucrative offer of her career: $350,000 to play the lead, plus ten percent of the gross.

"I made a terrible mistake," Debbie confessed. "I flew to New York to see Barbara Bel Geddes star as Mary McKellaway, as the divorced spouse of Bob McKellaway (Barry Nelson)."

The Yorkshire-born British actor, Michael Rennie, was cast in the Broadway production as a jaded Hollywood star, Dirk Winston, who has a date with Mary. Although both Nelson and Rennie were invited to replicate their stage roles in the upcoming film, Warner wanted a bigger name than Bel Geddes as the female lead.

"Barbara was a real actress, and I was not," Debbie said. "I was cute and adorable on camera, but that was not enough. I feared that *Mary, Mary* might show me up, revealing to my fans just how untalented I was as an actress. I had never felt so insecure in my career."

To prepare for the role in *Mary, Mary,* she turned to her former acting coach, Lillian Burns Sidney.

She coached Debbie in a run-through of every scene. After several days, Debbie became convinced that she could play Mary. Then, based partly on her insecurities as an actress, she asked Jack Warner to hire Burns as her acting coach for the duration of the shooting of the film.

"That really pissed off Mervyn LeRoy, our director," Debbie said. "After all, he was one of the most famous movie-makers in Hollywood."

"Actually, LeRoy was of no help to me," Debbie said. "At the twilight of his career, he stayed in his office most of the time. When he did come onto the set, his directions were vague. He would interrupt a scene to race to the john. He seemed to have a bladder problem like Marjorie Main."

It was Richard L. Breen who adapted Jean Kerr's original theatrical script for the screen. It was the story of a divorced couple, Bob and Mary, who come together for a reunion when he's being audited by the IRS.

Her former spouse doesn't want to see her again, but he needs her help. His tax lawyer, as portrayed by Hiram Sherman, needs Mary to help explain some of Bob's tax deductions. Complicating matters, Bob has a new

As she'd done, and would do again, Debbie appears furiously packing and leaving in this movie still from *Mary, Mary* with Michael Rennie watching impassively.

woman in his life, Tiffany Richards (Diane McBain). Also, in her role of Mary, Debbie displays an obvious romantic interest in the Hollywood star, Dirk Winston (as played by Rennie).

During the course of their IRS audit, Bob and Mary get caught in a snowstorm and have to spend the night in an apartment together. That leads to a discovery that they truly love each other.

As one critic noted, there is much talk about "income taxes, marriage, alimony, divorce, remarriage, extramarital relations, diet, exercises, and just plain sex."

All this talk was dismissed by critics as "conversational fuzz."

In the role of Tiffany, Diane McBain played Debbie's on-screen rival for Nelson. McBain's career peak came in the 1960s with the hit TV series, *Surfside 6*. She was also one of Elvis Presley's girlfriends in *Spinout* (1966).

"Barry Nelson was sorta cute, but I didn't feel that the two of us would heat up the screen with our sexual chemistry."

"I had to smoke in the role of Mary," Debbie said. "Michael Rennie taught me how it was done. I went through several coughing spasms before I finally learned to inhale. He didn't really do me a favor. I became addicted to cigarettes, and it took me years to shake the habit."

Bosley Crowther, in *The New York Times,* panned it. "Debbie Reynolds is her usual pint-sized hothead as the irritably retiring wife, flowery and flushed in her furies, but why she's retiring is hard to grasp. Barry Nelson is doltish and dyspeptic as her dissatisfied husband, and Michael Rennie is practically sarcastic in his silken portrayal of the Hollywood star. A sleek and conventional female rival is poured into slacks by Diane McBain, and the Broadway clown Hiram Sherman makes the lawyer a waspish stock character."

***

Debbie's greatest film role, an MGM Technicolor extravaganza released in 1964, was *The Unsinkable Molly Brown*. Its screenplay by Helen Deutsch was a fictionalized account of the life of the real-life Margaret Brown, who had famously survived the 1912 sinking of the RMS *Titanic*. The movie was based on the book for the theatrical musical, which opened as a play on Broadway in 1960. Its musical score was composed by Meredith Wilson, whose other most famous work was the 1957 Broadway hit, *The Music Man*.

Debbie flew to New York to do some shopping and to take in the latest Broadway hits. During her time there, she met with her friend, Marge Champion, who urged her to see *The Unsinkable Molly Brown*, starring Tammy Grimes and Harve Presnell. "You've got to see it!" the dancer urged. "You'd be perfect for the film role of Molly Brown. You could eat up the scenery with a part like that."

That very evening, Debbie was seen entering the theater for an overview of the hit play.

The reviews for Grimes had been terrific. One critic wrote: "She speaks in a voice like a buzz saw and has a lyric baritone singing voice, a low, throaty quiver, a hum that takes wings. She has the stage personality of a daffy but endearing pseudo-English eccentric."

Debbie was enthralled at Grimes' buoyant interpretation of a rough-hewn, turn-of-the 20th Century social climber, a Rocky Mountain mining millionairess who didn't go down with the *Titanic.*

"Ironically, Grimes was really named Tammy, whereas I was just Tammy on the screen and in that song." Debbie said. "As good as she was, she did not have a screen following, and I did, so I knew I had a chance at it."

Lawrence Weingarten, *Unsinkable's* producer, had previously produced *The Gazebo,* in which Debbie had co-starred with Glenn Ford. *Unsinkable's* director, Charles Walters, had previously helmed both Debbie and Frank Sinatra in *The Tender Trap.*

As soon as she returned to Hollywood, Debbie called Weingarten and set up a meeting at his office. He was not optimistic about her getting the part, telling her that Walters wanted Shirley MacLaine for the character of Molly, with Robert Goulet playing Molly's husband, Johnny Brown, nicknamed "Leadville."

"There is a slim chance you might get the role if Hal Wallis, who has Shirley under exclusive contract, won't release her."

As the days and weeks went by, Debbie grew increasingly agitated. Harry Karl said, "She was going around the house like her life depended on that damn role."

Finally, in desperation, she phoned her agent, Al Melnick, ordering him to call Weingarten and let him know she'd play Molly for free.

It took two weeks before Melnick got an answer. When he did, he phoned her at once. "You made a very generous offer to work for free, but Walters is set on Shirley."

Horribly disappointed, and with no more film roles in sight, Debbie decided to develop a stage act for Las Vegas. Over the past few years, many casino owners had tried to book her there, but to no avail.

During mid-January of 1963, her doctor told her she was pregnant again, even though she had taken precautions not to be. She believed her pregnancy would not start to show until April of that year, so she moved ahead with her act.

She lined up top talent to assist her with her gig in Vegas. Robert Sidney developed the choreography, and Rudy Render operated as her musical director. She worked with the talented Roger Edens to stage the show, as he so often did for Judy Garland. *[In fact, he'd written Garland's famous number, "Born in a Trunk."]*

In an attempt to "test" the act before its premiere in Vegas, Debbie decided to open it at the Shamrock Hotel in Houston in her native state of Texas. Her opening number was "I Want to Be Happy," climaxing it with her dressed as a clown singing "Make 'Em Laugh," a gig that had obviously been inspired by Donald O'Connor. She sang "Tammy" as an encore.

From Houston, she flew to Vegas and opened her act in the Versailles Room of the Riviera. Old friends such as Red Skelton and Jack Benny flew in for her spectacular opening, which generated raves. After the engagement, she flew to Miami Beach to perform her show at the Eden Roc.

Business had been so robust that the management of the Riviera invited her back to Vegas for a two-week gig.

It was now April, and she could no longer conceal her pregnancy. "Good news came at the wrong time," she said. "Melnick phoned, telling her that Wallis was threatening to sue MGM if they went ahead and cast MacLaine as Molly Brown.

Debbie's dream of playing Molly Brown had come true. Only her very closest friends knew that she had actually considered an abortion. "I want the role that bad," she confided to both Thelma Ritter and Agnes Moorehead.

Otherwise, her hope lay in Weingarten postponing the shoot until after her child was born.

She got a phone call from an outraged MacLaine on the day she was notified that the role of Molly was hers. "You dirty little bitch," MacLaine shouted. "Behind my back, you stabbed me. Weingarten told me you agreed to do the damn role for free.:"

As casting began for the character of Molly Brown, Shirley MacLaine was the leading choice. She later denounced Debbie for "stealing the role right out from under me."

In this photo, she looks like the least likely actress in Hollywood to play Molly.

"That's not the whole story," Debbie protested. "Wallis is threatening MGM with a lawsuit if it casts you."

"I can deal with any shit coming from Wallis," MacLaine said. "Got that?"

"Shirley, please understand," Debbie said. "This is probably my last chance for a great role. You're hot, in real demand. You'll be offered many great parts in your future. I know I won't. Maybe a few more silly little romantic comedies before I fade from the screen."

"Don't give me that Tammy bullshit," MacLaine said. "I'm warning you: DON'T CROSS ME!"

The next day, Walters called and asked to visit her at her home. That sounded ominous. Over a drink in her living room, he was very blunt. "Let's face it: You and Doris Day are increasingly *passé*. Your type of romantic comedy is fading fast. I want Shirley for the role if I can break Wallis' hold over her. And let's face it: You're too short to play Molly. Just take that number in a saloon of the Old West. In the center of the room, Molly belts out 'Belly Up to the Bar, Boys.' Can you imagine Tammy singing that?"

"I'm not Tammy," she answered, flashing anger. "I'm an actress. I can be your Molly, and a damn good one at that."

The tone of their meeting grew more hostile as Walters began his second drink. "The studio is insisting on signing you, and I can't talk them out of it. But there is a way out: You can turn down the role."

"If Larry Weingarten wants to sign me, and I'm told he does, then I'm going to play Molly—and that's that."

"I'm not sure of that," he said. "If I can't get Shirley, I'm considering three other actresses, each of whom would be better than you. Let's face it: Tammy Grimes has already shown she'd be the greatest Molly of them all."

Debbie stood up to signal that the interview was over. "Charlie, I'm looking forward

A few months after the sinking of the *Titanic* in April of 1912, Margaret Brown, the heroine who restored order in Lifeboat #6, participated in an award ceremony where 320 commemorative medals were given as an expression of appreciation from the survivors to staff, crew, and personnel instrumental in the rescue of the endangered passengers.

In this historic photo, the real life "Unsinkable Molly" is shown with Sir Arthur Henry Rostron, the captain of the *Carpathia*, who rescued the passengers who fled from the sinking transatlantic liner.

to being your Molly. Let me show you to the door."

***

At long last, the role of Molly in *The Unskinkable Molly Brown* was awarded to Debbie, who received a final version of the script. In the plot, an infant girl was rescued from the Colorado River by Seamus Tobin (Ed Begley, Sr.) who names her Molly. The setting is the early 20ᵗʰ Century. She grows up a tomboy, wrestling ferociously with her three younger brothers. Her ambition is to learn to read and write, and to marry a rich husband.

When she's grown, she journeys to the Saddle Rock Saloon in Leadville, Colorado, where Christmas Morgan (Jack Kruschen) hires her as a saloon singer.

Here, she meets the virile, handsome, and dashing J.S. ("Leadville") Johnny Brown, who falls in love with her, promising to give her whatever she wants ("I'll Never Say No"). He sells his claim to a silver mine for $300,000. In an attempt to hide the money, Molly hastily stores it in an iron stove, where it is accidentally burned. Johnny's fortunes are restored, however, when he discovers the richest gold mine in the state's history.

Hugely enriched, Molly demands that Johnny take her on a trip to Europe, where, as a free-spending couple with buckets of homespun charm, they're embraced by fringe royalty. Homesick, she invites some of them back to Denver, where they are introduced to local society. Johnny's rough-and-tumble friends barge in to ruin Molly's social pretensions.

She decides to return to Europe, but Johnny wants to remain behind in Leadville. While abroad, she is wooed by Prince Louis de Lanière (Vassili Lambrinos) who is after her money. But eventually, she grows bored and wants to return to Leadville and to Johnny.

During the Atlantic crossing aboard the RMS *Titanic*, it sinks when the vessel collides with an iceberg. Molly becomes a heroine when she rescues several of her fellow passengers. Back in Denver, she falls into the arms of Johnny once again, and is warmly welcomed

As Molly, Debbie claimed that she adored working with her co-star, Harve Presnell, finding him "very sexy, very talented, with a lot of male flash and charm."

by the local citizens.

When it became clear that Debbie wasn't scheduled for the shooting of *Molly Brown* until October of 1963, she and Harry Karl decided to fly to Europe, combining some of his business affairs with a vacation.

In England, Debbie experienced another miscarriage. She claimed that she felt the baby drop a few inches inside her body. In what seemed to be some of the same horror she'd experienced in Rome, she described the experience as a recurring nightmare.

She asked Karl, "Why is God doing this to me?" He had no answer, of course.

He immediately booked her on a flight back to Los Angeles, where she checked into St. Joseph's Hospital in Burbank. Once again, she was told she'd have to carry the baby to term.

"I refuse to do that," she said. Three doctors went into a conference, during which it was decided to abort the dead fetus.

A liquid solution, its contents unknown to her, was injected into her veins. It caused her body to swell into what she described as "a blimp," forcing her to reject the unformed infant.

For fourteen hours, she endured intense pain until the dead matter was ejected from her body. Fortunately, the sac had not broken. If it had, she might have died from peritonitis.

Although she really didn't want to know, she was told it would have been a boy. *[Her previous stillborn had been a girl.]* Karl took charge of the burial, and she didn't even ask the location of the grave.

Four days later, Karl arrived at the hospital in a station wagon with Carrie and Todd and put her into the back seat for the ride home, where she would try to recover and build up her strength before filming began.

During her summer of recovery *[1963]*, she read in the papers that Jacqueline Kennedy had given birth to her third child, Patrick Bouvier Kennedy, and that the infant had lived for only a few days. Debbie spent all day composing a six-page letter of sympathy to the First Lady, who was devastated by her loss, as Debbie herself was, too.

When Debbie was feeling better, she invited her producer, Lawrence Weingarten, and his wife, Dr. Jessie Marmorston, to dinner. During the meal, she fainted and had to be carried back to her bedroom by her staff.

The doctor came up to examine her and gave her something to make her sleep. Then, she arranged for a series of tests, scheduled for the following day. The results were horrifying. One doctor, who studied the results, didn't know that they pertained to Debbie, and assumed that that data had been collected from a seventy-five-year-old woman.

Her body seemed drained of everything: vitamins and minerals and estrogen. For the next few months, she received daily shots to build up her system. She later credited Dr. Marmorston with saving her life.

Shooting began that October, as Debbie journeyed with Todd and Carrie, along with their nursemaid, to Telluride, Colorado. She was already familiar with the terrain, based on the scenes she'd previously filmed for *How the West Was Won*.

During the early days of the shoot, her director, Charles Walters, was of no help to her whatsoever. He still resented her in her role, often commenting to other members of the cast, "Shirley MacLaine would have been brilliant as Molly."

Before she performed on camera, Walters came up to Debbie. "The scene we're about to shoot is very difficult. I don't know how in hell you're going to pull it off."

Debbie performed brilliantly. Time after time, after watching her act, he slowly changed his mind about her. Before leaving Colorado, he approached her. "You're doing great, kid."

After all the scenes in Colorado were wrapped, and she was heading back to Los Angeles, Walters approached her. "I've finally decided you're not too short for Molly."

Ed Begley, Sr., one of Hollywood's most talented character actors, had the third lead. He'd won a Best Supporting Actor Oscar for his role as the political boss in Tennessee Williams' *Sweet Bird of Youth* in 1962. He told Debbie he'd dropped out of school in the fifth grade, making a living working in carnivals, fairs, and small circuses.

She claimed she just adored the English actress, Hermione Baddeley, who had been cast as "Buttercup Grogan."

"If the role were bold, brassy, and blowsy, Hermione could play it," Debbie said.

On November 23, 1963, shooting was abandoned for the afternoon. Rudy Render, the musical director, came onto the set to announce that President Kennedy had been shot in Dallas while riding with Jacqueline in an open convertible. Reportedly, he was still alive, although another broadcast announced an unconfirmed report that his brain matter

No one could play an aristocrat like Marita Hunt, who's depicted here as the Grand Duchess.

"She could be queenly even when drunk, which was most of the time," Debbie said.

had been splattered all over the back seat of the limousine.

"I was shocked and saddened," Debbie said. "I had met JFK, but didn't know him as well as some actresses, notably Marilyn Monroe. But I always found him handsome and charming."

When shooting resumed, she got some bad news. MGM was putting much of its production money into filming the very costly *Dr. Zhivago* (1965). Walters had been told that day that one million dollars had been taken from their film's budget.

Debbie had lobbied to have the role of the Grand Duchess assigned to her intimate friend, Agnes Moorehead. But Walters turned her down, preferring Marita Hunt instead.

Born to English parents in Buenos Aires, she had first made a name for herself on the London stage. When Debbie met her, she'd been recently signed to appear as the regal Queen Matilda in *Becket* (1964).

One afternoon, following a three-martini lunch, Hunt, in a tiara and white satin gown, had to descend the stairs at Molly's mansion for her introduction to Denver society.

She fell down the steps, but got up unharmed, before trying the stairway descent again. Once again, she fell down, and then staggered to her feet again. Walters decided he knew what to do.

"A stagehand put a leather belt around Marita's waist," Debbie said. "It was concealed by her white satin gown. They cut a slit for the hook to which they would fasten a wire. She was suspended like a fish hooked on the end of a fishing line, and it worked perfectly."

***

Screenings of *The Unsinkable Molly Brown* ran for ten weeks at the Radio City Music Hall in Manhattan. For one year, Debbie was the number two box office attraction in the world and was asked to put her small hands and feet into wet cement in front of Grauman's Chinese Theater in Hollywood.

As an additional honor for her film, astronauts John Young and Gus Grissom named their spaceship *The Molly Brown* before blasting off into outer space.

In yet another review in *The New York Times,* A.H. Weiler called the movie "big, brassy, bold, and freewheeling. The tones are ringing, but often hollow. Molly is a colorful character all right. But Molly in the person of Miss Reynolds often takes vigor for art."

Variety observed, "In essence, it's a pretty shallow story since the title character is obsessed with a very superficial, egotistical problem of getting accepted by Denver high society. At times, Reynolds' approach to the character seems more athletic than artful."

Time Out London noted that Debbie as Molly "is as ebulliently energetic as ever and makes the brash social climbing both funny and touching. But the film itself gets trapped in two minds between satire and sentimentality."

TV Guide rated the film three out of four stars, claiming that "a rambunctious and spirited effort from Reynolds saves this otherwise weak script musical... from the long list of forgotten pictures."

At Oscar time, Debbie was nominated for Best Actress, competing with Kim Stanley in *Séance on a Wet Afternoon;* Sophia Loren in *Marriage Italian Style,* and Anne Bancroft in *The Pumpkin Eater.* Julie Andrews as *Mary Poppins* walked off with the gold.

Today, the American Film Institute rates *The Unsinkable Molly Brown* as one of the "greatest movie musicals."

***

Debbie had known the stately actress, Agnes Moorehead, for many years, but really became close friends when they made *How the West Was Won.* Ever since seeing her in Orson Welles' *Citizen Kane* (1941), Debbie had admired Moorehead's talent, which in many of her films, was not used to full advantage.

She'd seen this scene-stealer from Massachusetts play spinster aunts, intimidating moms, biddies, crones, grande dames, and comical secretaries. Nominated for many top awards, including the Oscars, the Golden Globes, and six Emmy nominations, Moorehead only became a household word after she was cast as the mortal-loathing, quick-witted witch mother in the hit TV series, *Bewitched,* which ran for eight seasons from 1964 to 1972.

In addition to Debbie, Moorehead had worked with some of the most talented actors in the world, including Welles, Bette Davis, Olivia de Havilland, Charles Laughton, Henry Fonda, and Lucille Ball.

Moorehead was one of Debbie's neighbors, a coterie of stars who included James Stewart, Jack Benny, Rosemary Clooney, and Eddie Cantor, each of whom occupied beautiful homes near Roxbury Drive and Lexington above Sunset Boulevard in

Out for a night on the town, Debbie and the formidable Agnes Moorehead were constant companions. But were those rumors about them really true?

310

Beverly Hills.

Debbie, along with Harry Karl, Carrie, and Todd, always attended Moorehead's annual Christmas party. Moorehead and Debbie would often go over to the home of another neighbor, Lucille Ball, and spend the evening dishing the dirt on other Hollywood stars.

Debbie claimed, "Lucy always had the best stories to tell, including shocking revelations about Henry Fonda ('He wore a jockstrap that Joan Crawford had given him'); Orson Welles ('He said that his favorite sex was to masturbate as two beautiful women get it on'); Milton Berle ('He claimed to have the biggest ding-dong in Hollywood'); and George Raft ('he called his thing The Blacksnake')."

At times, Moorehead would show up for dinner at Debbie's house two or three times a week. "She got along with my husband, Harry, because they were the same age. Often, he was gone, so Agnes and I spent the evening watching movies, gossiping, and just hanging out."

She and Moorehead discussed the failures of their respective first marriages. In 1930, she had wed actor John Griffith Lee, divorcing him in 1952. In 1949, they had adopted an orphan boy, Sean, although it was never clear if the adoption was actually legally authorized.

"I never wanted to criticize Agnes because with me, she was a kind and loving person. But as far as Sean was concerned, she was a terror. When the hippie era of the 1960s came in, he let his hair grow long, which absolutely infuriated Agnes. She demanded that he cut his hair or leave her house. He was gone for three weeks, but came back on her doorstep claiming that he was starving."

"She took him in and personally gave him a crewcut after killing the lice in his hair," Debbie said. "But things went downhill. She found a gun in his bedroom and feared he was going to use it on her. She kicked him out of her house again, and he disappeared, never to return. She was not a cruel person, but with Agnes, it was her way or the highway."

Over the years, there has been much speculation about Moorehead's sexuality, and she was widely suspected of being a lesbian. When Orson Welles had worked with her during their days with the Mercury Theater, he once revealed that she was romantically involved with one of the other female players.

A homophobe, Joseph Cotten, knew her back then, too. "That form of sex between Moorehead and her girlfriend repulsed me. I was never a devotee of oral sex, even among straight couples. Mother Nature intended that sex be only in the missionary position. Any other way is a crime against nature."

"I knew that Agnes was a lesbian," Thelma Ritter said." She had worked with her on location during the filming of *How the West Was Won*. "I ain't got nothing against gals like her. But personally, it was obvious to me that Agnes had the hots for Debbie and was quite possessive of her. She even resented my getting close to her. They spent a lot of time together. Who knows what happens when the lights go out in Hollywood? I can only imagine. I also heard lots of stories about Debbie's friend, Rock Hudson, who got drunk with me on camera in *Pillow Talk* (1959). If he was enjoying it, so much the better. Have a good time, I say. Life's just too fucking short."

After Moorehead's death in 1974, many articles appeared suggesting her lesbianism and linking her to Debbie. Most of them candidly admitted, however, that the suggestions were mere speculation.

The gay actor, Paul Lynde, who often co-starred with her on *Bewitched*, said, "Well, the whole world known Agnes is a lesbian—I mean, classy as hell, but one of the alltime Hollywood dykes."

Debbie, in contrast, always denied that her best friend was a lesbian. She claimed that the rumor-mongering began during Moorehead's divorce from John Griffin Lee.

Lynde's advice to both Debbie and Moorehead was, "If you gals have the name, why not play the game?"

Eddie Fisher was a firm believer in a possible lesbian relationship between Debbie and Moorehead—in fact, he prepared a chapter on it for insertion into his final memoir, *Been There, Done That*, published in 1999 by St. Martin's Press. Getting wind of it before the book came out, Debbie had her lawyer threaten her former husband with a million-dollar lawsuit. Subsequently, he omitted the chapter from his autobiography's ultimate release.

Dying of uterine cancer in the spring of 1974, Moorehead was said to have outed her same-sex orientation to a reporter, Greg Taylor, who never published the interview. "I'm in good company," Moorehead confessed. "I'll name only a few of Hollywood's other lesbians: Joan Crawford, Tallulah Bankhead, Kay Francis, Alexis Smith, Mary Martin, Janet Gaynor, Spring Byington, Lizabeth Scott, Marjorie Main, Claudette Colbert, Barbara Stanwyck, and Patsy Kelly."

Fisher was not only suspicious of Debbie's link to Moorehead, but of her close friendships with both Jeanette Johnson and Camille Williams. However, there is no real evidence to suggest a lesbian link to "my two best pals" (Debbie's words).

Carrie Fisher once said, "My father's claim that his marriage to Debbie failed because she was a lesbian is without foundation. Mother, however, did admit to me that she was rather cold and frigid during her ill-fated marriage to my dad, who claimed that she felt sex was only for making babies. That, of course, was not true. As she confessed to me, she was far more responsive to certain other men than she had been with Eddie."

***

Other than Moorehead, Camille Williams and Jeanette Johnson remained Debbie's lifelong friends, always willing to rush to her side in an emergency, or just to have fun.

Williams had comforted her after her breakup with Fisher, when reporters and photographers were camped outside her door. She was still around to testify on Debbie's behalf during her divorce proceedings from him.

Williams had flown to Spain to be with Debbie when she went there for location shooting for *It Started with a Kiss*. Williams, an actress and dancer, had to cut her trip short to fly to London to dance with Dan Dailey when his dance partner died suddenly from a heart attack.

Debbie had flown to Las Vegas to see Williams perform with Dailey again when he was trying for a comeback of sorts after he'd been exposed as a cross-dresser by *Confidential* magazine.

Ironically, Williams had once held the title of Miss Burbank, as Debbie had, and she made a few film appearances; including a bit part in *Tammy and the Bachelor*. Debbie claimed that her girlfriend was a "voluptuous brunette who was forever being chased by men."

Debbie was also very close to Jeanette Johnson, her former gym teacher. Ironically, she was in the profession that Debbie had originally aspired to before becoming a movie star.

Johnson often traveled with Debbie to such locations as Mexico and Paris. She was also with Debbie during key moments in her life, including her being maid of honor at Debbie's wedding to Fisher.

After an exhausted Debbie finished *Singin' in the Rain,* she and Johnson drove together to Lake Tahoe where she recovered, with Johnson cooking and then serving her breakfast in bed. After she was rested, Debbie and Johnson played tennis or else went water skiing.

Biographer William J. Mann was one of the few writers to reveal the link that existed with Debbie and her two close friends. He wrote, "Whatever the truth of Debbie's sexuality, and it's likely to be far more nuanced than any one label can describe—the fact of her artificial, largely sexless marriage to Eddie radically altered the narrative that seemed so sure, so true, in the fall of 1958."

***

On Broadway in 1959, *Goodbye Charlie* was a most improbable script by George Axelrod. He'd had bigger hits with *The Seven Year Itch* (1955), with Marilyn Monroe, and with *Will Success Spoil Rock Hunter?* (1957) starring Jayne Mansfield.

In a nutshell, *Goodbye Charlie* is the story of a

GIRLS WHO MARRY GAY MEN: How, everyone wondered, did the aggressively ugly, aggressively queeny, aggressively egomaniacal Vincente Minnelli, ever manage to marry Judy Garland?

callous womanizer, who is fatally shot and comes back, reincarnated, as a female.

The play on Broadway had starred Lauren Bacall as the reincarnated Charlie opposite Sidney Chaplin.

Although Fox had acquired the film rights and slated it for a November, 1964 release that would star Marilyn Monroe, she was dead before filming began.

Darryl F. Zanuck had at first offered its direction to Billy Wilder, hoping that he could repeat the box office success of *Some Like It Hot* (1959) with Marilyn Monroe and Tony Curtis. Wilder turned him down, defiantly telling the Fox chief, "No self-respecting picture maker will ever want to work for your company."

Nearing the end of his career, David Weisbart (he died in 1967), became the producer. He is best remembered for the James Dean classic, *Rebel Without a Cause* (1955). He'd also produced Elvis Presley's film debut, *Love Me Tender,* in 1956. At the time of his death, he was producing *Valley of the Dolls,* based on Jacqueline Susann's bestseller.

He offered the lead role (that of the "reincarnated-as-a-woman" Charlie) to Debbie, and cast Tony Curtis as Charlie's best friend, George Wellington Tracy.

At that time, Debbie still had director approval, and she asked for Vincente Minnelli, the former husband of Judy Garland and the father of Liza Minnelli. Debbie later regretted that decision.

She'd seen all his big hits, including such movies as *Meet Me in St. Louis* (1944) with Garland, *An American in Paris* (1951) with Gene Kelly, and *Lust for Life* (1956) with Kirk Douglas.

Minnelli had not seen the Broadway play with Bacall, but was told that she had played the reincarnated Charlie in a very masculine way, smoking cigars and swatting women on their butts.

"I wanted the female lead to be more feminine than that," Minnelli said. "Certainly, Monroe could have done that. Debbie, of course, was no Monroe. I never thought she was right for the part. She combines self-possession with a tendency to cuteness, which was not the quality I was looking for."

"Minnelli was always fussing with me over my scenes, telling me I was always off the mark," she said. "I think he was showing the beginning of Alzheimer's when we made that silly little comedy. He was very vague at times, and on several occasions,

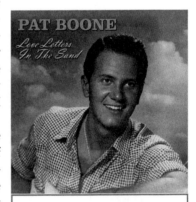

"Love Letters in the Sand," by Pat Boone, Mr. Goodie Two-Shoes.

he called me Judy, obviously remembering his marriage to Garland. He just couldn't convey what he wanted. One afternoon, he called me to the set, but didn't set things in motion. He must have spent two hours arranging black bobby pins on a black sofa."

"Obviously, his glory days in Hollywood had come and gone. He was now working for Fox. Up to then, he had made movies for MGM since 1942. It's sad to see a great director at the end of a fabulous career."

In addition to Curtis and Debbie, Minnelli lined up a talented cast: Pat Boone as Bruce Minton III; Ellen McRae (she was later billed as Ellen Burstyn) as Franny Salzman; Laura Devon as Rusty Sartori; Martin Gabel as Morton Craft; and Walter Matthau as Sir Leopold Sartori.

Curtis noted that Burstyn and Minnelli "practically declared World War III on each other, and he was always riding Debbie's ass. As for me, he had nothing but praise. He seemed to beam when I walked on the set. He told me that of all the pretty boys of the 1950s, I was at the top of the list, beating out Robert Wagner, Rock Hudson, and Tab Hunter. Music to my ears."

"In every scene I did, he said I was wonderful. He often came to my dressing room to help me get dressed. I knew he had the hots for me. He asked me to go away with him to Palm Springs at the end of the shoot, and I said I would. Of course, I had no intention of doing that. When the time came for a wrap, he asked me when we could leave. I told him some urgent business had come up, and I could not take a vacation with him. But, as I kissed him on the cheek, I said 'I'll take a raincheck.'"

Harry Kurnitz was assigned the difficult job of bringing this supernatural story to something resembling a probable screenplay. According to the plot, Charlie Sorrell (Harry Madden) is a skirt-chasing cad caught trying to seduce Rusty (Laura Devon), the wife of a Hungarian film producer, Sir Leopold Sartori (Walter Matthau), obviously based on the fabled British film producer Sir Alexander Korda. Catching Charlie with his wife, Sir Leopold fatally shoots him, and he falls into the sea.

Miraculously, he is reincarnated as a soaking

In *Goodbye Charlie*, Debbie, seen above with her co-star, Tony Curtis, has been reincarnated as a woman. Before that, he had been Curtis' best friend, a notorious womanizer.

According to Curtis, "If I have the hots for her new body, would that make me gay?"

wet blonde wandering along the beach. It's Debbie cast in her new role of Virginia Mason, but she is really Charlie reincarnated. She is discovered by a wealthy playboy, Bruce Minton III (Boone), and taken to the only address she can remember—Charlie's home.

She finally realizes who she is and calls Charlie's best friend, George. It takes some doing, but she finally convinces him she is his old pal, Charlie.

Expect all sorts of confusion, complications, and plot devices. George develops a sexual attraction to his best buddy, now in Debbie's appealing and shapely figure. In ways that evoke *Some Like it Hot,* there is a sexual ambiguity here.

"In the plot, I am really falling in love with my best male friend," Curtis said. "If you think this sounds like a perfect movie for a gay audience, you wouldn't be wrong."

Debbie announces she is "Mrs. Charlie Sorrel," and reverts to her Charlie character, as she blackmails society wives whom he has seduced. George is horrified by her behavior.

Ironically, Sir Leopold, who murdered Charlie, is sexually attracted to "Mrs. Sorrel." However, Rusty, his wife, gets wind of that and shoots the character played by Debbie.

This time, she comes back as a dog, who has a pretty owner bearing a striking resemblance to Mrs. Sorrel. George and the woman strike up a friendship while the dog (formerly Charlie) laps up some vodka.

Debbie and Curtis had previously co-starred together in *The Rat Race,* at which time he'd shown the first romantic interest in her, spending a lot of time privately in her dressing room. But there was no love lost between the stars when they reunited on the set of *Goodbye Charlie.*

"Several friends told me that fucker was spreading a rumor all over Hollywood that I was a card-carrying lesbian, carrying on a torrid affair with Agnes Moorehead," Debbie said. "He got that wrong piece of information from Eddie Fisher."

"Eddie is one of my best friends, and he has never lied to me," Curtis said. "Debbie was spending nearly every night with Agnes Moorehead."

"Eddie also told Curtis that I was a lousy lay, and he was spreading the news," Debbie said. "I was not a lesbian, but I admit I might have been a lousy lay. Eddie could have been more patient with me and taught me things that brought him sexual pleasure, but he didn't."

Curtis disappointed me," Debbie said. "At first I thought he was a friend… of sorts. But he had chosen to join Eddie's camp like a lot of other people who knew both of us. In a Hollywood divorce, it is not unusual for friends to take sides."

"Curtis and I pulled off our scenes together in spite of Minnelli's inept direction," she said. "My talk with Curtis made no difference. After the picture was wrapped, he continued to spread the lesbian and the 'lousy lay' rumors."

During the shoot, Carrie Fisher came onto the set and met Curtis. As she grew older, she would attack him as one of "the difficult Jewish fathers."

"Carrie blamed Eddie for the breakup of his marriage to her mother, Debbie," Curtis said, "much in the same way Jamie Lee was angry at me for breaking up with her mother, Janet (Leigh). According to Carrie, it was the fault of the Jewish fathers that the marriages went belly-up."

"Debbie was not without blame for our failed friendship," Curtis said. "She spread the word that I was Princess Tiny Meat. I think she was also jealous of all the publicity Janet and I got when we were hailed in the fan magazines as the ideal couple. We got an avalanche more publicity than Eddie and Debbie. By comparison, those two could have been our maid and butler."

The third lead in *Goodbye Charlie* was played by singer Pat Boone, who was more famous as a pop singer in the 1950s, selling more than 45 million records, including 38 "Top 40" hits. He was topped only by Elvis Presley.

As Sir Leopold, Walter Matthau was one of the most talented character actors of the latter 20th Century. "He stole every scene he was in," Debbie claimed. "He was even better at accents than I was."

Debbie arranged for her brother, Billy Reynolds, to work on the set of *Goodbye Charlie* so he could complete his seven-year apprenticeship as a makeup artist, allowing him to join the union.

In the U.S. and Canada, *Goodbye Charlie* made $3.7 million, but had cost $3.5 to make. Reviews were generally bad. *The Hollywood Reporter* wrote, "Curtis lends the proper anxious note to the whole proceedings. He and Debbie Reynolds make their work count as much as the script will permit under Vincente Minnelli's direction."

The Daily Worker claimed, "Miss Reynolds tackles the role manfully, and Curtis, as the dead man's best friend, flaps around, game to the end."

Bosley Crowther of *The New York Times* delivered the harshest attack, calling the movie "a bleak conglomeration of outrageous whimsies and stupidities."

Minnelli fared better in *Films and Filming*, which defined *Goodbye Charlie* as "a victory of décor over dialogue, of directorial control over a script that is as wild as all getout. Dialogues range erratically from the funny to the desperate, but is well reined in, and so is the entire cast, especially Debbie Reynolds."

***

As Carrie Fisher grew older, and began to write books and talk to friends, she revealed what life was like at the Karl/Reynolds household when she and Todd were growing up.

In the early years, both children saw little of their mother. As Carrie remembered it, she worked long hours and when she came home, she wanted to sleep. "Since Todd and I wanted to be with her, we invaded her bedroom and slept with her." Todd claimed the mauve-colored sofa by the window, and Carrie slept on the white carpet under a red blanket beside Debbie, who occupied the bed with Karl.

Surprisingly, their stepfather allowed that. One would imagine that he would want to be intimate with his wife, away from the prying eyes of his stepchildren. But the shoe manufacturer had his reasons.

After Debbie had two miscarriages, he falsely told her he was impotent. The facts were that he had a prostitute visit every day Debbie wasn't at home, passing the woman off as his manicurist. His nails were the only part of his body she didn't touch.

Carrie always claimed, and Debbie privately agreed, that she never loved Karl. The middle-aged man was the complete opposite of the boyish Eddie Fisher.

Carrie remembered the large, embassy-like mansion they occupied. "It had the warmth of a plant manufacturing disinfectant."

In the early days when he was courting Debbie, Karl paid attention to the kids, taking them places and purchasing presents for them. But after a few months, he grew bored in his role of a stepfather.

Carrie remembered him smoking five packages of cigarettes a day "on the road to getting cancer. Every time I saw him, he was engulfed in a cloud of smoke. In the living room, he hid behind a newspaper, always picking at that nose of his, extracting some big ones."

He slept in his pajama tops, since he was suffering from hemorrhoids and sometimes bled. He placed a large monogrammed pink towel under him at night. Carrie, in a memoir, recalled "his horrible, flaccid elephant trunk of a penis." As he headed to the bathroom, she took in the view of "his saggy buttocks and, when his legs opened, that withering gray ball sac."

In contrast, Todd and Carrie rarely saw their real father. Sometimes, Fisher phoned the nursemaid and told her to get the children ready to go on an excursion with him. Dressed and ready, they would wait by the picture window in their living room. On most occasions, he never showed up.

"At their young age, I thought they needed a mother more than a father," he said. "Besides, my love for Elizabeth took precedence over everything else, and she wanted me by her side night and day."

During chance encounters with Debbie, he found her hostile and always filled with criticism. "Years after the fact, she always had to remind reporters that I had deserted her and our children for Elizabeth."

"She forever reminded me that I no longer gave her child support," he said, "and that was true. "I was making no money at the time because of my wrecked career, and she was hauling in one million a year."

Carrie claimed that whereas Karl spent most of his time in bed sleeping, Fisher spent most of his time in bed not sleeping. After Elizabeth dumped him, he began many long years of a promiscuous lifestyle and used condoms except on rare drunken occasions. He had a steady supply shipped from a manufacturer in Tokyo, where he had first discovered them while patronizing an exclusive geisha resort. What made these condoms so special was that each contained a picture of that fiery redhead, Susan Hayward, on its wrapper.

***

In October of 1964, following the completion of her latest movie, *Goodbye Charlie*, Debbie and Karl decided to sail aboard the *Queen Elizabeth* to England.

In New York, they checked into the Regency and then went shopping along Fifth Avenue, where he bought three expensive designer gowns for her to wear abroad.

On her first night in Manhattan, a call came in from columnist Earl Wilson, who was the first member of the press to learn about Eddie Fisher's affair with Elizabeth Taylor.

He warned her that Richard Burton and Elizabeth were also sailing aboard the same Cunard vessel. "There will be at least a dozen reporters aboard, and they'll be hoping for a catfight between Elizabeth and you."

"They are not going to get it," she said. "Harry and I will fly to London."

Later that night, Karl talked her out of flying, claiming there would be so many passengers aboard *Queen Elizabeth* that chances were strong that they'd never encounter Burton or Taylor.

"I finally agreed," she said. "Let's face it: I no longer loved Eddie—perhaps I never did. I merely married him. Elizabeth, too, had moved on from him and perhaps found true happiness with Burton, although Roddy McDowall, our friend, told me that the Welshman was a notorious womanizer."

The Karls came aboard with a minimum of luggage, no more than the average tourist would carry. As Debbie boarded, she noticed a mountain of baggage, even animal cages, being loaded onto the ship, "at least the weight of the equipment the Allies needed for the landing on the beaches of Normandy in 1944," Debbie said. "I was told it was for Elizabeth Taylor."

Karl had booked one of the ocean liner's six suites for Debbie and himself. The steward told them that the other five suites had each been reserved for the Taylor/Burton party.

"We're bound to run into them," she told Karl. "I'm going to send them an invitation to visit our suite at nine tonight for champagne and caviar."

"Fine with me," he said.

[When Elizabeth and Burton had flown to Rome for the filming of Cleopatra (1963), she was still married to Fisher, and Burton was still married to Sybil.

Before the movie was completed, Burton and Elizabeth had fallen in love, and Fisher got dumped, as did Sybil. Debbie followed their exploits in the world press with fascination. "It serves Eddie right. I knew their marriage wouldn't last."

"Eddie left Rome, flying to New York on March 19, 1962," Roddy McDowall said. It would be two years before he saw Elizabeth again. I went to the airport to see him off. He downed three vodkas with Seconals before boarding. He said it was all over between Elizabeth and himself, except for the divorce, which he predicted would go on for years as they fought over money."

"He also accused both Elizabeth and you of destroying his career," McDowall told Debbie. "He's really in bad shape."

"Couldn't happen to a nicer guy," she answered, sarcastically.]

Debbie and Karl were resting in their suite when the last two passengers and their entourage came aboard. Reporters and photographers were there to record the arrival at the pier of Elizabeth and Burton.

Later that afternoon, Elizabeth sent word to Debbie that she and Burton were accepting the invitation to drinks.

To prepare for their arrival, Karl spent more time getting ready than Debbie did, and he even applied some of her makeup. He then fussed with room service about the Iranian caviar and the chill factor of the Dom Pérignon.

At exactly nine o'clock, Burton and Elizabeth were at their door. She looked radiant in mauve, pink, and purple.

Debbie rushed to greet her. "I see you've kept your figure, perhaps added a few pounds to it." No sooner had she made that remark than she regretted it. She had not seen Elizabeth in six years, not since the death of Mike Todd.

Elizabeth appraised Debbie with a skeptical eye. "I see that Tammy has emerged from the Louisiana swampland after fighting all those alligators," she said. "And who is this divine shoe salesman you married? He doesn't look like Eddie at all. Perhaps you'll hang on to this one."

"Now, girls," Burton said. "This is not a bitchfest, but a friendly gathering. I'll take over and entertain you with amusing stories—say, what Vivien Leigh and Larry Olivier are like in bed, or the night Princess Margaret came on to me, perhaps the time I took a shower with Sean Connery, and we got into an argument about which bloke had the bigger dick."

"All those stories sound absolutely delicious," Debbie said.

In his published diaries, Burton remembered the encounter, although erroneously putting it aboard *Queen Mary*, not *Queen Elizabeth*. "When I first met Harry Karl, I practically kissed him firmly on the mouth," he wrote. In a memoir, he revealed his disdain for Debbie by asserting, "Karl showed a lack of taste in marrying her."

Later, he said to Roddy McDowall, "I know you see a lot of Debbie, but I find her shallow and too cute for my tastes. I'd rather run off with the Serpent of the Nile."

After finishing three bottles of champagne and all of the caviar, Elizabeth suggested that "we shock the world and parade into the dining room as a friendly quartet."

Over dinner and over more champagne, their party turned raucous. "Who in the fuck cares about Eddie Fisher anymore?" Elizabeth asked. "Boring, boring!"

"When we were making *Cleopatra* in Rome, I came to Elizabeth's villa," Burton confessed. "I grabbed the little runt and hauled him upstairs to the bedroom, where I fucked hell out of him. I showed him who was the man."

"I think he enjoyed it," Elizabeth said. "I know Eddie has had some gay encounters on the road."

"Who hasn't?" Burton chimed in.

"By the way, Debbie darling, Eddie has spread rumors that you're a cold-hearted lesbian," Elizabeth said. "Are they true?"

"No, they're a god damn lie," Debbie said.

"I know you made a movie with Bette Davis," Elizabeth said. "I heard she was a lesbian, too. When you made the film, did the old bitch make a pass at you?"

"Bette told me she'd never had a lesbian affair, although Joan Crawford once propositioned her."

"Crawford hits on everyone without gender bias," Burton said.

"I know, I know," Debbie said. "Been there, done that."

The reunion between Elizabeth and Debbie was duly reported in the international press. "I don't know why all that fuss about me running off with Eddie should have gotten so much attention," Elizabeth said. "Husband-stealing is a time-honored condition in Hollywood. That's been true since the days of the silents."

Later, when Debbie returned to New York, she had dinner with McDowall, who was living there at the time. She reported to him what had happened: "That Burton is one charismatic guy, full of charm. His stories are so outrageous that I don't know if they're true or not. When we were walking back to our suites, Karl and Elizabeth were in front. Burton took the opportunity to pinch my butt."

"It feels delectable," he said to her. "Why not sneak off with me tomorrow to one of the linen closets, where we can knock off a quickie?"

"How did you handle that?" McDowall asked.

"I told him never to extend such a tantalizing invitation unless he meant to carry through with it."

***

Debbie, as was widely known,

Marie MacDonald died young, leaving Debbie as a surrogate mother for her three children.

321

was the mother of Carrie and Todd Fisher. But her husband was the father of three kids with Marie ("The Body") McDonald, whom he'd married and divorced twice, first in 1947 and again in 1955. Whereas a son, Harrison, known as "Bo," and a daughter, Denice, known as Dede) had each been adopted, their youngest, Tina Marie, was their biological child.

Because of their link through Karl, Debbie kept up with the press reports on McDonald, including her later marriages—one to TV executive Louis Bass in Las Vegas, the union lasting ten months, and another to Edward Callahan, an attorney and banker. That marriage survived only two nights.

McDonald's final marriage was to Donald Taylor, the producer of *Promises, Promises,* a show in which she was starring, in 1963.

After her second divorce from Karl, she had received generous monthly payment for child support. But she constantly phoned to complain that the money was never enough. "She hounded Harry all the time, wanting more and more money," Debbie said. "She had also taught her children to hate their father, so he never visited her home during my entire marriage to him."

Early one Christmas Eve in 1964, Karl was in London, and Debbie was home alone, wrapping presents. Carrie and Todd were at a party at the home of friends. A maid answered the door and, without checking, ushered McDonald into the living room. There, she encountered Debbie arranging presents around a tall, lavishly decorated evergreen from Oregon.

Debbie was startled to see her. Of course, she knew who she was, having known her before her own marriage to Karl. "She looked frumpy with her hair in rollers. She wore no makeup, but she'd kept her figure, so she could still be called 'The Body.'"

McDonald arrived with her daughter, Tina, a sad, desolate-looking child. Karl had told Debbie that he never believed that Tina was his biological daughter, but Debbie did. "She looked just like Harry, which was no compliment for a girl."

As Debbie had predicted, the actress had arrived hoping to meet with Karl and to press her demands for "a bundle of money to buy last-minute Christmas present for his children."

After a tense thirty minutes, during which McDonald requested a scotch—"and don't be stingy, honey"—she pleaded with Debbie to wring more money from Karl. Tina never said a word but stared intently at Debbie throughout the encounter.

This visit would be the last time Debbie ever saw the fading star. On October 21, 1965, McDonald's sixth husband, Taylor, discovered her body slumped over her dressing table. She was dead at the age of forty-three.

The police arrived at her house and began an intense questioning of Taylor, perhaps trying to determine if he murdered his wife.

When Debbie heard the news of McDonald's death as it was broadcast over the radio, she decided she had better go over and transport the three children back to her home. She feared that Taylor would be in no shape to take care of them. She was concerned about how Karl would relate to his kids, since he was deeply alienated from them.

Within the hour, Debbie had arrived at McDonald's home in Hidden Hills in the San Fernando Valley. Reporters and photographers were stationed in the front yard.

Inside, the police were questioning Taylor to see if he were implicated in a possible murder of his wife. Perhaps it hadn't been suicide after all...

The coroner eventually ruled that McDonald's death was caused by "active intoxication due to multiple drugs."

[Three months later, Taylor committed suicide by overdosing on Seconal.]

Back at her own home with the McDonald children, Debbie phoned Karl in London. Actually, as it was learned later, he was in bed with a prostitute he'd picked up on Piccadilly Circus.

She had already told the children, "Marie is gone now. I'm your new mother."

Karl's reaction was furious. "How dare you bring those kids into my house without my permission! I don't want them. Send them to boarding school. Don't let them be there when I fly home from London."

His demand was unreasonable. Whereas the adopted kids might eventually be sent to boarding school, it seemed clear that Tina would be their responsibility. Within a few hours of their arrival, it had become obvious that the new brood's presence was "a nightmare." *[Debbie's words.]*

Debbie learned that the McDonald/Taylor home had been a madhouse in an almost constant state of war. One evening, McDonald had cut herself with a knife and smeared her blood across the white walls of her living room. She and Taylor staged nightly fights, usually based on her sleeping with other men.

"Tina was desperate for love, and she started screaming if I had to leave her," Debbie claimed.

The newly arrived trio had been under the care of the same pediatrician as Carrie and Todd. Dr. Wile told Debbie that Tina had been born an addict because McDonald was heavy into drugs during her pregnancy. Tina had already spent six months in rehab.

In the months ahead, Tina became more and more of a problem. Karl was angered when he returned home "and found those brats living in my house." He became withdrawn from Debbie and moved out of their bedroom, installing a bed in his study. It had direct access to the outside, a design that allowed daily visits from his barber and his "manicurist" without forcing either of them to pass through the other areas of the house.

As time went by, he seemed more or less resigned to the positioning of Debbie as the principal caretaker of his children from a previous marriage. Once or twice, he had tried to dine with the children from his reconfigured family, but Tina had thrown food in his face.

Night after night, she had run out the door, racing toward the fast moving traffic in the street until Debbie rescued her.

"I didn't want to chain her to the bed like Joan Crawford did with her children. What to do? That god damn Harry was no help at all."

In loud, accusing tones, he told her, "YOU brought these juvenile delinquents into my home. YOU take care of them. Let me alone!"

One night, Tina told Debbie that Taylor, her stepfather, did not love her. "My mother got me a little puppy, and I loved him. But Taylor got mad at me and strangled him to death."

Tina did not get along with Harrison. One afternoon, she sank her teeth into him and wouldn't let go. He was bleeding. Finally, he broke free of her and slugged her in the face, bloodying her nose, and then started to choke her. Debbie rushed to poolside, but wasn't strong enough to tear them apart. "He almost killed her. I had to rush both of them to the hospital. I was beginning to feel like Nurse Ratchett in *Cuckoo's Nest.*"

Debbie consulted a child psychiatrist, who had three sessions with Tina. At their conclusion, he met privately with Debbie, telling her that her stepdaughter was not only mentally disturbed, but dangerous. She became alarmed when he told her that Tina might take a butcher knife and stab her one night within her home. "Better keep your bedroom door locked. She could also be a potential threat to your own children, whom she violently hates, especially Carrie."

"How to handle this?" Debbie asked such friends as Agnes Moorehead and Thelma Ritter.

Moorehead's advice was to force Karl to find another home for his brood. Ritter facetiously recommended that Debbie "take to the bottle."

"I followed Thelma's advice, and began to belt down a few at night," Debbie said. "I'd only had a few vodkas and 7-Up before that."

"It was one of the most confused periods of my life," Debbie said.

After phoning Ritter and telling her of the latest disaster, the older actress delivered some final advice: "Take another drink, kid."

Chapter Eleven

TO HER HORROR, DEBBIE DISCOVERS

SHE'S BROKE

HARRY KARL, THROUGH GAMBLING & BAD INVESTMENTS,
HAS SQUANDERED HIS MILLIONS AND HERS, TOO.

She Feuds with Shelley Winters in a Movie So Unprofitable
It Ends Her Status in Hollywood as a Leading Lady

TRUE GRIT

QUESTION: "WHAT'S LEFT FOR ME NOW?"
ANSWER: "A BARE-KNUCKLED FIGHT FOR SURVIVAL"

These two scenes in Debbie's latest picture, *How Sweet It Is!* had her co-starring with "that handsome hunk *[her words]*, James Garner."

"I had long envied leading ladies like Doris Day who got to work with him."

In the two scenes above, Debbie's role reflected what was going on in her real life. She had begun to drink heavily. In the other scene, she appears bare-breasted before Garner, hoping to lure him into bed. She was allowed to wear pasties, but later that night, she assured him, "You can have me without the pasties...and without anything. It's your play, big boy."

After the success of *The Unsinkable Molly Brown,* Debbie received several film offers in rapid-fire order. The one she eventually accepted was the relentlessly wholesome *The Singing Nun.* Scheduled for a release through MGM in March of 1966, it marked her return to her former home studio.

The Berlin-born director, Henry Koster, was assigned the task of pulling the package together. Born a Jew in Berlin, he fled from the Nazis in 1933 after he assaulted an SA officer in a bank.

He teamed with Joe Pasternak, who organized his transit to Hollywood and assigned him—despite the fact that he did not yet speak English—to direct the 14-year-old Deanna Durbin in *Three Smart Girls* (1936). A resounding hit, it was later credited with saving Universal from bankruptcy.

Eventually, Koster helmed such stars as Bette Davis, Richard Burton, Ava Gardner, and Loretta Young. He was also known for discovering Abbott and Costello at a nightclub in Manhattan. One of his biggest successes had been his direction of James Stewart in *Harvey* in 1950.

The plot of *The Singing Nun* was very, very loosely based on the life and career story of Jeannine Deckers, "The Singing Nun," also known as "Sister Smile."

Deckers was the bespectacled nun who, based on her worldwide hit, "Dominique," beat the Beatles to the top of the U.S. charts. The convent novice became the Grammy award-winning guitar-strumming singer known as Belgium's "Elvis Presley in a habit."

To populate *The Singing Nun,* Koster lined up an impressive cast that in-

Creative and suicidally desperate: Displayed above are two views of Jeannine Deckers, aka "Soeur Sourire/Sister Smile/The Singing Nun."

The guitar-strumming nun desperately wanted to conceal from the world that she was a lesbian.

cluded Ricardo Montalban, Greer Garson, and Debbie's close friend, Agnes Moorehead, along with such supporting players as Juanita Moore, Chad Everett, Katharine Ross, and Tom Drake (Judy Garland's Boy Next Door from *Meet Me in St. Louis;* 1944). Ed Sullivan appeared in the film as himself.

In real life, Deckers was known as a rebellious, unstable trouble-maker and a punk before her time, a fragile egotist full of repressed aggression and savage brutality. But based on pressure from the studio, Koster ordered scriptwriters John Furia and Sally Benson to compose a saccharine version of the nun's story. In real life, Deckers became depressed, alcoholic, and destitute. After the worldwide success of her song and her transformation into a pop icons, Deckers, in league with her lesbian lover, a fellow nun, Anne Pecher, abandoned the convent and spent years battling Belgian tax authorities for taxes allegedly owed on their music's profits. They both committed suicide in 1985.

One French author compared Deckers' rollercoaster life to that of a true rock star, Nirvana's Kurt Cobain. Near the peak of her fame, Deckers shocked her Catholic fan base by releasing a supportive ode to contraception entitled "The Golden Pill."

"I would like to have starred in the true story of that nun," Debbie said, "and not the vanilla version."

"The role of the Sister Ann I played was naïve and virginal. I was the perfect nun, idealized to the point of fantasy. I think of nothing but service to God and humanity. My co-star, Greer Garson, could have played the role fifteen years before."

The plot for *The Singing Nun* has Sister Ann arriving at the Samaritan House, a Dominican Convent in a depressed neighborhood in Ghent, Belgium. She doesn't impress Sister Cluny (Moore-

In the photo above, show-biz maestro Ed Sullivan appeared on the set to congratulate Greer Garson (left), Agnes Moorehead (center), and Debbie.

head), but wins support from the Mother Prioress (Garson), who believes that Sister Ann, with time and training, will become a welcome addition to the order.

One day, Father Clementi (Montalban) hears her sing and thinks she should record her music. He persuades Robert Gerarde (Everett), a partner in a recording firm, to make a recording of "Dominique." [*Five years earlier, he had been her classmate when she was broke and hungry and had posed for provocative photos. He had been attracted to her then, and his attraction for her is now rekindled.*]

Her recording becomes a spectacular hit worldwide, prompting Ed Sullivan and his TV crew to haul themselves off to Belgium to televise her singing.

Ann is overwhelmed with the raucous adulation that comes with fame. In the end, however, she surrenders her guitar to another nun and goes to work in an African village among depressed natives.

The British actress, Greer Garson, in *The Singing Nun's* second lead, had reached the peak of her career during the war years, winning an Oscar for her role in *Mrs. Miniver* (1942). What amused Debbie was that Greer had married her co-star, Richard Ney, who had played her son in that movie. She was 39 at the time, and he was 27.

The Mexican actor, Ricardo Montalban, charmed Debbie with his richly seductive voice. "I fell in love with Ricardo, but we didn't have an affair," she said. "Why not?" Because he was a priest, and I was a nun."

Early in their filming, Montalban had told Debbie, "Mexico is my mother, the United States my best friend."

In 1944, he had married Georgiana Belzer, an actress and model, and the half-sister of Loretta Young. He was still married to her at the time of her death in 2007.

Although Debbie's singing drew praise, *The Singing Nun* got mixed reviews. Most critics labeled it "syrupy," and Deckers herself dismissed it as pure fiction. One fan wrote, "All this movie needs is Bing Crosby as the priest."

Another critic, under the headline "The Singing Virgin," posted this: "The movie gives Debbie Reynolds the chance to do her finest singing to date. Here is also Greer Garson at the twilight of her career, and Ricardo Montalban, famous for swimming with Esther Williams in musicals. Agnes Moorehead looks like she's ready to cast a nasty on Darrin in *Bewitched,* and Chad Everett still looks like Dr. Gannon in his hospital TV show."

***

Months and months had passed without any expression of sexual intimacy between Harry Karl and Debbie. They were man and wife in name only. "Occasionally, I'd get a peck on the cheek—and that was that. He was more or less my escort when I needed him to take me to a Hollywood party or a premiere, or hopefully to one of my movies. But my list of films was growing fewer and far between. No longer did I rush from one picture to another."

Her doctor had warned her that after two stillborns, having another child might threaten her life. Karl reacted to that with a visit to his own doctor, who performed a vasectomy on him.

"I don't know why he bothered," Debbie said. "He wasn't screwing me, so there was no fear of my getting pregnant unless some other man was involved."

When a lull came in her work schedule, she asked Ray and Minnie to move in and look after their grandchildren while she and Karl flew to her favorite resort (Acapulco) for a three-week vacation.

Karl booked a suite for them at the Acapulco Towers, where many movie stars (including Lana Turner) had stayed. On her fourth night there, Debbie emerged from her shower and toweled herself dry. Then she spotted Karl on their terrace, which opened onto a view of the Pacific. He was having a tequila cocktail and watching the sun go down. "It was a beautiful and romantic setting," she said, "calling for a Ricardo Montalban type, not Harry. But I decided to make do with what was at hand."

She dropped the towel and, totally nude, walked onto the balcony and plopped down on his lap. He put his arm around her waist, but soon rose to his feet. "Excuse me while I make you a drink."

"That was that!" she said. "I felt like a little fool throwing myself at him. Never again would I approach him for sex. I was still a vital woman in need of some love-making. In the future, I would have to turn elsewhere for that. I suspected that was what he was already doing."

After her return from Mexico, she developed a nightly routine: After putting her children to bed, she would go downstairs and have several drinks, disguising the taste of the vodka with ginger ale or Seven-Up. At around midnight, she'd stagger up to her bedroom, where she'd collapse in a stupor.

On many nights, she'd spend an evening with her neighbor, Agnes Moorehead, or else drive to the home of Lillian Burns Sidney, her drama coach.

Other nights were spent with Rudy Render, her African-American musician friend. They would laugh, sing, play music, and gossip a lot. She loved evenings with him. If she weren't scheduled for filming the next day, she stayed up until three or four in the morning. Many nights he slept over, especially when she interpreted his condition as unsuitable for driving.

***

In the early spring of 1966, the canny, very talented Norman Lear, a producer and writer, phoned Debbie to ask her to drop by his office to discuss a new picture deal. He was both the producer and writer of a comedy, *Divorce American Style*, set for a 1967 release by Columbia.

"When she heard the title, she asked Lear, "Is the story about my current marriage to Harry Karl?"

"Not quite, but I heard you're in a marriage from hell, and that's why you came to mind."

Their next meeting, in his office the next day, did not go well either. To a keyed-up Debbie, he said, "At first, I thought of you as the female lead, but after a few sleepless nights, I'm having my doubts. I fear you're not quite right for it."

He knew she wanted and even needed the role, as her movie career had been in low gear for months. She also knew he believed in throwing up roadblocks and spinning unhurriedly through "The Art of the Deal" as a means of getting her price down.

This became evident in four successive interviews, one of which led to a shouting match. The price he offered for her services was lessened after each conversation. "I don't think you're worth the money," he bluntly told her at one point.

She never revealed the salary they ultimately reached, although she claimed that it was less than what she actually got, and far less than what she usually received for one of her night club appearances.

"As I began work on *Divorce American Style*, I thought it might be a dress rehearsal for the day I'd finally divorce Harry."

A progressive liberal born in Connecticut, Lear was on the dawn of his greatest fame, something that would make him a household word. In the upcoming 1970s, he would produce one hit TV series after another, including the hugely profitable *All in the Family* (1971-79). It elevated the character of Archie Bunker into part of the national vocabulary.

Others of his sitcom hits included *Sanford and Son, One Day at*

Debbie found Dick Van Dyke amusing to work with both on and off the screen, viewing him as a virtual Renaissance man—an actor, comedian, singer, writer, and producer.

When Debbie met him, he'd just come from his great success developing the hit TV sitcom, *The Dick Van Dyke Show*, which ran from 1961 to 1966. He'd also had great success as Bert, the chimney sweeper, in *Mary Poppins* (1964).

a Time, The Jeffersons, Good Times, and *Maude.* Highly controversial, they mostly dealt with social and political issues of the day.

Lear put his wife, Frances, in charge of wardrobe. "I don't know what kind of budget her husband gave her, but I think she purchased my entire wardrobe at a secondhand dress shop in the seedier part of downtown Los Angeles," Debbie said.

Frances divorced Lear in 1986, walking off with $120 million. "When I divorced Harry, I ended up bankrupt and millions in debt. Some gals have the luck. Not me!"

Lear hired Bud Yorkin to direct it. A former graduate in engineering at Carnegie Tech, he preferred the role of a Hollywood producer instead. He joined Lear in turning out many of his hit TV sitcoms, and he also produced TV shows for such stars as Tony Martin and Tennessee Ernie Ford.

As established in the script of *Divorce American Style,* an affluent suburban couple, Richard (as played by Dick Van Dyke) and Barbara have been married for seventeen years. But the union has grown stale, and they bicker all the time. The suggestion is that they haven't had a good roll in the hay in years. They are clearly bored with each other, and they agree to separate. The next day, they accidentally encounter one another at their bank as each of them attempts to withdraw money from their joint account.

After his separation from Barbara, Richard, subjected to heavy alimony and confined to a small apartment, struggles along on his take-home pay of $87.50 a week. Soon, he meets Nelson Downes (Jason Robards), a divorced man also making heavy alimony payments to his ex-wife Nancy (Jean Simmons).

Nelson (Roberts) wants to end his alimony payments by getting his ex-wife Nancy married off. There's another problem: He needs to marry his pregnant girlfriend.

Nelson also devises a similar scheme for Barbara (Debbie), trying to fix her up with an

Jason Robards, a combat veteran of World War II, was the son of a well-known actor, Jason Robards, Sr.

At the time Debbie worked with him, he was married to Lauren Bacall. "I became great friends with Jason and Dick on the set, and we liked each other so much, we spent weekends together in Malibu."

"Jason was a frustrated Broadway musical star, and he sang and danced for us. Mostly we drank, cursed, ate spicy food, farted, and sang. But no sex, please. We were married. I think our spouses were not amused, perhaps thinking we were having a three-way.

After Jason put on a show, Dick would take over before I came on. Dick and Jason were as much fun as a barrel of jackrabbits."

obnoxious millionaire car dealer, as portrayed by Van Johnson.

One complication after another, often comedic, transpires before Barbara and Richard get back together on the night before their divorce becomes final. Don't expect the typical Hollywood ending.

Before THE END flashes on the screen, Richard and Barbara are bickering again.

Lear and Yorkin, his director, hired a number of major-league actors to appear in supporting roles: Joe Flynn, Shelley Berman, Martin Gabel, Lee Grant, Tom Bosley, and Eileen Brennan.

On the set of *Divorce American Style*, Debbie had a reunion with Van Johnson, whom she'd known since her early days at MGM. His star had fallen a long time before.

"No longer were he and that nympho, June Allyson, known as America's sweethearts," Debbie said. "He was given fifth billing in an unattractive role. He eased his pain by inviting two studly members of our crew to his dressing room for love in the afternoon."

Originally, Debbie had been jealous of Jean Simmons, the English actress, when she took the lead in *The Actress* (1953), a role that Debbie had coveted. The effervescent Simmons had brought grace and style to movies well into the 1950s. She told Debbie, "Audrey Hepburn and Deborah Kerr, my chief rivals, got many of the parts I was best suited for." She had been nominated for a Best Supporting Actress Oscar when she played Ophelia opposite Laurence Olivier in *Hamlet* (1948).

Simmons continued with major roles in such films as *The Robe* (1953) opposite Richard Burton: *Guys and Dolls* (1955) with Marlon Brando, and *Elmer Gantry* (1960) with Burt Lancaster.

During a candid lunch with Debbie in the commissary, Simmons was frank and surprisingly graphic. "My marriage to Stewart Granger would have been more successful if his penis had been an inch and a half longer. Of all my lovers, including Olivier, Burton and Lancaster, only Nicky Hilton hit the hot spot."

According to Debbie, "She made that revelation with all the class she might have had inviting me to tea."

As was the case with almost any film in which Debbie starred, Bosley Crowther of *The New York Times* panned it. He called *Divorce American Style* "rather depressing, saddening, and annoying, largely because it does labor to turn a solemn subject into a great big American boob joke." Debbie fared better than one of her male co-stars. Crowther wrote, "Dick Van Dyke is too much of a giggler, too much of a dyed-in-the-wool TV comedian for this serio-comic husband role."

Variety noted that the film "pokes incisive, sometimes chilling fun at U.S. marriage and divorce problems."

The Chicago Sun-Times claimed that *Divorce American Style* was "a member of that rare species, a Hollywood comedy with teeth in it. The cast, including

Debbie Reynolds, among others, seemed unlikely on paper, but came across splendidly on screen."

In spite of many bad reviews, Lear and his assistant Robert Kaufman, were nominated for a Best Original Screenplay Oscar, losing to William Rose who wrote *Guess Who's Coming to Dinner?* which had starred Katharine Hepburn and Spencer Tracy in his final role.

***

Debbie's last big role as a major Hollywood player was in *How Sweet It Is!*, a romantic comedy she shot with James Garner, an actor she'd always called "a handsome hunk, the man of my dreams." Set for release in the summer of 1968, it became the first movie made by a new Hollywood studio, National General.

[After that, she would have only one more star role, this one a low-budget quickie, a horror movie (What's the Matter With Helen?) *that hoped to capitalize off the success of* What Ever Happened to Baby Jane? *which had co-starred those battling divas, Bette Davis and Joan Crawford.]*

"Most major stars in Hollywood live to see the sun set in the West on their careers," Debbie said. "I always knew that was in store for me. But fortunately, I had the talent to find a second act, which was in live appearances. Of course, the lucky few continued to work until they died with their boots on. Clark Gable was at death's door when he made *The Misfits* (1960) with Marilyn Monroe. Katharine Hepburn was one of the few survivors who found work even as the hearse outside was waiting to haul her away."

"When I started to work on this movie *[How Sweet It Is!]*, I knew it might be the last of those starring roles in romantic comedies of the 1950s. Doris Day and I were running out of time playing perpetual virgins. In fact, when I was making it, I decided to quit being a virgin in my private life, too. I didn't exactly become the whore of Babylon, but I got screwed in the future more than fans ever imagined."

Jerry Paris was assigned to direct Debbie and Garner in a script written by the two producers, Garry Marshall and Jerry Belson. As an actor, Paris had played the dentist, Jerry Helper, on *The Dick Van Dyke Show*. As a director, he had helmed such hit TV sitcoms as *The Odd Couple* and *The Mary Tyler Moore Show.*

Debbie developed a great friendship with one of the film's producers, Bronx-born Garry Marshall, who was best known later in his life for his hit TV series, *Happy Days* (1974-1984). "He had one of the best comedy minds in the business," she said.

In the script, Debbie was cast as a housewife, Jenny, married to Grif (Garner), a professional photographer whose magazine assigns him to accompany a group of American students during their tour of France. Grif decides to take his perky wife, Jenny (Debbie) along, too.

Their son, David (Donald Losby), is disappointed, as he'd hoped to travel—without parental supervision—with his girlfriend.

Debbie books passage for herself and her family aboard an ocean liner and arranges accommodations for them on the French Riviera, ignorant of the fact that her travel agent, Gilbert (Terry-Thomas), is a shyster.

Aboard the ship, Grif and Jenny are frustrated when they learn that they'll have to sleep in a dormitory where males and females are rigorously segregated. They are each hawkeyed by the ship's prissy purser (Paul Lynde). *[Before shooting began, Debbie sternly chastised Lynde for spreading lesbian rumors about Agnes Moorehead and herself.]*

Debbie is the first to arrive, days in advance before Grif and her son can join her on the Côte d'Azur. As it turns out, the accommodations she's booked for them aren't within a hotel, but in the private mansion of a handsome, rich, and charming attorney, Phillipe (Maurice Ronet). He arrives unexpectedly to discover Debbie, an attractive American tourist, living in his mansion. He allows her to stay, then tries to seduce her one night beside the pool.

Meanwhile, Grif (Garner) is being romantically pursued by Gloria (Alexandra Hay), the attractive, hot-to-trot chaperone of the student tour group.

Various screwball antics follow. In one of them, Jenny gets arrested and jailed with a coven of prostitutes. A pimp gets all of them released, and unsure of what to do next, she's taken to a house of prostitution masquerading as a conventional hotel. She's shocked to discover her son there in "a party mood."

Never mind: Her husband, Grif, in a stolen bus, comes to her rescue, eventually transporting Jenny and Davey back to the safety of their home in America. By the end of the movie, everyone involved is perhaps a bit more sophisticated, thanks to their summer of "European decadence."

To throw readers off the scent of what was really going on, Debbie in a memoir, described her attraction to the handsome French actor, Maurice Ronet. "He really did it for me," she claimed. "Yet even if I had romantic ideas about Monsieur Ronet, I wouldn't have acted on them, because I was still married. Besides, Maurice was gay and I wasn't Elizabeth Taylor." *[She*

How Sweet It Is! was based on a novel, *The Girl in the Turquoise Bikini*, by Muriel Resnik. Indeed, Debbie on screen wears a turquoise bikini for several of her scenes.

"Knowing that I was to appear in such a flimsy garment, I got into really good shape before facing the camera," she said.

was referring, of course, to her rival's penchant for seducing gay men such as Mont-gomery Clift and Rock Hudson.]

[She was wrong, as Ronet was not gay—bisexual would be a more apt description. He'd been married once, but quickly separated. However, he lived in homes in Paris and Provence with his companion, Josephine Chaplin, from 1977 until his death in 1983. Their son, Julien, was born in 1980.]

***

Debbie had long been attracted to the macho charm of James Garner, whom she'd seen on the screen in such pictures as *The Children's Hour* (1962) with Audrey Hepburn and Shirley MacLaine. She told him she'd been terribly disappointed not to have co-starred with him in *The Thrill of It All* (1963), a role she lost to Doris Day.

That same year, she'd also gone with her friend, Thelma Ritter, to see Day and Garner in *Move Over Darling*. Ritter had a supporting role in that movie, a remake of *My Favorite Wife* (1940) which had starred Cary Grant and Irene Dunne.

Actually, that film had been set to co-star Marilyn Monroe and Garner, but whereas he bowed out and was replaced by Dean Martin. Marilyn was fired from the project and died that August in 1963.

The only time Debbie had a disagreement with Marshall during the shoot was when he asked her, with Garner, to strip nude and pile under the sheets together for a romantic scene in bed. She refused to get completely naked and demanded that she retain her panties and be allowed to stick pasties on her nipples.

Garner also chose not to be nude, climbing into bed wearing a pair of tight-fitting jockey shorts that "left little to the imagination" *[Debbie's words]*. "He should have been hired to pose for underwear ads," she later said. "The sight of him in underwear was one of the thrills of my life."

As the scene unfolded, she suddenly heard a buzzing sound, and soon discovered that Garner had brought a vibrator into the bed with him and that he had, as a spoof, switched it on. She grabbed it

In *How Sweet It Is!*, James Garner and Debbie frolic on the beach. When work finished for the day, they continued to frolic under the sheets at night.

"I had to get it from some man," Debbie confessed to friends. "I certainly wasn't getting it from my husband."

from him and, in her panties and pasties, chased him, clad only his shorts, across the set, trying to hit him over the head with it.

As she later told Marshall, "James and I finally pulled that scene off, but you didn't know what was really happening. This time, he didn't need a vibrator. He took my delicate little hand and placed it against his crotch. I felt something hard as a rock. It was like feeling a baseball bat."

In a vanilla, highly "sanitized" accounting of her relationship with Garner, she did admit that sometimes co-stars fell for each other during the making of a film.

She went on to admit that he often showed up at her house, ostensibly to go to Todd's room to play "slot cars."

What she left out was that after putting Todd and Carrie to bed, he went to her bedroom, timing his secret rendezvous to coincide with Karl's frequent absences.

Sometimes, they had time for "Pillow Talk." He told her that he'd once had the world's most awful stepmother, who constantly beat him. Once, he fought back, knocking her down onto the floor and trying to choke her to death. "She fled from our family that night and never came back."

Garner insisted that before sex, she smoke a joint with him. She didn't really like it, but went along for the sex that followed.

He confessed to his pot smoking in his 2011 autobiography, *The Garner Files: A Memoir.*

In it he wrote, "I drank to get drunk, but ultimately didn't like the effect. Not so with grass. It had the opposite effect from alcohol: It made me tolerant and forgiving. I smoked marijuana for fifty years, and I don't know where I'd be without it. It opened my mind."

Carrie Fisher once wrote that her mother gave her a plastic bag of pot when she was only thirteen years old.

That was true, but Debbie didn't have to deal with a drug pusher to get it. One night, Garner left her bedroom when it was revealed that Karl had driven back from San Diego and was on the verge of returning to the house. In his haste, Garner left the plastic bag and its contents behind.

Debbie discovered it as she heard Karl coming up the stairs. She darted out into the hallway and stashed the pot in Carrie's room. Her daughter, in time, became a pothead.

When *How Sweet It Is!* opened, it got poor re-

Garner had been a gym teacher, an occupation that Debbie had once aspired to. He was eventually spotted by the owner of a modeling agency, who, after checking out his physique in a locker room, hired him at $25 an hour to model Jantzen bathing suits.

"I eventually quit," he told Debbie. "Too many gay photographers wanted my dick, and they were always trying to get me to pose nude."

views and did not do well at the box office. Many of the critics were hostile. Writing in *The New York Times,* Howard Thompson claimed: "This tired, aimlessly frisky comedy is about as sweet as a dill pickle."

***

After wrapping both *Divorce American Style* and *How Sweet It Is!,* several months passed before Debbie got another film offer. In the meantime, she wanted to put together a night club act—billed in some instances as *The Debbie Reynolds Revue*—and take it on the road.

Over the years, several offers had arrived from Las Vegas casinos, but she had never pursued any of them. Now, through her agent, she did, and she was overwhelmed at the positive response she received. As it happened, the best deal had come from the Riviera in Las Vegas, which made an offer of $80,000 a week for a three-week booking.

During the days that followed, additional offers came in from Houston, Miami Beach, Lake Tahoe, and Reno. Her agent accepted many of them, and also signed for her appearance in two TV specials for ABC.

Her act went over big at the Riviera, playing to full houses. As Christmas of 1967 was rapidly approaching, she wanted to buy cars for two dear men in her life, neither of whom could afford one. *[The men in question included her brother, Billy, and her friend and accompanist, Rudy Render.]*

As was her custom, she went to the cashier at the Riviera and asked to withdraw the money as an advance against her salary, with the understanding that at the end of her engagement there, she'd be paid nearly a quarter of a million dollars.

She was shocked when she learned that Karl had already withdrawn the full amount of her salary to settle a gambling debt. At first, she could not believe it and confronted him at once. He told her he had to have immediate cash, and promised to reimburse her for the money as soon as he returned to Los Angeles.

After her gig in Vegas, she flew for an appearance at The Continental Room in Houston at around the same time as Karl's return to Los Angeles. She needed money for various

As her film career dwindled, Debbie found another gig, and a lucrative one, as a nightclub performer.

She launched this new career at the Riviera in Las Vegas, for which she was paid $80,000 a week.

337

payments and salaries that had come due, but she was unsuccessful at getting Karl to reimburse the money he'd withdrawn.

Before returning to Nevada, she completed a highly successful engagement at the Eden Rock on Miami Beach. From Florida, she flew to New York to promote *Divorce American Style.*

Within a week, she was opening at Harrah's at Lake Tahoe, beginning a relationship with the owners that would last for a quarter of a century.

"I was spending more and more time away from my children," she said. "But being away from Harry didn't matter. I was his wife in name only."

While she was away, her family had shrunk by one. Denice (Dede), aged seventeen, wanted to get married to a 27-year-old man. Karl at first refused permission because of the ten-year difference in their ages, but he finally relented.

"Dede detested both Harry and me, so I, for one, was glad to see her leave," Debbie said. "Living with her was miserable. We'd figured she'd be better off living under some other roof."

During her time away, two movie scripts had been sent to Debbie by her agent. In one, entitled *Night Stalker,* she would play a Tammy-like creature who conceals the homicidal nature of her true personality. [*At night, she becomes a lesbian serial killer.*] The other script was the story of a sister in love with her brother. She sabotages his two marriages and runs over one of his offspring. "The title was subtle," Debbie said. "It was called *Incest.*"

There was an occasional highlight in her marriage, as when Karl, on her 35th birthday, presented her with a bracelet studded with three dozen small diamonds. "It was stunning, but he forgot to give me a birthday kiss on the cheek. Months later, I received the bill for it. The bastard had charged it to me at Cartier, and they were demanding payment."

Both Debbie and Karl were invited to a gala dinner at the White House, receiving an invitation from Lady Bird to "Join Lyndon and me for a banquet honoring Harold Wilson" (i.e., the Prime Minister of Great

Lady Bird and Lyndon Johnson, seen at his 1964 inauguration, invited Debbie to the White House for a gala.

"LBJ flirted with me," Debbie said. "He didn't pinch my butt, but he stood real close to me, almost a huddle, telling me that Texas gals are the hottest that God ever put on the face of the earth."

He also complained that since he became president, he can't scratch like he did back home. "My god damn tailors never give me enough crotch room in my pants."

Britain). Debbie, along with Janis Paige and her husband, musician Ray Gilbert, were the only entertainers invited.

Shortly after Debbie's return to California, two agents from the F.B.I. knocked on her door, wanting to see Karl. He was away, but she invited them in anyway. "I hope nothing's wrong. He's completely honest."

"That's not why we're here," one of the agents explained. He revealed that a scandal was about to break about the Friars Club, where Karl gambled two or three nights a week, along with Dean Martin and Jack Benny.

[Karl had been one of the founding members of the Friars' Club, an exclusive circle of movie stars and some of the leading businessmen and attorneys of the Greater Los Angeles area.]

"We have proof that your husband, night after night, was cheated out of thousands, $50,000 on some nights, even $100,000. We think he has lost millions to a scam. A spy was concealed in the ceiling overlooking the hands of the various players, mainly Karl. A card shark positioned on the gaming floor received and acted upon the radio signals that the spy transmitted, a very complicated thing to pull off."

The agent explained that the reason he was revealing so much to her was because she'd co-signed two mortgages on her homes, part of a well-intentioned attempt to pay off his gambling debts.

"What a fool I was," she said. "I just signed any documents he presented to me."

That night, she informed Karl of conversation she'd had with the FBI, and he chastised her for letting them in. During the upcoming weeks, they appeared at her door three more times, always demanding to speak to him. Each time, he refused to interact with them and ordered Debbie to send them away. Finally, he was forced to deal with the issues they'd been presenting when a subpoena was served, demanding that he testify before a Grand Jury.

The scandal made the frontpages, the articles citing Karl as the member with more gambling losses than anyone else at the club. At that time, Debbie didn't know that he'd gone through his own millions and that he was now gambling away her life's savings. "When she charged him with what she'd learned, he turned on her in anger. "It's my own god damn money. I guess I can spend it any way I want."

"Well, Buster," she said. "You'd better sell a hell of a lot of shoes."

***

After many weeks had passed without the arrival of any movie scripts, not even bad ones, Debbie began to listen to her agent and to her friends who had "crossed over" into television.

Dick Van Dyck, her recent co-star, urged her to join the rush of fading Hollywood stars migrating from the big screen to the little black box. He claimed that Ronald Reagan would be in oblivion had he not appeared in a TV series for General Electric.

Friends who included Eva Gabor and Donna Reed urged her to negotiate a TV deal.

Finally, Debbie sent word to her agent, "Get me on TV in the best deal possible." Two weeks later, he did just that.

"It was like a dream come true, the deal of a lifetime," she said. NBC offered her *The Debbie Reynolds Show,* with the understanding that it would broadcast nine episodes during the autumn of 1969. She would receive $25,000 a week for a minimum period of two years, and a fifty percent ownership of the series.

She would be in partnership with Jeff Oppenheimer, a TV writer, producer, and director, who was known for his mega-TV hit series, *I Love Lucy,* the original of which ran from 1951 to 1957, with later spinoffs.

Debbie phoned Lucille Ball, who urged her to accept and sign "this honey deal." She went on to praise Oppenheimer's ability to work with major stars, citing Jack Benny, Judy Garland, Bob Hope, Bing Crosby, and Ginger Rogers, among others.

NBC went out of its way to cater to Debbie's demands, even building a sound stage at MGM, her former home studio. "I wanted to bring back memories of where I got my start in films. Now, I'm getting a new start in a different medium."

She was even given final approval of her commercial sponsor, suggesting she wanted something wholesome and American, as befitted her image. She recommended Coca-Cola, which had sponsored Eddie Fisher's TV show, and General Foods.

When she read the first script, she phoned Ball again. "Jeff has me doing zany things like you do in *Lucy.*

"So, now I must view you as my screwball competition?" Ball said.

In her new television series, she'd be cast as Debbie Thompson, a housewife married to sportswriter Jim Thompson (Dan Chastain). Her screen

It was publicized, it was promoted, and it was pre-announced with a barrage of ads, two of which are displayed above.

But when it was pulled from the air, Debbie could only blame herself.

husband—who doubled in real life as a screenwriter and jazz singer—was three years younger than she was.

Tom Bosley had the second lead. She was already familiar with him, having emoted onscreen with him on *Divorce American Style*. Actress Patricia Smith also became a regular on the show, cast as Charlotte, Debbie's sister.

After the series was shot, it opened that year's fall season, airing on September 16 at 8PM. Sitting in her living room with her family, she was horrified when *The Debbie Reynolds Show* aired.

"I had made it clear that I did not want a tobacco company sponsoring my show," she said. "But when my program came on, there was a commercial for Pall Mall cigarettes. NBC completely went against my requests. In fact, there was more smoke on that screen than the San Francisco fire. They had fucked me really good."

The American Tobacco Company had been founded in 1890, but had been acquired by American Brands, which owned Pall Mall and an array of other products. "I had learned to smoke on the sets of *The Rat Race* and *Mary, Mary* and I became addicted to cigarettes," Debbie said. "They are habit-forming. Harry smoked between three and five packages a day, and we've heard that it causes lung cancer."

Against the advice of both Karl and her drama coach, Lillian Burns Sidney. Debbie decided to "raise hell." She put through a call to Mort Werner, who, since 1962, had been head of programming for NBC. Her secret lover and co-star, James Garner, had told her how easy Werner was to work with. He'd been the executive producer of Garner's hit TV series, *Maverick*.

At one time, Werner had been the vice president for broadcasting for the Young & Rubicam *[its name was later changed to Y&R]* Agency. He had been the executive responsible for promoting cigarette sponsorships, especially by Pall Mall, for Debbie's show.

Werner was in his office at the time, but he didn't accept Debbie's call. He instructed his secretary to tell her that her boss was in conference.

Debbie felt that she had a strong bargaining chip, and her agent agreed. "My two-year contract was iron-bound, even if my show went off the air," she said. "NBC still had to pay me."

In a fit of anger, she fired off a letter

For every woman who has been over-washing her hair...

A shampoo so rich
you only need to 'lather once'!

NEW!

NEW 'Lather Once', Lustre-Creme, Shampoo

A girl's gotta make a living...

Confronted with a barrage of bills, Debbie "got commercialized" as shown in this 1964 advertisement for shampoo.

to Werner, warning him that after she completed her most recent episode, "I will not return to the studio unless you agree to yank those offensive tobacco ads." News of her defiant stand was leaked to the press, angering both NBC and American Brands. One executive there referred to Debbie as "that aging Girl Scout cunt."

Then an executive for American Brands phoned Werner. "Miss Crusader can't tell us how to spend our advertising dollars. Who in hell does the bitch think she is?" Then he added, "I never saw *Singin' in the Rain*, and I wouldn't be caught dead watching a *Tammy* movie."

A final word came in from the president of American Brands: "We will not give in to the demands of Miss Reynolds. If she insists on being unreasonable, we will yank all advertising from your network." Werner was horrified, knowing that a decision like that would lead to millions of dollars in lost revenue.

Acting on bad advice from her agent, Debbie and her attorneys met with the opposing lawyers from American Brands. She signed a waiver, releasing them from their two-year option for sponsorship of *The Debbie Reynolds Show.*

When he heard that she'd signed the waiver, Werner called her "a silly little fool. That leaves NBC with a sitcom costing a fortune with no sponsor."

He met the next day with NBC lawyers, who had carefully studied the waiver and concluded that by signing it, Debbie had also released NBC from its option. Werner immediately sent word to Oppenheimer to cancel the second season of the show. "I thought it was a stupid piece of fluff anyway," he barked.

Debbie was informed that she'd received her last paycheck, and that her contract was null and void. She was mortified, later writing, "If I had paid attention to my work, instead of taking a stand against smoking, I might have been a rich woman today. I had made the stupidest mistake of my entire career."

***

By 1970, MGM was swimming in a lake of red ink, losing $8.5 million on movie production. Emergency measures had to be taken. The owners decided to sell off acres of real estate on their historic back lot. On it, iconic scenes had been filmed which included the burning of Atlanta in *Gone With the Wind.*

Debbie persuaded Harry Karl to go with her to meet with Al Hart, the president of City National Bank. She convinced him that for five million dollars, she and Karl could buy the back lot and turn it into an amusement park where thousands of people could visit the street scenes from dozens of movies they'd seen. Consequently, Hart began negotiations to buy the lot, too, with the intention of reconfiguring it, with Debbie's participation, as the centerpiece of a yet-to-be-defined tourist attraction.

MGM executives, however, suppressed any investment in tours of their back lot, asking her, "Who in hell would be interested?"

Ironically, MGM eventually sold its backlot to a group of real estate developers for about the same price Hart had offered. Today, the land which the backlot occupied is awash in condos.

MGM not only sold its backlot acreage, but held an auction, selling props and costumes from some of its famous movies, including many of the iconic outfits worn by Gable and Crawford. Judy Garland's ruby-red slippers from *The Wizard of Oz* (1939) were auctioned off, as was Jean Hagen's elaborate gown from *Singin' in the Rain*. Props from Luise Rainer's *The Good Earth* (1937) were also consigned to the auction block.

Debbie borrowed $180,000 from a bank and bought as many costumes as she could afford. Among her purchases were Marlon Brando's cape from *Désirée* (1954), and the hand-painted green-and-white checked suits that Gene Kelly and Donald O'Connor had worn for their "Fit as a Fiddle" number from *Singin' in the Rain*. Another acquisition that was later defined as a particular favorite of hers was the ravishing black-and-white gown, with a matching picture hat, that Audrey Hepburn had worn to the Ascot races in *My Fair Lady* (1964).

Other purchases included costumes from two of the MGM's movie versions of *Cleopatra*, including Cecil B. DeMille's 1934 version with Claudette Colbert; and the 1963 remake with Elizabeth Taylor and Richard Burton.

Jane Ellen Wayne, in her book, *The Golden Girls of MGM*, wrote: "Debbie went on a crusade to preserve the studio's backlot of memories before they were demolished. She had a solution but was overruled by power and greed. While other stars, who owed their fame to MGM, did nothing, Debbie bought costumes and relics at the MGM auction in 1970, hoping to preserve them in a Hollywood museum."

Her dream never came true.

***

Debbie felt financially secure, despite the fact she'd had no film work in a while. After all, her expenses were paid for, and she'd amassed a fortune of $10 million, all of which she'd entrusted to her business manager, Irving Briskin, who also handled the business affairs of Harry Karl.

Briskin had been instructed to invest her money wisely. In ways perhaps inspired by the investment successes of Mae West, she had told him that she was particularly interested in acquiring real estate.

When she heard he'd purchased a hospital in Santa Monica, she approved. "People always get sick," she told Karl. She assumed that she had been designated as one of the stockholders, who, along with Briskin and Karl, owned the hospital.

One afternoon, while arranging Karl's monogrammed underwear neatly in his chest of drawers, she noted slips of paper with notations for various amounts of money ranging from $250 to, in one instance, $850.

When he returned from the golf course, and as she was mixing his favorite cocktail, she asked him what all those financial notations meant.

He told her they represented bank withdrawals for cash which Briskin had given him as reimbursements for personal expenses. "Why are you asking? Do you need money? You know I always give you a hundred-dollar bill when you really need it."

"That you do," she said sarcastically. "And how generous of you. Once when you were in London, I asked Briskin for pin money, and he sent over $25 for the week."

Up until then, she had trusted Briskin to manage her money, but she was getting suspicious. She depended on the men in her life to look after her affairs, and had signed over powers of attorney not only to Briskin and Karl, but to Al Hart at City National Bank, too.

Her suspicions were further aroused by Rip Taylor, the flamboyant comedian she'd hired to co-star with her in live shows in Lake Tahoe, Reno, and inevitably, Las Vegas. She was drawn to his outrageous personality and exuberance, including his wild mustache and his habit of showering everyone, including herself, with confetti during his stage act.

In *My Fair Lady* (1964), Audrey Hepburn appeared at Ascot wearing this stunning black-and-white gown with a large picture hat.

It ended up in Debbie's wardrobe collection.

He needed a business manager, and she recommended Briskin. Taylor phoned to arrange an appointment. He called her the next day to report on what happened: "There's no way in hell I'm going to sign with that money-grubbing hog. He wants a quarter of all my earnings instead of the usual ten percent. Why in hell are you turning over 25% of everything you make to him?"

"I didn't know I was," she answered. "I thought he took the regular percentage."

That night when Karl returned from the golf course, she confronted him with Taylor's revelation. He admitted that Briskin "is a twenty-five percenter, but he's not only your business manager, he's a producer, too."

"Producer of what?" she asked. "He's never gotten me a job. That 25% has got to go—in fact, Briskin has got to go, too. I'm firing him and forcing him to turn over the millions he's holding for me."

"I don't understand you," he said. "He's managed your affairs for years, and this is the first time I ever heard you complain."

"I haven't known what was going on until now," she said.

Accompanied by her attorney, she descended on Briskin's office that Monday morning, demanding that he turn over all of her assets. "It was a showdown," she told Karl.

"I not only wanted my ten million back, but all the money he'd made by investing it. Up to now, he took every one of my paychecks. I also wanted to know about my financial stake in that Santa Monica hospital and in two apartment buildings he was told to buy for me. Then came the shock of my life."

All of her money had gone to pay Karl's gambling debts. Not only that, but he had gambled away his own millions, too. Briskin owned the hospital outright. She had no interest in it. Not only that, but there had not been enough money left to buy the apartment buildings. All she had left was $300,000 in government bonds.

"I've been robbed," she'd shouted at Briskin. "By you and by Harry."

The circumstances reminded her of what had happened to Doris Day, who had made millions in recordings and films. After her husband, Marty Melcher, died, she'd learned that all her hard-earned millions had evaporated.

When she returned home, Debbie headed to the bathroom and vomited. "What a fool I was!" she later lamented. She had to go to work and soon, that same evening, decided to accept more bookings for her act and to take in on a tour across the country.

She also had children to rear and household help to pay. Tina was growing more difficult by the day, and Harrison (Bo) had dropped out of high school and was wandering aimlessly around the house. Todd and Carrie, however, were doing fine, despite the fact that they were expensive to maintain.

In April of 1970, Karl presented her with an urgent request. He needed her to turn over the government bonds to him so he could use them as collateral to secure a much-needed business loan. At first she refused, telling him, "That's all the money I have. What if something happened to one of our kids?"

He finally prevailed, and the next day she went to her bank and transferred the bonds to an account all his own.

She had to have money, too, as the first payment for her own loan of $180,000 was coming due. She'd spent all of it on the acquisition of MGM props and costumes. She was still Debbie Reynolds, the movie star and the wife of a millionaire shoe manufacturer. She went to the bank and secured an additional loan for $140,000 to help pay her current expenses and to put together a live show to take on the road.

On looking back, she said, "What a silly little dope I was. On several occasions, I had told the press that I was on the verge of retiring. Now it seemed I'd be working until the day they haul me off to Forest Lawn. Perhaps not that exclusive graveyard. Perhaps some pauper's grave. My daddy always said that a fool and his money are soon parted. How true, so many of life's clichés."

"The curtain was going up on my second act. It was called *The New Debbie Reynolds Show.*"

***

As a young girl, Carrie Fisher was the family "bookworm." The library in her home was filled with volumes of literature which no one but she had read. She preferred the classics, her favorites being Charles Dickens, Edgar Allan Poe, and D.H. Lawrence. She also had a talent for writing, composing her first poem at the age of eight.

Debbie sent her to Beverly Hills High School, where she mingled with the sons and daughters of other movie stars, musicians, directors, and producers. When she was fifteen, she dropped out to appear in a Broadway musical with her mother.

Before that, however, Carrie had excelled in her studies, earning straight A's. "I didn't have much competition in my class. All the other kids wanted to grow up to become a dumb movie star. A few of the smarter boys hoped to become directors, and some of the boys had rich daddies, so they envisioned the life of a playboy."

"Many girls told me they wanted to marry a multi-millionaire like Debbie did. A few girls said their mothers had had a crush on Eddie Fisher in the 1950s."

"Debbie said I had a better voice than hers," Carrie said. "and she was always comparing it to the deep, rich sounds of Eddie in his heyday. I didn't want to go into show business. I thought I might become a writer, perhaps a novelist."

"Whatever my mother wanted me to do, I objected. I did the opposite. I wasn't trying to be difficult. I told her how I felt. She wanted me to be a fucking Girl Scout. I hated the Girl Scouts. Of one thing I was certain: I did not intend to be another Debbie Reynolds."

"I hated growing up the daughter of a movie star," she said. "It was not the kind of life I wanted for myself. One day, I told her the truth. 'Celebrity is just obscurity waiting to happen.'"

She revealed that as a teenager, she once had encountered Elizabeth Taylor, and blamed her for taking away her daddy when she was just a toddler. "I hated you for what you did to me," she said to Elizabeth.

The star turned to her and smiled. "You didn't miss much."

Over Carrie's objections, Debbie arranged for her to join her troupe during their summer tour of 1970, giving her a part onstage in *The Debbie Reynolds Revue [Editors Note: In some contexts, it was designated, like the TV series she'd been working on, as The New Debbie Reynolds Show.]* "It was a family affair. I wanted my kids with me. Todd had learned to play the guitar, and I also worked him into the show. Minnie was one of two women assigned to wardrobe. My mother was still the best seamstress in Hollywood. For years, she'd made all my clothes."

Carrie did not like her grandmother, referring to her behind her back as "that old broad." As part of a humiliating putdown of Debbie, Minnie told Carrie, "God didn't give your mother many brains. There's nothing in her head. He put what brains he gave her in her ankles."

"It took me a minute to decipher the Texas bitch," Carrie said. [She was referring to her daughter's ability to dance.]

Every night on stage, Carrie sang "I've Got Love" from *Purlie,* the 1970 Broadway musical that had featured such stars as Ruby Dee and Alan Alda. The book was based on Ossie Davis' 1961 play, *Purlie Victorious,* set in an era when Jim Crow laws prevailed in the Deep South.

Most nights, Debbie came out and sang Harry Belafonte's "Where Are You Going, My Little One," to Carrie, who sat on a stool beside her. Todd then emerged with his guitar, performing a number with his mother and sister.

In addition, most nights Carrie sang the Simon and Garfunkel song, "Bridge Over Troubled Water."

"Carrie's voice was sweet and airy at the beginning of the song," Debbie said, "But at the end, it gathered force, and she used all her vocal power for a climactic chorus. Every night she got a standing ovation."

[The song had been an instant smash across the country, topping the "Hot 100" chart for six straight weeks. Ironically, Carrie would later marry Paul Simon, the composer of the song. She had learned to sing it by listening to Simon & Garfunkel's recorded versions.]

"I was a show stopper," Debbie said. "I sang, I danced, I did my impersonations, including Zsa Zsa Gabor, Bette Davis, and Katharine Hepburn. I even did my Betty Hutton number—the one that won me the title of *Miss Burbank of 1948.*"

One of the show's touring highlights was the appearance of five overweight singers known as "The Weight Wotchers."

"Those diet people at Weight Watchers were pissed off at me," Debbie said, "and threatened to sue."

To pay for cast and crew, Debbie had to meet a weekly payroll of $30,000. That included her dear friend and sound man, Rudy Render; her lighting director, a drummer, and her hairdresser, "Pinky," who fretted endlessly over her coiffure.

From July to September of 1970, Debbie took her show across the country, on occasion playing cities she'd never visited, including Toledo, Ohio. "Every show was sold out," she said. "Everyone, it seemed, wanted to hear me sing 'Tammy.'"

"We lived in dreary roadside motels and ate a lot of fried chicken and gravy, or else salami-studded pizzas. Lunch was always hamburgers and

French fries. In honor of her father's long-ago Coke-sponsored TV show, Carrie always ordered that soft drink."

When the show's gig in Valley Forge, Pennsylvania ended, its props and costumes were loaded onto a truck with the understanding that they'd be hauled on to their next engagement, in this case, in Westbury, Long Island.

During their transit to Westbury, as their car cruised ahead of the rented truck that carried the costumes and props for their gig, Carrie, along with Todd and her mother, heard a loud crash. Their rented truck had slid off the road and then disastrously crashed into an electric pole.

**

By having accidentally crashed into that electric pole, Debbie's rented truck had cut off the electricity to the Valley Forge Theater from which Debbie's cast and crew had just exited. The power outage lasted for two full days and nights.

Its owner of the theater, Lee Guber, had to refund ticket holders as they arrived for the upcoming shows. He blamed Debbie for the situation and refused to pay for her company's otherwise successful engagement. Infuriated, she sued him and won, but the case wasn't settled until six months later, when—after applying heavy pressure and under duress from her creditors—she finally got the money she was owed

In dire need of money as a means of keeping her nightclub gigs up, running, and on the road, Debbie phoned Karl, asking for a return to her of some of the $300,000 in government bonds she had lent him. He told her that wasn't possible, because the bonds were still being held escrow against his loan.

She didn't believe him and called the bank. During her conversation, she learned that Karl had already cashed in all the bonds.

"I had to beg, borrow, and steal, robbing hen houses at night for chickens and stealing candy money from kids JUST JOKING!" she hastened to add. Eventually, James Garner came through with a $50,000 loan. Of course, he would be the first I'd pay back when I opened on Broadway in *Irene.*"

**

It was while she was touring with her stage revue that Rudy Render signed on as her musical director, a gig that lasted for the next twenty-two years. He also became her *confidant* as part of what continued to evolve into an intimate, rather gossipy private relationship. "She could dish boyfriends with me, and there were far more of those than her fans knew about."

Debbie's father, Ray, had long gotten over his racial prejudice of African Americans, and the two men had remained friends, even attending some sporting events together.

348

"Uncle Rudy, as I called him, became part of my family," Debbie said. "He often slept over at my home. We'd stay up having fun, dancing, singing, until the wee hours."

She became even closer when she took her show on the road, and they visited boring towns and stayed in dreary roadside motels. "I always found the best place for fried chicken with lots of cream gravy and mashed potatoes, and I got Debbie addicted to the dish, too."

He spoke to her of his past when he was born in Terre Haute, Indiana. It was there that he started to play the piano at the age of three. His mother had named him Rudolph Valentino Render after her favorite heartthrob of the silent screen.

One night at an all-white night club in Terre Haute, when he was performing at the piano, he was discovered. The man who spotted and began to promote him as a talented entertainer was Bill Hays, son of the notorious Will B. Hays, a hated puritanical censor who created a Draconian picture code, dictating what could and could not be depicted in films.

Render's big moment came in 1949, when he got to record Jessie Mae Robinson' song, "Sneakin' Around," for London Records. He watched it become No. 2 on *Billboard's* R&B chart, where it remained in that spot for six weeks.

Before he could solidify his recording career, he was drafted into the Army. When he returned to Hollywood, he had to start all over again, with a cameo in Joan Crawford's 1953 film, *Torch Song.* "To see Joan perform in blackface as 'Caribbean Woman' was worth the price of admission," he said.

In the Army, he had served with Billy Reynolds, Debbie's brother, who introduced Render to the Reynolds family. During the years ahead, Debbie got Render jobs in movies, beginning when he wrote the title music for *It Started With a Kiss,* the film in which she had co-starred with Glenn Ford. "I saw the affair between Glenn and Debbie blossoming," Render said. "Ford was so handsome and sexy, he could turn a straight man gay."

Billy was a frequent visitor to the set, and Debbie suspected that "something was going on between my brother and Rudy, but I don't know if Rudy ever acted

THE DEBBIE REYNOLDS SHOW
DEBBIE REYNOLDS

Life on the road was tough on Debbie, now that she was no longer one of the biggest box office attractions in Hollywood.

"I was the hardest-working and most marketed gal off, off off, and more off Broadway."

The poster advertises her sold-out gig at Long Island (NY's) Westbury Music Fair, which booked acts that also included Tom Jones and Connie Francis.

on his impulses. At any rate, he had a powerful crush on Billy. He just worshipped him."

"You have the greatest brother on earth," he told Debbie. "He's so mother fucking good looking, a living doll. Better keep him away from your buddy, Rock Hudson. Rock would go ape-shit if he laid eyes on Billy."

As her musical director, Render worked with her on the set of *The Unsinkable Molly Brown*. He was also involved in her road shows and night club appearances in such cities as Reno, Lake Tahoe, Houston, and Miami Beach.

One night in Vegas, he told her of his first experience there. "I worked alone at this club in Vegas, but was not allowed to sit in the audience. My dressing room was down in the basement I shared with rats. Vegas in those days was terrible. Lena Horne and Sammy Davis, Jr. did much to break down the barriers."

She assured him, "You certainly won't be treated like that in any club in which I appear. Bobby Short, your first cousin, certainly doesn't have to put up with shit like that."

Debbie helped him to secure a home in a segregated section of West Hollywood. At his home one night, she had to use the bathroom, but the ground floor toilet was out of order. "You can use my john upstairs," he told her. "I won't even let my mother go up there."

At the top of the stairs, she spotted an open door leading to his bedroom. Curious, she peeked inside. One wall was filled with candid snapshots of Billy, including one taken in the Army for which he posed shirtless.

In the toilet, she spotted an 8"x10" black-and-white photograph of a limp, uncut penis. She wondered if her brother Billy had posed for that—perhaps not. She'd seen Billy in the nude when they'd shared a bedroom in El Paso as they were growing up, but she certainly hadn't seen him nude since they'd become adults.

"Frankly," she said, "I didn't want to know if that were Billy's penis. I was told that a lot of black men prefer white boys and vice versa. In the future, the musical *Hair* would sing the praise of interracial love."

Render left the music business in 1972, telling Debbie, "I've had it." He got a job as an elementary school teacher in North Hollywood, but he still worked with Debbie on her future musical numbers. On rare occasions, she'd make a surprise appearance at one of his classes. "Since these kids didn't know who I was, Rudy had to introduce me as Princess Leia's mother."

***

It was while traveling with Minnie, Carrie, and Rudy Render, all of them together on the road with her Debbie Reynolds Revue, that she collapsed one night in Toledo, Ohio.

"My whole body felt numb all over, and I could no longer remember where I was. At first, I thought I had had a stroke, and would have to face the rest of my life paralyzed."

Minnie came to her aid and called for Render, who immediately secured a local doctor. While waiting for him to arrive, Minnie told Render, "I warned my empty-headed daughter not to go into show business. I knew something like this would happen, with her singing and dancing—and strutting her body before live audiences like a brazen whore pedaling her wares."

By the time Dr. Tiles rushed to her side, he found her hyperventilating. He spent most of the night watching over her after he'd given her some shots. At one point, she asked him, "Where is Dr. Needles now that I need him?"

[He didn't understand, of course, that she was referring to Dr. Max Jacobson, who had rendered all those shots to Eddie Fisher before he went on stage.]

By the next morning, she had rallied and could continue on the road again. However, in Westbury on Long Island, she collapsed again after a show. This time, a doctor from Manhattan, Dr. Morrill, was summoned to her bedside. He spent three hours with her, also administering shots. He told Minnie and Render that she was in a weakened, rundown condition. When he discovered that she did not remember going before a live audience the night before, he diagnosed her condition as "Transient Global Amnesia," a term she'd never heard before.

He suggested that she travel to Manhattan for some neurological tests.

[Transient Global Amnesia is a neurological disorder characterized by a temporary, almost total disruption of short-term memory. Its duration usually lasts from two to eight hours. Persons suffering from it believe they have had a stroke, as did Debbie. The condition is often intensified by anxiety, which had consumed Debbie ever since she'd learned that Karl had squandered her lifetime savings.]

She was not convinced of the doctor's diagnosis of her condition, and, in the words of Minnie, "She turned to astrological stars instead of to God."

Debbie remained convinced that she was going to die at the age of thirty-eight. She recalled that her grandmother had had a stroke at the age of thirty-seven.

She wanted to know if she had a future—or not. For a long time, she had been familiar with the growing reputation of Jeane Dixon, who defined herself as "the nation's leading psychic and astrologer." Her syndicated column on astrology was read by millions, and her fans eagerly awaited her end-of-the-year predictions about what the upcoming twelve months had in store for America.

In 1956, Dixon had predicted that a Democrat would win the election, but that the new president would be assassinated in 1963. Once at a party at the home of William Holden, Ronald Reagan told Debbie that Dixon had predicted that one day in the distant future he would be elected President of the United States.

Debbie called Dixon in Washington and set up an appointment for the following afternoon for a late lunch, with the understanding that she'd drive down to D.C. for the event.

Over lunch, Dixon delivered her good news first: "You are not going to die, at least not for several more decades. You are in good health, but plagued by anxiety. You do not have cancer or any such deadly disease. Your collapses, as I interpret them, were caused by stress and not by any medical disorder."

"But I see a lot of trouble, pain, and sorrow on your horizon. You are living through the beginning of the worst decade of your life, the 1970s. To begin with, you are married to the wrong man. He will almost destroy you, especially any financial security you had to protect yourself and your children. You must divorce him. Whatever you do, don't sign any papers such as a mortgage that he might fraudulently present to you."

"Your present husband is a far worse choice than your first one. Incidentally, in case you still care a bit, I see only a bleak future for Eddie Fisher."

"Will my present husband survive?" Debbie asked. "He quit having sex with me because he claims he has this awful infection."

"He is lying to you," Dixon said. "He told you that because he doesn't want to have sex with you anymore. During your marriage, he has turned to other women for sex, lots and lots of women."

"Do you see that I still have a future in show business, or that I will ever remarry?" Debbie asked.

"Your career will continue in the future, but you'll get minor parts in both feature films and on TV," Dixon said. "You'll make a good living in personal stage appearances, including on Broadway. But your married life is doomed to failure. The one man you should have married is Robert Wagner. His marriage to Natalie Wood was a big mistake. I see her consumed by murky waters deep at night. You will marry again, but be aware. Your third husband will plot to murder you. I suggest you go to see the Joan Crawford movie, *Sudden Fear* (1952), in which Jack Palance and Gloria Grahame plot to murder her for her money. The same fate awaits you."

Debbie later claimed that as she flew out of Washington, "I was overwhelmed by Dixon's predictions for my future. I decided she was wrong. After all, she had predicted the outbreak of World War III in 1958. She could be wrong about me, too. I decided that from that day forth, I would become Molly Brown...*UNSINKABLE!*"

Debbie's next offer was a minor one, involving a flight to London for an appearance at one of the episodes of *The ABC Comedy Hour.* The series featured a team of comedy impressionists called *"The Kopycats."*

She was invited as a guest host—one of the few women included—in a talented lineup of otherwise mostly male guest hosts. They included Orson Welles, Tony Curtis, and Ed Sullivan. Her appeal for the gig, she was told, was based on her ability to deliver satirical imitations of, among others, Zsa Zsa Gabor, Bette Davis, Mae West, and Katharine Hepburn.

The hosts were encouraged to spoof famous highlights, iconic films, or noteworthy personalities in the entertainment industry within a venue that's been cited as a forerunner to the parody skits of *Saturday Night Live.* Each of the other hosts were also noted for their skills at impersonations of celebrities. Frank Gorshin was known for his impressions of Kirk Douglas, Burt Lancaster, and *Columbo's* Peter Falk. His most famous, however, was his takeoff on Richard Nixon.

"Rich Little could impersonate almost anyone," Debbie said, "and I truly envied him. He did my friend Jim Nabors as Gomer Pyle, and even the baritone of Glen Campbell, who once raped me, and Frank Travalena could imitate everyone from Elvis Presley to Michael Jackson."

Debbie had flown to London with Carrie, leaving Karl at home to take care of the other children, including Todd.

After London, mother and daughter embarked on a spontaneous detour to Madrid, where they stayed within a suite at the landmark Palace Hotel. She'd tried to get accommodations at the Ritz, but the manager had come onto the phone, telling her, "I'm sorry, Miss Reynolds, but we don't rent to American movie stars. Their fans, the press, and photographers cause too much disruption."

Debbie embarked for Madrid with the secret intention of meeting secretly with Gregory Peters, one of Karl's business partners. Based during part of every year in Spain, Peters had accompanied Karl on some of his trips, including several to Europe and to Las Vegas. Without informing Carrie about the motive of her visit, her aim involved getting the lowdown on Karl. She wanted hard evidence, not just the psychic readings of Jeane Dixon.

On her first night in Madrid, Debbie left Carrie at the hotel and headed out to meet Peters at the exclusive Jockey, then the best restaurant in town. He had ordered a limousine to pick her up at her hotel and to return her there later.

It was a painful subject to bring up, but over dinner, she pumped Peters for information about Karl's adultery. "My hands were ice-cold and my insides were shaking, but I pressed forward."

She knew that Karl had taken many business trips to Europe with Peters, and she finally got him to confess that during those interludes, Karl had seduced a number of women, and that despite those adulterous affairs, he didn't have one in particular that he defined as his mistress.

"He doesn't have a steady, preferring instead the most expensive prostitutes in whatever town we visit. And as you know, he's a gambler."

"I heard he's lost as much as $100,000 in one night," she said.

"You don't know the half of it," Peters answered. "On one occasion, he lost half a million dollars in just four hours. He told me he's gone through as much as $25 million in a lifetime of gambling. One night he won $150,000, but that occasion was a rare as a heat wave in an Arctic winter."

Near the end of their evening together, Peters delivered yet another blow to Debbie when he told her, "Harry owes me $1.8 million."

A while later, she returned to her hotel suite, where Carrie was asleep. She didn't want to tell her what she'd learned about her stepfather. But Peters had given her plenty of reasons to file for divorce.

Landing in Los Angeles with Carrie beside her, Debbie knew that Karl would be waiting for her at the airport. She dreaded having to confront him.

Suddenly, she burst into tears, and her daughter tried to comfort her, asking her what was wrong. Although she hadn't planned to inform Carrie about Karl's many infidelities, she found herself doing just that, but between sobs.

Carrie did not seem surprised, causing Debbie to think she might have known all along. "My Carrie was one hip little girl," Debbie later recalled.

Finally, she rose to her feet and, with Carrie, disembarked.

As expected, Karl, with his carefully trimmed gray hair and mustache, was waiting for them. When he went to kiss Debbie, she averted her lips, reducing her exposure so that all he could deliver was a peck on the cheek.

During their ride back to Beverly Hills, Carrie and Karl did all the talking. Remaining silent, Debbie rode in the back seat. Under orders from Debbie, no mention was made of their secret detour to (and revelations in) Madrid.

Within a few days of her return home, she visited her neighbor, Agnes Moorehead, who had always liked Karl. But her attitude changed when she learned that he'd gambled away Debbie's fortune and that he'd been a steady patron of prostitutes.

Burying herself in the arms of the older actress, Debbie said, "I'm going to divorce the creep."

"When will you learn that men are no damn good? Moorehead asked.

***

NBC had managed to extricate itself from its financial obligations to the ill-fated TV series, *The Debbie Reynolds Show*. But, according to the terms of its contract with her, the studio still had to provide one half of the financing for two feature films that would configure her as their star. As the uncredited co-producer, she would be responsible for lining up additional producers who would contribute the remainder of the funds.

No scripts were being offered, so she went on a personal search for her own material. "Let's face it," she said. "I was no longer the new kid on the block, and I needed a script suitable for a 40-year-old woman. In Hollywood, that's the age at which most Margo Channings are buried." *[She was referring to Bette Davis, who had interpreted (and perfected) the character in All About Eve in 1950.]*

Quite by chance, she received a call from Curtis Harrington, a young director, who told her that he was sending her a script entitled *The Best of Friends*. It had been written by Henry Farrell, who had scored such a big hit in 1960 with *What Ever Happened to Baby Jane?* starring Bette Davis and Joan Crawford.

At last, Debbie was reading a script with a character she wanted to bring to the screen. The role she coveted was that of Adelle Bruckner. Adelle and her female friend, Helen, watch as their respective sons, Leonard and Wesley, are loaded into a paddy wagon and sent away to prison in the wake of a sentence of life in prison for the murder in Iowa of a character named Ellie Banner.

Harrington told Debbie that Shelley Winters, whom she knew only slightly, was ready to accept the co-starring role of Helen.

Horrified by death threats they receive for what their sons have done, the women decide to head west and start life anew in Hollywood. There, they open a dance academy with Adelle (Debbie), teaching dance and Helen (Shelley) playing the piano.

Their sales schticks are aimed at young girls of the 1930s who want to become the next Shirley Temple. *[That child star at the time of the movie's setting was at the peak of her nationwide box office clout. The era is evoked within the film by historically accurate wardrobes, decors, settings (including automobiles) appropriate to the 1930s, and archival footage of Franklin and Eleanor Roosevelt at the White House.]*

Adelle meets Lincoln Palmer (Dennis Weaver) and begins to date him, arousing the jealousy of Helen. (Yes, there are lesbian overtones here.) Licking her wounds, Helen takes solace in her faith, listening to the radio broadcasts of a religious evangelist, Sister Alma, as portrayed by Agnes Moorehead.

Tension mounts as Helen objects more and more strenuously to Adelle's romance with Lincoln, and Adelle eventually orders the meddlesome Helen to move out. But that night, as Adelle is out on a date with Lincoln, a mysterious intruder enters their dance studio. Helen pushes him, and the intruder falls down the stairs, plunging to his mangled death.

When Adelle returns home, she's horrified both by the corpse and its potentiality for bad publicity. Together, they drag it outside, then throw it into an open hole on the neighboring lot. A construction crew arrives the next morning and discovers the body.

As tension builds between Helen and Adelle, their relationship erupts.

With a butcher knife, Helen fatally stabs Adelle in the back.

Later that night, Lincoln drives up to escort Adelle on their scheduled date. He hears someone playing the piano and heads upstairs. There, he discovers Helen at the piano. He gasps in horror. She has dressed Adele's corpse in her signature dance costume and suspended it from a ladder onstage.

Debbie bonded with her director, Harrington, from the moment he arrived at her home one afternoon. As reporter Eric Myers once wrote, "Driven by unabashedly queer sensibility, one steeped in the decadence of such influences as Edgar Allan Poe, Josef von Sternberg, and

Aleister Crowley, Harrington was one of Hollywood's near-misses, a man whose feature credits seemed to consist almost entirely of films butchered, bungled, or, in some cases, barely released. One of them had been *Killer Bees* (1974) which featured an appearance by Gloria Swanson."

Harrington's life was documented in a memoir, *Nice Guys Don't Work in Hollywood*, published in 2013 by Drag City, about six years after Harrington's death in 2007.

Debbie had liked the film's original title, *The Best of Friends*, but Otto Preminger objected. He had shot *Such Good Friends* in 1971 and thought that the titles were too similar. Subsequently, the title was changed to *What's the Matter With Helen?*.

NBC agreed to put up $750,000 of the budget, and Debbie turned to producers George Edwards and Edward S. Feldman to raise the rest of the loot. Feldman had previously worked with Shelley Winters before, in 1962, during the filming of *Lolita*, based on Vladimir Nabokov's controversial novella about an adult male's aesthetic obsession with a female child. Edwards had produced a slim repertoire of films, including the curiously titled *How Awful About Allan* (1970). In 1978, he produced *Harper Valley PTA*.

When raising money for their film's production, Debbie learned that Universal had rejected Farrell's script because it could not get two name stars to appear in it. Debbie and Winters were considered as "not sufficient box office." United Artists agreed to release it.

In her private life, Debbie was virtually love starved when she met Dennis Weaver, finding him handsome and sexy. He was mainly known for his work on TV, where he interpreted such notable roles a Marshal Matt Dillon's trusty helper in *Gunsmoke*.

"Dennis was a great kisser, better than Frank Sinatra," she claimed. "I thoroughly enjoyed our love scenes. But he was not a party player and remained faithful to his wife, Gerry Stowell, whom he'd married in 1945."

In an interview he delivered in 1998, Harrington said, "In our script, Shelley is supposed to kill Debbie. But in real life, Debbie wanted to kill Shelley, who was making every day on the shoot living hell. Shelley was not only playing a psycho…she WAS a psycho!"

"She was overweight and always complaining about it. She was jealous of Debbie, who weighed in at 104 pounds."

Barely concealing her resentment, Winters once asked Harrington, "Who in hell does Tammy think she is? Wearing a slinky Jean Harlow gown with nothing on underneath it."

According to Harrington, "Shelley was always bitching about her weight, but at lunch, she'd devour big pasta dishes or fried chicken with lots of gravy and mashed potatoes. She also bitched to me that I was deliberately trying to make her look fat and ugly, preferring to photograph Debbie looking glamourous."

"Shelley constantly criticized her wardrobe," Harrington said. "At one point she ripped off her dress and rushed completely nude to confront me in front of the crew. She pounded her fists into my chest. 'I'm not ugly,' she shouted at me. 'Some of the most desirable men have seduced me, finding me beautiful. Clark Gable, Errol Flynn, Burt Lancaster, Howard Hughes, William Holden, Sean Connery.'"

"Wasn't that in a day gone by?" he asked her. "Those prime specimens are going to seed too."

"You dirty bastard," she shouted at him. "I could kill you." Then she stormed off the set.

Debbie approached Harrington and suggested that Winters be replaced with Geraldine Page, but he told her that the film would run way over budget if her scenes had to be reshot.

The next day, someone on the crew—a grip who had overheard Debbie—went to Winters and told her that Debbie had wanted to replace her in the role.

Winters immediately barged into Debbie's dressing room and began to toss anything she could find. The objects she hurled included a box of Girl Scout cookies and Debbie's makeup kit. Debbie had to call the security department to restrain her.

This photo of a distraught Shelley Winters shows that, indeed, there's something the matter with Helen.

Throughout the filming, Winters invented her own dialogue, often creating it spontaneously in her head as the camera was aimed at her. Again and again, Debbie faced the challenge of having to develop dialogue that corresponded to the words her co-star was saying.

Not only that, but when a scene was being rehearsed, Winters kept her record player blasting away at full volume. "It was very hard for me to remember my lines with a loudspeaker blaring *Brünnhilde.*"

When Harrington tried to direct Winters, she'd stop and shout at him. "Listen you cocksucker. I've won two Oscars. Don't you forget that. I'll do it my way, and you can think of the dick you sucked last night."

On another day, Winters appeared on the set wearing a gown. As Debbie walked by, she spotted Winters seated on a stool, but with a lot of movement going on under that gown. As she later realized, two members of the crew, with their heads buried beneath the fabric, were taking turns orally servicing Winters' genitalia.

When shooting was finally wrapped, Harrington approached Debbie and said, "I'm a total idiot. Guess what I've done? I've cast Shelley in my next picture, *Whoever Slew Auntie Roo?* She'll play a demented woman who keeps a mummified corpse of her daughter in the attic."

"Shelley will be great playing another psycho," Debbie said.

At the end of the picture, Winters was all smiles when she approached Debbie to bid her farewell. She spoke to her as if they'd had no differences.

"In my career, I was drowned by Monty Clift in *A Place in the Sun* (1951), run over in a car and crushed to death by James Mason in *Lolita* (1962), and discovered at the bottom of a lake again, compliments of Robert Mitchum, in *The Night of the Hunter* (1955). It's about time I was shipped off to the crematorium."

"I couldn't agree with you more," Debbie said, turning her back to the star and walking off the set.

What's the Matter With Helen? bombed at the box office, crushing Debbie's career as a leading star. It was the last time she'd ever be offered another leading role in a major-league Hollywood movie.

Chapter Twelve

DEBBIE DUMPS THE CZAR OF RETAIL SHOES

(Harry Karl, Husband #2)

Before Storming The Stages & Bright Lights of Broadway

The Early, Dysfunctional Stages of Debbie's

Troubled Revival of the Vintage Musical *Irene*

Bachelorette Debbie and her Affair with the Star of

Wild in the Streets Christopher Jones

Carrie Lays Claim—True or False—

to Losing Her Virginity to Warren Beatty

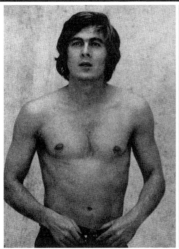

In an unofficial poll, Christopher Jones (left) and Warren Beatty were voted the two sexiest men in Hollywood. It was rumored that at least three-quarters of the poll came from votes cast by gay men.

"Chris had this 'little boy lost' appeal," Debbie said. "He set out to conquer me, but I really was after him. I was an easy conquest for him."

According to Jones, "When I met Debbie, I was going around with a lump in my pants. I could be had by both men such as Tennessee Williams and by women. I ejaculated for the first time when I was ten years old, and have been going at it ever since."

"Sex is Warren's hobby," said his sister, Shirley MacLaine. His former lover Joan Collins said. "Three, four, five times a day every day was not unusual for Warren, and he was able to accept phone calls at the same time."

Debbie defined it as "the last straw" in her disastrous marriage to Harry Karl.

One afternoon, he came to her with a document from the bank that he wanted her to sign. "What is this?" she asked. "You want me to sign my life away, or at least what's left of it?"

"We're short of money and have bills to pay," he said. "I want you to sign this extension on the mortgage on our house in Malibu."

"What's this 'our house' crap?" she demanded. "I'm the sole owner of that house. I paid every dime of it with money I earned from *The Unsinkable Molly Brown.* It's in my name—not yours."

"But you signed a document some time ago, allowing me to take out a mortgage on the property," he said. "We've paid off a lot of it. This document will give us ready cash to extend the mortgage."

"Put it on the coffee table," she commanded. "I'll read it later."

"You've never done this before," he said.

She didn't answer but looked on skeptically as he placed the document on the table. She noticed that he already had a drink in hand, as he usually did. "Get me a vodka and Seven-Up. On a day like this, I need a stiff one. Let's celebrate our going broke together."

When he returned with her drink, she rose from the sofa, looked down at the mortgage document for a final time, and said, "I'm not going to sign this fucking paper, or any other document you present to me. I've given everything I have to you. There's no more. Got that, Harry?"

Then she walked out of the living room and into her garden, which looked overgrown since she'd had to dismiss her caretaker. As she gazed up at the sky, a sudden noise sent a flock of birds flying from her tree, where they had nested.

As she later told Agnes Moorehead, "At that moment, I wanted to fly away with them. Like the bluebirds Judy Garland sang about. I didn't know where, perhaps somewhere over the rainbow."

***

Before she divorced Harry Karl, Debbie launched a number of affairs with a series of men. "I was looking for love in all the wrong places, as so many of us do. I wasn't sex-crazed, but at times I just wanted to be held in a man's arms and hear words of love, even if my boyfriend of the moment would forget them when morning came."

"Some of the men I meet," as she told Rudy Render, "were also married and trapped in the same loveless marriage I was. In Hollywood, marriage is an endangered species. The most gorgeous young men and women are thrown together, often making love on camera, or at least simulating it. Things happen when you least expect it. Even when you're not specifically looking for a man, he might suddenly walk through the door."

That was exactly what happened when Render invited her to a jazz joint, a favorite of his, on Sunset Strip. "He was cruising that night for a man. I wasn't. However, plans can change."

After the filming of *What's the Matter with Helen?*, Debbie had vowed she'd never speak to her co-star, Shelley ("The Killer") Winters again. "But a girl's allowed to break a vow," Debbie said.

At around ten o'clock that night, Debbie looked over at the door, along with all the other eyes in the club. In a low-cut, fire-engine red dress, Winters was making a spectacular entrance, earning a few wolf whistles.

Yet Debbie hardly noticed her, her eyes feasting instead on what she told Render was "the sexiest, handsomest boy I've seen since R.J. (Robert Wagner)."

"Who is he?" she asked Render.

"That's Christopher Jones, the boy movie star, the next James Dean. Don't you ever go to the movies?"

Spotting Debbie, Winters headed for her table followed by Jones. Without an invitation, she plopped down in a chair opposite her, inviting Jones to take the seat beside her.

When Christopher Jones met Debbie, he whispered in her ear, "Want to have some fun? I'm God's gift."

"Debbie, darling," Winters said. "I've missed you so. I've been meaning to call. It was fabulous working with you. Let's make another picture. Oh, by the way, this is Christopher Jones."

"Hiya, beautiful," he said.

After ordering drinks, Winters launched into a monologue about how she'd met Jones. "He was one of the beach boys on stage in Tennessee's *The Night of the Iguana*. I took over the role after Bette Davis bolted. As you can see, Chris is blonde, and the Mexican he played was supposed to have black hair, but Tennessee insisted Chris keep the role. We won't go there. We formed a friendship, although he's the most mischievous devil who ever entered my life—and a druggie, too."

"Friendship, hell!" he said. "The first night I met her, she wanted me to fuck her."

Debbie and Render fell silent.

"If you haven't already, you must see *Wild in the Streets* (1968), the picture in which I co-starred with Chris," Winters continued. "It's already on its way to becoming a cult classic, aimed at Baby Boomers working through their rebellion issues."

"I missed that one," Debbie said.

"Chris wears pants so tight you can see that he's uncut." Winters said.

"I believe that if you've got it, flaunt it," Jones said.

"My kind of man," Render added.

Jones turned to Debbie. "You are my favorite movie star."

"What am I, then?" Winters snapped. "Chopped liver?"

Jones turned to Winters again. "You're more than a film star. You are a goddess. Occupying a throne of your own, doll."

"I've seen all your movies," he said, turning once again to Debbie, "and loved every one of them. Of course, I have my favorites."

She'd heard that line before. She asked, perhaps with the intention of trapping him, "Which are your favorites?" She fully expected him to give the familiar response: *Singin' in the Rain, Tammy and the Bachelor,* and *The Unsinkable Molly Brown.*

But his answer surprised her: "*The Rat Race,* which is the story of my life, and *The Catered Affair.*"

Then Winters interjected once again with, "I introduced Chris to his wife, Susan Strasberg, even though her father, Lee, opposed the marriage."

"Susan and I are now divorced, but we had a daughter, named Jennifer, after Jennifer Jones."

Debbie looked skeptical but then said, flirtatiously, "You should have named her Debbie after your favorite actress."

"I wanted to, but Susan was hot for Jennifer."

After downing two vodkas, Winters excused herself to go to the women's room.

Jones quickly moved to occupy the chair she'd vacated, facing Debbie. "I'm on the Coast for two weeks, and I'd love to spend them with you."

"Doing what?" she asked, provocatively.

"Talking about love, marriage, the movies vs. the theater, why affairs go wrong, why stardom is overrated, why men can't be honorable and true to their women. How, if you really love someone, you can grow with her and make it last a lifetime, even as you face the final curtain together."

"My God, that will take days and days to cover all those subjects," she said. "I'm leaving for Palm Springs in the morning, and I think you should come with me. Write down your phone number and address, and I'll pick you up at six in the morning. You can drive."

"Hey, kids," Render interjected as a warning. "Grandma Winters is coming back."

"She's to know nothing of this," Debbie warned.

"My succulent lips are sealed," Jones said. "God, I could grab you and kiss you right now. I mean, really, really kiss you the way a girl should be kissed."

***

For ten days in Palm Springs, Debbie got to know Chris Jones intimately, finding him not only devastatingly handsome, but a tender, virile, and profoundly satisfying lover, too. "He makes Eddie Fisher look like a little boy, and Harry Karl evoke Pa Kettle."

She wanted to know anything and everything about where he'd come from and what he did. Blossoming under her attention, he talked candidly about his life.

Born in 1941 in Jackson, Tennessee, he had survived a rough boyhood. One afternoon, his mother (an artist) caught his father (a grocery clerk) in bed with another woman, who fled through an open window. Retrieving a firearm from the hallway, she threatened to kill him. In retaliation, he had his wife committed to a mental asylum in Bolivar, Tennessee. Jones was sent to Boys Town in Memphis.

"The accommodations in that virtual prison were better than the shack I grew up in with its coal-burning stove and the 'shithouse' out back."

Debbie shared her own memories of her poverty-stricken days as a child in El Paso.

At the age of sixteen, with the intention of escaping from Boys Town, he signed up to join the U.S. Army, receiving permission from his estranged father.

"Every time I went to take a god damn shower, there was a stampede of gay guys following me. I developed quite a following in the Army. One of the guys told me I should become a movie star. I said, 'Why not?'"

While assigned to an Army Barracks on Governor's Island in New York Harbor, he longed to explore Manhattan. But the military police caught him trying to escape, and he was imprisoned for going AWOL.

"The bastards threw me in jail. There, from a jail cell on Governor's Island, I got to see Manhattan through bars."

After his release from the Army, he explored Manhattan in depth, dreaming of becoming a Broadway actor. "Money was in short supply," he said, admitting that—in part because of the appeal of his dynamite body encased in skin-tight jeans—he'd become a hustler.

Eventually, an agent who had picked him up introduced him to Tennessee Williams. That led to his debut in December of 1961 in a small role in the Broadway production of *The Night of the Iguana* and his introduction to Shelley Winters (who had replaced Bette Davis) and eventually to Lee Strasberg of the Actors Studio and his daughter, Susan.

In time, he made it to Hollywood, where he won the title role in the ABC TV series, *The Legend of Jesse James*. That ran for 34 episodes during the 1965-66 season. That was followed with the feature film, *Chubasco*, filmed with Susan in 1968. *["Our marriage didn't survive that film," he told Debbie.]* Also in 1968, a year noted for its waves of anti-government protests, he'd played presidential aspirant Max Frost in *Wild in the Streets* with Winters.

Soon after that he was featured alongside Yvette Mimieux as the leading man in *Three in the Attic* (1968), a titillating sex comedy permeated with the free love context of the Swinging Sixties. He then made two films in Europe before director David Lean cast him in *Ryan's Daughter* (1970) with Robert Mitchum and Sarah Miles.

During the course of Christopher's sojourn with Debbie in Palm Springs, Rudy Render arrived for a weekend visit. When he got there, he learned that whereas Debbie was resting inside, Jones was lying nude beside her swimming pool.

"He knew I was gay, but he didn't rush to put a beach towel around his midriff like a lot of straight guys do. I got to enjoy him and the sight of that 'baby's arm' nestled between his legs."

Later, when Jones retired to his bedroom, Debbie joined Render beside the pool. "The time had come for the two of us to talk dirty about Chris," Render said.

She told him that her new discovery was the sexiest man she'd ever slept with. "In bed, he oozes masculinity from every pore. He looks great in those tight blue jeans with a shirt unbuttoned to the waist, but he looks even better without them."

"I can vouch for that," he said.

"Hands off, boy," she said, jokingly. "He likes to lie in the sun because he says it bleaches streaks of gold in his brownish hair. In bed, his deep brown eyes look into mine like a lovesick puppy. His face, with those high cheekbones, was surely created by a sculptor, and that mouth has the most kissable lips on the planet."

"You sure got it bad, gal," he said.

"Last night, he said he wanted to marry me," she confessed.

"Did you say YES YES to this Greek god descended from Mount Olympus?"

"Not yet," she answered. "I know he has a roving eye and isn't ready to settle down and be the father to my ready-made family. I told him what Esther Williams said to Fernando Lamas when he proposed to her. She told him, 'You've still got a lot of fucking to do. When you're ready to settle down, come back to me.'"

Back in the Los Angeles area, Render and Debbie were invited to the home of Minnie and Ray, her parents. Render had once lived in the cottage behind her family's house. Although Ray was friendly with him, engaging mostly in dialogues about sports, Render couldn't help but notice that he never even spoke to his wife, even though she took great pains to produce tasty meals for them.

After Debbie's parents had retired early to separate bedrooms, Debbie sat in the living room talking about the future of her career. "That is, if my career even *has* a future."

Then, Rudy asked about the stony silences that frequently prevailed between Ray and Minnie.

"In many ways, I'm repeating some of the patterns of my mother, Minnie," Debbie confessed. "She used to sit in the backyard and cry because Ray paid her no attention. He'd go for weeks without speaking to her. It probably set the pattern of my own marriage to Harry. Unlike Minnie, I was determined to look for love outside the house, since I sure wasn't getting any at home. Otherwise, I was the dutiful, perfect wife in an imperfect marriage."

***

[*Karl didn't show up at their home to celebrate the New Year of 1971, claiming he had urgent business in New York.*

While he was gone, 14-year-old Carrie presented Debbie with her rough notes for an essay she was writing on Debbie and her marriage. Since their visit to Spain, she'd been made emphatically aware of Karl's many affairs and how he'd drained Debbie of her life savings.

Convinced that her teenaged daughter would one day become a published author, Debbie read the first draft of Carrie's essay, finding her insights remarkable:

"You've got a lot of life in you, Miss Debbie Reynolds, and you're wasting it on a man who doesn't give a shit about you. We were the ideal family until he ruined everything with his lies and endless deceits. His gambling debts ate up the family's millions, which no doubt will bring an end to our comfortably secure life."

"Your giving and giving to him is not an act of love on your part, since you're not doing it for love but out of guilt. He spends your hard-earned money on his whores, his manicurists, his daily barber visits, his hopeless addiction to gambling. Giving to Harry makes as much sense as banging your head against a wall. You are miserable. Harry is miserable, and I am miserable. There is only one way out: DIVORCE. DIVORCE. DIVORCE."

Although Carrie would eventually tweak and polish these notes into a more formal essay, she'd already made her point to Debbie.]

***

As Debbie continued her dialogue with Render that night, she felt she'd done enough for Karl, and that she had not been rewarded. Instead of loving her for her sacrifices, he had stopped loving her at all. The time had come for her to tend to her own needs, and those needs were being satisfied by Christopher Jones, who revived memories of her brief involvement with James Dean.

When Jones roared into her driveway on his Norton 650 motorcycle, the same that Dean had ridden, Debbie was eager to accept his invitation to go on a ride with him through the Hollywood Hills.

Karl was still out of town, and Minnie was looking after her kids in Burbank. When she saw Jones' bright, shining, handsome face, she feared she was falling in love. She resisted, knowing that in time it would lead to heartbreak.

As she told Render, "Chris, like Dean, has that defiant walk with the pelvis thrust forward. He's a bundle of uncontrolled energy, so vibrant, so eager for his next adventure. And, yes, he's high most of the time."

"He took me on a hair-raising ride of a lifetime before we came to a secluded spot ideal for a picnic," she said. "He'd gone to a deli and brought along the makings of our lunch. In a quiet, secluded spot, we could talk, and he did just that, opening up about himself."

Their evening meal for that day was consumed in the dimly lit restaurant of a local motel. He told her that a writer from *Variety* had predicted that he would "take Hollywood by storm and become the next *Rebel Without a Cause.*"

"But that's not going to happen," he told her. "Not at all."

Author Randall Riese wrote: "Christopher Jones comes closer to resembling James Dean than all the other imitators. He wears the Rebel band energetically on or off the screen. He updated Dean's role by wearing his hair longer and donning bell bottoms. But something doesn't click. Jones made it to the threshold, but not to the throne that Dean vacated."

As Debbie later told Render, "That night, after he made wonderful love to me, he cuddled in my arms."

"I don't think I can go on," he confessed to her. "Whatever it takes to become a movie star like you, I don't have. I think you have to have a fire in your belly to become a movie star. I'm sure Marilyn Monroe would have agreed with that. I think *you* have it. But I fear my fire burns on a very low flame."

"My marriage to Susan failed almost from the beginning," he said. "My so-called father-in-law was partly to blame. He once called me 'a prick, the most detestable punk' he'd ever met."

"The same was said about Jimmy," she said, "and that guy's heading for immortality."

"The comparisons of me to Jimmy Dean have come to an end," he said. "I'm not going to be him, or anything like him. To begin with, I don't have a death wish. I want to live. I don't want to be James Dean anymore. I want to be Christopher Jones."

"And who is *he*?" Debbie asked.

"It may come as a surprise to you," he said, "but I plan to abandon acting altogether. I'm thinking I want to be a painter, perhaps a sculptor. I don't want people looking at my image on the screen and judging me."

"I've already judged you, and I find you a special young man who can be whatever he wants to be. If you change your mind and decide to continue appearing on the screen, I think you'll end as a far greater legend than Dean. You could dwarf his image with a distinguished body of films. If you want to be an artist, that can happen to you. You've got whatever it takes, Chris. And whatever it is you've got, I want."

***

With bills mounting and with her bank account almost empty, Debbie was in despair. She wondered how she could support her family. She hadn't received any money from Karl in years.

As a last resort, she went to the safe in Karl's den to remove her stash of diamonds and emeralds. She planned to hock at least some of them to help pay household expenses and the maintenance of her children.

To her shock and horror, she discovered that every piece of her jewelry was gone, even her diamond cross, and whatever gems Eddie Fisher had given her. She had never had all of her jewelry appraised, but she knew that it amounted to hundreds of thousands of dollars.

She went into a deep depression and began to drink heavily.

Then, during the depths of her despair, she received a call from an executive from Howard Hughes' Summa Corporation, the entity that owned the Desert Inn in Las Vegas. He set up an appointment to meet with her and her attorney or agent (or both) in Hollywood for the following Monday. She spent two or three hours getting ready, wanting to appear both businesslike and seductive.

The executive from the Summa Corporation was a young man in his thirties who booked talent for the Desert Inn. She was surprised, actually shocked, by his offer. The casino wanted to sign her to a two-year contract for her live shows, with an annual guarantee of $500,000. Her hand was shaking as she signed the contract.

That week, when the publicist for the inn announced the deal, The Las Vegas papers labeled her "The Million Dollar Baby." Beginning on March 11, 1972, she would appear for nightly appearances at the Inn over the span of a month.

Rudy Render tracked down and assembled the various members of her company for rehearsals; handled the musical arrangements; and hired an orchestra with a conductor, two dancers, and nine singers.

A wardrobe woman was also needed. Rudy didn't hire Maxine, Debbie's mother, this time, because Debbie needed her in Los Angeles to look after her family. It was determined, however, that "Pinky," her faithful hairdresser, would be part of her entourage.

Jones was high on the list of friends Debbie invited to her show's opening. He was in New York at the time. In theory, at least, he was auditioning for stage work, but she wasn't sure. He never explained what he did for money. He was, however, spotted at the Waldorf Astoria with her longtime friend, Rock Hudson, whom she hadn't seen in months. "Do you think Chris has become Rock's kept boy?" she asked Render.

"Stranger things have happened in Hollywood," he said. "I wish I was Rock's kept boy. What a stud!"

Her friends from Hollywood included one guest she didn't want: her errant husband.

When Karl checked into the Desert Inn and asked to be shown to her suite, he was told that a single room had been booked for him. When he was shown to it, he was very disappointed. It was small and dreary, overlooking a parking lot, a room usually reserved for servants or chauffeurs.

Later, he stormed into her dressing room as she was applying her makeup for her opening number. He angrily accused her of humiliating him. "Do you want the whole god damn world to know I don't sleep with my wife?"

"I'm your wife in name only, as you damn well know. That's been the case for months on end, and that's the way it's going to be. Now get out while I get ready to go on. You don't have to pay for your liquor and the room. They're on me. But tonight, you sit at a table in the rear, not at ringside. Those tables are reserved for my friends."

"I know you like to gamble," she continued, "but don't get the bright idea that you can go to the cashier and draw an advance against my salary. I've blocked that."

"You're acting like a bitch. Don't you trust me, your own husband?"

"You're no husband, you two-timing shit. Speaking of bitches, if you still have any ready cash on you, you'll find the lobby overpopulated with whores. Vegas is crawling with them. Take your pick. For a hundred, they'll even go to bed with a decrepit, decaying, gray-haired relic like you. Tell them you're Mr. Debbie Reynolds. That will surely impress them."

Without saying a word, he turned and walked out.

After he'd gone, there was a knock on her door as a stagehand opened it and said, "Miss Reynolds, you're due on stage in ten minutes."

"I'll wow them!" she said. "Tonight, *Tammy* becomes *The Unsinkable Molly Brown*."

A few days later, at the Desert Inn in Las Vegas, Debbie performed her show "but my heart wasn't really in it." After her closing number, she retired to her suite where she downed three vodkas with Seven-Up. Bored and depressed during the darkest hours of a dreary night, she needed someone to talk to, so she phoned Render's bedroom and asked him to come and sit with her for a while.

Sleepy-eyed, he knocked on her door, and she invited him in, giving him a drink. She shared a story with him that night about Christopher Jones and herself that never made the tabloids:

She told Render that one night, Jones had invited her to where he was living at the time: a guest cottage behind the house occupied by his manager, Rudy Altobelli. The address became notorious: 10050 Cielo Drive in Benedict Canyon, the setting for one of the most gruesome murders in the history of Hollywood. The director, Roman Polanski, had lived there with his wife, actress/model Sharon Tate.

She had read endless stories about the address and it came as a total surprise that Jones was staying there.

Polanski and Tate had met when she was cast in his *The Fearless Vampire Killers* (1967). They married a year later. Debbie had met Tate at a Hollywood party. If she remembered correctly, Pat Boone, her former co-star, had introduced them. *[They were fellow Texans: Tate had been born in Dallas.]*

She had already seen Tate on the screen in *Valley of the Dolls* (1967) based on Jacqueline Susann's bestseller. Near the end of 1968, Tate had become pregnant.

Jones confessed to Debbie that he suspected that he was the father because he had had unprotected sex with the emerging starlet, even though she was married at the time to Polanski. "I continued to have sex with Sharon during her pregnancy. Call me weird, but some guys get off on having sex with pregnant women. Jayne Mansfield told me she had sex with John F. Kennedy while she was pregnant."

He also told Debbie that "Sharon always had this premonition of her early death. Sometimes, or so I've heard, people seem to know of their impending doom."

In 1969, starlet Sharon Tate, her unborn baby, and several of her friends were stabbed to death by members of the Charles Manson gang at 10050 Cielo Drive in Benedict Canyon.

A few years later, before the notorious house was demolished and rebuilt with a different street numeration. Christopher Jones and Debbie Reynolds used it as a love nest.

On August 6, 1969, while Polanski was in London, Tate had dined with her best friend, Jay Sebring, the leading hairdresser in Hollywood. He had once proposed marriage to her. Other guests included her friends Wojciech Frykowski and Abigail Folger. After their meal, she invited them to return to her home to keep the party going.

Shortly after midnight, members of the psychotic Charles Manson family broke into the house and stabbed them to death. Postmortem, her doctors had estimated that Sharon was only two weeks from giving birth. Manson's "family" members, aiming directly for her stomach, stabbed her sixteen times.

Jones explained to Debbie that the cottage he occupied had at the time been the residence of the property's caretaker, William Garretson. For a brief moment he, at first, had been suspected of committing the murders.

She remembered the murders all too vividly, as they'd an impact on her own life. In the wake of the slayings, many Hollywood stars rushed to hire security guards. There was such a demand for them that many flew to Los Angeles from as far away as Miami. Fearing for the safety of her family, Debbie, too, hired security guards.

"The property was eerie and spooky," she told Render. I told Chris I thought the place should be torn down and rebuilt."

[That is exactly what happened in 1994 when the house and its cottage were demolished and built anew. Since the address had become so widely and gruesomely publicized, and for years attracted curiosity seekers, its street numeration was changed from 10050 Cielo Drive to 10066 Cielo Drive.]

"I spent the weekend there with Chris and, as always, I adored his lovemaking. Yet I was afraid to be living near the scene of those gruesome murders. I urged him to move out as soon as he could make other arrangements, and he took my advice."

"I'll say this: If Sharon's son or daughter had been born, I bet it would have been the most beautiful boy or girl in Hollywood. Both Sharon and Chris were the most gorgeous things walking."

"For months after spending time there, I was haunted by memories of the Manson murders," she continued. "I'd wake up at night imagining I'd heard some intruder breaking in. I was always worried about the safety of my children."

"Every Hollywood star has to think of the safety of their offspring. Instead of murder, the major fear is kidnapping. Frank Sinatra had plenty to say about that when Frank Junior was kidnapped and held for ransom. Such fears of a parent are one of the prices you pay for stardom."

***

Debbie had first met Warren Beatty in 1960, when she was in the MGM beauty parlor, getting her hair done, under a dryer, reading a book.

He lifted the lid. "Hi! I'm Warren Beatty, the new kid on the block. I've been longing to meet THE Debbie Reynolds."

"Now you've had the honor," she said, "you picked an odd occasion, catching me without makeup and with my hair in curlers."

"Your natural beauty shines through," he said. "My sister told me you're sweet and almost virginal. I can alter that state."

She knew he was referring to Shirley MacLaine, whom Debbie viewed as a friend, but not a very close friend. "We were so different," she said. "Shirley once told me that she had only one vice: Fucking! Her brother seemed just as forward as his older sister."

"How about a dinner date tonight?" he asked.

"He'd practically just arrived in Hollywood, and already, I'd heard he'd broken a string of hearts. I didn't want to become another notch on his belt."

To answer his invitation, she told him the biggest lie of her career. "You're not my type."

He looked dejected. "You're missing out on something special." Then he walked out of the salon.

"Anyway, he got along very well without me," she said. "His string of conquests became legendary."

She was referring to an array of stars who included Cher, Jane Fonda, Barbra Streisand, and, almost inevitably, in time, Elizabeth Taylor, who told Rock Hudson, "He's much better in bed than Eddie Fisher ever was."

"Years later, I heard that Warren seduced both Jackie Onassis and her sister, Lee Radziwell." Debbie said. "He didn't stop there. Throw in Christina Onassis, too."

"Then imagine my surprise," Debbie revealed, "when Carrie showed up one day with a script and told me that Warren wanted to cast her in his next picture. She was seventeen at the time and had always told me that the last thing on earth she wanted to be was an actress."

The script was for *Shampoo,* a satirical comedy-drama about sexual and social mores in the late 1960s. Written by Beatty and Robert Towne, the film was directed by Hal Ashby, and its release, by Columbia, scheduled for 1975. Ashby had already selected Julie Christie, Goldie Hawn, and Lee Grant as the female leads, as well

"Warren was real sexy and beautiful," Debbie later told Render. "He was definitely my type, in the same category of Christopher Jones. I must have been a fool turning him down."

"In time, Beatty earned a reputation as the sexiest man in Hollywood. No girl in her right mind would reject a stud like that. I've always regretted not going out to dinner with him, or whatever. Surely I must have been the only female star in Hollywood who didn't know what it was like to get fucked by Beatty."

as most of its other female players. It was clearly understood that Beatty would portray the male lead, the character of George Roundy, a desirable Hollywood hairdresser, who some husbands interpreted as gay, even though he's secretly seducing their wives.

Debbie read the script, taking it for a porno film. In the opening, Christie is having an orgasm that's interrupted by a phone dialogue with Beatty. As they continue their conversation, she crawls under a table muttering, "I want to suck your cock...oh, God, I must suck it."

"I can't imagine a scene like that making the final cut," Debbie told Carrie. After she continued reading, she said, "Warren's character sounds like he's a modern-day Don Juan."

Carrie described the role she'd been offered as that of "the pissed-off daughter of Lee Grant." Her character of the

The hippest teenager in Hollywood played the hippest teenager in Hollywood.

The photo above shows Carrie Fisher as a *strumpette* in *Shampoo*.

spoiled daughter of dysfunctional, mega-wealthy Hollywood mogul is precocious, angry, and promiscuous, and choreographs sex with her mother's hairdresser-lover, as played by Beatty. After a few moments of conversation, Carrie says to him, "Wanna fuck?"

Debbie objected so strongly to that that Beatty came over to her house that night. It had been years since she had last seen him, but he charmed her, even sitting at the piano with her, singing and joking.

She politely suggested that the word "fuck" be changed to "screw." He finally persuaded her, however, that the impact and the artistic value of the scene would be diluted. He cited the closing line of Clark Gable playing Rhett Butler in *Gone With the Wind*.

"If he told Scarlett, 'Frankly, my dear, I don't give a 'darn' instead of 'damn,' the whole dramatic impact would be like weak tea."

Before leaving, Beatty promised Debbie, "I won't take her virginity. You have my word on that. During her brief shoot, I'll come by and pick her up in the morning and drive her home faithfully every night."

Carrie didn't understand why Debbie had raised any objection to the word "fuck. As you, of all people know, I say fuck at least eighty-nine times a day, never ninety."

When Carrie spoke privately with Beatty, she immediately told him, "I'm not like my squeaky-clean mother, or at least the way she's depicted in the fan magazines. I use every four-letter word I know, but I'm still a virgin waiting for a knight in shining armor to ride up on a white horse, hellbent on deflowering me. I'm the most foul-mouthed virgin you're likely ever to meet."

"Warren liked hearing that and immediately offered to alleviate my virginity. I probably should have taken him up on that offer."

Years later, whether it was true or not, Carrie confessed to Debbie that "Warren took my virginity. I think it's known as making a woman out of me. He was Adam and I was Eve. We tasted the forbidden apple. But it wasn't in the Garden of Eden. It was in his dressing room."

"I don't know if Warren took her cherry or not," Debbie told Render. "He says he didn't and she says he did. Perhaps she confessed just to make me mad. Over the years, she's told me she went to bed with a lot of stars. I know she went to bed with some. I really can't believe half of what she says. She makes up a lot…But then, she's a novelist, so I should overlook it. Sometimes, a mother is the last to know."

After Eddie Fisher went to see *Shampoo* in New York and witnessed Carrie's performance, he said, "I turned beet red hearing my daughter say 'fuck' on the screen. Movies have sure come a long way since Debbie and I made *Bundle of Joy.*"

Shampoo was a big success and helped elevate Carrie to the status of a movie actress. Incidentally, she casually met the composer who crafted the music for *Shampoo*. His name was Paul Simon, and he would eventually marry her.

***

Debbie continued to receive bad financial news. She thought the time had come for her errant husband to sell his chain of retail shoe stores. She was at home the day a bid came in from Abraham Marks of Hartfield-Zodys, a department store chain. His corporation was willing to purchase Karl's Shoes for $5 million. As a contingency to their proposal, the buyers wanted Debbie to appear in TV commercials for free. She refused.

Later, during meetings with her lawyers, she learned horrible news: Not only had Karl squandered his millions and hers, but he had put up his stores as collateral, and owed every penny of the $5 million, plus $3.5 million more, to the State Street Bank of Boston.

At first, Karl tried to get Zodys to assume the debt as part of its purchase price, but they refused. Before the sale could go through, he'd have to settle the debt.

"It wasn't his money any more, and it certainly wasn't mine," she said. "I had to get out there on the front lines, not only as the breadwinner, but as a woman who owes millions of dollars in debt because I had signed those papers, making me his equity. It was now my debt as much as his. Maybe Susan

Hayward was right. She once told me all men should be deep-fried in hot oil. At that point I wanted to kill Harry. Perhaps stab him in the back one night like Shelley Winters had stabbed me in *What's the Matter With Helen?* Now, the question was, 'What's the Matter With Harry?' He was probably mentally ill when it came to gambling. The only thing Eddie Fisher left me was some jewelry, and Harry had sold it. What to do?"

***

Debbie had another daughter, Tina Karl, to worry about too. Compared to Carrie, Tina was completely out of control, a true child of Beverly Hills, a city known for its pampered brats.

Tina had been jealous when Carrie was cast opposite Warren Beatty in *Shampoo*. "It's always Carrie, Carrie," she said to Debbie. "Never Tina, Tina. The world seems to rise and set in Carrie's ass."

One day when she was sixteen, Tina decided that her entire wardrobe was too much that of a schoolgirl. She got into the secondhand Porsche Debbie had recently purchased for her and drove to Theodore, on Rodeo Drive. It was one of the most expensive and elegant stores for young women in Beverly Hills and was frequented by daughters of movie stars. Karl had given Tina a credit card, and she spent most of the day there, ordering a vast wardrobe with dozens of accessories.

The problem arose when the bill was sent to Karl, who could not pay it. As was his habit, he turned it over to Debbie.

She was finding it increasingly impossible to live under the same roof as Tina. Fortunately, she was away at a private school most of the time.

When she wasn't at school, she was often running wild with a group of teenaged Hollywood kids. "The sexual revolution was fully launched, and that meant sex and drugs," Debbie said. "I constantly warned her, but she wouldn't listen. Harry was of no help. He couldn't discipline himself, much less a young girl."

"Tina had been born an addict to a drugged-out mother. Even as a teenager, she was on the road to being a drug addict. So far, I didn't have to face this problem with Carrie...not yet!"

"Some of the parties Tina attended didn't get started until after midnight," Debbie said. "I absolutely refused to let her go, but she slipped out of the house anyway."

She tricked Debbie one time by telling her that she'd be spending the night with a girlfriend. Debbie asked her to leave a phone number at which she could be reached, but she rushed out the door without doing that.

By the following afternoon, she still hadn't returned home. Debbie was frantic. At around 8PM, the doorbell rang. A man who evoked Wally Cox was ushered into her living room, carrying a passed-out Tina in his arms.

"Here's your daughter," he announced, lowering her down onto the sofa. "She passed out."

Debbie checked her pulse, affirming that she was still alive, but just barely.

Before she could question him, the stranger was moving hurriedly toward the door. As he departed, he called back to her, "Good night! You're still hot, Tammy!"

She immediately rushed to call a doctor. In the meantime, Tina was carried upstairs and tucked into bed. Before a doctor arrived, she bolted upright and vomited green bile. With the aid of a servant, Debbie cleaned her off and had the bed linens changed. No sooner had she finished than Tina vomited again.

By the time the doctor arrived, she was vomiting into the toilet bowl.

After examining her, the doctor informed Debbie that she had overdosed on drugs, asserting that it was no used pumping her stomach because the drugs had already been absorbed into her system. For the next three days, Tina could hold down nothing in her stomach and remained violently ill. Debbie was forced to sleep in her room, not that she got much rest.

It was later ascertained that Tina had attended a party in Beverly Hills at which older men met young starlets. "Every casting couch in the house must have been in use," Debbie said.

Unclear about what to do, Debbie took Tina to a psychiatrist. When they got there, Tina refused to talk to him.

The following week, as Debbie was leaving for New York, she turned to Karl. "You've got to take care of Tina. I can't anymore. She's your responsibility—not mine. Her life is a mess. Your life is a mess. You've made a mess of my life. You got us into this jam, so try to get us out of it." Opening the door, she looked back at him. "You're a god damn rotten son of a bitch. You fuck up everything you touch. I detest you! I'm starting all over again. I'm too young to die."

***

"One afternoon in my overly mortgaged home in Beverly Hills, I wondered where my next dollar was coming from," Debbie said. "Almost out of nowhere, I got this phone call that changed my life. It was from producer Harry Rigby, who had a voice somewhere between a flute and Phyllis Diller."

In 1971, Rigby had been the driving force behind the hit revival of *No, No, Nanette* that had brought both Ruby Keeler and Busby Berkeley out of retirement and launched the nostalgia craze on Broadway. Bolstered by this success, he had decided to launch a Broadway revival of a musical that had been a huge success with jazz-age audiences in 1919, *Irene*. He envisioned that it would star Debbie.

Irene had originally starred Edith Day, a long-forgotten stage celebrity of yesteryear, who helped it rack up an impressive 675 performances. Its plot had already been recycled for two feature movies, the first a silent in 1926 starring Colleen Moore; the second a 1940 release with Anna Neagle.

The script arrived at Debbie's house before 7PM, and she read through it at once. She was to play Irene O'Dare, a humble, hard-working, and ambitious Irish lass who runs a small music store in Manhattan alongside her widowed mother. She is sent to tune a piano for a young tycoon, Donald Marshall III (Monte Markham), a Long Island society gent. Irene, of course, is captivated by his good looks and charm.

She took the script and drove it over to the home of her friend and acting mentor, Lillian Burns Sidney. Together, they talked into the early morning hours, with Burns eventually advising her to "go for it. It's about time you made your Broadway debut."

Debbie was taken by surprise when Rigby phoned her and asked her if he could drop by with her new Broadway director. He didn't identify him, although she hoped it would be Gower Champion or someone of his stature, perhaps Gene Kelly, who by this time in his career had evolved into a director.

To her shock, however, Rigby arrived with Sir John Gielgud, who was in Hollywood at the time. "Debbie, meet your new director, Sir John."

"We've met," she said, embracing him. When George Cukor had originally cast her as the female lead in *The Actress* (1953) opposite Spencer Tracy, he had asked Gielgud to rehearse her in a scene which called for her to recite some lines from Shakespeare. He recommended her for the role. "She can do it," Sir John had said. *[Despite Gielgud's approval, the role was later re-assigned to Jean Simmons.]*

Rudy Render arrived and was introduced to Sir John and to Rigby. In front of the producer and director, Debbie performed six numbers with Render at the piano. Sir John said that he liked the numbers and agreed to direct the musical.

Although she personally liked Sir John, she privately wondered if he could direct a romantic Broadway musical. He was, after all, one of the three greatest actors on the English stage, along with Laurence Olivier and Ralph Richardson. She'd never seen it, but his interpretation of *Hamlet*, a role he was famous for having "perfected" as a young man in the 1930s, had long ago been defined as the stuff of theatrical legend.

"I didn't know how he'd do as my director. After all, none of the lines in *Irene* had been written by the Bard. But I put on my brave face. I told him, 'With the Dynamo Duo of Debbie Reynolds and Sir John Gielgud, we'll have them lining up for a mile around the box office.'"

Then she made a major decision to take Carrie out of the Beverly Hills High School, even though she was only fifteen. Rigby promised to give her a minor role in *Irene* as a debutante and singer. Since Todd got along so well with Karl, she decided to allow him to remain behind in the house with his stepfather and Tina until he finished his school year. She knew that if Karl didn't look after the kids, her housekeeper, Mary Douglas French, would.

In her first memoir, Debbie presented a sanitized account of her departure from Beverly Hills for New York. She has Karl lying in bed watching Katharine Hepburn and Humphrey Bogart in *The African Queen* (1951). She even alleged that she kissed him on the cheek.

"I was there, and that's not what happened," Render said. "She called him a son of a bitch and accused him of messing up her life, driving her into bankruptcy, messing up his own life, and the lives of his children."

"I'm leaving you in charge," Debbie shouted at him. "Can't you do one god damn thing right in your whole wasted life?" Then she stormed out the door.

She later told Render that she didn't want to describe in print what actually transpired. "I hoped to retain the sympathy of my public and didn't want to appear too much of a bitch."

***

It was a cold, wet, and windy day in October of 1972 when Debbie arrived in Manhattan for rehearsals of *Irene*. "It was one of the many low points in my life. Because of Harry Karl, I was flat broke with bills piling up every day. I needed a hit on Broadway."

"I didn't expect a grand reception when I walked into the creaky old Broadway Arts Studio to meet my supporting cast. I'd heard that Broadway actors resented Hollywood stars flying in to take roles from them."

The first person she met was Monte Markham, her leading man. He was three years younger than she was. She had hoped that Rigby would have hired a name actor with a solid Broadway reputation; otherwise, she felt that she'd have to configure herself as the project's sole star power, commissioned with the responsibility of drawing acolytes and fans from off the streets.

She was unfamiliar with Markham's work. He was known for playing the dual roles of Luke and Ken Carpenter in ABC's 1967-68 sitcom, *The Second Hundred Years*; and for interpreting the role of Harry Kellem in the original version (1968-1980) of *Hawaii Five-O*.

The Florida-born actor was polite and rather courteous during their introductions. "He didn't seem impressed by my repertoire, and I was completely unfamiliar with his work, which seemed rather limited to me. I wondered if he could sing and dance."

Debbie would head the cast as Irene O'Dare, a perky, down-on-her-luck Irish immigrant with the grit and determination Debbie displayed years before as *Tammy* and *Unsinkable Molly*.

In vivid contrast, Markham would portray a young tycoon, Donald Marshall III, who lives on a Long Island estate propelled by his domineering mother. Through one of Donald's connections, Irene, pretending to be a society girl, becomes a model at Madame Lucy's, assigned with the task of luring rich patrons into Lucy's elegant shop.

The next actor Debbie met was Billy De Wolfe, the man with the pencil mustache known for his ability to play pompous bureaucrats. *[De Wolfe became known for his portrayal of fussy, petty men. In reference to his performance in* Isn't It Romantic? *(1948) The New York Times said: "He rips up the place with great delight. The material is at his mercy. Likewise the scenery. And he chews it to bits."]*

De Wolfe was slated to play a flamboyant French couturier, a biological male ("Madam Lucy") who appeared during some of his scenes in drag.

Sadly, two weeks into rehearsal, De Wolfe received something akin to a death notice from his doctor. Medical tests showed that he was soon to die of lung cancer. He left the cast and was replaced with George S. Irving, who embraced the crossdressing role of Madame Lucy.

Patsy Kelly, a stage, radio, film, and TV actress, was cast as Debbie's mother, Mrs. O'Dare. She was known for playing brash, tactless eccentrics, and was hailed as "The Queen of the Wisecracks."

"Patsy was a hoot—screwball crazy, and drunk most of the time," Debbie said. "She had been the longtime lover and companion of Tallulah Bankhead, and now seemed somewhat lost after the death of her beloved."

"No one could be more different from my real mother than Patsy," Debbie said.

In 1971, Kelly had appeared on Broadway in *No, No, Nanette* with Ruby Keeler, playing a wise-cracking, tap-dancing maid. For her efforts, she'd won the "Best Supporting Actress in a Musical" Tony Award.

"She was openly gay, and often referred to herself as a dyke," Debbie said. "She even offered to introduce me to lesbian sex, an invitation I declined."

Debbie, as Irene, is not the only one who finds love at the end of the play. Mrs. O'Dare (Kelly) crashes a chic society party being hosted by Mrs. Marshall (Ruth Warrick), only to discover that Madame Lucy is really her old flame, Liam O'Dougherty. At long last love. The mother-daughter acts ends happily— in marked contrast to the real life mother-daughter act of Debbie and Carrie.

Warrick excelled in her role as a rich society lady, Emmeline Marshall, the mother of Donald Marshall III. Debbie had seen her in *Citizen Kane* (1941), the iconic film conceived and directed by Orson Welles. In it, she had played the lonely, embittered, and hard-drinking wife of the *über*-rich protagonist (Kane), a figure who'd been inspired by the press baron, William Randolph Hearst. Decades later, Warrick had become familiar to millions of TV soap opera fans during her stint as an imperious matriarch, Phoebe Tyler, in *All My Children*, a perennial staple which made its debut in 1970.

She told Debbie, "People criticize me for dressing like a 1940s movie star. Hell, I WAS a 1940s movie star." Debbie had seen her in *Daisy Kenyon* (1947), which had starred Joan Crawford and Henry Fonda.

For accommodations, Debbie rented a brownstone in Manhattan for the run of the show and set up housekeeping with Carrie and Todd when he finished his school term. Her female hairdresser, "Pinky," also moved in to help her run the house. Rudy Render was there most of the time too, since she viewed him as a member of her family.

Except for brief roles that would crop up in the future, Debbie knew that her movie career was virtually over. To replace it, she envisioned becoming a Broadway musical star. "A stage actress can have a longer career than a film actress. Most women after forty are washed up in Hollywood. But I thought that on the Broadway stage, I could vastly extend my career, perhaps becoming the next Mary Martin."

During rehearsals for *Irene,* Sir John was assigned to direct scenes from the book, and Peter Gennaro was charged with staging and choreographing the musical numbers. These included "Alice Blue Gown" and the more engaging "I'm Always Chasing Rainbows," both of which were sung by Debbie. Together, Debbie and Markham sang, "You Made Me Love You."

She worked smoothly with Louisiana-born Gennaro, who had choreographed her dancing in *The Unsinkable Molly Brown.*

"It soon became obvious to me that our book and our musical numbers were not a cohesive whole," Debbie told Render and Pinky. "It's as if Sir John and Peter are operating on different planets. Sir John really seems to be struggling with the pacing of *Irene.* Musical comedy is obviously not his *forte.*"

Rigby booked *Irene* into the Royal Alexandra Theatre in Toronto for a four-month run. Over this period, the cast and crew hoped to work out and fine-tune the problems that plagued their musical. When it ended, Debbie pronounced the Canadian portion of their tour a disaster.

"The musical seemed to sink into an open grave," she said. "Nothing seemed to work, a new opening number, a fresher finale, one song added, another yanked. I, along with the rest of the cast, was on the verge of collapse from sheer exhaustion."

On top of it all, Debbie came down with a dangerously severe sore throat. She and Sir John asked the theater owner to cancel the show, but he refused, since he didn't want to be forced to refund ticket holders. "Haven't you heard? The show must go on!" he said to Debbie.

A compromise was reached: Whereas Debbie would appear, silently, in costume and onstage, for the dance numbers, Sir John, also onstage, would read aloud both her lines and the lyrics to her songs. During the presentation of this "arrangement," many in the audience booed, and some of them walked out before the final curtain.

The Toronto press was cruel the next day, many critics predicting that *Irene* would never make it to Broadway.

Then, as part of an unprecedented and spontaneous decision, Debbie, during an evening performance, signaled for the orchestra to stop playing in the middle of Markham's number, "You Made Me Love You." Then she signaled for the orchestra to start the number again, from the beginning.

"He was eight bars late on this familiar pop standard."

After the show, he barged into her dressing room. "How dare you stop the play! Are you crazy? You embarrassed the hell out of me. As for you, I don't think you can act your way out of a paper bag."

"Dear, you were singing in the wrong key," she said in her soft voice.

Markham continued to rant, even though she had asked him to leave. She reminded him that her contract allowed her to terminate his status as the play's leading man and replace him. After hearing that, he left immediately. The next performance, he sang on time in the right key.

*****

"At times we didn't know if Patsy Kelly would be able to go on or not," Render said. "After the curtain, she would drink until she passed out. Debbie ordered me to get her a wheelchair.

"We had rooms on the same floor of the same hotel. Often, Pinky and I had to wheel Patsy to her room, undress her, and put her to bed. She did little to boost the morale of the cast, telling all the actors that *Irene* would never make it to Broadway, and echoing most of the Toronto critics."

"One night, an almost unbelievable scene took place on our floor," Render said. "A spectacular horror. Pinky and I were sitting with Debbie in her suite, drinking, when we heard this awful scream coming from the hall. It was Patsy. We rushed out to see what was the matter. Patsy was lying nude in front of the elevator. Well, not completely nude. Her vagina was covered with dill pickles and crackers dressed with anchovy paste. Her breasts had a 'brassiere' of salmon sandwiches and stuffed olives."

"I've been raped!" Kelly shouted. "Raped! Call the police!"

"We didn't call the police," Render continued, "but carried her back to her room and put her to bed after we washed the food off her. The next day, we learned what had happened."

"Jaybird naked, Patsy had walked out of her bedroom, moved through the hall, and pressed the elevator button. For reasons known only to her, she was heading for the lobby in her condition. When the elevator opened onto our floor, a waiter carrying a tray of *hors d'oeuvres* for a party still going on at 4AM encountered her and fainted. As he fell, he dropped the tray and covered her with the *hors d'oeuvres*. That's when she started to scream rape, and the waiter fled. Just another day in the ongoing saga of Patsy Kelly."

Cast and crew, "in disgrace" after their shortcomings in Toronto, migrated to Philadelphia to continue their pre-Broadway tour of *Irene*. By this time, even Sir John knew that the production was in trouble, yet he didn't know how to fix it. To Debbie's embarrassment, some almost-forgotten members of Eddie Fisher's Philadelphia-based family turned out to see the show and have a reunion with Carrie, who didn't seem all that glad to welcome them.

In the midst of it all, Todd phoned from Beverly Hills. "There's no food in the house. Harry's gone all the time, and there's nothing for us. No money."

The arrangement had been that Harry was to provide the housekeeper with money for groceries. At this task, he had abjectly failed.

Debbie immediately wired the housekeeper $600 for emergency supplies. She complained to Render, telling him, "My weight is now under a hundred pounds. As you know, it's one sleepless night after another. I'm a nervous wreck."

Carrie told her, "You're the only mother I know who can continue to work while having a nervous breakdown."

In desperation, Debbie called Gower Champion in Malibu, where he was enjoying a beach holiday between jobs. She explained in detail what was going on and how desperately *Irene* needed him to rescue it. He said that in the morning, he would fly to Philadelphia.

She greeted him warmly at the airport, and was surprised when he gave her a long, lingering kiss at the gate. He agreed to slip into the theater without alerting Sir John in advance, and to sit through two evenings' performances, and then to slip out before the lights went on.

On the morning of his third day, he had a long meeting with Debbie and Rigby in her suite, telling them in detail what he thought was wrong with the show and how he could fix it.

Both Debbie and the producer listened in fascination and agreed with him.

"You're our new director," Rigby told him. "As of this afternoon."

Debbie knew he'd have to fire Sir John. She dreaded that upcoming moment of confrontation.

Fifteen minutes before the curtain went up on *Irene* in Philadelphia that night, there was a soft knock on the door to her dressing room. From a position at her makeup table, she rose to open it, grabbing a robe to cover her body.

It was Sir John, and he was in tears. "Rigby has fired me," he said, walking in. "On some days I put in eighteen hours trying to save this show. I did everything in my power...and now this. It's so terribly unfair. I'm flying out tonight."

"Sir John...it's been a wonderful privilege to work with you," she said. "I'll always remember your kindness and sensitivity to me. You are truly among the most talented actors of the 20th Century. You deserved so much better material to work with."

"A lovely sentiment," he answered. "If only it were true. Goodbye, my dear. I'm going back home to the comfort of my lover, Martin Hensler. I always return to his arms when I suffer a cruel blow."

[Years later, she heard from him again. He sent her a note from London. "You must go see Peter O'Toole and myself in Bob Guccione's Caligula *(1979). It's my first porno film."]*

Immediately, Gower set about to rescue the show, and asked Rigby to postpone the New York opening for a month of tryouts and a gala opening in Washington, D.C. before facing the harsh critics of Manhattan. The producer agreed.

Night after night, Gower worked with Debbie and the rest of the cast, perfecting the dance steps and sharpening the dialogue. He dropped current songs and subbed new ones, including a catchy opening number.

He completely restaged the finale, making it more spectacular. Years before, he and Debbie and his wife at the time, Marge Champion, had worked together during the filming of *Give a Girl a Break* (1953). Marge had become a friend, and Debbie had admired Gower from a distance. "He was the man of my dreams," she told Render. "But you don't unzip the pants of your friend's husband."

After midnight on her third night in Philadelphia, after Carrie had retired to their suite's second bedroom, there was a knock on her door.

She looked through the peephole and saw that it was Gower standing in the hallway. She opened the door. "Come in." He looked distressed. "Is something wrong?" she asked. Her first thought was that Rigby had shut down the show. He had been constantly fretting and complaining.

Gower stepped inside, shutting the door behind him. He looked soulfully into her eyes and said, "Without meaning to, I've fallen in love with you." Then he reached for her and held her tightly in his arms, kissing her deeply and long, arousing her passion.

"It was like a dream come true," she later told Render.

Before she could feel any guilt, he interrupted his kissing of her to announce, "I'm divorcing Marge. How could you and I have been so foolish? Both of us married the wrong spouses. I've got to have you. Right here, tonight. I can't wait any longer."

"Neither can I," she said. "I need you."

Chapter Thirteen

DIVORCE AMERICAN STYLE

DEBBIE'S ELDERLY EX-MILLIONAIRE SPOUSE DEMANDS HALF OF HER FUTURE EARNINGS PLUS ALIMONY

SUSTAINED BY THE FORCE OF DEBBIE'S PERFORMANCE, *IRENE* STAGGERS ON TO A BROADWAY OPENING

THE DEATH OF AGNES MOOREHEAD, THE SELF-DESTRUCTION OF CHRISTOPHER JONES, AND DEBBIE'S DEBUT AS AN ANIMATED SPIDER IN *CHARLOTTE'S WEB*

BOB FALLON (AKA "BOB PHALLUS") BECOMES DEBBIE'S NEW LOVER, LAUNCHING AN EIGHT-YEAR AFFAIR, SEX TOYS AND ALL

An old-fashioned and upbeat musical, *Irene* starring Debbie appealed to the reigning "Moral Majority" of its day, the out-of-towners as opposed to hip New Yorkers. From the first sound of a banjo, the audience knew they were being transported back to an era where father's walrus mustache was chic.

With Gower Champion as its new director, *Irene* was taken to Washington for four weeks, right after Richard Nixon was inaugurated for a second term as President of the United States, during the early stages of a burgeoning Watergate scandal.

On February 22, 1973, Debbie learned that Nixon, his wife, Patricia, and his daughter, Tricia, would attend a performance.

Backstage that night, a coven of Secret Service agents surveyed the scene at the theater in Washington, even inspecting Debbie's dressing room.

"Fearing assassination, they wanted to check everything," Rudy Render said. "One of them was a blonde Viking God, and he could have checked out anything I had."

After the performance, Nixon came backstage to congratulate Debbie and the cast. She felt honored because during his first term in office, Nixon had never attended a theatrical performance. He told Debbie that his wife had launched herself as a (minor) actress in the 1930s, "but I derailed her career."

Nixon predicted that *Irene* would be a big success on Broadway. *[Later, the play's publicist worked hard to distribute that endorsement. The ballyhoo helped spur Irene to $1.5 million in out-of-town business, plus an advance sale of $1.5 million waiting for them before its Broadway opening.]*

Debbie and Carrie were invited to the White House the next day. "I had to drag Carrie there, kicking and screaming. She was not a great fan of the President." Debbie herself had previously met Nixon when, as Eisenhower's vice president, he'd been made an honorary member of her beloved charity, the Thalians.

Nixon gave them

At the White House, Carrie Fisher shakes the hand of Richard Nixon, the President unaware that she loathed him. All smiles, Debbie looks on.

After seeing *Irene*, the President had endorsed the show for his supporters as a fine and decent musical that Republican parents could safely take their children to see.

The politically liberal *Village Voice* proclaimed "If you like Richard Nixon, you'll just love *Irene*."

384

autographed photographs of himself. On Carrie's he wrote, "May all your dreams come true." Carrie later told Debbie, "I wanted to write the fucker and tell him my biggest dream would come true when he was impeached."

***

In the midst of Debbie's affair with Gower, she received the bad news that Karl and "Mama Karl" (his mother) were flying to New York for the opening of *Irene*. He wanted to stay at the brownstone she'd rented for herself, Carrie, and Todd, but she refused.

"You and your mother can stay at a hotel," she told him. "You're not welcome in our temporary home."

"Do you want all of Manhattan to know we're separated?"

"Like I give a fuck," she said. "Tell people your mother's in bad health. And YOU have to look after her." After saying that, she slammed down the

"Even my enemies came to see me in *Irene,*" Debbie said. "They wanted to see Tammy fall on her face, but I was the Unsinkable Molly."

"A bubbly piece of nostalgia, the show was a big success, and the audiences applauded wildly. The music and relics were old-fashioned, set in an era when young people kept their clothes on in public."

phone.

By the time *Irene* went into two weeks of previews, Debbie hugged and kissed Gower "from his earlobes to his toes. I was grateful. He'd saved the show and also saved my life. I needed the money."

"Gower would make a great husband for me," she told Render at the time. "We speak the same language. We're both stars. We love the movies and the theater. The two of us can dance better than Fred Astaire and Ginger Rogers in the 1930s. He's also great in bed. I think I'm really falling big time for this guy. He's also very handsome with a trim, lean body and all the equipment in the right place. He fucks as well as he dances."

Opening night on Broadway, March 13, 1973, was a gala, star-studded event, with many famous personalities filling the seats.

The next morning, an early call came in from a happy producer. Gower was in bed with Debbie, and Harry Rigby's call woke both of them up. After speaking with him for about four minutes, Gower put down the phone and kissed Debbie. "Rigby said that the line for the opening of the box office this morning stretches a mile along 45th Street."

Clive Barnes of *The New York Times* found Debbie "a game trouper who works with a ferocious friendliness. Her face is a little bland, and her voice a little character-less, but she is clearly willing to do anything for the sake of the show—even baton-twirling, which she does awfully well. *Irene* is undemanding, rau-cous, frequently cheer-ful, and the best 1919 musical in town."

She had been shocked when the Tony Award nominees were announced: She'd been tapped for Best Actress in a Musical. The nom-inations were an-nounced right before the play's official open-ing night, a sequence of events that in the his-

A KISS FROM MOM — Debbie Reynolds kisses son, Todd Fisher as daughter, Carrie Fisher, whose engagement is rumored, looks on at the Minskoff Theater following the opening of "Irene".

Irene's opening night was widely reviewed across the country, as shown by the clipping above.

Carrie, who was shacked up with one of the men in the chorus, had a bit role in it.

Todd flew in to congratulate Debbie on her success, for which she rewarded him with a kiss.

tory of the Tonys had never transpired in quite that way before.

Also nominated for Best Supporting Actress in a musical was Patsy Kelly. "Who said a drunk can't make it in show business?" she quipped.

George S. Irving was nominated for Best Supporting Actor in a Musical, and Peter Gennaro was up for a Best Choreography Award.

Debbie lost her bid to win a Tony, bowing to Glynis Johns for her performance in another hit musical, *A Little Night Music*.

[*Irene continued as a wildly popular Broadway play for fourteen consecutive months, grossing nearly $8 million, which for the time broke all box office records. It was so successful that road show offers came flowing in from Chicago, Dallas, Los Angeles, and other cities.*

After its run on Broadway, Debbie took it on the road, proving "there's life in the old gal yet" (her words). She would remember arriving in Chicago in heavy rain, wind, and cold. Her most avid fans braved the weather, standing in line for tickets. On an impulse, she got a yellow raincoat like the one she'd worn in Singin' in the Rain, *went outside onto the drenched sidewalk, and performed the song in front of her water-soaked fans.*]

After attending the opening of *Irene* with his aging mother, Karl returned to California. Debbie pronounced it "good riddance. My thirteen years of horror were coming to an end, although I feared it would take months for me to get rid of the bastard."

"At least I had Carrie and Todd with me in New York. And I had Gower, or at least I thought I did. There was a backstage rumor that he was slipping around and seeing this cute little 23-year-old dancer named June or something or the other. I had never spoken to the bitch, but every time I walked past her, she glared at me."

"I was an aging actress, trying to compete with a chorus girl cutie. And I had a number of other problems, too, most of them financial. I feared that banks were ready to close in on me and force me out of my heavily mortgaged homes. I also feared I wouldn't be able to afford college for Todd, or even further education for Carrie. Worry, worry, worry."

"What if no more jobs opened up for me after *Irene* closed, as it inevitably would? I hate to admit this, but I started turning to the bottle after curtain call. I never showed up for work drunk like Patsy Kelly, but I did drink on nights I felt alone after Todd went to bed. I never knew where Carrie was. She was very independent."

"When Gower was with me, I felt all right and loved. But he didn't show up every night. I never dared ask him where he was. After all, he was still a married man, not quite divorced. He also had big plans for other Broadway shows. He would be around less and less. He'd done what he could for *Irene*."

"I know he said he loved me, but he looked at love differently from how I did. He once told me that love could last a week, a month, a year, and even for several years. But to love someone did not mean a lifetime commitment.

He cited Elizabeth Taylor as an example of someone who falls in and out of love."

***

In Manhattan, Carrie, even as a teenager, began to hang out with an older crowd, the youngest of whom was ten years her senior. She seemed like a girl desperately trying to become an adult before her time.

"After leaving California, my life as a girl came to an end," Carrie said. "I wanted to be grown up, and that included adult pleasures. I think you know what that means."

Rudy Render was the first to let Debbie know that Carrie was having an affair with a 25-year-old dancer in the chorus. "His name is Albert, and he's gay…well, not that gay."

Debbie opted not to interfere, even though Carrie was clearly "jailbait" (i.e., underaged).

Weeks later, when Carrie and Debbie talked about her affair, she shocked her daughter when she suggested that she was too inexperienced to have sex.

According to Carrie, "Instead of trying to stop me from having sex with Albert, she delivered a bombshell. She suggested that she be allowed to watch us having sex so she could give me tips. Call it 'eccentric mother love' or whatever. With a certain revulsion, I turned down her offer. Besides, Albert would not be able to keep an erection with Debbie watching."

When Todd came to live with her in New York, Debbie found him a great comfort. In all her turmoil, he stood by her side, expressing his devotion and love. "When there was no one else, I had my son, who would comfort me through some dark hours. With Carrie, you never knew where she might be— probably out seducing some gay guy, a trick she no doubt picked up from Elizabeth Taylor."

***

One night, Debbie arrived home in a state of total exhaustion, having sustained both a matinee and evening performance of *Irene.* It was growing late, but Todd was in her bedroom playing with a gun, one of the MGM props she'd bought. It had been used in MGM's 1950 musical, *Annie Get Your Gun,* starring Betty Hutton.

On television, he was watching *A Place in the Sun* (1951). In a memoir Debbie referred to that picture as having starred Montgomery Clift and Shelley Winters. Still holding a grudge, she had pointedly ignored the real star of that picture, Elizabeth Taylor.

"When I came in, Monty was drowning Shelley, something I wanted to do when we shot *What's the Matter with Helen?*"

388

After getting undressed for bed, she collapsed onto its mattress. Then Todd playfully pointed the gun at her. She sternly lectured him, "Never do that!"

"But it's only a prop with blanks!" he responded.

Breaking for a commercial, the TV screen showed a group of tap-dancers advertising some product. Todd told her he wanted to be a tap dancer, but she warned him, "You've got to have loose knees and loose legs if you want to be the male version of Ann Miller."

All this talk about knees somehow led him to point the gun at his own knee. He pulled the trigger, and the gun exploded against his kneecap. Blood spurted through the air.

She screamed, fearing his kneecap had been blown off. Ripping off her sheet, she formed a tourniquet. There was no one in the house to summon for help.

In desperation, she phoned her answering service, demanding that the woman who answered send a taxi to her home at once. Then she rushed back to tend to Todd before throwing on a house dress to race down the stairs to let in the taxi driver when he rang the doorbell.

She later told Render, "I must have looked like Elsa Lanchester on a bad night. No makeup. My hair a mess, sprayed red in part because of the wig I wore in *Irene*. Amazingly, he recognized me."

"Debbie! Debbie Reynolds!" he said. "We meet again. Korea. On your tour. You kissed my cheek. Don't you remember?"

"Of course I do," she said. "My son. Upstairs. He's shot himself."

Racing up the stairs, the driver hoisted Todd up into what Debbie described as "a fireman's hold," carried him down the steps, and placed him into the back seat of his cab.

Arriving at the entrance to New York Hospital, she watched as Todd was placed onto a stretcher and wheeled inside. Murmuring some shared memory of their meeting in Korea, she offered the driver a ten-dollar bill and kissed him on the cheek. He refused to accept it.

In the emergency room, there was only a young intern. He was authorized to clean the wound, but he was not authorized to perform surgery. In a state of panic, she placed a call to Jerry and Margaret Minskoff, the show-biz moguls who owned the theater where *Irene* was being staged. Within the hour, they arrived at the hospital with a surgeon.

They were followed by six policemen, who appeared on the scene. They'd learned about the incident, and they'd come to place Debbie under arrest. The first news that was leaked to them was that Debbie had attempted to murder her child.

As she was dragged out in handcuffs, she yelled, "You can't arrest me! *I'm Tammy!*"

"I don't give a fuck who you are," one of the cops said. "We're taking you to the local precinct."

She was placed in a large holding cell with about two dozen prostitutes rounded up from around Times Square. Even in her disheveled condition, she was immediately recognized. Word had spread about Todd being shot.

"I once tried to shoot my daughter," one of the hookers said. "I told her I wasn't going to raise no fucking whore."

Others wanted to know who was the best-hung man in Hollywood.

"John Ireland," Debbie said.

"Who is known as Rooster Meat?" another asked.

"Monty Clift," Debbie answered.

Then, as the Minskoffs stayed out front arranging for her release, she was ordered to wait within a small, locked room which also held two men charged with rape.

One of the men unzipped his pants and pulled out his penis. "Get an eyeful of Jumbo," he told her.

Before leaving the precinct, she learned the name of the restaurant and bar where Carrie and a lot of the cast had gone. She placed a call there, and a reluctant Carrie came to the phone.

"Todd shot himself in the kneecap with one of those guns I have from MGM," she said.

"At least he didn't shoot off his penis," Carrie said, flippantly.

"Cut the crap!" Debbie said. "The police are going to search our home. Get there right now. Remove any incriminating evidence, Yes, flush your pot down the toilet. Hide any other guns I have among those props."

Carrie rushed home, following instructions. Pinky arrived from a date to help her. "It was a sad moment when I flushed that valuable weed down the crapper," Carrie said. "Pinky suggested we hide two other guns from that Betty Hutton movie in the washing machine. No copper would ever think of looking there."

"When I went into Debbie's bedroom, it looked like a scene from a movie based on the Sharon Tate murders," Carrie said. "Blood everywhere."

By the time the police arrived, Debbie had put on makeup and slipped into a seductive gown. She adorned her head with a blonde wig.

"The policemen, one of whom was kinda cute, grilled me," Debbie said. "So many questions. They wanted to know what Clark Gable was really like. Was Mickey Rooney small all over? Did Lana Turner stab Johnny Stompanato? Did Marilyn Monroe sleep with all three of the Kennedy brothers? Finally they left."

Suddenly, a *Daily News* reporter was at the door, barging in as the cops were filing out.

"Is it true, Miss Reynolds, that you deliberately shot your son to get publicity for *Irene?*"

"That's absolutely true," she said. "Now I've got only one daughter left to shoot for more publicity. Get the fuck out of here!"

From Montego Bay in Jamaica, Eddie Fisher called. "What have you done to my son? The word is out that you tried to kill him, you dirty little bitch. I'm thinking of getting a court order declaring you an unfit mother and taking both Carrie and Todd away from you. Taking out your hatred of me on poor Todd."

Without answering, she slammed down the phone.

The morning papers arrived on her doorstep. "Pablo Picasso had died that night, but Todd, photographed in his hospital bed, crowded him off the front-pages," she said.

***

One night Debbie returned from the show alone, entering her brownstone. The housekeeper had left a note which revealed that Todd was feeling tired and had gone to bed. That afternoon, a doctor had examined him and reported to her that he was recovering nicely.

She felt lonely, needing someone to talk to. Usually, it would have been Pinky or Rudy Render, but on this particular night, they were gone. "I can't expect them to devote their entire lives to me," she'd told Carrie. "Rudy is probably out cruising, and Pinky is…God only knows what Pinky is up to."

After the show, Carrie and her boyfriend, Albert, had visited Debbie's dressing room, telling her they were going to this hot little club in Greenwich Village. Albert kissed Debbie on the cheek, calling her "Mother."

After he'd retreated back into the hallway, Carrie whispered to Debbie, "I don't need you to instruct me in sex. Albert has taught me all the tricks, and I mean *all* the tricks."

Later, at home in her bedroom, which had its own bar, Debbie poured herself her first vodka of the evening, fearing that she'd be consuming many more. She looked at herself in the mirror. Even before removing her makeup, she appeared older than she actually was.

As she confided to Render the next morning, "I just sat there looking at myself. A forty-two-year old former Hollywood movie star who in middle age is willing to take any job offer that came along."

Before the end of the month, two men, each of whom she already knew, would re-enter her life. There was also Gower Champion, popping in and out of her bed on occasion.

"I was still wanted, still desirable," she'd later say. "A man doesn't have to love you or pledge fidelity to go to bed with you. That's such an old-fash-ioned concept, and I'm no longer the girl who rode the cattle train in from El Paso."

***

In New York, after a night of sex, Gower Champion sat in Debbie's breakfast nook, eating bacon and eggs as prepared by her housekeeper. He expounded on his views of marriage. "Too many men and women rush into marriage the very year they either divorce or break up. That's not how it's done. You and I are doing it just right. Playing the field. When time comes to settle down, and both parties want to set up housekeeping, then it's time to head for the altar."

"My sentiments exactly," she said, not meaning a word of it.

She was eager to learn about his new Broadway musical, *Mack and Mabel*, with lyrics by Jerry Herman of *Hello, Dolly!* fame. Set in Hollywood during the silent era, the musical was the story of Mack Sennett, fabled for his Bathing Beauties, and actress Mabel Normand.

As he related the plot to her, she deeply regretted that she was not free to take on the role of Mabel. But she wasn't, and he'd already cast Bernadette Peters, with Robert Preston as Sennett.

After that night with her, their relationship cooled a bit, and he called her less frequently, in part because of his involvement in taking *Mack and Mabel* out of town for pre-Broadway tryouts. One of the stops *en route,* was Los Angeles.

Debbie flew back to New York for the show's Broadway opening on October 6, 1974. Later that evening, she raved about the show to Champion, with special praise for the visual effects and the spectacular dance sequences.

The morning after the play's opening, Champion was disappointed by its reviews. She had to fly back to Los Angeles and was sad to learn that the show had closed after only eight performances. It was nonetheless nominated for eight Tony Awards, including Best Musical. In time, the show—based on its presentation in locales outside New York—developed a cult following.

This photo, snapped years before as a publicity photo for their film, *Give a Girl a Break*, shows Marge and Gower Champion still married at the time, with *ingénue* Debbie as a third member of their dance trio.

Now, years later, Marge and Gower had divorced, and Gower could at last seamlessly express his perhaps long-suppressed love for Debbie.

[After their time together in New York, Debbie saw Gower very infrequently, and often not for months at a time. After a string of big Broadway hits, his career went into decline.

He didn't tell her, but she read in the papers that in 1976, he'd married Karla Russell.

Debbie attended one of his later Broad-

way musicals, Rockabye Hamlet, *which opened on February 17. 1976 at the Minskoff Theater, where he had staged* Irene *in 1973.*

Meeting him backstage, he thanked her for coming, but told her he had to meet with his backers and wouldn't be able to spend any time with her.

She didn't bother to attend his final musical, the disastrously named A Broadway Musical. *She read that the plot was about the attempt of a sleazy white theater producer to adapt an African -American writer's serious play into a commercial stage musical. "It's just as well I didn't show up," Debbie said. "After fourteen previews, it lasted only one night after its opening on December 21, 1978."*

She never heard from him again and was saddened to learn of his death on August 25, 1980. The year before, he'd been diagnosed with a rare form of blood cancer. Against his doctor's advice, he signed on to direct a new musical, 42nd Street, *based on the classic film (1933) with the same name. On the very evening of its opening, he collapsed and died.*

Ironically, the play ran for 3,486 performances, even beating the record of Hello, Dolly!.

"Poor, darling Gower," Debbie said. "He just wasn't around to carry off his eighth Tony."]

***

James Garner, Debbie's "handsome hunk," flew into New York. He phoned Debbie and told her he'd come backstage after seeing *Irene,* and he hoped she'd be free to have dinner with him.

"I'm checked into a hotel, but if I'm invited for a sleepover, I don't have to return there tonight."

"You can come and sleep over with me, although I don't know how much sleep you'll get."

"I've never seen so much energy on stage as you displayed in *Irene,"* he said. "I hope you saved some of that energy for me."

"You're on, big boy," she said. "Watch me go."

Over dinner, she found him in a career funk, complaining about his last three pictures. "The less said about *They Only Kill Their Masters* (MGM, 1972), the better. Your friends, Peter Lawford and June Allyson, were in it, but they couldn't save it—neither could I."

For Disney, he'd also starred in *One Little Indian* (1973). "I've done pictures I'm ashamed of—and this is one of the duds. The only bright spot in it was a cute little ten-year-old, Jodie Foster."

"After that clunker, Disney hired me again to star as *The Castaway Cowboy* with Vera Miles and Robert Culp. They are no better in it than I am. The scenery in Hawaii stole the picture from us."

Smoking endless cigarettes, he told her he was turning to television for better luck. "I'm going to star in something called *The Rockford Files.* There's hope for it."

She told Rudy Render how thrilling she found Garner as a lover. "He told me I have the most beautiful breasts of any star in Hollywood. He's a real breast man and can make love to a girl's knockers all night long. Of course, he can do other things, too."

With the money she'd made in *Irene*, Debbie wanted to pay Garner back the $50,000 he'd lent her when she was desperate. For *Irene*, she was drawing $15,000 a week. Despite her staggering expenses, she had managed to save $160,000.

After her financial wipe-out, Debbie had gone to the most prestigious accounting firm in Los Angeles and arranged for agents there to handle her affairs. Every week, she'd send them her paychecks from *Irene*.

But when she went to draw out a cashier's check for $50,000, she found that her account was drained. She could not believe that, and at first feared that Karl had somehow managed to get his name attached to her account, as he'd done so often in the past.

When the firm refused to return her money, she hired people to investigate. They found that a female associate of the firm had forged Debbie's name onto the back of her paychecks, and had cashed them for herself and absconded with all her funds.

"I wanted to go and kill myself," she said. "How could any hard-working girl like myself be so unlucky with money? I'd wanted to build up a nest egg to pay off debts—and now this!"

To her shock and outrage, the accounting firm sided with its employee. "To me, it was an open-and-shut case," Debbie said. "But the firm didn't see it that way. I had to sue the bastards to get my money back, and that took months and lots of legal fees. The ordeal nearly caused me to have a stroke. I finally prevailed in court."

"The firm didn't lose any money, as their insurance covered it. The thief who made off with my dough didn't even have to go to prison."

In New York, Garner came and went quickly from her life. It was some time before she heard from him again. She'd seen him on TV in *The Rockford Files*, which became a big success.

When he phoned again, he told her he'd made two movies with Lauren ("Betty") Bacall.

"What a beautiful woman—and so damn feisty. I just love her."

Bacall herself once spoke to the press about Garner. "Jim is a great guy. Everyone who works with him is crazy about him. He's an appealing creature and an adorable man."

Debbie asked, "I wonder if Jim's wife knows about all his nocturnal habits?"

***

In September of 1973, Debbie ordered her lawyers to end her thirteen-year-marriage to Harry Karl. Because of complicated financial matters she expected it to be an uphill battle that might consume the next months of her life.

She agreed to let him stay at their home on Greenway Drive in Beverly Hills until the property was sold. That way, for the moment at least, it would provide a home for Tina and Harrison (Bo). She would remain in Manhattan with Todd and Carrie until *Irene* closed.

Todd had bounced back from the gunshot wound to his knee. She had made a mistake in enrolling him in a private school in Manhattan, where nearly all of his fellow students wanted to be some kind of artist, perhaps a ballet dancer, a Broadway actor, a chorus boy, a stage designer. It was rumored that half of the boys in his class were gay.

"My son liked to build things," she said. "Perhaps he might become a great architect one day, like Frank Lloyd Wright. He also had an interest in photography. Who knows? Maybe he'd become Hollywood's greatest cinematographer, learning to catch me on film looking like a twenty-year-old."

One afternoon, Debbie returned to her rented Manhattan townhouse. "My boy was growing up. At the age of fourteen, it appeared that he was showing an interest in the opposite sex. He was sitting on the floor with this girl who had lovely red curly hair that came way below her neck."

"Hi, baby," she said. "Care to introduce me to your sweetie?"

When the redhead turned around, Debbie met Richard Friedlander, who was fifteen years old. "He was definitely a boy, a true Viking with that red hair."

As it turned out, he'd bonded with Todd at his school, as each had been relatively shunned by the other boys in their class.

"Richard had a rebellious streak in him and was having trouble with his parents. In a few weeks, he moved in with us. I'd found yet another child to mother."

In time, Richard dropped out of school and went on the road with *Irene*, learning how to be a sound technician. By the age of seventeen, he had mastered the profession.

In the beginning, Todd traveled with them, but in time, he grew bored and returned to school. "I practically adopted Richard, and he and Todd developed a long-term relationship. They were there for me when I was forced to live through the upcoming nightmare years."

***

During her stint with *Irene* on Broadway, Debbie grew closer and closer to Agnes Moorehead, who at the time was starring at the Uris Theatre *[which was rechristened "the Gershwin Theater" in 1983]*, in a stage musical, *Gigi. [The story of Gigi originated as a novella in 1944 by Colette. It was adapted into a movie musical, a huge hit, in 1958.]* In the Broadway production, Moorehead was cast as Aunt Alicia, alongside Leslie Caron, Maurice Chevalier, Louis Jourdan, and Hermione Gingold.

To ring in the New Year of 1973, Debbie had hosted a party for the combined casts of *Irene* and *Gigi* on the top floor of the Minskoff Theatre. "Agnes was in great shape that night, or so it seemed, but as the year wore on, she began to complain of stomach trouble. When she came over for dinner, she would eat only mashed potatoes."

"On many a night, Agnes liked to walk down memory lane, telling me stories of her life," Debbie said.

"I have played so many authoritative and strong figures that some people are nervous at the prospect of meeting me for the first time," Moorehead said. She told stories of her Broadway triumphs in such plays as *All the King's Men,* and *Don Juan in Hell* with Charles Boyer and Charles Laughton.

In collaboration with Orson Welles and Joseph Cotten, she'd been a founder and charter member of the Mercury Theater. She'd made some 100 films and received five Oscar nods, including one for her performance in *Hush, Hush, Sweet Charlotte* (1964) starring Bette Davis.

One night, she told Debbie, "I think an artist should be kept separated from fans to maintain glamour and a kind of mystery. Otherwise, it's like having three meals a day. Pretty dull. I don't believe in the girl-next-door image like you promoted for a while. What an actor has to sell to the public is fantasy, a magic kind of ingredient that should not be analyzed."

The two actresses often discussed the joy and pain of being a performer. Moorehead told Debbie, "It's a terribly discouraging business, a sorrowful business, a critical business. You're up there, and the people can take off your skin, bit by bit, and enjoy it. If you get anywhere, there's a strange kind of human tendency to tear you down. You have to keep on developing and maturing and being sincere in your work, and just go right on whether audiences or critics are taking your scalp off or not."

Moorehead said, "I've been in movies and played theater from coast to coast, so I was quite well known before *Bewitched,* and I don't particularly want to be constantly identified as a witch."

Before flying back to Los Angeles, Moorehead asked Debbie for permission to designate her as executrix of her will. "I agreed and thought no more of it at the time," Debbie said. "I didn't take it as a signal that Agnes was dying. I thought she was just arranging her business affairs in case something happened to her. I was wrong."

***

Debbie needed to take a hiatus from *Irene* to fulfill a gig in Las Vegas at the Desert Inn. Her contract for the Broadway musical had allowed her to take a temporary leave of absence and to designate her replacement.

She selected Jane Powell. "I was once the supporting player in those long-ago musicals we made. Now our fortunes were reversed. I was the star. She went over very well in the show, although she wasn't quite as zany as I was. That was not Janie's style."

Back in Vegas in the casino showroom, Debbie played to full houses. Sammy Davis, Jr. and Dean Martin, among other celebrities, came to see her. "Dean really hit on me, and I had always found him charming and even sexy. But I had been friends with his wife, Jeanne Biegger, and it didn't seem right for me to sleep with him."

Her most persistent suitor was Davis. "Sammy was far too short for me, and I certainly didn't turn him down because he was black. I figured that it would be a tough act to follow if I went to bed with him. You name 'em: Marilyn Monroe, Ava Gardner, Kim Novak, and even the stripper, Tempest Storm. He'd even bedded the era's two leading female porn stars—*Deep Throat's* Linda Lovelace and *Behind the Green Door's* Marilyn Chambers.

[Carrie wrote that Behind the Green Door *made Chambers "a household name, then a whorehouse-hold name. I had seen it at fifteen, not having heard the phrase 'blow job' before."]*

After completing her gig in Vegas, Debbie flew back to her home in Beverly Hills, where Karl was still in residence. Tina and Harrison (Bo) were also living there with their father.

When her taxi pulled up at 813 Greenway Drive, Debbie was shocked. Not only was her driveway filled with cars, but every parking space on the block was taken.

As she approached her front door, she heard loud music blaring from inside her house. The front door was wide open. As soon as she walked inside, she was greeted with bedlam. "There must have been a hundred kids there in various stages of dress," she said. "Some were dancing, some were necking, and all of them seemed on drugs."

She shouted, "Get out! Get the hell out of my house! I'm calling the police!"

From the center of the room

"Sammy Davis tried to get me to go with him to rituals at the Church of Satan," Debbie said.

"I was shocked to discover that he was a Devil worshipper. But he couldn't turn this little girl raised in the Church of the Nazarene into Satan's Mistress."

emerged an enraged Tina. "Like hell you're kicking out my friends! This house belongs to my father. I'll have whoever I want here!"

"THE HELL YOU WILL!" Although she was a tiny person, Debbie was a powerhouse when it came to emptying a room. After she slammed the door on the last intruder, she raced toward Karl's bedroom. She found him with earphones, listening to music while reading the latest edition of *Playboy*.

She yanked the earphones from his ears and confronted him. "You fucking bastard! You turned our home into a flophouse."

"Oh come on, Debbie," he said. "Those are Tina's friends, just trying to have a little fun—that's all."

"You're hopeless!" she said. "I can't trust you to do a fucking thing right!"

Then she stormed out of his bedroom and went to her own. "It looked like Berlin in 1945," she said. "all the locks had been broken on my closets and everything had been looted. I'd been cleaned out, including my three minks. Everything in the room had been taken except for the bed. Dwight and Mamie Eisenhower had given me two commemorative plates. They were gone." The rest of my jewelry, or whatever was left of it, had also been stolen from a hidden drawer in my vanity."

"I felt so desperate, so violated, so outraged," she said. "In that moment, I wanted to murder both Karl and his rotten little brat."

Once again, she barged into Karl's bedroom, this time to tell him about the robbery. "Oh well," he said. "It's in all the papers. A lot of juvenile delinquents. It's a big problem across the country."

"You're a hopeless relic, rotting in bed waiting for the undertaker," she said.

The next morning, she set about finding an apartment for Tina. She located a furnished one in Beverly Hills and moved Tina into it. "You're eighteen now, kid, so you're on your own. You are no longer my responsibility. Your father can take care of you. Of course, he can't even look after himself."

After the house on Greenway Drive home was sold, Karl was forced to move out. He found an apartment in Century City close to Hillcrest.

His first child, Judie Karl Anderson, the offspring of a union with his first wife, Ruth Lamb, showed up to assist him with his move. She seemed aware that her father needed help in his readjustment.

Debbie met with her at Century City, going into detail about how Karl liked his custom-made shirts pressed and his alligator shoes shined.

Judie protested that she wasn't going to do that. However, when Debbie demonstrated how to cut out cotton squares for applications of some form of healing oil he'd bought as treatment for his hemorrhoids, she agreed to do that. In reference to his hemorrhoids, Debbie said, "They looked like myriad mounts on a lunar landscape."

"Like Scarlett O'Hara, I would think about my post-Karl life tomorrow, because tomorrow is another day," Debbie said. "In the meantime, I had to return to Broadway to take back my role in *Irene*. I hoped that Janie Powell hadn't latched onto it and wanted to hang around. As she and I were finding out, there were no more movie roles for two washed-up cuties from those harmless MGM musicals of the 1950s. The Eisenhower era was over. We were living in the age of Nixon."

***

Debbie casually knew Marie Wilson, an actress who made a career out of playing noodle-brained "ultra-blondes" onscreen. Her large eyes and big mouth, along with her high-pitched voice, had been familiar to movie fans since 1934, when she appeared with Laurel and Hardy in *Babes in Toyland*. Debbie had seen many of her movies, including *My Friend Irma* (1949), a picture made with Jerry Lewis and Dean Martin, when she was cast as a good-hearted but clueless legal secretary.

"On the screen, the well-stacked Marie was a delight, evocative of the zany Gracie Allen," Debbie said. "Marie sometimes discussed her greatest disappointment. It was when she lost the role of Billie Dawn in *Born Yesterday* (1950). The Oscar-winning part went instead to Judy Holliday."

One night, Debbie was invited to what was known back then as a "hen party," this one hosted by Celeste Holm. Debbie was usually the show-stopper at parties, but this time, Wilson told more amusing and often personal stories, revealing that both Lewis and Martin had seduced her.

"Jerry has a little prick and Dean a big Italian sausage," Wilson claimed.

Wilson often attended the same Presbyterian church in Hollywood that Debbie did. It was at one Sunday service that she was introduced to the actor-producer, Bob Fallon, whom Marie had married in 1951. He'd turned out such pictures as *Flight* (1958), *Mr. Blackwell Presents* (1968), and *St. Patrick's Day* (1969), a TV special. Debbie often sat at the same table as

"After Marie Wilson died, I went bigtime for her husband, Bob Fallon," Debbie said. "One night when he followed me into my bedroom, I found he was well-equipped for lovemaking."

Wilson and Fallon at charity events for the Thalians.

In 1972, a few months before *Irene* opened on Broadway, Debbie read in the paper that Wilson had died of cancer. Although Debbie had sent a sympathy note to the late Marie's husband, Bob Fallon, she hadn't seen him since.

A mutual friend, Phyllis Pollack, brought Fallon and Debbie together again during the Broadway run of *Irene*. Phyllis had become one of Debbie's closest friends. With Eddie Fisher, Debbie had honeymooned at Phyllis's Thunderbird Hotel in Miami. She and Phyllis had much in common: both of them were shopping addicts.

Phyllis flew from Miami to New York to see Debbie in *Irene*. One day, when Debbie was performing in a matinee, Phyllis went shopping at Bloomingdale's. Here, she encountered Fallon, whom she'd met before. Configuring him as an ideal date for Debbie now that he was a widower and available, she invited him to see Debbie in *Irene* that night, suggesting he come by the Essex House (Phyllis had rented the presidential suite) at a designated time to escort them to the theater.

[Debbie was staying at the Essex House with Phyllis for two days. She had left her children in her rented townhouse to be looked after by the housekeeper.]

"He was good looking, and Debbie was beautiful, so I thought they would make a perfect match," Phyllis said. "I thought he might help Debbie get over the horror of her divorce."

At Essex House, to which Debbie had already returned after her matinee performance, Phyllis was between floors, ascending in the elevator. According to Phyllis, "A strange man who looked like the actor, John Ireland, got on the elevator and began to stare at me intently. Apparently, he noticed that I had pressed the elevator's button to the presidential suite. He gave me a final look before exiting at a lower floor."

Ten minutes later, the phone rang in her suite, and Phyllis answered it. A strong, masculine voice came over the line. "I want you to put my cock in your mouth. I want to feel your lips around it."

Phyllis immediately called to Debbie, "Dear, it's for you!"

Debbie picked up the receiver and heard the stranger repeat the same request. She slammed down the phone and laughed raucously.

Early that same evening, Fallon arrived right on time at the Essex House and escorted them both to the theater. After the show, Phyllis returned alone to the Essex, and Debbie invited Fallon back to her brownstone for the late-night supper her housekeeper had prepared.

He seemed eager to accept the invitation. Over potato salad and cold cuts, they laughed and joked and seemed most compatible.

As she later told Phyllis, "I didn't exactly invite him into my bedroom. It was getting late, and it was time for me to turn in. He followed me in there and started to undress. I really enjoyed the sex. Bob became one of my great all-time lovers. Not Eddie, not Harry, but Bob taught me what it was like to really feel like a woman. He was very experienced and a most unselfish lover."

***

"At last, I was making a return to the screen," Debbie said. "Or at least my voice was. The picture was *Charlotte's Web,* and I was 'typecast' as a spider." Based on the 1952 children's story by E.B. White, *Charlotte's Web* was an animated musical drama set for a release by Paramount in 1973.

Like the book that inspired it, the film tells the story of a piglet named Wilbur, who befriends an intelligent spider *[whose voice was that of Debbie],* who saves him from being slaughtered.

Music and lyrics were by the Sherman brothers, who had written the music for *Mary Poppins* (1964). Debbie, at the Academy Awards ceremony that year, had presented the brothers with an Oscar for their song "Chim Chim Cher-ee" from that movie.

"That year I was also up for a Best Actress Oscar for *The Unsinkable Molly Brown,*" Debbie said. "But Todd and Carrie were rooting for the winner, Julie Andrews, for *Mary Poppins,* a picture they'd loved. There's nothing like having loyal children."

The Sherman Brothers felt Debbie had done a brilliant job in creating and defining the voice of Charlotte. Other voiceovers were supplied by her friend, Agnes Moorehead, as the Goose; Henry Gibson as Wilbur, the piglet; and Paul Lynde as an egotistical rat. "Talk about type casting," Debbie said, in reference to Lynde.

The film did moderate business at the box office, but over the years has become something of a cult classic. E.B. White, however, called the movie "a travesty. It's Disney World with 76 trombones. But that's what you get when you become embroiled with Hollywood. I would have preferred Mozart to the Sherman Brothers. I don't care for jolly songs."

***

After kicking Karl out of the house on Greenway Drive in Beverly Hills, Debbie, with Carrie and Todd, moved into it temporarily until the banks seized the property.

The period that followed her last performance on Broadway in *Irene* was a time of great turmoil in her life. "I was drinking heavily, knowing that every day of my life would bring some new humiliation."

One night at around 1AM, a call came in for Debbie from Rock Hudson, who said it was an emergency. Knowing what a good friend of hers he was, the housekeeper decided to wake her when the actor told her, "It's a matter of life and death."

On the phone and with a sense of urgency, he told Debbie that she should go at once to the apartment he'd rented for Christopher Jones in West Hollywood. "Our 'love machine' has overdosed," Hudson told Debbie. "I think he's in desperate shape. Please rush there and take charge, perhaps get him to a hospital. I can't take care of him here at The Castle. I have film people coming over early tomorrow. A scandal could destroy my career, as you well know."

"I'll do what I can," she said, "but I don't know how good I am in these situations."

"You're the only person I know who's close enough to him to help him." Hudson then gave her the apartment's address and told her that the key was above the door frame. "Please hurry!" he said. "I'll owe you one for this."

Within the hour, Debbie was in West Hollywood, going to a dingy apartment and letting herself in with the key, right where Hudson had said it would be.

She found Jones lying nude on his bed in a pool of vomit. Grabbing a bath towel, she lifted his head and tried to awaken him. His eyes opened and then shut. He seemed in a kind of stupor, breathing heavily, as if he were having difficulty sucking air into his lungs.

She immediately phoned for an ambulance, informing the dispatcher that the patient's name was "William Parker." Like Hudson, she, too, wanted to avoid a scandal. As a means of covering his nudity, she struggled to shove his motionless body into a pair of pajama bottoms.

Two hours later, at a hospital, a doctor, after examining him, wanted to talk to her. He had never seen one of Jones' movies and didn't know who he was. Debbie explained that she was a friend of the family.

"He overdosed on drugs," the doctor said. "We get many cases like that these days. I think he'll be all right, mostly because you got him here on time. He might have died."

For the next three days, while he was recovering in a hospital room, which she paid for, she visited him regularly. The doctor and nurses let her visit and stay with him as often and for as long as she wanted.

He recovered quickly, explaining, "I took some bad shit." Having no one else to talk to, he poured out his anguish to Debbie, who feared that he was suicidal.

"Chris's world seemed to have fallen in on him, and he had horrible stories to tell about his ill-fated marriage to Susan Strasberg and the abuse he took from her father, Lee. He spoke lovingly of his daughter, Jennifer, of whom Susan had custody. "I fear I was not cut out to be a father."

Working those long, dreary months in Ireland during the filming of *Ryan's Daughter,* directed by David Lean, had traumatized him. "Making that fucking movie nearly killed me."

"It took a toll on me," he said. "I don't think I'll ever appear on the screen again. Some critics removed layers of my skin, leaving me raw. Then Lean hired another actor to dub my voice in every scene. He said my voice isn't compelling enough—something every actor wants to hear. Since then, he's told half of Hollywood that I had to be dubbed. That means it's unlikely that I'll be swamped with film offers. The point is that now, even if some director wants to take a chance on me again, which is highly unlikely, I think I'll say 'no.'"

When he left the hospital and moved back to his Hollywood apartment, Debbie visited Jones every night, and their sex life resumed. She brought in her housekeeper to give it a thorough cleaning. When they discovered bedbugs, Debbie tossed out his mattress. That very afternoon, Debbie went out and purchased a new, deluxe mattress for him with new bed coverings.

During her final night with him, he expounded on the glories of LSD and mescaline. "You've got to break free of your Tammy image, oh so sweet," he advised. "You're too tight-assed, too conventional. You've got to run *Wild in the Streets* like the title of the movie I made."

"By the time I left that night," she later told Rudy Render, "he looked so angelic, asleep on the pillow. But that was a mere mask to conceal what was roiling around inside that head of his."

After I left him, I didn't know if Chris would survive or not," she said. "But it was time for me to bow out of his troubled life and face my own troubled life. Call it an affair—better yet, an interlude, a detour. Frankly, I feared his whole life would be a detour, with him never reaching the main highway. Except for our love-making, he and I lived on different planets."

Then she asked Render a question: "Besides, would you want to wake up every morning and look at the sleeping head of your boyfriend on the pillow next to you and realize that he was prettier than you?"

***

"Unlike Christopher Jones, Bob Fallon and I were compatible in and out of bed," Debbie claimed. "He was fun to hang out with. He liked to dance as much as I did, and we often went to Cocoanut Grove or other clubs along Sunset Strip."

One night at the Grove, Fallon had three dances in a row with his alltime favorite screen goddess, Lana Turner.

"He liked to go to the movies as much as I did," Debbie said. "Even if the film starred my alltime crush, Robert Wagner. So I figured that if he could dance with Lana, I could daydream about my fantasy man, R.J., if only on the screen. Bob Fallon was a lot of fun, and he was good to my children."

Behind his back, Carrie and Todd called him "Bob Phallus," because early in his love affair with their mother, he'd arrived at their house with a bag of sex toys and exotic creams for love-making.

"That Christmas, he brought me and my grandmother vibrators," Carrie said. "I put mine to use, but Minnie was afraid to use hers. She told me she had not had an orgasm in so many years that she had forgotten what one felt like. She was also worried that the vibrator might short-circuit her pacemaker."

"When Bob wasn't around for stud duty, my mother sometimes borrowed my vibrator but told me, 'The damn gadget is no substitute for the real thing.'"

She continued to praise the sexual prowess of Fallon, both in a memoir and to her closest friends.

After her last and final appearance as *Irene* on Broadway, he returned to Los Angeles, He had a home there, the one he had lived in with Marie Wilson.

"I always felt uncomfortable there," Debbie confessed. "He hadn't changed one thing since she'd died. Her pictures were all over the place, including a photo of her with Dean Martin and Jerry Lewis that hung in the bathroom. I told him I'd help him redecorate, since he couldn't go on living with a memory. Besides, I was now his girl."

"With Bob, it was a celebration of the flesh between a man and a woman. Sometimes, I was the aggressor, demanding and getting satisfaction. As a girl, Minnie had taught me that sex was something a woman had to endure for the pleasure of the male. Not so with Bob."

"He and I could have written a book. A popular cookbook at the time was *The Joy of Cooking*. We'd call ours *The Joy of Love-Making.*"

"I treated him like he was my husband, seeing that he had three meals a day, freshly laundered shirts and underwear, his favorite shampoo in the shower, and freshly squeezed orange juice in the morning."

"I treated his son, Greg, like he was my own. What a wonderful boy."

In time, Fallon began to negotiate business deals for Debbie. He was very macho, a most commanding figure, and he sometimes pissed people off by being so bossy. But I liked to be dominated by him. It was a turn-on. We never married, and he had no intention of being called Mr. Debbie Reynolds, unlike so many other Hollywood husbands wed to stars. You were always hearing some man being called Mr. Hedy Lamarr or Mr. Gene Tierney."

Debbie may not have re-read her first memoir before releasing her third autobiography. In the first, she claimed that Fallon never took advantage of her financially, but made his own living, occasionally producing some film script, but more often as a contractor for the renovation of homes.

In her final memoir, she had a different take: "From Day One, Bob Fallon found my Diners Club card a big attraction. He lived beautifully off it. In time, I paid for everything, including taking many world cruises with him to such places as Italy, Bali, or Australia."

"Whatever, our love affair lasted for eight of the most tumultuous years of my life."

***

A friend told Debbie that Agnes Moorehead had been aboard a train to Rochester, Minnesota, where she'd checked herself into the Mayo Clinic. The actress didn't want Debbie to know of her illness. Remembering all those complaints in Manhattan from Moorehead about her stomach pain, she feared that she had cancer.

She phoned her at the clinic, where, at the age of 67, Moorehead had been hospitalized since April 9, 1974.

She refused to discuss her illness. "I didn't want you to know. You have enough grief of your own right now, and I hoped to avoid adding to your load."

Debbie phoned every day for the next three weeks, noticing that Moorehead's voice was growing weaker and weaker. She'd lost all her hair from chemotherapy.

Finally, during one of Debbie's last phone calls to her, the aging actress admitted, "My dear friend, I can face it now. I'm dying. Pray for me."

Moorehead's death occurred on the last day of April 1974, when the news flashed around the world. The cause of death was diagnosed as uterine cancer.

As executrix of her will, Debbie followed Moorehead's instructions, resisting calls from her friends who wanted to stage a funeral. "Agnes didn't want that and was rather adamant about it."

After her death, Moorehead's 94-year-old mother, the former Mary Mildred McCauley, flew to Los Angeles. Debbie met her at the airport, finding her still sprightly and alert. Before she died, Moorehead had informed Debbie that her will amply provided for her mother. It stipulated that she'd receive all the money from the sale of her house, plus future residuals from her TV hit, *Bewitched.*

Debbie, with Mary Mildred, met with Moorehead's attorney to learn the devastating news: The lawyer produced a new will, telling them, "Agnes left me everything and made no provision for either of you."

Debbie didn't believe him. When she checked the will he handed her, it had been signed by Moorehead. Although the first and last pages were exact replicas of the copy Debbie had been working with, three newer sheets had been inserted; pages which called for a vast giveaway to the attorney. Her immediate impression was that those unsigned substitute pages were frauds.

According to the new will, even the gift of a large sapphire ring—a token which Moorehead had specifically designated as Debbie's—were claimed by the attorney. In addition, all the stocks and bonds, the jewelry, the proceeds from the sale of Moorehead's house, and all of her artwork and household items, now belonged to the lawyer.

After the attorney left, Debbie urged Moorehead's mother to sue, but she refused, fearing that prolonged litigation would damage her heart.

Back within Moorehead's home, Debbie went to her safe. *[Moorehead had given her a copy of the key many months earlier.]* All the jewelry was gone, even a series of antique watches that Debbie had purchased for her over the years, knowing how much she liked to collect them.

When news of the will reached the press, a rumor arose that Moorehead and the attorney were lovers. "That was a damn lie," Debbie said. "At that time in her life, Moorehead told me she had absolutely no interest in sex."

In defiance of a threat of a lawsuit from the attorney, Debbie forged ahead and sold Moorehead's furnishings at auction, netting $30,000, which she turned over to the mother.

Later, the lawyer sold Moorehead's home for one million dollars, pocketing the money for himself.

There were other rumors: After Moorehead's death, gossips once again claimed that the older actress and Debbie had long been engaged in a lesbian love affair.

"That was the final blow," Debbie said. "Another humiliation. Most of Agnes' estate was looted, and her reputation had to suffer this final indignity. I'm not opposed to lesbianism in general. Everyone has a right to love. But Agnes tried three straight marriages, each of which failed. After that, she retired from the love game."

According to Debbie, "In the years ahead, Agnes, in an apparition, stood over me, looking down at me in my bed. She was as real to me then as she had been in life. I know it sounds crazy, but I swear I saw her face. She was like a guardian angel, telling me there was a better place in the afterlife than it was on earth."

Debbie spoke to the press: "Agnes Moorehead was known as a character actress. She could never really be typed. Her work ranged from comedy to tragedy, from portrayals of young girls to old ladies, from heroines to villains, parts she played with conviction and artistry. Ironically, after all that, her fate was to have a part on *Bewitched* become her most watched role."

"Whatever her legacy, I know this: She will be missed, not only by me, but by dozens of her friends. Her death is a blow to our hearts."

***

"It was time for *The Gunfight at the O.K. Corral* between Harry Karl and me," Debbie said. "Our estates had to be settled even though he'd squandered all our millions."

To confront her, he'd hired one of the most celebrated divorce lawyers in Hollywood, Albert Crowley. While Karl glared at her, Crowley read her husband's demands: "Everything is to be split in half, and that includes all the debts, especially that big loan held by the State Street Bank in Boston."

In Spain, during the dinner she'd shared with Gregory Peters, her husband's business partner, she had learned that the debt that Karl owed Peters had, with interest included, swelled to $2 million. Karl also owed multiple other millions to banks for mortgages he'd taken out on his shoe stores.

Her attorney suggested that she and Karl declare bankruptcy, but she stubbornly refused. "I was raised by my daddy to pay your debts, and I intend to, come hell or high water."

She later said, "Bankruptcy in 1973 was a disgrace. But in time it became fashionable. Even a future President of the United States once filed for bankruptcy to escape the massive debt from his Atlantic City casinos. "

Speaking for himself, and not through his lawyers, Karl presented his own demands. "I want fifty percent of everything you earned from *Irene*. I've talked it over with Albert here, and he agrees that's only fair. I also want ten percent of all your future earnings, a typical agent's fee. In addition, I'm seeking $25,000 a year in alimony until 1978."

At that time, she was already paying between $10,000 and $12,000 a week to the Boston bank, based on her having co-signed the original loan application.

After hearing his demands, Debbie rose to her feet and glared at Karl. "You're a disgusting reptile," she shouted at him. "You've stolen everything I have and gambled it away. Is there no end to your greed? Let's see what a divorce court judge has to say about this extortion of a penniless woman trying to support her children!"

At the divorce hearing, the judge sided with Debbie, ruling that none of her future earnings could be attached by Karl. However, she was still responsible for $2 million in debts, since she'd co-signed several of Karl's loan applications.

In the weeks ahead, she watched everything she owned—with the exception of the props she'd personally acquired at an MGM auction—seized by creditors. "Gregory Peters got our home on Greenway Drive for $450,000 and later sold it for $7 million. The only piece of jewelry I'd saved from that thief Karl, a large diamond ring, went for $75,000. It had cost $200,000."

"In the weeks ahead, my life evoked one of the opening scenes from *Sunset Blvd*. William Holden, as Joe Gillis, is fleeing two auto salesmen who want to repossess his car for back payments. The same thing happened to me. Two men arrived and seized my emerald green Rolls-Royce."

"I still had my old Cadillac, and when I found myself without a home, I slept in the back seat a few times before I could find lodgings," she said. "But then, a different set of men arrived and took the Cadillac too."

Bob Fallon came to her rescue, locating a $1,500, 1968 secondhand Chevrolet for her.

"The morning after I got it, I found it under the tree where I'd parked it. It was covered with bird droppings. From then on, Bob called it 'The Bird Turd Car.'"

During her final hour at the house on Greenway Drive, Debbie took a farewell stroll through the property, the setting for so many unhappy memories. "It would be suitable as a post office in any large American town. It had things a normal house doesn't have—eight little pink refrigerators, for example, just in case Snow White and the Seven Dwarfs showed up."

"Everything I had was gone except for my MGM props," she said. "The sun had set on my *Titanic*, except it went down in the Pacific Ocean, not the Atlantic. I think I'll entitle my memoirs, *We Used to Live in Beverly Hills*."

"In time, Julie Andrews and Blake Edwards bought the house," Debbie said. "I'd vacated it in such haste, I left valuable papers in a downstairs storage room and a closet full of linens. Mary Poppins returned all my stuff. When she did, I congratulated her for stealing my Oscar. The Academy obviously went for her Mary Poppins instead of my Molly Brown."

[On July 29, 1982, Harry Karl checked into the Cedars Sinai Medical Center in Los Angeles. In failing health, his body was deteriorating rapidly. He underwent heart bypass surgery on August 6 and died the following night at the age of sixty-eight. His survivors included his son Harrison (Bo) and three daughters, Judie, Denice, and Tina.

Debbie did not attend the funeral.]

ON THE ROAD WITH ANOTHER SHOW

THE EL PASO TOMBOY, NOW A FADED MOVIE STAR, STRUTS ACROSS THE STAGE

AGAIN & AGAIN & AGAIN

"THE LEGS ARE THE LAST TO GO."

CARRIE'S COMING OF AGE IN THE 70S WITH THE

DRUGGED-OUT GLITTERATI

FREDDIE MERCURY & DAVID BOWIE

SEX, DRUGS, & ROCK 'N ROLL: "WHAT'S LOVE GOT TO DO WITH IT?"

David Bowie (left) was already a world-class legend when the teenaged Carrie entered his life.

He had astonished the entertainment industry with his androgynous persona and his flamboyant outfits, some of which were ridiculed in the press as "swish drag."

"Freddie Mercury (right) had an apt last name," Carrie said after their first night together.

The leading light of *Queen*, he was an extroverted and flamboyant showman on stage. In private, he suffered through hellish depths of heartbreak and tragedy, haunted by nightmarish fears.

"Fortunately, in 1974, there was plenty of work for an aging El Paso cowgirl like me," Debbie said, joking that "Although a 'relic' of the 1950s, I was still a name to an older crowd, who flocked to the casinos to lose their money—shades of Harry Karl. When I wore a beautiful gown and lots of makeup, I was still hit upon. I always wore gowns slit up to my crotch—after all, the legs are the last to go."

"Vegas had become the burial ground of stars of yesterday," she said. "I was always having a reunion with some star whom I had known casually and, like me, had lived a brighter day."

Vegas memories came flooding back, all lost in the stardust of yesterday," she said. "I remember Mitzi Gaynor at the Versailles Room, still sexy, still seductive, with all that brassy show-biz pizzazz. She'd go on to play to audiences as long as there was someone out there. I decided to make her my role model and to carry on until I could no longer sell a ticket."

"After I got rid of that bank robber and jewel thief, Harry Karl, I was transformed into *The Gay Divorcée*," Debbie asserted. "Is there a nobody around who remembers that vintage film?"

She was referring to the 1934 movie starring Fred Astaire and Ginger Rogers.

"To tell the truth, my life wasn't all that gay," she said. "It had its low points: a dead body decomposing in the apartment of my stepdaughter; children hooked on drugs; my teenage son screwing around with a much older woman; a dying Joan Crawford; and, lest we forget, a thing called *Star Wars*. After that, and forever more, I became known as 'The Mother of Princess Leia.'"

"Dinah Shore might show up at the Landmark Theatre, packing 'em in. She never aged, wearing fabulous gowns and still every inch a star. She could get the most out of a song, especially when she sang that wistful, lovely 'Windmills of Your Mind.'"

"And Elvis, there was always Elvis. After his show, we'd get together for a few laughs. He no longer made passes at me, since I was not sixteen anymore, and he liked 'em young. Natalie Wood told me I didn't miss out on much. The gyrator still could put on a pair of 'Blue Suede Shoes' and shake that hillbilly pecker (his words) of his before a screaming pack of girls."

"Even my former rival, Jane Powell, put together a Vegas act. A review claimed she looked just as good as she did when she stepped from a soundstage at MGM. In flowing chiffon, her favorite, she still had that tantalizing vocal range, and this dazzling radiance, especially when she sang 'I'll Never Fall in Love Again.'"

"One night, I had dinner with Donald O'Connor," Debbie said, "My old buddy from *Singin' in the Rain*. We were younger then. I was innocent. Donald was never innocent. I think he started chasing pussy at age seven."

"I was still doing my Mae West impressions," Debbie said: "Guess what? Diamond 'Lil herself showed up one night. She was in town rehearsing her act with her 'Zodiache-Men.' She cast them only if they had big cocks."

"Lots of rumors about future acts were printed in the local rags," Debbie said. "Many were announced, but never made it from Los Angeles to the desert. Natalie Wood was slated to come into Vegas with a musical. Bette Davis was reported to be arriving to perform in a theatrical adaptation of Gore Vidal's *Myra Breckenridge* (1970). Bette would take the role that Mae West essayed on the screen. Mae wasn't happy about that, but it never came to town."

The wildest rumor of all was that Marlon Brando had signed to bring *A Streetcar Named Desire* to Vegas, with him resurrecting the part he's played on Broadway back in the days when I was a virgin. I'd believe that only when I saw it."

"I read that Elizabeth Taylor was in town for some fun and games, perhaps with Warren Beatty, although I'm not sure. That duo appeared in the disaster, *The Only Game in Town* (1970), where Elizabeth played an overweight showgirl. What a mistake that was! She told reporters that she was heading for Broadway to star in *The Devil and the Good God*—and that it would be her swan song. Not bloody likely!"

In the summer of 1974, Debbie, like a gypsy caravan, loaded up her self-styled "flotsam and jetsam" and flew to London. She'd been booked for a three-week gig at the Palladium in the heart of the West End's theatre district. She'd have to perform two shows a night. "It was standing room only. Everybody in London came to see it—everyone except the Queen. I don't have a clue as to what she was up to."

Debbie gave Carrie a star solo spot, and her every performance was followed with a standing ovation. Even Carrie's mother gave her a rave review: "My little girl—now big girl—was like an American Edith Piaf…well, not quite, but she was really good, and the audiences loved her. I often stood in the wings crying when she was on stage. Why was I doing that? Pride for my daughter? Or else the realization that the show business torch had passed?"

A review in *The London Times* claimed, "Debbie Reynolds is the gold of vaudeville, Carrie Fisher the platinum of vaudeville."

"What could I say after reading

411

that?" Debbie asked. "I told Rudy Render to get me a vodka and to make it a double."

At the age of thirteen, Carrie had first appeared on stage with Debbie. Now she was seventeen and on the road to stardom. "Frankly, I think mother was jealous. Right from the beginning, she sabotaged my first big offer."

Agents were so impressed with her performance that they came backstage and offered to sign her for a nightclub act of her own. One of the agents had been the power behind igniting the career of Anthony Newley, the second husband of Joan Collins.

The agent told Carrie that he wanted her to replicate the success of Liza Minnelli, who went from being the daughter of Judy Garland to becoming a star in her own right. When Debbie heard about the offer, she stubbornly refused to allow her daughter to enter into negotiations with the London agents.

"You're jealous that I might become a bigger star than you," Carrie shouted at her before storming out of her dressing room.

Debbie, however, had a different plan for Carrie, wanting her to try to get "appointed" (as the British called it) to the Royal Central School of Speech and Drama. Founded in 1906, it had a list of distinguished alumni, members of whom included Laurence Olivier, Vanessa Redgrave, Judi Dench, and Harold Pinter. After being called back twice for auditions, Carrie was accepted, but then she shocked Debbie by refusing to enroll.

She later said that when she countermanded her daughter and demanded that Carrie attend, "We staged the battle royal. Much of our confrontational dialogue could have been ripped from the pages of the script for that movie Elizabeth Taylor made with Richard Burton, *Who's Afraid of Virginia Wolff?*."

Debbie finally prevailed, although it caused a great strain in their relationship.

"I'm glad mother won out," Carrie said, later. "The time I spent in London was the most memorable of my life. At long last, I was an adult, partaking of all the pleasures that entailed. I even developed an English accent and could do a dead-on impression of

Debbie and Carrie's joint stage performances were perhaps inspired by, or a reaction to, the entertainment industry's other most famous mother/daughter team, Minnelli and Garland, shown here singing "Happy Days/Get Happy" at the London Palladium in November 1964.

Princess Margaret."

"One night," Carrie continued, "I got Tom Jones' private phone number and, imitating Margaret, called him. I said, 'Mr. Jones, I saw you on stage. I'm very impressed with that big package I saw in your skin-tight pants, and I want you to come over to Kensington Palace at midnight so we can get better acquainted.' I don't know if Tom showed up for that or not."

***

Bright Lights
Starring Carrie Fisher and Debbie Reynolds

After their show's finale one night at the London Palladium, Carrie brought her father, Eddie Fisher, backstage for a reunion with Debbie in her dressing room. He found her sitting at her makeup table, removing her "stage war paint" (her words).

She barely glanced up at the man Carrie had invited in to see her. "At first, it didn't register that this was the man I was once married to, the father of my children," Debbie said. "I hadn't seen Eddie in years. He looked like an old, beaten-down man, not my *Bundle of Joy* co-star from the mid-1950s."

Appearing on stage together, the mother/daughter act of "Carrie and Debbie" was a big hit with audiences.

"I could sing better than Debbie, but even at her age, she had better 'gams' than I did, and she never minded putting them on display. She kept showing those dynamite legs of her until she turned 80."

"Instead of hatred and resentment of him for his desertion of me and his children, I felt sorry for him in a way. Maybe marriage to three stars had done him in."

[She was referring to herself, Elizabeth Taylor, and Connie Stevens, his most recent wife. He'd wed Stevens in 1967 and divorced two years later.]

Debbie had been humiliated when he'd dumped her for Elizabeth, and he'd been even more humiliated when Elizabeth had dumped him. That had happened in Rome during the filming of *Cleopatra* (1963), starring Richard Burton. "Elizabeth obviously made the more virile, more manly choice," Debbie had said at the time.

Since Carrie wanted her to, Debbie reluctantly agreed to invite Fisher to her suites at the Savoy for a late supper, with the hope that Ray, Minnie, and Todd had retired for the night. Carrie had already sustained a reunion with Fisher that afternoon, and she bowed out, claiming that she was meeting friends later. That left Debbie alone with her former husband.

Although she already knew quite a bit about his ill-fated marriage to Eliz-

413

abeth Taylor *[it had morphed into a media circus]*, she knew less about his marriage to Connie Stevens, with whom he had two girls, Josely and Tricia, each a future actress.

Debbie hadn't really followed Stevens' career as either a singer or an actress. She knew that in 1960, she'd scored a big hit with her recording of "Sixteen Reasons." She'd also seen two of her movies, *Parrish* (1961) with her co-star, Troy Donahue, and *Susan Slade* (1962) in which she'd played an unwed mother. Stevens was mainly known to the greater American public for her inclusion as the character of Cricket Blad in the hit TV series *Hawaiian Eye* (1959-63).

"My marriage to Connie ended before it had begun," he said. "I would never have married her, but I learned she was pregnant."

"You certainly spent a lot of time divorcing Elizabeth," Debbie said. "I assume that held up your marriage to Connie?"

"I was holding out for a million-dollar settlement which I felt I was entitled to. I didn't get it but ended up with half a million. God, there have been so many rumors, only a few of them flattering," he said. "One had me seducing Elizabeth twelve times a day."

"I can certainly vouch that that wasn't true," she said.

"Yes, I had sex with her a hell of a lot more than I did with you, but hardly twelve times a day. I'm not that much of a stud."

"The press has been rough on you," she said.

"The *Los Angeles Times* wrote that it became a blood sport to tell Eddie Fisher jokes at Hollywood parties," he said. "Deejays liked to play my song, 'Call Me Irresponsible.' *Silver Screen* came out with an article headlined WHAT LIZ KNOWS ABOUT EDDIE AS A LOVER THAT CONNIE FOUND OUT TOO LATE. It suggested that I made a better lover than a husband."

"I'm sorry to hear about your third divorce," she said, even though she suspected he didn't want to talk about it.

"I'm sorry to hear about your second divorce," he said. "I understand Harry Karl cleaned you out, even stealing the diamond ring I gave you. At least that's the way Carrie tells it."

"She's absolutely right," Debbie answered. "But I didn't want to declare bankruptcy. I'm too proud for that."

"That's a pride I can't afford," he said. "I guess you read that in 1970, I declared bankruptcy. After Elizabeth kicked me out, my career revived for a brief interim in the mid-60s, but now it's almost over. By the end of the '60s, my throat was more gold-plated than gold. My gigs in Vegas dried up, but I heard you can still pack 'em in along the Strip. Everybody says I've become a recluse. One thing I try to keep active, though: I always have a woman with me, even if I have to pay for it."

"Are you still on drugs?" she asked. "Still flying in Dr. Needles?"

[Her reference was to Dr. Max Jacobson.]

"For years it was Max, Max, Max, Max," he said. "But that's over now, although for a while I turned to his son for injections. He's also a doctor. I came to know that Max was a killer with a needle."

"For a long time, I considered Jacobson a hero after he injected JFK with some juice so that he could confront Khrushchev in Vienna."

"Our relationship ended one night at the Diplomat Hotel in Miami Beach. He wanted to inject me in my solar plexus, and I bolted. 'Like hell,' I told him, and ordered him out of my suite."

"There are other doctors, other drugs," he said. "I can get all the drugs I need...or don't need as the case may be. I really slipped up badly one afternoon when I flew into San Juan with drugs in my luggage. Usually, the customs men just waved me through—but not that afternoon."

"They arrested me and hauled me into this small room where I was forced to strip naked," he said. "There were two guys, one of whom inspected my asshole to see if I had stuffed any drugs up there. Before they were done with me, at least a dozen other men from customs came in to get a look at me. One of them admitted why they were there: They wanted to see what kind of dick it took to satisfy Elizabeth Taylor."

"How humiliating," she said. By now, she'd heard enough, and it was time to end the supper. She needed her sleep but couldn't resist a final jab: "Let's face it: You were a lousy lover and a lousy father."

"I take that as a signal for me to leave," he said. "Thanks for the supper and for being such a good mother to our kids."

"You're welcome," she said. "No trouble at all." Then she had reverted to her El Paso accent, the one she'd had as a teenager in Texas. "Now don't you go and make yourself no stranger."

She shut the door behind him firmly, not forcefully. Eddie Fisher was yesterday. She had today to think about.

After leaving the Savoy, Fisher later recalled, "I felt worse than before. Debbie always made me feel more guilty than I actually felt. She made me ask myself what kind of man I was. I wanted to change for the better, but somehow, I couldn't. I wanted Carrie and Todd to be proud of their father, but I knew they weren't. What was there to be proud of?"

"I also suspected I was a bad father to Joely and Tricia, the kids I had with Connie. I was heading for a time when I would have almost no contact with my children, and I was afraid they would see what their father had become. I didn't want to be judged!"

On looking back, Fisher said, "I'd been the golden *boychik* of the 1950s, the dimpled Philly troubadour, but I was declared a war criminal of domesticity when I bolted from Debbie's dollhouse."

Near the end of his life, when Fisher was asked what he'd learned from his five marriages, he answered: "Don't marry Debbie Reynolds." When he was asked about Taylor, he said, "She had the face of an angel and the morals of a truck driver."

***

Bianca Jagger, the first wife of Mick Jagger (The Rolling Stones), visited the London Palladium to catch Debbie and Carrie's mother / daughter performance. When it was over, the Nicaragua-born actress came backstage to congratulate them.

She invited them to a party, that Saturday afternoon, at the townhouse she shared with Jagger, with whom she'd been married for almost four years. [*She later reported, "My marriage ended on my wedding day."*]

When Todd, only sixteen years old at the time, heard about the party, he wanted to come along, too.

After the curtain went down at the Palladium, Debbie, Carrie, and Todd headed for the party, which was already in full swing.

Mick Jagger warmly greeted her downstairs in the townhouse's foyer, hugging and kissing her. She introduced him to her children. Noting their ages, he called her aside and whispered, "Better keep the kids downstairs. A lot of shit is going on upstairs, where I've placed bowls of coke. My guests…how shall I say this? They indulge in adult pleasures."

"Will do," Debbie promised. "I don't want them to grow up too soon!"

Carrie and Todd seemed thrilled to meet members of the Rolling Stones [*Keith Richards, Ian Stewart, Charlie Watts, and Bill Wyman*]. Bianca and one of the members of the band cautioned Debbie about the sexual dramas being played out upstairs.

She already knew some of the party's guests from Hollywood, and had a reunion with her former co-star, Tony Curtis. Another visitor from Hollywood, Ryan O'Neal, allegedly flirted with Debbie, although Mick denied it. "Carrie would have been more his speed."

Debbie worked the room and was seen chatting with Elliott Gould, Rod Stewart, Lou Reed, Ringo and Maureen Starr, Sonny Bono, Jeff Beck, Dudley Moore, Peter Cooke, and Britt Ekland. She also spent part of the evening in a "huddle" with Cass Elliot, who had achieved fame as the key singer with "The Mamas and the Papas."

"She spoke to me about her life, focusing on disappointments and her bad health, which largely seemed to be caused by her gross poundage," Debbie said. "She sounded like some performer at the end of her life and on her death bed, although she

"All women are groupies," Mick Jagger told Debbie. "There's really no reason to have women on tour unless they've got a job to do. The only other reason is to fuck. Perhaps you'll let Carrie tour with us?"

416

was nearly ten years younger than me."

Elliot told Debbie that she'd lost out on the stage role of Miss Marmelstein on Broadway in 1963 for *I Can Get It For You Wholesale.* The director had preferred a fast-emerging actress in her early twenties at the time: Barbra Streisand.

"One day I was walking by this construction site, and I was hit on the head by some copper tubing," Elliot told Debbie. "It increased my vocal range by three notes, and that sounds ridiculous, but it's no shit."

Debbie told her that two of her favorite recordings were "California Dreaming" and "Dream a Little Dream for Me."

Both of them discussed giving solo performances in Las Vegas. Like Debbie, Elliot, too, had been offered $40,000 a week.

"I went on a crash diet," Elliot said. "Lost one hundred of my three hundred pounds. Then I went on a diet of thick cream and butter pecan ice cream and gained back fifty. I also suffered throat problems. My opening night in Vegas was a disaster. I had no voice…well, almost no voice. I embarrassed myself in front of Sammy Davis, Jr., Liza Minnelli, Mia Farrow, Joan Baez, Peter Lawford, and Jimi Hendrix. I was running a high fever and ended up in the hospital."

"Like your former husband, Eddie Fisher, I'm an addict, a closeted junkie. One of the reasons I like London is that you can go into a drugstore and get pharmaceutical heroin. Coke is great, and I'm on intimate speaking terms with Miss Dilaudid, Mr. Demerol, and Madam Percodan."

Mama Cass's gig had preceded Debbie's at the Palladium, but, unlike Debbie, she had often appeared before rows of empty seats.

By 2AM, Todd and Carrie left the party, each of them with someone they had met and picked up there. Debbie was unaware that they had left, and when she realized they were gone, she was "pissed off" that they didn't tell her goodbye or where they were going.

Within the hour, Keith Richards was removed from the townhouse on a stretcher by two men from a medical team. He was said to have overdosed upstairs.

At around 3AM, Mama Cass left the party alone. "I felt sorry for her, so alone and in such bad health," Debbie said.

She, too, had left alone and was asleep in her suite at the Savoy before dawn. She waited and waited for Todd and Carrie, but they hadn't

The Mamas and the Papas in 1967. Cass Elliot, the group's best singer, hovers, in psychedelic cacophony, over the other members of her group.

417

returned by the time she fell asleep.

She woke up around 10AM, when a room service waiter served her breakfast, which she had pre-ordered. She called for the maid, who informed her that a woman was asleep and with Todd in her son's room. Apparently, Carrie had returned to their suite alone and very late. She was asleep in another bedroom.

When the newspapers arrived, Debbie was shocked to read that Mama Cass, who was 32 years old at the time, had died in an apartment near Shepherd's Market. The apartment belonged to Harry Nilsson, the singer and songwriter.

In the medical reports associated with her death, a London pathologist asserted that "Miss Elliot weighed twice what she should have. One of heart muscles had turned to fat."

In the wake of her death, an urban legend arose that she had choked to death either on a ham sandwich or on her own vomit, or both, but no food was found in her windpipe.

Ironically, in 1978, Keith Moon, drummer for *The Who?*, died in the same bedroom of the same apartment. He, too, was only 32.

***

"Carrie was growing up before my eyes," Debbie said. "And I soon noticed that the same thing was happening to my sixteen-year-old son, Todd. At a party at the home of Mick Jagger, he'd met this woman in her thirties. Her name was Elizabeth. (The Fisher father and son had this thing for women called Elizabeth.) She must have been in her thirties, but she and my son began an affair that lasted throughout his time in London."

"We were staying in suites at the Savoy, and Elizabeth moved in with us. My mother, Minnie, objected almost violently, but there was nothing she could do."

"As for my dad, Ray, he was having a good time checking out the London showgirls," she said. "He even ended up on the frontpage of one newspaper staring down into the bosom of Bianca Jagger."

Elizabeth owned several restaurants in London, and Todd was not just her appetizer, but her main course, too. Debbie sometimes noticed that after any of his many nights with her, he appeared the next morning looking pale, but smiling.

"I'm only guessing here, but from the sounds coming from Todd's bedroom, I gathered he was learning about both oral and vaginal sex."

"Todd and I returned to Hollywood, but Carrie established a new life for herself in London. She never told her own story—only parts of it. It was pieced together from some of the older guys and dolls she hung out with. She had affairs there with some big-name stars."

418

***

At the end of Debbie's gig in London, Carrie remained there for another 18 months, enrolled as a student in the Central School of Speech and Drama. "It prepared me for the worldwide stardom that was about to descend upon me."

Todd, however, returned to Los Angeles with Debbie where he was graduated from Beverly Hills High School in 1976, along with a number of other boys and girls, many the offspring of stars like himself.

After graduation, he enrolled in the Southern California Institute of Architecture in Los Angeles. It was during Carrie's exile in London that Debbie began to fear, "I've lost my daughter, perhaps forever. She never calls or writes."

Once, eager for a reunion with Carrie, Debbie flew to London to stay with her in her flat. "Carrie virtually ignored me," Debbie said. "No mother-daughter talks. Once she had friends in from her drama class but asked me to stay in my bedroom for the duration of the party. Finally, I could take it no more, and I flew back to California."

Before she left for the airport, Carrie told her, "please don't come back. Stay out of my life."

***

The party she attended with Debbie at Mick Jagger's townhouse marked a turning point in Carrie's life. She made contacts that led to her hanging out with some of the hippest Londoners in town, mostly those in show business, especially music.

She revealed few details of her London sojourn, but those who met and befriended her during that time have, over the years, provided certain clues.

Somehow, for an interlude, she entered the world of the charismatic and dynamic singer, Freddie Mercury, who—although he was mostly gay—managed to sustain a few intimate relationships with women. The singer/songwriter, who was of Parsi descent, had been born in 1946 in the sultanate of Zanzibar (now Tanzania). *[Parsees are members of a well-defined community, in India, of the Iranian prophet Zoroaster.]*

Carrie became enchanted with him, even though he told her he'd never seen one of Debbie's movies, and that he thought Eddie Fisher as a singer "was a pile of lovesick mush."

She asked why he'd chosen the name *Queen*. "When I first heard the name, I thought it referred to a bunch of drag queens."

"I'm aware of that, of course, but I liked the sound of *Queen*—so regal, so splendid, so strong, so immediate."

419

"Whether you go for it or not, it's my own piss-take," he said. By hanging out with him, she was learning a new vocabulary.

In addition to an endless parade of boys and young men on the side, Mercury occasionally seduced a young woman and had a long-time relationship with Mary Austin, who was two years older than Carrie. Austin managed a shopping outlet called Biba Boutique, which had enjoyed its heyday in London during "The Swinging Sixties." Mercury referred to Austin as "my lover and soul-mate."

Carrie said she didn't want to interfere with his ongoing love affair, but he dismissed her concerns. "A bloke like me needs extra quim on the side." Evidently, she'd already figured out what "quim" meant.

During her short involvement with Mercury, she was fascinated with his wardrobe, especially his skin-tight, black-spangled "catsuit," for which the fingernails of one of his hands (the one that was sheathed in silver chainmail) had been lacquered in black. The sound of his voice thrilled her during his appearances at the Marquee, a popular performance space in the center of London. Jagger and the Rolling Stones had also performed at the club.

As described by biographer David Bret, "Mercury's voice had a wide range, escalating within a few bars from a deep, throaty 'rock-growl' to a tender, vibrant tenor, then on to a high-pitched, almost perfect *coloratura*, pure and crystalline in the upper reaches."

She'd been surprised at the way Mercury thrust his crotch forward in front of screaming audiences of young women and gay men. She soon became familiar with that crotch. He even indulged in "penis talk" with her, explaining that most young men in England had their foreskins intact, which made the head of the penis more sensitive during sex. "Of course, I know your father is Jewish, so his dick must have been mutilated."

Although she was hanging out at the time with a lot of cutting-edge young musicians, she protested, "I'm no god damn groupie, not the kind of girl you haul back to your hotel room, throw a fuck job to, and then rush out the door while you're still zipping up your pants."

She asserted that Mercury had a particular fetish for the 1950 film noir, *Sunset Blvd.* In it, Gloria Swanson played a has-been silent film star, Norma Desmond, who moves a gigolo into her life and later shoots him in the back."

In 1970, in collaboration with guitarist Brian May and drummer Roger Taylor, Freddie Mercury formed the rock band known as *Queen*. As a songwriter, he wrote numerous hits for the group, including "Killer Queen" and "Crazy Little Thing Called Love."

In time, he would become known as one of the greatest singers in the history of popular music.

"Freddie said he owned the gown that Swanson wore in the closing scene of that movie, when she descends the steps at the murder house. I didn't know if the gown was authentic or not, but he made me up to look like Norma Desmond, and even had me deliver her final lines."

"I wanted boyfriends, not husband material," Carrie told her friends. "There is no way I'd become a rock 'n roll wife. Frank Sinatra once warned my mother not to marry a singer. Good advice. If I get married one day, you can bet your left ball it won't be to a god damn crooner."

After Mercury went on tour to music venues that included the United States, she never heard from him again. "I was told that in every city he visited, he checked out the gay scene," she said. "An interview he gave in Ohio told me how much he'd changed."

In Ohio, reporter David Hancock had visited Mercury's hotel suite to interview him for *Record Popswop*.

"I found him in his hotel bedroom lying on a pile of cushions," Hancock said. "He reminded me of a sultan in some *Arabian Nights* fantasy. He was tended to by three muscled young men in transparent jockstraps. They were serving him drinks, even lighting his cigarettes."

"I expect to be waited on hand and foot, dear," he told Hancock. "Of course, the boys here have other duties, but we don't need to go into that."

When the article came out in the magazine, it was headlined: FREDDIE MERCURY THE QUICKSILVER GIRL.

"Freddie did leave me with a motto that helped me get through some of the darker decades of my life," Carrie said.

He'd once told her, "I am what I am, so is a stone. Those that don't like me can leave me alone."

The photo above depicts Gloria Swanson as the delusional has-been, Norma Desmond, in the classic *film noir*, released in 1950, *Sunset Blvd.*

Within the context of that film, she delivered some of the most iconic and "dementedly campy" lines in the history of film, words that Freddie Mercury asked Carrie to repeat while flamboyantly dressed in garments that might have once been worn by (or at least evoked) Swanson herself.

According to Carrie, here's a transcript of the bone-chilling speech that Mercury asked her to replicate, perhaps when both of them were high:

NORMA, descending the steps of her Hollywood mansion, as medics prepare her immediate transfer to an insane asylum:

"I just want to tell you how happy I am to be back in the studio, making a picture. I promise you I'll never desert you again, because after *Salome*, we'll make another picture, and then another, and then another!"

" You see, this is my life. There's nothing else, just us, and the camera, and those wonderful people out there in the dark."

"All right, Mr. DeMille, I'm ready for my closeup."

"He moved on and so did I," Carrie said. "In London, another singer entered my life. These men were but stepping stones to what I was becoming, except I didn't know what I wanted to be. Certainly not a pale imitation of Debbie Reynolds."

***

Soon after Debbie's return from London to Los Angeles, she had to fly to Dallas. In her native Texas, she was slated to star in *Irene,* her Broadway hit. "I could act the part in my sleep by now," she said.

At the time of her divorce from Harry Karl, she had moved her stepdaughter, Tina, out of her house, finding and paying for the apartment she'd live in. Debbie had hoped that this would free her from her troubled stepdaughter and her problems.

But that was not to be.

Tina had crashed the car Debbie had bought for her at the junction of Wilshire and Westwood Boulevards. At the age of eighteen, she had miraculously survived without serious injury.

Months after that crisis, Tina called Debbie in Dallas and asked if she could fly there for a visit. Although suspicious, Debbie agreed, fearing that the real reason for her visit was to announce that she was pregnant. It later became clear that pregnancy wasn't a factor in the reason for Tina's visit, and for three days, she acted uncharacteristically like a dutiful daughter.

During Tina's stay, she occupied one of the bedrooms in Debbie's suite. At around 3:30AM, an emergency call came in from Los Angeles. It was Tina's brother, Harrison (Bo). A sleepy Debbie heard him blurt out: "There's a corpse, all black, rotting in Tina's apartment. The Beverly Hills Police found it and they're looking for Tina to question her. Maybe she murdered the girl?"

Debbie told her stepson that she'd call him back. Rushing into the bedroom next door, she shook Tina awake. "You're wanted by the police in Beverly Hills," she shouted at her. "It seems you left a corpse in your living room!"

Tina began screaming hysterically until Debbie calmed her down and got her version of the story.

"I wasn't at home," she said. "I was in London visiting Carrie. While I was away, I let a friend use my apartment, and he threw a big party. Lots of drugs. It seemed that the girl overdosed and died. Everybody fled. When I got back from England, I just looked in through the window and saw the body. I was afraid to go inside. I called you, and here I am."

"How thoughtful of you," Debbie said sarcastically, "to pay me a visit at this time."

Tina flew back to Los Angeles and, with an attorney Debbie had hired, met with the police. After an interrogation that established that she'd been in London at the time of the girl's death, she was released without any charges. Debbie then paid a contractor to repaint the apartment "and remove that horrible stench of death."

Rudy Render, to whom Debbie had confided, asked her why Tina hadn't turned to her father.

"Because he's completely worthless," Debbie said. "Besides, he probably has no money to give her."

More trouble awaited Debbie when she flew back to California. She learned that Harry Karl's mother, affectionately known as "Mama Rose," was barely surviving. Her son had gone to her, claiming that he feared for his life because of death threats from a member of the Mafia. He'd run up a large gambling debt and didn't have the money to pay for it. Mama Rose turned over her entire life's savings of $30,000. That left her completely broke. Debbie had to assume responsibility for her welfare, including paying for a part-time nurse, since the elderly woman was bed ridden.

"When I was in town, I visited her every week, watching her condition getting weaker and weaker," Debbie said. "One Saturday, when I came by for my weekly visit, I noticed that she was barely clinging to life. I phoned a doctor. Later, he took me outside her bedroom and told me she'd probably not last the night. She slipped into a coma."

Debbie didn't want to speak to Karl again, but phoned him and told him, "Get your ass over here. Mama Rose is dying."

"I can't," he said. "I have a bad back, and it's too painful for me to ride in a car."

Within a few hours, his mother was dead. At her bedside, Debbie had held her hand until she sighed her last breath. "That fucking bastard never showed up, not even for the funeral, which I had to pay for," Debbie said.

In the meantime, she had to find a place to live. All the vacant homes for rent in her old neighborhood were far too expensive, sometimes asking $5,000 a month or more. On Oakland Drive, in a less expensive section of Beverly Hills, she found a small house "tacky as hell." She rented it for $1,500 a month.

In the driveway of her new home, as she was unloading her clothing, a gunman suddenly appeared from the bushes, seemingly out of nowhere, and pointed a gun at her head. "Get into the fucking house or I'll shoot you!"

At that very moment, Bob Fallon, her lover, pulled into the driveway and got out. At first, he didn't realize it was a robbery. Then the gunmen pointed his weapon directly at Fallon, ordering both of them into the house.

In the living room, he demanded that Debbie and Fallon get down on their knees. Within minutes, a second gunman appeared, also pointing his pistol at them. When he heard noises from the kitchen, he rushed toward it, returning with Mary Douglas French, Debbie's African American housekeeper.

She got on her knees, too, screaming, "Please don't shoot. Don't kill me!"

"I'm not going to shoot you, sister," he said. "Only this rich white bitch if she doesn't turn over all her money and jewelry to me."

Fallon had $200 in his wallet, and Mary had $160, money that Debbie had provided to buy groceries. The second gunman raced up to Debbie's bedroom looking for jewelry. He returned with the fake gems that Debbie had used in her act impersonating Zsa Zsa Gabor and Mae West. Then he ordered her to empty her purse. It contained the remaining pieces of jewelry that Karl had not managed to steal: Only some pearls and two small diamond clips. She nonetheless managed to convince the gunman that they were also fake.

Before the gunmen left, they manhandled Debbie, Fallon, and Mary into a "powder room" with a toilet and a sink under the stairwell. It was all that the three of them could do to fit in.

"At any minute, we expected bullets to come through the door, killing all of us. We waited an hour, afraid to venture out. Finally, we did. The men had fled."

Mary got them two glasses of brandy, as Debbie and Fallon sat on the floor, discussing what had just happened. "This is a helluva way to begin life in a new home," Debbie said.

In about thirty minutes, Todd and his friend, "Zinc," pulled their car into the driveway. When they were inside, Debbie told them what had happened. "I knew that Zinc always carried a gun," she said. "If he and Todd had come in the last half hour, I bet there'd have been a gunfight like you see in the movies. TV stations across the country would be interrupting their regular broadcasting to announce that FILM STAR DEBBIE REYNOLDS MURDERED.

"What can I say? All of us missed the bullet and didn't make the front pages like another Charles Manson massacre."

***

Back when Debbie was still performing in *Irene* on Broadway, Jack Haley, Jr. came backstage to escort her to a late supper at Sardi's.

She'd been friends with him for years, admiring his talent as a film director, producer, writer, and a two-time Emmy Award winner. Later, he'd become the second husband (1974-79) of Liza Minnelli. A true Hollywood insider, Haley's celebrated father, Jack Haley Sr., had played the Tin Man in Judy Garland's *The Wizard of Oz* (1939).

Debbie was offered a role in his next picture, *That's Entertainment!* Set for release in 1974, it was a celebration of highlights of MGM musicals from the 1920s through the 1950s. Debbie would be one of the hosts, narrating and introducing the sequence of famous musical numbers. Her fellow hosts would include Elizabeth Taylor, James Stewart, Bing Crosby, Frank Sinatra, Gene Kelly, Fred Astaire, Mickey Rooney, Peter Lawford, Donald O'Connor, and—as a representative of Judy Garland—Liza Minnelli.

Whereas most of the host's narrating shots were filmed on MGM's decaying backlot (the part that hadn't yet been sold off), Debbie's segment was shot backstage at the Minskoff Theatre on Broadway.

She defined the movie as "a love letter to film history. I was taken out of mothballs and flashed on the screen singing 'Aba Daba Honeymoon' with Carleton Carpenter in *Two Weeks with Love* from 1950," she said. Also included in the anthology was her schtick from *Three Little Words* (also 1950), in which she hoofed her way through "I Wanna Be Loved by You." *[In that one, in postproduction after its original filming, her voice had been dubbed by Helen Kane.]*

Her alltime favorite dance number was included in the anthology, too. It depicted Fred Astaire and Eleanor Powell in *Broadway Melody of 1940.* Together, they tap-danced to Cole Porter's "Begin the Beguine."

"A whole new generation got to see MGM's musical highlights, many of them filmed long before some members of the audience were born. The array of stars was dazzling—June Allyson, Astaire, Leslie Caron, Joan Crawford, Clark Gable, Ava Gardner, Garland, Cary Grant, Jean Harlow, Gene Kelly, Mario Lanza, Jeanette MacDonald, and Esther Williams."

The premiere of *That's Entertainment!* unfolded at Westwood, near the UCLA campus. There, Debbie experienced "one of the most embarrassing moments of my life at a party" during the reception that followed the screening.

On stage, Fred Astaire (then in his mid-seventies) with his sister, Adele, were gamely replicating a dance number they had premiered in the 1920s. "In the middle of their routine, my old pal, Donald O'Connor, staggered on stage and tried to join in their dance, much to Fred's horror," Debbie said.

From her seat in the audience, Edie Wasserman, the wife of Lew Wasserman, head of Universal, begged Debbie to lure him off the stage. At first, she resisted, but finally acquiesced. After climbing up onto the stage, she grabbed O'Connor's shoulder and spun him around in an attempt to get him to dance with her. That made him furious, and he tried to strike her, the blow narrowly missing her face.

By that time, two security guards had rushed onstage and carried O'Connor out of the theater, putting him into the back seat of a waiting limousine.

"It took Donald three years before he would speak to me again," Debbie said. "But I'm sure Fred and Adele were grateful. I came very close that night to getting into a fistfight on stage."

***

Any time Debbie was in New York, she always considered it imperative that she visit Joan Crawford, now in retirement there. "Joan had befriended me in my early days in Hollywood, and I was always grateful for that. Yes, she did have a sexual interest in me back then, but I brushed that aside and turned it into a lifelong and enduring bond. For the final years of her life, I either called on her personally or else spoke to her on the phone."

"Like Marlene Dietrich in Paris, Joan answered the phone, pretending to be her maid," Debbie said. "I always knew who it was. I called her 'Hazel the Maid' after that character Shirley Booth played in her hit TV series in the 1960s."

Debbie had been embarrassed for her friend when she'd gone to see her recent (and final) movie, *Trog*, released in 1970. In that one, Crawford's co-star had been a horrifying, eight-foot troglodyte (cave dweller).

Crawford told Debbie that she thought that at least one more great film role might materialize for her. "I didn't give up the movies, the movies gave me up. But there's always such a thing as a comeback. Gloria Swanson—as Norma Desmond in *Sunset Blvd.*—hated that word, preferring instead to simply call it, 'a return to pictures.'"

"In the early 1970s, before she became an almost total recluse, Joan and I, dressed to the nines, would make a spectacular entrance at the restaurant '21.' She always reserved a corner table on the second floor, which was strategically positioned so that all diners coming or going would notice her."

"Her last husband, Alfred Steele, the CEO of Pepsi-Cola, had died in his 50s and she was alone, her adopted children having long ago bolted from the nest."

In the spring of 1973, Debbie visited with Crawford shortly after the board of Pepsi dismissed her. She'd been drawing a salary of $40,000 annually, generating publicity for the company and appearing as a celebrity at the opening of new bottling plants. "After firing me, they gave me a pension of $50,000 a year, which was more than I'd been getting as a salary. But they took away all the fringe benefits, including a 24-hour limousine in Manhattan, free flights to anywhere aboard a private plane, and a personal secretary to help me with all the fan mail I received."

According to Debbie, "Sometimes, we'd just sit in her apartment and talk about lovers we'd known. Glenn Ford had screwed both of us."

"Her own life was greater and probably more tragic than any drama in which Joan had

"Joan Crawford and I were such different types on the screen," Debbie said. "But in so many ways, she was my favorite actress—so dramatic, so forceful, so camera-ready."

Here's Joan, as she appeared in the 1949 *Flamingo Road* as Lana Bellamy, a carnival dancer and hooker.

appeared. At times, she could get quite personal, even telling me of three actors she'd seduced who had the largest endowments in Hollywood—John Ireland, Steve Cochran, and Rock Hudson."

According to Debbie, Crawford said, "Among the men I married, Franchot Tone was the clear winner. He demanded that I pay daily homage to his ten-inch shaft. We nicknamed it 'The Jawbreaker.'"

"One night, Joan told me her greatest sexual thrill, and I was surprised," Debbie said.

"It was when Kirk Douglas played a boxer in *Champion* (1949)" Crawford confessed. "He'd shaved his armpits, and I found sucking them most delightful."

Crawford expressed great interest in Debbie's plans to open a museum built to exhibit the props she had acquired at the MGM auction. She promised Debbie that she would donate props or costumes she'd worn in several of her movies, including *Flamingo Road* (1949). "Perhaps you'll have a whole room devoted just to me."

Debbie told her that Jack Haley, Jr. was featuring both of them in *That's Entertainment!* "He's running that sequence of you singing "Got a Feelin' for You" from *The Hollywood Revue of 1929.*"

"Oh, my god!" was all that Crawford said.

Learning that Debbie needed financing, Crawford told her that she knew a real estate developer, Donald Trump, who might put up the money to open a museum—"either his own

When Joan Crawford saw this picture of herself snapped at a party with Rosalind Russell, she said, "I looked demented. After that humiliating photograph, I decided never to appear in public again. I went into seclusion."

Joan Crawford arranged a meeting between Debbie and Donald Trump, a real estate developer in Manhattan. She was seeking a financier to back her opening of a museum devoted to Hollywood memorabilia.

She later called the future President of the United States "a man of broken promises."

money or an investor's. I'll set up a luncheon for us," she promised.

She was not known for making idle promises. That Saturday afternoon, with the understanding that she'd be there, too, she arranged for Debbie to meet him at "21," which just happened to be his favorite restaurant.

At the time, Debbie was only vaguely aware of who Trump actually was. When she was introduced, she found him courteous and gracious. He paid acute attention as she shared her dream of opening a museum of Hollywood costumes and memorabilia.

At first, he didn't comment. When she'd finished her pitch, he delivered his own opinion: "I think it should be two Hollywood museums, one in the hometown itself and another in Las Vegas. I suggest an admission of $10 to $12 per head. You could have a spectacular opening. I'm sure all the stars of the Golden Age would come out of retirement to make personal appearances. And you'd make a great mistress of ceremonies."

"I noticed that he and Joan flirted in a harmless way, suggesting that at one time, they had been intimate," Debbie said. "He didn't flirt with me but treated me with great respect, like a business woman."

"When Donald left that afternoon, he promised he'd get back to me within the month after he made a few investigative phone calls," Debbie said. "When a lot of time went by and I hadn't heard from him, I phoned him. He told me something was cooking. After two more calls, his promises got a little more vague. During the fourth phone call, his secretary told me he was unavailable. She said that when something came through, 'He'll phone you in the future.' I know a kiss-off when I heard one."

[Years later, according to Debbie, "By the time Trump was elected president in November of 2016, my dream of a Hollywood museum had faded with the love affairs of yesterday. He did the impossible and became President of the United States. My daughter was very outspoken about Trump. 'Maybe he'll fuck the American people like he fucked you!' Carrie told me."]

***

At a party in London hosted by friends of Mick Jagger, Carrie met David Bowie, one of pop music's great chameleons, an artist whom she later referred to as "The Starman Who Fell to Earth."

In many of his acts, he'd bounce onto the stage wearing skintight, sci-fi outfits that included platform boots and glitter. More than any other entertainer, he virtually defined "glam rock" of the turbulent mid-1970s. Carrie had played his 1972 album, "The Rise and Fall of Ziggy Stardust" over and over.

At the time Bowie met Carrie, he was married to Angie Barnett, but he never discussed her during his on-and-off six-week interlude with Carrie.

She'd heard rumors that he was bisexual. Ava Charry, his former backup singer, later revealed, "I was the tasty filling in the cookie between Bowie and Jagger." Her phraseology, of course, suggested a three-way.

Bowie himself had told the press, "I am a closet heterosexual." Even the conservative *Wall Street Journal* wrote, "Bowie's outrageous characters have made it acceptable to come out as gay, bisexual, or different."

It was Bowie who truly introduced Carrie to the world of drugs. "He seemed to survive for days on brain-sizzling cocaine, drinking only milk for nourishment, nothing solid," she said.

"Some nights were torture for him as he sank into a cocaine pit of hell," she said. "He could be ruthless, mean, jealous. At other times, he conquered his demons and could be sweet and tender, wanting and needing love."

He told her, "I'm adored by millions of fans, but I feel at times like I'm all by myself out there on the edge of a cliff that is slowly giving way and that I'm about to fall into the raging waters below."

"Nights could be torture for Bowie, depending on his mood," she said. "He often sank into a deep depression and would cry for hours, bitter tears drifting into soft moans. He drank too much and took too many drugs. I took drugs with him. I have no one to blame but myself for my future addiction, but he certainly led me to the water to drink. I think we had sex. Or did I fantasize about it? At least we woke up in bed naked together."

"That was only on weekends," she said. "On weekdays, I had to get up early and go to school. He usually slept until noon. I learned to prepare his breakfast. He always preferred the same thing: black coffee and a fag. The first time he requested a fag, I thought he wanted me to procure a boy hustler for him, but Brits call a cigarette a fag."

"On many nights, he had nightmares, but on occasion, a sex dream," he said. "He woke me up one time and told me he'd just had a three-way with Chopin and his lover, the novelist, George Sand."

"He'd pull himself together for his music, a true professional," she said. "As a boy, he'd told his teachers that he wanted to be the British Elvis."

"I want my music to reflect my new-found freedom," he told her. "I've removed the shackles that bind me to earth. In the future, I'll explore a synthesized sound, create poems that reflect a wide range of emotions—wonder, sorrow, terror, and the absolute bewilderment of the mystery of life and death itself."

"Sometimes, he'd just disappear for two or three days and not call," she said. "When he did show up, he never explained where he'd gone. I knew he had another life, even a wife, whom he seemed to neglect."

"Once, we went on bikes to explore London, ending up in a section called Fulham," she said.

"We dropped into this seedy pub for truck drivers. David called them lorry drivers. I ordered apple

"I was drawn to David Bowie," Carrie said, "because he had made the world a better place for rebels, oddballs, and misfits like me."

cider. He stood next to a lorry driver who looked like Wallace Beery, that old-time movie star from the 1930s. Ignoring me, David chattered with him and bought him a lager. They had another lager and another lager. At some point, they had to empty their bladders and headed together toward the 'loo.' They were gone and gone, and I gave up waiting. Those two buggers must have slipped out the rear door into the alleyway and disappeared. I biked home alone. David showed up three nights later, and I never asked him where he'd gone, like I didn't know. We picked up where we'd left off, but it didn't last for long after that."

"David entered my life, but like a flash of lightning, he was soon gone," she said. "I would remember Ziggy Stardust for the rest of my life. When I left London, he was set to make a movie, *The Man Who Fell to Earth,* in which he would be cast as a lost space alien."

"Unknown to me at the time, I was getting ready to return to California where I, too, would be wandering into Outer Space, but I'd be a Princess."

***

A new musical, *Follies,* a nostalgic play about ex-showgirls, opened on Broadway on April 4, 1972, and instantly morphed into a smash hit. *Follies* was directed by Harold Prince and Michael Bennett. It dusted off some stars from yesteryear and brought them back, including Alexis Smith, Yvonne De Carlo, and Fifi d'Orsay.

The plot of *Follies,* as written by James Goldman, centered on a reunion of the long-ago cast of a girl revue evocative of the Ziegfeld Girls. They'd scheduled a rendezvous within a crumbling Broadway theater that's slated for demolition. The troupe had flourished between the wars with such standards as "Broadway Baby," "Too Many Mornings," "Could I Leave You?," and "Losing My Mind." Its most memorable song was De Carlo singing "I'm Still Here."

Producer Jerry Springer, along with his financial backers, acquired the film rights. He wanted to change the setting from Broadway to the sound stages of a fading movie studio just before its demise.

Springer envisioned an all-star cast, every member of whom had outlived their expiration date as a compelling public figure. Heading the roster would be "that scandal of yesterday," Elizabeth Taylor, otherwise known as *Cleopatra* (1963) and her Marc Antony (Richard Burton). *[It had been during the filming of that movie that Elizabeth had dumped Eddie Fisher.]*

Springer's picture would include the depiction of a reunion of two feuding stars, Bette Davis and Joan Crawford, who had (with many conflicts) co-starred together in the 1960 horror film, *What Ever Happened to Baby Jane?* Davis would be asked to sing, "I'm Still Here," and Crawford would be assigned the number, "Broadway Baby."

Springer called Debbie and asked if she'd joined the cast, and, without

430

reading the part, she immediately accepted. "She was thrilled with the offer and called me every god damn day, asking me when we'd be ready to start shooting," Springer said.

The cast would be rounded out by Gloria Swanson, who, as Norma Desmond, had achieved screen immortality in *Sunset Blvd* (1950). "I'll do it," Swanson told Springer, "but it seems all the scripts offered these days have me cast as a has-been."

Shelley Winters, Anne Jeffreys, and Fredric March (in a wheelchair) were also cast, the latter playing an aging producer.

When Debbie heard that Winters had been included, she phoned Springer. "Must you cast that bitch? She's a god damn horror." Memories of making *What's the Matter With Helen?* flooded her mind.

When she came to New York, Debbie spent the weekend with Crawford in her apartment. Although Crawford was excited to be cast in a picture again, she admitted that she was afraid to face the cameras. "Time, that relentless old bag, is unkind to us ladies who have known greater days. Would you believe it? I used to represent glamour on the screen."

"You still do," Debbie assured her.

Two weeks later, Springer phoned both stars and passed on the bad news. His major financial backers had pulled out, and without him, *Follies* would be too expensive to produce.

A week later, he phoned again with another offer, asking Crawford to appear for one night at Manhattan's Town Hall. It was for one of his "Legendary Women of the Screen" stage shows, which in the past had featured Myrna Loy, Sylvia Sidney, and Lana Turner. And whereas Jean Arthur had been slated to appear, too, five days before she was to go on, she bowed out. Springer had rushed to replace her with Crawford.

Reacting to the fast-changing roster of her fellow cast members, Crawford told Patricia Bosworth of *The New York Times:* "I still want to be an actress. I want to act. To quote from that song in *Follies,* 'I'm Still Here.'"

At Town Hall, every seat was sold out. When Crawford walked on stage, the audience, consisting mostly of gay men, poured out a standing ovation that lasted for ten minutes. When everyone quieted down, she blew kisses at them. "I never knew there was so much love."

At the end of the show, Debbie was waiting for her in the wings. Crawford fell into her arms, sobbing.

"You pulled it off, babe," Debbie assured her.

The elation was short-lived. Springer phoned once again and asked Crawford if she'd appear at a book party as a co-host with her longtime friend, Rosalind Russell.

The two women had known each other since the 1930s, and both of them had co-starred in the MGM classic, *The Women* (1939.

Crawford agreed and showed up wearing a brown wig, a red chiffon dress, and $100,000 worth of glittering diamonds. There, in the Rainbow Room at Rockefeller Center, she saw Russell and—although she was shocked by her appearance—she artfully concealed it.

Her friend's face was horribly bloated, as she'd been taking cortisone injections for her rheumatoid arthritis.

When she saw the tabloids the next day, Crawford phoned Debbie. "Rosalind and I looked horrible. I'm humiliated. You once told me a photographer snapped you when you were looking like Elsa Lanchester. I looked like *The Bride of Frankenstein* myself. I'll never make another public appearance. If that's what Joan Crawford, once known for her 'timeless glamour,' looks like today, the only way the world will see me in the future is in one of my old pictures."

***

Back in the United States after many months in London, Carrie wasn't certain what she wanted to do with the rest of her life. Unlike her mother Debbie, "who was always 'on,' day or night," she was not innately or single-mindedly devoted to a life as a performer.

According to Carrie, "Some movie stars discourage their children from going into show business, knowing what a rocky road it is. Not so Debbie. Even at her funeral, she'll rise from the coffin if somebody yells 'LIGHTS! CAMERA! ACTION!'"

To her daughter, Debbie continued to cite the example of Lisa Minnelli, who had become a star on her own, despite her status as Judy Garland's daughter. "Do you want to go through life known only as the daughter of Debbie Reynolds and Eddie Fisher?"

She arranged an appointment for Carrie with the boy wonder director, Terrence Malick, of Waco, Texas. His 1973 movie, *Badlands*, had been hailed in some quarters as "the most assured first film by an American since Orson Welles' *Citizen Kane.*"

He was hoping to repeat his success with *Days of Heaven*, which would not be released until 1978. Set against the dramatic scenic backdrop of a Midwestern wheat harvest at the turn of the 20th Century, the movie was the moody saga of a turbulent love triangle.

Initially, John Travolta had been designated as the male lead. Carrie had seen his hit TV sitcom, *Welcome Back, Kotter*, in which he had played "the sweathog dandy," Vinnie Barbarino. "He was mesmerizing," she said.

During the first and second of their appointments, Malick just listened as Carrie talked about her life. During their third session, Travolta showed up for a reading with her.

"We had great chemistry," she said. "Two beakers containing flammable liquid. We bubbled along together like beef in a stewpot."

She was very disappointed a day or so later when she showed up for additional run-throughs with Travolta. He had dropped out. Richard Gere had been contracted to replace him.

"What can I say? I bombed in my reading with Gere. He stayed on as the lead, and my part went to Brooke Adams, hardly a household name."

A new chance for her to costar with Travolta rose up again when he phoned her to suggest she test for a role in his next film, *Grease,* set for release in 1978. Ironically, Gere—cast as Danny Zuko—had starred in the hit Broadway version with the same title and theme.

Director Randal Kleiser faced the daunting task of bringing this fantasy of 1950s teenage life to the screen.

"Once again, I had several readings with Travolta, and in my view we really clicked," Carrie said. "I understood the part. This time I felt I'd made it. But my role went to Stockard Channing. She's a fine actress but, my god, she was born in 1944. That was back during World War II. I was young, vibrant, alive. But I was rejected."

"In the days to follow, I was filled with self-doubt," Carrie said. "Was something wrong with my left tit? I knew I had talent, both as a singer and an actress, and I could fart on cue if demanded. I decided to give acting one final try before I entered a convent or went to work on street corners for the Salvation Army."

Mike Nichols was casting *The Fortune* (1975) and had already lined up his two charismatic male stars, Jack Nicholson and Warren Beatty.

"This time around," Carrie said, "I thought I should agree to lie on the casting couch. I already knew Warren from *Shampoo,* and I'd told Debbie that I had 'surrendered the pink' to him. I was willing to do the same for Jack Nicholson. I was told he walked around with a perpetual hard-on. I didn't think Mike Nichols would want any action from me because I'd heard that

Carrie disagreed with the reviewer who critiqued John Travolta's performance as a disco dancer in *Saturday Night Fever* (1977):

"Travolta had all the anodyne sexual thrust of virginal horniness. He has a mother's boy face, a gaunt, narcissistic horse's head flabby with self-pity, and butterfly lips."

"During our reading, Richard Gere gave me nothing as a performer," Carrie said.

"He was a symbol of self-love with a grimly passive male beauty, of which he was well aware. I felt I was trying to emote with a mannequin. Unlike Travolta, Gere and I had no chemistry at all."

he was a closeted gay."

[It was later revealed that the director had a ten-year affair with the photographer Richard Avedon.]

The Fortune was a dark cinematic comedy about two fumbling friends involved in a *ménage à trois* with a dizzy heiress to a sanitary napkin fortune. The men had ineptly schemed to drown her so that they could collect her inheritance.

"The triangle aspect of our movie was partially influenced by Warren and Jack's reputation for sharing women," Nichols said. "It was type casting. Both actors were known as 'Lions of the Loin.'"

"I got along fab with Warren and Jack," Carrie said, "but Mike wasn't sure I was right for the part. But what did he know?"

"He turned me down for *The Fortune* and went for Stockard Channing instead. That bitch! She took my role in *Grease* and now this. An outrage!"

"I went to see *The Fortune*. Jack was terrific, and Warren was…well, Warren. But Channing was all wrong for the role. I could have done it better and made a fortune for the studio. But no, Nichols thought he knew better than me."

"I had to face facts: Three strikes and you're out. I couldn't contemplate spending the rest of my life getting turned down for movie roles. I had to plot some other dazzling existence."

"Although I didn't want to marry one of those rock stars in England. I had not ruled out marrying one of the royal princes created in Queen Elizabeth's belly. If not that, what was left for me? Rocket scientist? A potential First Lady if I married the right crooked politician?"

"Then one day I get this phone call from a guy named George Lukas. He was dredging around, trying to come up with a cast for this sci-fi B picture he was peddling. He asked me to come in for a reading and, just for the hell of it, I said okay. For my role, I'd be blasted off to some remote galaxy in Outer Space."

"When I told Debbie that I was going to try out for a role in *Star Wars*, do you know what my bitch mother asked?"

"What is it about, dear? Is it a script about your parents, Eddie and me?"

434

Chapter Fifteen

CARRIE FISHER & HARRISON FORD

THOSE STAR WARS LOVERS DESCEND TO EARTH TO MAKE WILD, PASSIONATE LOVE

HOW CARRIE, "THE HIPPEST CHICK IN TINSELTOWN," ORCHESTRATED A RECONCILIATION WITH HER SUICIDAL, STRUNG-OUT FATHER

GETTING HIGH WITH EDDIE FISHER:

CARRIE REVEALS DEBBIE'S SECRET OF SURVIVAL IN SHOW BUSINESS—
"SHE DRINKS BAT'S BLOOD FOR BREAKFAST
AND SMEARS BUG BRAINS ON HER SKIN"

LEAPING LIZARDS! IT'S LIBERACE!

AND HE PROPOSES MARRIAGE TO DEBBIE
(SEPARATE BEDROOMS, OF COURSE!)

"I Smelled Future Stardom When My Intergalactic Tongue Explored Every Inch of That "Space Pirate and Perfect Specimen" Harrison Ford"

—Carrie Fisher

"Millions of Teenage Boys Masturbated to My Princess Leia Picture with the Cinnamon Bun—Or Lost Their Virginity to That Underground Sex Doll With My Face On It."

—Carrie Fisher

STAR WARS

The Evolution of a Franchise

Princess Leia Organa, the character developed and portrayed in at least six of the films in the *Star Wars* franchise was, as defined in the Star Wars Database, "one of the Rebel Alliance's greatest leaders, fearless on the battlefield and dedicated to ending the tyranny of the Empire. But the road she traveled for identification with the brand reads like a case study in the Agony and Ecstasy of movie development and marketing during the latter decades of the 20th Century.

When it became obvious that there was ample room for spinoffs from Lucas' original vision, he articulated the feasibility of three separate Star War Trilogies (a total of nine separate films). Three were conceived as "prequels," five more as continuations of the original 1977 theme. Applauded today as a brilliant way to create a sense of anticipation for future installments, what Lucas did nearly 40 years ago has been copied and refined by movie marketers ever since.

The evolution and growth of the Star Wars franchise was articulated by Denise Worrell in her 1993 book entitled "Icons: Intimate Portraits." It quotes Lucas as saying, in the early 1980s, that he intended to make three "Star Wars" trilogies: one dealing with political and social issues (the set that fans believe covers the movies released from 1999 through 2005); another would examine personal growth and self-realization (topics covered in the original trio of films, those issued between 1977 and 1983). The final trilogy (two of which were released in 2015 and 2017, respectively, plus one presently envisioned for release in 2019) examined and/or will examine moral issues and philosophical problems.

What's included immediately above does not include the astonishing roster of spinoffs (anthology films, animated films, comic books, TV films, games, toys, theme park attractions, and radio dramas) that evolved from the first film (1977).

Star Wars holds a Guinness World Record as "The most successful film merchandising franchise." In 2015, after its acquisition by Disney in 2012, its total value was estimated at US $42 billion, making it the second-highest-grossing media franchise in history. Equivalent contenders include, at #1, the Pokémon (aka Nintendo) franchise, and at #3 and #4, the Harry Potter and James Bond franchises, respectively.

One thing is certain: Princess Leia, played by Carrie Fisher, will forever be indelibly associated with the brand.

"The girl with the cinnamon bun hairdo"

The *Star Wars* franchise launched a great American movie empire and turned Carrie Fisher as Princess Leia into a legend, far surpassing the fame and the money of her mother, Debbie Reynolds.

The 1977 *Star Wars* (later retitled *Star Wars: Episode IV — A New Hope*) became the highest-grossing film of its day, but the road to its eventual filming was rocky, with a few boulders placed in front of its writer and director, George Lucas.

"Unlike all the carpetbaggers who descended on Hollywood, I was its native son," Lucas said. "Born in Modesto, California, a home movie-maker. In junior college, I was intrigued by special effects and camera tricks. I was from that generation of filmmakers inspired by comic books, machines, and shaved-head creatures. My mentor was Francis Ford Coppola."

Lucas' first big hit was based on his experience of growing up with other teenagers under the glaring sun of California. *American Graffiti* (1973), which Lucas co-wrote and directed, was an insightful mosaic of teenagers coming of age after graduation in 1962. Its stars were Ron Howard and Richard Dreyfuss, whom the picture made a star. In a small role was Harrison Ford, who would shoot to international fame as Han Solo in *Star Wars* and as the title character in all those *Indiana Jones* adventure sagas.

Of course, during the course of a career that ultimately spanned six decades, he starred in several other blockbusters, including *Blade Runner* (1982). In that, he was cast as Rick Deckard in this neo-noir dystopia sci-fi film. As of 2017, his films had a worldwide gross, toppling the $6 billion mark, making him the second-highest grossing U.S. domestic box office superstar.

Lucas had not set out to make *Star Wars*. His favorite comic strip when he was growing up had been *Flash Gordon,* and although he wanted to adapt the hero into an adventure serial and/or franchise, he failed to obtain the rights.

Working feverishly, he created the concept of *Star Wars,* an original intergalactic adventure, in January of 1973. Both Carrie and Debbie had seen *American Graffiti,* and Carrie had hailed it as a masterpiece. Debbie later said she wished she'd been cast in it. "Although it was set in 1962, it was really inspired by the 1950s and I still looked young enough to play a teenager."

The movie received five Oscar nods, including one for Best Picture.

According to Lucas, "My reason for wanting to make *Star Wars* was to entertain young people with a picture that depicted honest, wholesome fantasy life, the kind my generation had. We had our westerns with Gary Cooper and John Wayne, our swashbuckling adventures with Errol Flynn, and all kinds of great things. I want a simple plot which boils down to good vs. evil, the kind of stories that had enchanted me as a kid. The word for *Star Wars* was fun."

"My picture had no points of reference to Planet Earth. It is not about the future, but some galactic past which human creatures, not earthlings, once inhabited. It was set in a time when outer space hardware was taken for granted."

For Lucas, getting *Star Wars* financed was more than a boulder in the road to reality. "It was more like a mountain to climb. Producer after producer told me that as America moved deeper and deeper into the 1970s, science fiction had gone out of style."

One producer told him, "We've stopped making those flicks like *Queen of Outer Space* (1958) with Zsa Zsa Gabor."

Then Lucas turned to Walt Disney, thinking that that studio had the finances and the imagination to create a medley of high-drama, high-tech societies within a galaxy far from earth. "I wasn't exactly thrown out on my ass, but I was shown to the door," Lukas said.

He went from studio to studio, meeting rejection after rejection from United Artists, MGM, Warner Brothers, and Paramount. Universal's refusal to finance *Star Wars* was especially painful, because it had released Lucas' previous success, *American Graffiti,* and wanted a similar movie, perhaps a sequel. The studio chiefs there found the concept of *Star Wars* "too weird."

Finally, Lucas found a sympathetic ear at 20th Century Fox, Alan Ladd, Jr., son of the famous actor of the 1940s and 50s, thought it might work. The studio had had a recent string of flops, and Ladd was looking for a blockbuster to get them out of debt. "Elizabeth Taylor's *Cleopatra* (1963) almost bankrupted us," Ladd told Lucas.

"He green-lighted it but put me as writer and director on a starvation yearly salary of $150,000. I wanted $18 million to finance the movie, but he shaved ten million off that. Eventually, I got $11 million, and had to manage on that."

Before casting his project, he set out to find suitable geographic locations, finally settling on the deserts of Tunisia and the Mayan temples at Tika, Guatemala, which served as the rebel base for the film he envisioned.

"I wanted the film to have an ethereal quality, yet be well composed and, also, to have an alien look. I sought a combination of the strange graphics of fantasy, yet the feel of a documentary. Gilbert Taylor, the British cinematographer, came to the rescue."

Back in England, a total of three dozen sets depicting *faux* planets, starships and their control rooms, caves, cantinas, and Death Star corridors were created on at least nine sound stages near London, many of them at Shepperton Studios, the largest in Europe at the time.

Star Wars was set for release for Christmas of 1976 but had to be postponed to the summer of 1977 because of production delays.

Its future star, Carrie Fisher, as Princess Leia, claimed, "All of us in the cast and crew thought *Star Wars* would be a big hit. There was only one dissenter: George Lucas himself."

***

When the locations and many of the production problems that plagued his film were resolved, Lucas set about casting, especially the key roles of Han Solo, Luke Skywalker (originally devised as Luke Skykiller), and Princess Leia.

The male lead in *Star Wars*, Han Solo, was a cynical smuggler hired by the characters of Obi-Wan and Luke to take them in his spaceship, *Millennium Falcon*, to the outer world of Alderaan.

Lucas drew up a list of the actors he'd most prefer to play Solo. Ironically, he hired Harrison Ford, whom he'd previously directed in *American Graffiti,* to read lines during tryouts to the other actors. In all the readings—from Lucas' point of view—Christopher Walken performed the best. Lucas was also impressed with the talents of Burt Reynolds, Jack Nicholson, Al Pacino, Steve Martin, Chevy Chase, Billy Dee Williams (who later played Lando Calrissian in the sequels), and Perry King, who was cast as Han Solo in the radio plays of *Star Wars*. At the bottom of the list was Ford. Lucas explained, "I wanted a fresh face I hadn't directed before."

At the last minute, and for reasons not clear, he decided to cast from the bottom of his list. In the end, the career-making role went to Ford.

As regards the casting for *Star Wars'* second-most-important male character, the heroic Luke Skywalker, Mark Hamill grew up in Oakland, California and later attended Los Angeles City College as a drama major. Before *Star Wars*, he had a recurring role in the soap opera *General Hospital.*

"From the moment I met Mark, I knew he was my Luke," Lucas said. "The role made him a teen idol, adored by thousands of American teenagers. He popped up on dozens of covers of magazines such as *Tiger Beat.* During filming, however, he had a serious car accident on the Los Angeles Freeway, requiring several hours of surgery. His nose had been crushed but was restored. He later faced rumors that his face had been smashed in and had to be virtually reconstructed. He denied all such gossip."

On the casting roster appeared the names of Sissy Spacek, Glenn Close, Angelica Huston, Kathleen Turner, Amy Irving, the singer, Terry Nunn, Cindy Williams, and Karen Allen. Lucas rejected all of them and offered the role instead to Jodie Foster. She had to turn it down because she was under contract at the time to Disney and owed them two other films.

Actually, Carrie showed up during a casting process associated with the director Brian De Palma, who was auditioning for actresses to perform in the horror film *Carrie,* released, like *Star Wars*, in 1977. "I figured that with the name like *Carrie*, the role would be mine," she said. When she showed up, she found that Sissy Spacek was also trying out for it. "That bitch was no sissy, trying to take food from my mouth."

"De Palma, that motherfucker, didn't want me," Carrie said. "He gave the role to—guess who?—Miss Spacek."

However, Lucas, who was in communication with De Palma at the time and who later summoned Carrie back for auditions, "thought I would be ideal for Princess Leia, and he hired me, providing I would lose ten pounds. 'You're fat in the face,' he told me."

Mark Hamill (left), Carrie as Princess Leia, and Harrison Ford as Han Solo.

As regards the casting of her own character, Carrie said, "It seemed that every damn actress in Hollywood was trying out for the role of Princess Leia, the leader of the Rebel Alliance and member of the Imperial Senate."

"I could have cared less at the time. But I had to admit that the competition was formidable. Would you believe that Meryl Streep tried out for it?"

"How very flattering!" she said later, when he was out of earshot. "My thick jaws would be ideal if I gave blow jobs as a sex worker."

Debbie had heard good things about a fat farm in her native Texas and sent Carrie there for some weight-loss and spa treatments. There, Carrie met and chatted with other "inmates," notably the advice columnist, Ann Landers, and Lady Bird Johnson.

"The former First Lady told me amusing stories about her marriage to Lyndon, and also the tragic ones. She emphatically disputed the claim that her husband had ordered the assassination of John Kennedy in Dallas."

After she began her work filming *Star Wars,* Carrie objected to having to sit for two hours every morning while her hairdresser fashioned a "bagel bun" for her.

"I called in the 'Buns of Navarone,' and thought it would be ideal for a transvestite. Looking at myself in the mirror, I didn't realize at the time that thousands upon thousands of teenage boys across America would masturbate to my picture as Princess Leia."

The "blaster-wielding" teenager was only nineteen when, on camera, she ordered the dashingly handsome 33-year-old Harrison Ford as Han Solo to "jump into the garbage chute, fly boy." Then, based on her character's status as the no-nonsense leader of an intergalactic rebellion, she had to fight her way out of an imperial prison.

"George (Lucas) was a sadist," Carrie said later. "But like any abused child wearing a metal bikini and chained to a giant slug, I kept coming back for more. In the years to come, he provided Harrison and me with a merry band of stalkers to keep us entertained for the rest of our unnatural lives."

"George was a director who didn't direct. All he did was say, 'go faster' or 'look more intense.' He was more concerned with that white dress I wore. He directed me to remove my bra, claiming that there is no underwear in outer space. He said that in space, the body becomes weightless and expands. "Your bra does not, and it might strangle you," he told her.

"Within the year, a rumor was spread that some shit was secretly manufacturing a Princess Leia sex doll. You could fuck her to orgasm. Who knows how many of those creepy sons of bitches were out there banging me every night? Debbie tried to buy one for Eddie (Fisher) as a Christmas gift, but I don't know if she pulled that one off. What a sick idea."

"Don't let anyone know this, but I have a weird fucking mother," Carrie said. "She got stranger as time went by. I'll say one thing for her: She is god damn resilient. That button-nosed, *boop-boopie-doo* girl is a show business survivor. What's her secret? She drinks bat's blood for breakfast and smears bug brains on her skin. That keeps her engine roaring at all times."

"She looks so normal at times, but really isn't. Remember, this is the mother who gave me a bag of weed when I was only thirteen and wanted to supervise the sex act between Albert, my gay lover of long ago, and me when

I was still in diapers…well, almost."

***

Another key role was played by the English actor, Peter Cushing. Cast as the Grand Moff Tarkin, one of the most malevolent villains in *Star Wars* history, he portrayed the Governor of the Imperial Outland Regions and Commander of the spaceship *Death Star*, a doomsday weapon "as big as a dwarf planet."

During his stellar career, Cushing had made a reputation for himself in British horror films, interpreting such roles as the sinister Baron Franken-stein, the vampire-hunting Doctor Van Helsing, even Sherlock Holmes.

When Cushing met Carrie, he said, "Don't be alarmed. I'm not a real monster. I won't be grabbing one of your boobies. I'm a gentle soul, a keen bird watcher."

"You're adorable, Baron," she answered. "Just so long as you don't make me the Bride of Frankenstein."

[Cushing died in the cathedral city of Canterbury in England in August of 1994. However, he appeared on the screen again in 2016, reprising his role as Grand Moff Tarkin in Rogue One, *defined by its producers as one of the Star Wars "Anthology Films." His likeness was digitally repurposed on the body of actor Guy Henry.]*

The role of the noble patriarch Obi-Wan ("Ben") Kenobi, the aging Jedi Master," went to Alec Guinness. *[The part was initially offered to Toshiro Mifune, the memorable Japanese actor who had starred in Akira Kurosawa's The Hidden Fortress (1958), but he rejected it.]*

Carrie admitted to making "the mistake of my life when I signed the original contract. I surrendered all rights to the merchandizing of my image."

"I never got any of the loot from the sale of all those Princess Leia dolls," she said. "I protested to Lucas only once. On one doll, a voyeur could see all the way up my dress to my anatomically correct—though shaved—galaxy snatch."

She confronted him. "You know what? Owning my likeness does not include rights to my lagoon of mystery."

442

Guinness, of course, was one of the "British Knights" of the English stage and screen, sharing honors with Laurence Olivier and John Gielgud. He'd won a Best Actor Oscar in 1957 for David Lean's *The Bridge on the River Kwai.*

Guinness was offered $150,000 for his involvement in the film. Ironically, that was what Lucas had been paid for writing and directing it. Guinness was also given two percent of the producer's profits, which made him a very rich man.

On June 16, 1976, Guinness finished his work on *Star Wars* and told Carrie goodbye. "Safe journeys through Outer Space. As for me, I feel deflated and demoralized."

Later, when he went to see the movie on Leicester Square in London, he reported that it was "pretty staggering." He did complain, however, about the performance of Tony Daniels as C-3PO, the taller and more articulate of the two Robots (aka "the protocol droid").

"I found him fidgety and overly elaborately spoken. But when the money starts rolling in, I'm sure I'll be most satisfied. As for Princess Leia, she doesn't act like one of our fine English princesses, except maybe with a trait or two of Princess Anne."

The role of the villain, Darth Vader, went to David Prowse, a 6'5" weightlifter and character actor from the West Country of England. *[Previous acting gigs had included the role of an eccentric bodyguard in* Clockwork Orange, *and a stint as "Jack the Ripper" on English comedy shows in which he ripped up phone books.]* "His voice sounded like a farmer from Cornwall," Carrie said. "The cast nicknamed him Darth Farmer."

At first, Lucas decided to dub his voice with that of Orson Welles. Later, fearing that Welles' voice would be too familiar to audiences, he hired James Earl Jones for the voiceovers.

At first, Lucas had cast Peter Cushing as Obi-Wan, the "force-sensitive human male Jedi Master."

Lucas later concluded, however, that Cushing's lean, ascetic-looking physique would be better suited for the role of the malevolent Imperial General instead.

"Peter will be making fans for the next 350 years," Lucas predicted.

***

The first time Carrie met her co-star, Mark Hamill, she told friends, "He's so cute, the most adorable creature wandering around in Outer Space. He's only five years older than me, and he's a bachelor, free as a bird, as am I. Perhaps two birds will flock together. I smell husband material here."

She had yet to meet the star of the picture, Harrison Ford, who was equally as handsome. "Both guys are gorgeous," she said. "The only problem with Harrison as a possible beau is that he's fourteen years older than me…and married."

But as she was soon to learn, love does not always select convenient partners. Since 1964, Ford, a Chicago native, had been married to Mary Marquardt. The couple had two children, Benjamin, born in 1966 and Willard, born in 1969. *[In 1979, based to some extent on the pressures of Harrison's role in* Star Wars, *the couple would divorce.]*

Guinness frequently complained to Carrie, "The dialogue I've been given is pure rubbish. It doesn't make my character clear or even bearable."

"And I have to put up with that moron, Harrison Ford, whoever the hell he is. He mocks me by calling me 'Mother Superior.' Obviously, he's heard rumors of my alleged homosexuality."

Whereas Lucas and Hamill were the first to discover that Carrie was having an affair with Ford, most of the rest of the world had to wait until 2016 when she published her last and final book, *The Princess Diarist.* Within it, Carrie revealed the details of her adulterous love affair.

Shortly before she died, she discovered the journals she'd written in 1976 during the filming of the first *Star Wars.* She wrote those notes when she was

a naïve, vulnerable young woman on the brink of stardom.

Readers' reactions to the entries in Carrie's journals, were widely varied, some of them miles off base. "I was not shocked that Carrie had an affair with a married man," wrote one reader.

David Prowse's face was hidden behind the ominous-looking Darth Vader mask throughout the course of the film.

Years later, Prowse claimed he was originally told that he would be seen and heard at the end of *Return of the Jedi,* when his mask was removed.

Instead, during that long-awaited moment, the face of actor Sebastian Shaw was substituted for his own. Consequently, in years to come, despite the dramatic importance of his role, Prowse emerged as the least-recognized major player in the entire cast of *Star Wars.*

444

"What shocked me was that Debbie Reynolds was her mother. How did Carrie and Debbie keep that secret for so long? Not only that, but I learned that Eddie Fisher was her father. Hollywood does like to keep its secrets. Did Elizabeth Taylor, the wife of Eddie, learn of his illicit affair with Debbie and that her husband had impregnated her?"

One reader captured the Ford/Fisher liaison in a nutshell. "Harrison wouldn't talk to her, looked down on her, made her feel insecure, ignored her during the work week, and then every weekend did some mattress dancing with her."

Another referred to her affair with Ford as "a snooze fest."

Carrie wrote, "I was obsessed with Harrison long before it became fashionable. I was a trend-setter in that sense. I started a craze among *Star Wars* fans."

"When I got the part of Princess Leia in this goofy little sci-fi film, I thought it's would be fun to do. I'll hang out with a bunch of robots for a few months, then return to my life and try to figure out what I wanted to do when I grow up."

Movie reviewer Tasha Robinson, after Carrie's death, wrote, "The younger version of [*Carrie*] Fisher is painfully, miserably obsessed with Ford. She repeatedly spins elaborate fantasies about him leaving his wife to be with her. She blames herself for his remoteness and tries to figure out what about herself she can change to make him more engaged. She pours out her heart with a rawness that eclipses any humor, later-life analysis, or nostalgia she brings to the story."

***

According to Carrie, "I decided to let *Star Wars* groupies know that Harrison and I crawled beneath the sheets weekend after weekend during the shoot in England. What I didn't' reveal in my diaries is that Harrison has a wonderful cock, most satisfying to a woman or even to a person of another gender, but he does not drift in that direction."

Carrie was not a porn writer, and she is not descriptive like Terry Moore writing about her affair with Howard Hughes. Carrie did admit, however, that under the glare of the movie cameras of the sets of *Star*

When Carrie saw this picture of Mark Hamill, cast as Luke Skywalker, she said, "It looks like he's getting humped by Yoda."

At first, at least until she met Harrison Ford, she'd set her romantic sights on Hamill.

Wars, "We did soft porn on the screen for hardened sci-fi fans."

"From the moment I met him, I was stunned at how handsome he was. I told Lucas, 'It'll be a lucky girl who gets him.'"

"He's already taken," Lucas responded. "He's married. With two boys."

"That was like hearing there was no Santa, no Tooth Fairy, no Easter Bunny. But my luck was about to change."

According to one of her memoirs, "It was a night in May of 1976 when I became intimate with my cinematic lover. My candidate for seduction was a shining specimen of manhood and oh, so handsome. He could give a girl an orgasm just by staring intently into her eyes."

Their affair began in a seedy pub in the London suburbs near where *Star Wars* was being filmed. It seemed that everybody in the pub was drunk, except Carrie, who at that time, didn't drink. When she entered, she was surrounded by "sparks" (the British term for electricians) from the nearby sound stages. "Those bastards finally got me to down more than one drink, and the alcohol immediately went to my head. I wasn't in complete control. Three of the sparks were leading me out the back door into the parking lot."

One of them told her that the four of them could get better acquainted in the back of his van. According to Carrie, "The taste and effects of alcohol make me stupid, sick, and unconscious really fast. But I wanted to fit in," she said. "I had no idea what these burly men planned to do with little ol' me. I have to believe not much, but they were going to make a great deal of noise while they didn't do it."

Before she could be gang-raped, it was Ford who came to her rescue. He grabbed her and escorted her rapidly out the front door, where he put her into the back of a studio car and ordered the driver to take them to her residence in central London.

"In the rear of that car, I got to taste the tongue and luscious lips of this dreamboat for the first time. It was better than devouring a whole box of chocolates. I was getting felt up. Perhaps he wanted to determine that I was, indeed, female. I did some groping myself, only to discover that he was a man—and what a man!"

"Not only did I ascertain his gender, I decided he had a rocket that felt like it was ready to take off to the moon."

Suddenly, a car pulled up alongside them and blew its horn. Inside it was Mark Hamill. Peter Kohn, a member of the crew, was there too, at the wheel, escorting a beautiful young woman.

There ensued an animated dialogue through each of the cars' open windows about where the occupants might hang out together for a while. Within a few moments, the name of a nearby Italian restaurant was agreed upon for dinner.

With that settled, Ford resumed "his tongue exploration of my back molars."

At the *trattoria,* Carrie was introduced to the American actress, Koo Stark, who had a small role (that of Camie Loneozner) in *Star Wars.*

[Her scene was later cut, but it didn't end up on the cutting room floor. It was filed within the Star Wars *archives and, in 1998, was inserted into a documentary about the franchise's saga,* Star Wars: Behind the Magic.*]*

No one knew it that day as they ate their lasagna, but Koo Stark, a New Yorker born to two writers in Manhattan, was about to become infamous.

"She was far more beautiful than I was, and I was afraid she was going to walk off with both Mark Hamill and Harrison after dumping her date, Peter," Carrie said.

After the meal, the three men—-"blessed with a bounty of backed-up semen" (Carrie's words)—fought over the check. After telling the party goodbye, Ford hailed a taxi for himself and Carrie. After getting her to reveal her address, he instructed the driver to take them to Esmond Court, off Kensington High Street.

That was the first of many weekends Ford and Carrie spent together in bed. "Michael Jackson would call it a 'sleepover,'" she said. In her journals, Carrie avoided going into the intimate details of what occurred between Ford and her in bed. She remembered waking up the next morning and staring into his sleeping face. "My god, he was gorgeous."

Although their affair would mostly play out as part of summer weekends, she later observed, "It was like a long-enduring one-night stand that lasted and lasted—wonderful sex with a wonderful man. We never talked of our future together. He was a man of actions and few words. I didn't know if we'd even have a future."

"If he'd asked me to walk down the aisle with him, after his divorce from Mary, my answer would have been in the affirmative. Actually, if

Harrison Ford as Han Solo.

In Las Vegas one night, Mae West advised Debbie to "keep a diary while you're young, because when you get older, it will keep you."

According to Carrie, as revealed to Lucas, "When I discovered my journals about my affair with Harrison, I wasn't really following Miss West's advice. But in a way I was, profiting from book sales about my love affair with Han Solo so long ago."

"Shameless literary hussy that I am, I revealed it to the world after being silent for decades."

we got married, I'm sure he would have preferred a private ceremony, as he was a very private man."

"He didn't blab a lot," she said. "Don't get the wrong idea. His tongue was most active in his journeys across my body. No words were coming out, but his tongue was an instrument to communicate."

"The worst part of our summer romance was a dream I had one night. In my dream, Harrison and I were having a three-way with Debbie. What a nightmare!"

"Our rendezvous point was the North Star Pub in St. John's Wood, midway between the studio at Elstree and Central London. "Our faces had not been plastered around the world at the time, so no one paid us any attention. I had been introduced to the pub by David Bowie when I was studying drama in London."

"I wasn't as good at impressions as Debbie. But one night at the pub, I gave a demonstration of Harrison and how he walked with a John Wayne swagger. He wasn't insulted, but amused."

***

"In August, Harrison was in tears when he told me he'd fallen in love with me, but he also claimed that he was still in love with his wife. He was so in love with her than in a few months, they were headed for the divorce court."

"You are my soulmate, the only person who really understands me," he told her one night after intense love-making. That weekend, he slipped a gold band on her finger, with diamonds spelling out CARRISON, a combination of their names.

"Pot played a big role in our weekends together," she said. "His weed had a brutal strength. I don't know where in London he got his stash."

"Frank Sinatra sang about love fading with the summer winds," she said. "There was another song about Autumn Leaves starting to fall. It was in the fading days of autumn when the winds started to blow down from Scotland and *Star Wars* was wrapped. It was time to escape to California where it was still summer. We sat in seats together on the long flight west."

After they landed at LAX, he kissed her and had parting words: "You have the eyes of a doe and the balls of a Samurai warrior."

***

[Months before her death, Debbie read her daughter's memoir, The Princess Diarist. In it, Carrie had claimed that her affair with Harrison Ford was her first.

After reading that passage, Debbie commented to her daughter, "Dear, you know he was not the first. There were others before Han Solo flew you away in his spaceship."

"It's true," Carrie answered. "But the others were just for sex. With Harrison, it was a real affair. Just when I was being created in your gut from Eddie's semen, Harrison was already a teenaged boy working overtime with his fist for sexual relief."

"What a lovely image, dear," Debbie said. "No romance writer will ever fear competition from you."]

* * *

George Lucas was slow to comprehend the enormous future success of his *Star Wars* franchise. "I got the point when I went into a record store in Los Angeles to buy an album. *Star Wars* fans attacked me and ripped off my shirt to cut up as souvenirs."

Carrie was initially amazed and later thrilled at the international reception of *Star Wars*. "The role made me something I thought I'd never be: It turned me into a legend."

Star Wars eventually replaced *Jaws* (1975) as the highest-grossing film in North America. It made $220 million, an amount equivalent to $875 million, adjusted into 2016 dollars. That—if inflation were figured into the equation—made it second in sales only to *Gone With the Wind* (1939).

The critics raved, or at least most of them did "except for the snipers" (Carrie's words). Roger Ebert of the *Chicago Sun-Times* called it "an out-of-the-body experience." Vincent Canby of *The New York Times* labeled it "the most elaborate, most expensive, and most beautiful movie ever made."

Variety called it "the biggest possible adventure fantasy," and *The Washington Post* defined it as "a space swashbuckler."

Of course, Lucas and his stars expected the usual attacks. One that was particularly acerbic came from John Simon writing in *The New Yorker:* "Strip *Star Wars* of its often striking images and its highfalutin' scientific jargon, and you get a story, characters, and dialogue of overwhelming banality." He also wrote, "Carrie Fisher is bovine and unappealing, having inherited the worst qualities of both of her parents." Pauline Kael, also writing in *The New Yorker,* stated, "there's no breather in the picture, no lyricism."

In *The New Republic,* Stanley Kaufmann stated: "*Star Wars* was made for those (particularly male) who carry a portable shrine within them of their adolescence, a chalice of Self that was better back then, before the world's affairs—or in any complex way—sex intruded."

Peter Keough of the *Boston Phoenix* detested the movie. He found it a "junkyard of cinematic gimcracks, a heap of purloined, discarded, barely functioning droids."

Time, however, named it "Movie of the Year." In that magazine, Gerald Clarke wrote: "It is a grand glorious film, the smash hit of 1977 and certainly the best movie of the year. It is a remarkable confection: a subliminal history of the movies, wrapped in a riveting tale of suspense and adventure, orna-

449

mented with some of the most ingenious special effects ever contrived for film."

At the 50th annual Academy Awards ceremony, *Star Wars* won numerous accolades. Lucas was nominated for but did not win Oscars for Best Original Screenplay, Best Director, and Best Picture. (*Star Wars* lost in that latter category to Woody Allen's *Annie Hall*.) Alec Guinness was nominated as Best Actor in a Supporting Role, losing to Jacon Robards for *Julia*. However, the film won Oscars for Best Art Direction, Best Costume Design, Best Film Editing, Best Original Score, Best Sound, and Best Visual Effects.

Over the years, some critics attacked both Lucas and his sometimes rival and collaborator Steven Spielberg for shifting the focus away from such subtle films as *The Godfather* (1972), or *Taxi Driver* (1976) to lavish and spectacular indulgences of juvenile fantasy. "Lucas and Spielberg returned the 1970s audience, grown sophisticated on a diet of European and New Hollywood films, to the simplicities of the pre-1960s Golden Age of movies," wrote one critic. "They marched backward through the looking glass."

Tom Shone, another critic, claimed that Lucas and Spielberg didn't betray cinema at all. "They plugged it back in the grid, returning the medium to its roots as a carnival sideshow, a magic act, one big special effect, all of which was a kind of rebirth."

As late as March of 2002, *Vanity Fair* was describing how Lucas handled a love story: "The closest he got to romance was in the original *Star Wars* trilogy in a flirty badinage and casual liplock between Harrison Ford's Han Solo and Carrie Fisher's Princess Leia, who seemed more like cocksure Maxwell's Plum singles than two virginal hearts beating as one."

[The reference to Maxwell's Plum was to a chic pickup bar that flourished in Manhattan in the 1970s. Donald Trump picked up his future first wife, Ivana, one night in that bar when she was in town on a modeling assignment.]

In her writings, Carrie maintained a blunt, "tell-it-like-it-is" *persona*, claiming "I'm a fierce truth teller." She also attacked feminists who pointed out that Leia was for a time depicted as a slave.

"These women are asinine," Carrie charged. "Leia is a prisoner of a giant testicle, who has a lot of saliva going on. She does not want to wear that metallic bikini, and it's ultimately that chain which you're now indicating is some sort of accessory to S&M, that is used to kill the giant saliva testicle."

[EDITORS NOTE: Was she high when she wrote this? Only the most devoted Star Wars fans will find meaning here: others need not bother.]

"I will forever be Princess Leia. That's a very, very light cross to bear."

***

Debbie's faded film career had gone the way of the jitterbug and Veronica Lake movies. But she did appear again in 1976 when MGM put together a sequel from archival footage, entitling it *That's Entertainment! Part II.*

Gene Kelly not only directed it, but, along with Fred Astaire, was one of the hosts. Debbie had been one of the hosts for the original *That's Entertainment,* a roughly equivalent anthology released in 1974, two years before.

This time around, the producer was Daniel Melnick, known today for such films as *All That Jazz* (1979; it had starred Debbie's sexual harasser, choreographer, Bob Fosse), and *Altered States* (1980), which marked the film debut of William Hurt. In all, Melnick's films eventually won more than 20 Oscars based on 80 nominations.

For the *That's Entertainment* sequel, Melnick and Kelly dug deep into MGM's archives, including some scenes that had been saved but did not appear in the original release.

Clips from two of Debbie's films were included in the revue: *Singin' in the Rain* (1952) with Gene Kelly, and *The Tender Trap* (1955) with Frank Sinatra.

Other clips in the film included scenes with Clark Gable, Judy Garland, Lana Turner, Mickey Rooney, Greta Garbo, Bing Crosby, Grace Kelly, James Cagney, John Barrymore, Doris Day, Vivien Leigh, and Elizabeth Taylor. ("Of course, they had to include that one," Debbie said.)

Debbie gave her review of *That's Entertainment Part II* to the press:

"The movie has the greatest all-star cast in the history of cinema, not likely to be equaled again, because there aren't that many stars anymore."

Fred Astaire and Gene Kelly in *That's Entertainment.*

"It was worth the price of admission just to see Gene and Fred dance together," Debbie said. "Fred was 76, and this was the last time he'd dance on the screen."

"For a good part of the 1970s," Debbie said, "I traveled some forty weeks a year, appearing in night club acts or musical plays. I became a regular in Nevada, especially Vegas, but also in Tahoe and Reno."

"By this time, *Irene* had become my bread and butter, as I bounced onto stages in such places as Salt Lake City, Westbury (Long Island), Houston, Atlanta, Phoenix, and Valley Forge (Pennsylvania)."

"For my night club gigs, I updated some of my impressions," she said. "Of course, I did Mae West and Zsa Zsa Gabor, but I also added Barbra Streisand and Dolly Parton. For Dolly, I had to stuff my bra until I was top heavy. I also nailed Dr. Ruth perfectly and gave raucous sex advice to my audience."

"My moment of truth came every night when I had to sit at my makeup table and stare at my image in that god damn cruel and unforgiving mirror. My challenge was to reverse the ravages of time."

"One night I got a call from one of the most famous entertainers in America. He would soon propose marriage to me."

***

On evening in 1975, Debbie's show in Vegas had played before a packed audience. When it was over, she wanted to return to her suite and collapse. So when the phone in her dressing room rang, she cautioned her maid, "I don't want to speak to anyone."

Answering the phone, the maid heard Liberace's gushing voice on the other end. "It's Liberace!" she whispered to Debbie.

Startled to be getting a call from him, she took the receiver. After the familiar raves about each other's talent, he invited her to a late-night birthday party for singer Tom Jones.

After she accepted, he told her he'd retrieve her in thirty minutes, and she was to come in full makeup and wearing the shimmering gown she'd worn on stage. "I, too, will be dressed up, perhaps a little flashy for some tastes. After all, I have more diamonds and minks than Elizabeth Taylor."

He lived up to his word, arriving in front of her hotel in a chauffeur-driven white limousine, wearing a floor-length ermine coat with a white suit, white shoes, and diamonds, everything matching the color of his vehicle. In marked contrast, she wore a black strapless gown and a black velvet coat.

Before she got into the back seat, he introduced her to his handsome, blonde-haired chauffeur, Scott Thorson, who wore a white uniform with gold braid. She detected a certain intimacy between Liberace and Thorson, and she suspected that Thorson was more than his driver.

En route to the party, which was being hosted at a private home, she settled back to get to know "Mr. Showmanship." His glass-topped piano thrilled millions of his fan base, to a large extent composed of blue-haired ladies over fifty.

He was always dazzling. His show business outfits were called the most outrageous on the planet. A consummate performer, he used a lavish gold candelabra as his most celebrated prop. Of course, he faced many cruel jibes from critics who labeled him, "The Wizard of Ooze." But, drowning in a sea of sequins, he shot back, "I'm crying all the way to the bank."

Although acting "so very, very gay," (Debbie's words), Liberace was always sensitive about rumors of his homosexuality. The most famous case was a libel judgment against the *Daily Mail* in London. A reporter from that paper had written: "Liberace is the summit of sex—the pinnacle of masculine, feminine, and neuter. Everything that he, she, and it can ever want, this deadly, winding, sniggering, snuggling, chromium-plated, scent-impregnated, luminous, quivering, giggling, fruit-flavored, mincing, ice-covered heap of mother love has had the biggest reception and impact on London since Charlie Chaplin arrived at Waterloo train station in 1921."

Liberace denied that he was a homosexual and immediately hired a law firm in London to sue the newspaper. He told the press, "If I was as degenerate as the *Daily Mail* claims, and as unmanly as they say, explain all the interest that women have shown in me over the years."

It took three years before the case came to trial. He won a libel award of £8,000, or around $25,000 in the U.S. dollars at the time. In today's currency, that would be worth about $190,000.

At the party with Debbie, a sea of women crowded around Tom Jones, as if they wanted to undress him, which they probably did. "Tom's pants are so tight you can tell that his Welsh dick is uncut," Liberace said.

Although the most outrageously dressed, flamboyant, and "queenie" entertainer in America, Liberace tried (but with ever-decreasing success) to remain in the closet.

Finally, Debbie and Liberace made their way to the "birthday boy," where he kissed her on both cheeks. Yet when Liberace tried to kiss him, he backed away. "If not a kiss, can I cop a feel to see if you've got a sock stuffed in there?" Liberace asked.

Jones laughed. "It's for real, baby. My motto is, 'If you've got it, flaunt it.'"

With his megawatt smile, Liberace worked the room. At the piano, he played what sounded like a brilliant combination of Beethoven and "The Beer Barrel Polka."

After the party, Liberace dropped Debbie off at the Desert Inn for much-needed sleep. Since both of them had the following night off, he invited her to his home for dinner.

The next evening, he showed up again at her hotel. This time, she was dressed more simply, and he wore a pair of "hot pants" showing off his legs. His Rolls-Royce was painted pink, and so was Thorson's chauffeur's uniform.

At the beginning of their second evening together, members of the press spotted Liberace's distinctive car as it pulled once again into the driveway of Debbie's hotel.

"Got a date with Liberace?" reporter called to her.

Using her best Mae West imitation, she said, "I'm going over to Liberace's home to see his gold organ. I've seen every other kind, but never a gold one."

It wasn't surprising that within the surreal context associated with Liberace, she had borrowed a line from Mae West. The aging sex goddess had used an almost identical quip when she herself had faced reporters before one of her own rendezvous with the singer.

Liberace's residence was spectacularly furnished, with a grand piano in every room except the bathroom. Surveying the predictable lushness, Debbie said, "I used to live like this until my husband took all my money."

There were treasures everywhere, including a lot of gold chairs, 16th-century tapestries, art works, and antiques, with luxury and elegance around every corner. Overhead were chandeliers in 18-karat gold and Baccarat crystal.

His objects of pride included a stunningly beautiful onyx table which had a crack in it. "This cameraman asked me if he could put his heavy equipment on my table. I told him I welcome heavy equipment, but wouldn't it be better to display it in my bedroom? How did I know he meant his big movie camera, which cracked my table?"

He even showed her his gold and marble bathtub. "I'd feel like a queen taking a bubble bath in that," she said.

To that, Liberace responded with a giggle, "That's exactly how I feel every time Scott and I swim around in it." That was her first confirmation that he and Thorson were lovers.

During dinner, Liberace amused her with stories about his life, and an enduring friendship was launched. He revealed that Elvis Presley, "dressed like a country hick," had bombed when he first played Vegas. "But I invited him home and stripped him down. He had to drop his jockey shorts and reveal his hillbilly pecker. To return the favor, I designed a whole new wardrobe for him, everything from gold *lamé* to white leather with sequins. He became the biggest hit in town. He owed it all to me. I turned Elvis into a Rhinestone Cowboy."

In the weeks and months ahead, Thorson not only joined them during their dinners together, but intruded brusquely into their conversations, often dominating them.

That irritated Debbie, and she became quite harsh with him. "Why do you keep interrupting us?" she asked. "Why don't you go out for a stroll and walk the dogs?"

After he'd stormed out of the room, Liberace said, "I'm glad you told him that. He's so young and doesn't yet know that he's supposed to listen."

"You shouldn't have people around who don't know how to behave," she answered.

"I know, I know," he said. "But you know how lonely life is on the road."

"I have a funny feeling that this young man will mean nothing but trouble for you. He's out for your money…big money!"

"It's a cross I'll have to bear," he answered.

One evening, in preparation for Debbie's imminent arrival, Liberace remained at home cooking the meal and sent Thorson, as his driver, to pick her up. He asked her to ride in the front seat with him, which she agreed to do. He seemed to have forgiven her for snapping at him, and even spoke to her confidentially.

"I'm having some problems with Lee," he confided. "He's a sex maniac, wanting it six times a day. I don't think men, regardless of their sexual preference, should act like a dripping sissy faggot."

In Liberace's lavish living room, Debbie was introduced to the honored guest of the evening. It was Michael Jackson. He was with a 12-year-old boy whom he didn't bother to introduce.

Liberace served a series of dishes, which he would later feature in his book, *Liberace Cooks!* The dinner began with *zuppa di pesce* followed with Rock Cornish hen with wild rice stuffing, topped off with *crêpes Suzette*. It was one of the most delicious dinners she'd ever had.

She found Jackson very respectful. And he'd seen many of her musicals, his favorite being the obvious: *Singin' in the Rain.* Her dinner with him that evening was before he submitted to plastic surgery, on the dawn of his worldwide adulation. He told her that in October of 1978, he'd be appearing as the scarecrow in *The Wiz.*

Whenever he was on the road, Liberace sometimes invited Debbie to stay at his house, which was fully staffed even during his absences, as a break from too constant a diet of hotels. During one of her sojourns within his house (he had flown to

In his 1988 memoir, *Behind the Candelabra*, Thorson remembered Debbie fondly:

"She is so down to earth, a warm, funny lady. She often worked in the same hotel as Lee, and we came to know her quite well. She had a vitality to her and a sense of the ridiculous."

L.A. for a week to attend to some business), he opted to not let Thorson accompany him. As he told Debbie, "I've met this new trick I want to audition. Besides, Scott has turned to drugs, and I'm getting tired of him."

As she was alone, resting on a *chaise longue* beside Liberace's pool, Thorson appeared on the patio stark nude. He approached her saying, "Hi, babe. I guess it's obvious now what the big attraction is for Lee."

"I can hardly miss it. Now, don't try to get a job posing nude for a centerfold. The magazine would have to insert an extra page."

"Thanks for the compliment," he answered. "If you'd like to visit my bedroom, I'll show you that I know how to use it."

"As tempting as it is, I'll pass on this one."

"I don't want you to think I'm a fag. I like girls. I just seduce guys for the money."

"Scott, we both know you're a whore, so go find your bathing suit, and we'll get along just fine. Thanks for the show."

***

Based to some extent on the many magazine exposés such as those in *Confidential,* and after all the "faggot jokes," being bandied around about him in the media, Liberace began to panic about his career. He feared he'd lose his fan base if he got into a sex scandal. His manager, Seymour Heller, kept urging him to enter into a "lavender marriage" with an understanding woman. His first recommendation for such a marriage partner was Debbie, whom he used to manage until they had a violent falling out.

"Seymour was a problem for Debbie," Liberace said. "Because of our friendship and his managing my life, she was always encountering him. Any time the two of them were in the same room together, I could feel the Arctic chill."

Liberace had become famous during the relatively innocent Eisenhower era of the 1950s. From the beginning reporters consistently badgered him about why he had never married.

Along the way he had invented some *faux* romances with women he sometimes escorted. He was famously linked at one time to the aging Olympic ice skater from Norway, Sonja Henie. Fleeing from some nagging early associations with the Nazis, she had arrived in Hollywood in the early 1940s and appeared in some cheerful ice-skating movies for Fox.

Henie was known for her many affairs, most notably with Tyrone Power. She referred to his penis as "Jimmy," and he referred to her vagina as "Betsy."

Henie's other affairs included sexual interludes with Desi Arnaz, "cocksman" Greg Bautzer, Dick Haymes, the (usually) gay actor Van Johnson, and many other ice skaters, ski instructors, and Fox crewmen. Her most celebrated affair was with a young naval lieutenant, John F. Kennedy.

She once told the press she'd fallen in love with Liberace and that they were engaged, but instead, she ended up marrying Niels Onstad, the Norwegian shipowner, multi-millionaire, and visionary art collector.

For a while, Liberace was even linked to Christine Jorgenson, the world's most famous transsexual. When reporters clustered around her and asked her to name the date they'd be wed, she answered, "When a cow jumps over the moon." On another occasion, Jorgenson said, "Lee is a very nice man, but a bit weird."

As Heller continued to put pressure on his famous client, Liberace set up a dinner with Debbie within his famous residence in Los Angeles. He served it on the sprawling balcony of his luxurious apartment because of its view of the moon and stars. He had carefully rehearsed, in advance of her arrival and with his formally dressed staff, every elegant detail.

When the meal was over, he made his pitch, proposing marriage to her and holding out to her the largest diamond she'd ever seen, with the exception of the ones associated with Elizabeth Taylor.

At first, she didn't answer, listening to him promise her "three Rolls-Royces, a mint of jewelry, all the furs needed for a prolonged stay at the North Pole, and a Helen Rose gown every other night."

He told her he was on the verge of kicking Thorson out of his house, and in the future, he'd arrange for some "really hot numbers" to arrive regularly at his house. "I'll make sure they're bi- so that they can satisfy me one night,

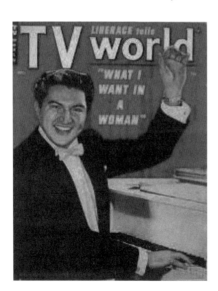 

Liberace represented one of the most artful and strong-willed balancing acts of his day, a career that veered between self-satirization and artful denial of an alternative sexuality. Debbie stumbled into a friendship with the entertainer....

you the next. As my wife, you'll be the beard for me. No one will suspect when they see the three of us, whoever the third guy is to be, dining together. That's done in Hollywood all the time!"

"Dear, your proposal sounds absolutely delightful," she said. "And I love you a whole lot. But I want it to be as your friend. Besides, I'd have to get permission from Carrie and Todd about their new stepdad."

"I'll give each of them a Cadillac, a great wardrobe, an elegant apartment, and I'll send them to the best schools."

"They'll love living in the lap of luxury, but I don't think it'll work out," she said. "I just don't. I'm not that decadent."

[Her assessment of Thorson as a trouble-maker came true. In 1982, he filed a palimony suit against Liberace after he was dumped. Asking for $113 million, he testified in Los Angeles Superior Court, claiming that Liberace had made massive financial commitments to him in return for his sexual favors. The case was eventually settled out of court for only $95,000.

Liberace died of AIDS on February 4, 1987 at the age of 67. A memorial service then unfolded in Las Vegas at St. Anne's Roman Catholic Church.

Debbie attended with her friend, Donald O'Connor. After the memorial service, she told reporters, "Lee was a wonderful man and should be remembered as a dear, loving person—and not for any other reason."

Of course, her reference was to all the AIDS controversy that was raging at the time in the newspapers, particularly after the death of his long-time lover, Rock Hudson.

Ironically, in Debbie's last feature film, Behind the Candelabra *(2013), based on Thorson's memoires, she was cast as Liberace's mother.]*

***

In the wake of the crescendo of fame that resulted from the release of *Star Wars*, Carrie saw less and less of Debbie. "She had fled the nest to start a new life in New York," Debbie said. "As for me, I was on the road for most of the year, rarely at home...that is, if I had a home. I'd become a gypsy."

As regards lodgings, and before she moved into her small new home in unfashionable North Hollywood, Debbie sometimes didn't have a roof over her head. "Of course, I could

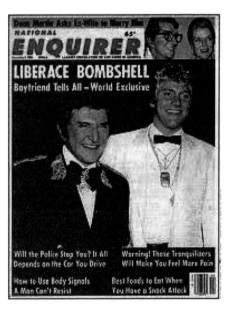

have gone to Todd's house, but I didn't want to intrude into his life."

He would soon marry his high school sweetheart, Donna Freberg, the daughter of Stan Freberg. He was also becoming deeply religious and had morphed into a Born Again Christian. In 1982, he was ordained as a minister.

In 1972, as an investment, Debbie had bought a dance studio, DR Studios, and began renting it to actors as rehearsal space. "I was tired of filthy dressing room, dance halls, and foul-smelling toilets. I wanted a clean, nice environment for performers to work out their routines. My investment paid off. I had it rented for most of the time."

Located in North Hollywood, the studio space evoked the one she had operated with Shelley Winters in the movie, *What's the Matter with Helen?*

For a while, Todd used her dance studio as the setting for his Sunday sermons. Most of his congregation were members of the film colony. During interludes between his sermons, the congregation listened to Henry Cutorne's rock band, *Gentle Faith.*

In time, Todd's church was moved to the Beverly Theater in Beverly Hills. Debbie occasionally attended, not for spiritual guidance, "But to see what in hell that son of mine was up to."

She used the money from the rental of her beach house to pay her mortgage on the dance studio. She charged the students for dancing lessons, which paid for the salaries of her instructors.

All of her possessions, including the props she'd purchased from the MGM auction, had been placed into storage.

"I could have rented a hotel room, which I did sometime, making use of its bathroom facilities, lingering for an hour or two in a bubble bath. Sometimes, when I left a restaurant, a Hollywood party, or a night club, I stood on the sidewalk with no place to go. On such nights, I drove to a quiet street in Beverly Hills and slept on the back seat of my car."

In financial stress, Debbie opened the DR Dance studios in North Hollywood. Michael Jackson preferred it to all other rehearsal halls.

"I was tired of ratty studios and stinking toilets," she said. "I wanted a fine and decent place for performers."

"I was making fairly good money, but all of it was used to pay long-ago bills. I'd lost everything through reckless spending and being cheated out of all I had worked so hard for. Harry Karl comes to mind as the culprit."

"When the weather was awful, I sometimes drove over to the home of my dear friends, Bob and Margie Peterson. He was the president of *Hot Rod* magazine, and he always extended his hospitality. While I soaked in their bathtub, they prepared a home-cooked meal for me."

At times, I felt I was ready to die, but I didn't really want to die. I wanted to live. For me, suicide was not an option."

She even came up with a philosophy of life. "Life is both faith and love. Without faith, love is only one dimensional and incomplete. Faith helps you to overlook other people's shortcomings. Faith helps you to love them as they are. If you ask too much of any relationship, you can't help but be disappointed. But if you ask nothing, you can't be hurt or disappointed."

***

In post-recovery from her ill-fated love affair with Harrison Ford, Carrie fled to New York to start a life anew. Her *Star Wars* fame had catalyzed the development of a whole new array of friends, most of them in show business. Nearly all of them were much older than she was. "But I was rushing to grow up…and fast."

Although mainly separated from her traveling mother, Carrie woke up one morning and decided it was time for her to seek a reunion with her father, Eddie Fisher. As a child growing up, he had more or less abandoned her, but she was nevertheless ready for a reconciliation. The question was, was he?

He'd already gone through three marriages *[to Debbie, to Elizabeth Taylor, and to Connie Stevens]*. His fourth marriage *[to Terry Richard]* would be his shortest. Wedding her in 1975, he divorced her a few months later. Terry was half his age and had been Miss Louisiana in the Miss World beauty pageant. She'd come to Hollywood to pursue a career as a singer and actress. As a teenager growing up, "she'd worshipped Eddie for his good looks on TV," and had collected all his records.

No longer involved with "Dr. Needles," Fisher had switched to tranquilizers. "My little bottles went with me everywhere."

One night in Baja, California, tanked up on Gatorade and vodka, Fisher had married the beauty queen, but "after

When he saw this picture of himself, Eddie Fisher told Dean Martin and others, "This is what a singer looks like when he warbles off tune and marries Debbie Reynolds, Elizabeth Taylor, and Connie Stevens, and gets raped one night in Rome by Richard Burton."

460

three weeks of marriage, I became dangerously close to committing suicide, I was so depressed," he said. "Lack of money, a career in serious decline....I couldn't even afford to get Terry's teeth straightened," he later told Carrie.

"Eddie's marriage to Terry came and went so fast I didn't get to know my new stepmother," Carrie said.

Terry Richard and Eddie Fisher divorced on April 1, 1976. Their Mexican marriage might not even have been legal: The seal on their wedding certificate was an exact copy of the seal associated with *Good Housekeeping* magazine.

At the age of fifty, in failing health, Fisher had fallen into a repetitive pattern of desperate breakdowns followed by quick recoveries. He suffered laryngitis, extreme fatigue, and bronchitis. At one point, a physical and emotional wreck, he checked into Los Angeles' Cedars Sinai Hospital, where Todd, now twenty years old, visited him every day. After his release from the hospital, Todd invited him to come live with him and his girlfriend. They were soon to get married.

According to Fisher, "For the first time I got to know my son, who was now a computer wizard and electronics genius. He didn't inherit that from me. I didn't know how to turn on a TV."

"As a Born Again Christian, he tried to convert me and my wicked, wicked ways, but he did not succeed. 'Born a Jew, I'll die a Jew,' I told my son."

Everything he had was stored in a warehouse, but he had fallen behind in paying the rent for his storage units. "My worldly goods were sold at auction before I realized what was happening. All the precious mementos of my life were gone."

"In my moment of great despair, a call came in from Carrie, who was living at the time in New York. She wanted me to come and join her and start life anew."

***

After a long absence, Carrie and Eddie Fisher were reunited, and he moved into her Manhattan apartment. He was somewhat surprised to meet actress Joan Hackett, who was having a hard time financially and who had also moved in with Carrie.

During one of their first meals together, Carrie confided to her father that Hackett "is teaching me a lot, especially about love-making and the philosophy of lip gloss."

He quickly surmised that Hackett was becoming a surrogate mother for his daughter. He had seen her in only one film, *The Group* (1966), alongside such co-stars as Candice Bergen and Larry Hagman. This native of East Harlem, New York, was avidly seeking work and in the early 1980s would be nominated by the Academy Awards Committee as Best Supporting Actress for her work in *Only When I Laugh* (1981).

461

In Manhattan, Carrie had developed a new coterie of friends, many of them appearing as regulars on NBC's *Saturday Night Live,* a long-running comedy review which had premiered in 1975. The show parodied contemporary culture and politics, based on the monologues and interactions of regulars interspersed with a rotating cast of stars. In 1978, Carrie herself would be one of the guest hosts.

As a welcoming event for her father, she staged a party in her small apartment, inviting her newly minted friends. Director Mike Nichols showed up with his lover, the photographer Richard Avedon. Her father was also introduced to John Belushi, whom he did not particularly like until he learned that the actor/comedian was supplying Carrie with drugs. Belushi was soon offering drugs to Fisher, too. Carrie later said, "Eddie and I took drugs together; otherwise, we would not understand each other."

Belushi's best friend and artistic partner was *SNL* star, Dan Aykroyd, whom he'd met when they were both working at Chicago's *The Second City* comedy club. Soon, Carrie would be co-starring in a hit movie with Belushi and Aykroyd.

Fisher met a number of other performers he didn't know. Buck Henry was an actor, director, and writer who had been nominated for a "Best Adapted Screenplay" Oscar for his script for *The Graduate* (1968) starring Dustin Hoffman and Anne Bancroft. More recently, in 1979, he'd been nominated for a Best Director Oscar for his direction of *Heaven Can Wait.*

Tom Schiller was another close friend of Carrie's. He would have a long-term stint writing and directing episodes of *SNL.* Fisher engaged in long talks with the actor Richard Dreyfuss of Brooklyn. He had seen several of his films, including *The Goodbye Girl* (1977) for which he'd won an Oscar for Best Actor.

With the possible exception of Joan Hackett, Carrie's best girlfriend was Penny Marshall, the street-smart, "in your face" character actress from the Bronx. She was a hit on TV playing Lavern DeFazio in *Laverne & Shirley,* which had premiered in 1976.

"I was glad to meet Carrie's friends," Fisher said. "Belushi had a wry wit. He came up to me and asked, 'Didn't you use to be somebody?' Carrie's friends were brilliantly inventive, and some of their energy rubbed off on me. If they seemed older than their years, they made me, at fifty, feel younger than mine."

He was most impressed with the two young musicians—Paul Simon and Art Garfunkel—whom Carrie and her friend, Penny Marshall, were respectively dating.

According to Carrie, "When we spotted these guys at a party, I told Penny she could take Garfunkel, and I'd be the one to fuck Simon."

Whereas Carrie's involvement would lead to marriage, Marshall sustained only a brief relationship with Garfunkel He later credited her for helping him get through a depression. He said, "Everything changed. Penny is a sweet human being who can bring anybody down to earth. We had a lot of laughs, great sex, and a ton of party nights."

Fisher liked this folk rock duo of Simon & Garfunkel, who had been known as that since 1963, their first hit being "The Sound of Silence." He had also been intrigued by their album, *Parsley, Sage, Rosemary, & Thyme,* and by their hugely successful *Bridge Over Troubled Water.* When Carrie sang it, he was moved to tears.

He knew that Simon & Garfunkel had contributed to the soundtrack of *The Graduate* (1967), the iconic film from Mike Nichols in which Dustin Hoffman, as a disillusioned college graduate, is emotionally torn between his older lover and her daughter. Garfunkel told him that the original title of the film's theme song was "Mrs. Roosevelt."

When she wasn't dating Simon, Carrie and her father went everywhere together: The Stork Club, Broadway openings, and restaurants in Chinatown and Little Italy. "She wanted to invigorate my career, and friends of hers supplied new songs for me so I wouldn't sound like a relic of the 1950s. For the first time, I became aware of how right and rewarding a father-daughter relationship can be…Carrie was even working on a movie script about a father and daughter. Like everything else she wrote, it was semi-autobiographical. I didn't tell her that I disliked the plot. The father in the movie was a latent homosexual."

He eventually decided it was time for him to develop a gig for a return engagement at Grossingers in the Catskills. To his chagrin, two days before he contacted the resort's booking director, a tabloid exposé was published. It hit the newsstands with the fake revelation that Todd, now a Born Again Christian minister, had converted his father to Christianity. Although it was not true, Jennie Grossinger had died, and her daughter, Elaine, was in charge.

"Grossingers had once been my second home, but now Elaine told me she couldn't use me anymore because of all those Born Again stories."

"So what did I do? Carrie helped me get a booking at The Concord, Grossingers major competitor." *[Located in Kiamesha Lake, New York, the Concord was the largest resort in the region until its closing in 1998.]* "She later came on stage with me, and we got a standing ovation when we sang 'If I Loved You.'"

Back in New York, he asked Carrie to accompany him to dinner at Sardi's, which was still a theatrical hangout for stars. The *maître d',* perhaps with a touch of malice, seated them two tables away from Elizabeth Taylor, who was dining with her longtime friends, Peter Lawford and Roddy McDowall.

As he later recorded in a memoir, "I sent her a bottle of Dom Pérignon, and she raised a glass to me with a 'Mazel tov.' We spoke a few friendly words, and looking into her eyes and her still beautiful face, I realized that the painful memories had gone long ago. We had changed over the years, and I wished her well. We spoke again as I left the restaurant."

"*Shalom,* Eddie," she said.

"*Shalom,* Elizabeth."

On the West Coast, Debbie, too, having turned fifty, was having to reinvent herself. To an increasing degree, she faced the ghosts of yesteryear, knowing it was time to move on. Her lover, Bob Fallon, had already moved on, the relationship ending without bitterness. She was lonely on the road and after she moved into her small new home, she wondered if there would ever be another Fallon in her life. "In the romantic department, I felt I had an 'expired' date stamped on me."

"But life is nothing but full of surprises. How does that song go? On 'Some Enchanted Evening' you'll see a stranger across a crowded room...or something like that."

Debbie Reynolds
Younger Days, Happier Times

Chapter Sixteen

PRINCESS LEIA BECOMES A DRUG ADDICT

"When mother heard I was heavy into LSD, she did what any sensible parent would do: She phoned Cary Grant."

"GALAXY SNATCHING" WITH JOHN BELUSHI, GEORGE HARRISON, & JAMES BROWN

CARRIE AND PAUL (SIMON) GET MARRIED CROSSING A BRIDGE INTO TROUBLED WATER

UNSINKABLE DEBBIE AS ANNIE OAKLEY
SHOOTING UP THEATERS ACROSS THE WILD WEST

BURYING MOMMIE DEAREST (JOAN CRAWFORD)
DEBBIE FACES HER OWN MORTALITY DURING HER FINAL MONTHS AS CARETAKER TO A GREAT STAR

Carrie once summarized her relationship with Paul Simon: "Paul and I dated for six years, were married for two, divorced, and then began to date again."

The famous movie star and the famous singer started dating in 1977 with "lots of sleep-overs." Married on August 16, 1983, she filed for divorce in July of 1984. During a call to her father, she said, "It was a great wedding—you were there—but it was a bad marriage. I should have learned from Debbie not to marry a Jew Boy."

In all, the sexual liaison between Simon and Carrie lasted for twelve years.

George Lucas himself was the creator of the original scenario for the second installment of *Star Wars*. Entitled *The Empire Strikes Back,* and released in 1980, it was cast with the original trio of actors who had made the first installment internationally famous: Harrison Ford as Han Solo; Mark Hamill as Luke Skywalker; and Carrie Fisher as Princess Leia.

This time around, however, Lucas tapped Gary Kurtz to produce it; Irvin Kershner to direct it, and during the project's initial phases, Leigh Brackett to adapt the screenplay.

Supporting players included Billy Dee Williams as Lando Carlissian, the administrator of Cloud City; Anthony Daniels as a humanoid "protocol droid" with the Rebel Alliance; David Prowse as Darth Vader; Kenny Baker as an "astromech droid"; Frank Oz as Yoda; and Peter Mayhew as Chewbacca, a Wookiee *[i.e. a species of intelligent bipeds from the planet Kashyyyk]* and friend of Han Solo.

Alec Guinness appears again too, albeit briefly, in *The Empire Strikes Back,* as Obi-Wan, Luke Skywalker's deceased mentor. Obi-Wan guides Luke to Yoda.

The action in this latest series unfolds three years before the timeline of the original *Star Wars* that was released in 1977. Led by the villainous Darth Vader, "The Galactic Empire" is in pursuit of Luke Skywalker and what's left of the Rebel Alliance.

Led by Princess Leia, the rebels have established a new base on the ice planet of Hoth. With murderous resolve, Darth Vader has ordered his new fleet to track down and annihilate the rebels across the galaxy.

George Lucas was disappointed with Brackett's first draft of the screenplay. But before he could review and revise the script with her, she died of cancer. Immediately, Lucas made some strong structural changes, specifying Darth Vader as the father of his enemy, Luke, and leaving Han Solo imprisoned in carbonite and left in limbo before his rescue.

Shooting began in March 1979, amid the bleak landscapes near Norway's Hardingerjøkulen Glacier. Shortly after they arrived, the cast and crew encountered the worst storm Norway had endured in fifty years, delaying production.

Later, the very elaborate interior shots were filmed at Elstree Studios outside London. They required the design and construction of fifty sets. Costs rose rapidly. The management of 20th Century Fox blamed the additional expenses on the company's president, Alan Ladd, Jr., the rancor from which eventually led to his resignation.

Recognized everywhere as a major production whose implications would affect filmmaking for years to come, its world premiere was staged in May of 1980 at the Kennedy Center in Washington, D.C. It received mixed, often negative, reviews.

Vincent Canby of *The New York Times* panned it. David Denby of *New York*

Magazine called it "a Wagnerian pop movie—grandiose, thrilling, imperiously generous in scale, and also a bit ponderous." Judith Martin of the *Washington Post* attacked the film for having no particular beginning or end, which—with the understanding that additional sequences were on their way— was true.

But as the decades moved along, and as the film was re-released several times, its reputation and its profits grew. Lucas had used the $33 million he'd made from his 1977 film, bolstered with bank loans, to finance it. By the second decade of the 21st Century, its worldwide gross approached $600 million.

Reviews also got better. Roger Ebert called it "the most thought-provoking of the *Star Wars* Trilogy." *Rotten Tomatoes* described it as, "Dark, sinister, but ultimately even more involving than *A New Hope. The Empire Strikes Back* defies viewer expectations and takes the series to heightened emotional levels."

In 2015, *Empire Magazine*, based on reviews submitted by its fans, defined *The Empire Strikes Back* as the greatest film ever made.

***

During the making of *The Empire Strikes Back*, Carrie's summer affair with Harrison Ford was fading into memory. "But we became friends and even played love scenes on camera."

Beginning at the age of sixteen, she'd become "addicted to weed, compliments of Debbie. But after six years of going up in smoke, pot became creepy, dark, and scary for me."

During the making of this latest *Star Wars* adventure, she turned to drugs that included cocaine, painkillers, and ultimately LSD, a psychedelic holdover from the Swinging Sixties.

Through memoirs and interviews Carrie gave over the years, one can reconstruct the condition of her troubled mind at the time.

"Through protracted use and over time, drugs became mind-relievers and pain expanders—a place where everything hurt and nothing made sense. The drugs helped me to dial down my erratic and sometimes angry or sad moods. I don't mean to tattle tales, but during those location shoots on that god damn glacier in Norway, cast and crew, at least many of them, were stoned. We were living in a

Some viewers suggested that the optics of *The Empire Strikes Back* were inspired by the psychedelic colors and movements of LSD.

In the upper photo, the Evil genius, Darth Vader (right) pits his "Force" against one of the "good guys"

In the lower photo, a computer graphic replicates the undulating, hypnotic effect of an LSD trip.

world of our own on that ice planet. You couldn't take a crap without feeling the cold. Drop your pants and icicles formed around your rosebud."

"Unlike my fellow actors, I didn't dig coke all that much, at least not as much as my co-workers. But I snorted it anyway, hoping to fit in."

"Before the shoot was over, I faced a cold, dark fact: I was taking more drugs than all the rest of them."

"One reason I turned to drugs was that I could not handle fame. I saw what fame did to both my mother and father. In many ways, it destroyed Eddie's life."

"Debbie," Carrie continued, "suffered tragedies worthy of a Shakespeare heroine. She was constantly having her life destroyed and forced to reconstruct it. After she passed fifty, that became harder and harder to pull off. She also became harder and harder, having long ago attended the backwoods funeral of 'Tammy, The Beloved.'"

By the time she turned twenty, Carrie had become more and more dependent on drugs, including LSD. When cast and crew of *The Empire Strikes Back* descended on London for interior shooting, word reached Debbie about her daughter's increasing addiction.

"When mother heard I was heavy into drugs, she did what any sensible parent would do: She phoned Cary Grant."

[Carrie's statement would make no sense unless you're familiar with the life of that matinée idol. As Cary Grant admitted himself, after completing An Affair to Remember *(1957), he began a supervised use of LSD at the recommendation of two psychiatrists in Beverly Hills. They were pioneers (of sorts) in the therapeutic use of psychedelics, hoping to treat severe depressions such as those that plagued their famous movie star client.*

Under careful supervision, Grant was administered LSD at the Hartman and Chandler Psychiatric Institute in Beverly Hills. Throughout the rest of the 1950s, he would continue this controversial and experimental form of therapy.]

Debbie, during her conversations with Grant, confided, "My daughter, Carrie Fisher, is taking LSD, 'mainlining' the stuff, if that's the right word. I don't know much of the druggie lingo. I'm a vodka gal myself."

Grant was in London at the time that Carrie was finishing her latest *Star Wars* installment. As such, he promised Debbie that he would call

"Turn on, tune in, drop out," or so said LSD user Cary Grant.

468

her and talk to her.

He did not know it at the time, but he was her ultimate movie idol, some critics calling him "the most important actor in the history of cinema."

"I was not awed by most celebrities," Carrie said, "Cary Grant being the exception. After all, I was born the daughter of two celebrities, and I grew up knowing Fred Astaire, Judy Garland, and a host of other stars. For a time, Elizabeth Taylor was my stepmother. How's that for name dropping? In time, I would even marry a celebrated singer, Paul Simon."

"Cary just killed me," Carrie said to Alec Guinness. "We even had the same first name, only spelled differently. I was completely blown away by him. He had it all—an easy-going class, quiet confidence, a sharp wit, all in a handsome package. If he'd ever asked me, I would immediately have surrendered to him my galaxy snatch."

When he first phoned her in London, she thought that some Cary Grant impersonator was pulling a telephonic joke. "Oh, Tony [Curtis], cut the shit. I know you're not Cary Grant!" she said to the voice on the phone.

The voice on the phone responded with its distinctively crisp accent: "On some days, I don't know if I'm Cary Grant either. Archie Leach was sitting in an office at Paramount one afternoon in 1932 when he decided he was henceforth going to become Cary Grant. A man can't go through life being known as Leach."

Somehow, that self-deprecating humor convinced her that the voice on the phone was really that of Cary Grant. She doubted if sex was what he wanted from her. Within the entertainment community, he was widely perceived as a legendary bisexual. She'd heard that the love of his life, especially during the 1930s, had been Randolph Scott.

Cary Grant had also seduced two of the world's richest women, the tobacco heiress Doris Duke and the Woolworth heiress, Barbara Hutton, whom he eventually married.

A parade of some of the most desirable (or well-connected) men and women on the planet had visited his bed, including Grace Kelly, Ginger Rogers, Gary Cooper, Howard Hughes, and Cole Porter.

After the mandatory chitchat, the two stars began discussing psychedelics. "Before I took LSD, I had this policeman who lived inside me, keeping me from facing the truth about myself and my desires," Grant told her. "It was through acid that I finally freed myself from his prison to become the man I really was. I was able to piece together a whole man who had been divided into parts. I emerged as a fully formed person, a union of mind, body, and soul."

He relayed to her much of what he'd already written in his diary: "I learned to accept the responsibility for my own actions, and to blame no one but myself for the circumstances of my own creation. I learned that no one was keeping me from being happy but myself. You cannot judge the day unless you experience the night. It takes a long time for happiness to break through barrier walls."

Debbie may have hoped that Grant would talk to Carrie and wean her from LSD, but, if anything, he seemed to endorse the drug for its allegedly therapeutic effects.

"I wanted to love and be loved," he said. "But that cannot happen until you love yourself."

He defined his ingestion of LSD as "a rebirth. I passed through changing seas of horrifying and happy sights, through a montage of intense hate and love, a mosaic of past impressions assembling and reassembling through terrifying depths of dark despair replaced by glorious heavenlike religious symbolisms. I am better for having used it, and I believe that there is a curative power in the drug itself."

"Everybody wants to be Cary Grant," he continued. "Even I want to be Cary Grant. I have spent the greater part of my life fluctuating between Archie Leach and Cary Grant, unsure of either, suspecting each. I pretended to be somebody I wanted to be until finally, I became that person, or he became me."

"Your dreams under the influence of LSD can be rough, but ultimately liberating," he told Carrie. He cited a dream in which "I became this enormous penis which I used painfully to rape the matinée idols of my day—Clark Gable, Robert Taylor, Errol Flynn, Gary Cooper, and Tyrone Power."

"In another dream, I defecated all over the rug in my psychiatrist's office. In yet another dream, I shot like Princess Leia into Outer Space, escaping Earth, which was being blown into oblivion."

Responding to his dialogue, Carrie shared details with him about some of her own LSD-induced hallucinations. "In one dream, I was sailing all the seas of the world. At first, I faced an ocean filled with prehistoric monsters that once inhabited the planet, those that didn't survive the Ice Age. In some dreams, I had to battle dragons. But in others, I was in a peaceful meadow of daffodils surrounded by lambs. At times, I would see a light show of dazzling colors— purple, sunflower yellow, bright orange, chartreuse, magenta, fire engine red. One night, I had a sword fight with Darth Vader."

"Sometimes I would flush a toilet and it became Niagara Falls. When I looked in the mirror 'under the influence,' a monstrous green iguana was staring back at me."

"At times, I was visited by a fairy godmother like the type Billie Burke played in *The Wizard of Oz*. Before the dream ended, she had morphed into the threatening Wicked Witch of the West, none other than Margaret Hamilton menacing Judy Garland."

"In my most horrid nightmare, I was covered with menstrual blood. One night, I screeched in horror as I gave birth to *Rosemary's Baby*, who began to eat at my flesh."

In all, Grant made three very long phone calls to Carrie. She later wrote, jokingly, "I could have accused him of stalking me."

470

When she heard in the paper that he was going to celebrate his birthday on January 18 (born in 1904), she went to a liquor store and bought an expensive bottle of wine. He called to thank her. This time, the call was brief, and there was no talk of LSD. He did say, however, that he had never really liked wine.

"After all the talk about LSD, I came to my own conclusion," she said. "For the rest of my life, I knew in some way or the other that I would be dependent on what Jacqueline Susann called 'dolls' in that bestseller, *Valley of the Dolls.* Those little devils would always be waiting for me in my medicine cabinet or beside my bed whenever I wanted to alter reality."

***

Debbie had known Ava Gardner since their early days at MGM when both of them were contract players. They had to roll out of bed in the pre-dawn hours to report to the studio's makeup department at 6AM. Gardner liked Debbie but told her, "You're too square to hang out with my crowd." *[Elizabeth Taylor had previously told Debbie much the same thing.]*

Debbie saw less and less of her when Gardner moved to London and eventually settled in an apartment in Kensington.

Motivated by her perception that the last time she had spoken to her daughter, her voice had been slurred, and even included moments when she'd been incoherent, Debbie, from L.A., had been trying to get Carrie on the phone. She kept dialing the telephone in her London accommodation until well after midnight, local time, but with no answer. Soon, she began worrying that her daughter might be suffering from, or dying from, a drug overdose.

The only person she knew in London who might be awake during the wee hours of the morning there was Gardner herself, perhaps drinking too much champagne and listening to Frank Sinatra records. Debbie phoned her and found her wide awake. She explained the situation to the fading star, who agreed to help.

"I've dealt with drunks all my life, including Dean Martin," Ava said, "so I guess I can handle a druggie."

Thirty minutes later, a taxi deposited Gardner in front of the St. James Hotel *[London SW1]*, where the desk manager welcomed her and led her upstairs to Carrie's room, using a passkey to gain entrance.

"From bullfighters to Mexican beach boys, from Clark Gable to Richard Burton, I've had them all. That's why I'm the tattered relic you see before you," Ava Gardner said to Debbie.

They found Carrie fully dressed and passed out on the floor, face down. The windows were open, blowing in the cold night air, and her TV set was blaring.

After checking to see if she were alive, Gardner phoned her own doctor, who rushed to the hotel. After examining her, he reported that whereas Carrie had not overdosed in a way that might immediately threaten her life, she had definitely ingested too many drugs.

Carrie was undressed and tucked away in bed. Gardner promised that she would sit up all night to ensure that nothing went wrong.

As Carrie reported the following day, "Imagine waking up and staring into the face of the beautiful Ava Gardner. I knew at once she'd been sent here by Debbie. I felt embarrassed and humiliated."

After hearing Carrie's profuse thanks, and after Carrie's assuring her that she'd be all right, Gardner exited from her apartment, telling her, "Now for god's sake, call your mother."

Carrie promised she would. Within two days, she'd flown back to Los Angeles where her faithful, loving brother, Todd, was waiting to welcome her home.

[For the remainder of her life, Debbie was grateful to Gardner for coming to Carrie's aid. Every time she visited London, she made it a point to call on her at her apartment.]

"Like all of the 1950s MGM girls, we were fighting our worst enemy: Time," Debbie said. "In her heyday, Ava, along with Hedy *[Lamarr]*, was hailed as the most beautiful woman in the world. But a life of heavy drinking and heavy living had taken its toll on her face. She was also in poor health."

"During my last visit, we spoke of drugs and Carrie. She told me she was never turned on to drugs. Her second husband, Artie Shaw, and Robert Mitchum, her former co-star, had tried to turn her onto pot."

"Of course, I've had more than my share of booze," Gardner confessed.

"And I've been known to drink more than one vodka at night," Debbie admitted.

Gardner was in such poor health that when she flew to Los Angeles in the fall of 1989, she was immediately transferred by stretcher from the airport to an ambulance heading for St. John's hospital in Santa Monica.

Both Carrie and Debbie visited her there, where she reported having trouble breathing. She confessed to them, "I don't think I have long to live. Would you believe it, Frank *[Sinatra]* hasn't visited me? He'd been such a faithful friend until now."

"Does he know you're here?" Debbie asked.

"I'm sure he does," Gardner said. "It's that god damn bitch of a wife. She hates me. Jealous as hell." *[Ava, whose stormy marriage to Sinatra had lasted from 1951 to 1957, was referring to his fourth and final wife, Barbara Marx, whose marriage to the singer endured from 1976 until his death in 1998.]*

Both Debbie and Carrie urged her to remain in California for its better weather, but Gardner nonetheless flew back to London. It was there that she died on January 25, 1990, her obituary appearing on frontpages around the world.

Debbie faced the press: "Ava Gardner was one of the most striking and genuine stars of all time. She never relied on her great beauty to carry a picture, even if the script was mediocre. My heart is broken, and all of her friends are so very sad to hear of the passing of this fine and noble lady."

Carrie also addressed the press: "The Hollywood legends are dying out. Who's next? Will I live to bury two legends, Eddie Fisher and Debbie Reynolds? Or will they bury me?"

***

Even in moments of despair, Debbie could always "lose myself in my work." In distinct contrast to most of the female movie stars of her generation—many of whom were retired or had retreated from view, a few of whom had married rich men—she would continue to receive job offers of some sort until the day of her death. "After all," she frequently said, "I was the 'Unsinkable Tammy.'"

In the late 1970s, the Broadway producers Cy Feuer and Ernest Martin hired Debbie to star in a revival of *Annie Get Your Gun,* which had been a hit Broadway musical (1946-49) and an even bigger success as a movie adaptation (1950) starring Betty Hutton.

A noted scriptwriter of her era, Dorothy Fields, had long wanted to update the story of Annie Oakley (1860-1926), a female sharpshooter who had toured in Buffalo Bill's Wild West Show and sustained a romance with her fellow sharpshooter, Frank Butler. Fields originally shopped her vision for a Broadway revival to producer Mike Todd, but he rejected it. "No one wants to see a play about a fucking dyke cowgal," he told her.

Undaunted, Fields turned to Richard Rodgers and Oscar Hammerstein II, who agreed to produce it as a lavish new musical that retained Irving Berlin's original music and lyrics. Born in 1888, Berlin had written his first hit in 1903, and Debbie al-

Debbie as Annie Oakley in *Annie Get Your Gun,* a revival of the famous musical.

"Okay," she said. "So Im not as good as Ethel Merman or Betty Hutton."

ways considered him the greatest songwriter in the history of America.

Ethel Merman had virtually defined the character of Annie in the original (1946) Broadway version of *Annie Get Your Gun,* which ran for 1,147 performances. Its 1950 adaptation by MGM into a movie musical at first starred Judy Garland, who was fired and replaced with Betty Hutton. Howard Keel was cast as Frank Butler. Many hits emerged from the show, the most celebrated of which was "There's No Business Like Show Business."

Debbie was granted her choice of director, and she wanted her former lover, Gower Champion. He guided her through the numbers smoothly, as he always did, although she began to sense he was fading a bit. Both of them agreed that Harve Presnell, her co-star from *The Unsinkable Molly Brown,* would be ideal in the role of Butler.

Martin and Feuer wanted to take the musical to Broadway, but Debbie turned down the chance. She told them that her voice was light and that Merman, with whom any adaptation would be compared, had been a "real belter. I feared that the Broadway critics would roast me and compare me unfavorably to Merman."

Yet two weeks later, she got a call from Berlin, who at first had to convince her he was real. (She thought someone in the cast was playing a joke on her.) He told her he was too old to ever leave New York, and that she "would make one songwriter very happy to see you play Annie on Broadway." Even with such a powerful request from the composer (Berlin) of the music himself, she was still reluctant, and turned him down.

Both Champion and Debbie realized that some of the lyrics to "I'm an Indian Too" might offend present-day Native Americans or their champion, Marlon Brando. With the hope that they might be revised, she phoned Berlin and within a day, he had come up with new, less offensive lyrics.

The final decision not to take the play to Broadway was made by the producers themselves. As such, Debbie's revival of *Annie Get Your Gun* toured sporadically through the American West, especially in and around L.A., but never made it back to Broadway in Manhattan.

Berlin survived long enough to be *fêted* on his 100th birthday, dying in September of 1989. Television and radio station across the country played his major hits, including "Easter Parade," "There's No Business Like Show business," and Kate Smith's "God Bless America," first performed in 1938. Many other famous artists also performed renditions of his songs, including Judy Garland, Bing Crosby ("White Christmas"), Frank Sinatra, Elvis Presley, Billie Holiday, and Barbra Streisand.

"What a send-off to a great man," Debbie said, mourning his loss.

***

Joan Crawford had befriended Debbie since she'd been a starlet in the

1950s, and Debbie had remained forever grateful. She continued to visit her every time she flew into New York, and they often talked together over the phone.

In 1975, Debbie was at Crawford's side as the megastar of the 30s, 40s, and 50s made a grand entrance into the fashionable dining club, "21," in Manhattan.

The following year, Debbie phoned Crawford and invited her as her guest to a charity event in New York for the Thalians, which she had continued to support. The venue was in the penthouse apartment of Martin Kimmel, a rich New Yorker who had once been married to Gloria de Haven, a fixture in many MGM musicals of the 1940s.

Debbie met Crawford at the door of Kimmel's apartment, and immediately rushed her into a nearby bedroom to repair the older star's makeup. Her eyesight had been failing, and one of her false eyelashes was about to come loose. Debbie quickly repaired it and steered Crawford back to the party. "Joan looked stunning in her large picture hat and with a midnight black taffeta dress. She could still pull off a star's entrance."

In April of 1977, Debbie flew once again to New York, where Crawford was one of the first friends she called. It was a different Crawford who answered the phone this time. Her voice was weak, and, in Debbie's words, she seemed disconnected.

Debbie invited her out, but the star turned her down. "I'm not seeing anybody," she said. "I want my friends, and, of course, my fans, to remember me the way I used to be—perhaps in *Torch Song* (1953), where I showed off my still shapely gams."

After about ten minutes of conversation, Crawford seemed to want to get off the phone. She told Debbie that she'd given away her beloved dog, Princess. She also said that she was mailing her a gold pin that Alfred Steele, her last husband *[1955-59]*, had given her. "I want you to have it as a token of our long-enduring friendship."

Three weeks later, back in California, Debbie received another phone call from another life-long friend, Bette Davis, whom she still referred to as "Mother."

After Crawford's death, Debbie learned about how she'd spent her last night on earth:

Along with her housekeeper and a female fan, she'd watched on TV *The Damned Don't Cry* (1950), a film she'd made for Warner Brothers. During the shoot, she seduced both of her leading men, Steve Cochran and David Brian.

Her housekeeper told a reporter that on the day before she died, Crawford had received two letters, one from Barbara Stanwyck, another from Katharine Hepburn.

"Have you heard the news?" Davis asked. "Joan Crawford is dead! We're supposed to speak only good of the dead. Good!" As Davis put down her phone, Debbie burst into tears.

Born in 1904 in San Antonio, Texas, Crawford had died white-haired, wide-eyed, and looking gaunt, suffering from pancreatic cancer.

The New York Times wrote: "Joan Crawford was the quintessential superstar, an epitome of timeless glamour who personified for decades the dreams and disappointments of millions of American women."

In June, Debbie attended a remembrance for Crawford at the Samuel Goldwyn Theater at the Academy of Motion Picture Arts and Sciences. Sponsored by director George Cukor, film clips were screened from throughout the course of the star's career, including her Oscar-winning performance as *Mildred Pierce* (1945).

The presentation ended with blow-ups of portraits of Crawford during the different phases of her career.

Reporter Bob Thomas wrote about "Joan Crawford's patrician brow that belied her beginnings, the pencil-line eyebrows with an air of *hauteur*, the bones almost visible beneath the sculptured cheeks, the firm, determined chin, and the sensuous painted mouth. Most of all, those eyes. Those huge, luminous, omniscient eyes that had known much agony, not all of it self-inflicted, and the endless, unrealized pursuit of love."

After Crawford's death, her adopted and disinherited daughter, Christina Crawford, wrote a vindictive and accusatory autobiography entitled *Mommie Dearest* and published it in 1981. "It was a cruel, heartless treatment of poor Joan," Debbie said. "The Joan in that book was not the Joan I knew over the years. It was filled with scurrilous tales, which two of her other children denounced as 'notorious lies.'"

"It was even made into a movie with Faye Dunaway who delivered an almost campy performance, treating it like a horror movie," Debbie said. "I'm grateful to Anne Bancroft for turning down the role."

"Joan was dead and didn't have to read this wicked gal's libelous attack on her. At least with my own daughter, Carrie, I was alive when she wrote *Postcards from the Edge* in 1987."

***

When Debbie was on Broadway starring in the musical, *Irene*, she met Bob O'Connell, who worked in the wardrobe department. His first words to her were, "I'm your new wardrobe mistress."

"He didn't look like any costumer I'd ever known," she said. "He was almost as tall as Rock Hudson, and looked like a rough, tough, ex-basketball jock."

"Bob could iron costumes and repair them," Debbie said. "He claimed he even sewed ballet slippers for Rudolf Nureyev on occasion. I suspect he'd performed other 'services' for Rudi as well."

O'Connell and Debbie bonded. "We became instant friends. He'd seen all my movies and raved about them. I didn't tell Carrie, but he didn't care all that much for *Star Wars.*"

"He liked musicals, especially those from the 1940s with Judy Garland and Mickey Rooney. He played the records of The Andrews Sisters and he had seen all of Betty Grable's movies at least three times each. On a drunken night, to amuse me, he did his impersonation of Carmen Miranda. Mickey did it better, however. *[The pint-sized star's drag impersonation of Miranda was seen around the world.]*

Bob O'Connell in a scene from the daytime TV series, *Dark Shadows.* Only a part-time actor, he worked as Debbie's costumer.

Before working with her, O'Connell had been hired by the ballet dancer Rudolf Nureyev as his dresser.

"I had the greatest job on the planet," he told her. "I had to fit Rudi into his ballet tights every night without a jockstrap. He liked to show off his endowment."

When Jane Powell took over Debbie's role in *Irene,* O'Connell was dismissed, but "I hired him when I took *Irene* on the road," Debbie said.

"Bob Fallon had split from my life, and a new Bob came to live with me. Of course, there was a big difference between these two Bobs—Fallon for sex, O'Connell for companionship. He didn't go without sex, however. He always managed to slip off somewhere with one of the stagehands, preferring those who were married."

"In Los Angeles, we attended premieres together, Hollywood parties, and endless movies. For food, we patronized little dives. I had developed this passion for Mexican food, especially tacos, and he always wanted pickled pigs' feet followed by strawberry ice cream."

"I came to adore him. He was my guardian angel."

O'Connell had wanted to be an actor but got only minor roles, nearly all of them uncredited. His two biggest gigs were in TV serials.

He began with his role as a bartender on *Dark Shadows,* where he appeared in 56 episodes from 1966 to 1970. That was followed by another stint for thirteen episodes on *Ryan's Hope* from 1976 to 1977. Once again, he had to use his bartop dishrag to clean beer mugs on camera.

The only starring role O'Connell ever got was that of a gangster, Johnny Scaro, in the 1968 soft-porn flick, *Some Like It Violent.* The character he portrays commandeers an online dating service to use as a front for a prostitution ring.

O'Connell invited Debbie to go with him for a screening when his film opened in Los Angeles. Surprising for an XXX-rated film, he got some good reviews. One critic wrote that he was a *"tour de force* as a hardened gangster." Another claimed, "He is simply fabulous in his monologues." Yet another noted, "He must have seen James Cagney's *White Heat* (1949) too many times."

Their friendship endured for several years but ended disastrously. It happened in a way Debbie would never forget. At O'Connell's request, he asked his doctor to phone her. "Your friend has cancer," the doctor stated bluntly. "He's got about six months to live, if that."

Back home that afternoon, he came into her living room. "Those were the saddest blue eyes I've ever seen in my life. "I'm gonna die. Why me? I thought I would live forever."

She recalled that in spite of his size, he sat down on her lap. "Bob and I sobbed for hours."

In the weeks that followed, his condition worsened, and his weight dropped drastically, almost ten pounds at a time. Soon, he was a skeleton of himself, weighing only ninety pounds. Subjected to chemotherapy treatments, he vomited a lot and his hair began to fall out in patches.

"I kept up his diet of morphine," she said. "He wanted to stay with me until the end, but in his final weeks, I could no longer give him the 24-hour care he needed. He was reluctant, but I checked him into Cedars Sinai and spent hours every day by his bed."

Finally, death came to this good-hearted man, age 48, who had been born into an Irish Catholic family in the Bronx.

"He wanted to be cremated," Debbie said. "With a friend, I rented a small plane and we took off, heading to Catalina. I tossed his ashes to the winds. I looked out the window as I watched what was left of my best and most loyal friend disappear into an unforgiving sea."

***

In the early years of "the Reagan era," (i.e., the 1980s), now launched as an independent young woman leading her own life without her mother's interference, Carrie began a series of film roles and assorted affairs that she later referred to as "sordid."

Despite his status as a married man, John Belushi and Carrie began a brief affair. He had married Judith Jacklin, his high school sweetheart, in 1976, and remained married to her until his death in 1982. It is not known if his wife ever learned about her husband's affair with Carrie, but she must have suspected.

"We made passionate love," she confessed. "At least I think we did. Both of us were too stoned to know. John and I did a lot of drugs...and I mean a lot."

Some sources claim that it was not Belushi, but his partner, Dan Aykroyd, who was Carrie's lover. Once, when asked about that, Carrie said, "How in the fuck am I supposed to know that? I know this: It was either John or Dan, one of them. What in hell does it matter? A dick is a dick is a dick, as Gertrude Stein might have said."

John Belushi, Dan Aykroyd, and Carrie in a moment of relaxation during the shooting of *The Blues Brothers*.

Carrie could sing about a woman torn between two lovers.

From her beginnings, Carrie was perhaps the most candid celebrity in Hollywood about her drug habits. "I want to get one thing fucking straight: Religion is called the opiate of the masses. Well, get this...I took masses of opiates religiously. But I was a virgin druggie compared to John *[Belushi]*. He did not have a substance abuse problem. He was an abuser of substances."

Both Belushi and Aykroyd became refugees from *Saturday Night Live,* using it as a stepping stone for future gigs as screen actors. As a team, they launched their respective film careers in the same movie, a flop called *1941,* released in 1979 and directed by Steven Spielberg. That was followed by *The Blues Brothers* (1980). According to Carrie, "Since John was enjoying my galaxy snatch, he felt obligated to give me a role."

Its director, John Landis, agreed to the casting. He had previously directed Belushi and Aykroyd in *National Lampoon's Animal House* (1978), a spoof of college life in the early 1960s.

In *The Blues Brothers,* Carrie was cast as the unnamed "Mystery Woman," Belushi's vengeful, probably psychotic ex-*fiancée* who repeatedly tries to kill him. He survives her action-adventure volley of bullets from her M-36. Landis and Aykroyd had collaborated on the screenplay, and supporting players, in addition to Carrie, included Henry Gibson, John Candy, and Charles Napier.

Carrie became especially fond of Gibson, an actor, singer, and songwriter best known for his recurring appearance in the long-running TV series, *Rowan & Martin's Laugh-In* (1968-1971). In *The Blues Brothers,* his role was that of "Head Nazi" or "Illinois Nazi."

The leading male characters in *The Blues Brothers* evolved from some of the skits presented on *Saturday Night Live.*

The fanciful tale is a story of redemption, beginning when Jake (Belushi) is released from prison and finds his brother Elwood (Aykroyd) waiting for him at the gate. Together, they set out on a "mission from God" to prevent a bank's foreclosure of the Catholic orphanage in which they were reared. They decide to raise $5,000 in back taxes by reuniting the R&B band for a fund-raising performance. Along the way, they are targeted for death not only by "Mystery Woman," played by Carrie, but by Neo-Nazis and a competing Country-Western band, all the while in hot pursuit by the Chicago police. In the pursuit of their task, the brothers nearly destroy Chicago.

The film's producer Robert K. Weiss "was nearly driven out of my mind." As costs mounted, Universal applied increasing pressure to trim them.

A staggering roster of stars had been cast in the film. They included musicians, many of them African American, and famous performers making short but expensive cameo appearances.

Belushi's partying and drug addiction caused costly delays. Destructive car chases and special effects [mostly machine-gun fights and explosions] ballooned the budget as well, making it one of the most expensive comedies ever filmed.

In addition to the cast, more than 500 extras were hired, including 200 National Guardsmen and 100 state and city police officers. In addition to that, two dozen horses had to be rented for the mounted police scenes, along with a fleet of helicopters, fire engines, and a trio of Sherman tanks.

When he wasn't filming, Belushi escorted Carrie to haunts in his native Chicago, especially Wrigley Field and the Old Town Ale House. "John not only made me a card-carrying drug addict, but a god damn alcoholic—think Ray Milland in *The Lost Weekend* (1945)."

Landis once went to Belushi's dressing trailer where he discovered "a mountain" of cocaine on his coffee table. Belushi broke down and sobbed in his arms. "I know drugs ae going to kill me sooner than later. I'm one of those guys facing early death."

"Drug use was common among cast and crew," Carrie asserted. "We even had our own bar on the set. We called it The Blues Club, and its staff doubled as drug dealers. What fun! Movies should be about having fun." Carrie enjoyed meeting and talking to the cast, most of whom appeared in abbreviated cameo roles.

In addition to a host of other actors, singer Steve Lawrence was cast as a booking agent; the iconic British model, Twiggy, was a "chic lady in a Jaguar";

Homicidal Carrie, playing Belushi's vengeful ex, in *The Blues Brothers*.

Spielberg played a county clerk; Landis, a state trooper; Paul Reubens (later Pee-Wee Herman) a waiter.

Soul and R&B entertainers included some of the biggest names in music at the time: Aretha Franklin, James Brown, Ray Charles, and Cab Calloway.

In 1980, in the week following its opening across America, *The Blues Brothers* ranked second in attendance, nationwide, surpassed only by *The Empire Strikes Back*. Carrie, with a profound sense of irony, found herself starring in the two highest-grossing films in the country. Landis claimed that *The Blues Brothers* was also the first American film to gross more money overseas than it did in the United States.

Reviews, for the most part, were positive. *Rotten Tomatoes* asserted that it was "Too over the top for its own good, but ultimately rescued by the cast's charm, director John Landis' grace, and several soul-searching numbers."

Time magazine wrote, "The movie is a demolition symphony that works with the cold efficiency of a Moog synthesizer gone sadistic."

Empire magazine defined *The Blues Brothers* as "an amalgam of urban sleaze, automobile crunch, and blackheart rhythm and blues with better music than any film has had for many years."

Over the decades, the movie has become a staple of late-night cinema. In the second decade of the 21st Century, it was still a cult classic.

***

[On the morning of March 5, 1982, a health and fitness trainer, Bill Wallace, arrived at bungalow 3 at the Chateau Marmont Hotel on Sunset Boulevard in Hollywood. He'd come for a workout with Belushi. When he did not answer the door, Wallace tried the knob and found the door unlocked. He entered the darkened interior only to discover that its movie star occupant—John Belushi—was dead, lying face down in a pool of vomit, He was 33 years old.

The coroner determined the cause of death as a "speedball," i.e., an injection combining both cocaine and heroin.

In the early morning hours before his death, Belushi had had three visitors. They included Robin Williams, Robert De Niro, and Catherine Evelyn Smith, who had been the last to leave.

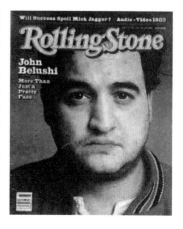

Two months later, Smith, during an interview with the National Enquirer *admitted that she had administered Belushi's fatal injection. Above the article was a banner headline: "I KILLED BELUSHI."*

After the appearance of that article, the case was reopened, and Smith was charged with first degree murder and extradited from Ontario. In a plea bargain, the charge was reduced to involuntary manslaughter, and she served fifteen months in jail.

In 2004, Belushi was posthumously honored with a star on the Hollywood Walk of Fame. Carrie visited it privately, placing a lone rose on the sidewalk. Soon after, it was trampled upon by a passerby.]

***

Of the many musicians Carrie met during her involvement with *The Blues Brothers,* James Brown intrigued her the most. "Cab Calloway is old enough to be my grandfather, and Roy Charles is blind, so he can't be enthralled by my beauty."

"I decided, at least for the week and as a dare to myself, to see what Jane Fonda and Jean Seberg, plus hundreds of other adventurous women, found it so delightful in getting seduced by black men. Seberg and Fonda went for members of the Black Panthers, but I preferred more cuddly teddy bear types."

"James was just a year younger than my mother, but he had a strong, masculine appeal," she said. "I had long appreciated his music, and I was soon calling him by his nickname of 'Hi De Ho Man.'"

She later confessed to her roommate, Joan Hackett, "Carrie Fisher spent the weekend with the Godfather of Soul. Go figure!"

Brown is credited for his role in changing the implications of the word "black" into an affirmation. Two of his songs that come to mind include "Black Is Beautiful" and "I'm Black and I'm Proud."

One Saturday night, Brown invited Carrie to a jazz club in South Chicago, promising her that it regularly presented the best jazz outside of New Orleans. There was no sign outside; its aficionados just knew the address. Brown said that the club's former patrons, fans, and performers had included Louis Armstrong, Nat King Cole, Billie Holiday, and Ella Fitzgerald, who was escorted there one night by Frank Sinatra.

When Calloway heard of their plans, he asked if he could accompany them. In *The Blues Brothers,* he'd sung his most famous song, "Minnie the Moocher," which he told her he'd first recorded in 1931. *[He'd been born on Christmas Day in 1907 in Rochester, New York.]*

When Carrie had first moved to New York City, she'd gone to the Cotton Club in Harlem to hear him perform.

During her evening with him in South Chicago, Carrie asked Calloway if he'd contribute one of his zoot suits to Debbie's museum *[it was still in its planning stage]* of Hollywood props and costumes.

When she got to the club, Carrie was one of only three white women visiting it that night. "No one paid me much attention, but patrons treated Cab and James like beloved figures."

After an intensely creative interaction with the music and the setting that night, Brown invited Carrie to a late-night party ten blocks away. Calloway bowed out and headed back to his hotel.

After leaving the club together, Brown told her that they were lucky that there were no photographers lurking outside. "Otherwise, I can just see the headline— PRINCESS LEIA IN LOVE TRYST WITH THE GODFATHER OF SOUL. Sammy Davis, Jr. has that kind of trouble with the press all the time. My god, that black boy sure likes to grab peaches from the top of the tree—take Ava Gardner or Marilyn Monroe, for instance. That Sammy!"

At the decaying apartment building where the party was jiving, they climbed four flights of stairs before entering an apartment with about a dozen couples in various stages of heavy petting.

Brown and Carrie left the party when he proposed that they visit an apartment two floors below, telling her that it belonged to a musician friend of his.

James Brown performs in Hamburg in 1973.

Brown, a son of South Carolina, was a progenitor of funk music and a major figure in pop music.

Perhaps salaciously, Carrie wondered if he lived up to the title of one of his hit songs: "Get Up. I Feel Like a Sex Machine."

"Going down the stairs to that apartment, I knew what was going to happen," Carrie related to Hackett. "I thought not so much about Jane Fonda and Jean Seberg, but of Doris Day, of all people. I had heard that she'd once had a black lover. I figured that if Doris could go for chocolate, so could I."

"Once we were inside the apartment, he didn't go ape-shit over me, attacking me and doing it right on the floor," she said. "Instead, we sat talking for a long time."

"I want to live in a world where if doesn't matter if you're black or white," he said. "Where it doesn't matter who you sleep with, even if it's with someone of the same sex. Faggots and drag queens have a right to love like the rest of God's children."

"I don't go down Sammy's road," Brown continued. "I'm more of a one man, one woman kind of guy. Sammy likes Satanic orgies, occasional homo sex, and plenty of sessions with two or three gals at a time. He told me his ultimate sexual fantasy was to fuck with a black bitch, a white bitch, a Chinese bitch, and an Indian squaw, all at the same time. But I don't want to sound too moral," he said. "I'm not a perfect man."

"Who is?" she asked.

"I live on the edge and to hell with the consequences," he answered.

"That's the way I live, or want to live, too," she said. "I'm not my mother's daughter."

"The Black Panthers, at least most of them, don't worship me," he said. "Some of them call me a jive-ass joke because I appeal to white audiences. They seem to think all white men are mean-spirited and bigoted. But some black guys are also bigots."

"I don't want to tear down America, where I've become a big star and can have all the money and all the gals I want. Not bad for a kid like me who grew up po' and made it big."

When they parted early the next morning, he turned to her. "I don't know when or if we'll meet again. But I had a good time. How about you?"

"I was truly, truly satisfied," she said.

"No black man ever likes to leave a woman's bed until he satisfies her," he said.

"I'll have to pass that along to my mother. She's been married twice, and neither man satisfied her."

Suddenly, he was gone. She later referred to her weekend with him as "an interlude."

"Now," she later wrote, "the time had come for this alleycat to get on with her life. Before marriage, I was entering my most promiscuous period, most ready and raring for my next adventure. My time with Brown had given me something spicy to record in my diary."

***

Director Steve Rash was assigned to direct Carrie, Chevy Chase, and Eve Arden in a comedy, *Under the Rainbow* (1981), to be distributed by Warners. Rash had previously been involved with only a limited repertoire of films, one of which was *The Buddy Holly Story* (1978).

Five separate writers had laboriously devised the screenplay, whose plot was loosely based on a gathering of the Munchkins, those cheerful "little people" from *The Wizard of Oz* (1939).

Under the Rainbow was peopled with assassins, spies, and tourists, even two characters loosely based on the Duke and Duchess of Windsor. Eve Arden played the Duchess and Joseph Maher was the Duke.

Before the last reel, Annie (Carrie) and Bruce (Chase) were supposed to fall in love. "That was pure fiction," Carrie said. "In real life, Chevy and I got along like a house on fire."

"My character was assigned the task of taking care of all those little people and also finding a dog like Toto, Judy Garland's beloved dog in *The Wizard of Oz.*"

During the making of the movie, Carrie heard that Chase was scheduled to be on the popular TV show *Tomorrow,* hosted by Tom Snyder.

Cary Grant had once expressed his admiration for Chase, who in time became known for his portrayals of Clark Griswold in five of the *National Lampoon's* vacation films. During the context of his TV show, Snyder asked Chase what he thought of Grant.

Chase's answer shocked everyone, including Grant, who was watching the show that night. "He's really a great physical comic," Chase said, "and I understand he's a homo. What a gal!" He delivered those lines in a lisping, effeminate voice while making a limp-wristed gesture.

The millions of viewers who had tuned in were shocked and horrified, especially Grant. The next day, he filed a $10 million libel suit against Chase. But after a few weeks, faced with the reality that he'd have to face depositions from Chase's lawyers, he let the lawsuit drop, probably because he feared that many embarrassing incidents from his past would otherwise be aired. One of the incidents he wanted to avoid talking about involved his arrest in the men's room

Retro/nostalgia is the theme in this trio of publicity shots from *Under the Rainbow.* Depicted are its co-stars, Chevy Chase and Carrie Fisher.

One critic summarized its plot like this: "The film poses the question of what if 150 people auditioning to play the Munchkins in MGM's *The Wizard of Oz* were staying at the same hotel as some Nazis and a group of spies?"

Another reviewer wrote, "What a peculiar career choice for Carrie Fisher, otherwise known as Princess Leia."

of a Los Angeles department store, where he'd been charged for soliciting sex from a teenaged boy.

According to Carrie, "I don't know if Chevy knew how offended I was by his attack on Cary Grant, whom I considered my friend. But he and I managed to finish the picture."

Upon its release, *Under the Rainbow* barely broke even at the box office. It received extremely negative reviews, some of them based on its depiction of the Munchkins, who were configured as objects of ridicule. Carrie, however, found the film riveting and marvelous, except for the musical score.

***

In 1981, Donald S. Cramer and Aaron Spelling, the same team who had produced *The Love Boat* TV series (1977-87), approached Debbie and of-fered her the lead in a roughly equiva-lent but newer series. Tom Greene had created the story line for *Aloha Paradise,* scheduled to be filmed in Hawaii and aired every Wednesday night on NBC.

Debbie eagerly accepted the role of Sydney Chase, the manager of a re-sort, Paradise Village, on the (fictional) U.S.-administered island of Kona. Her co-star, Bill Daily, portrayed her assis-tant. Each episode was about people in love, people out of love, and people looking for love.

A wide range of guest stars was booked for appearances on the show, including Ralph Bellamy, Ray Bolger, Joan Fontaine, Louis Jourdan, Dana Wynter, and two of Debbie's friends, Van Johnson and Jim Nabors. Debbie also found herself working alongside Connie Stevens, who had married and divorced Eddie Fisher after he'd been dumped by Elizabeth Taylor.

As described by Debbie, "One of my dearest friends, Phyllis Pollack, the owner of the Thunderbird Hotel in

Aloha Paradise was panned by critics and it bombed with TV audiences. Premiered on February 25, 1981, it was canceled two months later.

"ABC presented me with the worst scripts I'd ever seen," Debbie complained. "I to-tally disliked every one they gave me, but bravely carried on. They accused me of in-terfering with my ideas of how to improve the comedies."

Miami, flew to Honolulu with me. She'd lost her husband."

"While in Hawaii, I began dating Lloyd Beckett. I found him a total bore, talking golf all the time. He also went after Phyllis, but I warned her how dull he was. As it turned out, Phyllis was an avid golfer, and the two of them had a great time. I was a matchmaker! The last I heard, they were in their fourth decade of wedding bliss."

***

Carrie's rendezvous with an ex-Beatle began in 1981 with a phone call from her agent, who informed her that Bob Dylan wanted to get in touch with her to discuss something. "Please stay close to your phone this afternoon. He said he'd call. This could be either a major boost to your career, or else he wants to screw you. I'm sure you'd be willing, whichever way the wind blows," *[an obvious reference to the lyrics of "Blowin' in the Wind."]*

She later articulated the immediate response she wanted to tell the agent. "FUCK YOU! You get that stalker away from me. I don't want any 1960s icons fucking up my life." But she never said that, assuring her agent that she'd be waiting eagerly beside her phone.

It rang at 3PM: "Dylan's third line to me was something about where he was off to with his girlfriends. He wanted something else from me other than my galaxy snatch."

During their phone conversation, Dylan's question struck Carrie as bizarre: Apparently, he'd heard from someone that she was clever, and he wanted her advice for a catchy name for a brand of men's cologne he was on the verge of launching.

"I hoisted three names up the flagpole to see if he'd salute one," she said. "He went for all three—*Ambivalence* for the scent of confusion; *Empathy* for men to smell like other men; and *Arbitrary* for the guy who doesn't give a shit about how he smells."

Although Dylan liked all three of the names she'd proposed, he wasn't certain about which of the three he preferred. He told her that he was also considering opening an exclusive beauty salon, for which she suggested the name *Tangled Up & Blown.*

As a reward for her creative input, he invited her to a dinner party honoring George Harrison, who was visiting Hollywood at the time, ostensibly to buy some vintage automobiles for his collection of antique cars. Finding herself seated next to Harrison at dinner, Carrie told him about Dylan's plan to launch a new cologne.

Harrison replied that Dylan had previously approached him with a proposal to set up a partnership for the development and construction of a hotel, with the provision that it would be named "The Traveling Wilburys."

The Beatles had arrived on the international music scene when Carrie was just a kid, but she soon became an avid fan of their music, and was sorry to read, in 1970, that they had broken up.

After that, she remained avidly up-to-date with gossip about the former "Fab Four," and was aware of Harrison's marital status. In September of 1978, he'd wed Olivia Trinidad Arias. *[Their son had been born a month before that.]* The papers had run stories about his first marriage, in 1966, to model Pattie Boyd, with Paul McCartney designated as his best man. Pattie had been cast in the Beatle's movie *Hard Day's Night*, playing a schoolgirl.

In 1974, Pattie and George Harrison separated. Their divorce became final in 1977, three years later.

During the course of their marriage, Harrison had taken advantage of many of the groupies who flocked around him. His wife also learned about his affair with Maureen, the wife of Ringo Starr.

Pattie had told the judge at their divorce hearing that "the fuel for our marriage was not his love for me, but for liquor and cocaine."

When Carrie read that, she'd said, "Sounds like my kind of man."

In 1979, Pattie married Eric Clapton.

Harrison was staying in a bungalow behind the Beverly Hills Hotel. It had once been a hideaway for Howard Hughes.

"When not rolling around and trying to make babies (just joking), George and I had long talks about Indian culture and mysticism. He was really into all that shit. He had nothing but raves for his guru, Ravi Shankar. I'd read about him, considering him no more than a money grubber, trying to bilk the Beatles out of their millions. But I didn't let on a word."

[Carrie did not keep her "conquest" of a Beatle a secret, and over the years made several references to it, both to friends and as on-the-air revelations.]

"I was a better audience when he spoke of psychedelic drugs, particularly LSD, which he claimed fueled his meditation and his pursuit of Hinduism. I could jive with him on LSD."

"Over dinner the previous night, I'd learned that he was a vegetarian. On our second dinner at the hotel, I ordered a sirloin, rare, but tried to keep the blood from running from the corners of my mouth like a

In 1988, George Harrison had been instrumental in the formation of a musical group called *The Traveling Wilburys*. Its members included Bob Dylan, Tom Perry, Jeff Lynne, and Roy Orbison.

They recorded an album in Dylan's garage, each using a pseudonym, and each posing as half-brothers named "the Tilburys."

Harrison's rationale (or lack thereof) for all this was, "Let's confuse the buggers."

vampire."

"The sex wasn't bad," Carrie later confessed to Rudy Render. "Rudy was gay and gay men liked to pump star fuckers like me about the size of a man's dick. I told him that George was a bit of a disappointment when he first stepped out of his jockey shorts. A piece of okra—uncut, of course, and me a Jewish girl. But I was pleasantly surprised when he rose to the occasion. Quite competent in the sack. We spent four days together screwing around, listening to music, and taking drugs."

"He didn't talk much about the Beatles, other than saying, "John Lennon was a saint and definitely heavy duty. And he's just great, and I loved him. But at the same time, he's such a bastard—but that's the great thing about him, you know."

She didn't know, or completely understand, but nodded her accord anyway. Actually, she got a better description of Lennon when she picked up a copy of his latest biography, written by Albert Goldman. She read the blurb on its back cover:

"Behind this fabled figure, however, there was a sick and suffering human being. The real John Lennon was not his image. In fact, there was no real John Lennon, only an endless succession of masks that he spent his tortured and tragic life impulsively donning and doffing. He was, by turn, man, woman, and child; moralist and immoralist; idealist and cynic; solipsist and exhibitionist; ascetic and junkie; creative genius and plagiarist; master and slave; murderous criminal and crucified victim. Yet he had the talent and courage to embody his jagged and fractured personality into an unforgettable man."

According to Carrie, "During my sexual tryst with George, I played my favorite of his songs, 'Here Comes the Sun,' at least eighteen times, until he got tired of it."

"When it came time to say goodbye to Harrison, as was inevitable, he was like a soldier saying farewell before heading for the battlefield," she said to Render. "He warned me that it would not be wise for us to be photographed leaving the hotel together."

Away from prying eyes, and embracing her for a final time, he said, "When we come back in another life, we'll start all over again, just you and me against the wind."

***

Bob Dylan appeared for a final episode in Carrie's life when she invited him to a party at her home in Los Angeles. Arriving with his girlfriend, he wore sunglasses and a parka.

After a brief talk with him about Harrison, she introduced him to her new friend, Meryl Streep. She had been assigned to play the young, aspiring protagonist in Carrie's semi-autobiographical novel, *Postcards from the Edge* (1990), a thinly disguised portrait of Debbie and Carrie herself.

"I introduced Dylan to Meryl, and he monopolized all her time, raving movie by movie, about nearly all of her films, beginning with his favorite, *Ironweed* (1987) with Jack Nicholson."

***

When Carrie was only fourteen, Eddie Fisher had gone to see her, with Todd, perform with Debbie at the Desert Inn in Las Vegas. He later wrote that when his daughter sang "Bridge Over Troubled Water," "Tears of joy came streaming down my cheeks—my girl could sing. I had no idea that she would grow up to marry the singer of that hit record."

Ever the gentleman, Simon asked Debbie for her daughter's hand in marriage. According to Debbie, "I could see how much they loved each other, and I said yes."

The coincidence that Carrie was marrying a Jewish man who happened to be one of the most popular recording artists in America did not escape Debbie. "However, I felt the similarities between Paul and Eddie ended there."

In discussions about the groom-to-be with his fiancée (her daughter), Debbie said, "Paul can be charming—if he wants to be."

According to Carrie, "When Eddie learned the news, he immediately wanted Paul to write him an album of new songs to record, Dad was hoping that that might make for a big comeback for him."

The wedding was conducted at Simon's apartment in Manhattan on Central Park West. Penny Marshall, the lover of Art Garfunkel, was Carrie's bridesmaid, and Lorne Michaels was Simon's best man. Other guests included Mike Nichols, actress Terry Garr, Billy Joel, Randy Newman, Robin Williams, George Lucas, and Christie Brinkley. A reporter asked Simon if he'd seen *Star Wars.* He said that he had. "Carrie's really got the goods, and the Force is with her."

According to Carrie, Art Garfunkel, during one of his conversations at her wedding said, "I thought Paul was going to name me as his best man, but he didn't. I was supposed to conclude that Paul was the cutest guy I know. I guess that was the message."

Carrie found his statement made no sense.

At the wedding, Eddie Fisher rendezvoused with his wife of long ago. "I hadn't seen her in years. She came up to me and told me how wonderful I looked. She was such a liar. Both of us knew I looked like shit. Time had been cruel to me. I was no longer the cute bugger who'd hawked Coca-Cola on TV."

"Then she told me to get lost while she had a woman-on-woman talk with my mother, 'Mama La Fisher.' Believe me, getting away from Debbie always made me happy."

He then approached Carrie to kiss her and wish her all the happiness in the world. "She told me I should get back with Debbie. She also reminded me that her mother still has great tits."

After the ceremony, and after Mama La Fisher's conversation with Debbie, Eddie's distressed mother, Katharine (aka Mrs. Max Stupp), approached her son, urging that they leave at once. In the elevator, as it descended to the ground floor, Katharine claimed "Debbie has cancer. It's eating away at her. She'll die soon!"

"She didn't believe me when I told her that Debbie was in perfect health. Every now and then, she comes up with that 'I-have-cancer' line. When I first met her, she told me her mother, Minnie, had cancer. Minnie is still going strong after all these decades. You can't believe a word Debbie says."

The honeymoon that followed Carrie's wedding to Simon was a disaster. According to Carrie, "In a fit of anger, I told him, 'Not only do I not like you, I don't like you *personally*. From then on, I knew our marriage was doomed to failure. The divorce came when I was twenty-eight years old, and ready for rehab. Actually, I was drugged throughout the months I was married. I'd come back to the apartment with those 'dolls' (her word for pills) sizzling inside my feverish skull."

"Throughout our marriage, we'd make love, then have a fight. In that sense, our marriage evoked that of Frank Sinatra and Ava Gardner. She said she and Frank were great in bed. Their fights began when she was on her way to the bidet."

There were plenty of good times, however, and she enjoyed performing with him. She appeared with him when he'd hosted Lorne Michaels' *Saturday Night Live*. Sometimes, when Simon was singing on stage, Carrie rose up from the audience and joined him. In one of the best sequences from *SNL*, he played a henpecked Abraham Lincoln and she impersonated a "bitchy" Mary Todd Lincoln.

In a bizarre attempt to save their marriage, Simon and Carrie flew together to Brazil, where they traveled up the Amazon to meet with a *brujo* (spiritual healer) in the jungle. He chanted some incantations and prayed to the gods in the air, on the ground, and in the sea. Then he served them an infusion brewed from plants with psychedelic powers,

Two of America's most popular singers, Paul Simon (left) and Art Garfunkel.

"I married Paul and presented Art to my best friend, Penny Marshall," Carrie claimed.

promising them that a giant anaconda would appear to them in a vision.

The motivation for their efforts was to confront the monsters that lurked within Simon. During his drugged state, he lovingly rested his tired head on Carrie's lap and seemed to drift off into another realm of consciousness.

"I felt pinned beneath him," she said. "I was under his control in every situation, and I wanted to be free."

After their return to New York, she filed for divorce. He used the experience to create a new album, *Rhythm of the Saints,* and dedicated it to Carrie.

She wrote, "I think Paul had me in mind when he later wrote a lyric, 'My heart is allergic to the woman I love.'"

After their divorce, Carrie returned time and time again to his side "for a nostalgic bout of sex." In 1990, she published a novel, *Surrender the Pink.* Its main characters—Dinah Kaufman, a writer/producer of soap operas and her companion and later husband, playwright Rudy Gendler—were surely based on Simon and herself.

Enigmatic, disorganized, subjective, and occasionally confusing, the novel contained these unashamedly autobiographical passages about her marriage to Paul Simon, to whom she applied the pseudonym of Rudy:

"To Dinah, the more valuable trophy in a man was for him to be rich, to be powerful, to be talented. And the men you looked up to tended to need looking after. These were the men worth winning and getting behind. Men looked for a breeder, woman looked for a provider, and she figured that you have to accept the way things were before you could change them. Could you change them?"

Carrie told her friends, "I was in diapers when the boy from Queens had his first hit record in 1957, just after Elvis Presley had ignited the rock era. My love affair with Paul can be summed up in the title of his songs, 'Bridge Over Troubled Water,' 'Fifty Ways to Leave Your Lover,' 'Still Crazy About You After All These Years,' and 'The Sound of Silence.'"

Chapter Seventeen

SENATORS & SEX

CARRIE'S AFFAIRS WITH TEDDY KENNEDY AND CHRIS DODD,
EACH OF THEM A PRESIDENTIAL CANDIDATE

WAS CARRIE SEXUALLY HARASSED?

HOW THE DIRECTOR OF A *STAR WARS* SEQUEL SOLICITED A
MOTHER/DAUGHTER THREE-WAY

CARRIE GOES CRAZY

BIPOLAR & "SHOCKAHOLIC" PRINCESS LEIA FLIES OVER THE
CUCKOO'S NEST, THEN DESCRIBES HER BIPOLAR SYNDROME,
DEBILITATING DEPRESSIONS, & ELECTROSHOCK THERAPIES

HER FALL FROM HOLLYWOOD GRACE:

CARRIE ACCEPTS WHATEVER FILM ROLES SHE'S OFFERED

*"Bit parts as a Mother Superior. A Boyfriend Poacher.
A Vengeful Hairdresser. A drug-addicted writer. It's all OK by me."*

ROMANCE IN VEGAS

DEBBIE MEETS HUSBAND #3

"Me Hamlett, You Ophelia"

"There went my chance to become First Lady of the United States," Carrie said.

She was referring to her affairs with Senators Chris Dodd and Ted Kennedy, both of whom eyed presidential races.

After drastically scaling back on her expenses, Debbie experienced her most profound period of loneliness in her new home, a small, unimpressive bungalow in unfashionable North Hollywood. Her high-profile days of living in grand style in Beverly Hills were over.

Alone in the evenings, she began to drink heavily. At times, she exploded with unresolved fury at her memories of Harry Karl, who had gambled away her life savings. "On some nights, rage just bubbled over in me, spewing forth."

In an impulsive, reckless move, she phoned him one night. Suppressing her feelings, she engaged in a relatively civil conversation, and then agreed to meet him for dinner in Los Angeles at Trader Vic's, a pseudo-Polynesian restaurant.

Inside, he was seated at table waiting for her. "He was still dressed in his Savile Row suit, but he looked much older and had lost a lot of weight. I'd heard that he'd been in and out of hospitals."

Before their drinks were served, she told him, "I hate you, really, really hate you. Why did you destroy me?"

"It wasn't on purpose," he answered. "Gambling is like being an alcoholic. Sometimes, it's out of one's control." Then he shocked her by saying that he wanted to remarry her. "I know we can be happy the second time around."

"You must be out of your fucking mind," she said, sharply. "Never! Once was more than enough."

Trying to reassure her, he said, "Sex doesn't have to be involved. It could be a marriage of companionship."

"That's more or less what it was before," she said. "Remember, you couldn't perform with me, but you seem to do okay with your whores."

By the time the food was served, she'd lost her appetite and wondered why she had set up this dinner in the first place. "Harry, I'm leaving. For the first time in my life, I'm sticking you with the bill. The valet told me you gave him fifty dollars to park your Rolls, so I guess you can pick up the tab."

Reaching for her arm, he said, "I could make you happy. Sometimes love is better the second time around.

"This is goodbye," she said. "*Forever!*"

[On July 29, 1982, at the age of 68, Karl was rushed to Cedars Sinai Medical Center in Los Angeles. About a week later, on August 6, he underwent bypass surgery. He died the following night.

His three daughters and son survived him. His oldest daughter, Judie, died on May 24, 2010 at the age of 71.]

***

The romantic comedy, *Woman of the Year* (1942), had co-starred Katharine Hepburn and Spencer Tracy. Ring Lardner, Jr., and Michael Kanin had written the screenplay, a battle-of-the-sexes conflict between Tess Harding, an international affairs correspondent who had been honored as "Woman of the Year," and Sam Craig, a gruffly chauvinistic sports writer. They meet, fall in love, marry, and encounter numerous problems as a result of her refusal to compromise and her unflinching commitment to her career.

Debbie in *Woman of the Year:* "What kind of fool am I? Little Miss Debbie Reynolds stepping into the shoes of Katharine Hepburn, Lauren Bacall, and a candidate for a *Playboy* centerfold, sexy Raquel Welch."

Audiences dwindled nightly.

In 1981, that vintage film was adapted into a hit Broadway musical. Its producers hired Lauren Bacall as the female lead. Her hard work and pizzazz as *Woman of the Year* eventually won her a Tony award.

When Bacall took a leave of absence for a two-week vacation, with the understanding that her absence would be temporary, she was replaced by Raquel Welch. Later, after Bacall had completed her contract, Welch replaced her once again, this time on a longer-term basis.

By February of 1983, audiences had dwindled, allegedly because of Welch's inability to "draw them in." The producers reacted by replacing her with Debbie Reynolds, whose star power had been amply displayed during her blockbusting appearances in *Irene.*

To everyone's regret, after an enviable 770 performances, the re-designed but somewhat overtired production, this time featuring Debbie, closed about a month later. Most of the publicity associated with her premiere was never released because of a devastating newspaper strike that stifled what might normally have perked up box office sales.

***

Around the same time, Carrie was launched into Outer Space again for *The Return of the Jedi.* Released in 1983 as the third installment of the original *Star Wars* trilogy, it positioned George Lucas as executive producer and as one of the screenwriters, but not as its director. After seriously reviewing the qualifications of three different men, he awarded the job to Richard Marquand because he'd been impressed with his 1981 drama, the critically acclaimed romantic thriller, *Eye of the Needle* (1981).

Returning to their by now familiar roles were Harrison Ford as Han Solo, Mark Hamill as Skywalker, and Carrie as Princess Leia. Supporting players included Billy Dee Williams, Anthony Daniels, David Prowse (as Darth Vader), Kenny Baker, Peter Mayhew, and Frank Oz.

Once again, Alec Guinness returned as Obi-Wan, Luke's deceased Jedi Master, who continues, even from beyond the grave as a "Force Ghost" to teach his pupil. James Earl Jones was brought in once again, too, as the voice of Darth Vader.

In this newest plot, the Galactic Empire, under the direction of the ruthless Emperor (Ian McDiarmid), has built a second *Death Star* to crush the Rebel Alliance once and for all.

Location shooting was successfully concluded between January and May of 1982 in England, Arizona, and California.

Because Marquand was relatively inexperienced as a director, Lucas seemed to hover over the set. Marquand later said, "It was like trying to direct *King Lear* with Shakespeare in the next room."

Part of the film was shot in Arizona's Yuma Desert, where cast and crew replicated the landscapes of the desolate (fictional) planet of Tatooine.

During several of their phone calls, Carrie had complained to her mother that Marquand was sexually harassing her. In the aftermath of those calls, Debbie flew to Arizona for a reunion.

On the afternoon of the day of her arrival, she met Marquand, the Welsh-born director, who was five years younger than she was. She found him handsome in a rugged, blue-collar way. He invited her for dinner that evening, and she accepted.

In her first memoir, Debbie inserted an episode from her visit, but did not specifically name either the director or the title of the film.

Over dinner, he surprised Debbie by telling her, "As a boy growing up near Cardiff, you were my girlfriend. I saw all of your movies. I collected publicity pictures of you to decorate my bedroom walls."

She jokingly asked, "You didn't use those images of me for 'self-abuse,' did you?"

"Guilty! Night after night," he said. "Now, I'm not only dining with the real thing, but directing her daughter in a movie, too. I find Carrie very, very sexy, and I'm delighted to see that you've lost none of your appeal. In fact, during your time here, I'd think it would be a delight if you and Carrie bunked with me. We could get to

The Welsh director, Richard Marquand, helmed Carrie as Princess Leia in *The Return of the Jedi.*

In Arizona, Debbie visited the set, finding the director "ruggedly good looking and oozing masculine charm."

But she had to reject his offer to set up a *ménage à trois* with her and her daughter.

know each other so much better."

"Are you suggesting that Tammy and Princess Leia hop into bed with you?" she asked.

"Great jolly fun," he answered. "What a night (or nights) that would be!"

Debbie later said, "If Richard had asked me to sleep with him alone, I might have said yes. I missed having a man in my bed. I'd known plenty of better looking men, but never one so ruggedly sexy."

"If we make it," Marquand continued, "I could have fulfilled those long-ago desires I had as a boy. A fantasy come true for him."

According to Debbie, in retrospect, "My age didn't seem a problem for him, and I appreciated his interest after all these years. But his proposal that Carrie join us for a three-way was too much."

"I told him I was perfectly capable of taking care of his sexual desires without the help of my daughter. But he insisted on a three-way, so I rejected him. Before I left Arizona, I asked some members of the crew to look after Carrie, and they promised that they would."

Two or three years later, Debbie went to see the courtroom thriller *Jagged Edge* (1985), starring Glenn Close, Jeff Bridges, and Peter Coyote, and was impressed with Marquand's direction. "I admired his professional abilities, but regrettably was never able to judge his talents in the boudoir. However, he must have had a good sperm count, because he fathered four children."

Return of the Jedi received mostly positive reviews, grossing $475 million in the United States, and $572 million worldwide.

***

In 1983, Debbie flew to Reno with Bill Cosby, her dear friend Jim Nabors, Suzanne Somers, and Sammy Davis, Jr. They were in Nevada to tape a TV special being sponsored by Chrysler, *Classic Cars & Classic Stars,* a star-studded tribute to Bill Harrah, the head of Harrah's Hotels. It took all day and into midnight to shoot the special before a wrap was called.

A gala party followed, but she wanted to excuse herself because she was exhausted and her ankles were swollen. But her friends, Rip Torn and publisher Bob Petersen, went to her suite and persuaded her to attend the festivities.

At the lavish late-night cocktail party, she was introduced to the chairman of *Time-Life* and the governor of Nevada, who kissed her on the lips. She was also introduced to the CEO of Chrysler, who suggested that they might want to hire her for a TV commercial: "Pretty gals still sell cars," he told her.

At around 1AM, a man she called "Mr. Beautiful Blue Eyes" approached her table and asked if she would pose for a photograph with him. She consented.

After the photo, he asked her to dance, and in spite of her aching feet, she agreed. He held her tightly in his arms and swept her across the floor. Then he invited himself to join her table, introducing himself as Richard Hamlett, "like Shakespeare with an extra T."

As she got up to leave at around 4AM, he gave her his card with an address in Roanoke, Virginia. It seemed he was a real estate developer. She reciprocated by writing down her own private phone number.

He was returning to Virginia, and she was flying back to Los Angeles. "Actually, I didn't think I'd ever see him again. An actress meets so many beautiful men, soon gone and forgotten unless you marry one of them."

Three months later, Hamlett made use of that phone number and called her. At first, she didn't remember him, but he jogged her memory. After getting re-acquainted, they made plans to meet in Las Vegas in ten days. Their point of rendezvous would be the Desert Inn, where she had often been the star entertainer. The reason for her return to Las

"For the rest of the evening, Richard Hamlett didn't take his eyes off me. He seemed enchanted. I didn't know who in hell he was, a perfect stranger, but he had oodles of charm. He kept staring at me with this 'I want to fuck you, babe' look in those blue eyes of his."

Vegas was because she'd been scheduled for an appearance at a physical fitness convention, where she planned to promote her fitness and exercise video *Do It Debbie's Way.*

[One of Debbie's startup businesses at the time, their short, videotaped promotional prototypes included cameo participation from Dionne Warwick, Shelley Winters, and Teri Garr, and sometimes included wisecracking jokes bandied around on stage, including (from Debbie) "I was at MGM studios for years in musicals so I thought we'd do it up in sorta pink, not brown." And (from Shelley) "How many of the girls here slept with Howard Hughes?"

In reference to the exercise concept's title, Debbie quipped "The title of my exercise video is not to be confused with that porn flick, Debbie Does Dallas.*]* □

On the date and time of their pre-arranged reunion, she had misunderstood where they were to meet, so she stood in the lobby waiting for him. She noticed that a lot of men were coming and going, heading off into the night with their lady of choice.

Finally, she saw him emerging from the bar that adjoined the dining room. He kissed her on both cheeks, and both of them later shared a laugh that she was standing within a pool of hookers waiting to meet their johns for the evening. "I guess no one wanted to fuck Tammy," she said.

No longer joking, he looked into her eyes and said. "Except for me."

Over dinner, they bonded once again, joking and laughing. Before their Baked Alaska was served he said, "I am Hamlett and I want you to be my Ophelia. In other words, I want to marry you."

She was stunned, since she didn't know him very well.

"You might not know me, but I've known you for years, ever since I saw you in *Tammy*, I fell in love with you then, and I've followed your career ever since, learning everything I could about you."

"I'm very flattered by your offer, but I can't marry you on a sudden impulse."

"Something I've been thinking about for years could hardly be called an impulse."

Then she held out the promise that she might become his girlfriend, perhaps his traveling companion, sharing the same hotel suites.

He didn't like that. "I'm an old-fashioned country boy, and I want a wife—not a mistress. They're a dime a dozen."

She later wrote, "Richard was sexually intoxicating, putting my other husbands to shame. He was brave, loving, and loyal, a tiger in bed. Days turned into weeks and I had not heard from him. Then I picked up the phone one night and dialed his number."

"My answer is yes," she said.

He seemed dumbfounded. Had he forgotten he'd proposed marriage? "Yes to what?" he asked.

"Yes to becoming your wife."

Suddenly, he remembered. Before he could speak, she said, "Is your offer still valid?"

"You bet your sweet ass it is. Tomorrow your Hamlett, in green tights, is winging his way West."

***

In 1984, Sidney Lumet cast Carrie in *Garbo Talks,* a comedy-drama starring Anne Bancroft, Ron Silver, and Carrie, with a cameo appearance by Betty Comden as Greta Garbo.

Sadly, *Garbo Talks* marked the last screen appearance of Hermione Gingold and Howard Da Silva. Dorothy Loudon and Harvey Fierstein had minor roles in it, too.

As Estelle Rolle, Bancroft played a hot-tempered social activist who had idolized Garbo throughout her entire life. Occasionally, Estelle's son, Gilbert (Ron Silver), has to go to the local police precinct to bail her out of jail for a street protest that became violent.

Gilbert loves his mother and wants to grant her deathbed request. She has been diagnosed with terminal brain cancer, and she's obsessed with her dream of meeting Garbo before she dies. His wife, Lisa (as portrayed by Carrie), sympathizes but loses her patience when her husband quits his job and embarks on a "Garbo

Always ready with a wisecrack, Carrie was shown this picture of herself with Ron Silver, her leading man in *Garbo Talks*.

"You'll note that at this point, my hand had not wandered below the belt."

hunt." Fed up, she abandons him.

With tenacity and persistence, Gilbert finally locates the elusive diva and explains his mother's circumstances. Reacting favorably, and deeply flattered, Garbo arrives at the hospital for a deathbed encounter with Estelle.

Distributed by United Artists, the film bombed at the box office, earning only $1.5 million. Vincent Canby of *The New York Times* was charitable, writing, "*Garbo Talks* has a number of comic scenes and lines that are played with great verve by Miss Bancroft and Mr. Silver."

Roger Ebert of the *Chicago Sun-Times*, however, panned it, writing "The film starts out as a great idea for a movie, and when it's over, it's a great idea for a movie, but the problem is, there are no great ideas in between."

***

During her later years, Carrie often made very negative and satirical comments about the roles she was assigned in feature films or on television. Many of her critiques, as relayed to her various co-stars or directors, have been rounded up and included in the final pages of this chapter, and reflect her changing opinions. Unlike her mother, who was less successful at snagging film roles as she aged, Carrie continued to find work in movies until the year of her death.

"*Star Wars* made me famous as Princess Leia, but I never achieved such success in any other film I made. An occasional hit, but a barrage of misses. Like Debbie, we took whatever offer that came our way. At least we were getting jobs, unlike some poor souls who became entertainers."

"Often I've appeared in a cameo in some series shown on TV. Such was the case when I popped up on *Laverne & Shirley* (1982). There were several dozen of these appearances, but I was too stoned at the time to recall most of them. Often, a director would hire me to play 'Carrie Fisher herself,' my favorite role. I was certainly versatile. I could play a vengeful hairdresser, a hostile mother-in-law, a flute-playing adultress (imagine that!), a drug-addicted writer (talk about type-casting), a boyfriend-poaching actress, a boy-hungry casting director, an unfaithful wife, and angry

Carrie, Hugh Hefner, and Penny Marshall in an episode of *Laverne & Shirley*.

"At last I got to play a *Playboy* bunny with floppy ears and a bushy tail. Hef, that horny bastard, asked me to expose my galaxy snatch to the voyeuristic horndogs of ogling readers."

boss, and even a nun (what a hard role for me to play). Debbie had played a nun who sang. I was a mere nun in *Jay and Silent Bob Strike Back* (what fucker came up with that title?). And in an episode on *Charlie's Angels,* a hit TV show, I was a Mother Superior."

Set for release in 1985, she starred in a comedy entitled *The Man With One Red Shoe* with Tom Hanks and Dabney Coleman. Carrie's role was that of Paula, married to a man named Morris *[played by Jim Belushi, the younger brother of her former lover, John Belushi].* Directed by Stan Dragoli, it was a remake of the wacky French comedy, *Le Grand Blond avec chaussure noire* (1972).

"That was the role I mentioned where I was a flute-playing adultress. The movie, I think, was about a CIA agent arrested in Morocco on a drug-smuggling charge. I tried for some real acting coming on to Tom, virtually begging him to sample my wares. Would you believe him? That fucker didn't even try to fuck me. He's a fine actor, but even he couldn't save this turkey."

"I could have gone for our director, Stan Dragoti, although he was probably out of my league. From 1970 to '79, he'd been married to supermodel Cheryl Tiegs. She was the hottest thing heating up the planet, a $2,000-a-day model, ABC-TVs 'Rookie of the Year,' and a major figure in the pinup poster sweepstakes."

Carrie claimed that Tiegs had sent her a note before filming began: "Consider yourself lucky. Stan is the most liberated man in the world."

"That may be true, but you can't prove it by me," Carrie said.

"Dabney Coleman was very talented," she said. He'd been in *Tootsie* (1982) with Dustin Hoffman in drag, and in *9 to 5* (1980) with Jane Fonda, Dolly Parton, and Lily Tomlin. He had also appeared in that bizarre soap opera on TV, *Mary Hartman, Mary Hartman* (1976-77).

"I remember one TV film called *Frankenstein* (1984). Mary Shelley must have been turning over in her grave when she watched it on some underground cemetery TV. Robert Powell played Victor Frankenstein, and David Warner was 'The Creature.' I was this character known as Elizabeth."

"You won't believe this, but the great John Gielgud took fourth billing, playing 'De Lacy.' He had been helpful to Debbie early in her career, and I thanked him for that. I admired him but was sorry to see such a great actor of stage and screen reduced to playing a role in our silly little crap. He showed his grace throughout but stooped low when he repeated that old chestnut, 'There are no small roles, only small actors.' Yeah, right!"

"Along comes another TV movie, *Sun-*

Carrie Fisher and Robert Powell playing romantic Victorians in *Frankenstein* (1984).

day Drive. In 1986, it was the feature on the program, *The Disney Sunday Movie.* I got co-billing with that closeted homosexual Tony Randall. Debbie had a horrible time when she had co-starred with him. I thought he was a jerk. When he made sarcastic remarks about my mother, I told him to go to hell. The film was about two drivers with identical cars who unwittingly take each other's vehicles. Disney had released greater films."

***

One day, a call that Debbie had long dreaded came with bad news about her father. At the age of 78, Ray Reynolds' health had taken a turn for the worse. He was quite sick and in need of medical care. He had long ago retired and spent most of his days in bed in the little house he occupied with his wife, Minnie, in Palm Springs.

For years, he had worked for the railroad, but had quit. Later, he got a job maintaining the retail shoe stores of his son-in-law, Harry Karl. When that post ended, he had retired, and seemed to be suffering from dementia as he neared his final days.

His love for Minnie had long ago died. Their passion had blown away with those long-ago tumbleweeds around El Paso. Yet through it all, they had remained together, even though they often went for days without speaking.

Sometimes, for hours at a time, the only things Minnie said to him were the words, "breakfast," "lunch," or "supper."

Even when Debbie was short of cash herself, she always provided for their needs, including their medical bills.

One afternoon, before Ray got very sick, he had phoned Debbie saying, "Mary Frances, I hate to say this, but my life is coming to an end. The trail has been long and rough, with a lot of rattlesnakes getting in my path. I can't wrap my mind around those films you made. But I remember in one picture, you was Tammy. That is my favorite song. You reminded me of this gal I knew back in Texas before I met your mother. I should have married her, but didn't. Even though my memory is fading, I still remember you winning the title of Miss Burbank of 1948.

In 1988, Debbie went on a book tour to promote her first memoir, *Debbie My Life.*

"It was the vanilla version of my life. I didn't want my remaining fans to know the real Debbie. Years later, I read the optimistic ending of that early memoir. I couldn't believe how naïve I was when I wrote it."

"But in a second memoir, *Unsinkable* (2013), I had to paraphrase Bette Davis in *All About Eve:* 'Fasten your seatbelts,' I've had a bumpy ride."

That was the best time in my life."

By 1986, Ray's condition had worsened to the point that he needed around-the-clock care. Debbie had hired a nurse to help Minnie look after him. Near the end, nearly all of his memory had gone.

Minnie called Debbie: "One morning when I went to tend to him and carry out his bedpan, I don't think he even knew who I was. Sometimes, he'll perk up and remember something. Some friends from the church called, and your name came up. He didn't seem to know who Debbie Reynolds was, but he told them he had a gal named Mary Frances, and that you would turn fifteen come April."

Death came to Ray less than a month after that conversation.

Debbie and Carrie rejected the idea of a traditional religious ceremony and designed their own program with the intention of including something that Ray, had he still been alive, might have enjoyed. Throughout the course of his life, he had been a baseball fan. In recognition of that, Todd had brought a recording of a highlight from a recent game to the funeral services, so, instead of words from a pastor, the mourners heard a sports broadcast—all in all, a most unusual funeral.

At his gravesite, Carrie read a poem she'd composed the night before. It referred to his leathery skin and his favorite refreshment, peanuts in a coke bottle, a treat that was also a favorite of Elvis Presley.

Minnie stood between Debbie and Carrie as she watched her late husband being buried. She looked stoic as he disappeared into the earth, the man with whom she had lived with, but not loved, for sixty years.

Debbie lost a father that day, but another man, a far different sort, was about to enter her life.

***

"I wasn't too proud to accept a role in a made-for-TV movie," Carrie said. "So after I read the script for *Liberty* (1985), I phoned and agreed to the role immediately."

"I would play the poet, Emma Lazarus (1849-1887), who wrote the sonnet 'The New Colossus' in 1885. Her words are inscribed on the bronze plaque on the pedestal of the Statue of Liberty. They include the words, 'Give me your tired, your poor…'"

"Emma had been born in a large Sephardic Jewish family, and I had been born in a small, half-Jewish family. I was also a poet, so I guess we had a lot in common. Peter Hamill, a famous journalist known for fucking Jackie Kennedy, wrote the script, so *Liberty* sounded like it had class to me."

Parts of the film would be shot in the city of Baltimore, a reasonable drive from Washington, D.C., "home to all those horny senators, some of whom were neo-Nazis, willing to send gays, Jews, and communists to the gas chambers if they could get away with it."

Liberty's script delivered a fictionalized account of the construction of the Statue of Liberty. *[The film's release more or less coincided with the Centennial of the statue's inauguration, a fact duly noted by its marketers.]* In the film, sculptor Frédéric Bartholdi (Frank Langella) presents the monument to the United States as a gift from the people of France. The teleplay depicts his use of the face of his mother, Madam Bartholdi (as portrayed by Claire Bloom), and enlists an immigrant American coppersmith, Jacques Merchant (Chris Sarandon) in the crafting of the copper sheathing of the massive statue. George Kennedy would co-star as a kindly shop owner, Seamus Reilly.

"Our director, Richard C. Sarafian, had lined up some real talent, and I was afraid their lights would shine brighter than mine," Carrie said. "Take Claire Bloom, for instance. Not only had she screwed Laurence Olivier, or so I'd heard, but she'd worked with him as well, co-starring in *Richard III* (1956). Of course, Larry had also fucked Noël Coward, Richard Burton, Danny Kaye, and Errol Flynn."

"Bloom was great in Shakespearean stuff, even *Hamlet* which she'd made with Burton, the object of her "long and stormy" first love affair. She'd made Tennessee Williams "exultant" when she'd starred on the stage as Blanche DuBois in *A Streetcar Named Desire*."

"George Kennedy was in one of my favorite movies, *Cool Hand Luke* (1967), which brought him a Best Supporting Actor Oscar."

"Frank Langella was a big deal on both the stage and in film," Carrie continued. "He told me that in 1977, he'd appeared on the Broadway stage in the title role of *Dracula*. At first, he didn't want to reprise the monster in the 1979 film version, since he didn't want to get typecast. However, when he heard that Olivier would be his co-star, he signed on."

"Another big talent was Chris Sarandon. A Greek born in redneck West Virginia, he'd divorced Susan Sarandon in 1979. My favorite of his films, the one that earned him an Oscar nomination, was his performance as Al Pacino's transgendered wife in *Dog Day Afternoon* (1975)."

According to Carrie, "I sat through the first screening of *Liberty* with its author, Hamill. He hated the picture, demanding that his name be removed and that authorship be credited to a pseudonym, Robert Mallo. He must have been right, because most of our reviews were negative."

People magazine found it "as pretentious as a high school sophomore trying to act like a college freshman."

Th critic for the *Chicago Tribune* described it as "turgid as well as ludicrous, drawing upon the device of meshing fictional and historical characters."

***

Pete Hamill, or so it was reported, may have been the link who suggested to Carrie that she date Senator Christopher ("Chris") Dodd of Connecticut. The implications intrigued her, and she agreed she'd go out with him. After speaking to him on the phone, it was decided that she would drive from Baltimore to Washington, D.C. and rendezvous with him in one of the Senate Office Buildings in the late morning. It was understood that he would then escort her on a tour of the city's monuments. All of this was scheduled on a weekend when neither of them was working.

She admitted that she knew nothing about Senator Dodd until she was told who he was. Before their first meeting, she called Paul Simon, her former husband, and asked about him. A native of Connecticut, Simon had worked for Dodd on one of his political campaigns. "Politically, Paul's heart always beats in the right places, so I knew Dodd was not one of those right-wingers."

Dodd had worked as a lobbyist, attorney, and later, beginning in 1981, as the Democratic Senator from Connecticut, serving a term that lasted for thirty years. *[A profoundly influential player in politics, he headed the Democratic National Committee (1995-97), and later operated as Chairman of the Senate Banking Committee. In 2006, Dodd would seek the Democratic nomination for President of the United States, but he found that support for that was lacking and dropped out of the race for the Oval Office. After his retirement from the Senate in 2011, he served as President of the Motion Picture Association of America, retiring from that position in 2017.]*

Simon told her that Dodd was single, having divorced Susan Mooney, whom he'd married in 1970, a union that lasted for twelve years.

Since she was not familiar with the skyline of Washington, on their first date he drove her around, pointing out the sights, providing nutshell histories of the White House, the Washington Monument, the U.S. Mint, the Supreme Court (he didn't approve of all those right-wing judges), and the Lincoln Memorial. According to Carrie, "As a high school dropout, my knowledge of the workings of the U.S. government could be put in a walnut."

Before the end of her tour, he suggested that she call him Chris. As she facetiously wrote later, "I guess that was better than 'Ball Sack,' although I suspected he had quite a bag, because he was a powerful man not afraid of his political enemies."

"Debbie had been invited to the White House on several separate occasions, so I fig-

Carrie admitted in print that Senator Dodd was not a handsome man, although during his 20s and 30s, he'd been considered so.

Now in his early 50s, he had what she called "the reddest of cheeks, the whitest of hair, and the bluest of eyes—an American face!—and there was a merry sort of force that twinkled out of those eyes."

ured she was a bit of an expert on government. I'd asked her how many senators there were. She told me, 'Every American knows that each state sends one senator to Washington.' Chris told me my mother was wrong. Each state has two senators."

"Driving around, it was clear to me that our middle-aged senator wanted to get laid, so he didn't denounce me for being a politically ignorant fool."

"At the end of the day, he drove me to this elegant and exclusive restaurant in Georgetown," she said. "There we were to meet two other couples for dinner." Arriving at the restaurant, the *maître d'* ushered them to table, where their four other companions were sipping wine as they waited.

She was startled to come face to face with the one senator she knew something about: Ted Kennedy, known as the "Lion of the Senate," and a Democrat from Massachusetts. "I was stunned to have a close encounter with a face I'd seen a thousand times on TV and in the newspapers. He introduced me to his woman *du jour*, Lacey Neuhaus, a very attractive blonde with perfect manners and a voice reflecting her good breeding."

"I forgot the names of the other couple, but remembered they lived on Hickory Hill, next to Ethel Kennedy and her brood. Before he was assassinated, Bobby must have been determined to let the world know that he did not believe in birth control."

She later recalled, "Chris and I were not the first to call for a union between Hollywood and Washington. Our President and First Lady were the most famous examples of uniting these two notorious meccas of decadence and chicanery. In addition to Ronnie and Nancy, Elizabeth Taylor had married Senator John Warner of Virginia, although the differences in their respective policies about gays was about as wide as the distance between Earth and the Moon. Linda Ronstadt was shacking up with that cute California governor, Jerry Brown, and Debra Winger was cuddling with the Nebraska governor, John Kerry."

"I suspected that Teddy Boy and Chris had gone on many a 'wench hunt' together. Some waitress in a restaurant at the Capitol had once accused them of sexual harassment. I'd heard that the two of them with their gals had often gone sailing together off the coast of Cape Cod."

"Teddy was quite eloquent at the beginning of the evening, talking about Nicaragua, claiming that it was a potential powder keg. The only thing I knew about that country was that it was somewhere in Central America, and had been the birthplace of my friend, Bianca Jagger, who married Mick Jagger of *The Rolling Stones*. I decided to listen

Teddy Kennedy in a photo that shows the famously glacial "Kennedy stare."

"But I melted his cold, cold heart," Carrie claimed.

like a little bimbo and keep my trap shut so I wouldn't reveal myself to be ignorant. Here I was sitting with two of the most powerful movers and shakers in Washington, and about to be fucked by one of them. I was a few cards short of a royal flush."

"I had just recently gotten off drugs, and I intended to stay cold sober, ordering only a bottle of coke. My mental condition was a bit shaky at the time. Inside me lurked a monster that I didn't want to break out of his cage. I wondered if Chris or Teddy had the nuts—or were nuts enough—to take me on in combat."

As the night wore on, the *politicos* switched from wine to more lethal vodka tonics, with Teddy outdrinking everyone at the table. "That Irishman really loved his booze, although John Belushi could have beaten him. Teddy was beginning to let his hair down. He wanted to get bawdy, talk a little rough."

"I'd like to address Princess Leia," he said. "Do you plan to have sex with Chris tonight?"

"Dumbfounded, I couldn't believe he'd asked me such a personal question in public. Before answering, I looked first at Chris to rescue me. He didn't seem to find the question out of order, since, by now, he was used to our naughty boy. Finally, I spoke up: 'No, not tonight, as Josephine said to Napoléon.' Thanks for asking, though. I appreciate your concern for Chris' libido.'"

"Why not? Do you think you're too good for him?" Kennedy asked.

"Perhaps not worthy enough," she answered. "I'm off drugs tonight. Usually, when I'm drugged, I would have had the senator's pants off by now. I'll perhaps say no even if he is a Democrat. I try not to fuck Republicans. They never bathe. I go wild on LSD."

"When you're zonked out on acid, do you have sex?" Kennedy asked.

"Acid is not an aphrodisiac,"

"Well, when you're on acid, do you masturbate?" he asked.

She picked up her fork as if to use it as a weapon. "If you don't mind, I prefer the term 'play with yourself.' It's less clinical."

"Teddy Boy and I seemed to be playing a game of who could shock who the most," she recalled. Our guests sat in stony silence."

"I understand you're the daughter of Eddie Fisher, that singer who used to hustle coke on TV," Kennedy said. "The bottled drink, not the drug, of course. Are you certain he's your father? With all the sleeping around in that town, I don't think any Hollywood brat can be sure who the father is."

"I would say that in this case, Hollywood and Washington have something in common," she said.

"Fisher ran off with Elizabeth Taylor who once fucked my brother John." Kennedy said. "And probably Bobby, too. Was your father a good influence on you?"

"I always turn to him for advice," Carrie answered sarcastically. "Before I married Paul Simon, I phoned Eddie. He told me I had a great ass and should be marrying him."

"So much for *Father Knows Best*," Kennedy quipped.

"The party was getting rough," Carrie said, "and I was surprised when he asked me to sing. I could have turned him down, and should have, but I obliged. I burst into the lyrics of 'If I Loved You,' from *Carousel* by Rodgers & Hammerstein. I sang the whole song, and the table, including Senator Kennedy, clapped politely. Music would have helped."

"After the bill was settled and Senator Dodd had privately invited me back to his quarters, we three couples stood outside, waiting for our cars. Teddy Boy leaned close to me, and at first I thought he was going to trap me in a liplock or else grab my galaxy snatch. He did neither. He wanted to ask me another of his damn questions."

"Would you like to have sex with Chris in a hot tub?"

"That was his farewell to me," she said. "After that send-off, I thought Teddy Boy was out of my life forever. I didn't think I was going to become his Marilyn Monroe, since he'd made it obvious that he didn't like me. How wrong I was!"

She later admitted to friends, "I had sex with Chris—not bad. This was not his first time at the rodeo. He's a fine and decent man, and I started to date him. Even though they were the best of friends, he had far more manners than Teddy Boy, who, when drunk, acted like a Harvard frat boy."

"Before I got really serious about Chris, and proposed marriage to him, a thought crossed my mind. The press would surely say that I was marrying a father figure. He was not a father figure, as he was only twelve years older than me. Most twelve-year-old boys don't have kids, although I'm sure some of them do if they're really horny."

"What screwed up my relationship—perhaps 'screw' is not the right word—came when I found the two-timer was slipping behind my back and messing around with my friend, Bianca Jagger, who was no longer married to Mick. That put a strain on my romantic illusions about Chris. Time and distance caused us to drift apart. I wouldn't have outed our affair in my book, *Shockaholic*, had he not talked to the press about it. A reporter asked him about us."

According to Dodd, "Our courtship was long ago. "It was on a galaxy, far, far away."

When she heard that, Carrie said, "Surely Chris didn't say something that lame."

***

"Long before Teddy Kennedy and I became fat and bloated, both of us were two hot pieces of ass. In many ways, when he was in his twenties, Teddy was better looking than Jack or Bobby. Even Rose Kennedy said so. But, as

Marilyn Monroe sang, 'We all lose our charms in the end.'"

Months after she'd stopped seeing Senator Dodd, Carrie encountered Senator Kennedy at a Hollywood party hosted by his friend, Jack Nicholson. The embarrassment of that testy night around a restaurant's dining table in Washington had faded. "It was a different Teddy Kennedy I met in California. He was fun and flirtatious. Those exchanges we'd had were just our sexual chemistry bubbling over. He flirted with me, and I flirted right back."

"The last time, when he'd asked me if I wanted to have sex with Chris in a hot tub, he was asking for himself, as I was soon to find out during that torrid weekend of passion. I was anxious to become another notch on his well-worn belt."

"There was something about this charismatic figure that appealed to me, and it went far beyond sexual chemistry. I identified with him in some way. Like my own life, his, too, had been a kaleidoscope of roles, from thrill seeker one moment to a constructive senator at times, championing the poor and advocating civil rights for all people. Like his brothers, he had an eye for a shapely woman. Actresses seemed a favorite of all three brothers. Teddy was the baby of that trio, but what a big baby. He was football player size."

"Although there were other people at the party, Teddy spent most of his time in a huddle with me. The first thing he told me was that he had been a *Star Wars* fan, and that he really dug Princess Leia. After telling me that, I would have run off with him into the night, but it became clear that after this cocktail party, he had already lined up some other tail for his dessert."

"However, he did invite me to go with him to Palm Springs for the weekend, where he'd been given the use of a private villa. He didn't tell me who owned it, and I really didn't want to know."

"He was a bit older than me, but no more than a country mile. He'd been hatched the same year Debbie was. I think FDR was running for President. I'd read that he had divorced his first wife, Joan Bennett (no, not the fabled brunette screen goddess)."

"I had dropped out of high school, and he'd gone to Harvard, so we weren't going to spend the weekend talking politics, of which I am vastly ignorant. There had been some scandal about him cheating on his exams. Why not? I would have done the same thing. By the time Teddy got around to porking me, he had already failed in his 1980 presidential bid."

In her skinny memoir, *Shockaholic*, Carrie wrote about her first meeting with Kennedy, but left out details of her subsequent affair with him on the West Coast. Over time, she told others of her fling, including Anne Bancroft, who had become her friend when they had co-starred together in *Garbo Talks*. Carrie also confided details of her affair with Kennedy to Maureen O'Sullivan, Rudy Render, and director Michael Winner.

"Late the following morning, when I got into his car to drive to the desert, I made a stupid joke. I told him I was relieved to know that there were no bridges between Los Angeles and Palm Springs. The joke fell flat, and well it should," she said. "He was obviously disturbed to hear me say that. I should have apologized, but I thought that might make his hurt all the worse. He drove for another thirty minutes before he broke through the stone wall of silence."

"Before we got to Palm Springs, we were laughing and talking again, and looking forward to a fun weekend."

[Carrie had been referring to Kennedy's negligence in the death of Mary Jo Kopechne at Chappaquiddick on Martha's Vineyard in Massachusetts on July 20, 1969. She also remembered that as the day Neil Armstrong performed his Moon Walk. But instead of focusing on that memorable milestone in America's space program, newspapers had headlined the drowning of Kopechne as its major story of the day.]

"It seemed that the entire world had heard of Teddy's heavy boozing, his dare-devil driving, and his chasing after any hot dame in a dress," Carrie said. "But I didn't see that as any reason to boycott him."

"We didn't take drugs during the weekend I spent in his august presence," she claimed, "but we drank a lot. I learned that Teddy was a binge drinker. He told me he could go for days without one drop, but then he'd have one drink and couldn't stop belting down more. Liquor seemed to emancipate him the way drugs did for me."

"I will not pretend that Teddy was a great lover because he wasn't," she said. "He was proficient in the sack, as many men are, but nothing to brag about. He was better as a senator than as a lover. Women were drawn to him because he was a Kennedy, and a charismatic figure, a son of Camelot carrying on the legacy of his brothers."

"In the tabloids, he'd been linked to many prominent playmates. I hoped I could be added to that distinguished list."

[Carrie was referring to Countess Lana Campbell; socialite Helga Wagner, British debutante Louise Steel; ski champion Suzie Chaffee, and the German princess Angela Wepper; even a saucy blonde, Claudia Cummings, the former Miss Alabama. Reportedly, he'd also had flings with two of the most fabled women on the planet and the wife of a prime minister. He'd seduced Jacqueline Kennedy after the assassination of his brother, Bobby, in Los Angeles in 1968. He was also said to have seduced Margaret Trudeau, the wife of the prime minister of Canada, although that has never been confirmed.

Following in the footsteps of his brothers, JFK and Bobby, Teddy had crawled between the sheets of Marilyn Monroe during the course of one long weekend. Marilyn told Shelley Winters, "If you go for one, chances are you'll go for the rest of the brothers, too."]

Critics claimed that Kennedy, when not pursuing social justice in the Senate, "broke loose and behaved like a drunken toot."

"That weekend in Palm Springs, we indulged ourselves with booze, nude swims, and lobsters transported from Los Angeles. That same seafood restaurant sent three quarts of clam chowder for his breakfasts."

After their weekend tryst, she saw him on two other occasions, "but by then he'd moved on to other vaginas and didn't pay my galaxy snatch any more attention."

***

At long last, Carrie got cast in a hit movie outside the *Star Wars* franchise. Woody Allen was impressed with her acting talent and cast her in his 1986 comedy, *Hannah and Her Sisters*. Written and directed by the master himself, he lined up an all-star cast, headed by his mistress, Mia Farrow, the former wife of Frank Sinatra. The British actor, Michael Caine, at the time the 12th highest-grossing actor in the world, was cast as Hannah's husband, with Barbara Hershey and Dianne Wiest as her sisters.

Carrie interpreted the supporting role of April, a friend of one of the sisters. Playing the trio's parents were Maureen O'Sullivan (who happened to be Mia Farrow's real-life mother) and Lloyd Nolan, who would die four months before the movie's release. Other players included Max von Sydow and David Stern. A pre-adolescent Soon-Yi Previn appeared in an uncredited role, too. In 1997, she would marry Allen.

The script revolves around the intertwined stories of an extended family over two years that begins and ends with a Thanksgiving dinner. Carrie appears in scenes with Holly (Wiest). After borrowing money from Hannah, Holly starts a catering business with April, her friend and fellow actress. But in time, the two women become rivals in love and competitors for the same role in a Broadway musical. Both of them are also in pursuit of Sam Waterston, cast in an uncredited role as an architect.

Carrie bonded with O'Sullivan during the filming. In addition to many other roles, she was known for playing Jane in *Tarzan* movies with Johnny Weissmuller. "We talked about men and the complications they bring into our lives," Carrie said. "Maureen told me that Frank Sinatra should have married her instead of Mia, who was just too young to deal with him."

According to Carrie, "In London one night, Ava Gardner said to me, 'I always knew Frank would

In the Woody Allen hit comedy, *Hannah and Her Sisters*, Carrie flirts with Sam Waterston.

Allen was at his peak when he made this movie, with his current lover, Mia Farrow.

He cast his Mia's adopted daughter, Soon Ye Previn, in a minor role, too. Later, when he married her, it caused a worldwide scandal.

one day end up with a boy.' Naturally, she was referring to Mia."

"When Carrie met the much-lauded Caine, "I decided to be a bitch. I asked him what it was like to fuck Bianca Jagger. They had dated in London in 1968."

Farrow complained to Carrie that she did not like Allen's script. "He took many of the serious themes of our lives together, distorted them, and made us cartoonish. But he's my lover, and I'm grist for the mill."

Hannah and Her Sisters became one of Allen's highest-grossing films. Vincent Canby of *The New York Times* hailed it "for setting new standards for American movie makers." *Slant* magazine wrote of its "brilliant balancing act of conflicting desires and feelings."

"Compared to all this talent and honors, I feel like a wallflower at the ball," Carrie said.

Michael Caine won a Best Supporting Actor Oscar, with Wiest winning the Best Supporting Actress gold.

***

After *Hannah and Her Sisters,* Carrie, throughout the rest of the 1980s, appeared in a number of forgettable pictures before she was cast in another hit.

First, she was offered fourth billing, the role of rookie undercover cop, Betty Melton, in the lurid but slow-moving *Hollywood Vice Squad* (1986), which its producers promoted with the slogan: SEX, DRUGS, BLOOD, AND GUTS—IT'S ALL IN A NIGHT'S WORK.

Its director, Penelope Spheeris, hired a cast that included Trish Van Devers, the wife of actor George C. Scott. She played Pauline Stanton, who travels to Hollywood in search of her daughter Lori, who has become involved in the hard-core porn industry.

Lori, Pauline's drug-addicted daughter, was played by the very talented Robin Wright in one of her earliest screen roles. In time, she would marry Sean Penn after his divorce from Madonna, and would become a household word when she starred in the hit TV series, *House of Cards* from 2013 to 2017 opposite Kevin Spacey.

The male leads were played by Ronny Cox as Captain Jensen and Frank Gorshin as Walsh, who amused Carrie between takes with his on-target

Michael Caine in *Hannah* was at the peak of his appeal—"that is, before he became old and withered like me," Carrie said.

"This ex-porter at *[London's]* Smithfield Meat Market tended to be as cold and barricaded as his spectacles. I was tempted to take away the horn rims he often wore and discover what Cockney love was all about. Bianca Jagger had already staked him out."

impressions of Kirk Douglas.

Spheeris, a native of New Orleans, was also a producer and screenwriter best known for her trilogy entitled *The Decline of Western Civilization.*

After that, Carrie moved on to one of the most bizarre films she ever made, *Amazon Women on the Moon* (1987), a satirical comedy that parodied the low-budget movies then being broadcast on late-night television. Five directors were hired to helm three dozen comedy skits with all-star ensemble casts. The title derived from a particularly campy sci-fi movie, *Queen of Outer Space* (1950), that had starred Zsa Zsa Gabor.

Making a cameo appearance was Rosanna Arquette, who by 2018 would be making headlines with her claim that Harvey Weinstein had sexually assaulted her. *["Weinstein landed my career in the gutter by telling directors and producers that I 'was a pain in the ass,' but I escaped his clutches."]*

Other cameos were executed by Hollywood personalities who included Ralph Bellamy, Steve Forrest *[According to Carrie, "He once fucked my mother"]*, Steve Guttenberg, Michelle Pfeiffer, Henry Silva, Bryan Cranston, Steve Allen, Henny Youngman, B.B. King, Rip Taylor *[Debbie's co-star in various night club acts]*, and a host of other public figures.

Carrie's relatively minor role was that of Mary Brown within a segment devised as a spoof of *Reefer Madness* (1936), an antiquated anti-marijuana propaganda film that was frequently screened for pot smokers at late-night movie theaters.

With a wry sense of irony and the ridiculous, Carrie later said, "When I die, I'm sure the *Los Angeles Times* will headline my obit STAR OF AMAZON WOMEN ON THE MOON DIES.

That was followed with an equivalently hokey role in another dubious film, *The Time Guardian* (1987), another sci-fi fantasy. Directed by Brian Hannant, and in addition to Carrie, it starred Tom Burlinson, Nikki Coghill, and Dean Stockwell.

[In the year 4039, survivors from the Neutron Wars travel through time and space to escape from the deadly Jen-Kiki, a race of cyborgs intent on wiping out humanity. Ballard (Tom Burlinson) and Carrie (as Petra) are transported to the Southern Australian Outback, where it is 1988, to prepare for a landing site for the other survivors. Petra is wounded, as an advance party of Jen-Kiki also lands in Australia to pursue their prey.]

The lead actor, Burlinson, was also a singer and TV host. Before working with Carrie, he had starred in *The Man from Snowy*

"What can I say about my appearance in *Amazon Women on the Moon?*" Carrie asked.

"I knew it would not immortalize me as a screen icon. But what the hell?"

River (1982). A "coming of age" film set on the Outback in the 1880s, it was one of the highest-grossing and most internationally successful Australian movies ever made.

His voice evoked that of Frank Sinatra. In fact, Tina Sinatra used Burlinson's singing voice as that of a young Sinatra in a miniseries she produced about her father.

A son of Hollywood, Dean Stockwell had originated as a child star in such movies as *Anchors Aweigh* (1945) and *Kim* (1950). After working with Carrie, he would go on to his next picture, *Married to the Mob* (1988) in which he would win a Best Supporting Actor nomination from the Academy Awards.

Carrie with Tom Burlinson in *The Time Guardian*, a commercial flop whose sci-fi premises evoked some aspects of *Star Wars*.

She found the Australian actor "hot and sexy, and very handsome."

The Time Guardian was poorly received, with critic David Stratton writing, "The film had the wrong producers, the wrong deals, the wrong budget, the wrong cast, and in the end, the wrong script."

"I had high hopes for my next picture, *Appointment With Death* (1988)," Carrie said. It was a British mystery film shot in England and Israel by Golan-Globus Productions and directed by Michael Winner."

Its script was based on an adaptation of a mystery novel by Agatha Christie that featured the Belgian detective Hercule Poirot, as interpreted by Peter Ustinov. His co-star, Lauren Bacall as Lady Westholme, had previously appeared with him in *Murder on the Orient Express* (1974).

Rounding out the cast were Carrie, Piper Laurie, John Gielgud, Hayley Mills, Nicholas Guest, Jenny Seagrove, and David Soul. Both Carrie and Gielgud had previously appeared together in the TV film, *Frankenstein.*

In the plot, the greedy Emily Boynton (Piper Laurie) wants all of her husband's money after he dies. She's the stepmother of the three Boynton children—Lennox, Raymond, and Carol. *[Cast as the third lead, Carrie as Nadine, plays her daughter-in-law.]* Emily blackmails the family lawyer, Jefferson Cope (David Soul), into destroying a more recent will of her late husband that would have freed her stepchildren from her dominating influence.

Some questions become immediately obvious to most viewers: How long will it take before Emily is murdered? And how long will it take for the master detective, Hercule Poirot, to nail the guilty culprit?

"Our director, Michael Winner, was fabulous," Carrie said. "In London, we dined out nearly every night. As he was the food critic for *The Sunday Times*,

514

he took me to some of the city's finest restaurants. Before he worked with me, he was also known for hanging out with movie stars—Marlene Dietrich and James Stewart come to mind. He'd directed Marlon Brando in *The Nightcomers* (1971).

"Peter Ustinov was one of the grandest creatures ever put on the planet," Carrie said. "He was an intellectual, a diplomat, a distinguished actor, director, screenwriter, columnist, and broadcaster—a true Renaissance man."

"One night, he escorted me to this exclusive party in Mayfair where Princess Margaret was the guest of honor. I was riding high that night and not responsible for my actions. When I greeted Meg, I said, 'So, one princess meets another princess.' I also asked her, 'Is it true that my father, Eddie Fisher, once screwed you?' Her Majesty turned and walked away without answering me, and she avoided me for the rest of the evening—and rightly so. Me and my big mouth! Sometimes I go wild when I take drugs."

"*Appointment With Death* was a dud at the box office, the least successful of all the Hercule Poirot films. It earned only a million dollars but cost six million to make."

Many of the critics hated it, *Variety* summarizing it as "A Loser for Director Winner. Ustinov looked a bit jaded in his third big screen appearance as the sleuth. Winner's helming is lackluster, the script and characterizations bland, and there simply aren't enough murders to sustain interest, even from the most avid of Agatha Christie fans."

"In my next film, *The 'Burbs* (1989), a comedy thriller, Tom Hanks and I did a hell of a lot better box office than we did with *The Man with One Red Shoe*," Carrie said.

Directed by Joe Dante, it poked fun at

In *Appointment with Death*, based on the Agatha Christie thriller, Carrie was cast with Peter Ustinov in his familiar role of the Belgian detective, Hercule Poirot,

"Not even the very talented Mr. Ustinov, or even John Gielgud, could save this dud," Carrie said.

Nicholas Guest appears with Carrie in *Appointment with Death*.

She later claimed that after the film was released, "I got a note from Debbie. It read simply, 'Hello, dear. I saw you in your latest movie.'"

suburbanites and their sometimes eccentric inhabitants. Ron Howard was one of the producers, and other co-stars included Bruce Dern, Corey Feldman, Carrie's friend Henry Gibson, and Gale Gordon, forever associated with Lucille Ball's antics on TV.

Screenwriter Dana Olsen told Carrie that he was inspired to write the story based on his own middle-class upbringing in the suburbs. "Most of the people were normal, but, of course, every neighborhood has the resident psycho. I was going for a medley of horror, comedy, and reality that might have been titled *Ozzie and Harriet Meet Charles Manson.*"

Hanks played Ray Peterson, who's suspicious of his next door neighbors, the Klopeks, because he hears strange noises coming from their basement. His wife, Carol (Carrie), grows tired of her husband's snooping, and so he sends her and his son Dave to visit her sister, while he and his buddies try to find out what is going on at the Klopek's home.

On a budget of $18 million, *The 'Burbs* grossed $50 million.

"Tom puts his own spin on every role he plays, and I struggle along in my usual thankless part," Carrie said.

She hardly remembered making her next movie, the 1989 film, *Loverboy.* *[Confusingly, other movies also have that same title.]* Director Joan Micklin Silver cast Patrick Dempsey, Kirstie Alley, and Carrie in the three leading roles.

"Randy was the right name for the Dempsey character as he had to fuck his way from woman to woman throughout the film," Carrie said.

Dempsey plays a rebellious college slacker whose studies don't seem to be going anywhere. His father demands that he return home and get a job. He takes a job as a pizza delivery boy, in the course of which he meets a rich and horny Italian woman, Alex Barnett (Barbara Carrera). The middle-aged vamp showers Randy with expensive gifts, each of which come with a card that's signed "Love, Alex." His father reads the cards and thinks Alex is a man and that his son is gay and hustling.

Among the other women in whose beds Randy performs is

"No one seems to remember that I was once a co-star of Tom Hanks, as I was in *The Burbs,* a sendup of suburban life in America," Carrie said.

"Tom was amiable, decent, and non-threatening, hardly a sexual menace. He'd dropped out of Cal State to become an actor, which was the best decision of his life. He even survived getting cast in ten hopeless duds."

"My friend, Penny Marshall, did a hell of a lot better with him when she was cast with Tom in *Big* (1988). He played a twelve-year-old who finds himself in a man's body, looking down to see what he saw in his jockey shorts for the first time. For that, he got an Oscar nod."

Monica Delancy (Carrie), cast as an isolated and aspiring photographer. Of course, a conflict ensues when angry husbands learn about their wives' affairs with "Randy Randy."

Distributed by TriStar Pictures, *Loverboy* grossed around $4 million after its nationwide release.

After that, Carrie went on to play the female lead in another 1989 release, *She's Back.*

Cast as Beatrice, in a Joe Gage film not specifically aimed at gay men, Carrie has been killed and returns as a ghost to goad her henpecked husband, Paul (Robert Joy), into avenging her attackers. As an electrician, he comes up with some inventive methods of revenge.

A Canadian actor, he amused Carrie with stories of his co-starring with Madonna, playing her punk musician boyfriend in *Desperately Seeking Susan* (1985).

The director of *She's Back*, Tim Kincaid, had previously been widely known by the name of "Joe Gage," and to a lesser degree as "Mac Larson." Through the previous release of films that included *Kansas City Trucking Co.* (1976) and *L.A. Tool & Die* (1979), he'd already had a significant impact on the gay male culture that developed in the 1970s. The "Gage Men"

"I liked the original script for *Loverboy* (1989) rather than the final cut," Carrie said.

"I played an older woman, a photographer, having an affair with a younger man, Patrick Dempsey. I was to have appeared in a segment where he posed for me in the nude, a sort of *Playgirl* centerfold. But it was viewed as too *risqué.*"

depicted in some of his erotic films tended more toward hairy and hunky "Average Joes," instead of the archetypal, preppy-looking clones for Abercrombie & Fitch seen in stereotypical gay porn before that. In the words of one sociologist and critic, "Gage is the first artist who dared to suggest that sex between men was more about camaraderie than romance, more about hot action than a lifestyle."

A TV station in the Twin Cities of St. Paul and Minneapolis regularly showed some really bad movies every Monday to Friday night. *She's Back* was selected one night. A critic wrote, "Carrie Fisher as Beatrice irritates her husband endlessly…and the viewers, too. She is just so annoying. The plot is silly; the acting bad; the story…well, you get my drift. Anyway, if you wanna see a really bad movie—really, really bad, check out *She's Back*."

***

Before 1989 came to an end, and after her involvement in a stampede of

517

unmemorable films, Carrie was finally cast in a hit, *When Harry Met Sally...*, a romantic comedy by Nora Ephron directed by Rob Reiner and starring Billy Crystal as Harry and Meg Ryan as Sally. Carrie had the third lead playing Marie Fisher, Sally's best friend, falling for Harry's best friend, Jess (Bruno Kirby).

Still in wide circulation and originally released by Columbia, *When Harry Met Sally...*, in time became what was called "the quintessential contemporary feel-good relationship movie that still rings true."

The plot follows two friends, male and female, over twelve years of chance encounters. It raises the question: Can men and women ever be just friends? As is to be expected, after all these years of knowing each other, having long talks and being supportive of each other, they finally have sex, coming (so to speak) together for the first time. As Harry later says, "The sex part got in the way of our friendship."

The most famous scene in the movie took place in Katz's Deli in Manhattan. The character of Sally (Meg Ryan) claims that men can't tell if a woman is faking orgasm. To prove her point, and fully clothed, she fakes an orgasm at a public table in the deli. A nearby patron (actually Reiner's real-life mother) tells the waitress, "I'll have whatever she's having." *The New York Times* referred to the scene as "one of the most memorably funny lines in movie history."

Carrie had long known Reiner because he'd been married to her best friend, Penny Marshall. The marriage, which began in 1971, lasted a decade. She liked working with him and with Crystal, a TV host, comedian, director, writer, and producer. He'd achieved national recognition when he'd first appeared on the ABC sitcom *Soap*, playing Jodie Dallas, one of the first unambiguously gay characters in the cast of an American TV series (1977-81).

Although Carrie was jealous of her for having landed the better part, she also liked Meg Ryan, confessing to Reiner, "I would have liked the role of Sally myself."

He responded that Ryan had not been his first choice. He'd considered hiring Susan Dey, Elizabeth Perkins, Elizabeth McGovern, and Molly Ringwald before finally selecting her.

Ryan's career took off in the 1990s in such hits as *Sleepless in Seattle* (1993), and *You've Got Mail* (1998). At one time

Carrie (left) in a scene with Meg Ryan in *When Harry Met Sally...*

"I wanted the lead role of Sally for myself, but lost out to Meg," Carrie claimed. "One scene became iconic where Meg's face has to express her faking an orgasm. I could have played that perfectly, having already done that in my real life so many times already."

518

(1991-2001), she was married to actor Dennis Quaid.

Carrie bonded more with Ephron than with any other member of the cast. Both of these writers had much to talk about. They agreed that that ex-husbands, providing that the author changed their names, could be interpreted as legitimate inspirations for the characters depicted in their film scripts and novels. Ephron had been married to reporter Carl Bernstein who, along with Bob Woodward, helped expose the Watergate scandal that led to the resignation of Richard Nixon.

After the collapse of her marriage to Bernstein, Ephron published a 1983 novel, *Heartburn,* in which he was depicted as "capable of having sex with a Venetian blind." Enraged, Bernstein threatened to sue but never did.

Following in her footsteps, Carrie would write about Paul Simon in her 1990 novel, *Surrender the Pink,* in which he is clearly the inspiration for the character of Rudy. She also wrote about her second husband, Bryan Lourd, in her 2003 novel, *The Best Awful,* again assigning a pseudonym to the character he'd inspired.

When Harry Met Sally… was a big hit, taking in around $95 million at the box office, a hefty profit from its initial cost of $16 million.

Reviews, for the most part, were positive. Roger Ebert praised the sexual chemistry of Crystal with Ryan, and lauded Reiner as "one of Hollywood's very best directors of comedy." Caryn James, in *The New York Times,* characterized it as "the sitcom version of a Woody Allen film, full of amusing lines and scenes, all infused with an uncomfortable sense of *déja vu.*"

Rotten Tomatoes declared that *When Harry Met Sally…* set a new standard for romantic comedies. *Newsweek,* however, sounded a sour note, interpreting Crystal as not suitable as a romantic leading man.

Carrie read all the reviews and became distressed that she hadn't been singled out for any particularly effusive individual praise. "What about me! I was in the movie, too, playing a character whose last name was Fisher."

***

As Carrie revealed in her 2011 autobiographical book, *Shockaholic,* and in numerous television appearances, she suffered from a bipolar disorder *[then known as manic depression].*

This condition, with its lofty peaks which could descent into deep gutters, adversely affected her life, her career, her two husbands, the daughter she would eventually have, and her relationship with Debbie, which for almost a decade, entered a "blackout" when they didn't speak.

"There were days when I was so desperate I couldn't get out of bed, and other days when I was overwhelmed by a giddy euphoria."

"I was given a challenging illness, and there is no other option than to face up to that challenge. Call it confronting my demons. I was long addicted to

519

Percodan, my drug of choice. It could, at least momentarily, make me feel I was the happiest woman on the planet. Of course, it was known to have its downside; heart palpitations, or even a heart attack. The shadowy figure of death in some cases came knocking on the door. So we're talking major risk here."

"One of its side effects was sudden weight gain or loss. On many occasions when I couldn't stop binge eating, I ballooned up to look like a cow with sagging tits, the size that could nurse a herd of baby cattle."

"At first, I didn't know the reasons for my sudden mood swings," she said. "I was told they came about because I was an alcoholic. So, that was what was the matter with me. Maybe I should give up booze, perhaps go to an AA meeting, although the dread of sharing my affliction with strangers overpowered me."

"As an alcoholic, I was in good company. John Barrymore was a drunkard when he came to Hollywood and made all those bad pictures. In the years leading up to his death, F. Scott Fitzgerald, the author of *The Great Gatsby*, was an alcoholic. So was the Welsh poet, Dylan Thomas."

"If I want to drop even bigger bipolar names, I must cite Abraham Lincoln, a closeted gay, or Winston Churchill, who called his condition, 'The Black Dog.'"

"When you're manic, every urge is like an edict from the Vatican. In my worst condition, I could stay awake, if you called it awake, for six days. Instead of really being awake, you existed in some foggy limbo, moving about but unable to shut down your brain waves for welcoming sleep. I was like a crippled woman stumbling down a steep stairway to a dark gulf. Staying awake for six days is like being in training to become a psychotic."

She first told the world she was bipolar when she was interviewed on TV by Diane Sawyer.

"When I married for the second time and had this little girl, I, as a mother, had to confess to her, 'Your mother is bipolar; your father is a homosexual; your grandmother is a tap dancer; and your grandfather, a redneck Texan, shoots speed.'"

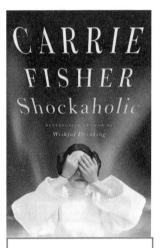

Carrie received mixed reviews for her autobiographical *Shockaholic.* It relayed her struggles with bipolar disorder. *The New York Post* claimed that she was "unafraid to write brutally but vividly." *USA Today* called it "wickedly funny," and *Publishers Weekly* hailed it for "juicy confessions and outrageously funny observations."

In the book, she reveals that the electro-convulsive shock therapy that she's been regularly undergoing is threatening to wipe out what's left of her memory.

Through it all, she was so candid that she shocked people. One time, during a period of binge eating and rapid weight gain, she said, "My tits are so big that they had to add extra letters to the alphabet to come up with my bra size."

One night, Carrie was rushed to Cedars Sinai Medical Center in Los Angeles. Todd checked her in, and she registered under the name of "Shame."

"When I came to, I felt I was in the loonie bin. When I met my doctor, I was convinced of it. Was he my doctor or a patient himself? He was this John Steinbeck character, walking in and announcing, 'Finally, here's someone who can tell us what it's like to get his cock sucked.' Had I heard right? 'His cock?' Did he think that with tits like mine, I was a man? I'm sure when he examined me, he would see how wrong he was when confronted with the Grand Canyon."

"What I knew about mental hospitals is what I learned watching Olivia de Havilland emote in *The Snake Pit* (1948). *Frances* (1982), a film starring Jessica Lange, was like taking a course labeled 'Mental Asylum 101' in college. It told the tragic life of that oldtime actress, Frances Farmer. When she was in the asylum, she was raped by both lesbians and male interns. Would that happen to me?"

"It was at this time in the hospital that electroshock therapy was recommended to me. It was later given the less foreboding name of electroconvulsive therapy (ECT). It had to be explained to me. When I first heard about it, I viewed it as a nightmare descended from hell. I imagined that the electric shocks that shot into my body were like bolts of lightning. I thought for a while I would be insane to agree to such a horrendous experience."

She was given pamphlets and printouts to read, the material explaining that ECT was a psychiatric treatment in which seizures are electrically induced in a patient to provide relief from mental disorders. The procedure is viewed in some quarters as the last line of intervention for major depressive disorders, mania, and catanoia [*i.e., a state of immobility and stupor*].

"In spite of my personal problems, I always managed to straighten out my tits, iron the wrinkles out of my ass, and get that god damn hairdo set right for another appearance as Princess Leia opposite that darling man, Harrison Ford, as Han Solo."

"I was afraid of it. I knew that Ernest Hemingway committed suicide in 1961 shortly after he'd been administered electroshock at the Mayo

521

Clinic, and I'd read Sylvia Plath's *The Bell Jar* three times."

"Not only that, but I had seen Jack Nicholson's performance in *One Flew Over the Cuckoo's Nest* (1975). He went crazy."

But eventually, as a last-ditch effort, she submitted to the treatment. "I was desperate to get rid of those clouds of depression. Psychotherapy had not worked, and more medication left me drifting into this dense fog. ECT was like a blast of cement walls to the brain. It erased many of my past memories, especially the painful ones. But regardless of what its critics say, ECT is a hell of a lot better than lobotomies like the one old Joe Kennedy gave to one of his daughters and like Katharine Hepburn tried to convince Monty Clift to perform on Elizabeth Taylor in *Suddenly, Last Summer* (1959)."

"First of all, when I woke up, I didn't remember one fucking thing. For all I knew, I was dressed in a ballgown, surrounded by dancing dolphins, and getting ready to be married off to Rush Limbaugh."

"At first, my treatment was three times a week for three weeks, and then it tapered off. But it seemed to work for me, although not always. It was sort of like getting your nails done if your nails were in your cerebral cortex."

When Simon & Schuster released *Shockaholic*, it promoted it with a strange blurb: "Get ready for a shock. Not only does Carrie Fisher not mind paying for that second electric bill, she loves the high-voltage treatments. In fact, she gets a real charge out of them. She can't get enough. In fact, this might be a brand new addiction for her. But before she can truly commit herself to it in the long term, she'd better get some of those more nagging memories of hers on paper."

And that she did in this slim autobiography, which went over fairly well with fans of Princess Leia. From the blogosphere, "Mouthy Jenn" wrote that "Carrie Fisher, my dears, is fucking hysterical!!" "Bre V" claimed, "You either love Carrie Fisher or you're wrong."

"Heidi the Hippie Reader" wrote, "Who else could give us the inside scoop on ECT, Elizabeth Taylor, Michael Jackson, and Eddie Fisher? It's honest, raw, profanity laced, an unbelievable life written down without apology."

Of course, Carrie attracted critics, too, especially "Margot," who said, "I found this second memoir mildly annoying and something to be gotten through. Nobody's life is perfect and being famous and rich doesn't buy you happiness. But I found myself wanting to say: 'Suck it up a little, Carrie. You were not chubby as a young or middle-aged woman, but gorgeous. Boohoo that *Star Wars* became an instant classic and launched you into unwanted stardom. You made bank; set for life. And the Princess Leia hair and the metal bra really don't justify all the whining I'm hearing from you. So dudes like to see your picture as Princess Leia as they masturbate. DEAL WITH IT!"

Chapter Eighteen

REAL ESTATE ROULETTE
Lawsuits, Sabotage, & the Loss of Millions

TERRORIZING TAMMY
Debbie's Fear That She'll be Murdered by Her Embezzling (Third) Husband

TRAGIC HAMLETT
But in This Drama, He's No Prince
"I'll destroy you. I married you for your money, and I never loved you."

Debbie Fails in a Bid to Portray Herself in the Film Version of her Daughter's Memoir

Mommie Dearest to its Director, Mike Nichols:
"You mean, I'm not right for the part?"

Meryl Streep (left) and Shirley MacLaine starred together in *Postcards from the Edge*, a script written by Carrie Fisher and clearly based on her tumultuous relationship with her own mother, Debbie Reynolds.

"I played a lot of softball when I was younger,"

Debbie said. "It was three strikes and you're out. Now I was up at bat for the third time, hoping to score a home run. My marriage to Mr. Blue Eyes (Richard Hamlett) was my chance to reverse my losing streak with husbands. In the first game, my husband ran off with the world's most desirable woman, and in my second playoff, my spouse, the loathsome shoe huckster, left me flat broke."

Hamlett had proposed marriage, and she'd taken her time before accepting. "He was great in the sack," she told friends, "and he seems to have his own money. He's also good looking for a middle-aged man, not exactly Robert Wagner in the 1950s, but even R.J. doesn't look that good anymore."

"It had been twenty-six years since Eddie Fisher dumped me for Elizabeth Taylor's big tits. I can't even speak of Harry Karl, the bank robber, without exploding in rage."

"I'm now fifty-two, a hard thing to move on the marriage market, since I have a 'sell by' date stamped on me. Along comes Richard. I figured I'd better jump at the chance. Husband material is as rare as film roles for me these days. I was facing a lonely widowhood, ending up looking like Bette Davis in *What Ever Happened to Baby Jane.*"

"One morning, I woke up determined, directing myself "to go for it—what the hell!"

The wedding took place in May of 1984 in Miami. "Carrie couldn't make it. She was drugged out in London. But my faithful brother Billy showed up with my faithful son, Todd. Minnie came too, finding things to criticize. She told me, 'I hope you don't make a mess of this like you did with the other two.'"

The day before the marriage, Debbie had presented Hamlett with a series of prenuptial agreements. "He studied them for hours and was very reluctant to sign them. But I told him that if he didn't, I would call off the wedding. After all, I had learned something from being married to that shit, Harry Karl. I didn't really think Richard was marrying me for my newly acquired money, but what Hollywood movie star, male or female, could ever be sure of a spouse?"

"In Miami, we stayed in a suite at the Ambassador Hotel," she said. "My friends, Joe and Nancy Kanter, allowed us to use their bayfront home for the ceremony. I was a vision of loveliness, or at least I hoped so, in my Bob Mackie lime green chiffon. Todd gave me away. At twenty-six, he'd become quite a man. Before the wedding, he had a man-to-man talk with Richard, warning him not to do me harm like Karl did."

"When I cut the wedding cake, I accidentally got some icing on my neck. Richard to the rescue. He licked it off and got applauded for doing so. When we went outside, we were greeted with a sea of reporters and paparazzi."

After the wedding, the married couple departed on an upscale cruise from Miami to Bermuda. "On the first day, I was exhausted and slept until well into the afternoon. When I woke up, there was no Richard. I dressed and went on a search party to find my man. I found him all right. He was on deck surrounded by three good-looking women. They were laughing and flirting with him, and he seemed to enjoy it bigtime. I couldn't help but notice that even the oldest was probably twenty years my junior."

"He introduced these hussies to me," she said. "All of them were magnolia-voiced friends of his (so he said) from Roanoke. Later, they watched him as he played tennis on the ship's court. He was known for his fast moves. I'll give him credit for one thing: He sure had the balls for the game."

"The cruise had its high and lows. At night, he made passionate love to me when he returned late from the gambling tables in the casino. During the day, he spent his time laughing with that trio of Scarlett O'Haras. I imagined he'd slept with all of them back in Virginia. One day, he was in the blazing sun so much he turned lobster red, but I wasn't in the mood to comfort him."

"At the end of the cruise, when it came time to pay the bill, I noticed he'd charged his gambling debts to our suite, and I was expected to pay for his losses. Shades of Harry Karl all over again. I paid up, since it was a honeymoon, but I hoped this wouldn't happen again now that I was putting away some of my hard-earned money."

Back in North Hollywood, a friend of hers, Phyllis Berkett, whom she'd known since 1957, hosted a "welcome back home" party for Debbie at her own home. Friends who included Florence Henderson and Tom Bosley were guests.

"The first part of the party went off beautifully," Debbie said. "A catered affair. However, at one point I noticed this anguish on Richard's face. He headed for the hall, and I followed him. He complained of an 'awful stabbing chest pain.' I got him into the bedroom and phoned a doctor."

"After a quick examination, he ordered me to rent a chauffeured limo to take him on a two-hour drive south to La Jolla. The doctor phoned and made arrangements to have him checked into the Scripps Medical Center, which specialized in diagnostics. The next day I learned he had a hole in his heart, and that it was leaking."

Treatment would take several weeks, and Debbie rented the room next door to be near him, providing love and comfort until he was able to return to Roanoke, where he checked into a local hospital for a few more weeks.

As Debbie told her friend, Phyllis, during a phone call: "Let's face it: My marriage is getting off to a rough start. That gambling debt aboard the cruise, those Southern belles, and now a heart condition. Who's writing the script of my life? I thought heart conditions were to occur at the end of a long marriage—not during the honeymoon."

***

525

With Hamlett in the hospital, Debbie spent lonely nights wandering around his mansion in Roanoke. It was on the summit of a hill with panoramic views in all directions. Once again, she began to drink heavily. But by the following morning, she had pulled herself together for a stint at Hamlett's bedside. He was gradually recovering.

"One day I encountered those Southern magnolia blossoms, and all of them welcomed me to Roanoke, referring to me as Ophelia in the Shakespeare play. I smiled faintly and made my escape. Their syrupy voices were insincere."

"Every day, I brought treats such as freshly baked chocolate éclairs or pecan pie. Apparently, Southerners devour it along with sweet potato pie. And I always brought him freshly laundered white jockey shorts. But I got tired of them and found some new jockey shorts on the market in more fashionable colors of black, green, blue, and even pink."

"When he got better and returned home, he took me on a driving tour of his properties," she said. "Often, we visited them, and I was impressed that he owned so much real estate—that is, until I found out they were heavily mortgaged."

"He suggested we might become partners in real estate, even acquiring some buildings together," she said. "Harry Karl had proposed the same thing, but I ended up with no real estate, not even the roof over my head. I had no idea how much money Richard was worth and was too afraid to ask. Looking back now, I should have."

"My other loser husbands never considered me great for a roll in the hay," she told Phyllis. "I decided I wouldn't make that same mistake with Richard, and became determined to learn more about how to pleasure a man. Up to now, I never knew they often hired whores to make love to their balls and do unspeakable things to their rosebuds. I thought all their erotic zones were centered in their penises. I also didn't know that men liked to have their tits sucked. I thought that was just something men did to women."

"At this charity party, I met this Linda Darnell lookalike. She was the mistress of the richest man in Roanoke, or so I was told. Gossip had it that she was an expert on sex. Apparently, that was how she held onto her John, who everybody referred to as 'Big Daddy.' She and I bonded, and I got invited to visit her home."

"I made it clear from the beginning that I wanted sex lessons from her, and she obliged. One room of her house seemed filled with sex toys—yes, even handcuffs, the works, with all sorts of lubricants. I couldn't believe that some men—certainly not Richard—got turned on by the insertion of a big dildo. Imagine that!"

"She even taught me the feather trick. She told me that U.S. servicemen had learned about it in the bordellos of China, especially Shanghai, in 1945 at war's end. She also claimed that the Duchess of Windsor had used it on the Duke's three-and-a-half-inch (when erect) dickie."

"Richard loved these sex toys—not all of them, but a woman over time learns what turns a man on."

"Our marriage was working, and our real estate dreams marched on."

"When I went on the road, I often phoned Federal Express and had my paycheck rushed to him to invest in real estate or to help pay off a mortgage. I know I was repeating a disastrous pattern like I did with Karl. But Richard was different. I knew I could trust him."

"Of course, when I was on the road, I couldn't help but wonder if those Virginia magnolia blossoms were giving him comfort."

"Even so, I was no lovesick fool. On the advice of my lawyers, I had him sign documents to pay me back—without interest, I might add—for the loans I was dispensing. We didn't talk a lot about money, because I saw how stressed he became."

Phyllis sent her an embarrassing item that appeared in one of the Hollywood gossip rags:

"Where do old has-been Hollywood movie stars go when there's no demand for them in Hollywood? They head for Virginia. Elizabeth Taylor started the craze when she married Senator John Warner and moved to his farm there."

"Now, Debbie Reynolds is following in Elizabeth's footsteps. She's living in Roanoke with some unknown real estate developer, Richard Hamlet" (sic)."

A week after his release from the hospital, and to celebrate the restoration of his health, Debbie, at Hamlett's mansion, threw "A Catered Affair," ripe with references to the movie she'd made with Bette Davis in 1956.

"There, I met Grandma Hamlett, who seemed like a survivor from the Civil War. I had the usual forks for a fancy dinner, but she didn't understand why."

"What are all these darn forks for?" the elderly woman asked. "I grew up using just one fork, and it sure was enough to feed me. I guess you Hollywood movie stars do things different. You are a movie star, aren't you? I've never seen one of those damn picture shows in my life. I hear all sorts of sinful things are shown in those movie houses. I sure hope you didn't make a lot of those dirty pictures."

During the days and weeks ahead, Hamlett shared his dream of creating a real estate empire with her. "Who knows? We may even end up as the king and queen of Roanoke."

"Richard was grateful for my cash flows to him," she said. "Sometimes, we indulged in *Pillow Talk*. Remember that old movie with Doris Day and Rock Hudson? He claimed that for the first time he was a free man, and that my loans had been used to pay off his mortgages, of which he had too many. He seemed happy to lie in my arms, and I avoided telling him that many of those loans came from my retirement fund."

"Todd and Carrie liked their new stepdad," she said. "One Christmas, they gave him this stunning alligator briefcase engraved 'TO THE BEST STEPDAD IN THE WORLD.'"

"We traveled together on occasion, once taking the Orient Express, visiting Venice and Rome. Todd had divorced his wife, Dona Freeberg, and had taken up with this lovely girl, Rene Russo."

Carrie even arranged a cameo appearance for Richard in her movie, *When Harry Met Sally…* (1989). He played her father.

When she wasn't working, Debbie—who was used to a fast-paced life—grew bored in Roanoke. "Looking after Richard, I was turning into a combo of a Stepford Wife and Florence Nightingale. Thrashing around for something to do, I proposed we become co-producers and take the theatrical version of *The Unsinkable Molly Brown* on the road again. We agreed, but I was a bit put off when he demanded $20,000 a week for his involvement in the project, telling me, 'I'm worth it!'"

During her development of the project, she phoned her former movie co-star, Harve Presnell, with a proposal, and he seemed delighted by the idea of working with her again. "Dear Harve never quite made it as a bigtime movie star, although he had the looks and talent."

"Our director, John Bowab, told us that audiences would expect those athletic dances we'd filmed for the movie, so he had reworked the script to include them. I was young when I made *Unsinkable,* and these resurrected dance routines, at my age, practically did me in."

It was during the development of this complicated road tour in the mid- to late-1980s that Debbie learned that Carrie was working on a semi-autobiographical novel entitled *Postcards from the Edge.*

***

Focusing on a show-biz daughter's relationship with her show-biz mother, the novel is obviously autobiographical. Carrie is the movie actress Suzanne Vale, who is trying to pull her life together after a drug overdose. During her struggles to come to terms with her drug addiction and rehab experiences, she keeps a detailed journal. Even as she works through a resolution to her horrors, she maintains a wry, wicked sense of humor.

One scene depicts her in a hospital, where she has been rushed after a drug overdose. Carrie writes: "Maybe I shouldn't have given the guy who pumped my stomach my phone number. But who cares? My life is over anyway."

The character that Carrie crafted of the actress, Doris Mann, was clearly based on Debbie.

In one scene, Suzanne reflects: "My mother is probably sort of disappointed at how I turned out, but she doesn't show it. She came by today and brought me a satin and velvet quilt. I'm surprised I was able to detox without it. I was nervous about seeing her, but it went okay. She thinks I blame her for my being in rehab. I mainly blame my dealer, my doctor, and myself, and not necessarily in that order. She washed my underwear and left."

"It's hard growing up with a really dynamic mother, especially one that a lot of people admired," Carrie said. "Not only does she have the gift of always knowing exactly what she wants, she's really beautiful. Even when she dances like Mary J. Blige, or takes those classic 'Mom selfies' with her head cocked to the side, she's stunning and charismatic."

Carrie admitted to having drawn upon Debbie for her character of Doris. "Debbie came up in the MGM studio system, and she doesn't know how to temper her personality to give another person, namely me, some room."

In one episode of Carrie's novel, Doris asks Suzanne, "How would you have liked to have Joan Crawford for a mother? Or Lana Turner?"

Carrie's first novel, *Post-cards from the Edge*, was published in 1987 by Simon & Schuster. It was eventually designated as "a single woman's answer to Nora Ephron's *Heartburn*, a less sexual version of Erica Jong's *Fear of Flying*, the smart successor to Joan Didion's *Play It as It Lays*."

"Oh, please," Suzanne responds. "Those are the only options? Joan or Lana?"

At times, however, Carrie backed away from her assertions that she had used Debbie as a model for Doris, telling a reporter at *Entertainment Weekly*, "I wrote about a mother actress and a daughter actress. I'm not shocked that people think it's about Debbie or me. It's easier for them to think I have no imagination for language, just a tape recorder with endless batteries."

Part fiction, part memoir, *Postcards from the Edge* takes readers on an emotional roller-coaster of highs and lows: Self-pity gorging, making bad decisions, drug overdoses, casual sex, Hollywood Party Terror, and much more, including falling in love…sort of.

Reviewers at the *Los Angeles Times* interpreted it as "intelligent, original, focused, insightful, and interesting." A.O. Scott in *The New York Times* claimed that it "bristles with a bravery and candor."

Tom Robbins wrote: "With surprisingly literary artistry, Carrie Fisher swims through relationship-infested waters, braves cocaine blizzards, glitz spills, sushi tsunamis, and *bon-mot* attacks to show us what despair is like when it refuses to take itself seriously."

Readers, many of them fans of Princess Leia, posted their impressions of the novel on the web. Comments ranged from "hilariously witty and amazingly devious" to "mother-fucking goddamn shit." One fan described Carrie as "a wonderful nutbag." Another wrote, "It is truly fascinating to listen to her voice spewing out the most intricate, absurdist, intellectual, and insightful witticisms."

***

Shirley MacLaine had known Debbie since they'd each been in their twenties. They had remained friends, though not terribly close. Their relationship became tense when MacLaine lost the leading role in *The Unsinkable Molly Brown*.

Now, during the casting for the film adaptation of Carrie's novel, the situation was reversed. Debbie desperately wanted "to play myself" (a reference to the mother figure in *Postcards from the Edge)*, but MacLaine got the role instead.

According to MacLaine, "Debbie was pert, perky, precocious, and punctual. She was bubbling with enthusiasm and right on the button with every comedic assessment she made. It was a surprise when our lives converged again, and I had to become the screen *persona* of her as Doris Mann, which was obviously based on her."

Shortly after Carrie sold the movie rights to her novel to Columbia, Mike Nichols was designated as its director. Debbie, who had known him for years, called him, met with him, and even read through parts of the script with him, "trying out" for the role of Doris.

Nichols listened patiently and then informed her, "Sorry, kid, you're not right for the role."

"Excuse me?" she protested. "Nor right, you say? You mean I can't play myself? The role of Doris Mann is *me*. It's a part I've been creating—admittedly unwittingly—for decades."

"The answer is *no*," Nichols answered. "I want Shirley MacLaine for Doris and Meryl Streep to play your daughter Carrie." Carrie is already adapting it to the screen for us."

Two weeks later, MacLaine phoned Debbie to relay gossip, talk about the casting and discuss her development of the role. She asked Debbie if she had wanted the mother role, and Debbie denied it, not revealing that she'd discreetly rendezvoused with Nichols behind her back during the casting process. "Oh no, dear," Debbie lied. "I can't play myself. Besides, it isn't really me. It's not like me at all. You'll be great as Doris."

Then MacLaine asked if she could move in and spend the weekend observing her, with the intention of better developing her understanding of the character she'd be playing. With some reluctance, Debbie agreed.

She later said, "As my guest, Shirley put me under a microscope, watching every move I made. The way I talked, my facial expressions. She trailed me everywhere, even into the bathroom. I couldn't turn around without bumping into Miss Sherlock."

In their "girl-on-girl" talks, MacLaine surprised Debbie with her candor. Debbie always tried to hide her secrets if they contradicted or diminished her image. But MacLaine spoke with frankness and honesty, confessing, "I have only one vice: Fucking. And I don't have to worry about my husband getting tired of me, because I never see him." She was referring to her thirty-year marriage to Steve Parker, a film producer living in Japan.

Many people in the industry adored MacLaine, but, like all stars, she had her critics.

Debbie admitted, "We did not have a deep friendship because there was always a certain rivalry there. I'm fond of her, however."

A film critic wrote: "MacLaine and Streep have a mother-daughter chemistry that crackles with energy, like the *Gilmore Girls* with glamour, or *Freaky Friday* on speed. Every line from Doris is punctuated with an eye roll or an inflection of theatricality. They're mother and daughter, but also kindred spirits, two control freaks who are out of control."

One of her detractors, a Hollywood producer named Martin Rackin, told the press: "Shirley MacLaine is a disaster, a fucking ovary with a propeller who leaves a trail of blood wherever she goes. (She's) a half-assed chorus girl, a pseudo-intellectual who thinks she knows politics, thinks she knows everything, and wears clothes from the ladies of the Good Christ Church Bazaar."

MacLaine confessed to Debbie, "I had many love affairs—and a lot of awful lovers. I wasn't into 'sexcapades' but I did try it once…I had three men in one day."

"I had affairs with so many men…," MacLaine continued. "Even Robert Mitchum and Yves Montand, although Marilyn Monroe got there before me. Jack Lemmon and Jack Nicholson never turned me on, but I find Frank Sinatra hot. Jack Lemmon reminded me of my Aunt Rose, and Nicholson was just too much for me. He is authentically dangerous."

Once filming began, MacLaine admitted that she was in awe of Streep's amazing acting ability. "I respected her but never became close. With my other leading ladies, I developed much more intimate friendships, notably with Audrey Hepburn, Anne Bancroft, Shirley Booth, Debra Winger, Sally Field, Dolly Parton, and Julia Roberts."

Carrie was impressed with the amazing array of talent Nichols had assembled for the supporting roles in *Postcards*—Dennis Quaid, Gene Hackman, Richard Dreyfuss, Rob Reiner, Mary Wickes, Annette Benning, and Gary Morton.

Debbie wrote, "When I went to see the movie, I wasn't thrilled to see how they showed me with no hair near the end of the movie, or me putting vodka in my breakfast drink, but that's part of their script—it isn't me."

***

In spite of her problems with drugs and her self-described "imprisonment" in rehab, Carrie was able to pull herself together and continued staying involved, one way or another, with the making of films. This was not work of which she was proud, "but I made a living," she said.

In 1990, she appeared in a comedy directed by Carl Reiner entitled *Sibling Rivalry*. Kirstie Alley had the lead as Marjorie Turner. Marjorie has become tired and bored with her husband Harry, not only for his neglect, but for the strain imposed on her by his snooty relatives.

At a supermarket, she picks up a stranger for a "quickie," but he dies during his strenuous exertions with her in the saddle, and to her horror, she finds herself naked and in bed with a corpse. Even more horrifying, as it turns out, her recently deceased sex partner is the long-lost brother of her husband, Harry.

Carrie had a very small part in *Sibling Rivalry*, interpreting the secondary role of Iris Turner-Hunter. Released by Warners, the movie earned only $18 million and did nothing for Carrie's career.

Also in 1990, Carrie landed a more substantial role in *Sweet Revenge,* a made-for-TV comedy in which she plays a lawyer ordered to pay alimony to her divorced husband. She hires Rosanna Arquette, with whom she had worked before, to try to woo her former husband to the altar so that Carrie could then cut off those alimony payments.

The 89-minute film, directed by Charlotte Brandstorm, was aired on Turner Home Entertainment. Soon after that, it just faded away.

In the following year, 1991, Carrie continued in minor roles, beginning with *Drop Dead Fred,* a British-American black comedy released by New Line Cinema. It was billed as suitable for children, although it dealt with such adult themes as mental illness, emotional abuse, and was littered with profanity.

The English actor Rik Mayall *[described at the time as a pioneer in the field of "alternative comedy"]* starred in the title role, playing an anarchic and devilish imaginary friend of a young girl named Elizabeth (Phoebe Cates). Carrie had fifth billing in a minor appearance as Janie. Even though no one but Elizabeth can see him, Mayall causes chaos in the neighborhood. Her domineering mother, Polly, was essayed by Marsha Mason.

Drop Dead Fred managed to break even at the box office and was panned by critics. Leonard Maltin claimed that "the appealing Phoebe Cates can't salvage this putrid mess, which is recommended only to those who think nose-picking is funny." Gene Siskel named it the worst film of 1991. *Entertainment Weekly* wrote, "It is supposed to be hilarious, but is really, really a depressing story about the long-term effects of child abuse."

Next on Carrie's agenda was *Soapdish* (1991), in which Sally Fields starred as a mature soap opera star, and which was co-produced by Aaron Spellman. Director Michael Hoffman lined up an impressive cast of supporting players: Kevin Klein, Robert Downey, Jr., Whoopi Goldberg, and Carrie in a very minor role as Betsy Faye Sharon.

With mostly positive reviews, it grossed nearly $38 million at the box office. *Entertainment Weekly* gave *Soapdish* a Grade C rating, claiming, "It makes the tackiness of soap operas seem far more desperate than funny."

Roger Ebert awarded it three-and-a-half stars, ambiguously and unenthusiastically defining it as "the kind of movie that is a balancing act, really."

The *Washington Post* described it as "a pure joy, a lemon-fresh spoof of daytime TV drama, an uproarious look behind the scenes of the making of a soap opera—mirroring life and all that."

Supplementing her income from acting, Carrie sometimes got involved in script doctoring, too. Steven Spielberg hired Carrie in that capacity for *Hook* (1991), a fantasy adventure film starring Dustin Hoffman as Captain Hook. Supporting players included Robin Williams as Peter Pan, Julia Roberts as Tinker Bell, and Maggie Smith as Wendy Darling.

Spielberg didn't like the first drafts of Tinker Bell's dialogue, and he commissioned Carrie to "make it more enchanting."

One day, another refugee from *Star Wars*, George Lucas, appeared on the set of *Hook* to talk to Spielberg. He came up with an idea that featured Lucas and Carrie appearing uncredited as faceless, anonymous, lovers kissing on a bridge. "That's as close as I ever got to making love to George," Carrie said. Tinker Bell sprinkles Pixie dust over the lovers before briskly escorting Peter Pan to Neverland.

On another afternoon, Dodi Fayed, one of the most famous Egyptians of his generation, visited the set of *Hook* and was introduced to Carrie. He controlled some of the rights to the Peter Pan film, and he'd made a deal with TriSar to be credited as an executive producer.

Fayed flirted with her, and she found him attractive—not handsome—but charming and attentive. She accepted his invitation that night to dine with him at Chasen's. He arrived to pick her up, and then hauled her away, in a chauffeur-driven Rolls Royce.

At the dinner table, he presented her with a Jaeger-LeCoultre wristwatch, which after many years, eventually disappeared from her jewelry box. She was astonished at his generosity, realizing for the first time that he might be richer than she had originally understood. After dinner, as she later recalled to Rudy Render, "We headed for a night of enjoying lines of cocaine."

Dodi was the son of the Egyptian billionaire, Mohamed El Fayed. Among many other possessions, he was famous for his ownership of Harrod's in London, the most famous department store in Europe. His father had set him up with a movie company, Allied Stars, and designated him as its executive producer. Dodi's first movie was the prestigious *Chariots of Fire* (1981), which she had not seen. According to his reputation, Dodi had already dated numerous actresses, especially "the name ones."

Tina Brown *[editor of* Vanity Fair *from 1984-92]* accurately described his home in Beverly Hills, as "party central, a magnet for freeloaders, gold-diggers, and deal jockeys exploiting Dodi's childlike generosity. He threw, on the average four parties a week."

When Carrie arrived at his residence, the only people in the house were servants. His lavish living room was scented with candles.

"It was an *Arabian Nights* adventure for me," she told Rudy Render. "Right after midnight, I knew what was coming, and I went with him to his bedchamber. I'd never been fucked by an Arab before. Frankly, it's not much different from getting fucked by a Jew or a Gentile. That guy knew what to do. As a teenager, he must have spent a lot of time in a harem, learning all the right moves."

The next day, sometime after noon, she woke up, alone. The butler had an elegant breakfast waiting for her, which she enjoyed. He told her that Mr. Fayed had had to fly at once to London for a business emergency.

Before exiting from his house later that day, she left her phone number, which she'd already given him. She wanted to make absolutely sure that he had it in the event he wanted a repeat. He never did.

As the 90s moved on, Carrie was surprised to read about Dodi's romance with the by-then-divorced Princess Diana.

But her shock came in a television news bulletin announcing that on August 31, 1997, in Paris, Dodi Fayed had died in a car crash. With him in the demolished car was the Princess of Wales. Barely alive, she was rushed to the hospital for emergency procedures. Under the glare of the frenzied publicity associated with the controversial and murky event, and with global speculation hawkeyeing the reactions of Britain's Royal Family, she died at 4AM the next morning.

"I sampled Dodi Fayed before Princess Di latched onto him," Carrie claimed.

***

Nothing so memorable as meeting Fayed

534

happened to Carrie during the crafting of her next picture. She did have a re-union, however, with Nora Ephron, co-writer of the screenplay for *This Is My Life*. Released in 1992, it was a romantic comedy based on the book of the same name by Meg Wolitzer. This film production marked Ephron's directorial debut.

Its plot centered on Dottie Ingels (Julie Kavner), who works behind a cosmetics counter but aspires to be a stand-up comedian. Her career takes off with the help of Arnold Moss (Dan Akyroyd) and his assistant Claudia Curtis (Carrie).

On the set, Carrie was also reunited with Aykroyd, whom she had dated during the making of *The Blues Brothers* with John Belushi. It was during their latest picture that she revealed that her former relationship with Aykroyd—and not just Belushi—was more intense than she had at first suggested

"Dan and I were briefly engaged in 1980,": she admitted. "He proposed marriage to me on the set of *The Blues Brothers*. We had the rings, we got blood tests, the whole shot, but then I got back together with Paul Simon and called it off. As the world knows, my other lover, Belushi, was found dead of a drug overdose."

Released by 20th Century Fox in 1992, *This Is My Life* met with a lukewarm response both from the critics and movie audiences.

***

Carrie then had a very minor role playing a therapist in the 1997 spy action-adventure, *Austin Powers: International Man of Mystery*. A spoof of the James Bond 007 films, it was the first to star Mike Myers in the title role of Austin Powers, "the shagadelic super spy." Director Jay Roach lined up a strong supporting cast which included Elizabeth Hurley, Seth Green, Will Ferrell, Mimi Rogers, and Robert Wagner ("Debbie's long-ago fling.")

Many stars appeared in it in cameos, including Burt Bacharach as himself; Christian Slater as a security guard; and Rob Lowe as "A Guy at a Bachelor Party."

The movie collected nearly $70 million at the box office, "but no one came to see it because of my appearance," Carrie said.

She also wrote the screenplay for an episode of the hit TV sitcom, *Rosanne* (1988-1997), entitled *Arsenic and Old Mom*. Debbie made a guest appearance in that episode.

Carrie's reputation as a script doctor blossomed. She was tapped to work on *Lethal Weapon 3* (1992), rewriting some of Rene Russo's dialogue. She also worked on the disaster film *Outbreak* (1995, also starring Russo); Adam Sandler's *The Wedding Singer* (1998); and the Sylvester Stallone "buddy cop" comedy, *Stop! Or My Mom Will Shoot* (1992).

***

In the 1990s, Carrie also published two additional novels: *Surrender the Pink* (1990), and *Delusions of Grandma* (1993).

Many critics found *Surrender the Pink* talky, drawn-out, and rambling. In it, her heroine, Dinah Kaufman, a soap opera writer/producer, is working through her divorce from her longtime companion/husband, the playwright Rudy Gendler. During its crafting, she was clearly inspired by her relationship with Paul Simon.

The Library Journal viewed it as "a disappointment." Unlike Suzanne in *Postcards from the Edge*, many readers did not find her newest character of Dinah very sympathetic. "You don't root for her flaws at all," wrote one consumer. Others found Dinah "amusingly flawed, sharp-witted, and refreshingly daring."

Obviously aging, but with a knack for finding ongoing film roles in Hollywood, Carrie played an attentive therapist in *Austin Powers, International Man of Mystery*

Dr. John T. Webbon was impressed with how Carrie "made lemonade from the lemons (that) fate handed her."

Carrie received raves from major news outlets. *Time* compared her narrative voice to that of Holden Caulfield in *Catcher in the Rye*. *The New York Times* interpreted the novel as "at once harrowing and hilarious." *Vogue* called *Surrender the Pink* "sensationally acute, searingly funny."

Four years later, Carrie released another book, this one with the rather odd title, *Delusions of Grandma*. Marketed as a romantic comedy, it was—like all her novels—semi-autobiographical.

Its heroine is Cora Sharpe, a Hollywood screenwriter who's about to give birth to a child whose unmarried father (a lawyer) had drifted off downriver. Believing that she will not survive childbirth, she writes a series of long letters to her unborn kid.

Cora sustains complicated relationships with a string of other characters, including her zany mother, a retired musical comedy star, a "showbizzy" grandma-to-be. *[That reflected Debbie's status at the time after Carrie's one-and-only child was born.]* Cora's friend and co-author, Bud, is gay and bipolar, and her friend, William, is dying of AIDS.

Barbara Graham, writing in *People,* said, "Cora's vulnerability bursts through in spite of herself, and we can't help but root for her."

Kirkus Reviews wasn't kind: "Even for admirers of Fisher's many skills, her letters to her unborn child are not very funny. Admirers of her will find *Delusions of Grandma* a vaporous as an HBO movie you wished you'd never watched."

536

***

Richard Hamlett wanted to expand his real estate empire and focused on Las Vegas. He alerted real estate agents there to alert him whenever a bargain hotel property came on the market.

He had long talks with Debbie about it, eventually selling her on the idea. What ultimately convinced her to agree was when he said that she could have her own showroom. "You can be singing *Tammy* to aging Baby Boomers until you croak." Not only that, but he promised that a section on the ground floor would be converted into a nostalgia-soaked museum of her Hollywood memorabilia.

Finally, Hamlett received the phone call he'd been waiting for when he was advised that the Paddlewheel Hotel and Casino, standing on six acres of arid, sunblasted terrain near the Las Vegas Strip, was on the market, and had been for some time. He flew to Vegas to check out the property and learn about its history.

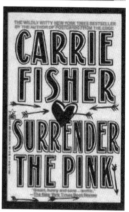

[Conceived and constructed with 200 rooms as the Royal Inn, a name it retained for a decade, it had originally been built in 1970. Late in 1979, the owners sold it to the fast-food chain, Horn & Hardart, which paid $7.4 million and redecorated it with a theme that evoked New York City, rechristening it as the Royal Americana (1980-1982).

In 1982, after many losses, Horn & Hardart sold it to an investment group for $15.4 million. After additional renovations, which at first focused on a kid-friendly venue with rides and amusements, it was recycled as the Paddlewheel Hotel & Casino (1983-1993). During the decade it retained that name, it switched its marketing outreach to attract more mature audiences. During one period of its checkered history, it even featured a late-night, all-male revue.

By the time it attracted the interest of Richard Hamlett in 1993, it had been on the market since 1990, with no offers.]

As Debbie was shown around the property, "Unsinkable Molly" came to believe that the hotel could be redesigned and reconfigured as her showcase, and that her cherished dream of having her own showroom and her museum of Hollywood memorabilia might be coming true at last.

At Studio City in Los Angeles, she reached out to the Great Western Savings & Loan on Victory Boulevard and withdrew her life's savings of $200,000. She was saddened that Hamlett had no money to invest. Both of them were

537

hoping that theirs would be the highest bid at the ensuing auction.

After her errand at the bank, she drove to North Hollywood to handle some policy decisions at the business she had established in 1979. DR Studios, located within what had been a branch of the U.S. Postal Service on Lankershim Boulevard, had been transformed into dance studios and rehearsal spaces, each rentable by the hour or long-term. With six big rehearsal halls with springboard hardwood floors, changing rooms, and huge mirrors, it had attracted actors, dancers, and such stars as Bette Midler, Janet Jackson, and Madonna. Even Michael Jackson had rehearsed some of the dance routines associated with his spectacularly successful album, *Thriller* (1982).

Then she flew to Las Vegas with a cashier's check. Hamlett greeted her in her small, two-bedroom apartment, which she had been renting since 1973, mainly as a place to store the wardrobes and accessories for her many appearances within the resort's casino hotels. Her apartment was on the 12th floor of a residential apartment building near the Strip.

When Debbie bought her Las Vegas hotel, she transformed its giant decorative paddlewheel into an enormous movie reel, with a simulated strip of celluloid stretching around the entire facade, each frame of which contained a huge color image of different stars from the Golden Age of Hollywood.

Those photographic images had originally been part of the decor of Bally's Hotel and Casino from back when it had been the MGM Grand.

That night during dinner, she and Hamlett carefully reviewed their scheme. If they won the property at auction, they'd still face the daunting hurdle of having to convince a bank to loan them $2 million. There was also another formidable challenge: They had to be granted a gaming license. He suggested, "Your buddy, Frank Sinatra, might help you out."

It was clearly understood at the time that if a bank refused to advance a loan of $2 million, Debbie's $200,000 deposit on the property was non-refundable, and would be forfeited. "I knew the risk I was taking," she said. "But I was doing it for Richard and myself, of course."

The next day, about two dozen bidders showed up at the auction. It opened with a low bid of slightly more than $1 million. Debbie kept raising the bid until most of the other contenders dropped out, except for one determined investor from L.A. After he placed his final bid of $2.1 million, she raised her paddle, thereby agreeing to a purchase price of $2.2 million, and won.

After several long and tedious negotiations, she got a bank to extend a $2 million loan. Now, the real work began—the task of radically restoring and renovating the site's battered décor and infrastructure. They hoped to have it ready before June of 1993. Whereas Hamlett took charge of the restoration, she was assigned the task of redecorating.

She wanted a Hollywood theme throughout. To do so, she brought in her close friend, Jerry Wunderlich, a set designer who had created the sets for her movie, *The Singing Nun,* way back in the mid-1960s. He remained on site, nursing the project through to its completion. Her showroom was positioned on one of the building's upper floors.

Todd quit work on his ranch and flew to Vegas to help out and was assigned to handle the lighting—his expertise.

In the lobby, Debbie placed Harold ("Speedy") Lloyd's Steinway player piano, which cheerfully rattled out nostalgia-soaked piano adaptations of show tunes. Lloyd, a comedian from the silent screen, had died in 1971 at the age of 78. She commissioned an effigy that depicted him during his heyday and seated it in front of the keyboard.

One of the biggest headaches during the hotel's refurbishment were the kitchens. A total mess, they frequently flooded. Rats infested the blocked-up sewage pipes. Debbie herself, wearing yellow rubber wading boots, joined the efforts of the cleanup crew.

Gambling czar Steve Wynn visited one day. She knew that he did not consider her venture as direct competition to his bigger, better-accessorized blockbuster properties. He alerted her to an impending auction of the chairs and booths from the former showroom at the once-legendary Dunes Hotel. *[The Dunes was sold and demolished in 1993. At the time of Wynn's conversation with Debbie, he was involved with plans for his spectacularly splashy Bellagio Hotel, being constructed at the time. Inaugurated in 1998, it was eventually cited as the most expensive hotel/casino ever built.]*

Meanwhile, without asking Debbie or including her in the arrangements, Hamlett began selling time shares in their precarious new property. He also subcontracted the administration and maintenance of the hotel's restaurants, retail spaces, and dining rooms, signing leases to outside purveyors. Even more controversial, he signed a contract with a gaming concern for their operation of the in-house casino, with the provision that he and Debbie would receive only eight percent of the take.

"He was working so many deals, I couldn't keep up with what was happening," she said. "I couldn't think straight…it was hectic. I lived to regret that."

Then, in lieu of relying on the local labor force, he imported workers from Roanoke. The paint strippers poured their gunky wastes directly into the hotel's drainage pipes. When they reached Las Vegas' sewer system and solidified, the entire neighborhood was flooded.

The owners of neighboring properties summoned inspectors from the Nevada Division of Environmental Protection, who demanded that the hazardous wastes blocking the city's sewage system be removed, and Debbie was fined $52,000. A few days later, the FBI arrived to arrest the workers, who were extradited to Virginia to face felony charges there.

Hamlett brought in another contractor to redesign and rebuild the swimming pool. When they ordained that it was ready, Todd was the first to jump in. At the bottom, he discovered gray guck which eventually floated to the top. It seemed that the contractor had used stucco instead of waterproof cement as its sheathing. Another $30,000 had to be spent to correct the problem.

On several occasions, Debbie confronted Hamlett, but whenever he perceived that his authority was being questioned, he exploded into violent rages. She wanted Todd to design the upstairs showroom, but Hamlett objected. A major battle ensued, with Todd and Debbie emerging as the bloodied winners.

Before the showroom could open, a run-of-the-mill cocktail lounge on the hotel's lobby level was designated as the "Jazz and Jokes Club." Debbie brought in her former nightclub partner, Rip Taylor, who moved into an accommodation within the hotel. Nightly, as a team, they performed as a lounge act where no one imposed or collected a cover charge. Insiders came to view their regular appearances there as one of the great "undiscovered staples" of Las Vegas.

"One night, Robert Wagner, the love of my life, showed up," Debbie said. "I could easily forgive him for drowning Natalie Wood back in 1981. There were times I wanted to drown her too. Just joking, folks."

"R.J. came with his host, Steve Wynn, and his girlfriend, Stephanie Powers. She looked young and lovely," Debbie said. "Frankly, I was jealous. If only I had let R.J. take my cherry on that summer night so long ago. He greeted me warmly as he always did. Every time I saw him, there was a tingle of heartbreak, but both of us had moved on."

"One night, Eartha Kitt dropped in to perform a number or two. Norm Crosby also showed up to do his act," Debbie said. "It was all so very informal. I invited Frank Sinatra. Although he didn't show up, he sent me a note: 'Sorry, Debbie, I don't work for free.'"

Meanwhile, Todd continued his labors on the 500-seat upstairs showroom, always with the widely publicized intention of inaugurating it as *Debbie Reynold's Star Theater* in October of 1993.

But for no apparent reason, inspectors from the Las Vegas Building and Safety Department kept appearing on site because they were being bombarded with complaints about building code violations.

Finally, Todd asked one of the inspectors why they were searching for violations to the building code so frequently. One of them said, "We keep getting calls from this guy named Richard Hamlett. Have you heard of him?"

"I sure have," Todd answered. "He's my stepdad, married to my mother, Debbie Reynolds."

That night, she confronted her husband, demanding to know why he was trying to sabotage the opening of the Star Theater. He didn't answer but stormed off the property and disappeared for two days and nights.

By now even more suspicious, Todd one day asked one of the inspectors about who owned the title to the hotel. He was told that it was Billy Walters, a business associate of Hamlett.

Todd immediately relayed this to Debbie, who said, "I knew Billy. He had lent me money to keep the restoration going. When I was away, on the road and touring, I sent him my paychecks to pay back my debt to him."

Debbie immediately drove to Walters' home in Vegas, demanding information about why his name—and not hers—was on the title. After much arguing, he finally admitted, "Richard told me to do it."

That night, in a confrontation with Hamlett, Debbie threatened to fly out of Vegas and never come back until Walters' name was removed from the deed and replaced with her own. After many complaints and much resistance, he acquiesced.

At the last minute, days before the long-awaited opening, Hamlett demanded major structural changes to the bar behind the theater, including a complete reconfiguration of its elevations. Todd responded that the radical changes would take weeks and delay the hotel's opening. Debbie was called in to arbitrate the dispute, and ultimately agreed with Todd. A big fight ensued, but the opening proceeded as announced nationwide and as advertised in the local newspapers.

Always strapped for cash, Debbie needed money to pay her musicians and dancers for the act she'd prepared for her opening night. She set up a luncheon with Phyllis McGuire, a member of the long-ago singers, the McGuire Sisters, and asked for a $20,000 loan. The ex-singer agreed, as she had lent Debbie money before, and had always been paid back.

Debbie's theater was packed on opening night. Rip Taylor was on hand, prepped and ready to open the show as Todd frantically struggled to complete the lighting. Because it wasn't ready, he signaled to Taylor to "vamp" for another hour.

Finally, the lighting was ready, and so was Debbie. Taylor, who had kept the audience entertained and laughing at his campy routines, finally announced: "Debbie Reynolds is set to go on, but first she had to deal with a crisis: Eddie Fisher left her for Elizabeth Taylor. Screw him!"

A postcard from the edge? Debbie's Star Theater, site of so much striving and so much pain.

Even as a grandmother, Debbie could still reveal a shapely leg.

541

"I did—twice!" Debbie shouted back at him from the wings, obviously suggesting that she'd had sex with him only two times, each instance of which led to the births of Carrie and Todd.

In the front of the audience was a series of seats known as Kings Row, usually reserved for casino high rollers, "*über-VIPs*," and long-standing personal friends of Debbie. Behind them was another row of seats known as Queens Row. "You can guess who filled up those queenie seats," Debbie said. "My loyal gay fans, God love 'em."

Midway through her act, she spotted Hamlett, sitting in the middle of the room. He rose from his seat to leave the theater. Although she was dismayed and a bit shocked by his early departure, she soldiered through with the continuation of her act, telling the audience, "They say sex is a bridge. If you don't have a good partner, you'd better get a good hand." The audience roared with laughter. After the show, she threw a "wee hours" party for cast and crew.

The next day, Todd talked to Frank Basso, who had poured the concrete for the hotel's swimming pool. "Hamlett bet me ten thousand dollars that the Star Theater would not open on time. That's why he tried to sabotage its opening. At least that's what I heard that he did."

Then Basso continued with: "Last night, when your mother was performing, he tried to run out on me, knowing I was in the audience ready to collect. I followed him into the parking lot. I had to bounce him off the turf a few times, but I got my money."

When Debbie was informed of this, she was horrified. "I can't believe it. For ten thousand dollars, he was willing to fuck up my hotel. Some god damn partner this Southern gent of Virginia is. He's not Ashley Wilkes. More like that Victor Jory, 'evil carpetbagger' character in *Gone With the Wind*. Let's face it, son. Debbie has gone and done it again. I've married another shit!"

After the cast party, she returned to her small apartment near the Strip to await the return of Hamlett. The sliding glass doors that accessed the balcony were open, and she sat outside, drinking wine, waiting for the sun to come up over Las Vegas. Only two days before, someone had alerted her that her husband was seen making frequent stopovers, including overnights, in one of the rooms at the Stardust Hotel. It was occupied by a woman named Jane Parker from Roanoke, Virginia. She was much younger than Debbie.

Waiting impatiently for the return of her errant, philandering husband, Debbie riffled through her mail, eventually opting to open an oversized envelope from her lawyer in Bel Air, where she had hoped to erect her dream house and share it during her old age, supposedly with Hamlett.

The envelope contained a copy of the deed to her Bel Air propery. She quickly ascertained that Hamlett's name was on the deed, positioned immediately, as co-owner, next to hers. She had bought and paid for the property herself.

Finally, at around 5AM, she heard the key turn in the lock of her apartment's front door. After Hamlett entered, he looked her over skeptically and said, with contempt, "You're drunk."

According to Debbie, "He looked like he smelled of sex and with his tousled gray hair, appeared to have just emerged from Parker's bed after a workout."

She didn't ask why he'd walked out on her show, since she already knew, so she confronted him with the lawyer's deed, demanding an explanation. "That is my land."

"It's *our* land," he shouted at her. "I'm your husband."

"In name only, you bastard. My lawyer has sent me a copy of the deed," she said with fury, "along with a document you're to sign, surrendering your part ownership."

"Come on, Debbie," he answered. "Let's go get some fresh air and talk things over sensibly."

"Like hell I'm going out on that three-foot balcony with you," she said. "I know why you walked out of my show. I also know you have a mistress, Jane Parker, stashed at the Stardust. Now sign the fucking paper and return the land to me. Your name on the deed is a fraud. My attorney will sue you."

"Okay," he said. "I'll sign the blasted thing." Then he quickly scribbled his name. "Please, Debbie, come out on that balcony with me and let's make sense of all this mess. On the balcony, you can clear your boozy head. We'll be friends and business partners, even if we didn't quite make it as husband and wife."

It was clear to her why he wanted to get her out onto that balcony. In case of her death, he had a million-dollar insurance policy on her life. She'd seen what Robert Wagner had done to Joanne Woodward in *A Kiss Before Dying* (1965). He'd shoved her off the roof of a tall building. "I could just see myself meeting poor Joanne's cruel fate. I feared that he'd push me, and I'd plunge twelve stories below."

As she stated in her memoirs, she then ran out of the living room into the kitchen, where she opened (and left unlocked) the service door to indicate that she'd escaped through the public corridor.

Debbie wrote, "I opened my closet door and quietly closed the door behind me, then shimmied up a pole to the top shelf, where I kept my big baggage and quilted bags, and slid behind the bags, arranging them in front of me so that I was completely hidden."

It was dawn by the time she heard him walking around the apartment, repeatedly calling her name. Then she heard the kitchen's service door slam shut.

She waited a while longer before she believed it was safe to climb down from her hiding place. Her so-called drunken suicide plunge would have been fodder for the tabloids. She was terrified that he'd had it all planned.

"I didn't want to do myself in like Marilyn Monroe. Or was she murdered? Probably it was murder, just what my god damn husband had in store for me."

She called security. "This is Debbie Reynolds. I want you to remove the name of Richard Hamlett from the parking garage list. Also send out an order that he is not to be allowed in this building ever again. He tried to kill me this morning." Then she put down the phone.

***

Three days later, not having heard form Hamlett, Debbie called the Stardust Hotel and learned that he was not formally registered there. "Give him a message from Debbie Reynolds. Put it in Jane Parker's letterbox. He's living in her room as her guest."

Late that afternoon, he phoned Debbie, and she told him she wanted to meet with him. Not in her apartment with that balcony twelve stories above ground level, but in one of the public areas on the ground floor of her hotel—in the coffee shop.

When he showed up about an hour later than the agreed-upon time, she was quite angry but tried to control her temper. Unwilling to indulge in small talk, she bluntly got to the point: "I want a divorce."

"There's no way in hell I'm gonna give you a divorce," he shot back. "I'm in this thing for the long haul. Right from the beginning, I saw you as a meal ticket with the possibility of becoming a cash cow. Emphasis on *cow*. Let's face it: You're going on sixty You're beyond the age to give a man a hard-on. I married you only for the dough—nothing else. I had to fake passion for you. I never loved you. I'm in love with someone else."

She looked at him with amazement. Eddie Fisher had once uttered almost those same words to her. But in his case, he'd substituted "Elizabeth Taylor" for "someone else."

"You mean your mistress, Jane Parker?" she said. "I know about her. You're paying her bill at the Stardust with my money."

"She is not my mistress. She's the woman I love."

"So let me get this straight," she said. "You want to continue in a marriage to me, while spending your nights in bed with this Parker dame?"

"You've got that right, kid. Trying to get rid of me would be so expensive, you couldn't afford it. It'd cost millions you don't have. *SO LIVE WITH IT!* I'm your husband in name only, and I plan to continue in that role. There are many advantages to being married to a movie star. If you try to get rid of me, I predict you'll be homeless again, living in your car and sleeping in the back seat every night. But I might even take the car away from you, too."

"I'm sure that with 200 rooms here, I'll be able to find a bed for the night," she said, "At my *own* hotel."

"It's not your hotel," he answered, furiously. "It's *our* hotel."

"We'll see about that," she said. "I want you out of my life forever. I loathe you. The sight of you sickens me. To think I thought I loved you. You've de-

544

stroyed that feeling in me, leaving only hate."

Abruptly, he rose to his feet and reached for her hand, kissing it lightly in a courtly gesture.

She later told Todd, "Who would believe it? Hamlett is the only man on the planet who can make a kiss on the hand and turn it into a sign of contempt."

"I'll say this for Eddie Fisher. When he walked out on me, he didn't take any of my money. Of course, he never provided child support either."

Several days later, she had dinner with Phyllis McQuire, describing her incidents and encounters with Hamlett. "If it weren't for Todd, I don't know what I'd do. Even at his age, he's become the man in my life. He's learning fast how to survive in this world. He loves me and is always fighting for my interest, which is now being threatened by Hamlett and a barrage of lawsuits. Unlike Carrie, Todd has never been alienated from me. Unlike those beasts I married, I know I can always count on him."

***

After finishing her Sunday matinee performance in her showroom, Debbie chartered a small airplane to fly to Roanoke to recover her possessions there. Her friend, Margie Duncan, and Duncan's son, Mark Rich, an employee of Debbie's, agreed to fly there with her to help her pack and load her belongings into a rented truck during her "Retreat from Virginia." Todd, along with one of his friends, Fred Pierson, also agreed to accompany her.

Although she was supposed to have been part owner of at least a dozen pieces of Virginia real estate, she feared that Hamlett had played "deed roulette" and juggled the registered names of the owners.

On Monday, after her arrival in Roanoke, she headed for the office of Hamlett's accountant, where he let her make photocopies of all the transactions she'd had with him, including documents associated with loans she'd made to pay off his mortgages and promissory notes.

She also visited Hamlett's home, where it became instantly clear that the locks had been changed, as she'd fully expected in advance. As she recalled, "I had paid for the house three times over, and I wasn't afraid to break into it. Todd found a vulnerable window in the rear of the home and broke in."

She and her helpers set about carting off her fine china in crates, as well as many of the costumes she'd showcased in *The Unsinkable Molly Brown*, especially that red dress she'd worn in her athletic dance number with Harve Presnell.

In the bedroom where Hamlett had made love to her, she found that Jane Parker's wardrobe had replaced her own. All her wardrobe, everything from wigs to dresses and gowns, had been carelessly piled in a corner.

To aid her in her divorce, she discovered in a desk some business documents and some passionate love letters describing the graphic details of Hamlett's sex life with his mistress. Many of them attested to his self-image of what a lion he was in bed.

After the truck was fully loaded, Pierson agreed to drive it back, alone, to California.

At no point did Hamlett show up to confront her. She later learned that he and Parker were away in Europe at the time. Later, charges for the trip they'd taken appeared on a credit card for which she was responsible for payment.

The business papers she'd taken away from Hamlett's home did not match the ones she'd retrieved from his bookkeeper, but it soon became clearly evident that ownership of the properties, as noted on the deeds, had been changed, and nothing was listed in her name. Some of the deeds had been backdated, and in some cases, Parker was listed as the owner of real estate that Debbie had paid for. Other properties bore as owners the names of Hamlett's relatives, including his brother.

She knew how expensive it would be for her California lawyers to wade through this mess of falsified documents in the determination of who owned what. One of the documents showed that Hamlett's first wife had sued Parker over the loss of the Peters Creek property, which Debbie thought she owned. "I bought that property in 1984, and now a former wife and a mistress were suing one another for ownership."

Something she found among his documents was very clearly listed in her name: A bill from the municipal treasurer of Roanoke, demanding payment of $35,000—maybe more—in back taxes. She'd given Hamlett the money, but he had not paid the taxes. Liens had therefore been placed on the properties affected.

Although recognizing that Hamlett would have made a great actor, she was overcome with an awful sense of betrayal. He had been deeply convincing during his proclamations of love.

"I didn't sleep a wink during that flight back to Vegas," Debbie said. "I arrived just in time to get ready for that evening's show. After all, the show must go on. I was bubbling and bouncy that night. I don't think one person in the audience knew I had a broken heart."

"That night, back in my hotel, I took a long, leisurely bubble bath before washing that cheating bastard out of my hair."

"The divorce was going to be long and messy, and I'd be tabloid fodder again. I could just see the headlines—HUBBIE NO. 3 DUMPS TAMMY."

***

Despite all her personal and financial woes, Debbie occasionally appeared on the big screen, if not with her image, at least with her voice. It was as a voice actor that she was cast in *Kiki's Delivery Service* (1989), an animated Japanese fantasy written, produced, and directed by Hayao Miyazaki and released by his studio, Ghibli. Miyazaki was a master storyteller and widely renowned as one of the world's best directors of animated feature films. "This was my first feature film in fifteen years," Debbie said, "and I was the voice of a witch—how fitting! Kiki was a young girl who runs an air courier service."

"Women of my age were lucky to get film work. As I've said so many times before, musicals more or less came to an end with the Fifties. The Hollywood Hills were peopled with former movie legends waiting for the phone to ring. In the decade about to begin, the 1990s, I would become a grandmother. But that's a story for another day."

"My next appearance on the screen was shot in a day," she said. She was referring to *The Bodyguard* (1992) starring Kevin Costner and marking the film debut of Whitney Houston. Costner phoned Debbie and asked her to appear as herself on the red carpet at a presentation ceremony of the Academy Awards.

Originally conceived as a vehicle for Ryan O'Neal and Diana Ross, its plot concerned a former Secret Service agent hired to protect a big music star from an unknown stalker who is sending her death threats.

"I was not only surprised, but a little bit shocked when Oliver Stone, the director and producer, wanted me for the mother role in his third and final film in his Vietnam War trilogy, *Heaven & Earth* (1993). She was pleased to be working with such an acclaimed director, who had already won an Oscar for his direction of *Platoon* (1986).

"At long last, I appeared onscreen wearing a gray wig in *Heaven & Earth* for Warner Brothers, playing Eugenia, the mother of Tommy Lee Jones, cast as a Gunnery Sergeant in the U.S. Marine Corps."

"I got bad news after the film was edited," she said. "Most of my footage ended up on the cutting room floor, since the movie was running too long."

"Both Oliver and Tommy treated me with great respect. I had long admired Tommy for his screen appearances, including when he'd played a U.S. marshal in that thriller, *The Fugitive* (1993). He was a very masculine man, and like me, a fellow Texan. He was born in 1946, the first year of the Baby Boomers, which meant I would have been only fourteen years old when I gave birth to him."

***

In 1994, Debbie expressed her displeasure when *That's Entertainment III* was released in celebration of MGM's 70th anniversary.

Its producers and director had raided the studio's film vaults to come up with musical sequences that had not appeared in the original releases. They included several musical numbers by Judy Garland.

Debbie's sequence was "You Are My Lucky Star," something that had been rejected from the final cut of *Singin' in the Rain*. "The key was too high for me. The number should have been cut."

She also appeared singing an alternate rendition—one which had been shot in a farmyard—of "A Lady Loves." *[The more famous rendition—the one which had actually appeared in* I Love Melvin—*was set against an opulent indoor background.]*

She was fascinated to hear a voice recording of Ava Gardner singing "Can't Help Lovin' That Man" from *Show Boat*. In the original version, her voice had been dubbed by Annette Warren.

As part of the retrospective, Gene Kelly, in his final appearance on the screen, asked Debbie to be one of the hosts, along with June Allyson, Cyd Charisse, Howard Keel, Ann Miller, Mickey Rooney, and Esther Williams. "For Esther, it marked her first appearance in a feature film in thirty years," Debbie said. "Gene Kelly sure rounded up that old gang of mine. All of us looked worse for wear. But we were holding ourselves together with spit and glue and lots and lots of makeup to conceal the ravages of time."

***

Divorce papers were served on Richard Hamlett in September of 1994. "It was going to be messy, but it was long overdue. My one bright spot was the opening of my Hollywood museum in Las Vegas, a brilliant creation of Todd."

To make her museum a reality, she'd had to borrow nearly a million dollars. "This time, I was swamped with lawsuits for nothing I had done personally. But Richard had done plenty, and now I was left to pick up the pieces."

"Oh, those sleepless nights in Las Vegas pacing the floor... Sex? What was sex? At least I didn't have to wake up in the morning and face that former husband of mine. I was borrowing money from everybody who would lend it to me. Getting deeper and deeper into debt, I was advised to designate Todd CEO of the company, although hotel management was not his expertise. We met with Steve Wynn at his hotel, The Mirage. After a talk with Todd, who was now thirty-four, Steve determined he was the man for the job. "At least you can trust your son," Wynn told her. "Everybody else seems to be robbing you blind. I think Todd will do a super job."

To assist in her procurement of a gaming license, "Wynn placed a call to the head of the gaming commission, a man whose last name was Bible. I found out from him that a gaming license would cost me $2 million. That would mean more borrowing. I was beginning to feel that this time, Molly Brown was on the verge of going down with the *Titanic*."

In the face of all this, she held onto her dream of opening her Hollywood museum, perhaps reconfiguring it as a larger venue that wasn't associated with a gambling resort—perhaps in Los Angeles. But in the end, her negotiations with the city fell through.

Despite the many setbacks, she attended more studio auctions, including

548

one at 20th Century Fox. There, she invested in some of the costumes Marilyn Monroe had worn in her films in the 1950s. "I knew they'd be valuable one day."

She managed to obtain space at the Garden Court Apartments on Hollywood Boulevard and moved her collection into storage there. Actress Anne Baxter and her former lover, George Peppard, helped her move. Later, when she went to retrieve them, she learned that security was lacking in the storage rooms, and that some of her valuable costumes, props, and furniture had been stolen.

"On many a tear-streaked night, I wanted to throw in the towel. Give everything up and go hide somewhere…perhaps in Nebraska. No one on the planet would ever think of looking for me in Nebraska."

***

Eventually, after months of stress and tedious preparations, she found herself facing Richard Hamlett in a Vegas divorce court. There, in front of the judge, he engaged in rounds of bitter confrontations with Debbie's female lawyer, who confronted him with many incriminating allegations of "deed roulette." In the end, Debbie emerged with an $8.9 million dollar judgment in her favor, plus reimbursement of $1.4 million in legal fees.

"On May 14, 1996, I became a free woman again. Single at last, and this is how I planned to remain for the rest of my days. Of course, a woman of my age was not in big demand on the marriage market."

Her legal battles with Hamlett were far from over. He filed an appeal in his home state of Virginia, a venue where it was more difficult for her to fight. She referred to the ensuing months as a "firestorm."

Late one night, she picked up her phone and heard his voice. "You'll never get a god damn cent out of me," he fumed. "If I have to, I'll go after you and all the people around you." After a lot of additional angry words, he slammed down the phone.

In the end, she paid him $270,000 for his share of the hotel but was forced to settle for only $300,000 from all the millions that the Vegas court had ordered that he pay to her. Her nightmarish dealings with Hamlett became a thing of the past, but her legal woes in Vegas were heating up. "I needed money and more money…so much that I was delighted when someone finally offered me some dough for my first starring role in a good picture in years. Debbie was going back to work before the cameras."

***

Albert Brooks was ready to cast his next film, simply entitled *Mother*, a film eventually released by Paramount in 1996. In it, he would play a neurotic sci-fi writer who moves in with his strong-willed mother, Beatrice, after his second divorce. His character wonders why his relationships with women are so unsuccessful. The script defined interchanges with Beatrice as filled with bickering and power struggles. She frequently complains that she's unfairly blamed for her son's failings.

The actress he first wanted as the domineering mother was Nancy Reagan. The former First Lady hadn't made a movie in decades. Ronald Reagan had married her in 1952 and within a few years, took her off the screen. "She had ruled the White House, and perhaps the Free World, too, so she could be more than adequate in dominating her son," Brooks said. "As for box office, her enemies would certainly flock to see it."

When Carrie rendezvoused with Brooks [*she had known him since he'd made a guest appearance on* Saturday Night Live] she recommended Debbie for the role. His ears perked up. "Casting against type! I like that! Tammy as a hell-on-wheels mother. Great casting!"

Two days later, he met with Debbie and found her bossy enough to fulfill the demands of the role. He hired her on the spot, without an audition.

It was hard for her to escape her hotel management problems and her legal woes in Las Vegas, but she wanted to accept the role, and to make it possible, a massive load of responsibility was transferred onto Todd. He promised to book, during her absence, a winning revue into her Star Theater.

She was not particularly familiar with Brooks or his career, but Carrie filled her in, comparing him to a second Woody Allen—"in other words, an anxiety-ridden wreck."

Shortly before the beginning of filming, Debbie suffered a ruptured stomach and was rushed to the hospital. She feared that Brooks would recast her role during her stint in the hospital, but he held it open for her.

In a weakened condition, she reported for work as soon as she could and performed exactly as he'd hoped she would. She told Brooks that X-rays of my stomach revealed that "I've been drinking Drano instead of champagne."

The director and the film star worked smoothly together, and *Mother* emerged as one of Debbie's favorite movies in years. Andrew Sarris defined it as the best film of 1996. Although not as lavish in their praise, other critics weighed in with favorable reviews, too.

Debbie claimed, "I've worked with a lot of shits in my day, but Albert was not one of them. He was talented and brilliant, and we worked smoothly together. I sort of hated when filming came to an end, fearing that this would be my last big role. But I had to return to the nightmare waiting for me in Las Vegas."

Chapter Nineteen

THESE OLD BROADS

Embrace their Status as Geriatrics in Show-Biz

Satirizing their Fading Allure as "Hoofers and
Heifers," Elizabeth Taylor, Debbie Reynolds,
Shirley MacLaine, & Joan Collins
Resolve their Feuds, Celebrate Life, &
Strut Their Stuff

Collectively, They're 269 Years old with 16 ex-husbands

Their Fans Go Wild

CARRIE MARRIES BRYAN LOURD

He's Handsome! He's Charming! He's Connected!
He's Successful! And He Wants a Husband of His Own!

The Unholy Quartet: (left to right) Joan Collins, Shirley MacLaine, Elizabeth Taylor, and Debbie Reynolds showed the world they were "timeless wonders" when they appeared together in *These Old Broads*.

They'd betrayed each other, stolen each other's husbands or lovers, and vied for the same roles, but at twilight time, they reconciled and joined forces.

In the late 1980s, Carrie met talent agent Bryan Lourd, and they started dating on and off for a period of three years. In 1991, they married. It was a troubled union that lasted until 1994.

"It took some time to get to know him," she said. "Unlike all those show business types I knew, like my mother Debbie, Bryan didn't go around day and night promoting himself. He hyped the talents of others."

Eddie Fisher met him and liked him, calling him, "a calm and quiet man, like the eye of a hurricane."

Gradually, some of the details of his early life emerged: Four years younger than Carrie (born in 1956), Lourd was born November 5, 1960 in New Iberia, Louisiana.

As a high school student, he'd appeared in a number of musicals, perhaps wanting to go on the stage professionally. But after enrolling at the University of Southern California, he studied journalism and communications, graduating in 1982.

He decided to remain in the Los Angeles area, not as an actor or director, but as a talent agent, working himself up the rungs of the ladder to a top position in management.

Mike Nichols said, "Bryan was a young man on the rise. He was very ambitious but concealed it behind a courtly façade. He was the farthest thing from a Darryl F. Zanuck puffing on a cigar and barking orders to starlets."

Whatever faults Bryan might have had as a husband, no one criticized him as a father.

Debbie had been present at Cedars Sinai Hospital during the birth of her grandchild. She claimed that before the birth of Billie Lourd on November 17, 1992, Carrie went off drugs based on her fear that they would adversely affect her child. She also stopped her regime of anti-depressants, which led to horrific mood changes in her.

In the hospital, Debbie said she'd always remember the scene of Bryan with his new daughter. "He took the infant and bathed her with such love and tenderness. The first time I saw Billie, I thought of the Stevie Wonder song, 'You Are the Sunshine of My Life.' After that, I

Carrie's second marriage was to Bryan Lourd, a genius of a talent agent.

For three years, she failed to comprehend the source of his increasing dissatisfaction. "It was like life was going by before him, and he was missing out on it, missing something vital to his inner desires."

called her 'My Sunshine Girl.'"

Two days after giving birth, Carrie telephoned her father, Eddie Fisher, in New York: "You weren't a good father, but I'm going to give you a chance to be a good grandfather. I'm naming my daughter Carrie Fisher Lourd, honoring you. Please don't disappoint."

According to Eddie, "When I first saw Bryan with his daughter, I was amazed at what a wonderful father he was. He was as good a parent as Carrie. Frankly, I was kind of jealous because the importance of my role as a grandfather suddenly grew smaller."

Whereas Debbie, in her memoirs, wrote many negative observations about each of her three husbands, Carrie delivered only a few abbreviated details about her affair with Bryan. A few additional insights were provided in her novel, *The Best Awful*, in 2003. In it, she re-introduces her heroine, Suzanne Vale, the messed-up actress who had first appeared in *Postcards from the Edge.*

In *The Best Awful*, the protagonist falls in love and marries a young man she calls "Leland Franklin" who is clearly Bryan. "He forgot to tell me he was gay, and I forgot to notice," she wrote.

Her not knowing that important detail came as a surprise to those who knew her. "Both Carrie and Debbie had great gay radar which extended for at least a mile," said Mike Nichols. "They had many gay friends and were very hip to the scene. Debbie, in particular, was a bit of a fag hag."

Carrie dedicated *The Best Awful* to Bryan and their daughter, Billie Lourd, since she had clearly used them as inspiration.

In that memoir, Leland is a studio executive, which Bryan became in real life. According to the novel's protagonist, "He helped me find my real self"— that is, before he left her for a male lover when their daughter, "Honey," was three years old. Sharon Vale (i.e., Carrie) is depicted as a successful TV talk show host with a gay ex-husband and an "aging starlet" mother from the 1950s.

Many pages of *The Best Awful* deal with Carrie's (aka Sharon's) status as a recovering drug addict. After weaning herself from OxyContin, she's plunged into a recurring series of manic episodes, which eventually help land her in "Shady Lanes" (a mental asylum). "I was the latest patient to hit this looney bin."

She credits her movie star mom and her ex-husband, plus a circle of friends, for helping to guide her "on that long journey back to sanity."

In Carrie's novel, Leland at first doesn't tell Vale why he's leaving her. "He told me it was because I was crazy, keeping him up all night with talk, talk, and more talk." *[It has been surmised that that reflected Carrie's erratic behavior during the aftermath of stopping her medication for bipolarism.]*

Weeks after she was dumped, Vale (or Carrie's) ex-husband called her and told her the real reason he'd flown over the cuckoo's nest: "You turned me gay, and you did so by taking all that cocaine."

She apologized to him. "I didn't read the warning on the label of that bottle of Percotin. It warned about using heavy machinery after taking the pills. It did not mention that it causes homosexuality in your husband."

After he left her, Carrie admitted going through "a bright, phosphorus glow of a gnaw of pain glowing in the hot spot of my chest. The winds of hurt and blame were storming out of Cape Fear."

During talks with Debbie and others, Carrie said, "Somehow, he kept me at arm's length even though fucking me, admittedly a neat trick to pull off. He had this subtle way of patrolling my borders. He was a miracle of care, concern, and control. He was the kind of man who would tuck you into bed for the night and wake you up with juice and coffee."

"Month after month of my marriage, I should have become suspicious, but I wasn't," Carrie said. "Those calls late at night from young men who would not give me their names should have alerted me."

"I had come to depend on him like oxygen. Then I found out he was missing Southern Comfort in the arms of a lover who was more adequately equipped than I was."

In her novel, she has her husband tiptoeing out the door "in search of something saner and more sensible for himself." That was exactly what Bryan did. He found what he was looking for in the arms of another.

As soon as Debbie learned that Carrie's latest relationship had failed, she rushed to her side. "Dear, let's face it: You and I don't know how to pick husbands."

Carrie agreed with that, having once described the Debbie character in her novel, *The Best Awful,* as "a famous 1950s movie icon whose three marriages had left her publicly humiliated, bankrupted, and bankrupted again."

"Now that Bryan has broken out of prison, perhaps you'll get your next husband to pledge allegiance to the flag of straights," Debbie quipped.

In the weeks following Bryan's departure, Carrie really wanted him back, thinking that they could work something out in their marriage. "I not only missed him, but I desperately needed him. I was willing to allow him to date other men. After all, this is common practice among many of the wives of European husbands. It's most acceptable to them. Most Americans seem to have crazy objections to this perfectly normal arrangement."

Bryan's prognosis about the possibility of patching up their marriage was stated very clearly: "I will return for a visit as the father of Billie—but never as your husband. I have a husband of my own now to love and to care for. Whatever we had is a memory growing dimmer day by day. I've found what I always wanted. I hope the same for you."

***

[The great career highlights of Bryan Lourd emerged after he left Carrie. His career

554

zoomed skyward, and in 1995, he became the managing director and co-chairman of Creative Artists Agency (CAA). The film colony—at least most of them—seemed to adore him for his behind-the-scenes talent and skill.

Soon, he'd made friends with such luminaries as Gwyneth Paltrow, Sarah Jessica Parker, power mogul David Geffen, Jimmy Fallon, Anne Hathaway, even Madonna.

The New Orleans-born Reese Witherspoon said, "He's just a humble, nice boy from my home state of Louisiana, which he and I bonded over. He has all those beautiful southern manners. He is the one person in Hollywood who still understands the power of the hand-written thank you note."

Liam Neeson also commented on Bryan's unassuming persona. "He keeps it a mystery, which I like. He doesn't unzip and say, 'This is me!'"

Whoopi Goldberg said, "He was never the cliché of the slick Sammy Glick abusive agent. He tells the truth. This is more important than anything, especially in our business, where lying is an art."

According to Carrie, "I dated him and made love to him, but I never really knew him, in spite of our long talks, sharing our hopes and dreams. Perhaps he didn't want to share his dreams with me. I always felt he was holding something back that he didn't want me to know. Debbie, with her gossipy friends, had heard certain rumors about Bryan, but I discounted them. I didn't believe a word of them."

She is said to have married him in 1991, but in 2004, sources claimed that they were never legally or formally wed.

Bryan serves on the Board of Directors of the Lincoln Center for the Performing Arts in New York City. In 2009, President Barack Obama appointed him to the President's Committee on the Arts and Humanities, followed four years later by his appointment to the Board of the John F. Kennedy Center for the Performing Arts.

In 2014, a gala was hosted in his honor in New York at Lincoln Center. Some 750 guests showed up to honor him. "Half of them, it seemed, had been a cover subject for Vanity Fair*" said actress Ellen Barkin, who called the event "a royal coronation for Bryan." Holding a champagne glass, she stood on stage, introducing Bryan as her best friend. "And right now," she said wryly, "there are about 300 people out there staring daggers at me, thinking* '**What** *is she talking about?* **I'm** *Bryan Lourd's best friend.'"*

On October 12, 2016, Bryan married Bruce Bozzi, a co-owner of The Palm, a famous steakhouse in Manhattan. The two husbands divide their time between a penthouse apartment in New York's Greenwich Village and a home in Beverly Hills.

Bryan's daughter, Billie, was born in Los Angeles but studied psychology at New York University, graduating in 2014. After that, she headed for Hollywood, where she was cast in the horror comedy, Scream Queen *(2015). She wore earmuffs as an affectionate reference to Carrie's iconic "cinnamon bun" hairdo in the original* Star Wars.

Right before Christmas of 2015, she joined the cast of the TV drama, appearing in an episode eventually released in 2017, American Horror Story: Cult, *part of an ongoing horror anthology broadcast on FX. The role she played was that of Linda Kasabian, a former member of the Charles Manson Cult.*

In 2015, Billie was assigned the role of Lt Kaydel Ko Connix in Star Wars, the Force Awakens, *and in 2017, she reprised that character in* Star Wars: The Last Jedi.

"Billie will never need to look for work ever again after the death of her mother. Carrie's daughter inherited a fortune that should nurture her through at least three more lives," as phrased by a reporter at the time.]

***

Although Debbie's business and legal woes were swamping her in Las Vegas, she opted to take time off for the filming of her cameo appearance in *Wedding Bell Blues,* a romantic comedy released in 1996.

Directed by Dana Lustig, Debbie appeared as herself performing in her Star Theater within her hotel. The plot centers not on her, but on three beautiful young women who come to Las Vegas with the intention of finding husbands. Its trio of stars included Illeana Douglas, supermodel Paulina Porizkova, and Julie Warner, none of them household names.

This movie did not particularly help their careers. It was one of the worst-performing movies of the year, taking in less than $50,000 nationwide after it was released.

"At the time, I was barely alive, performing under great stress," Debbie said. "The girls in the film were trying to find husbands, while I was trying to get rid of one."

***

Back in Las Vegas, facing up to her massive debt and legal troubles, and with the memory of Richard Hamlett still "lingering in my gut," Debbie received a call from Frank Oz, an English-born actor, filmmaker, and puppeteer. Since she was onstage, performing, at the time of his call, he left a message. After receiving the message, she at first concluded that it had something to do with Carrie.

Oz had interpreted the voice and (aided by padding and a Yoda costume) physicality of Yoda in George Lucas' *Star Wars* series. He had added a lot of creative input to the character and was responsible for creating Yoda's unusual

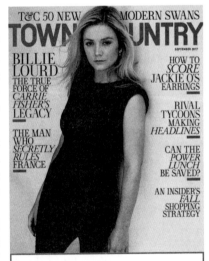

Instant Stardom: Billie Lourd as Cover Girl in the wake of the deaths of her mother and grandmother, for the September 2017 edition of *Town & Country*.

syntax.

Debbie returned Oz's phone call later that night. He told her he wanted her to play the mother of Kevin Kline in a romantic comedy, *In & Out*, scheduled for release by Paramount in 1997. In it, Klein would be cast as her character's gay son. Local wits interpreted the title of *In & Out* as a reference to quickie sex.

"My own son is not gay, but I've mothered enough gay men in my day," Debbie responded. "I accept, without even reading the script, providing the mother is not an aging stripper."

Later, although not exactly thrilled by her role, she found the script by Paul Rudnick amusing.

In the plot, Kline is a highly regarded teacher of English literature, living life in the closet in the imaginary town of Greenleaf, Indiana. His boss, the high school principal, Tom Halliwell, is played by Bob Newhart. Homosexuality frightens him, and as such, he is not exactly a champion of gay rights.

Howard's *fiancée*, Emily Montgomery (Joan Cusack), is also a teacher. In preparation for her role, and before the debut of filming, Cusack dieted aggressively and lost 75 pounds.

As the movie progresses, one of Howard's former students, Cameron Drake (Matt Dillon), is seen by millions on TV receiving an Oscar for playing a gay soldier in *To Serve and Protect*. In his acceptance speech, he specifically thanks Howard, adding "and he's gay."

The citizens of Greenleaf become hysterical, and Emily, along with Howard's students and their parents, are shocked. Debbie, playing Bernice (Howard's mother), is wed to Frank (Wilford Brimley).

Reporters wing their way to Indiana to cover a reception being hosted in Howard's honor in the wake of his (cinematic) "outing." One of the reporters, Peter Malloy (as played by Tom Selleck), remains behind after the others leave with the intention of getting to know Howard better. Malloy, too, is gay, and in one scene, he gives Howard a long, passionate kiss. The teacher seems to enjoy it.

During his wedding to Emily, Howard tells the minister, "I'm gay." In tears, Emily dumps him, and he's immediately fired from his job, yet he shows up for the graduation ceremony to support his students. Then, in an almost universal gesture of their support, the film ends with all the students proclaiming, "I'm gay, too!"

Then movie-star Cameron (Dillon) flies in to transfer to Howard the Oscar he'd won for his impersonation of a gay

In & Out. Debbie as a mother figure with her gay son, as portrayed by Kevin Kline.

solider. Howard's wedding-obsessed mother (Debbie), then celebrates her own wedding, renewing her marriage vows to Frank. At the end, students and teachers, including a skeptical Newhart, are dancing to "Macho Man" from the Village People.

During the course of their filming, Debbie developed a great admiration for Kline, who had made his film debut in *Sophie's Choice* (1982). According to Debbie, "He had wild comic energy, and was very versatile, able to play a number of roles."

During her filming of *In & Out*, trouble developed with her director, Oz. "He wanted me to play this pushy broad who is horrified that her son is gay." Resisting that interpretation, Debbie preferred to emphasize Beatrice's status as a supportive mother to her son, regardless of the lifestyle choices he made. After some artistic tension, the director and his actor compromised.

On a budget of $35 million, *In & Out* took in $65 million at the box office, and Debbie was besieged with letters of approval from her gay fans.

***

"Back in Las Vegas, I returned to my financial nightmares," Debbie said. "A board meeting of angry shareholders was announced, and I anticipated facing my alltime most hostile audience."

In 1996, her hotel had chalked up a negative cash flow of $6.5 million. *[In 1995, its losses had been much worse, totaling $8.5 million.]* The hotel needed more investors, and—as Todd soon learned—they were hard to find.

Debbie needed money and with that in mind, she paid a visit to one of her friends, a television actress named Crystal Bernard. Bernard was best known for her eight-year run in the sitcom, *Wings* (1990-97). Her role demanded that she speak in a Texas drawl. That came easy for her since she was born there.

In one of the episodes ("If It's Not One Thing, It's Your Mother") of *Wings*, Debbie had played Bernard's tight-fisted mother.

She found that she had much in common with Bernard, each of them having grown up in fundamentalist households. Bernard's father had been a televangelist, preaching and singing. As a young girl, Bernard had sung, onstage and accompanied by one of her sisters, Scarlett, during her father's Bible rallies.

As a young girl, in an act where she'd been joined by her older sister, Bernard had recorded a hit entitled "Monkey Song," a melodic objection to Charles Darwin's theory of evolution.

During their meeting, Debbie poured out her financial woes, and her friend responded by handing over a check for $100,000. Debbie vowed to pay her back, but it took a long time.

In preparation for her upcoming meeting with the board of directors, Debbie was given a letter written by a member of the board of directors. He had already distributed copies of it to every other member of the board.

He'd written: "Debbie Reynolds is a no-talent, has-been actress of the 1950s. She isn't worth the $25,000 we pay her to perform at the Star Theater where she manages to put the meager audience to sleep. Oh, my god, if I hear her sing 'Tammy' one more time, I'll croak."

"I was already on the verge of a nervous breakdown," Debbie mused. "But after reading that, I wanted to jump from the top floor."

She was shocked when the hotel's attorney, Edward Coleman, told the press that she had never earned so much money in her life. "I guess he didn't read the papers. In 1962, I signed a million-dollar contract for my appearance at the Riviera."

When other performers, such as the Smothers Brothers, filled in for Debbie, they were paid equivalent salaries. Her paycheck wasn't out of bounds for other stars, some past their prime, appearing at various venues along the Strip at the time. Many were drawing even higher fees for their gigs.

As audiences dwindled at the hotel during the slow months, Todd came up with a scheme to drum up more business. He'd read in the papers that his father, Eddie Fisher, was in town, so he phoned to arrange a reunion.

Over dinner that night, Todd pitched his idea: Eddie would become an off-season headliner at the Star Theater, thinking it would draw crowds, at least as a curiosity, if not for any other reason. "You still have your voice. You'll go over great," Todd assured him.

At first, Eddie appeared on the verge of accepting. "Sure, I'll do the show. Perhaps your mother will trick me into having another baby like she did when she got me drunk and seduced me, which led to her giving birth to you."

"Don't worry about that," Todd said. "She's had a hysterectomy."

"All joking aside, I'd love to help you out, kid, but frankly, I don't have the stomach for it."

When Todd failed to extract a commitment from him, he pursued another goal, and that was to get his father to become a Born Again Christian.

"I can't do that," Eddie said. "I couldn't let Sammy Davis, Jr. be a better Jew than me."

Later in the same evening, at the same time, they each had to visit the men's room. Standing side by side at urinals, Eddie used the moment to check out his son's penis, wondering if Debbie had ever had him circumcised.

Todd also checked out Eddie's penis. Then he told him, "Carrie's is bigger than yours."

***

Board members arrived three days in advance of their confrontation with Debbie, occupying suites on her hotel's top floor. She met some of them, including a "worm farmer" operating outside Vegas. Later, she was told that the shareholders had hired a coven of prostitutes during their stay.

Realizing what a hopeless enterprise her hotel was, Jackpot Enterprises had waited long and fruitlessly for the hotel to get a permanent gambling license. When it appeared that such a license would never be forthcoming, two enormous trucks arrived to confiscate some two hundred slot machines and two blackjack tables. To fill the empty spaces, Todd moved in displays of more of his mother's Hollywood props and costumes.

As the tense board meeting was called to order, Debbie—who was the last to arrive—sensed a palpable tension. Her chief antagonist was a giant of a man, Joe Kowal. He addressed the assembled crowd like this: "Miss Reynolds is not in the control of this hotel. In case she doesn't know this, WE are the ones in charge here. She works for us. Her attempts at management have grossly failed. I attended her show. What a bore! A tired old broad singing 'Tammy' for the 100,000th time. She's sucking up all her profits with her salary demands. She should pay us to sit through one of her disaster performances."

At the time of her attack, she had been munching on an apple, of all things. She later said, "It was the apple that Eve tempted Adam with in the Garden of Eden. It was still juicy but a bit rotten."

I still had my pitcher's arm, the one I demonstrated at high school softball games, and when I tossed that big cake into Jean Hagen's face in *Singin' in the Rain*. I aimed my apple at his fat chest and scored a bull's eye with its juicy pulp on his pink designer suit. Then I lunged at him, pounding my little fists into his chest. That ugly hulk of flesh merely laughed at me. Then Todd and two other guys pulled me away from King Kong. I was escorted out of the room. Needless to say, this was the last board meeting I ever attended."

***

In the summer of 1997, Debbie faced a horrifying new reality and the failure of a cherished dream. Confronted with bills that mounted daily and a hotel that struggled to stay open, she had to declare bankruptcy

Her heavily mortgaged home in Los Angeles was being occupied by her brother, Billy Reynolds, who lived there as its caretaker.

Todd had already pink-slipped fifty employees and was operating the hotel with fewer than 100 staffers. That would dwindle to only twenty during the hotel's final days. The shareholders asked Debbie to resign. Shortly thereafter, she signed a letter of resignation without protest, only regret.

In the meantime, Todd searched frantically for a buyer, and finally came up with an interested party. He was David Siegel, a successful time-share salesman from South Florida. He flew in, inspected the hotel, and talked extensively with Debbie and Todd before placing his bid of $15.5 million. In return, he wanted 92 percent of the stock, and was willing to let Todd and Debbie retain control of entertainment and a possible casino, if they could ever raise $2 million for the gaming license.

As Todd computed it, Siegel's offer would almost pay off the most demanding of the creditors. After (and if) the deal were settled, Siegel would assume management of the premises.

Board members heard of Siegel's offer and rejected it with the belief that at public auction, they might generate $20 million. They even took Debbie to court to prevent the sale. The judge who heard the cased ruled in favor of the board. "Talk about a *good ol' boy* Vegas network," she said in disgust.

"I was forced to allow the auction to proceed," she said. "Oh, jolly, jolly... another public humiliation for me. It was unlikely I'd emerge with one cent in my purse."

She defined August 1, 1998 as her own private Doomsday. "At long last, Molly Brown, after several close calls in the past, was going down, this time as the Sinkable Molly Brown, with the *Titanic*. I expected to end up in the darkest, most shark-infested waters of the North Atlantic."

"On that day I had to face the bidders at the auction. Some members of the audience, I suspected, would be Peeping Toms come to see me humiliated yet again. I put on my Debbie Reynolds face, adorned myself with my brightest outfit (a number in luscious pink); strapped on my Joan Crawford fuck-me shoes (as they were called in 1945); and entered the auction room, flashing my best Tammy smile."

Todd told her there was a rumor going around that Richard Hamlett had flown in from Roanoke to witness the auction. "I knew he didn't have the money to bid, so he must have shown up just to see me go down."

Before the bidding began, she appeared on stage, giving a little speech in which she emphasized only the good times she'd had running the hotel. ("There had been few of those to talk about.")

She ended her speech with a lament: "I would have preferred to stay on for the rest of my days singing 'Tammy' every night." Then she glanced down at her watch. "That career ends at noon today."

There was only scattered laughter at what she had hoped would be interpreted as a self-effacing joke. As she exited from the stage, she noticed many members of her remaining staff shedding tears.

Bidding was brief and proceeded without much enthusiasm. The winning bid of $11 million went to the World Wrestling Federation.

Debbie stood up and faced some of the board members who had rejected David Siegel's offer of $15.5 million. "That was one sad-faced group of greedy bastards. The lower bid would mean they got nothing, the money having been earmarked for the front-line banks. I, too, had nothing to celebrate. After all my work and anguish, I would say farewell. What could I do except lift a finger to the shitheads I was leaving behind and storm out of the building for the final time?"

***

561

Accepting every role she was offered in feature films, regardless of how minor, Debbie signed to play the fourth lead in a romantic comedy, *Zack and Reba* (1998). Distributed by LIVE Entertainment, it starred Sean Patrick Flanery as Zack Blanton and Brittany Murphy as Reba. The third lead, "Oras," was cast with Michael Jeter.

As Beulah Blanton, Debbie played a grandmother who lives in a Victorian house and who, from inside her house and through her bedroom window, shoots birds. "The role reminded me of an old Molly Brown, except I had an awful wardrobe and sported an even worse hairdo."

Written by Jay Stapleton, the plot was bizarre, Zack's wife has died, and he carried around her skeleton as a constant reminder of his loss. All of that changes when he meets Reba (Murphy) whose boyfriend has recently committed suicide. "How romantic can you get?" Debbie asked the director, Nicole Bettauer.

She admired her director and working with her went smoothly. "In private life, Nicole did much social work and campaigned for mental health. She also made charming little films. In one, a duck saves a man's life."

Atlanta-born Murphy also won Debbie's approval. She had come from the Broadway stage, where she'd appeared in Arthur Miller's *A View from the Bridge* (1997).

"Years later, I was sorry to learn of her fate," Debbie said.

[She was referring to her unexpected, sudden death from pneumonia at the age of 32. Six months later, her husband, Simon Monjack, died of the same disease.]

Debbie had the highest praise for Michael Jeter. "He was always on the mark, a talented, clever, funny guy."

She had nothing but disdain, however, for the lead, Sean Patrick Flanery. Born in Louisiana, he was also an author and martial artist. "He grew up in my native state of Texas, but we had nothing in common. He refused to rehearse with me. He seemed to think of himself as the next James Dean. I knew Jimmy. He had talent. Sean didn't impress me as an actor. But he went on to marry a *Playboy* model (Lauren Michell Hill), so I guess he had some talent."

***

"Don't let anyone know this," Debbie said, "but I also worked on *Rudolph the Red-Nosed Reindeer: The Movie* (1998). I performed the voices of Blitzen's wife; Rudolph's mother; Mrs. Claus; and Mrs. Prance."

Other voiceovers were performed by such stars as John Goodman as Santa Claus; Eric Idle as Slyly the Fox; Bob Newhart as a polar bear; Richard Simmons as Boone; and Whoopi Goldberg as Stormella.

Legacy Releasing, the film's producers, thought their film would become a big box office draw at Christmas, but when it opened, the public stayed away. A spectacular flop, *Rudolph* earned around $115,000 when it premiered, having cost $10 million to make.

***

"I was very excited to receive a call from the director, Terry Gilliam," Debbie said. "He wanted to talk to me about his upcoming film, *Fear and Loathing in Las Vegas* (1998)." The movie, set to star Johnny Depp, was based on the cult novel of the same name by Hunter S. Thompson.

As two drug-addicted pals, Depp would play Raoul Duke, and the Puerto Rican actor, Benicio Del Toro, would be his pal, Dr. Gonzo.

Driving into Vegas with his pal while high on mescaline, Depp as Raoul imagines that he's being attacked by a swarm of giant bats. Then the two men pick up a hitchhiker, Tobey Maguire, who quickly realizes that Raoul is crazy.

"I was disappointed to learn that I was only to be a voiceover. At no point in the movie would there be a moving replica of myself. I would appear in the film only as a motionless image on a billboard advertising my stage appearance in Vegas. There were to be no hot love scenes with Johnny, whom I heard was called 'Donkey Dong' throughout Hollywood."

When Raoul, fueled with mescaline, sees Debbie's image on the billboard during his drive into town, he says, "That's a hot chick."

"I was flattered when I saw that segment in the movie," she said.

"I didn't get to meet Johnny, and later, I failed to once again when he rented my DR Studios as rehearsal space for his swordfighting scenes for one of his upcoming *Pirates of the Caribbean* movies. From what I hear, Johnny is quite the swordsman himself. I told everybody I was in a new Johnny Depp movie. Except I wasn't really there...let's call it 'my romantic life in a nutshell.'"

In *Fear and Loathing in Las Vegas*. Debbie appeared only as a name on a series of billboards, an archetype and symbol in front of which other cinematic events unfolded.

The movie, based on the Hunter S. Thompson novel, starred Johnny Depp. "But I didn't get to work with him," she lamented.

"I heard I missed out on a big thing," she quipped.

***

My roles, if they could even be called that, got more and more bizarre," she said. "Again, I wouldn't even be seen when I was offered a voice-over in an animated comedy drama. *Rugrats in Paris: The Movie* (2000) for Paramount."

[It was the second in a series of three animated movies released in 1998, 2000, and 2003, respectively. Collectively grossing about $300 million worldwide, each was a commercial success.

"I was the voice of Lulu Pickles. With a name like that, how could I turn it down? It was my voice that lured them into the theaters, and I'm certain of that," Debbie said.

***

As the 20th Century—Debbie called it "my century"—neared its end, she was offered her longest-running TV gig. From 1999 until 2006, she would appear as Debra Messing's mother in the hit TV comedy series, *Will & Grace*. Messing plays Grace, a heterosexual interior designer, who lives (platonically) in a New York apartment with her best friend, Will Truman, a (gay) lawyer, as portrayed by Eric McCormack.

Will & Grace became one of the most successful TV series with gay principal characters. They included Sean Hayes as their flamboyant neighbor across the hall. He played Jack McFarland, forever outrageous. For many years, Hayes refused to discuss his sexual orientation with reporters, but in 2014, he married his partner of eight years, Scott Icenogle.

U.S. Vice President Joe Biden asserted that the series probably did more to educate the American public about LGBT issues than almost anything has ever done so far.

Debbie joined the cast of the series in its second year, appearing in an episode called "The Unsinkable Molly Adler," which she defined as "an ego booster for me."

She makes her entrance into her daughter's apartment, mugging Ethel Merman singing "Everything's Coming Up Roses" from *Gypsy*. *[She had often impersonated Merman as part of her stage appearances.]* In another episode, she sang the chorus of "Good Morning" from *Singin' in the Rain* (1952).

She referred to the series' director, Jim Burrows, as one of the finest talents working in television, and she found both cast and crew friendly and respectful of her, unlike many of her experiences in feature films.

On camera and in their respective roles, Debbie and Messing were often confrontational, battling out issues as mother vs. daughter. In real life, however, they became admiring friends, "even though she grew up in Brooklyn, and I came from El Paso, two wide worlds apart."

In her "mother" role as Bobbi Adler, Debbie was a bundle of energy, ever bubbling, and imbued with theatrics. She likes to meddle in her daughter's love life, often trying to fix her up with unlikely men such as "Stanley Fink," a mortician. She wants her daughter to marry, even suggesting that she wed Will, despite his self-evaluation that he's gay.

Others of Debbie's episodes within the series were entitled, "Whose Mom Is It, Anyway?", and "Swish Out of Water."

[Messing was shocked and grieved by the news of Debbie's death in 2016 and issued a statement: "She was pure energy when she appeared. She was a loving, bawdy, and most playful woman, consummate pro—old school, and yet she had the work ethic and invested more in her craft than many a fiery 'up and comer.'"

"She was always running off to Vegas or somewhere else, always on the road, always the hoofer, singing and dancing to please her fans. She performed 340 days a year. She was an inspiration, a legend, the epitome of clean-cut American optimism, dancing with Gene Kelly as her equal, a warrior woman who never stopped working."]

***

Cary Grant, Carrie's LSD mentor, had once owned some landscaped acreage on which stood both a house and a fully independent cottage for his gardener. Grant eventually sold the entire parcel to Edith Head. *[Head was arguably the most famous costumer in Hollywood, having designed dozens of outfits for the film industry's biggest stars. Elizabeth Taylor had on occasion been her overnight guest.]*

After she sold it, the new owner had split the parcel into two separate entities, and the cottage now stood as a fully independent unit, completely separate from the larger house of which it

In the hit TV series, *Will & Grace*, Eric McCormack played a gay lawyer, the roommate of Deborah Messing, who portrayed a (heterosexual) interior designer. Debbie (*right figure in the upper photo*) played her bubbling, charismatic mother.

In the lower photo, Deborah points to the portrait of her screen mother, which hung in her New York apartment.

had previously been a satellite. Eventually, Carrie purchased the bigger of the two original buildings (i.e., "the main house') and had decorated it in her very eccentric style.

A few years later, the smaller of the two original buildings (i.e., "the cottage") came on the market, Carrie called Debbie and suggested it would be ideal for her, since she had been looking for a place to live after the Las Vegas fiasco. Adding to its appeal was the fact that Debbie liked the idea of living next to her daughter and her new granddaughter, Billie Lourd.

She arrived that afternoon and met with the owner. Although she was working almost constantly, she was deeply committed to repaying loans to friends who had helped her, financially, and she was still chronically short of cash.

Fortunately, the owner accepted a small down payment and also agreed to extend a mortgage to her directly, without the intervention (or approval) of a bank. And although it needed a lot of work, Debbie now had a new home.

She hired her brother, Billy, to restore the cottage, a job that would take an entire year. Billy also shouldered the responsibility of looking after their mother, Minnie, visiting her almost every night.

In the early part of 1999, Debbie wanted to escape from her ongoing financial problems and recover from the ordeal of Las Vegas. As a means to that end, she invited both Carrie and her granddaughter, Billie Lourd, to fly with her to Honolulu for a vacation. It was during her sojourn there that she caught up with the events in Carrie's life and got to enjoy Billie.

Midway through their vacation, her brother called with an emergency. An ambulance had rushed Minnie to the hospital. There, after some examinations, doctors had informed her that she had only a few days to live. It was important that Debbie return at once.

En route back to L.A., Debbie sat with Billie and Carrie, dreading whatever awaited them when they got there.

By the time they reached the hospital, Minnie had slipped into a coma and was fading fast. Alongside her brother, Debbie sat at her bedside until an attendant came in to check her. The attendant then turned to the siblings and said, "Your mother is gone."

At Minnie's request, the funeral was simple: As a preacher, Todd conducted the service and Carrie read a passage from the Bible. Debbie invited two of the male members of her nightclub act, Steve Lane and Shelby Grime, to end the service with their rendition of "Nearer My God to Thee."

She told her remaining family, "Minnie had a rough, unsatisfying life. I wished Ray could have loved her more. Perhaps she'll find a better and more fulfilling life upstairs."

When a friend phoned Carrie to ask about the death of her grandmother, she said, "Ding Dong! The witch is dead!"

***

As she began a new chapter in the frequently shifting saga of her career, Carrie took on the daunting challenge of writing an all-new film script for TV. She did it with the understanding that, if she completed it to their satisfaction, it would be distributed by Sony Pictures Television. She dared to entitle it *These Old Broads.*

Its director, Matthew Diamond, speculated that "no over-the-hill actress in Hollywood would ever want to appear in this as such an obvious has-been." He went on to remind Carrie that when Bette Davis had referred to herself and Joan Crawford as "old broads," she was threatened with a lawsuit.

Undaunted, Carrie forged ahead with her script, even creating a character within it (Piper Grayson) that was earmarked for Debbie. Despite the project's unflattering title, she accepted the role.

Then, although Julie Andrews, Lauren Bacall, and June Allyson were also offered parts, an involvement by those "vintage" stars never got off the ground. Subsequently, the roles went to Shirley MacLaine (playing Kate Westbourne); Joan Collins (as Addie Holden); and Elizabeth Taylor. *[Cast as Beryl Mason, Taylor would play their wily, tough-talking Hollywood agent.]*

These Old Broads would mark the final film of Taylor's spectacular career. Sadly, since she was having severe pains in her back, she could only be filmed from a sitting position.

"Someone calculated that the four of us will set some sort of record," Debbie said. "Our combined ages are 269 years and our ex-husbands totaled sixteen."

Carrie's film script revolved around a TV executive, Gavin (as played by Nestor Carbonell), who hopes to reunite three Hollywood stars who had feuded throughout most of their lives. As it happens, their (fictional) 1960s musical, *Boy Crazy*, has been recently re-released to wide public acclaim, and Gavin wants to cash in on the nostalgia it generated. It's clear that none of the aging, battle-scarred movie stars can stand each other, but all of them need money, and all of them accept their assignments.

Author Graham Lord noted that in Carrie's script, she had the actresses poking fun at themselves for their new,

Resolving their feuds, celebrating life, strutting their stuff, and embracing their status as geriatrics in show-biz: Debbie (left), Joan Collins (center), and Shirley MacLaine.

567

real-life status as aging harridans. "Joan Collins plays a man-eating bitch who had a red-velvet swing and has undergone plastic surgery every few years."

"You tramp!" Debbie tells her at one point in the script. "No wonder they call you the British Open!"

"Shirley MacLaine," Lord wrote, "mocks her own wacky New Age beliefs and superstitions. Debbie Reynolds is her own goody-goody image, accusing Elizabeth Taylor of running off with her husband: That was forty-two years ago. And she amazed everyone by ordering that she be called Dame Elizabeth. In her role, she has a pet called Cleopatra. All of them should have been amusing fun, but the film turned out to be slow, dull, and completely humorless."

Carrie exploded in anger when she read that. *[The authors of this book disagree with Graham Lord's assessment: We thought* These Old Broads *was charming, ironic, self-satirizing, and a lot of fun.]*

Debbie's friendship with Elizabeth dated from their early days at MGM, when both of them were enrolled in the studio schoolhouse together. The friendship thrived throughout the respective courses of their early marriages, especially in the era when Debbie was wed to Eddie Fisher and Elizabeth to Mike Todd.

Their friendship had conspicuously cooled, however, after the death of Mike Todd. *[Eddie, of course, left Debbie in the wake of Mike's death and took up with Elizabeth].* But within a few years of that, Debbie and Elizabeth had reconciled.

She commented on her reunion with Elizabeth. "It was like the good old days at MGM, where we were just getting started—young and virginal—in life. At least I was virginal. I didn't think Elizabeth was. There were rumors of teenage sex between her and John Derek, Ronald Reagan, Peter Lawford, and God knows who else. Robert Taylor comes to mind."

"Along the way, she and I had known great sorrow and heartbreak. Gals like us pack a lot of living in between being delivered 'through the snatch' and going on valiantly until we face the final curtain."

"The first time we lunched together, we had this morbid talk about which of us would be the first to die," Debbie said. "Elizabeth predicted that it would be her because she was in almost constant pain and had already had a series of near-death experiences, each a real hospital emergency."

According to Elizabeth Taylor, "It was Carrie, my stepdaughter, who most wanted me to star in

In this publicity pic for *These Old Broads*, Debbie and Elizabeth made it abundantly clear to the world at large that the painful years of their involvement with Eddie Fisher had ended a long time ago.

These Old Broads. I'm doing it as a favor to her," Elizabeth said, "Even though my doctors warned me against appearing in another movie. But I don't think I'll expire before the shooting on this one is finished."

According to Debbie, "Yes, she stole my husband, but she's done a few noble things, too."

[Debbie might have been referring to the gold armor that Richard Burton had worn in Cleopatra *(1963). It had become available at auction, and although Debbie desperately wanted it for her museum, she was short of cash. She called Elizabeth and articulated how eager she was for a section of her museum to be specifically devoted to the filming of that epic movie.*

Elizabeth listened with empathy and, at the end of Debbie's talk, she said she'd send over a blank check.

At the auction, Debbie placed the highest bid ($16,000) and bought the armor.

When she called Elizabeth to thank her, the brunette star responded, "Don't mention it. I don't need any souvenirs from the making of that bloody film."]

The two ex-MGM stars arranged a few final visits before Elizabeth died. "My life has had so many startling tomorrows that I don't think they'll ever stop. But in my heart, I know they will. I'm so very sorry to have taken Eddie. Sorry about what I did to you and your kids."

Both of them lamented growing old, Debbie defining it as "so shitty."

"Truer words were never uttered," Elizabeth responded. "To think I was the youngest girl ever to arrive in Hollywood."

After working with her, Debbie told director Diamond, "That Elizabeth Taylor reached out and grabbed life by the balls."

***

On the set of *These Old Broads,* Debbie greeted Shirley MacLaine. Both stars had maintained their friendship despite their frequent rivalries. MacLaine had never quite gotten over the fact that because of a previous contract, she had not been free to make *The Unsinkable Molly Brown* way back in the mid-1960s.

Debbie never revealed to MacLaine something that Elizabeth had told her in confidence: "It was me who was first offered the starring role in *Irma la Douce* (1961), but I turned it down because I thought that Shirley could play a whore better than I could."

[Debbie didn't remind Elizabeth that after she'd played a prostitute in BUtterfield 8 *in 1960, she'd won a Best Actress Oscar.]*

When Debbie greeted MacLaine, the red-headed star told her, "You look fabulous, Debbie, dear. And after all the crap you've been through." Then MacLaine turned and looked into her dressing room mirror: "I'm a shipwreck, too, like that scene in *Postcards from the Edge* with no hair."

In her memoir, Debbie was kind, claiming that MacLaine was "still a beautiful vixen but her looks had matured…Let's face it: All of us will live up to my daughter's title for our movie."

When MacLaine eventually discussed the aging process with Debbie, her remarks paralleled what she'd previously written in a memoir: "It's hard for me to look in the mirror and confront all this sagging skin. It seems I'm deteriorating. A woman cannot control time and gravity. Even an older woman who continues to exercise can't escape from the time machine. My memory is going. Of course, there's a lot I'd like to forget. Right now, my attention span lasts for twenty seconds. It amazes me when fans see me as a whirling dervish of disciplined overachievement. In truth, I prefer to do nothing. Fundamentally, I'm lazy. My body has served me like a workhorse, and I hate to see it go. But I'm not ready to be put out to pasture, at least not yet."

"You know, that whoring bitch, Joan Collins, is coming onto the set today," MacLaine said to Debbie. "She once had a torrid affair with my little brother [*Warren Beatty*]. I always wondered what it would be like to get fucked by Warren. Perhaps a director will cast us as lovers in a film one day, and at least I'll find out what kind of kisser he is."

***

In preparation for their upcoming work together in *These Old Broads,* Debbie arranged for a reunion with Joan Collins. She found her "still a glamour-puss and in great shape. She was the best preserved of all of us, doing a hundred situps every day."

"I'm not exactly looking forward to working with Miss Taylor," Collins said. "You may not know this, but originally, I was tapped to star in *Cleopatra,* but Skouras and the other brass at Fox decided I was not famous enough to carry the picture as Queen of the Nile."

"I heard at the time that Sophia Loren and Gina Lollobrigida were also in the running for the part," Debbie said, then continuing, cattily, "And so was Audrey Hepburn during the period they thought about starring her. Unlike Sophia and Gina, Audrey certainly wasn't going to be signed for her breasts. Imagine that! A no-tit Cleo!"

"It seems I'm always meeting women who went to bed with my all-time crush, Robert Wagner," Debbie said. "I heard rumors that Joan (Collins) seduced him in 1957 when they co-starred in *Stopover Tokyo*. She was rumored to have seduced Harry Belafonte when they made *Islands in the Sun,* also in 1957. It seems that Marlon Brando and Ryan O'Neal have crawled between her bedsheets, too. And although all three of us got up close and personal with Nicky Hilton, Elizabeth actually *married* him! At least Joan and I had better sense than *that*!"

"I'm fully aware that I have a certain reputation...," Collins said. "But I was a virgin until I lost it on my first date with Maxwell Reed, my first husband. He drugged me, and I passed out. When I regained consciousness, he was trying to push this strange, soft object into my mouth. He once tried to make me go to bed with this rich Arab oil sheik, who was offering £10,000 for one night with me. I divorced Maxwell after that."

"I always wanted to ask Joan something but never had the nerve," Debbie said. "My question would have been, 'Have you ever fucked Eddie Fisher?'"

***

On February 12, 2001, Debbie, vodka in hand, sat at her television, watching the premiere of *These Old Broads*.

Her verdict at the end of her screening?

"Time is running out for Elizabeth, Joan, Shirley…and me."

***

During the first decade of the 21st Century, Carrie worked steadily, not only appearing in an array of films, but also working as a script doctor on several movies. Directors told her, "You have a clever way with dialogue."

She wrote an original script for a TV pilot, *Esme's Little Secret,* hoping it would morph into a series. Throughout its 30-minute playing time, Andrea Martin remained in a hospital bed, her plight being relayed in the form of a voice-over narration. Debbie played Andrea's mother, holding vigil at her bedside.

In an appraisal of her daughter's efforts, Debbie said, "CBS didn't go for it. I think Carrie's plot was too advanced for its time."

The first film in which Carrie appeared in the new century was *Scream 3* (2000), a slasher movie—the third installment of the *Scream* franchise—that became a worldwide hit, grossing $162 million. Director Wes Craven offered her the minor role of an actress, Bianca Burnette, who quickly gets embroiled in the terror of its context. During its shoot, Carrie "polished" the dialogue she'd been assigned.

Plagued with production problems and last-minute revisions to the script, its stars included David Arquette, Neve Campbell, Patrick Dempsey, and Scott Foley.

Rotten Tomatoes claimed that "the movie has become what it originally spoofed. It seems to have lost its freshness and originality, falling back on the old horror formulas and *clichés*."

***

That same year, Carrie made a cameo appearance in *Lisa Picard is Famous* (2000), a comedy-drama starring Laura Kirk, Nat DeWolf, and Griffin Dunne, who also directed it. It tells the story of Lisa Picard (Kirk), an actress on the

571

verge of stardom.

First shown at the Cannes Film Festival, it was noted for the number of famous actors appearing in cameos: Spike Lee, Charlie Sheen, Buck Henry, Sandra Bullock, and, of course, Carrie.

***

Carrie made two films in 2001, beginning with *Heartbreakers,* a caper-romantic comedy about the elaborate con jobs perpetrated by a mother-daughter team who specialize in swindling men who respond to their sexual and emotional charms. It had a difficult time getting off the launching pad, with many combinations of well-known actresses agreeing, and then retreating, from an involvement in its production. It was eventually cast with Sigourney Weaver and Jennifer Love Hewitt as the mother and daughter (Max and Page), respectively, and Ray Liotta and Gene Hackman as men they eventually dupe with varying degrees of success and some surprising counter-plots and side cons.

One of the three or four scams they perpetrate include a conspiracy for Max to marry a rich man, and then arrange for her scantily clad daughter to seduce him, thereby establishing a motive for divorce and the ensuing settlement. Carrie was cast as Mrs. Surpin, Max's hard-hearted divorce lawyer.

Anne Bancroft makes a surprise appearance as Gloria (aka Barbara), a perpetrator in the film of a hoax-within-a-con. The film went on to gross almost $60 million worldwide. Its reviews were mixed but mostly favorable, *The New York Times* asserting, "At a time when most comedies go for your wallet, a kick in the groin, and a blackjack to the base of the head, this one delivers."

***

"What, me? Play a nun?" Carrie asked Kevin Smith, the director of *Jay and Silent Bob Strike Back* (2001). "Who do you think I am? Debbie Reynolds?"

Its stars included Jason Mewes and Kevin Smith, with several actors making cameos, including Ben Affleck, Will Ferrell, Chris Rock, Matt Damon, and Carrie's *Star Wars* co-star, Mark Hamill, cast as "Cocknocker."

Smith later complained that its star, Mewes, hampered production with drug and alcohol abuse, "He was a fucking time bomb."

When Carrie heard this, she said, "Been there, done that."

Receiving mixed reviews, the movie

Carrie was amused when the director, Kevin Smith, asked her to play a nun in *Jay and Silent Bob Strike Back*, released in 2001.

"Type casting, I'd say," she said, jokingly.

made $35 million at the box office, on a budget of $22 million. *Empire* wrote, "When it's good, it's very, very good, but when it's bad, it's offensive." *The New York Times* found it "the greatest picture ever made for 14-year-olds."

The title and its logo are direct references to *The Empire Strikes Back,* in which Carrie had been cast as Princess Leia.

***

Carrie moved into 2002 by accepting a minor role in *A Midsummer's Night Rave.* It transposes Shakespeare's *A Midsummer Night's Dream* into modern rave culture. *[In this instance,* Rave *is a reference to a large dance party with a seamless flow of loud electronic dance music and a consumption of drugs—especially Ecstasy— by most of the participants. In this film, it's made clear that the recreational drug of choice is "a green-glowing drug provided by a British mystic."]*

One critic suggested that "Whereas the love drug is not needed to view this film, cynics in the audience will find that it helps."

Its director, Gil Gates, Jr., assembled a cast that included Corey Pearson, Lauren German, Andrew Keegan, Chad Lindberg, and Sunny Mabrey. Cast in fifth billing, Carrie plays Mabrey's mother.

Many of the actors had previously starred in popular movies for young audiences. The plot involves a drug dealer (modeled on Shakespeare's character of Shylock); stolen drug money; an actor (Nick Bottom in a donkey costume at a daycare center); and a liberated lesbian, Elena, played by Lauren German in the lead female role.

One reviewer wrote: "It ain't Laurence Olivier or John Gielgud, not even Orson Welles."

R.S. White in Shakespeare's *Cinema of Love,* cited *A Midsummer's Night Rave* as a "conscious pastiche of Shakespeare's plays, showing irrational events caused by consciousness-altering drugs and the air of psychedelic fantasy created by a musical rave party."

***

Carrie phoned Debbie one morning when she was feeling provocative. "Guess what, mom? I'm going to make my first porn flick. Its plot involves John C. Holmes."

"Who is he, dear?" Debbie asked. "Never heard of him. I always preferred

Despite the youth-oriented, radical nature of the films she appeared in (in this case, *A Midsummer Night's Rave*), it was increasingly obvious that Carrie was aging.

573

the real thing to porn."

"John C. Holmes, sometimes billed as Johnny Wadd, is still the biggest porn star in America in terms of rentals. He's known for his 13 ½ -inch *schlong*."

"Are you sure you can take it, dear?" Debbie asked.

Her mother was just too cool for her, not raising one objection about her upcoming appearance in a porn movie.

"Holmes died of AIDS in 1988," Carrie said. "Val Kilmer is going to play him in our movie, *Wonderland* (2003). It's going to be directed by James Cox.

"Did Mr. Cox audition Val to make sure he measures up?"

"Val doesn't have to show his dick. Get real, mother."

The movie was based on the notorious Wonderland murders which had been committed in Los Angeles in 1981. They were the most grisly since the Charles Manson gang had massacred Sharon Tate and her friends in 1969.

Holmes had been one of the suspects in the ghastly multiple murders at the home of Eddie Nash. Carrie was cast as Sally Hansen, a screwed-up member of "The Wonderland Gang." The other actors included Kate Bosworth, Dylan McDermott, Lisa Kudrow, and Josh Lucas, with Paris Hilton aptly cast as "Barbie."

Trading on her ability to look dull, "normal," ordinary, and respectable: Carrie Fisher as she appeared in *Wonderland*.

The film grossed $5.5 million on a budget of $2.5 million. Reviews were mostly negative, Roger Ebert writing, "True crime can have a certain fascination, but not when they're jumbled glimpses of what might or might not have happened involving a lot of empty people whose main claim to fame is that they're dead."

***

"My good friend, Penny Marshall, and I found ourselves playing minor roles in a real dud of a movie," Carrie said. She was referring to *Stateside*, a romantic drama released in 2004 and based on a true story.

Reverge Anselmo directed a cast that starred Rachael Leigh Cook, Jonathan Tucker, Agnes Bruckner, Val Kilmer (no longer a porn star as he'd been in Carrie's previous movie), Joe Mantegna, Diane Venora, and Ed Begley, Jr.

The director, himself a former Marine, also wrote the script, which depicts and actress/singer with undiagnosed schizophrenia, Dorri Lawrence (as portrayed by Cook). Despite her many shortcomings, Mark Deloach (Tucker), the son of a wealthy family who's attending a Catholic School, falls in love with her.

Underage drinking leads to a car accident involving Sue Dubois (Bruckner). Her mother (Carrie) wants to bring charges against Mark, but in lieu of legal retribution, a deal is made allowing him to sign up for the U.S. Marine Corps instead.

On leave from his military service, Mark loses his virginity to Dorri. Her mental condition worsens, and she begins to lose touch with reality.

Now a Marine who has earned the respect of his tough and demanding platoon leader, Mark is sent to Lebanon, where he is injured in the bombing of the Marine barracks in Beirut in 1983.

A lot of other complications follow, and Mark ends up back in the States in a hospital bed. There, Dorri visits him as he recovers from his wounds. She's better now: they marry as a new life unfolds for them.

Stateside was a miserable failure at the box office, generating a negative response from critics and grossing only $115,000 in a nationwide release.

***

Opposite Kip Purdue, Carrie had the second lead, portraying a character also named Carrie in her newest movie, *Undiscovered* (2005). Its original title, *Wannabe*, might have been more apt, as it's the story of artists with big dreams of making it in an industry noted for its frauds, casting couches, and elusive fame.

A New York model, Brier (Pell James), flies to Los Angeles, trying to break into the movies. She wins the support of her agent (Carrie, playing Carrie) who becomes her surrogate mom. Carrie adds a certain panache to the film.

Brier meets Luke Falcon (Steven Strait), and the pair fall in love. Before the end of the film, they learn that fame carries a high price. Ashlee Simpson appears in a supporting role, singing two ballads, but she's not much of an actress. Kip Purdue does a good job as Luke's wacky brother. Most viewers agreed that Strait, as Luke Falcon, is very good looking.

***

In *Suffering Man's Charity* (2007), also known as *Ghost Writer,* Carrie had only a small role as an unnamed reporter. Alan Cumming, the picture's star and also its director, cast himself as John Vandermark, an eccentric music teacher. He takes in a struggling young writer, David Borananz, cast as Sebastian St. Germain.

John becomes erotically attracted to the young man and grows jealous when he starts to date women. In supporting female leads were Anne Heche and Karen Black.

John and Sebastian get into a fight, which leads to the younger man's accidental death. After the funeral, John discovers that he has completed the manuscript of a

Convincingly aging and convincingly predatory: Carrie Fisher as a cougar in *Cougar Club*.

book which has never been submitted for advance review or for publication. John decides to have Sebastian's book published under his own name. As expected, complications ensue.

***

On a budget of $2 million, producer and director Christopher Duddy pulled together a movie called *Cougar Club* (2007). Carrie, as an older college professor, Gladys Goodbey, is one of the cougars. Faye Dunaway, in a thankless role, is another cougar on the make for a young man who is married.

Two buddies, Marshall Hogan II (Warren Kole) and Spence Holmes (Jason Jurman), work for abusive divorce lawyers. They come up with a plan to make money by having sex with cougars [*in this context, sometimes predatory older women with a preference for younger men*].

Joe Mantegna, cast as Mr. Stack, portrays the most evil and malicious divorce lawyer in town.

Scenes include Hogan walking in on Spence having anal sex with the office's older secretary. In another scene, he's humiliated by having to cut one of the evil lawyer's dirty toenails.

The young men exact revenge on their mean bosses by sleeping with their wives, especially the one who is "lusty and busty." They are later arrested for pandering, but in a surprise ending, all ends well when Spence seduces the judge [*who, it's revealed, is also a cougar*] in her chambers, and she acquits both Hogan and Spencer of their crime.

***

Director, producer, and writer Diane English worked for fifteen years to craft and organize a remake of George Cukor's classic movie, *The Women*

(1939), a drama that eventually got released in 2008. The original featured an all-star and all-female cast: Norma Shearer, Joan Crawford (in one of her best roles), Rosalind Russell, Joan Fontaine, Paulette Goddard, even Ma Kettle (Marjorie Main) and Prissy (Butterfly McQueen), a refugee from *Gone With the Wind* (1939).

In the original script by Claire Boothe Luce, the women were mainly idle socialites thriving on afternoon cocktails and gossip. But English wanted to update the script, defining its women as career players in such fields as publishing and fashion design. To make it even more modern, she wrote in a lesbian character, Alex Fisher (Jada Pinkett Smith).

As in the original, there are no males represented in the cast, even in crowd scenes—that is, until the end, when a baby boy is born.

In 1994, Julia Roberts and Meg Ryan showed keen interest in the two lead roles, but both actresses wanted the same part, and the deal fell through. However, when *The Women* was eventually re-adapted for a newer version in the 21st Century, Ryan was assigned the leading role.

As time went by, other actresses wanted to sign on, too, including Sandra Bullock, Ashley Judd, and Uma Thurman. Whitney Houston and Queen Latifah expressed interest too as novel casting choices.

Although every major studio in Hollywood rejected it, their interest was revived after HBO's sitcom, *Sex and the City* (1998-2004), morphed into a major hit.

Finally, Diane English (its producer) found a co-producer in Mick Jagger, through his company, Jagged Films. In the updated version's final casting, Carrie emerged in the role of a gossip columnist, Bailey Smith, drawing her inspiration from Louella Parsons and Hedda Hopper.

English cast the leading roles with Meg Ryan, Annette Benning, Eva Mendes, and Debra Messing, with minor appearances by Cloris Leachman, Debi Mazar, Bette Midler, and Candice Bergen.

The film ends on an upbeat note, *The Women* talking about the "joys, heartaches, and unique trimphs of being a woman."

On a budget of $16 million, the movie, released after many setbacks in 2008, grossed

Carrie appeared as a gossip maven in the remake of the classic, *The Women.*

"I'm afraid all of us gals found Joan Crawford, Norma Shearer, Rosalind Russell, *et al.*, a tough act to follow."

577

$50 million at the box office.

For the most part, critics came down hard on the remake. Roger Ebert of the *Chicago Sun-Times* found it "well-crafted, well-written, and well-acted," but A.O. Scott of *The New York Times* attacked it as a "catfighter of a movie wandering and wallowing."

The youth-oriented *Rolling Stone* magazine was not impressed. "It is a misbegotten redo and a major dud, struggling with a script that resists being crowbarred into the 21st Century." Film historian Richard Schickel of *Time* magazine called it "one of the worst movies I've ever seen."

As a "reward" for their involvements, Meg Ryan, Annette Benning, Eva Mendes, Debra Messing, and Jada Pinkett Smith each were nominated for a Razzie, losing to Paris Hilton for her dismally critiqued satire of the dating scene, *The Hottie and the Nottie* (2008).

***

White Lightin' (2009) was one of the most bizarre films Carrie ever made. Directed by Dominic Murphy, it was inspired by the life story of Jesco White, a mentally challenged Appalachian mountain dancer born "on the white, trashy side of town." First shown at the Sundance Film Festival, it starred British actor, Edward Hogg, as the hillbilly protagonist, Jesco. He was known as "The Dancing Outlaw," which some film-goers thought would have made a better title.

Jesco had led a troubled life, beginning as a kid when he got high by sniffing gasoline, glue, lighter fluid, and airplane cement. He ended up in a reform school, but, once released, continued to find himself in trouble with the law. Appalachian dancing became a way "to keep me from losing my soul," he said. The movie has Jesco being shuttled between prisons and mental institutions, usually as a nut case. "I started to destroy my brain cells at an early age," he says.

In this dark, quirky film, Carrie plays the (perhaps incestuous) love of his life with a certain subtlety. As one critic phrased it, "Like everyone else in the movie, she hasn't much sense, but her seeing something in Jesco is the only humanity the movie gives him."

The relentlessly grim plot is permeated with brutality, torture, self-mutilation, and murder. Eventually Jesco encounters God and cuts and chops himself with a hatchet until he dies to expiate himself of his sins.

Carrie as a self-destructive Appalachian dysfunctional in *White Lightnin'.*

"The slash-and-burn reviews killed us."

The critics were harsh in their assaults on the film, one reviewer writing, "Why anyone wants to lavish real talent on such a pathetic character is a sick joke."

Another critic claimed, "The director can't get enough of the exoticism of Appalachian trailer park trash. He fixates on gross-out moments—an insane man defecates on the floor, and Jesco makes body tattoos with sharp objects that play like money shots in a porno."

***

Carrie's next film for 2009, her second released that year, was oddly linked to the fame she had derived as Princess Leia. It was *Fanboys,* a zany action/adventure/coming of age film in which she had only a minor role, that of a character identified as "The Doctor." Directed by Kyle Newman, *Fanboys* starred a host of minor actors, including Sam Huntington, Chris Marquette, Dan Fogler, Jay Baruchel, and Kristen Bell.

Some viewers interpreted it as a film deliberately aimed at *Star Wars* fans by other *Star Wars* fans. Eric Bottler (Huntington) reunites with his old high school buddies, including one known as "Windows" (Baruchel). To his dismay, he learns that they have not matured or grown emotionally in any significant way since their time together as teenagers. The only thing the old gang has in common is their devotion to movies in the *Star Wars* franchise.

According to the plot, the latest film in that series, *The Phantom Menace,* has been completed, and although it hasn't yet been made available for general release, a rough cut of the film is being safeguarded within the Skywalker Ranch. They therefore embark on a zany quest to infiltrate the property and steal a copy for an advance preview.

En route to the Skywalker Ranch, the young men stumble into a biker bar. One orders only a glass of water, but is hit with a $100 tab. Since they can't pay it, they are ordered to provide some "midnight entertainment."

Hutch strips to the music of Menudo, which goes terribly wrong when he displays what viewers come to understand as one of his physical quirks: He has only one testicle. Before they're beat up by the drunk and hostile audience, they're saved by a man named "The Chief," who fixes their van after they pass out from eating guacamole laced with peyote. Billy Dee Williams plays a judge who presides over their moment in court. Along the way, they meet up with *Star Trek* heavyweight William Shatner. Seth Rogan played an angry pimp (Roach), who tangles with the boys for an unpaid "escort bill."'

One of them is injured and is taken to a hospital where Carrie, a doctor, warns him to return home for the sake of his health.

Nonetheless, seemingly obsessed by their fixation on *Star Wars,* they continue their obsessive pilgrimage to the Skywalker Ranch and break in. Then they're apprehended by security guards.

At last, in an anticlimactic fulfillment of their adolescent dreams, the boys get to see the latest installment in the *Star Wars* franchise, which is screened for them after all they trouble they've caused to see it.

George Lucas was shown a rough cut of *Fanboys.* Perhaps interpreting it as beneficial for the future sales of his franchise, he bestowed upon it his stamp of approval. He even offered the filmmakers free use of the sound effects in the original *Star Wars* for use in future edits of the film. Having been budgeted at $4 million, the movie made only a million at the box office.

Rotten Tomatoes found it "a sop to *Star Wars* fanatics, but the uninitiated will find little to enjoy. Ben Mankiewicz claimed, "It devolves into nothing more than a silly road trip movie."

***

Carrie's third and final movie for 2009, *Sorority Row,* directed by Stewart Hendler, was another of those blood-soaked, sexually teasing slasher movies. It starred Briana Evigan, Leah Pipes, Rumer Willis, and Jamie Chung. As the mother of a sorority house, Carrie had only a minor role as "Mrs. Crenshaw."

Its plot focuses on a group of sorority sisters who—after covering up the accidental death of one of their sisters—are stalked and murdered on the night of their graduation.

When Carrie learns that the girls are being pursued, she orders them to lock themselves into their bedrooms while she calls the police. Then, as she attempts to re-load her shotgun, she is brutally massacred by a hooded figure.

Reviews were mostly negative, *Rotten Tomatoes* evaluating it as "slick and stylish but offering nothing new in the slasher genre and missing the mark in its attempts at humor and thrills."

Nevertheless, on a $12.5 million budget, the film took in a respectable $27 million at the box office.

***

Throughout the early part of the 21st Century, Carrie was one of the top "script doctors" in Hollywood, polishing the dialogues for George Lucas' 1992 TV series, *The Young Indiana Jones Chronicles* and the dialogue for the *Star Wars* prequel scripts.

Carrie also "voiced" the speech patterns of Peter Griffin's boss, Angela, on the animated sitcom *Family Guy*. *[One of the most durable TV sitcoms in enter-tainment history and broadcast on the Fox TV Network with many media tie-ins, it originated in 1999. In October of 2017, it inaugurated its 16ᵗʰ season.]*

In addition to these "off camera" career statements, her novel, *The Best Awful,* was published in 2001.

From 2006 to January 2007, she wrote and performed in her one-woman play, *Wishful Drinking*, during its staging at the Geffen Playhouse in Los Ange-les. After its run there, she transferred it to other towns that included Berkeley, San Jose, and Boston. Her autobiographical book, *Wishful Drinking* was re-leased in 2008.

In 2000, she appeared as herself in an episode of *Sex and the City* starring Sarah Jessica Parker, and in 2007, she was cast in the fourth episode *[it was en-titled "Rosemary's Baby"]* of the second season of *30 Rock*. She also made a cameo appearance as Princess Leia in an episode *[entitled Star Wars Episode II)* that was aired in 2008 within the TV series known as *Robot Chicken*.

She also starred as Edwina in the TV film, *Romancing the Bridge* (2005), and she played herself in the TV documentary *Bring Back...Star Wars* (2008).

***

Debbie continued to take her stage shows on the road, performing at least forty weeks a year touring through city after city. Despite her age, she held up reasonably well, although fatigue set in earlier and more frequently.

Unlike Carrie's thriving career in one or another aspect of the entertain-ment industry, Debbie's was sputtering to its conclusion. In the first decade of the 21ˢᵗ Century, she appeared in only two films, *Connie and Carla* (2004) and—only as a voice-cover— *Light of Olympia.*

Connie and Carla, which featured a corps of drag queens, was an offbeat comedy shot mainly in Vancouver. Michael Lembeck directed it, and Tom Hanks was one of its co-producers.

Nia Vardalos wrote the screenplay and also starred in it. Of Greek descent, the Canadian-American actress was best known for her 2002 movie, *My Big Fat Greek Wedding*, a film about a woman's struggle to find love. In supporting roles were Toni Collette and David Duchovny. Connie falls for him in his role of Jeff, the straight brother of Robert (Stephen Spinella), one of their drag queen friends.

Connie and Carla seemed inspired by Marilyn Monroe's 1959 classic, *Some Like It Hot*, in which Tony Curtis and Jack Lemmon played drag queens. Connie and Carla, each a biological female, are performers who dream of stardom in musical theater. For the moment, at least, they're resigned to their status as players in an airport lounge act as a means of earning some money for food and rent. In the Chicago airport, they are witnesses to a Mafia hit and go on the run, fleeing the killers. They end up in Los Angeles, where they decide to conceal themselves as men in drag, finding work in a gay club, The Handlebar. Eventually, they emerge as stars on the drag queen circuit. Everything eventually devolves into a roundelay of mistaken identities configured into a drag show spoof.

On opening night at the dinner theater where they're performing, killers from the mob appear and face bedlam. The drag queens prevail during the scratching and clawing fistfights that ensue, and Connie and Carla reveal their true identities to the (wildly applauding) audience.

After the film's director, Limbeck, complimented Debbie on her performance, she quipped, "Actually, I flubbed one of my lines twenty times. The line was, 'I've got the sheet music, gorgeous gowns, and a great underwire bra.' But every time I said that, the word 'sheet' came out as 'shit.'"

***

"I've always had glorious feelings about voice overs," Debbie said. "Remember *Singin' in the Rain?* In 2007, I was hired as the voice of 'Queen' in the animated feature *Light of Olympia* (2008). The businesspeople behind it, Santoon Productions, also hired Joey D'Auria, Phyllis Diller, and Tom Gibbs for the other roles."

Outside the recording studio, Debbie had a reunion with Phyllis Diller. "I loved her exaggerated laugh and her self-deprecating humor. She showed up for work looking like a drag queen. I accused her of being a refugee from *Connie and Carla.* Like me, Phyllis has a large gay following, men who appreciate her campy humor."

Another of the voice-over actors was Joey D'Auria, cast in a leading role as the Witch Doctor. According to Debbie, "This New York native had a long gig on TV as Bozo and was known for his improvisational skills."

As she aged, Debbie worked more frequently on TV than in major-release films. One widely touted appearance was as "Aggie" Cromwell in the made-for-TV movie *Halloweentown*, released in 1998. In 2000, she starred as Gwen in *Virtual Mom*, and in 2002, she had a role in another made-for-TV movie, *Generation Gap.*

"I ended up wondering if I'd ever appear in a feature film again," Debbie said. "For me, the leaves of autumn were falling, the fires of September had already burned out. Surely, if you're gay, you've already seen Joan Crawford emote in *Autumn Leaves* (1956), where Joan is lusting after a handsome younger man, Cliff Robertson, who once made a nether region of mine tingle."

"I was moving toward December," Debbie continued, "but I wanted to keep performing until the final curtain."

***

In 2002, the British singer-songwriter, James Blunt, flew into Los Angeles to record his first album, *Back to Bedlam,* which was released the following year. He met Carrie at a party at the home of its producer, Tom Rockroth.

Blunt was immediately attracted to her wit and charm, and she found him "manly, sexy, handsome, and appealing, although troubled."

Their time together was so successful that she invited him to check out of his hotel and come and stay with her, as a guest in her home, during his stopover on the West Coast.

At first, he must have assumed that this was a transparent attempt at seduction, but that did not turn out to be the case, even after she made her guest bedroom fully available to him.

He was eighteen years younger than her, but they seemed to speak the same language and understood each other's references in spite of the differences in their backgrounds.

Blunt had been born into a military family, his father having been a cavalry officer in the Royal Hussars. Blunt himself had become a captain and reconnaissance officer in the Life Guards, a cavalry regiment of the British Army, serving under NATO command during the Kosovo War of 1990. In April of 2002, after the death of Queen Elizabeth the Queen Mother, Blunt stood guard at her coffin and marched in her funeral procession.

During his 2002 sojourn in Los Angles, the singer spent his daylight hours recording at Rothrock's studio, but his nights were spent with Carrie in her home. Her two favorite songs from his upcoming album included "Goodbye My Lover," and "You're Beautiful." The album would sell eleven million copies. Carrie herself suggested a name for the album, *Back to Bedlam.*

In 2005, Blunt appeared on *The Oprah Winfrey Show,* and also as a guest on *Saturday Night Live* that same year as one of his songs was featured in Carrie's movie, *Undiscovered* (2005).

Her fans wanted to know if Princess Leia was ever sexually intimate with the charismatic young singer. She denied it, saying, "I was his therapist, and it's wrong for a therapist to sleep with her patient."

***

When a break came for Debbie in September of 2001, she flew to New York to attend a Michael Jackson concert at Madison Square Garden. She'd read in the papers that his close friend, Elizabeth Taylor, would be there to honor his 30th year in show business.

She didn't know or understand him like Eliza-

Recording artist James Blunt was a "sleepover" at Carrie's home.

"He was a delight, a real charmer, but he never invaded my bedroom—not even to rape me."

beth did, having only met him casually when he'd rented her DR Studio to rehearse for the videos associated with his release of "Thriller" and "Beat It!."

She didn't have a date for the gala event. The concert was going to be shown on television, and she'd heard that Elizabeth would deliver a brief speech. She hadn't seen her since "she'd gone blonde."

At Madison Square Garden, Debbie was seated a few seats away from Elizabeth and her entourage. It included the young blonde-haired actor, Macaulay Caulkin. Rumors had been circulating that Jackson liked young boys around and was—although she didn't believe it—in love with Caulkin.

"Guess who? It's me, Tammy. I'm still here!"

"File that with rumors that I'm a lesbian," she said to Tim Mendelson, Elizabeth's assistant, who got her a seat in the garden at the last minute.

Madison Square was packed that night, and she was a little embarrassed to be appearing there alone, without an escort. "After all, I could have called an escort service. Big stars such as Marlene Dietrich and Lana Turner had done as much when they got older, but it didn't seem right for me."

That night at the concert, Jackson family performed both alongside and separately from Michael, and collectively, they met with roaring approval from his worshipful fans.

"Elizabeth spotted me, and I waved to her," Debbie said. "Mendelson delivered a message to me that she was staying at The Pierre and wanted me to phone her and come by."

At the end of Jackson's performance, Debbie had hoped that the singer would invite her to a gathering he was sponsoring to honor Elizabeth. But no invitation was forthcoming.

In was the night of September 10, 2001, and feeling a bit lonely, she returned to her hotel alone, as the following day would be busy, three separate interviews having been scheduled.

Beside her bed was a phone and a notepad. She wrote down some points she wanted to make during the morning's interviews and then, at the top of the notepad, she scribbled the date: It was "9/11."

Chapter Twenty

BRIGHT LIGHTS
BEHIND THE CANDELABRA

As Liberace's Destructive Mother, "Tammy the Terrible" Plays a Haranguing Shrew.

THE END OF A DREAM

Debbie's Cherished Plans for a Hollywood Museum Hit an Iceberg and Sink. "Molly Survives" by Selling Its Components at Auction.

Marilyn Monroe's Dress from *The Seven Year Itch* Sells for $5.2 Million.

CARRIE PROFITS
From Her Status as a *Star Wars* Icon

WRAPPING THINGS UP
BEFORE THE BITTER END
Shuffling Along with Eddie Fisher, Michael Jackson, & Elizabeth Taylor

In her last feature film role, *Behind the Candelabra,* Debbie (left photo) was cast as the mother of Liberace. "That her son, the flamboyant Liberace, could have emerged from the loins of this archly conservative Polish farm girl staggers the imagination," she said.

As she aged, and as the *Star Wars* franchise moved forward with new installations and updates, Carrie Fisher (right photo) morphed from Princess Leia into General Leia.

Although at dawn on Tuesday, September 11, 2001,

New York City awakened as it would on most other days, within a few hours of sunrise, a living, screaming hell broke loose.

Whereas then-President Franklin D. Roosevelt had defined the Japanese attack on Pearl Harbor "a date that will live in infamy" (December 7, 1941), New Yorkers now faced their own date of infamy, referring ever after to September 11 by its abbreviated code letters "9/11."

From the relative safety of her midtown hotel suite, where she was in bed, Debbie woke up to the smell of something burning, fearing at first that the building was on fire. She immediately phoned the front desk and got a young male clerk who had just reported for his shift. In the background, she heard a TV broadcasting with the volume turned up loud.

He answered her concerns with a shaky voice: "A plane has crashed into a building in Lower Manhattan. I suggest you stay in your room until further notice. Our hotel doesn't appear to be in danger. We're far from the scene of this disaster."

She wasn't reassured. She jumped up and switched on her own TV to learn that Manhattan had been attacked by what was believed to be radical terrorists. As she continued to watch her TV, new footage revealed a second plane crashing into yet another Twin Tower at the World Trade Center. Fascinated and horrified, she remained glued to her TV in time to see both buildings collapse.

She tried switching to other channels for more information, but only one came on, presumably because the transmitters for the other networks had been destroyed. The news that followed was almost unbelievable: There were frenzied reports of a commercial jet that, from high above the nation's capital, had crashed into the Pentagon.

Then there was news of yet another plane that had crashed into a field near Shanksville, Pennsylvania. A few brave passengers had stormed the cockpit and diverted the plane away from its intended crash site, The White House.

Relatives and friends across

Debbie was in Manhattan as the World Trade Center was attacked by suicidal terrorists in control of highjacked commercial planes.

"As I slept, the whole country had gone crazy, showing how a few psychos could bring the most powerful country in the world to its knees. Everything was disrupted."

the country were posting messages and photos, frantically seeking information about their loved ones. She would try to get through to Carrie and Todd to let them know she was all right.

"The war had come to America, and in another awful decision on my part, I had flown to New York to attend a Michael Jackson concert. I think I'll entitle my next memoir *My Foolish Heart.* Remember that Susan Hayward picture from 1949?"

As she was trying to reach Todd and Carrie, her phone rang. It was from Tim Mendelson, Elizabeth Taylor's trusty, hard-working personal assistant who had procured for Debbie a seat the previous evening at the Michael Jackson concert.

[That's where and when Elizabeth had been alerted to Debbie's presence in Manhattan.]

"Miss Taylor is concerned about you," he said. "She understands that you're in the city alone."

"That I am," she said. "I'm also scared shitless. How is Elizabeth? Is she okay?"

"She's horrified about what's happening, and in tears in front of her TV," he answered. "She wants you to pack up and come join her at The Pierre, where she has an extra room available within her suite. All her children were safely back in California before any of this happened."

"That's an offer I accept," she said. "I don't want to be alone at a time like this. Has Elizabeth heard from Michael Jackson?"

"She learned that he and his family rented a private bus and are headed back to California," he told her.

Packing her two suitcases hurriedly, Debbie persuaded a taxi to take her through the ashen streets of Manhattan to The Pierre, at the corner of 5th Avenue at 61st Street. Elizabeth was waiting for her, in her suite, with outstretched arms. "Do you think this is the beginning of World War III?" she asked.

"I hope not," Debbie answered. Then she joined Elizabeth, who was still in tears, in front of the TV set. Debbie saw that instead of facing the surging flames inside each of the Twin Towers, some of their occupants had opted for (perhaps) less painful deaths by jumping through the shattered glass of the windows to their deaths hundreds of feet below.

Suffering from yet another attack of her persistent spinal pain, Elizabeth was enduring both mental and physical anguish, enough so that she had employed a full-time doctor to look after her and to administer painkillers. She had also hired an around-the-clock masseur. Despite her anguish, she appeared perfectly groomed. *[She had imported her personal hair stylist too.]*

A French butler from Amiens (France) served breakfast. Both of the movie stars preferred only black coffee and unbuttered toast. The other guests in the room sat in front of folding trays positioned in front of the TV.

After a while, Debbie retreated to her bedroom, where she tried to get calls through to her son and daughter. She reached Carrie first to tell her that she was with Elizabeth at The Pierre. She begged her to contact Todd, who might be asleep at this hour, not knowing that Manhattan and Washington had been attacked.

During her time at The Pierre, Debbie learned that calls coming in specifically for Elizabeth tied up the switchboard, as her friends and reporters wanted to know if she were all right. There was a rumor that Jackson had rented a limousine for her, and they both were making their way to California by car.

"With all this news coming out, the world was hardly concerned with the whereabouts of one *little ol'* Debbie Reynolds."

She explained to Elizabeth that she'd been scheduled to appear in Escondido as the focal point of a sold-out matinee of her one-woman show. She heard that planes across the Northeast had been grounded, and she didn't know what to do.

"I do," Elizabeth said before being wheeled into her bedroom. There, she placed a call to Senator John Warner of Virginia. Although she had divorced him, they had remained on good terms—or at least had remained reasonable.

Elizabeth returned to the living room to inform her that the senator could arrange a flight for them that would depart early on Saturday morning. "If all goes well, you can make it in time to your performance in Escondido, wherever in the hell that is."

"It's near San Diego," Debbie responded. "I'll be so grateful to you and the senator. It sure comes in handy to have been married to such a powerful man."

Rising early, Elizabeth and Debbie departed from the hotel, embarking with members of Elizabeth's entourage in two limousines headed for the Teterboro Airport

[Teterboro is owned and managed by the Port Authority of New York and New Jersey and positioned in the New Jersey Meadowlands, 12 miles from Midtown Manhattan. Because it was designed for aircraft weighing less than 100,000 pounds, it services mostly private and corporate aircraft.]

Along the way, they passed through nearly deserted streets. Everyone in Manhattan, except emergency vehicles, seemed to have opted to remain indoors,

In happier times, a married couple, Elizabeth Taylor and Senator John Warner of Virginia, were depicted on the cover of *People*.

This powerful politician was a man both Elizabeth and Debbie could rely on to get them out of the ashen streets of Manhattan.

awaiting news about how to react to a world that had fundamentally changed.

"At the airport, our private plane was the only one ready to take off. The others were grounded."

"Elizabeth told me our flight plan had been approved," Debbie said. "Flying out, we could look down at the smoldering ruins of Lower Manhattan, where some fires were still burning. Elizabeth started to cry again, even though those violet eyes were already swollen."

"I don't know how Senator Warner pulled it off, but our private plane seemed to be the only one winging its way across Continental America," Debbie said. "Someone on the plane speculated that we might be shot down, but Elizabeth shut him up."

Before disembarking, Debbie had phoned one of her best friends, Bob Petersen, the owner of the Petersen Publishing House and the publisher of *Hot Rod* magazine. He had a helicopter waiting for her, ready to fly her to San Diego. She hugged and kissed Elizabeth profusely, thanking her for everything before taking off.

She arrived at the matinee only thirty minutes before she was scheduled to appear on stage. "I just had time to put on a little warpaint before facing my audience."

When she stepped out into the glare of the lights, she got a standing ovation. It lasted for almost five minutes. The audience had been told that she might not appear.

Her show was different from others she had delivered and included fewer jokes. In front of her raptly attentive audience, she talked about the repair of her friendship with Elizabeth Taylor, and how they'd grown even closer during their co-starring film shoot of *These Old Broads*. She also fascinated the audience with "Tales of Manhattan," and what she'd gone through after learning about the attack on the World Trade Center. She also relayed the details of how Elizabeth had arranged to get them aboard that westbound private plane.

"I guess that sort of makes up for the Eddie thing," she said. The audience burst into laughter.

She ended her show with a rousing rendition of "God Bless America."

"I didn't have the voice of Kate Smith, but everybody in the audience joined in, and we practically raised the rafters with our voices."

***

Back within her home at last, Debbie confronted one of her most vexing problems: What should she do with her collection of Hollywood memorabilia? She turned to Todd for advice and help.

After the fiasco that ended her association with the hotel in Las Vegas, Todd had shipped her collection to storage facilities at his ranch in Northern California. He was all too aware that unless her treasures, especially the costumes, were carefully "archived and preserved" in an appropriate setting, they'd deteriorate, get moldy, and be reduced to rags. As a means of educating himself in the techniques of costume preservation, he arranged a meeting in London with curators at the Victoria & Albert Museum. They had successfully preserved clothing from four hundred years ago, including outfits from the Tudors, especially Henry VIII.

Back in California, he took elaborate precautions to preserve the outfits previously worn by movie stars. To his dismay, he learned how expensive his maintenance of the wardrobes would be, as they required consistently controlled temperatures and elaborate ventilation. "I hated to send my mother her first electric bill."

***

Debbie lacked the financial resources to open a museum to house her collection, and therefore, was most receptive to hear from TrizecHahn, an organization engaged in the acquisition, development, and operation of office properties. At the time, it was developing a shopping complex in Los Angeles at the corner of North Highland and Hollywood Boulevards. Debbie thought that location would be convenient for tourists, as it stood near Grauman's Chinese Theatre.

A redevelopment agency of the City of Los Angeles planned to issue bonds to pay for the construction costs of the multi-million dollar complex, with the understanding that it would shelter shops, restaurants, and attractions.

Todd hired Dianna Wong as his architect, and she set about devising a floor plan. The ground-breaking ceremony, which Debbie attended, was presided over by Johnny Grant, the honorary mayor of Hollywood.

Complications in Debbie's leased quarters began when it became obvious that pipes and structural elements would require major changes in the floor plan she had envisioned. Meeting with the developers, she signed a revised lease for "the nose" of the building, a glass-enclosed structure spread over four floors. That called for a radical redesign of Wong's original designs.

Debbie's expenses mounted rapidly, and in the months ahead, she grew increasingly frustrated as revised completion dates were announced, recalculated, delayed, and rescheduled yet again.

Her expenses became intolerable, and she needed more loans to keep operations going. She turned to a private investor, George Orman, who inspected the property and agreed to advance her $1.5 million. With that, she could pay off some overdue bills and still meet the payrolls of the workers she'd hired. She would later regret accepting that loan.

To raise even more cash, and with deep sorrow, she was forced to schedule an auction of some of her Hollywood props and costumes, with the understanding that special treasures would remain a part of her "permanent collection."

Newspapers of December 6, 2003, carried stories of her upcoming auction. The event was well attended, and she was saddened to part with some of her pieces, including a costume that James Cagney had worn in *Yankee Doodle Dandy* (1942). He had won a Best Actor Oscar for his role as showman George M. Cohan.

She sadly parted with costumes worn by Judy Garland in *Ziegfeld Follies* (1946), starring William Powell and Fred Astaire.

A little old lady from Sacramento, an avid movie fan, had been driven to the event. She had no money but wanted to see some of the props and costumes from movies she had loved from the days of her youth. She told Debbie, "I'm so sorry you have to part with pieces of your wonderful collection."

"Up to now," Debbie answered, "I've been selling myself. It's about time I sold objects instead of my tired old bones."

***

During the depths of Debbie's despair, an unexpected offer came in for her museum from a company called BIV Retail. Its administration was intrigued by the concept of opening a Hollywood Museum in Pigeon Forge, Tennessee, the site of Dolly Parton's Dollywood.

*[Set in the foothills of Tennessee's Smoky Mountains, near Knoxville, **Dollywood** is the biggest ticketed tourist attraction in Tennessee. Jointly owned by the Herschend Family Entertainment Group and Dolly Parton, and hosting around 3 million guests a year, it's the venue for country/western musical events, concerts, thrill rides, a water park, Dolly's Dixie Stampede dinner theater, and the Southern Gospel Museum and Hall of Fame.]*

After some letters and phone calls, Todd flew to Tennessee, where he was warmly welcomed by potential backers. He had been surprised to learn that Pigeon Forge attracted more visitors than the entertainment meccas at Branson, Missouri, cynically known as "the last showcase for has-beens."

He was driven to Belle Island to survey the backer's proposed building site. They showed him the preliminary architectural drawings, for which he proposed alterations that would focus the building's sightlines on props and costumes from Debbie's collection. There would be special emphasis on cos-

tumes from Elizabeth Taylor's *Cleopatra* (1963); Clark Gable's *Mutiny on the Bounty* (1935); Peter O'Toole's *Lawrence of Arabia* (1962); and Charlton Heston's *Ben-Hur* (1959). He even designed a sketch of what he wanted the entrance to look like—a re-creation of a showboat, evoking MGM's 1951 musical romance, *Show Boat*, starring Kathryn Grayson, Howard Keel, and Ava Gardner.

Despite the interest from the investors in Tennessee, Debbie still clung to the hope that she could get backing for the museum in its hometown of Hollywood. She arranged appointments with potential backers who included Steven Spielberg, David Geffen, and George Lucas. All of them rejected her proposals.

In lieu of that, a deal was finalized with financiers for placement of a museum at Pigeon Forge. They offered $12 million for its construction.

Building began almost immediately. Debbie flew to Tennessee for a "topping off" ceremony on May 27, 2008, during which a gigantic crane positioned the final steel beam to the top of the unfinished building's six-story skeleton. All the townspeople turned out to see her, in her capacity as the fabled movie star who presided over the event.

After four decades, her Hollywood museum showed positive signs of becoming a reality. But, as so frequently happened in her tumultuous life, disaster struck. She defined it as "the George W. Bush recession" that swept across the land in 2007 and 2008. Banks began foreclosures on properties across the nation, and Pigeon Forge and its unfinished Hollywood Museum were among the worst hit. Funds for its continuation dried up and vanished like smoke.

Interpreting this as a serious emergency, Debbie phoned the office of the governor of Tennessee, hoping he might authorize his certification of a state-sponsored bond issue. He treated her with no respect and wouldn't even come to the phone. Later, she said, "Maybe he didn't like *Singin' in the Rain.*"

***

In her attempts to recover from this newest fiasco, Debbie continued to accept most of the job offers that came her way, even appearing at an evening of entertainment backed up by the Omaha Symphony in Nebraska. In the audience was the billionaire financier, Warren Buffett ("The Oracle of Omaha") and his "lady friend," who each appeared backstage after her performance to congratulate her. Buffett had particularly enjoyed her impressions of other stars, among them, Barbra Streisand. During their conversation backstage, she accepted a dinner invitation from him for an

"The Oracle of Omaha," Warren Buffett, admired Debbie's impersonations, but had no intention of becoming her "angel"—that is, the backer of her Hollywood museum.

event the following night at his home.

After her return to Hollywood, she met with her son and discussed Buffett as a potential investor for her museum. Consequently, Todd set up an appointment with Buffett and presented his plan. Buffett listened respectfully, and then turned down the deal.

Confronted with desperately unfavorable odds, Debbie filed for Chapter 7 Bankruptcy protection in June of 2008. "I was still the Unsinkable Molly, but the rising waters had engulfed everything except my head. I still had my head above water, but just barely." She needed more time to find backers for her Hollywood Motion Picture Museum (her final name for it).

In March of 2010, an offer arrived for her to perform in England and Wales in a traveling road show billed as "Debbie Reynolds Alive and Fabulous." By April 1, on her 78th birthday, she was touring the U.K. in a double-decker bus with scheduled performances in Liverpool, home of the Beatles; Leeds, where Peter O'Toole had once worked; Bristol, the home town of Cary Grant; the industrial heartland city of Manchester; Norwich in East Anglia; and Cardiff, the capital of Wales. She ended her tour at the Apollo Theatre in London.

Five years had passed and she had defaulted on that $1.5 million loan from financier Greg Orman. She had not paid any interest (which had compounded) on the loan, and he was demanding a net payoff of $9 million, which, of course, she did not have. In league with Todd, she proposed a compromise, wherein she'd borrow $3.5 million and turn all of it over to him. He rejected the idea, and filed a lawsuit. "I think I'll spend the rest of my life telling it to the judge," she lamented.

The trial opened on September 8, 2010. After each side had presented its case, the judge rejected Orman's hoped-for $9 million, but also rejected Debbie's lower offer too. She ruled that Debbie would have to pay Orman $5.3 million within a period of five months before further action was taken.

The judge's ruling forced Debbie into making decisions she had always feared. She had to auction off the glittering remainder of her Hollywood treasures. There was no other way she could pay the Orman judgment. "It was the hardest decision of my life, but I had to make it."

When Todd approached Christie's, the legendary auctioneer in New York City, he was told that the entire collection would have to be shipped to Manhattan. Debbie resisted that, so a deal was forged with a newer, somewhat less prestigious, auction house ("Profiles in History") on the West Coast.

To publicize her auction, she launched a media blitz, even appearing to discuss the upcoming sale on *The Oprah Winfrey Show*. As the cameras rolled, she exhibited the celebrated white dress that Marilyn Monroe had worn in an iconic scene from *The Seven Year Itch* (1955). In that scene, as a means of cooling herself down during a midsummer heat wave, Marilyn stood, with her legs apart, above a subway grating as the air from the tunnel below made her dress billow up, revealing her panties.

For the auction's venue, a deal was struck with the Paley Center for Media in Beverly Hills. It was preceded with a two-week preview of the collection. It attracted "rubber neckers" from across the country and from abroad.

On the day of the auction (June 18, 2011), Debbie spent hours dressing and making herself up. "I put on my best and sweetest Tammy smile and ventured forth into the day. My face was all a mask. In my heart, I was in mourning. It's hard to give up a life-long dream." One by one, she watched as the items to which she had devoted four decades of her life were sold off to strangers.

First on the block was the "suit of lights" worn by Rudolph Valentino, cast as the dashing bullfighter in the silent screen version of *Blood and Sand*. (1922). She was astonished when it sold for $210,000. Buyers from all over the world, many of them anonymous, placed bids. Bidder no. 249 frequently emerged with the highest offer. Debbie later learned that the unknown party was from South Korea.

Her treasures from Judy Garland's *The Wizard of Oz* (1939) came on the block, including the ruby slippers. They were not the version filmed in that movie's final cut, but the pair that had been designed for Garland's wardrobe tests that prefaced the filming. *[Resembling something that might have been conceived for a pasha's daughter from* Arabian Nights, *their toes were longer and more pointed than the more stream-lined version that appeared in the film's final cut. Director Victor Fleming had rejected them in favor a more conventional pair. Even so, the "magic slip-pers" fetched $510,000. The "country-cousin" dress that Garland had worn throughout most of the film sold for an astonishing $910,000.]*

Overjoyed at the prices her items were fetching, Debbie grew increasingly nervous and finally excused herself from the auction floor. As she recalled, she was sitting on the toilet in the women's room when one of her favorite items went on the block: It was the red, silk-velvet Santa Claus outfit that Edmund Gwenn had worn in *Miracle on 34th Street* (1947). He'd won a Best Supporting Actor Oscar that year for playing Kris Kringle. The movie has since emerged as a classic, broadcast every year on television at Christmas.

The exhibit that attracted worldwide interest was, of course, Marilyn Monroe's white

At an auction of Debbie's memorabilia, she put on the block the white dress Marilyn Monroe had worn in *The Seven Year Itch*.

"Marilyn died with $23,000 in the bank," Debbie said. "Had she lived, she could have collected millions for this dress as well as blackmail money from the Kennedy family for not selling her tell-all memoir."

dress from *The Seven Year Itch*. "By the time that went on the block, I had begun to steady my nerves," Debbie said. "I already had made enough to pay Orman his millions, and even have a tidy sum left over for my old age pension. That way, I wouldn't have to end up playing every seedy honky-tonk in the world. Remember *Honky-Tonk,* that 1941 romance with Clark Gable and Lana Turner?"

The opening bid for Marilyn's dress was $1 million. After that, bids increased in increments ranging from $100,000 to $200,000 as bidders from around the world vied for the prize. The winning bid of $5,520,000 set a world record for the sale of a motion picture costume. The audience burst into applause.

For some reason, Debbie was once again seen leaving the room when the collection's second most-celebrated dress came up for auction. It was the whimsical but rigorously formal black-and-white "Ascot Dress." Designed by Cecil Beaton, and accessorized with "the world's most fabulous hat," it had been worn to the races by Audrey Hepburn in *My Fair Lady* (1964).

When Debbie was informed that the costume had sold for $3.8 million, she exclaimed, "Holy shit!"

Caught by a reporter as she was exiting from the auction, she told him, "I had saved my precious collections over the decades, and now they are saving me."

***

"I didn't know Michael Jackson very well," Carrie said. "But I knew 'The Gloved One' far better than Debbie. He was so mysterious that nobody really knew him. So I might rank among his closest friends, with the exception of Elizabeth Taylor."

"Of course, I was not built like Macaulay Culkin, so that may have detracted a bit from my allure. I became, for eighteen years, his Princess Leia, and he was my King of Pop."

Debbie had met Jackson during his use of studio space at her DR Studios. At the time, he was rehearsing the dances for videos associated with some of his albums.

"When I met Michael, I found that we had a lot more in common than I ever realized," Carrie said. "We bonded...sort of." Her introduction to Michael did not originate with Debbie or with her godmother, Elizabeth.

It was arranged through her derma-

Dr. Arnold Klein, "Dermatologist to the Stars," brought together an unlikely pair: Carrie Fisher and Michael Jackson.

tologist, Dr. Arnold Klein. One day, in Klein's office, Michael spotted a picture of Carrie with her six-month-old daughter, Billie Lourd. The year was 1993. He was so enthralled with the photograph that he telephoned Carrie, who was surprised to hear his distinctive voice on the other end of the line.

"I knew I wasn't his type, and he didn't want *that*," she said. "But he had a strange request: He wanted me to e-send him, electronically, some photos of my daughter, Billie. I asked him why he wanted them, and he claimed that she had the most innocent face in all the world."

"I adore innocence more than anything on this earth," he said, "and your daughter is the embodiment of innocence, unlike anything I've seen in my life. She is God's little angel, and I'm sure you agree. She reminds me of the innocence many of us have in the beginning, including me, and perhaps yourself. That is, we have it before the world corrupts us."

She agreed to send him some photos, but "I felt a little bit creepy doing it."

"If my child had been a boy, I would not have sent them, but since Billie is a girl, I thought it might be harmless enough."

Both of them continued their medical consultations with Dr. Klein, who was known as "the Dermatologist to the Stars."

"His injections of Botox extended many an actor's career," Carrie claimed.

Many in the medical profession defined Arnold Klein as the country's expert on skin disorders. He had been the first physician to diagnose a case of Kaposi's Sarcoma in Southern California.

"Back then, no one had ever heard of AIDS," Carrie said.

Klein eventually helped establish the Elizabeth Taylor Center for AIDS Research, Treatment, and Education at UCLA.

He was also the dermatologist to Elizabeth Taylor, Goldie Hawn, and Dolly Parton, who claimed at the Hollywood Bowl in 2011, "It takes a lot of money to look this cheap, and I owe it all to Dr. Arnie Klein."

He built up an A-list clientele of Hollywood icons, starlets, industry bigwigs, and Beverly Hills matrons who sought to obliterate crow's feet, firm up droopy jaw lines, and plump up smiles. He became known as "the King of Lips."

Elizabeth told Carrie, "He's a brilliant dermatologist, but he's so much more to me."

It was Klein who had introduced Michael Jackson to Debbie Rowe, a "motorcycle mama" working as his secretary at the time. Rowe eventually agreed to become a surrogate mother for two of Jackson's children, Michael ("Prince") Jackson and Paris Katherine. When Rowe announced that she was pregnant with Michael's heir, she did not reveal the biological father of either of them at birth.

"One day, Arnie (Dr. Klein) introduced me to Michael in his office," Carrie remembered. "I don't know what he was there for. His skin was changing color.

I guess, and I had developed a rash around my galaxy snatch. We got along fabulously once he stopped raving about Debbie's musicals. It turned out to be the beginning of a beautiful friendship, a case of Princess Leia meeting the King of Pop. We were royalty."

"He told me how much he adored *Star Wars*," she said. *["I'm into fantasy," he said.]*

"When you first meet Michael, you have to pretend not to notice how much he has transformed himself since I first saw him as a kid on TV," Carrie said. "Obviously, he didn't like being born a little black boy. He wanted to transform himself into a white woman like me. With his money, he could do amazing things to his appearance. I'd call it 'dysmorphic'—not a bad word coming from a high school dropout like me."

Soon, an invitation arrived from Michael for Carrie to visit Neverland, Jackson's ranch north of Los Angeles. "He knew I had a daughter, Billie, and she was invited, too. We went with Dr. Arnie and an assortment of his burly gay buddies. Homosexuals refer to guys like that as 'bears.' Arnie went for fleshy guys like himself. Riding with them, I felt I was extending Billie's knowledge of male sexuality."

Neverland was like a trip to Disneyland for Billie, who found all sorts of child-friendly attractions there, including a merry-go-round, a zoo, and a pizza parlor. "Mike was so kind and playful with the children, almost like a kid himself."

He looked so harmless," she said. "I had a hard time hearing all those revelations about child molestation and kiddie porn, shit like that. To me, Michael was still a kid himself trapped in a man's body…well, sort of a man's body. Of course, I soon realized that that was too simplistic a description of him. He was far more complicated."

"He had a secret life as one would expect, considering his perversions," she said. "He didn't always welcome company. He once told me that to escape from the world, his family and his fans, he often stripped naked in a dark room at midnight, put on his music, and danced until dawn."

"Don't you ever need a partner?" she asked.

"The music is my dancing partner," he answered.

"Michael and I found common ground in spite of our differences," she said. "We came from different backgrounds, but each of us was a child performer. And whereas he got started at the age of six, I appeared at the age of thirteen with Debbie on Broadway. From that age, he wanted to become the biggest name entertainer in the world, whereas I had to be dragged, kicking and screaming, into stardom."

***

In addition to the links they shared through their dermatologist and their equivalent histories as child entertainers, Carrie also shared a link to Michael Jackson through her dentist, Dr. Evan Chandler, known at the time as "Dentist to the Stars."

"Whenever I went in for even a checkup, Evan was always bragging about his son's friendship with Michael."

"They're very close," he told me. "Whenever Jordie isn't staying at Neverland, he and Michael talk on the phone for two or three hours a day. I can't imagine what they have that's important enough to justify three hours a day of chitchat."

She learned that the thirteen-year-old Jordan ("Jordie") had been born in 1980, making him twenty-two years younger than Michael. The dentist was Jewish and an aspirant scriptwriter. Jordie's mother, June, a former model, had come from the Caribbean island of St.-Vincent.

"Evan constantly talked to me about how good-looking Jordie is," Carrie said. "He went on and on."

"Michael thinks Jordie is the most gorgeous boy in Tinseltown, where the competition is stiff. Call me prejudiced, but I think that Jordie is far better-looking than Macaulay Culkin."

"Usually, fathers talk about how smart their boys are, or else that their boy is the up-and-coming Joe DiMaggio. Not Evan. It was all about how handsome he was, and that in Michael's opinion, he was 'so cute.' He told me that Michael finds him adorable. Those guys just dote on each other."

"For a smart medical man, Chandler seemed ignorant of the homosexual implications of such a friendship—even the implications of child molestation," Carrie said.

Elizabeth Taylor was also a dental patient of Chandler. At the home of her former stepmother, Carrie once asked her what she thought about Michael being sexually interested in young boys.

"It's a silly rumor, like hundreds spread about me," Elizabeth answered. "Michael loves children and likes to make them happy and play with them in his amusement park at

Michael Jackson's bizarre relationship with a young boy, Jordie Chandler, generated lurid media attention.

Neverland. But I can't believe his interest extends to sex. Of all the men I've known—and there have been plenty—I think Michael is asexual. In all the time I've known him, there has never been one sexual reference from him. That's so unlike your father. And so unlike Richard Burton."

Carrie even discussed it with her mother, who listened patiently before rising to her feet. "I was sexually molested when I was only six years old by these two older boys in El Paso. One gets over it, dear. Actually, it taught me a lesson."

"What lesson might that have been, dear?" Carrie asked.

"I learned for the first time that a man's penis undergoes a transformation when it become hard. I hadn't known that. I'd seen my uncles and brother nude, since we shared the same bedroom at the time, but their dicks were soft."

According to Carrie, "During my next visit to the dentist, Evan was all excited, claiming that Michael had bought his latest screenplay and was going to put up the money to produce it. Evan told me, 'I studied for years to become a dentist, and I think I'm very good at that, but in my heart, I want to write for the movies. I think I could do an updated version of *Casablanca*, or maybe another *From Here to Eternity* superimposed over the Vietnam War.'"

"Both of those ideas are a bit of a stretch," Carrie responded. "I mean, the Bogie picture had World War II as a backdrop, and the Burt Lancaster/Frank Sinatra film had Pearl Harbor. Tough acts to follow."

A short while after her appointment with Chandler, Carrie departed for an extended sojourn in New York. Many months later, after her return to L.A., she visited Chandler for additional dental treatments. "While probing around my back molars, he immediately started yakking about Michael and this Jordie boy, whom I had never met."

"Michael has practically adopted my son," Chandler confessed. "He takes him everywhere, buys him expensive clothes, even jewelry. Jordie wanted to learn how to use a computer, and Michael set up an office for him. They are so close! Jordie sleeps in Michael's bed at least three or four nights a week."

"Let me get this straight," she said. "But perhaps 'straight' isn't the right word. You're telling me that you have no objection to your son sleeping in the same bed with Michael Jackson?"

"Not at all, since Michael looked me right in the eye and told me that nothing wrong is going on."

She learned that Chandler had divorced his wife, June, the former model, in 1985. She had remarried a man named David Schwarz.

Chandler said, "June and David don't see anything wrong with the relationship either—in fact, June adores Michael. He buys her expensive clothing and jewelry. I don't know what he does for David, but he's all fired up about producing my latest screenplay about a serial killer."

"I can't wait to see it," Carrie said.

About three months later, Chandler, knowing that Carrie was a friend of

Michael's, phoned and asked to come over to see her.

When he arrived, he looked very stressed. Over drinks, he revealed that both he and his ex-wife, June, were filing a multi-million-dollar lawsuit against Michael. "We made Jordie confess. Michael, that bastard, frequently had sex with my son. He's into young boys, never older than thirteen. He's a child molester."

"I'm sorry you didn't see this coming," Carrie answered. "I hope it hasn't messed up your son's life forever."

"Well, I think it has, but he'll pay—and pay dearly. Not four or five million dollars. I want at least $20 million to settle the case out of court. Otherwise, he'll be exposed. He might even go to jail. He's smart. He knows the damage Jordie's confession in court can do to his career. Those so-called loyal fans will desert him in droves."

"It was on that night that I realized I needed to shop for another dentist," Carrie said. "I'm not taking up for Michael, and there seemed to be plenty of blame to go around. But Evan has to take some of the responsibility. Let's face it: He pimped Jordie to Michael."

As she had anticipated, the case and its *tsumani* of scandal went public. Press reports, filled with lurid accusations about Michael's "perversions," seriously damaged the singer—mentally, physically, and financially. His world tour was canceled, and he lost millions of dollars after lucrative sponsorship deals were abruptly terminated.

He escaped prosecution by settling around $25 million on the Chandlers. "Jordie would be fixed for life for letting Michael play with his peepee," Carrie said, sarcastically. "Ah, Hollywood…don't you love it?"

[Years later, in November of 2009, alone in a luxurious Manhattan apartment, Dr. Chandler gripped a snub-nosed revolver, placed it to his head, and pulled the trigger. His body had been dead for many days before it was discovered.

Almost a decade after that, in 2018, Jordie disappeared. Lawyers were seeking him with hopes of forcing him to serve as a witness in a postmortem $100 million sex-abuse case brought against Michael Jackson's estate by Wade Robson and Jimmy Safechuck. Both of them claimed that as young boys, they had been sexually abused by the late entertainer.

Jordie, whose whereabouts were unknown, had apparently fled from New York to avoid having to deliver court testimony in the new trials.]

"Sometimes, dating combos in Hollywood can get fucking weird," Carrie said. "Take the night I went to an AIDS charity event at the invitation of Michael Jackson. His date for the evening was Elizabeth Taylor, my former stepmother. My date for the evening was Shirley MacLaine, who had portrayed Debbie in *Postcards from the Edge*, based on my script."

"At times, I had doubted the sincerity of the Michael Jackson/Elizabeth Taylor friendship. I felt he was buying that friendship by showering her with jewelry. That was a sure way to Elizabeth's heart. At times, I privately referred to her as 'Diamond Liz'"

"When the limousine pulled up in front of the Beverly Hills Hotel, MacLaine and Carrie were virtually brushed aside. All the press and all the paparazzi rushed to photograph Elizabeth being escorted inside by Michael.

"Whereas Shirley and I were the 'merely famous,' they were the *über*-famous," Carrie explained.

"At times, Elizabeth invited me to other AIDS charity events, and I always went," Carrie said. "I saw Michael less and less but was delighted when he invited me to spend what became his last Christmas Eve on earth in 2008."

"I arrived at his house with our skin guy, Dr. Arnie Klein, and with two of his burly 'bears.' It was a wonderful night with Michael and his kids. At one point, he asked me to do my hologram from *Star Wars*. He was such a devoted fan."

"My favorite picture of him in all the world was taken of him reading my book, *Wishful Drinking*. I don't care what people say about him. I think he was a great father, perhaps not your regular All-American family guy, but there was love from him and his kids gave back as good as they got. He lavished presents on them."

"After that Christmas Eve, I heard from him only one more time. He phoned late one night, and his voice was only a whisper," she said.

"I'll soon be traveling like Princess Leia in Outer Space," he said. "I'm going to the Death Star, the one that twinkles and glows the brightest at night because its insides are on fire."

"All of that sounded like pretty dramatic stuff to me," she said. "A little theatrical. He may have sounded weak, but I was spaced out myself. 'Don't worry,' I told him. 'Princess Leia might be going on the journey with you.' I realize that that conversation sounds silly and ridiculous, but I had to say something."

"Good night, Carrie, and God bless you," he said.

On June 25, 2009, every major television network broadcasted the news of Michael Jackson's death from cardiac arrest associated with acute propofol and benzodiazepine intoxication.

Carrie later wrote: "Michael's death was a byproduct of his fame. He died because he could get doctors to give him something he had no business having. A combination of money and celebrity is a deadly surf and turf."

***

Stepmother Elizabeth Taylor's role in Carrie's life started down a shaky road but ended up on smoother turf toward the end. She continued to invite Carrie to her AIDS charity events, and occasionally to her elegant home for a pool party, or for an occasional lunch, sometimes including Debbie, too.

"One day, after she pushed me into her pool and then sent for a beautiful robe so that I could put something on my soaking body, we sort of bonded and became close."

"At first, I had blamed her for running off with my father," Carrie said. "Man, did I evolve over the years. In the end, I was thanking her for getting that train wreck out of our house."

"No one told better stories of old Hollywood than Elizabeth. She knew which closets contained which skeletons. Once, over lunch, she told Debbie and me that Marilyn Monroe had once come on to her."

"Did you allow Marilyn Monroe to give you lip service?" Debbie asked.

"That's a secret I'll take to the grave," Elizabeth said.

According to Carrie, "At first, Elizabeth used to call Debbie 'Miss Goody Two Shoes.' But in time, Debbie, herself a potty mouth, gave Elizabeth's vulgar tongue some competition."

"At one point, I asked Elizabeth a question that had been burning in my brain for a long time," Carrie said. "Were you ever in love with my father?"

"Hell no!" she answered. "We were just keeping alive the memory of Mike Todd."

"The last time I heard from her was when she called to get Eddie's phone number," Carrie said.

"I feel that your father and I will soon be moving on, and in some small way, if only to say 'I'm sorry,' I want to try to make amends," Elizabeth said. "I know it's impossible to heal wounds, but I still want to try."

Then she admitted, "I ruined his life and certainly his career. There is nothing I can do about that now, other than tell him how profoundly sorry I am to have caused pain of any sort."

Carrie later said, "I don't know if she ever got through to Eddie. He was soon to die, followed by Elizabeth herself. My regret, if I have any, is that I never really got to know either of them. I saw both of them as tragic figures who experienced some of the best and worst that life has to offer."

***

The last time Debbie ever spoke to Elizabeth was over the phone. It was a long chat, and she found Elizabeth in a reflective mood.

It was Elizabeth who ended the call by saying, "Everything I have done in my life that was a mistake, I will admit and answer for it. But I'm not going to answer to an image created by hundreds of people who do not know what's true or false. If I did, that would take me from here to eternity."

The legendary star died on March 24, 2011, at the age of seventy-nine.

***

[In the immediate aftermath of Elizabeth's death, Debbie—besieged with phone

602

***

"You haven't really lived until you wake up in bed one morning and find a corpse lying beside you," Carrie said. "That's only great if you're into necrophilia, which I'm not."

The man in bed beside her was Greg Stevens, a close friend and a gay man known as a Republican operative. "We both stumbled into bed drunk one night after attending an Oscar presentation. We were zonked out and had fallen asleep at once."

"When news of my dead bedmate leaked out, my closest friends weren't that concerned about his demise. They were more appalled to learn that he was a Republican. One of their most stinging judgments was, 'How could you, Carrie? A Republican, of all people?'"

"I can explain."

She'd met Greg at a party two years before his death. From the beginning, they morphed into instant friends…"like two soulmates. It was not a romance. He was gay and had plenty of boyfriends on the side, mostly Log Cabin Republicans. As a political operative, he worked behind the scenes on GOP campaigns."

"On our first night together, we tried to top each other with our tall tales. One incident he related took the prize."

[When he and the future president, George W. Bush, were young men, they had shared a small office together. "He had this annoying, rather smelly habit," Greg told Carrie. "Whenever I had a meeting in my office, he'd run in through the door, let out a big Texas fart, then disappear through a side door. When my clients arrived, they held their noses, smelling Dubya's odorous fart, blaming

By 2015, with only a year to live, Carrie had long ago found a lucrative new gig: She often appeared at conventions where she met fans of *Star Wars*. For a price, she would pose with them for pictures.

Here, she was at a "Comic-con" convention in San Diego, capitalizing off her role as Princess Leia.

me. No skunk was competition for Georgie boy. That guy could fart on cue. The poisonous gasses used in the trenches of World War I had nothing on Dubya."]

According to Carrie, "My time with Greg was far too short, as I was looking forward to a life-long friendship. At least he didn't die in the saddle the way John Garfield did. Some men told me that's how they wanted to die, croaking after giving one final blast of semen that would lead to the birth of triplets."

Greg had flown into Los Angeles with his friend, Judy, his GOP assistant, to escort Carrie to the Oscar presentations, and to attend some of the gala parties that followed. *[As was her custom, she didn't give the date (or year) of the Academy Awards ceremony she was describing.]*

"It turned out to be a riot in more ways than one," she said. "I invited Judy and Greg back to my house to spend the weekend. I had two choices for sleeping arrangements: In the guest cottage, or in my bed. Judy was a lesbian and Greg was gay. I thought he might be the safer bet, as I knew he would not be attracted to my galaxy snatch."

"So Judy slept in my guest cottage, and Greg slept with me in my bed. At least he bunked with me until somewhere in the middle of the night, when he decided to leave the Planet Earth. The next morning, I confronted dead male flesh already beginning to rot."

"The police were called and after a quick investigation, it was concluded that I did not kill Greg. Unlike Lana Turner, I never killed someone in my bedroom. He suffered from sleep apnea and had big trouble breathing at night, often snoring loudly and gasping for breath. That evening, he'd had an overload of OxyContin, nicknamed 'OxyCoffin.'"

Years later, when Carrie made onstage appearances, and later fielding questions about her past, spectators from the audience often asked two things:

"Why was the man in your bed?," and

"Were the two of you naked at the time?"

***

Carrie survived having a quirky mother like Debbie Reynolds, who was at least loyal. In contrast, her father-daughter relationship with Eddie Fisher had been turbulent since he had bolted from their household when she was a child.

"He was the absentee father who deposited his musical sperm after creating Todd and me, and then abandoned us. Debbie once told me that the best thing about Eddie was his sperm."

"As the world knows, he fell into the arms of Elizabeth Taylor and later, Connie Stevens, plus two other wives. When not seducing hookers, he went for world-class pussy."

Carrie read her father's second memoir, *Been There, Done That,* issued in

1999. "I called it *Been There, Done Them.* After reading it, I wanted to get my DNA fumigated."

"He'd had them all, from Mia Farrow to Judy Garland, and he survived on four thick joints a day. I nicknamed him 'Puff Daddy.'"

After the Fisher memoir came out, a reporter from the *Enquirer* phoned Carrie and asked her what she thought of her father alluding to the charge that Debbie was a lesbian.

"My mother is not a lesbian," Carrie said. "She's just a really, really bad heterosexual."

"I think my father was proud of me as a performer and that I'd risen as far as I had in the world. After all, I was descended from white trash in South Philly and even whiter trash in El Paso."

From 1970 to 1977 Carrie did not speak to her father. She'd also gone for a whole decade without speaking to Debbie, either.

But when Eddie and Carrie were each in New York during the same period, they bonded for the first time. He lived with her for several months before finding a place of his own. "Even so, my father showed up every three days or so, carrying with him a stash of drugs for me. We would get stoned out of our minds. He told me that he could relate to me better when both of us were zonked out of our heads."

Carrie saw the most of Eddie when he moved to San Francisco during his marriage (1993-2001) to Betty Young Lin, a rich Chinese businesswoman. During the final years of his life, Carrie visited him whenever she could.

"Although slipping into dementia, he often came around and talked about his 'glorious pussy past,'" she said. He revealed to her that one night in New York, he'd attended a dinner party at the home of columnist Leonard Lyons. Eddie's date that night was Margaret Truman, the daughter of Harry S Truman.

Lyons had staged the party as a venue for Marlene Dietrich to meet Democratic contender Adlai Stevenson, who had twice run for president (in 1952 and again in 1956) against the Republican candidate, Dwight D. Eisenhower.

"Marlene talked to Adlai for about five minutes before drifting off," Eddie said. "Later that evening, out on the terrace, she told me, 'The man is gay.'"

At that party, Fisher deserted the presidential daughter to chat with Honey Warren, the daughter of Earl Warren, the chief justice of the Supreme Court. Soon, he and Honey were not only dating, but traveling together.

Dietrich had not forgotten Fisher, and one night, she attended one of his night club appearances and came backstage to greet him. She followed that with a dinner at her apartment and an invitation to her boudoir. "The sex was incredible," he recalled. "I saw Marlene on and off after that. A lot of guys asked me why I was dating such an old woman. I told the bastards that Dietrich was ageless."

Carrie recalled one visit when she and her daughter, Billie, had come to see him. "He had purchased this miniature super-expensive hearing aid, two units, each the size of a lima bean. Not to lose them, he put them in his pillbox. Waking up one morning, thinking they were pills in his groggy state, he swallowed both of them. To get him to hear us, Billie and I had to talk to his stomach or else his ass."

"In the final years of his life, especially after his wife Betty died, I saw Eddie more and more frequently in San Francisco. In fact, I became his mother, offering what comfort I could. I didn't have to breast feed him, though he talked a lot about my jugs, comparing them to those of Elizabeth Taylor. He seemed to have a fixation on breasts."

In his final years, Fisher went through a rough time, suffering from back and knee pain, and an increasing loss of his hearing. After major cataract surgery, he grew increasingly blind. During his later years, he was frequently visited by his musician friend, George Michalski, who would play the piano and listen to music with him.

According to Carrie, "He remembered the old songs by The Andrews Sisters, Jo Stafford, Dinah Shore, Vic Damone, Perry Como, Dean Martin, Nat King Cole, and of course, Sinatra. But when I sang 'Yesterday' from the Beatles, he thought I had written it. He didn't know, or perhaps had forgotten, who John Lennon and the Beatles were. The music of the 1960s and the decades later just passed him by."

"One night, he told me that before dying, he wanted once more to have access to the recess between a woman's legs," Carrie said. "Call it a final lay before the grave. He'd been getting laid all his life, but times were different now."

"His passion for one last pass at pussy remained undiminished, if only his decaying body would cooperate," she said. "We talked over the idea that one really good prostitute might answer the call of nature. I sent him on different occasions two or three ladies, none of whom had ever heard of Eddie Fisher. Seeing the decrepit dying man in bed, they fled."

Once, at the end of a performance of her one-woman show, *Wishful Drinking*, in San Francisco, Carrie announced, "Does anyone in the audience know a really good prostitute, female, that is? For my father, not for me. If so, come backstage tonight and give me the details."

No one came backstage.

Eddie Fisher shortly before his death.

On his deathbed, he confessed to Carrie, "I failed as a husband, as a father, as a grandfather. After being a big shot in the 1950s, I even failed as a singer, my career deteriorating along with my senile bones."

Eddie had this Mongolian woman, Sarah, working for him, cooking and cleaning. Needing help, she brought in a teenaged girl in a miniskirt. But she soon left, complaining "that old man in bed is constantly harassing me sexually."

"Eddie became bed ridden throughout the final five years of his life. He also suffered three strokes, but kept puffing away on his weed," Carrie said. "His drug dealer made two visits a week."

He was often foggy but occasionally he'd emerge from his daze. He once told Sarah, "I flowed with my life like a raft on a river, going wherever the current took me. Carrie navigated through her own life. There was one lesson I could have taught my daughter, and that is that relationships often come to an end. She had to find that out for herself."

On September 9, 2010, Fisher, while trying to get out of bed, fell and broke his hip. He was taken to the hospital, where, two days later, he submitted to hip surgery. He never really recovered, and eventually drifted into a coma, dying on September 22 at the age of eighty-two.

In New York, Carrie was grief-stricken that she had not been with him at the time of his death. "In spite of all the bad times in our lives, Eddie was an unbelievably lovable man."

Normally, Carrie would have attacked the sentimentality of the following line, but she wrote it down and published it anyway: "I was not there to prepare to escort my dad to his last big club act in the sky."

***

During the second decade of the 21st Century, Debbie received only two offers for roles in feature films. In contrast, her daughter worked steadily and frequently.

One for the Money (2012) was a crime comedy based on Janet Evanovich's 1994 novel of the same name. Although its movie rights had been purchased, it had "languished in development hell" for years. Finally, TriStar Pictures seemed ready to move ahead with its film adaptation. As its director, they hired British-born Julie Anne Robinson, previously know for her direction of *The Last Song* (2008). It was she who wanted to cast Debbie, with the understanding that she'd have to inject a

In one of her final film roles, Debbie agreed to play a perky grandmother in *One for the Money.*

According to Carrie, "My mother was poppin' fresh but dotty."

low-end New Jersey accent into her speech patterns in her portrayal of the feisty family matriarch, Grandma Mazur. Katherine Heigl (the female lead) and Debra Monk were cast as her granddaughter and daughter, respectively.

"Here I was, Miss Burbank of 1948, in Granny roles," Debbie lamented. "Movies today were much faster in sound, staging, and lighting since my early days at MGM. It was hard for me to keep up. Also, my memory was not what it was when I could learn pages and pages of dialogue. Julie was a patient director with me."

The plot called for Stephanie (Heigl), out of work and out of money, to play a bail enforcement agent and bounty hunter. Her boss was the disreputable Cousin Vinnie (Patrick Fischer), who runs a gritty, low-end detective agency known as Vinnie's Bail Bonds.

She chases after Joe Morelli (Jason O'Mara), a former vice cop wanted on a charge of murder. He's the same guy who, way back in high school and in rapid-fire succession, had taken her virginity and dumped her. A few months later, perhaps accidentally, she had broken his leg in three places by "misdirecting" her car in his direction.

After intricate complications, the bounty hunter catches her man, only to learn that the charges against him won't hold up in court. Her ardor for her long-ago high school hero burns anew.

Heigl was a rising star born in the nation's capital. She had been a fashion model before turning to acting, making her debut in *That Night* (1992). Her greatest recognition would derive from her co-starring performance in the long-running TV medical drama that originated in 2005, *Grey's Anatomy*.

Jason O'Mara was a blue-eyed Dublin-born actor who had performed with the Royal Shakespeare Theatre in London. After Debbie met him, she told the director, "That is one masculine, good-looking guy. If I were only a century younger. Why didn't I hook up with a man like that instead of with my three losers?"

Of mixed ancestry, John Leguizamo, cast as Jimmy Alpha, was one of the most talented of the actors who appeared in Debbie's latest film. He became known after starring in the action comedy, *Super Mario Bros.* (1993), and was also a voiceover artist, a stand-up comedian, a producer, playwright, and screenwriter. When

Two of Hollywood's most visible heterosexuals, Michael Douglas (left) and Matt Damon signed to play "the outrageous queenie" Liberace and his studly hustler-lover, Scott Thorson, in the HBO release of *Behind the Candelabra*.

It was based on Thorson's scandalous memoir of his gay-for-pay affair with the pianist.

Debbie met him, he had already starred in 75 movies, had produced ten films, and had appeared on Broadway, even though born as recently as 1964.

One for the Money failed at the box office, but came close to breaking even, earning back $37 of the $40 million it had cost to make it.

Rotten Tomatoes labeled *One for the Money* as "dull and unfunny," and *Slant Magazine* criticized "the cartoonish portrayal of New Jersey and its various caricatures." The *Los Angeles Times* attacked it as "a strained attempt at hilarity, all delivered in an unconvincing *Joizy* vibe."

***

"Can you believe it?" Debbie asked her friends. "In his next film, Steven Soderbergh wants me to play Liberace's mother!"

She was referring to *Behind the Candelabra*, a 2015 TV dramatization of the last ten years of the life of "Mr. Showman" himself.

The plot focused on Liberace's gay affair with Scott Thorson, a studly teenager and animal trainer he met and invited to share the "canopied-bed-with-an-ermine-cover" in his gaudily decorated Las Vegas mansion. The title of the film was from Thorson's memoirs.

As depicted in the upcoming movie, the public was introduced to Thorson when he appeared onstage with Liberace as his elaborately dressed chauffeur, slowly piloting Liberace's Rolls-Royce as it rolled onstage. A few seconds later, Liberace—sequined, plumed, and bejeweled—would emerge with grandeur from the innards of the car as part of his razzmatazz opening act.

As time went by, Thorson's ongoing drug abuses contributed to the death of Liberace's ardor, and he began relationships with other young men. Debbie revealed that in real life, "Lee," as she called him, "bought up every available copy of *Playgirl* for its centerfolds of nude, good-looking men."

He would systematically acquire their contact information and send them half of a thousand-dollar bill. To retrieve the other half, they had to visit Liberace in Vegas and

"Even my most ardent fans didn't recognize me as Liberace's heavily accented Polish mother," Debbie said.

"I made *Candelabra* a year after the auction that broke my heart and saved my life. Lee, as I called Liberace, and his mother were friends of mine. I was happy for the chance to play someone I knew so well."

extend their favors.

"I always knew what I was getting because I'd already seen them nude in the magazine," Liberace told Debbie.

His affair with Thorson came to a crashing end when the hustler sued Liberace for $100 million dollars as part of a palimony lawsuit.

According to Debbie, in reference to her role in *Behind the Candelabra*, "I was surprised and delighted to work with such big-name stars like Michael Douglas as Liberace and Matt Damon as Scott Thorson. I knew Lee and Scott, too. These two manly men, Michael and Matt, must have had good pairs of balls to play such gay characters. Even in the relatively enlightened 1980s, many actors in Hollywood didn't want to be caught in a movie playing it gay."

"Mike worked hard on his character, and, miraculously, he *became* Liberace, with all his queenliness and quirkiness intact. And although the actual music was later dubbed, he learned how to move his hands across the keyboard of a piano. His flamboyant costumes were perfect."

"Matt has the most divine blue eyes," she said. "A real star and a man of dignity and charm, but with the ability to play a sleazy character like Thorson."

Soderbergh told her he had a lot of trouble finding a Hollywood producer who'd invest $25 million in this picture. Finally, HBO Films came through for him.

"Steve called me and set up a meeting at the Four Seasons Hotel in Beverly Hills," Debbie said. "To meet him, I dressed for the part in an outfit that included a wig, glasses, Minnie's granny dress, and little or no makeup."

"When Steve entered the bar, I waved him over to our table, but he took one look at me and moved on. I had to call him back and identify myself. I must have looked like a hooker servicing the men who fought in World War II. He liked it, telling me that all my look needed was a prosthetic nose."

When HBO eventually released it on TV, *Behind the Candelabra* attracted 3.5 million viewers. *The Guardian* defined it as "a black comedy, a portrait of celebrity loneliness that is very stylish and effective, with Damon and Douglas giving supremely entertaining performances."

***

John Cohan has been called "The Celebrity Psychic to the Stars." His yearly predictions are published by columnist Cindy Adams in *The New York Post*. Over the years, many famous stars have turned to him for his insights into their future and for his spiritual guidance. His clients have included Elizabeth Taylor, Elvis Presley, Burt Reynolds, Julia Roberts, Merv Griffin, Lana Turner, and an array of others who have called on him. So also did Sandra Dee, the love of his life.

Many vignettes of his life are encased in his memoir, *Catch a Falling Star*, which is filled with any number of surprising celebrity secrets.

One of its biggest revelations spins around Nicole Brown Simpson, the murdered former wife of O.J. Simpson. She was Cohan's friend. Before her death, she revealed to him that she was having an affair with Ron Goldman, a waiter, who was slaughtered alongside her on her doorstep

During the course of Cohan's career, Agnes Moorehead became his friend. *[Some movie fans remember her from her role in Orson Welles'* Citizen Kane *(1941); others remember her as Samantha Stevens' witchy, bitchy mother in the long-running TV series,* Bewitched *(1964-1972).]*

If anyone, during her later years, knew Moorehead back then, he or she eventually met Debbie, as the two women were best friends.

In Hollywood circles, Morehead was widely recognized and accepted as a lesbian and the centerpiece of widespread gossip. Those rumors were widely circulated by Eddie Fisher after he bolted from Debbie. "I left her in Agnes' arms," he claimed.

Cohan was aware of the close emotional links the actresses shared for each other. "If they provided love and comfort to each other, so much the better," he said. "We must lower the shades on what really went on between these remarkable talents."

According to Cohan, "In a town loaded with ambitious stars, career-conscious Debbie was one of the leaders of the pack."

She had approached him with concern about a role she'd been offered in a horror movie entitled *What's the Matter with Helen?* She didn't know it at the time, but it would be the last leading role in a feature film that she'd ever be offered. Scheduled for release in June of 1971 by United Artists, the movie would co-star Shelley Winters.

At the time, a lot of faded stars had made themselves available for the filming of horror flicks. The fad had been launched in 1962 when Bette Davis and Joan Crawford had campily co-starred together in *What Ever Happened to Baby Jane?*

With the intention of prolonging and perhaps enhancing her career, Debbie both wanted and feared an involvement in a genre (horror) that had never been associated with her before. In a discreet conversation with Cohan, Debbie confessed, "This is such a rad-

John Cohan was hailed as "The Celebrity Psychic to the Stars," and he became a close friend of Agnes Moorehead, Debbie's dearest companion.

During the years she knew him, Debbie confessed both her fears and her secrets to this insightful visionary who was always "gentle, thoughtful, and a special soul" to the stars, many of whom became his friend.

611

ical departure from *Tammy*. I don't know if I can pull it off. I feel insecure."

Cohan assured her that she could do it, and that the film—even if it didn't become a blockbusting success—would sharpen her acting skills.

On the set of *What's the Matter with Helen?*, during the first week of shooting, Winters got along fairly well with Debbie and asked if she could visit her that upcoming Saturday night. Acquiescing, Debbie invited her to her home for dinner. As Debbie later confessed to Cohan, "Shelley hit on me, and we exchanged words. I didn't know Shelley had a lez streak in her. Up to now, I'd heard she was strictly a stud seducer." *[She was no doubt referring to Winters' long string of lovers who had included Clark Gable, Errol Flynn, Burt Lancaster, Sean Connery, and among many others, Marlon Brando.]*

One night in Manhattan at Downey's Restaurant near Times Square, Winters told some of her male friends that when she had roomed with Marilyn Monroe during that actress's impoverished debut, they often had sex with each other. *[At table with her that evening were actors who included Winters' temporary lover, Christopher Jones; the vintage Hollywood film noir star, John Ireland; the novelist, James Leo Herlihy, author of* Midnight Cowboy; *and Darwin Porter.]*

That Saturday night within her home, Debbie resisted Winters' sexual advances, and—beginning the following Monday, as Debbie told Cohan—"It was living hell on the set of *Helen*."

Cohan also learned that J. Edgar Hoover had, over the decades that he'd been chief honcho at the F.B.I., accumulated an enormous dossier on Debbie.

[One of Hoover's most malevolent pastimes involved summoning members of his staff, behind the scenes, to document the bedtime preferences of Hollywood celebrities. A closeted homosexual himself, Hoover made arrangements to have many of these controversial files destroyed within a few days of his death. For more about this, refer to Blood Moon's 2012 release of Darwin Porter's J. Edgar Hoover & Clyde Tolson, Investigating the Sexual Secrets of America's Most Famous Men and Women.*]*

During the final years of her life, Debbie, according to Cohan, lived in fear that unsavory details associated with her private life might be exposed. From her (heavily whitewashed) memoirs, readers get the impression that she rarely slept with anyone outside the boundaries of marriage to her trio of husbands.

In vivid contrast to the image she projected, Debbie sustained affairs with a number of men, and certainly—in the years before her marriage to

As director of the FBI, J. Edgar Hoover of the bulldog face, ordered many of his agents in New York and California to investigate the private lives of celebrities for his own voyeuristic pleasure.

His G-Men accumulated a "fat file" on Debbie.

Eddie Fisher, got involved in what she called "heavy petting."]

The last time Cohan ever saw Debbie was associated with her entertainment gig within the Cabaret Theater within *The Mohegan Sun. [Located in Uncasville, in southeastern Connecticut, it's one of the largest casino resorts in the United States. When Cohan saw her there, she'd been drinking heavily as a patron at the on-site bar associated with Bobby Flay's Restaurant.]*

According to Cohan, "I had seen nothing but trouble ahead for her in her marriages. Even though her unions with Harry Karl and Richard Hamlett had led her to financial ruin, I predicted that she'd go out of her life with millions—and she did." *[Cohan was referring to the multi-million dollar selloff of her Hollywood costumes and props.]*

Although at the time he wondered if she'd be in any condition to go onstage, she miraculously pulled herself together and delivered her act wearing a dazzling smile and a sequin-spangled gown split up the left side. *[At the time, she was the unchallenged star of the company she'd formed to help stage and promote her acts, "Debbie Reynolds Ain't Down Yet Productions."]*

She moved rapidly forward on stage, romping through nostalgic, outrageous, and sometimes campy episodes of Hollywood history. Sometimes she shocked the sheltered members of her audience with her potty mouth—a manifestation of *Tammy* that some of them might not have expected. Projected on a screen behind her were clips from some of her vintage movies, especially the dance scenes from *Singin' in the Rain.*

The audience was especially impressed by her "impressions" of divas, including her favorite, Zsa Zsa Gabor.

["DAH-LINKS!" she projected toward the audience. "I was married to Conrad Hilton, but I spent most of my marriage getting fucked by his son, Nicky. But he finally dumped me and married Elizabeth Taylor."

The highlight of her show was Debbie's reprised medley of Judy Garland hits, especially "Over the Rainbow."]

After the show, she had a long conversation with Cohan, blaming herself for the turmoil in the life of her bipolar daughter, Carrie, which had had recently led to electroshock treatments in a mental hospital. He tried to relieve her of any guilt, blaming it on "that bad crowd" Carrie had been running

Onstage, she wore a blonde wig, an accessory she described as "perky." Then, with a style and panache that those who had been following her interpreted as self-deprecating and endearing, she said, "I'm glad that my fans are still alive. Many of you younger kids may never have heard of me. I'm Princess Leia's mother."

around with in Manhattan, especially John Belushi. "Hanging out with those guys 'poisoned' her," Cohan claimed.

In his view, Debbie seemed obsessed with the singer and actress, Connie Stevens, whom Eddie Fisher had married after Elizabeth Taylor had thrown him out of her life. "Perhaps Debbie was jealous of Connie, who was so much younger."

Connie had given birth to two children during the course of her marriage to Eddie Fisher: Joely Fisher and Tricia Leigh Fisher.

Debbie told Cohan, "They are now half-siblings to my Todd and Carrie, but I don't see us getting together for a family reunion."

Cohan had known Connie long before met Debbie, having attended grammar school with her. "Connie's was a Cinderella story gone bad. She went from a sweet, charming girl into an angry, thin woman, often frail-looking and bitchy."

During the last hour that Cohan ever spent with Debbie, her mood became reflective: "I've kissed frogs, but I've also smooched with princes, King Baudouin of Belgium and Robert Wagner, once the Prince of Hollywood. I've lived through it all and suffered the blows, and I plan to perform until my final moments, croaking onstage in the middle of my act, probably in a long-forgotten, dismal place like Broken Bow, Nebraska."

***

During the first decade of the 21st Century, Carrie continued to receive film roles, including parts in three more installments of the *Star Wars* franchise as Princess (or General) Leia.

Much of her time was spent writing, polishing, and performing her one-woman show, *Wishful Drinking*, which opened for a sold-out eight-week run beginning in November of 2006 at the Geffen Playhouse in Los Angeles. From there, it moved on to venues in Berkeley, Seattle, San Jose, Boston, and Hartford before arriving in Manhattan at Studio 54.

Her book, *Wishful Drinking* had been released in December of 2008 to a mixture of praise and criticism.

In 2012, HBO reformatted and filmed it as a full-length documentary-style overview of

In her autobiographical *Wishful Drinking*, readers got a glimpse into the world of Princess Leia. The book was filled with pills and booze...and a lot more.

Some readers attacked her "giddy girlie" writing style. Others found it "the story of a woman who had had a fair share of extreme highs and extreme lows."

her very special life. During her oft-repeated delivery of the material she knew so well, Carrie skipped around and across many of its details. Consequently, for a viewer to know something about her travails in advance of its screening is very helpful.

In HBO's televised version, Carrie presents a billboard, a weirdly instructional diagram of her complicated family tree, fully inclusive of her famous parents, her sibling spouses, step-parents (one of whom was Elizabeth Taylor), half-siblings, step-siblings, and more.

She talks very personally about scenes that include her recurring bouts with alcohol and drug abuse, and her history as a bipolar who had spent time in some mental institutions.

A fan wrote, "Hearing Princess Leia reveal all these tales is just priceless."

***

The cable TV film ran for 76 minutes and was released as a DVD in 2011. The *Los Angeles Times* said, "Fisher can be broad, but that is also the person she plays everywhere now: a little larger than life, worn but not worn out." A critic from the *Boston Globe* said that "Her obsession with her parents and step parents can be a little tiresome, but honest. She even seems boastful about her dysfunction. Her show is like a narcissistic screed."

***

A drama, *Maps to the Stars* (2014) was written by Bruce Wagner as an acerbic and satirical look behind the scenes of Tinseltown, what one critic described as "a tour into the heart of a Hollywood family chasing celebrity."

A hard sell, the script had floated around Hollywood for six years, and Carrie read it and wanted to appear in a cameo as herself within it. "To get cast, I made Bruce (Wagner), its scriptwriter, the godfather of my daughter, Billie Lourd."

Its director, David Cronenberg, had made most of his previous films in Canada. "Hollywood is a world that's seductive and repellent at the same time, and it's the combination of the two that makes it so potent."

Julianne Moore was cast as Havana Segrand, a once-famous, aging Freudian mess who lives resentfully in the shadow of her movie-star mother. Into Havana's orbit comes the younger, docile-looking Agatha Weiss, played by Mia Wasikowska, an estranged, barely controllable pyromaniac, who accepts a position as Havana's personal assistant. Carrie delivers a brief cameo performance as Havana's "best friend" who urges her, based on their encounter on Twitter, to hire the mysterious screwed-up newcomer as her assistant.

Other star parts were interpreted by John Cusack as a telegenic psychotherapist and head of the spectacularly dysfunctional Weiss family; and Robert Pattinson as a struggling limousine driver ("the only character in the film who's not going insane"), who yearns for stardom as an actor and screenwriter. Pattinson described the movie as a dark tale "about people who lie to themselves—right up until the end."

Maps to the Stars died a painful death at the box office, earning just $4 million on a budget of $13 million.

Carrie denied that *Maps to the Stars* exaggerated Hollywood culture. "It's hard to exaggerate an exaggeration. Being in Hollywood is like handling a grenade with the pin pulled out."

***

Star Wars: The Force Awakens (2015), another epic space opera, was the first installment of the *Star Wars* Sequel Trilogy, and the seventh main installment of the Star Wars franchise first launched by George Lukas. Like the others, it, too, featured Carrie, but not as "Princess" Leia Organa, but as the wiser and more mature "General" Leia Organa. Harrison Ford reprised his durable, long-standing character of Han Solo and Mark Hamill once again portrayed Luke Skywalker.

The Walt Disney studio was now in charge, having acquired the franchise from Lucasfilm in 2012. Director J.J. Abrams hauled his cameras to sites that included Abu Dhabi and Iceland, with principal photography in Ireland and at the Pinewood Studios in England.

Reporters greeted Carrie on her first day of work. "*Star Wars* has been my whole life," she said. "It wasn't like a deal made with the devil. It's now a deal with Disney. It's like a summer camp for droids, and it's nice to be back among droidkateers. The new actors in the series are great. Harrison, Mark, and I are now the old guard at a reunion. The new guys we call the freshmen. I should warn them that if they go over and the series continues, they're likely to be stalked by fans for the next forty years, as I was."

She was also asked about her claims that George Lukas had ruined her life. "I meant

Time marches inexorably on, both galactically and here on Earth.

In *The Force Awakens*, General Leia appears in a moment of vulnerability

that in only the nicest way possible. He certainly changed my life. But he couldn't ruin it. It was weird right from the beginning. No one had the power to ruin my life. But George had the power to transform it and do it fast."

"As for Leia, I am Leia, and Leia is me. We've overlapped each other because my life has been so cartoony. At my age, it would be ridiculous if I had a problem with it. Most of my fans are really nice, even if I am tattooed on their arm."

In the latest franchise, thirty years have passed since the last Galactic Civil War. A terrifying new union, The First Order, has risen from the fallen Galactic Empire, and it seeks to eliminate the New Republic. The Resistance, backed by the Republic, is led by General Organa (Carrie, that is). As the plot unfolds, Leia searches for her lost brother, Luke Skywalker.

Ford said he was comfortable once again as Han Solo, "Even though I'm attacked by gangs seeking to settle old debts with me. As I age, I do not aspire in future *Star Wars* to become some New Age Alec Guinness. There's a lot of the rogue still left in Han Solo. Some things don't change."

Carrie's General Leia was described by one critic as "a little more than battle weary, a little more broken hearted."

"Leia is as committed as ever to her cause, but I would imagine feeling somewhat defeated, tired, and pissed," Carrie said.

For their involvements, Ford was paid $25 million, plus 0.5 percent of the gross, with Carrie getting $1.5 million. "I guess Disney doesn't believe in equal pay," she said.

For the most part, the new *Star Wars* received positive reviews and became the highest-grossing film in North America that year. In all, it took in $2 billion during its worldwide release, making a profit of 780 million. It had been phenomenally expensive to produce.

***

Rogue One: A Star Wars Story (2016) was yet another epic space drama, but with a twist. This was the first installment what its producers designated as a "stand alone" film, the first in a new *Star Wars* "anthology" series.

Its chronology was adjusted to a time before the passage of events in the original *Star Wars* film. It depicts a group of rebels on a mission to steal the plans for the Death Star, the Galactic Empire's super weapon.

The new cast included the British actress Felicity Jones, playing Jyn Erso, a former criminal who aids the Rebel Alliance in a desperate attempt to steal the plans to the Death Star. She's backed up by Diego Luna, Ben Mendelsohn, and Forest Whitaker.

Grand Moff Tarkin and Princess Leia were portrayed by Guy Henry and Ingvild Deila with digital likenesses of Peter Cushing and Carrie superimposed over the faces of those newer actors. Archival audio of Carrie was used to replicate the voice of the character she was most associated with.

The film received fair praise, and garnered Oscar nods for Best Sound and Best Visual Effects, grossing $1 billion worldwide.

***

Star Wars: The Last Jedi (2017) would mark Carrie's final appearance in a *Star Wars* film. Contrary to reports, it was not her last feature film, however.

Written and directed by Rian Johnson, *The Last Jedi* was distributed by Disney. Like the others in the *Star Wars* franchise, it starred Mark Hamill as Luke Skywalker and Carrie as General Leia Organa. Carrie was assigned a larger part than she had had in *The Force Awakens*. At the end of the film, as a post-mortem tribute, there was a touching dedication to her. Director Johnson told the press that he did not tinker with Carrie's scenes after her death.

Most of *The Last Jedi's* plot centered on one single standoff between the Resistance and the First Order, a "historical space event" that, in the plot, unfolds over a period of 24 hours. At first, it appears that Carrie, as Leia, is going to be blown into Outer Space within fifteen minutes of the opening scenes of the film. But she comes back in full force after her body has gone spinning. She uses her dying energy for one big Force push.

In *The Last Jedi*, Carrie's daughter, Billie Lourd, was cast in a small role.

At the London premiere of *The Last Jedi*, the press caught up with Hamill, who, in reference to his late co-star, said, "I always think of Carrie in the present," he told reporters. "Never the past."

***

Carrie's final feature film, *Wonderwell*, had not yet been released at the time of her death in 2016, and at presstime, its opening had been scheduled for sometime in 2018. Its director, Vlad Marsavin, in his feature film debut, had cast her alongside Rita Ora, best known as a British pop singer and as the actress who played Christian Grey's sister, Mia, in *Fifty Shades of Grey* (2015).

Violet is a 12-year-old girl who is impish and awkward, living with her parents and her flashy, competitive older sister in Italy. She wanders into a nearby forest, where she meets a mysterious stranger (Carrie), who sends her on a mission of discovery armed with an intu-

Reporter Natalie Finn wrote, "Leia was brave, resilient, and magnetic, with a face that launched millions of crushes from young men, and a gold bikini so memorable it was re-enshrined in the lexicon via a classic *Friends* TV episode thirteen years later."

itive new gift: She can view herself in the future. During the course of the film, Violet transitions from girlhood to womanhood. Hers, however, may be a journey of no return.

***

Bright Lights: Starring Carrie Fisher and Debbie Reynolds (2017) marked their last screen appearance together as a mother-daughter team on this HBO TV special. "Two old troupers, bidding farewell to the screen, were shining for the last time in this almost embarrassingly intimate portrait," wrote one critic.

Its producers marketed this focus on the players' mother/daughter dynamic to fans of both Golden Age Hollywood and to fans of *Star Wars*—as well as to gossipy voyeurs in general. Home movie clips reveal Carrie and Todd as playful children growing up as the kids of celebrities. Debbie is shown having a friendly debate with Carrie. In real life, their debates were far more intense, sometimes leading to long separations.

Caught in the middle between these two divas, Todd appears as a reasonable anchor within the family, and not eccentric at all.

Directors Fisher Stevens and Alexis Bloom turned *Bright Lights* into a kind of reality show that was ultimately viewed as a "soul tango of past and present."

Debbie and Carrie are shown in bizarrely decorated homes, amicably co-existing as next-door neighbors. Carrie bakes a *soufflé* to feed to Debbie and herself, although a dog gets in on the act.

One critic called it, "Not a *Postcard from the Edge,* but more likely a smiley-faced *Grey Gardens* or else *All About Eve: The Golden Age."*

The viewer journeys back to Debbie's marriage to Eddie Fisher, viewed as a surrealistic disaster, or her second marriage to Harry Karl, a financial disaster.

Reporter Gwen Gleiberman wrote, "Through it all, Reynolds held onto her goodness screen image. She's never not 'on,' as Eddie Fisher once

Bright Lights: Starring Carrie Fisher and Debbie Reynolds was defined as "a portrait of two late stars and their loving and complex bond, a gem of documentary intimacy that, when viewed today, seems karmically timed."

charged. She's a more serene Betty White on the *Golden Girls*, speaking in soft-edged zingers."

In *Bright Lights*, clips are included of Carrie at a *Star Wars* convention. Devoted acolytes have waited patiently to have their picture taken and autographed by Princess Leia. This *schtick* became quite profitable for her, as she charged each fan $75 to have their picture taken with her. She erroneously referred to her posing for a photograph in these circumstances as a "celebrity lap dance."

On camera, Debbie shares her philosophy of life, explaining how her *Unsinkable Molly* persona had survived: "The only way you make it through life is to fight. You don't get there the easy way. If you feel sorry for yourself, and if you let yourself down, you'll drown."

"These two never went down," Gleiberman wrote, "and neither one of them got there the easy way. Watching *Bright Lights*, it doesn't seem too much of a stretch to presume that they're still together, and always will be, holding up their mirrors of love."

Epilogue

In December of 2016, Carrie Fisher was in London promoting her latest memoir, *The Princess Diarist*. It was based on recently "re-discovered" journals that she'd developed during the filming in England of the first installment of *Star Wars*.

At last, she formally admitted what many of her fans had suspected for a very long time: The then-married Harrison Ford and Carrie had been lovers off screen.

As she packed her suitcases in advance of her return flight to L.A. from Heathrow, Carrie had complained of being exhausted, and planned a long rest in California. She had endured a sleepless night and had swallowed some of her trusty pills, but that didn't seem to bring much relief. Perhaps, purely based on sheer exhaustion, she'd be able to sleep on the airplane.

Hours into the flight, she called out, alerting the flight attendant and the other passengers in first class that something was wrong. Then she passed out. Efforts were made to revive her, but she remained unconscious throughout the duration of that very long flight. She was still breathing, at least, although it was obvious that she'd suffered what the attendants thought was a massive heart attack.

The airport staff at LAX was alerted that a passenger aboard an arriving flight had suffered a stroke and that an ambulance should be waiting to rush her to a hospital as soon as her plane landed.

After it landed, four men boarded the plane to carefully move her onto a stretcher. From there, she was loaded into an ambulance. With dome lights flashing, it rushed to an intensive care unit.

By then, news of the incident had been tweeted and texted to the world at large by dozens of on-board passengers. Word spread to the press, and Debbie and Todd were among the first to be alerted. Even though she wasn't feeling well herself, she rushed, accompanied by Todd, to the hospital. Stricken with anxiety and grief, each of them feared the worst.

They maintained a vigil, making themselves available for any task required of them whenever they were allowed to visit. In her hospital bed, Carrie remained under an oxygen tent.

Her death came four days later, on December 27, 2016. Bulletins went out around the world, and some American newspapers printed obituaries beneath "Second Coming" headlines. *The New York Times* interpreted her death as an event so newsworthy that they featured it on its frontpage.

Tributes and sympathy calls poured in for Debbie about the passing of her daughter. Painfully, she and Todd began the funeral arrangements, with the understanding that in advance of her death, Carrie had clearly specified her wish to be cremated.

Hundreds of her fans expressed grief at the passing of Princess Leia. Harrison Ford weighed in with, "Carrie Fisher was one of a kind—brilliant, original, funny, and emotionally fearless. She lived her life bravely."

Steven Spielberg said, "I have always stood in awe of Carrie, and her suggestions always made me laugh and gasp at the same time. She didn't need The Force. She was a force of nature, of loyalty, and friendship. I will miss her very much."

The results of an autopsy were revealed to the press: Tests showed traces of cocaine, Ecstasy, heroin, morphine, methadone, and merperidine in her system, substances collectively capable of suppressing breathing and the respiratory drive.

Her official cause of death was diagnosed as "sleep apnea and other undetermined factors."

A doctor asserted that "Miss Fisher's use of legal and illegal drugs proved a deadly combination."

In the hours after Carrie's death, Debbie seemed to grow weaker, and often sighed with despair during the funeral arrangements she and Todd had organized for her daughter and his sister.

She wept in front of Carrie's casket, delivering her final farewell before the body was placed in a hearse for delivery to the funeral home. Documents associated with her last will and testament had revealed her clearly stated wish to protect Billie Lourd financially.

 Throughout the month that preceded her daughter's death, Debbie had complained of headaches, and she'd become unsteady on her feet. She had not slept well at night, and complained, "I'm tired when I wake up, tired when I go to bed. Oh, to be sixty again."

Even so, she bravely carried on, admitting, "My heart is broken."

After 6½ decades in show business, she was now eighty-four years old, with a birthday coming up on April 1. According to Todd, "The shock of Carrie's death had been too much for her to take. She told me she didn't know how much longer she could go on."

Debbie issued a statement aimed at the many Princess Leia fans who had expressed their sympathies: "I am so grateful to all of you for your condolences and prayers for Todd and me, who are left behind. They have given me renewed strength. Carrie is now on her way to her new home in the galaxy."

***

Death came to Debbie on December 28, 2016, a day after the death of her daughter.

There was much speculation that she had died of a broken heart. Todd said, "Mother told me goodbye until we meet again on some distant shore."

Since turning eighty, she had experienced a generalized decline in her health, and some days, she didn't want to get out of bed. One of her last disappointments involved not being able to attend the 2015 Academy Awards presentations. The Academy had announced its intention to present her with Lifetime Achievement Award, which they did, awarding it to her in absentia.

Fans and friends from around the world expressed their condolences. Many key figures from her past had already passed on, stars who included Agnes Moorehead, Elizabeth Taylor, and Judy Garland.

Albert Brooks, who had directed and co-starred with her in *Mother* (1996), told the press, "Debbie Reynolds is a legend and my movie mom. My heart goes out to Todd and Billie Lourd."

Bette Midler said, "Her death is hard to comprehend. She was beautiful, talented, and dedicated to her craft, and her legacy will live on."

The question most often asked was, "Did Debbie Reynolds die of a broken heart?"

Dr. Suzanne Steinbaum, director of the Women and Heart Health program at Lenox Hill Hospital in Manhattan, said, "The sudden loss of a child or a spouse, perhaps the foremost of life's cruelties, sets off an overflow of stress hormones, and on occasion, the heart collapses."

Reports from the American Heart Association assert that intense grief can lead to cardiac arrest, even if a patient has no history of heart disease.

On January 8, 2018, a joint funeral for Carrie Fisher and Debbie Reynolds was held at Forest Lawn. Arriving dressed entirely in black, Todd carried a Prozac-shaped urn containing Carrie's ashes, with the intention of placing them into the grave, beside his mother's coffin.

Billie Lourd had been designated as the sole heir to Carrie's multi-million dollar estate. She later spoke of the passing of her mother and grandmother: "I've always lived in their shadows, and now the time has come in my life when I must go on with my own life and stand on my own. I loved being my mother's daughter. That is something I will always have. But from now on, I will be just Billie."

Fans from around the word mourned their passings, sending out a message, perhaps to another galaxy:

FAREWELL
PRINCESS LEIA

&

FAREWELL
UNSINKABLE
DEBBIE

Princess Leia and Unsinkable Tammy in Hell:
ITS AUTHORS

DARWIN PORTER

As an intense nine-year-old, **Darwin Porter** began meeting movie stars, TV personalities, politicians, and singers through his vivacious and attractive mother, Hazel, an eccentric but charismatic Southern girl who had lost her husband in World War II. Migrating from the Depression-ravaged valleys of western North Carolina to Miami Beach during its most ebullient heyday, Hazel became a stylist, wardrobe mistress, and personal assistant to the vaudeville *comedienne* **Sophie Tucker**, the bawdy and irrepressible "Last of the Red Hot Mamas."

Virtually every show-biz celebrity who visited Miami Beach paid a call on "Miss Sophie," and Darwin, as a pre-teen loosely and indulgently supervised by his mother, was regularly dazzled by the likes of **Judy Garland, Dinah Shore,** and **Frank Sinatra.**

It was at Miss Sophie's that he met his first political figure, who was actually an actor at the time. Between marriages, **Ronald Reagan** came to call on Ms. Sophie, who was his favorite singer. He was accompanied by a young blonde starlet, **Marilyn Monroe.**

At the University of Miami, Darwin edited the school newspaper. He first met and interviewed **Eleanor Roosevelt** at the Fontainebleau Hotel on Miami Beach and invited her to spend a day at the university. She accepted, much to his delight.

After graduation, he became the Bureau Chief of *The Miami Herald* in Key West, Florida, where he got to take early morning walks with the former U.S. president **Harry S Truman**, discussing his presidency and the events that had shaped it.

Through Truman, Darwin was introduced and later joined the staff of **Senator George Smathers** of Florida. His best friend was a young senator, **John F. Kennedy.** Through "Gorgeous George," as Smathers was known in the Senate, Darwin got to meet Jack and Jacqueline in Palm Beach. He later wrote two books about them—*The Kennedys, All the Gossip Unfit to Print,* and one of his all-time bestsellers, *Jacqueline Kennedy Onassis—A Life Beyond Her Wildest Dreams.*

For about a decade in New York, Darwin worked in television journalism and advertising with his long-time partner, the journalist, art director, and arts-industry socialite **Stanley Mills Haggart.**

Stanley (as an art director) and Darwin (as a writer and assistant), worked as freelance agents in television. Jointly, they helped produce TV commercials that included testimonials from **Joan Crawford** (then feverishly promoting Pepsi-

Cola); **Ronald Reagan** (General Electric); and **Debbie Reynolds** (Singer sewing machines). Other personalities appearing and delivering televised sales pitches included **Louis Armstrong, Lena Horne,** and **Arlene Dahl,** each of them hawking a commercial product.

Beginning in the early 1960s, Darwin joined forces with the then-fledgling **Arthur Frommer** organization, playing a key role in researching and writing more than 50 titles and defining the style and values that later emerged as the world's leading travel guidebooks, *The Frommer Guides,* with particular emphasis on Europe, New England, and the Caribbean. Between the creation and updating of hundreds of editions of detailed travel guides to England, France, Italy, Spain, Portugal, Austria, Hungary, Germany, Switzerland, the Caribbean, and California, he continued to interview and discuss the triumphs, feuds, and frustrations of celebrities, many by then reclusive, whom he either sought out or encountered randomly as part of his extensive travels. **Ava Gardner, Debbie Reynolds,** and **Lana Turner** were particularly insightful.

It was while living in New York that Darwin became fascinated by the career of a rising real estate mogul changing the skyline of Manhattan. He later, of course, became the "gambling czar" of Atlantic City and a star of reality TV.

Darwin began collecting an astonishing amount of data on Donald Trump, squirreling it away in boxes, hoping one day to write a biography of this charismatic, controversial figure.

Before doing that, he penned more than thirty-five uncensored, unvarnished, and unauthorized biographies on subjects that included **Donald Trump, Bill and Hillary Clinton, Ronald Reagan and Nancy Davis, Jane Wyman, Jacqueline Kennedy, Jack Kennedy, Lana Turner, Peter O'Toole, James Dean, Marlon Brando, Merv Griffin, Katharine Hepburn, Howard Hughes, Humphrey Bogart, Michael Jackson, Paul Newman, Steve McQueen, Marilyn Monroe, Elizabeth Taylor, Rock Hudson, Frank Sinatra, Vivien Leigh, Laurence Olivier, the notorious porn star Linda Lovelace, Zsa Zsa Gabor and her sisters, Tennessee Williams, Gore Vidal,** and **Truman Capote.**

As a departure from his usual repertoire, Darwin also wrote the controversial *J. Edgar Hoover & Clyde Tolson: Investigating the Sexual Secrets of America's Most Famous Men and Women,* a book about celebrity, voyeurism, political and sexual repression, and blackmail within the highest circles of the U.S. government.

Porter's biographies, over the years, have won twenty-five first prize or "runner-up to first prize" awards at literary festivals in cities or states which include New England, New York, Los Angeles, Hollywood, San Francisco, Florida, California, and Paris.

Darwin can be heard at regular intervals as a radio and television commentator, "dishing" celebrities, pop culture, politics, and scandal.

A resident of New York City, Darwin is currently at work on a startling new biography of *Playboy's* Hugh Hefner.

DANFORTH PRINCE

The co-author of this book, **Danforth Prince** is president and founder of Blood Moon Productions, a publishing venture that's devoted to salvaging, compiling, and marketing the oral histories of America's entertainment industry.

Prince launched his career in journalism in the 1970s at the Paris Bureau of *The New York Times*. In the early '80s, he joined Darwin Porter in developing first editions of many of the titles within *The Frommer Guides*. Together, they reviewed and articulated the travel scenes of more than 50 nations, most of them within Europe and The Caribbean. Authoritative and comprehensive, they became best-selling "travel bibles" for millions of readers.

Prince, in collaboration with Porter, is also the co-author of several award-winning celebrity biographies, each configured as a title within **Blood Moon's Babylon series.** These have included *Hollywood Babylon—It's Back!; Hollywood Babylon Strikes Again; The Kennedys: All the Gossip Unfit to Print; Frank Sinatra, The Boudoir Singer, Elizabeth Taylor: There Is Nothing Like a Dame; Pink Triangle: The Feuds and Private Lives of Tennessee Williams, Gore Vidal, Truman Capote, and Members of their Entourages*; and *Jacqueline Kennedy Onassis: A Life Beyond Her Wildest Dreams*. More recent efforts include *Lana Turner, Hearts and Diamonds Take All; Peter O'-Toole—Hellraiser, Sexual Outlaw, Irish Rebel; Bill & Hillary—So This Is That Thing Called Love; James Dean, Tomorrow Never Comes*; and *Rock Hudson Erotic Fire.*

One of his recent projects, co-authored with Darwin Porter, is *Donald Trump, The Man Who Would Be King.* Configured for release directly into the frenzy of the 2016 presidential elections, and winner of at least three literary awards, it's a celebrity exposé of the decades of pre-presidential scandals—personal, political, and dynastic—associated with **The Donald** during the rambunctious decades when no one ever thought he'd actually get elected.

Prince is also the co-author of four books on film criticism, three of which won honors at regional bookfests in Los Angeles and San Francisco.

Prince, a graduate of Hamilton College and a native of Easton and Bethlehem, Pennsylvania, is the president and founder of the Georgia Literary Association (1996), and of the Porter and Prince Corporation (1983) which has produced dozens of titles for Simon & Schuster, Prentice Hall, and John Wiley & Sons. In 2011, he was named "Publisher of the Year" by a consortium of literary critics and marketers spearheaded by the J.M. Northern Media Group.

He has electronically documented some of the controversies associated with his stewardship of Blood Moon in at least 50 documentaries, book trailers, public speeches, and TV or radio interviews. Most of these are available on **YouTube.com**

627

and **Facebook** *(keywords: "Danforth Prince" or "Blood Moon Productions");* on **Twitter** *(#BloodyandLunar);* or by clicking on **BloodMoonProductions.com**.

He is currently at work writing and researching an upcoming biography focussing on *Playboy's* Hugh Hefner.

Do you want to meet him up close, personal, and on his home turf? Prince is also an innkeeper, running a historic bed & breakfast in New York City, **Magnolia House (www.MagnoliaHouseSaintGeorge.com).** Affiliated with AirBnb, and increasingly sought out by filmmakers as an evocative locale for moviemaking, it lies in highly desirable Saint George, at the northernmost tip of Staten Island, a district that's historically associated with Henry James, Theodore Dreiser, the Vanderbilts, and key moments in the colonial history of America.

Set in a verdant, large, and carefully terraced garden, and boasting a history of visits from literary and show-biz stars who have included Tennessee Williams, Gloria Swanson, Jolie Gabor, Ruth Warwick, Greta Keller, Lucille Lortel, and many of the luminaries of Broadway, the inn is within a ten-minute walk to the ferries sailing at 20- to 30-minute intervals to the Financial District and subway junctions of Lower Manhattan. Publicized as "a reasonably priced celebrity-centric retreat with links to the book trades," and the beneficiary of rave ("superhost") reviews from hundreds of previous clients, many of whom arrive from around the world, often as part of extended families, **Magnolia House** is loaded with furniture and memorabilia that Prince collected during his decades as a travel journalist for the Frommer Guides.

*Stay with Us! Learn more about "Celebrity-Centric Sleepovers" at Blood Moon's **Magnolia House**, a historic and moderately priced "Airbnb" in New York City.*

For more information about the welcome and hospitality that's waiting for you
at the Bed and Breakfast affiliate of Blood Moon Productions, click on
MagnoliaHouseSaintGeorge.com

Who Actually Writes These Books?

If You Want to Meet Them, Consider a Sleepover at their Headquarters in the Big Apple.

Magnolia House

Our publishing venture lies immediately upstairs from a reasonably priced, widely reviewed "AirBnB.com" Bed and Breakfast in New York City. In addition to overnight hospitality, it specializes in literary nostaligia, the history of pop culture, and the book trades. Elegant, historic, well-furnished, & comfortable, it's an architectural and literary landmark within the highly desirable neighborhood of St. George, Staten Island, a ten-minute walk from the departure point of the famous ferryboats to Manhattan.

As stated by its resident manager, **Danforth Prince**, "Magnolia House results from my 30-year role as co-author of many titles, and many editions, of *The Frommer Guides*, each of which included evaluations of the bed and breakfast inns of Europe. Whereas I'm still writing travel articles and celebrity *exposés* from the upper floors of this building, most of it now operates as a celebrity-centric AirBnb with links to the early days of the Frommer Guides, 'the Golden Age of Travel,' and Blood Moon's associations with Broadway, Hollywood, and the Entertainment Industry. The next time you visit New York City, COME STAY WITH US!"

Edgy media associations have always been part of the Magnolia House experience. Previous guests have included **Tennessee Williams** *("Magnolia House reminds me of Blanche DuBois' lost plantation, Bellereve!")*; golden age film personality **Joan Blondell** (a close friend of celebrity biographer and co-owner, **Darwin Porter**); **Lucille Lortel** (the philanthropic but very temperamental Queen of Off-Broadway); the very outspoken **Jolie Gabor** (mother of the three "Bombshells from Budapest" otherwise known as **Zsa Zsa, Eva, and Magda**); and a host of other stars, *starlettes*, and *demi-mondains* of all descriptions and persuasions.

For photographs, testimonials from previous guests, and information about availabilities and reservations, click on **www.MagnoliaHouseSaintGeorge.com**.

Magnolia House is the historic home in NYC where we research, write, & publish Blood Moon's Award-Winning Entertainment About How America Interprets Its Celebrities.

It's called "Show-Biz Hospitality," and it collaborates with AirBnB. Stay for a sleepover in Blood Moon's magnolia-scented Bed & Breakfast during your next trip to New York City. Stay at ***MagnoliaHouseSaintGeorge.com***

DONALD TRUMP
IS *THE MAN WHO WOULD BE KING*

This is the most famous book about our incendiary President you've probably never heard of.

Winner of three respected literary awards, and released three months before the Presidentail elections of 2016, it's an entertainingly packaged, artfully salacious bombshell, a scathingly historic overview of America during its 2016 election cycle, a portrait unlike anything ever published on CANDIDATE DONALD and the climate in which he thrived and massacred his political rivals.

Its volcanic, much-suppressed release during the heat and venom of the Presidential campaign has already been heralded by the *Midwestern Book Review, California Book Watch, the Seattle Gay News*, the staunchly right-wing **WILS-AM radio**, and also by the editors at the most popular Seniors' magazine in Florida, *BOOMER TIMES*, which designated it as their September choice for **BOOK OF THE MONTH.**

TRUMPOCALYPSE: *"Donald Trump: The Man Who Would Be King* is recommended reading for all sides, no matter what political stance is being adopted: Republican, Democrat, or other.

"One of its driving forces is its ability to synthesize an unbelievable amount of information into a format and presentation which blends lively irony with outrageous observations, entertaining even as it presents eye-opening information in a format accessible to all.

"Politics dovetail with American obsessions and fascinations with trends, figureheads, drama, and sizzling news stories, but blend well with the observations of sociologists, psychologists, politicians, and others in a wide range of fields who lend their expertise and insights to create a much broader review of the Trump phenomena than a more casual book could provide.

"The result is a 'must read' for any American interested in issues of race, freedom, equality, and justice—and for any non-American who wonders just what is going on behind the scenes in this country's latest election debacle."

Diane Donovan, Senior Editor,
California Bookwatch

DONALD TRUMP, THE MAN WHO WOULD BE KING
WINNER OF "BEST BIOGRAPHY" AWARDS FROM BOOK FESTIVALS IN
NEW YORK, CALIFORNIA, AND FLORIDA
by Darwin Porter and Danforth Prince
Softcover, with 822 pages and hundreds of photos. ISBN *978-1-936003-51-8*.

Available now from Amazon.com, Barnes&Noble.com,
and other internet purveyors, worldwide.

ROCK HUDSON EROTIC FIRE

Another tragic, myth-shattering, & uncensored tale about
America's obsession with celebrities, from Blood Moon Productions.

In the dying days of Hollywood's Golden
Age, Rock Hudson was the most celebrated
phallic symbol and lust object in America.
This book describes his rise and fall, and the
Entertainment Industry that created him.

Rock Hudson charmed every casting director in
Hollywood (and movie-goers throughout America) as the mega-star they most wanted to share
PILLOW TALK with. This book describes his
rise and fall, and how he handled himself as a
closeted but promiscuous bisexual during an age
when EVERYBODY tried to throw him onto a
casting couch.

Based on dozens of face-to-face interviews with
the actor's friends, co-conspirators, and enemies,
and researched over a period of a half century,
this biography reveals the shame, agonies, and
irony of Rock Hudson's complete, never-before-
told story.

In 2017, the year of its release, it was designated
as winner ("BEST BIOGRAPHY") at two of the
Golden State's most prestigious literary competitions, the Northern California and the Southern
California Book Festivals.

Rock Hudson Erotic Fire

Darwin Porter & Danforth Prince
Another Outrageous Title in Blood Moon's Babylon Series

It was also favorably reviewed by the *Midwestern
Book Review, California Book Watch, KNEWS RADIO, the New York Journal of Books,* and the
editors at the most popular Seniors' magazine in Florida, *BOOMER TIMES.*

ROCK HUDSON EROTIC FIRE

By Darwin Porter & Danforth Prince
Softcover, 624 pages, with dozens of photos, 6" x 9"
ISBN 978-1-936003-55-6

Available everywhere now, online and in bookstores.

This is What Happens When A Demented Billionaire Hits Hollywood

HOWARD HUGHES

HELL'S ANGEL

BY DARWIN PORTER

From his reckless pursuit of love as a rich teenager to his final days as a demented fossil, Howard Hughes tasted the best and worst of the century he occupied. Along the way, he changed the worlds of aviation and entertainment forever.

This biography reveals inside details about his destructive and usually scandalous associations with other Hollywood players.

"The Aviator flew both ways. Porter's biography presents new allegations about Hughes' shady dealings with some of the biggest names of the 20th century"
—New York Daily News

"Darwin Porter's access to film industry insiders and other Hughes confidants supplied him with the resources he needed to create a portrait of Hughes that both corroborates what other Hughes biographies have divulged, and go them one better."
—Foreword Magazine

"Thanks to this bio of Howard Hughes, we'll never be able to look at the old pinups in quite the same way again."
—The Times (London)

Winner of a respected literary award from the Los Angeles Book Festival, this book gives an insider's perspective about what money can buy
—and what it can't.

814 pages, with photos. Available everywhere now, online and in bookstores.

ISBN 978-1-936003-13-6

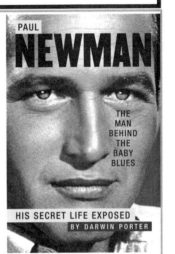

LANA TURNER

THE SWEATER GIRL, CELLULOID VENUS, SEX NYMPH TO THE G.I.s WHO WON WORLD WAR II, AND HOLLYWOOD'S OTHER MOST NOTORIOUS BLONDE

BEAUTIFUL AND BAD, HER FULL STORY HAS NEVER BEEN TOLD. UNTIL NOW!

Lana Turner was the most scandalous, most copied, and most gossiped-about actress in Hollywood. When her abusive Mafia lover was murdered in her house, every newspaper in the Free World described the murky dramas with something approaching hysteria.

Blood Moon's salacious but empathetic new biography exposes the public and private dramas of the girl who changed the American definition of what it REALLY means to be a blonde.

Here's how **CALIFORNIA BOOKWATCH** and **THE MIDWEST BOOK REVIEW** described the mega-celebrity as revealed in this book:

"*Lana Turner: Hearts and Diamonds Take All* belongs on the shelves of any collection strong in movie star biographies in general and Hollywood evolution in particular, and represents no lightweight production, appearing on the 20th anniversary of Lana Turner's death to provide a weighty survey packed with new information about her life.

"One would think that just about everything to be known about The Sweater Girl would have already appeared in print, but it should be noted that Lana Turner: Hearts and Diamonds Take All offers many new revelations not just about Turner, but about the movie industry in the aftermath of World War II.

"From Lana's introduction of a new brand of covert sexuality in women's movies to her scandalous romances among the stars, her extreme promiscuity, her search for love, and her notorious flings - even her involvement in murder - are all probed in a revealing account of glamour and movie industry relationships that bring Turner and her times to life.

"Some of the greatest scandals in Hollywood history are intricately detailed on these pages, making this much more than another survey of her life and times, and a 'must have' pick for any collection strong in Hollywood history in general, gossip and scandals and the real stories behind them, and Lana Turner's tumultuous career, in particular."

Lana Turner, Hearts & Diamonds Take All
Winner of the coveted "Best Biography" Award from the San Francisco Book Festival
By Darwin Porter and Danforth Prince
Softcover, 622 pages, with photos. ISBN 978-1-936003-53-2
Available everywhere, online and in stores.

KATHARINE THE GREAT

Hepburn, A Lifetime of Secrets Revealed

by Darwin Porter

Katharine Hepburn was the world's greatest screen diva—the most famous actress in American history. But until the appearance of this biography, no one had ever published the intimate details of her complicated and ferociously secretive private life.

Thanks to the "deferential and obsequious whitewashes" which followed in the wake of her death, readers probably know WHAT KATE REMEMBERED. Here, however, is an unvarnished account of what Katharine Hepburn desperately wanted to forget.

"Darwin Porter's biography of Hepburn cannot be lightly dismissed or ignored. Connoisseurs of Hepburn's life would do well to seek it out as a forbidden supplement."
—*The Sunday Times* **(London)**

"Behind the scenes of her movies, Katharine Hepburn played the temptress to as many women as she did men, ranted and raved with her co-stars and directors, and broke into her neighbors' homes for fun. And somehow, she managed to keep all of it out of the press. As they say, Katharine the Great is hard to put down."
—*The Dallas Voice*

"The door to Hepburn's closet has finally been opened. This is the most honest and least apologetic biography of Hollywood's most ferociously private actress ever written."
—*Senior Life Magazine, Miami*

The First Unvarnished Overview of the Empress Katharine, the First to Blow the Doors off the Closet of the Most Obsessively Secretive Actress in Hollywood

Softcover, 569 pages, with photos

ISBN   978-0-9748118-0-2
Available for E-Readers

LOVE TRIANGLE:
RONALD REAGAN
JANE WYMAN, & NANCY DAVIS

HOW MUCH DO YOU REALLY KNOW ABOUT THE REAGANS? THIS BOOKS TELLS EVERYTHING ABOUT THE SHOW-BIZ SCANDALS THEY DESPERATELY WANTED TO FORGET.

Unique in the history of publishing, this scandalous triple biography focuses on the Hollywood indiscretions of former U.S. president Ronald Reagan and his two wives. A proud and Presidential addition to Blood Moon's Babylon series, it digs deep into what these three young and attractive movie stars were doing decades before two of them took over the Free World.

As reviewed by Diane Donovan, Senior Reviewer at the California Bookwatch section of the Midwest Book Review: *"Love Triangle: Ronald Reagan, Jane Wyman & Nancy Davis may find its way onto many a Republican Reagan fan's reading shelf; but those who expect another Reagan celebration will be surprised: this is lurid Hollywood exposé writing at its best, and outlines the truths surrounding one of the most provocative industry scandals in the world.*

"There are already so many biographies of the Reagans on the market that one might expect similar mile-markers from this: be prepared for shock and awe; because Love Triangle doesn't take your ordinary approach to biography and describes a love triangle that eventually bumped a major Hollywood movie star from the possibility of being First Lady and replaced her with a lesser-known Grade B actress (Nancy Davis).

"From politics and betrayal to romance, infidelity, and sordid affairs, Love Triangle is a steamy, eye-opening story that blows the lid off of the Reagan illusion to raise eyebrows on both sides of the big screen.

"Black and white photos liberally pepper an account of the careers of all three and the lasting shock of their stormy relationships in a delightful pursuit especially recommended for any who relish Hollywood gossip."

In 2015, LOVE TRIANGLE, Blood Moon Productions' overview of the early dramas associated with Ronald Reagan's scandal-soaked career in Hollywood, was designated by the Awards Committee of the **HOLLYWOOD BOOK FESTIVAL** as Runner-Up to Best Biography of the Year.

LOVE TRIANGLE: Ronald Reagan, Jane Wyman, & Nancy Davis
Darwin Porter & Danforth Prince
Softcover, 6" x 9", with hundreds of photos.   ISBN 978-1-936003-41-9

PINK TRIANGLE

THE FEUDS AND PRIVATE LIVES OF

TENNESSEE WILLIAMS, GORE VIDAL, TRUMAN CAPOTE,

& FAMOUS MEMBERS OF THEIR ENTOURAGES

Darwin Porter & Danforth Prince

This book, the only one of its kind, reveals the backlot intrigues associated with the literary and script-writing *enfants terribles* of America's entertainment community during the mid-20th century.

It exposes their bitchfests, their slugfests, and their relationships with the *glitterati*—Marilyn Monroe, Brando, the Oliviers, the Paleys, U.S. Presidents, a gaggle of other movie stars, millionaires, and international *débauchés*.

This is for anyone who's interested in the formerly concealed scandals of Hollywood and Broadway, and the values and pretentions of both the literary community and the entertainment industry.

"A banquet... If PINK TRIANGLE had not been written for us, we would have had to research and type it all up for ourselves…Pink Triangle is nearly seven hundred pages of the most entertaining histrionics ever sliced, spiced, heated, and serviced up to the reading public. Everything that Blood Moon has done before pales in comparison.
Given the fact that the subjects of the book themselves were nearly delusional on the subject of themselves (to say nothing of each other) it is hard to find fault. Add to this the intertwined jungle that was the relationship among Williams, Capote, and Vidal, of the times they vied for things they loved most—especially attention—and the times they enthralled each other and the world, [Pink Triangle is] the perfect antidote to the Polar Vortex."
—Vinton McCabe in the NY JOURNAL OF BOOKS

"Full disclosure: I have been a friend and follower of Blood Moon Productions' tomes for years, and always marveled at the amount of information in their books—it's staggering. The index alone to Pink Triangle runs to 21 pages—and the scale of names in it runs like a Who's Who of American social, cultural and political life through much of the 20th century."
—Perry Brass in THE HUFFINGTON POST

"We Brits are not spared the Porter/Prince silken lash either. PINK TRIANGLE's research is, quite frankly, breathtaking. PINK TRIANGLE will fascinate you for many weeks to come. Once you have made the initial titillating dip, the day will seem dull without it."
—Jeffery Tayor in THE SUNDAY EXPRESS (UK)

PINK TRIANGLE—The Feuds and Private Lives of Tennessee Williams, *Gore Vidal, Truman Capote, and Famous Members of their Entourages*
Darwin Porter & Danforth Prince
Softcover, 700 pages, with photos   ISBN 978-1-936003-37-2   Also Available for E-Readers

THOSE GLAMOROUS GABORS

Bombshells from Budapest

Zsa Zsa, Eva, and Magda Gabor transferred their glittery dreams and gold-digging ambitions from the twilight of the Austro-Hungarian Empire to Hollywood. There, more effectively than any army, these Bombshells from Budapest broke hearts, amassed fortunes, lovers, and A-list husbands, and amused millions of *voyeurs* through the medium of television, movies, and the social registers. In this astonishing "triple-play" biography, designated "Best Biography of the Year" by the Hollywood Book Festival, Blood Moon lifts the "mink-and-diamond" curtain on this amazing trio of blood-related sisters, whose complicated intrigues have never been fully explored before.

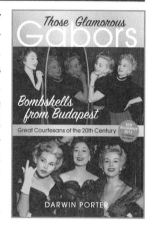

"**You will never be Ga-bored...this book gives new meaning to the term compelling.**
Be warned, *Those Glamorous Gabors* is both an epic and a pip. Not since *Gone With the Wind* have so many characters on the printed page been forced to run for their lives for one reason or another. And Scarlett making a dress out of the curtains is nothing compared to what a Gabor will do when she needs to scrap together an outfit for a movie premiere or late-night outing.

"For those not up to speed, Jolie Tilleman came from a family of jewelers and therefore came by her love for the shiny stones honestly, perhaps genetically. She married Vilmos Gabor somewhere around World War 1 (exact dates, especially birth dates, are always somewhat vague in order to establish plausible deniability later on) and they were soon blessed with three daughters: **Magda**, the oldest, whose hair, sadly, was naturally brown, although it would turn quite red in America; **Zsa Zsa** (born 'Sari') a natural blond who at a very young age exhibited the desire for fame with none of the talents usually associated with achievement, excepting beauty and a natural wit; and **Eva**, the youngest and blondest of the girls, who after seeing Grace Moore perform at the National Theater, decided that she wanted to be an actress and that she would one day move to Hollywood to become a star.

"Given that the Gabor family at that time lived in Budapest, Hungary, at the period of time between the World Wars, that Hollywood dream seemed a distant one indeed. The story—the riches to rags to riches to rags to riches again myth of survival against all odds as the four women, because of their Jewish heritage, flee Europe with only the minks on their backs and what jewels they could smuggle along with them in their *decolletage*, only to have to battle afresh for their places in the vicious Hollywood pecking order—gives new meaning to the term 'compelling.' The reader, as if he were witnessing a particularly gore-drenched traffic accident, is incapable of looking away."

—New York Review of Books

Those Glamorous Gabors, Bombshells from Budapest, by Darwin Porter.
Softcover, 730 pages, with hundreds of photos   ISBN 978-1-936003-35-8

PETER O'TOOLE

HELLRAISER, SEXUAL OUTLAW, IRISH REBEL

At the time of its publication early in 2015, this book was widely publicized in the *Daily Mail,* the *New York Daily News,* the *New York Post,* the *Midwest Book Review, The Express (London), The Globe,* the *National Enquirer,* and in equivalent publications worldwide

One of the world's most admired (and brilliant) actors, Peter O'Toole wined and wenched his way through a labyrinth of sexual and interpersonal betrayals, sometimes with disastrous results. Away from the stage and screen, where such films as *Becket* and *Lawrence of Arabia*, made film history, his life was filled with drunken, debauched nights and edgy sexual experimentations, most of which were never openly examined in the press. A hellraiser, he shared wild times with his "best blokes" Richard Burton and Richard Harris. Peter Finch, also his close friend, once invited him to join him in sharing the pleasures of his mistress, Vivien Leigh.

"My father, a bookie, moved us to the Mick community of Leeds," O'Toole once told a reporter. "We were very poor, but I was born an Irishman, which accounts for my gift of gab, my unruly behavior, my passionate devotion to women and the bottle, and my loathing of any authority figure."

Author Robert Sellers described O'Toole's boyhood neighborhood. "Three of his playmates went on to be hanged for murder; one strangled a girl in a lovers' quarrel; one killed a man during a robbery; another cut up a warden in South Africa with a pair of shears. It was a heavy bunch."

Peter O'Toole's hell-raising life story has never been told, until now. Hot and uncensored, from a writing team which, even prior to O'Toole's death in 2013, had been collecting under-the-radar info about him for years, this book has everything you ever wanted to know about how THE LION navigated his way through the boudoirs of the Entertainment Industry IN WINTER, Spring, Summer, and a dissipated Autumn as well.

Blood Moon has ripped away the imperial robe, scepter, and crown usually associated with this quixotic problem child of the British Midlands. Provocatively uncensored, this illusion-shattering overview of Peter O'Toole's hellraising (or at least very naughty) and demented life is unique in the history of publishing.

PETER O'TOOLE: HELLRAISER, SEXUAL OUTLAW, IRISH REBEL
DARWIN PORTER & DANFORTH PRINCE
Softcover, with photos. ISBN 978-1-936003-45-7

JAMES DEAN

TOMORROW NEVER COMES

HONORING THE 60TH ANNIVERSARY OF HIS VIOLENT AND EARLY DEATH

America's most enduring and legendary symbol of young, enraged rebellion, James Dean continues into the 21st Century to capture the imagination of the world.

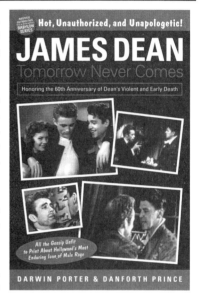

After one of his many flirtations with Death, which caught up with him when he was a celebrity-soaked 24-year-old, he said, "If a man can live after he dies, then maybe he's a great man." Today, bars from Nigeria to Patagonia are named in honor of this international, spectacularly self-destructive movie star icon.

Migrating from the dusty backroads of Indiana to center stage in the most formidable boudoirs of Hollywood, his saga is electrifying.

A strikingly handsome heart-throb, Dean is a study in contrasts: Tough but tender, brutal but remarkably sensitive; he was a reckless hellraiser badass who could revert to a little boy in bed.

A rampant bisexual, he claimed that he didn't want to go through life "with one hand tied behind my back." He demonstrated that during bedroom trysts with Marilyn Monroe, Rock Hudson, Elizabeth Taylor, Paul Newman, Natalie Wood, Shelley Winters, Marlon Brando, Steve McQueen, Ursula Andress, Montgomery Clift, Pier Angeli, Tennessee Williams, Susan Strasberg, Tallulah Bankhead, and FBI director J. Edgar Hoover.

Woolworth heiress Barbara Hutton, one of the richest and most dissipated women of her era, wanted to make him her toy boy.

Tomorrow Never Comes is the most penetrating look at James Dean to have emerged from the wreckage of his Porsche Spyder in 1955.

Before setting out on his last ride, he said, "I feel life too intensely to bear living it."

Tomorrow Never Comes presents a damaged but beautiful soul.

JAMES DEAN—TOMORROW NEVER COMES
DARWIN PORTER & DANFORTH PRINCE
Softcover, with photos. ISBN 978-1-936003-49-5

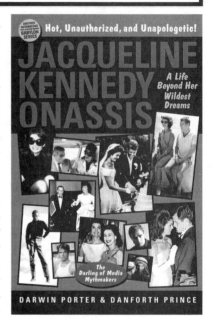

After floods of analysis and commentary in tabloid and mainstream newspapers worldwide, this has emerged as the world's most comprehensive testimonial to the flimsier side of Camelot, the most comprehensive compendium of gossip ever published about America's unofficial, uncrowned queen, **Jacqueline Kennedy Onassis**. Its publication coincided with the 20-year anniversary of the death of one of the most famous, revered, and talked-about women who ever lived.

During her tumultuous life, Mrs. Onassis zealously guarded her privacy and her secrets. But in the wake of her death, more and more revelations have emerged about her frustrations, her rage, her passions, her towering strengths, and her delicate fragility, which she hid from the glare of the world behind oversized sunglasses. Within this posthumous biography, a three-dimensional woman emerges through the compilation of some 1,000 eyewitness testimonials from men and women who knew her over a period of decades.

An overview of the life of Mrs. Onassis is a natural fit for Blood Moon, a publishing enterprise that's increasingly known, worldwide, as one of the most provocative and scandalous in the history of publishing.

"References to this American icon appear with almost rhythmic regularity to anyone researching the cultural landscape of America during the last half of The American Century," said Danforth Prince. "Based on what we'd uncovered about Jackie during the research of many of our earlier titles, we're positioning ourselves as a more or less solitary outpost of irreverence within a landscape that's otherwise flooded with fawning, over-reverential testimonials. Therein lies this book's appeal—albeit with a constant respect and affection for a woman we admired and adored."

Based on decades of research by writers who define themselves as "voraciously attentive Kennedyphiles," it supplements the half-dozen other titles within Blood Moon's Babylon series.

LINDA LOVELACE

INSIDE LINDA LOVELACE'S DEEP THROAT
DEGRADATION, PORNO CHIC, AND THE RISE OF FEMINISM

THE MOST COMPREHENSIVE BIOGRAPHY EVER WRITTEN OF AN ADULT ENTERTAINMENT STAR, HER TORMENTED RELATIONSHIP WITH HOLLYWOOD'S UNDERBELLY, AND HOW SHE CHANGED FOREVER THE WORLD'S PERCEPTIONS ABOUT CENSORSHIP, SEXUAL BEHAVIOR PATTERNS, AND PORNOGRAPHY.

Darwin Porter, author of some twenty critically acclaimed celebrity exposés of behind-the-scenes intrigue in the entertainment industry, was deeply involved in the Linda Lovelace saga as it unfolded in the 70s, interviewing many of the players, and raising money for the legal defense of the film's co-star, Harry Reems.

In this book, emphasizing her role as an unlikely celebrity interacting with other celebrities, he brings inside information and a never-before-published revelation to almost every page.

"This book drew me in..How could it not?"
Coco Papy, *Bookslut.*

THE BEACH BOOK FESTIVALS GRAND PRIZE WINNER FOR "BEST SUMMER READING OF 2013"

RUNNER-UP TO "BEST BIOGRAPHY OF 2013" *THE LOS ANGELES BOOK FESTIVAL*

Another hot and insightful commentary about major and sometimes violently controversial conflicts of the American Century, from Blood Moon Productions.

Inside Linda Lovelace's Deep Throat, by Darwin Porter
Softcover, 640 pages, 6"x9" with photos.
ISBN 978-1-936003-33-4

STEVE McQUEEN

A COOL BIOGRAPHY TOO HOT TO BE PUBLISHED DURING THE LIFETIME OF ITS SUBJECT.

"This book is potentially dangerous for middle-aged men."
—The Sunday Times (London)

The drama of Steve McQueen's personal life far exceeded any role he ever played on screen. Born to a prostitute, he was brutally molested by some of his mother's "johns," and endured gang rape in reform school. His drift into prostitution began when he was hired as a towel boy in the most notorious bordello in the Dominican Republic, where he starred in a string of cheap porno films. Returning to New York before migrating to Hollywood, he hustled men on Times Square and, as a "gentleman escort" in a borrowed tux, rich older women.

And then, sudden stardom as he became the world's top box office attraction. The abused became the abuser. "I live for myself, and I answer to nobody," he proclaimed. "The last thing I want to do is fall in love with a broad."

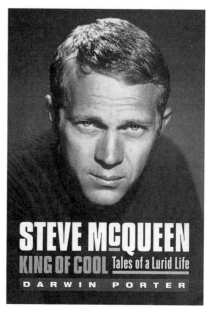

Thus began a string of seductions that included hundreds of overnight pickups--both male and female. Topping his A-list conquests were James Dean, Paul Newman, Marilyn Monroe, and Barbra Streisand. Finally, this pioneering biography explores the mysterious death of Steve McQueen. Were those salacious rumors really true?

Steve McQueen
King of Cool, Tales of a Lurid Life
Darwin Porter

A carefully researched, 466-page hardcover with dozens of photos

ISBN 978-1-936003-05-1

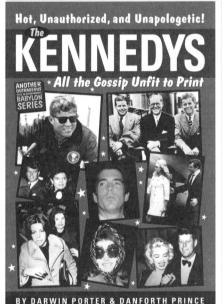

CONFUSED ABOUT HOW TO INTERPRET THEIR RAUCOUS PAST?
THIS UNCENSORED TALE ABOUT A LOVE AFFAIR THAT CHANGED THE COURSE
OF POLITICS AND THE PLANET IS OF COMPELLING INTEREST TO ANYONE IN-
VOLVED IN THE POLITICAL SLUGFESTS AND INCENDIARY WARS OF THE
CLINTONS.

BILL & HILLARY
SO THIS IS THAT THING CALLED LOVE

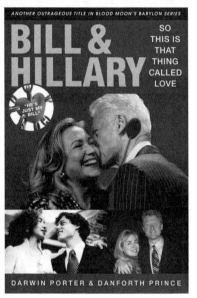

"This is both a biographical coverage of the Clintons and a political exposé; a detailed, weighty exploration that traces the couple's social and political evolution, from how each entered the political arena to their White House years under Bill Clinton's presidency.

"Containing gossip, scandal, and biographical sketches, it delves deeply into the news and politics of its times, presenting enough historical background to fully explore the underlying controversies affecting the Clinton family and their choices.

"Sidebars of information and black and white photos liberally peppered throughout the account offer visual reinforcement to the exploration, lending it the feel and tone of both a gossip column and political piece - something that probes not just Clinton interactions but the D.C. political milieu as a whole.

"The result may appear weighty, sporting over five hundred pages, but is an absorbing, top recommendation for readers of both biographical and political pieces who will thoroughly enjoy this spirited, lively, and thought-provoking analysis."

—*THE MIDWEST BOOK REVIEW*

***

Shortly after its release in December of 2015, this book received a literary award (Runner-up to Best Biography of the Year) from the New England Book Festival. As stated by a spokesperson for the Awards, "The New England Book Festival is an annual competition honoring excellence in books, with particular focus on projects that deserve closer attention from the academic community. Congratulations to Blood Moon and its authors, especially Darwin Porter, for his highly entertaining analysis of Clinton's double-barreled presidential regime, and the sometimes hysterical over-reaction of their enemies."

J. EDGAR HOOVER & CLYDE TOLSON

INVESTIGATING THE SEXUAL SECRETS OF AMERICA'S MOST FAMOUS MEN & WOMEN

DARWIN PORTER

This epic saga of power and corruption has a revelation on every page—cross dressing, gay parties, sexual indiscretions, hustlers for sale, alliances with the Mafia, and criminal activity by the nation's chief law enforcer.

It's all here, with chilling details about the abuse of power on the dark side of the American saga. But mostly it's the decades-long love story of America's two most powerful men who could tell presidents "how to skip rope." (Hoover's words.)

"Everyone's dredging up J. Edgar Hoover. Leonardo DiCaprio just immortalized him, and now comes Darwin Porter's paperback, *J. Edgar Hoover & Clyde Tolson: Investigating the Sexual Secrets of America's Most Famous Men and Women*. It shovels Hoover's darkest secrets dragged kicking and screaming from the closet. It's filth on every VIP who's safely dead and some who are still above ground."

—Cindy Adams, The New York Post

"This book is important, because it destroys what's left of Hoover's reputation. Did you know he had intel on the bombing of Pearl Harbor, but he sat on it, making him more or less responsible for thousands of deaths? Or that he had almost nothing to do with the arrests or killings of any of the 1930s gangsters that he took credit for catching?

"A lot of people are angry with its author, Darwin Porter. They say that his outing of celebrities is just cheap gossip about dead people who can't defend themselves. I suppose it's because Porter is destroying carefully constructed myths that are comforting to most people. As gay men, we benefit the most from Porter's work, because we know that except for AIDS, the closet was the most terrible thing about the 20th century. If the closet never existed, neither would Hoover. The fact that he got away with such duplicity under eight presidents makes you think that every one of them was a complete fool for tolerating it."

—Paul Bellini, FAB Magazine (Toronto)

Winner of Literary Awards from the Los Angeles & the Hollywood Book Festivals
ISBN 978-1-936003-25-9

SCARLETT O'HARA,

Desperately in Love with Heathcliff,

Together on the Road to Hell

Damn You, Scarlett O'Hara
The Private Lives of **Vivien Leigh** and **Laurence Olivier**

Here, for the first time, is a biography that raises the curtain on the secret lives of **Lord Laurence Olivier**, often cited as the finest actor in the history of England, and **Vivien Leigh,** who immortalized herself with her Oscar-winning portrayals of Scarlett O'Hara in *Gone With the Wind,* and as Blanche DuBois in Tennessee Williams' *A Streetcar Named Desire.*

Dashing and "impossibly handsome," Laurence Olivier was pursued by the most dazzling luminaries, male and female, of the movie and theater worlds.

by **Darwin Porter** and **Roy Moseley**

Lord Olivier's beautiful and brilliant but emotionally disturbed wife (Viv to her lovers) led a tumultuous off-the-record life whose paramours ranged from the A-list celebrities to men she selected randomly off the street. But none of the brilliant roles depicted by Lord and Lady Olivier, on stage or on screen, ever matched the power and drama of personal dramas which wavered between Wagnerian opera and Greek tragedy. *Damn You, Scarlett O'Hara* is the definitive and most revelatory portrait ever published of the most talented and tormented actor and actress of the 20th century.

Darwin Porter is the principal author of this seminal work.

"The folks over at TMZ would have had a field day tracking Laurence Olivier and Vivien Leigh with flip cameras in hand. **Damn You, Scarlett O'Hara** *can be a dazzling read, the prose unmannered and instantly digestible. The authors' ability to pile scandal atop scandal, seduction after seduction, can be impossible to resist."*

—THE WASHINGTON TIMES

DAMN YOU, SCARLETT O'HARA

THE PRIVATE LIFES OF LAURENCE OLIVIER AND VIVIEN LEIGH

Darwin Porter and Roy Moseley

Winner of four distinguished literary awards, this is the best biography of Vivien Leigh and Laurence Olivier ever published, with hundreds of insights into the London Theatre, the role of the Oliviers in the politics of World War II, and the passion, fury, and frustration of their lives together as actors in the West End, on Broadway, and in Hollywood.

ISBN 978-1-936003-15-0 Hardcover, 708 pages, with about a hundred photos.

ELIZABETH TAYLOR

There is Nothing Like a Dame
All the Gossip Unfit to Print from the Glory Days of Hollywood

For more than 60 years, Elizabeth Taylor dazzled generations of movie-goers with her glamor and her all-consuming passion for life. She was the last of the great stars of Golden Age Hollywood, coming to a sad end at the age of 79 in 2011.

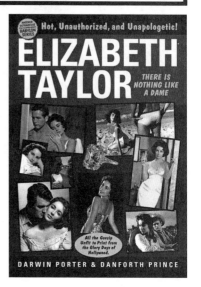

But before she died, appearing on the Larry King show, she claimed that her biographers had revealed "only half of my story, but I can't tell the other half in a memoir because I'd get sued."

Now, Blood Moon presents for the first time a comprehensive compilation of most of the secrets from the mercurial Dame Elizabeth, whose hedonism helped define the jet set of the tumultuous 60s and beyond.

Throughout the many decades of her life, she consistently generated hysteria among her fans. Here, her story is told with brutal honesty in rich, juicy detail and illustrated, with a new revelation on every page.

It's all here, and a lot more, in an exposé that's both sympathetic and shocking, with a candor and attention to detail that brings the *femme fatale* of the 20th century back to life.

"What has never been denied about Elizabeth Taylor is that the young actress, though small for her age, was mature beyond her years, deeply ambitious, and sexually precocious...Insiders agreed she always had a strong rebellious streak. Could the studio system's vice-like grip on publicity have stopped scandals about their most valuable child star from leaking out?

"A recent biography of Taylor claims that as a teenager, she lost her virginity at 15 to British actor Peter Lawford, had flings with Ronald Reagan and Errol Flynn, was roughly seduced by Orson Welles, and even enjoyed a threesome involving John F. Kennedy.

The authors—Darwin Porter and Danforth Prince—also allege Taylor was just 11 when she was taught by her close friend, the gay British actor, Roddy McDowall, the star of Lassie Come Home, *how to satisfy men without sleeping with them."*

Tom Leonard in THE DAILY MAIL, October 19, 2015

"Before they wither, Elizabeth Taylor's breasts will topple empires."

—Richard Burton

Softcover, 460 pages, with photos ISBN 978-1-936003-31-0.

JACKO, HIS RISE AND FALL

THE SOCIAL AND SEXUAL HISTORY OF MICHAEL JACKSON

Darwin Porter

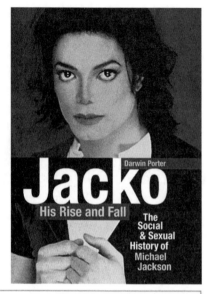

He rewrote the rules of America's entertainment industry, and he led a life of notoriety. Even his death was the occasion for scandals which continue to this day.

This is the world's most comprehensive historical overview of a pop star's rise, fall, and to some extent, rebirth as an American Icon. Read it for the real story of the circumstances and players who created the icon which the world will forever remember as "the gloved one," Michael Jackson.

"This is the story of Peter Pan gone rotten. Don't stop till you get enough. Darwin Porter's biography of Michael Jackson is dangerously addictive."
—*The Sunday Observer* (London)

"In this compelling glimpse of Jackson's life, Porter provides what many journalists have failed to produce in their writings about the pop star: A real person behind the headlines."
— *Foreword Magazine*

"I'd have thought that there wasn't one single gossippy rock yet to be overturned in the microscopically scrutinized life of Michael Jackson, but Darwin Porter has proven me wrong. Definitely a page-turner. But don't turn the pages too quickly. Almost every one holds a fascinating revelation."
—*Books to Watch Out For*

This book, a winner of literary awards from both *Foreword Magazine* and the Hollywood Book Festival, was originally published during the lifetime of Michael Jackson. This, the revised, post-mortem edition, with extra analysis and commentary, was released after his death.

Hardcover 600 indexed pages with about a hundred photos

ISBN 978-0-936003-10-5

BRANDO UNZIPPED

An Uncensored *Exposé* of America's Most Visible Method Actor and Sexual Outlaw

by Darwin Porter

BRANDO EXPOSED! This "entertainingly outrageous" (*Frontiers Magazine*) biography provides a definitive, blow-by-blow description of the "hot, provocative, and barely under control drama" that was the life of America's most famous Postwar actor.

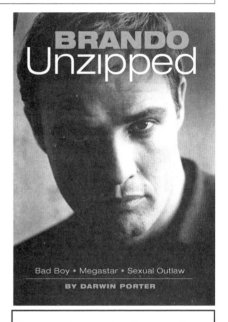

"Lurid, raunchy, perceptive, and certainly worth reading...One of the ten best show-biz biographies of 2006."
The Sunday Times (London)

"Yummy. An irresistably flamboyant romp of a read."
Books to Watch Out For

"Astonishing. An extraordinarily detailed portrait of Brando that's as blunt, uncompromising, and X-rated as the man himself."
Women's Weekly

"This shocking new book is sparking a major re-assessment of Brando's legacy as one of Hollywood's most macho lotharios."
Daily Express (London)

"As author Darwin Porter finds, it wasn't just the acting world Marlon Brando conquered. It was the actors, too."
Gay Times (London)

"*Brando Unzipped* is the definitive gossip guide to the late, great actor's life."
The New York Daily News

Extensively serialized in London's *MAIL ON SUNDAY*, this is history's most definitive biography of Marlon Brando.

An artfully lurid hardcover with 625 indexed pages and hundreds of photos, it's the book that redefined the icon who ALWAYS raised headlines, heartrates, and expectations of what a hot actor is supposed to be.

One of the most talked-about Hollywood bios ever, it's still available for E-readers

ISBN 978-0-9748118-2-6

HUMPHREY BOGART

THE MAKING OF A LEGEND

DARWIN PORTER

A "CRADLE-TO-GRAVE" HARDCOVER ABOUT THE RISE TO FAME OF AN OBSCURE, UNLIKELY, AND FREQUENTLY UNEMPLOYED BROADWAY ACTOR.

Whereas **Humphrey Bogart** is always at the top of any list of the Entertainment Industry's most famous actors, very little is known about how he clawed his way from Broadway to Hollywood during Prohibition and the Jazz Age.

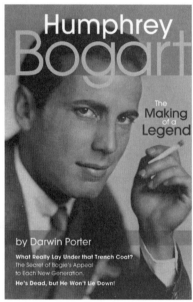

This pioneering biography begins with Bogart's origins as the child of wealthy (morphine-addicted) parents in New York City, then examines the love affairs, scandals, failures, and breakthroughs that launched him as an American icon.

It includes details about behind-the-scenes dramas associated with three mysterious marriages, and films such as *The Petrified Forest*, *The Maltese Falcon*, *High Sierra*, and *Casablanca*. Read all about the debut and formative years of the actor who influenced many generations of filmgoers, laying Bogie's life bare in a style you've come to expect from Darwin Porter. Exposed with all their juicy details is what Bogie never told his fourth wife, Lauren Bacall, herself a screen legend.

Drawn from original interviews with friends and foes who knew a lot about what lay beneath his trenchcoat, this exposé covers Bogart's remarkable life as it helped define movie-making, Hollywood's portrayal of macho, and America's evolving concept of Entertainment itself.

This revelatory book is based on dusty unpublished memoirs, letters, diaries, and often personal interviews from the women—and the men—who adored him.

There are also shocking allegations from colleagues, former friends, and jilted lovers who wanted the screen icon to burn in hell.

All this and more, much more, in Darwin Porter's *exposé* of Bogie's startling secret life.

WITH STARTLING NEW INFORMATION ABOUT BOGART, THE MOVIES, & GOLDEN AGE HOLLYWOOD

542 PAGES, WITH HUNDREDS OF PHOTOS **ISBN** 978-1-936003-14-3

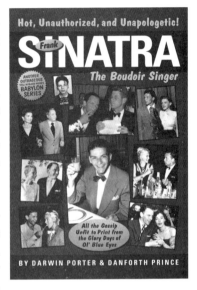